Sybase ™

Developer's Guide

Developer's Guide

SAMS
PUBLISHING

A Division of Macmillan
Computer Publishing

201 West 103rd Street,
Indianapolis, Indiana 46290

Daniel
Worden

*For my father
Who taught me that
the principles of
information manage-
ment are media
independent and
showed me how to
have a passion for my
work.*

*And for my mother
Who instilled in me
the discipline without
which I would never
have finished this, or
any other, project.*

Copyright ©1994 by Sams Publishing

International Standard Book Number: 0-672-30467-8

Library of Congress Catalog Card Number: 93-87172

97 96 95 94   4   3   2   1

Interpretation of the printing code: the rightmost double-digit number is the
year of the book's printing; the rightmost single-digit, the number of the book's
printing. For example, a printing code of 94-1 shows that the first printing of
the book occurred in 1994.

Composed in AGaramond and MCPdigital by Macmillan Computer
Publishing

Printed in the United States of America

Trademarks

Publisher

Richard K. Swadley

Associate Publisher

Jordan Gold

Acquisitions Manager

Stacy Hiquet

Managing Editor

Cindy Morrow

Acquisitions Editor

Christopher Denny

Development Editor

Dean Miller

Production Editor

Susan Christophersen

Editors

Cheri Clark
Angie Trzepacz

Editorial Coordinator

Bill Whitmer

Editorial Assistants

Carol Ackerman
Sharon Cox
Lynette Quinn

Technical Reviewer

Sybase Corporation

Marketing Manager

Gregg Bushyeager

Cover Designer

Karen Ruggles

Book Designer

Michele Laseau

Director of Production and Manufacturing

Jeff Valler

Imprint Manager

Juli Cook

Manufacturing Coordinator

Paul Gilchrist

Production Analysts

Dennis Hager
Mary Beth Wakefield

Graphics Image Specialists

Tim Montgomery
Dennis Sheehan
Susan VandeWalle

Production

Nick Anderson
Katy Bodenmiller
Ayrika Bryant
Steph Davis
Karen Dodson
Terri Edwards
Rich Evers
Greg Kemp
Stephanie J. McComb
Wendy Ott
Shelly Palma
Angela P. Judy
Linda Quigley
Ryan Rader
Michelle Self
Tonya R. Simpson
S.A. Springer
Becky Tapley
Elaine Webb

Indexer

Craig Small

	Introduction	xxv

1 Introduction to Sybase Client/Server

1.1	The Enterprise Client/Server Solution	3
1.2	The Benefits of Sybase Client/Server Computing	17
1.3	An Overview of the SQL Server Environment	51
1.4	Integrating Sybase with Existing Resources	69

2 Defining the Development Environment

2.1	Roles and Responsibilities in a Client/Server Project	95
2.2	Developing Application Specifications	111
2.3	Developing a Data Model	137
2.4	Modeling Queries	155
2.5	Defining Report Requirements	169
2.6	Data Integrity and Recovery	173

3 Installing and Configuring SQL Server

3.1	Installing Your SQL Server	189
3.2	Platform-Specific Issues	203
3.3	Configuring Your SQL Server	221
3.4	Memory and Configuration Options	231
3.5	Creating Tables, Views, and Indexes	239
3.6	Adding Groups and Setting Permissions	261
3.7	Defining and Using Dump Devices	271

4 Using SQL Server Features

4.1	Sybase-Supplied Stored Procedures	283
4.2	Database Integrity	309
4.3	TransAct SQL	319
4.4	Writing Stored Procedures	339

4.5	Triggers and Referential Integrity	347
4.6	Writing Transactions in SQL Server	355
4.7	Table Locks in SQL Server	369
4.8	The SQL Server Systems Tables	377
4.9	The Use of Cursors in SQL Server	387
4.10	Opportunities for Optimization	393

5 The Open Client Architecture

5.1	The Open Client DB-Library	431
5.2	Using DB-Library Calls in the C/C++ Programming Environment	453
5.3	Connecting Personal Computers to a SQL Server	525
5.4	Troubleshooting Net-Lib Connections	539

6 Front-End Tools and Utilities

6.1	Sybase-Supplied Utilities	551
6.2	Build Momentum	559
6.3	PowerTools for Microsoft Windows Development	569
6.4	Database Publishing	585
6.5	Using CASE Tools with SQL Server	593

7 New Products and Emerging Trends

7.1	What's New in SQL Server Release 10.0	609
7.2	Remote Client/Server Solutions	631

8 Glossary

8.1	Glossary	645
	Index	657

Contents

Introduction   **xxv**

1 Introduction to Sybase Client/Server

1.1   The Enterprise Client/Server Solution   3

In the Beginning 4
   A New Approach to Relational Systems 4
   The 1980's Market 5
Advantages of SQL Server 6
   The Programmable Database 6
   Event-Driven Triggers 7
   Multithreading 7
Rounding Out the Product Line 8
   Open Server 8
   DEFT CASE Tool 9
The Present 9
   Improving Support 10
   New and Improved Tools 10
   Developing New Server Products 11
Future Developments 11
The Emerging Client/Server Marketplace 13
Third-Party Products 14
Summary 15

1.2   The Benefits of Sybase Client/Server Computing   17

How to Identify the Benefits of Your Sybase Solution 19
   Open Architecture 21
   Scalability 22
   Interoperability 22
   Distributed Database Support 23
   Systems Administration Tools 24
Some Real-World Examples 24
   Case 1: SQL Server Supports Global Consulting 24
   Case 2: Sybase at the Stock Market 27
   Case 3: SQL Server and Risk Management 29
   Case 4: SQL Server and Health Care 30
   Case 5: SQL Server Helps Money Change Hands 31

Lessons Learned: Analyzing the Case Studies 33
    Rules 1 and 2: Situation Normal... 33
    Rules 3 and 4: Never Mind How... 34
    Rules 5 and 6: If you can't beat 'em... 35
    Rules 7 and 8: Which Came First... 36
The Benefits of Client/Server 37
    Relevance to the Business 37
    Short-Term Payback and Long-Term Value 38
    Integrating the Users 39
    Leveraging Existing Systems 40
    Learning from Experience 40
    Return on Investment 41
Build, Buy, or Both? 42
Pitfalls 43
    Using Obsolete Development Models 43
    Developing in Isolation 44
    Inadequate Specifications 45
    Insufficient Technology Transfer 46
    Underestimating the Complexity 47
Summary 48

1.3   An Overview of the SQL Server Environment   51

The SQL Server's Relationship to the Operating System 52
Installation of the SQL Server 54
    SQL Server Software 54
    Sybase Devices 55
    Databases and Logs 56
    Database Objects 57
    Data Dictionary 58
The SQL Server 60
    Net-Libraries 62
A Sample Query 64
A Sample Update 65
Summary 66

1.4   Integrating Sybase with Existing Resources   69

Integrating Systems with SQL Server 71

Integration Opportunities Across Departmental Lines 71

Traditional Systems Development Models 74

The Top-Down Approach 75

The Bottom-Up Approach 76

The Results 77

Lessons from the Past: What to Keep 78

What *Not* to Keep 79

Client/Server Development Models 80

Rapid Application Development 81

Joint Application Development 81

Object-Oriented Programming and Design 82

Side-by-Side Development Model 83

The Development Process 84

Eight Steps Toward Successful Development 85

Amalgamated Monoliths: A Case in Point 87

Summary 89

Section Summary 90

2   Defining the Development Environment

2.1   Roles and Responsibilities in a Client/Server Project   95

Why Define Roles and Responsibilities? 96

Project Sponsor 98

Project Manager 99

Project Leader 99

Technical Specialist 100

End User 101

End-User Developer 101

Systems Architect 102

Applications Analyst 103

Database Administrator 103

Data Administrator 104

Interface Designer 105

Network Architect 106

Documentation Specialist 107

Summary 110

2.2 Developing Application Specifications   **111**

Application Specifications: Form Follows Function 112

An Application Specification Model 114

Information-Gathering Techniques 116

   Defining the Business Practice versus the Existing System ... 118

   The Interview Process 119

   Data Flow Diagrams 122

   Entity Relationship Diagrams 124

   Object-Oriented Diagramming Techniques 127

A Sample Application 129

Summary 135

2.3 Developing a Data Model   **137**

How the Data Model Supports the Application 138

Integrating Multiple Applications with the Data Models 141

The Logical Data Model Defined 142

User Walkthroughs of the Data Models 143

Risks and Costs Associated with Modifying the Data Model 144

Description of the Physical Data Model 145

Determining Permissions for Creating Database Objects 149

Defining Database Objects as Part of the Physical
   Data Model 151

Mapping the Physical Data Model to the
   Server Environment 152

Summary 153

2.4 Modeling Queries   **155**

The Role of Queries in the Application 156

Translating User Data Requests into SQL Queries 158

Determining SQL Query Types 158

   The SELECT Command 159

   Using SELECT with Multiple Tables 160

   The JOIN Command 161

   Join Strategies and Options 162

   Using Views in Place of Joins 163

   The INSERT Command 164

Sample Queries 165

Summary 166

2.5   Defining Report Requirements   169

Batch Reports versus User-Generated Reports 170

   Questionnaires 171

   Forms 171

   Database Publishing 171

Retrieving Data for Reports 172

Summary 172

2.6   Data Integrity and Recovery   173

Threats and Perils...174

   Unauthorized Access 175

   Systems Failure 175

Threats to Data Integrity..176

   Column-Level Data Integrity 177

   Table-Level Data Integrity 178

   Database-Level Integrity 179

Transaction Logs 180

Incomplete Transactions 180

Application Logic Bugs 182

Addressing System Security with Sybase 182

   Stored Procedures as a Security Mechanism 183

   Security Through Backups 184

   Disk Mirroring 184

Summary 185

Section Summary 185

3 Installing and Configuring SQL Server

3.1   Installing Your SQL Server   189

Getting Started..190

The Release Notes 191

The Sybase User 191

The SQL Server Address 191

Character Set and Sort Order 192

Default Language 193

Ownership of Physical Resources 194

Installing Sybase from the Distribution Media 195

Error Logs and Messages 198

   Enabling Remote Server Communications...........................199

Files versus Raw Partitions 200

Physical Database Implementation Plan 200

Estimating Resource Requirements 201

Summary 202

3.2   Platform-Specific Issues   203

UNIX 204

SunOS 4.1.3 204

Sun Solaris 2.x 205

    IBM Risc System/6000 AIX 205

    SQL Server on an HP-UX Version 9.0 Platform..................205

Novell NLM 213

OS/2 SQL Server 214

    LAN Manager...215

SQL Server 4.2 Manual Installation 216

Summary 220

3.3   Configuring Your SQL Server   221

Configuration Rules 222

Segments 228

Summary 229

3.4   Memory and Configuration Options   231

sp_configure 232

Summary 237

3.5   Creating Tables, Views, and Indexes   239

Tables 240

    Altering Tables 243

    Datatypes..244

    Built-In Functions 249

    String Functions 249

    Substrings 250

    Converting Datatypes 251

Creating Views...252

    Using Views 252

    Modifying Data Through Views 254

Indexes 255

    Clustered Indexes 255

    Nonclustered Indexes...257

Summary 259

3.6   Adding Groups and Setting Permissions   261

Adding Logins to the SQL Server 262

    Aliasing 267

    setuser 268

Summary 268

3.7   Defining and Using Dump Devices   271

Defining Your Dump Device 272

Backing Up Your Data 274

Reloading a Database from a Dump Device 276

Restoring the Master Device 278

Summary 279

4 Using SQL Server Features

4.1   Sybase-Supplied Stored Procedures   283

Getting Around SQL Server 284

Manipulating Database Objects 293

    Systems Procedures for Documenting Key Relationships 304

Summary 307

4.2   Database Integrity   309

Ensuring Data Integrity through Rules and Defaults 310

    Defining Defaults 311

    Rules 312

Incorporating Rules and Defaults into
    User-Defined Datatypes 316

Summary 317

4.3   TransAct SQL   319

What Is TransAct SQL? 320

T-SQL Extensions and Enhancements 321

    Wildcards 323

    String Operations and Manipulation 325

    Datetime Functions 327

    Aggregate Functions 330

    Mathematical Functions 332

    Systems Functions 334

    Changing the Order of the Output 335

    Using COMPUTE BY in a SELECT Statement 337

Summary 338

4.4   Writing Stored Procedures   339

Stored Procedures Defined 340
The Benefits of Stored Procedures 340
Writing Stored Procedures 341
Returning Values and Status Messages
from Stored Procedures...343
Stored Procedure Restrictions 344
Remote Procedures 344
Summary 344

4.5   Triggers and Referential Integrity   347

Referential Integrity 348
Using Triggers 349
Trigger Syntax 349
Cascading Deletes 350
Trigger Behavior 352
Summary 353

4.6   Writing Transactions in SQL Server   355

Statement Blocks, Batches, and Transactions Defined..............356
Special Batches 357
Containing Batches within Transactions 358
Transactions 358
Incorporating Stored Procedures and
Remote Procedure Calls within Transactions.....................360
Rollbacks and Triggers...361
Nesting Transactions 361
Error Handling within Transactions 361
Transaction Restrictions 364
Two-Phase Commit 364
Summary 367

4.7   Table Locks in SQL Server   369

The Need for Concurrency Controls in SQL Server.................370
SQL Server Locks...370
Shared Locks 371
Update Locks...371
Exclusive Locks 371
How the Locks Interact 371
Deadlocks 373
Table versus Page Locking 374
Holdlocks 374

Browse Mode 374

Summary 376

4.8   The SQL Server Systems Tables   377

SQL Server Systems Tables 378

Accessing Systems Tables with Stored Procedures 381

Master Database Systems Tables 383

Summary 385

4.9   The Use of Cursors in SQL Server   387

Cursors Defined 388

Positioning within Cursors 389

Cursors and Concurrency 389

How Cursors Work... 390

Restrictions on Cursors 391

Incorporating Cursors into Open Client Applications 391

Summary 392

4.10   Opportunities for Optimization   393

The Importance of Good Design 394

Indexing Options 396

Query Structure 397

Defining and Monitoring Performance 399

Areas of Performance Impact 400

Rule #1: Give the User What He or She Wants 401

Rule #2: Give the User Something to Do 401

Rule #3: Explain Everything as a Benefit (But Don't Lie) 401

Rule #4: Take Advantage of the Environment 401

Rule #5: Second-Guess Your Assumptions 402

Performance of the Technology 402

Host Performance 403

SQL Server Performance 404

Using SHOWPLAN 404

Using FORCEPLAN 407

Rules of Thumb 408

Query Examples 410

Storing Redundant Data 410

Costs and Implications of Normalization 411

Denormalization through Redundancy 412

Denormalization through Table Segmentation 412

Contrived Columns 413

Database Objects and Performance 413

Calculating Table Size and Data Pages 414
Hardware Impact on Performance 423
Network Performance 425
Wide-Area Networks......................................426
Balancing the Load 427
Summary 427

5   The Open Client Architecture

5.1   The Open Client DB-Library   431
What Is Open Client DB-Library? 432
Establishing a Connection 433
   Assembling the Command Batch 435
   Sending the Commands to the SQL Server.............436
   Managing the Returned Results 437
   Closing the Connection 440
   Error Handling 441
Programming Functions Available with
   Open Client DB-Library............................442
Sample DB-Library Program 450
Summary 452

5.2   Using DB-Library Calls in the C/C++
Programming Environment   453
Installing Open Client DB-Library 455
Open Client DB-Library for PC/DOS 455
Compiling the Test Program 460
Incorporating Open Client DB-Library Calls
   into Windows Programs 465
Installing Open Client DB-Library for PC/Windows.............466
   Compiling the Windows Test Program Under
      Microsoft Visual C/C++ 1.0 (MSVC) 467
The SQLTEST3.C Application 468
Interpreting the Sample Program 484
Windows Templates 484
Other Capabilities Available through
   Open Client DB-Library............................497
Cursors through the Open Client DB-Library API 500
Bulk Copy Functions in DB-Library 520
Summary 524

5.3   Connecting Personal Computers to a SQL Server   525

Sybase Networks—A User's Perspective 526

How a PC Client Talks to the SQL Server 528

Communications Hardware 529

    Network Card Notes 529

    Communications Drivers 530

Application-Supplied Board-Specific Drivers 530

Sybase Net-Lib Explained 530

PC Communications Software Options 532

    Packet Drivers 533

    ODI (Open Data-Link Interconnect) 533

    NDIS (Network Data Interchange Specification) 533

    Named Pipes 534

Installation Scenarios 534

    Sybase Client Scenario #1:

      Novell Only with a DOS Client 534

    Sybase Client Scenario #2:

      Novell Only with a Windows Client 535

    Sybase Client Scenario #3: UNIX Host Only 536

    Sybase Client Scenario #4:

      Concurrent Access to a UNIX Host, NetWare,

      and SQL Server from a Windows-Based PC 537

    Summary 537

5.4   Troubleshooting Net-Lib Connections   539

Diagnosing Network Problems 541

An Example Case 544

    The Problem 545

    The Approach 545

More Problem-Solving Approaches 546

    Symptom 546

    Action Steps 546

Summary 547

Section Summary 548

6   Front-End Tools and Utilities

6.1   Sybase-Supplied Utilities   551

ISQL 552

BCP Bulk Copy 554

    Fast Bulk Copy 555

Slow Bulk Copy 555

Interactive Bulk Copy 556

defncopy 556

Summary 557

6.2   Build Momentum   559

Build Momentum and Object Orientation 560

Dynamic Compilation 562

Stratification of Systems Skills 562

Team Development Facilities 563

The Application Development Environment 564

Database Browser 564

Development Features 565

Applications Deployment 566

Summary 566

6.3   PowerTools for Microsoft Windows Development   569

Windows Client Development 571

Connecting PowerBuilder to a Database 571

The GUI Development Environment 573

PowerBuilder's DataWindows 574

Structures, Cursors, and Functions within PowerBuilder 577

Drag-and-Drop and Other Windows Features 577

A Practical Example 578

The PowerSoft Product Suite and Target Market 580

PowerBuilder and Third-Party Products 582

Summary 582

6.4   Database Publishing   585

The Requirement 586

Seamless Transparency 587

Third-Party Software 588

The Microsoft Office 588

Batch Printing 590

Summary 591

6.5   Using CASE Tools with SQL Server   593

Why Use CASE? 595

Where Do CASE Tools Fit in the Development Cycle? 595

Who Uses CASE Tools? 596

What Is a CASE Tool? 596

Using a CASE Tool 597

A Practical Example 598
   Using CASE to Model a Bookstore Application 598
   Defining Domains for the Column Values 599
   Generating Data Definition Language from a CASE Tool ... 600
   Designing and Documenting Referential Integrity 602
   Managing Multiple Databases 603
Summary 604

7   New Products and Emerging Trends

7.1   What's New in SQL Server Release 10.0   609

New Features 610
SQL Server Architecture Changes 611
   New Installation Utility 612
   Backup Server 612
   Security Features 613
   Audit Server 614
   Cursors 614
   Declarative Referential Integrity 614
   New Datatypes 615
   Changes to Keywords Allowed in Transactions,
      Triggers, and Stored Procedures 615
   Trigger Behavior 616
   Changes to Views 617
   Create Schema 617
   Datatype Conversion Changes 617
   Query and Data Modification Changes 617
   Set FIPS Flagger 618
   Chained Transactions 618
   Transaction Isolation Levels 618
   Other ANSI Standard Features 619
   Systems Administration 619
   Chargeback Statistics 620
   DBCC Option 620
   Kill Command 620
   Space Monitoring 620
   Create Index Performance Enhancements 620
   Query Optimizer Enhancements 621
   Bulk Copy Performance Improvements 621
   Set Options 621

Upgrading to SQL Server Release 10.0 628

Prerequisites for Upgrading 628

Changes to Existing Database Objects 628

Summary 628

7.2   Remote Client/Server Solutions   631

The Remote Client 632

The Significance of Bandwidth and Speed 634

The Relationship Between Speed and Capacity 635

Remote Client/Server Defined 636

Wide-Area Communications Options 638

Asynchronous Dial-Up Lines 638

Packet-Switching Networks 639

Private Packet-Switching Networks 640

New Products and Services 640

Frame Relay 640

Integrated Services Digital Network (ISDN) 641

Switched Multimegabit Data Service (SMDS) 641

Asynchronous Transfer Mode (ATM) 641

Designing for Remote Clients 642

Summary 643

Section Summary 644

8   Glossary

8.1   Glossary   645

Index 657

Acknowledgments

Having read about the great many people acknowledged in other books, I had no idea just how many people contributed to the creation and refinement of a project like this. I probably will forget someone in the following list, and if I do, please know that I appreciate all of your efforts, listed here or not.

I would like to thank Scott Jerome-Parks for his support, ideas, and feedback from the beginning. Likewise, thanks to Jim Munro for his help with DB-Library programming and Rob Quinn for stored procedures. And, thanks to Breck Carter for his curmudgeonly, but trenchant, observations and assistance.

Thanks definitely due to the Word N Systems, Inc. team—John Daum, Jim Blakely, Marie Worden, Jannette Anderson, and Sue Carter—for their infinite patience, support, and feedback, not to mention DBA@Win.

Sybase Toronto helped with the Build Momentum demonstration and tutorial. Thanks, Derek Molliet and Steve Reynolds, for your time.

Thanks go to my Florida SQL Server class who helped me gain insight into how to structure the book and make it relevant to experienced IS people moving to client/server. Thanks due to Norm Turnbull, Jr., Tim Nichol, Kynerd Coleman, Don Coy, Sharon Litz, Cheryl Taylor, Suzanne Simonel, Christine Huffman, Kurt Jefferson, and Andrew Blakeslee. You were great guinea pigs!

The editorial and production staff at SAMS were not only great to work with, supportive and enthusiastic, but really willing to work with me on up to the last-minute revisions, improvements, and deletions. Thank you Chris Denny, Dean Miller, Angie Trzepacz, Cheri Clark and Susan Christophersen.

Last but not least, thanks and acknowledgment to my family, especially Alexander, Tristan, and Marie, who gave up so much time while this project was completed.

Introduction

Because you are reading this book, I assume you have an interest in client/server computing generally, and Sybase SQL Server specifically. After that, it gets tough to make assumptions about you and your situation. Perhaps it will save time and help you gain a better insight into *Sybase Developer's Guide* if I simply tell you something about this book and what it is intended to be.

SQL Server applications invariably involve a convergence of many diverse technologies: relational database, networking, workstations, GUIs, CASE tools, development methodologies, various host platforms, staffing roles, project management techniques, and more. *Sybase Developer's Guide* was intended to cover *all* aspects of the client/server continuum as they relate to a SQL Server. This has proven to be an ambitious undertaking, indeed.

The key to integrating this wide range of topics can be found in a single question: What do I wish someone had told me the first time I designed and implemented a Sybase client/server system? Realistically, no one can prepare you fully for the challenge of implementing your first client/server system. The number of variables—and the range of unknowns—is staggering. At the same time, it is not necessary to hack your way through the client/server jungle entirely alone; some trails are already marked. The purpose of this book is to give you a guide through the first part of your journey into the brave new world of client/server systems. It should prove a useful tool to help shape your understanding of Sybase, and assist you in identifying specific aspects of your application that may need special attention.

Successful SQL Server applications are built on integration. More than merely systems integration, this integration also involves tying together users and developers, proven systems techniques with new capabilities, and leveraging investment in existing skill sets with new learning.

Sybase Developer's Guide provides an end-to-end view of client/server systems built using a SQL Server database engine as a core component. Necessarily, as it deals with all aspects of client/server applications, it is not intended as a "down and in" detailed reference on any particular aspect. This book will be of particular appeal to experienced systems people who are new to client/server technology and are preparing to work with their first Sybase (or Microsoft) SQL Server.

No matter what your particular role in that critical first project is to be—Architect, DBA, Project Leader, or Developer—this book was written with your requirements in mind. In preparing the materials for *Sybase Developer's Guide*, I met systems people with a wide variety of backgrounds and responsibilities. Some were mainframers who knew a great deal about data modeling and structured methodologies, but were struggling with integration of event-driven GUI-based client applications. Others had a great deal of experience building highly effective PC based solutions but had to grapple with the function and requirements of the back-end database. Frequently, both these groups had black holes where networking information needed to be. These professionals were also asked the question, "What did you wish someone had told you when you first got into Sybase client/server systems?"

This book is the result of that feedback. It is intended to be the first book you use on your project, not the last word on any aspect of client/server technology. The currently nonexistent *Complete Sybase Developer's Guide* will have to wait until the technology stops evolving at its current breakneck pace. But I wouldn't look for that slowing of technology to happen any day soon.

This book has been organized into the stages an organization would generally undergo as it evaluated, planned, and implemented its first SQL Server system.

Section One, "Introduction to Sybase Client/Server," introduces you to Sybase, Inc., its history and product line. This background will help you gain an understanding of the product's roots, and will clarify some of the reasons why Sybase SQL Server has emphasized certain architectural characteristics over its competitors. This should also give you some insight into what the company will do in the future, based on past behavior. Also, especially for those of you being thrown into the Sybase client/server arena for the first time, the section reviews why all the pain and effort of implementing Sybase SQL Server is worthwhile.

Additionally, you will be taken through several case studies, examples based on real-world experiences with the SQL Server product. These examples are intended to be representative of the nature and scope of Sybase projects everywhere.

Lastly, the first section will introduce you to the SQL Server architecture, paying particular attention to those features that make it unique.

Section Two, "Defining the Development Environment," walks you through the roles, responsibilities, and steps necessary to develop a plan or model from which you can begin to work with Sybase. We all know that the greatest temptation facing any technical person is to start work without a comprehensive plan. In this section, the preliminary planning processes are identified and discussed as they relate to a Sybase client/server project. Much of this material will be review for those of you with structured systems backgrounds; still, it may prove interesting and useful to see how much of the traditional approach is applicable to the new technologies.

This section will be of great utility for anyone involved in planning and managing an up-sizing project where your existing system is on an Xbase/PC LAN environment. Developers will benefit from reading this section to help them understand the modeling and specification process in order to determine what they will need to establish before beginning work on the project.

Section Three, "Installing and Configuring SQL Server," gets into the installation of SQL Server and platform-specific issues. Those of you working with a single SQL Server will no doubt focus on your particular configuration—although Sybase client sites increasingly are implementing SQL Server on multiple platforms—to take into account the support and processing requirements of each discrete group. Reading through the descriptions of each issue may give you a better appreciation of the distinctions and restrictions from one host to another.

Everyone involved in installing and configuring a SQL Server on any platform will get something out of the review of devices, resources and options covered in this section. Administration activities such as establishing users, groups, and permissions, as well as backing up and restoring databases, are also covered.

Section Four, "Using SQL Server Features," gets into the more meaty aspects of SQL Server from a developer's perspective. The Sybase implementation of SQL is covered, including each of its extensions and uses. Database objects such as stored procedures, triggers, rules, views, tables, and datatypes are also explored.

How these features can be used to implement business rules and enforce referential integrity is discussed. Also in this section, you are taken through the SQL Server approach to logging, locks, and transaction management.

At the end of this section you are taken through several methods of evaluating and optimizing SQL Server performance for your specific requirements.

Section Five, "The Open Client Architecture," moves outside the Sybase database engine itself and explains exactly how the open client architecture can be used to tie various client programs back to the SQL Server. The Sybase approach to connectivity is explored from the most simplistic level of connect read-only query tools through to writing C/C++ programs that access SQL Server data through Open Client DB-Library calls. Not only are these features covered conceptually, but there are several examples of C/C++ programs for DOS and Windows developers to use in developing your own applications.

This section provides developers, power users, and systems architects alike a grounding in the multitude of options available for meeting requirements for accessing SQL Server data from the myriad client platforms existing in the real world.

Section Six, "Front-End Tools and Utilities," deals with front-end tools and utilities, whether shipped with Sybase or acquired from third-party vendors. Along with introducing you to the popular development tool PowerBuilder, you also get a look at the direction of new object-oriented development tools from Sybase. Shrink-wrapped query tools are also covered, to round out the discussion of the various types of client programs that can be used in building a suite of applications accessing and manipulating SQL Server data. Particular attention is paid to how you can minimize the amount of time necessary to meet any given user requirement, which allows you to increase the time available to build high-profile custom applications. The integration and use of CASE tools for modeling and creating data-definition language scripts are also covered in this section.

Section Seven, "New Products and Emerging Trends," deals with the new features incorporated into SQL Server Release 10.0. Wherever possible, the book has been applicable to all versions of SQL Server currently on the market. By separating Release 10.0 into a separate chapter, you can review the new features and determine whether they warrant the upgrade immediately or if you will want to wait. For many platforms, SQL Server Release 10.0 is not yet available, so this chapter will give you a better sense of what you are waiting for.

Lastly, this section contains a discussion on emerging trends and their potential impact on your SQL Server applications. The hype over the information highway sometimes obscures existing communications options and the quiet strides that are continually being made in wide-area networks. This section gives you a frame of reference for watching these developments and helping you determine when and how to use them to provide SQL Server access to remote users and clients.

Not only have the syntax examples been provided to save you some typing, but several automated indexes and quick look-up utilities have been included so that you can quickly identify and retrieve relevant information.

And last, but by no means least, a front-end database tool has been provided so that you may be more productive in your access of SQL Server. As you get more experienced with Sybase, you will quickly get tired of the ISQL command-line interface, so we have thoughtfully provided a windows-based DBA and developers tool to replace it.

All in all, a great deal of effort has been put into this tome and its success is directly dependent on how useful the book is for you. I hope that after reading this, you find it that much easier to face the variables and unknowns of your particular project and that you will be able to say, "I was glad I found that out before I got started."

In closing, I should probably say something about the writing style used in this book. Many of you will agree that nothing is more tedious than a dry technical treatise. To alleviate this somewhat, I have elected to sprinkle bad puns, acerbic observations, and Groucho Marx asides liberally throughout the book. I hope this makes reading the book a more pleasant experience without detracting from the value of the technical points discussed.

Last, I would like to stress that all of us involved in creating this work recognize the importance of technical accuracy. To this end, and to keep you, the reader, up to date with changes and refinements regarding SQL Server as they occur, we are creating a topic area under the PHCP forum on CompuServe. I will be lurking on CompuServe to personally address any questions, comments, observations, or (heaven forbid) criticisms you may wish to note. Perhaps even more useful will be the updates and news that will be posted on this forum to keep you abreast of changes and revisions as they are identified. I am confident that this forum will prove to be a useful source of ongoing feedback and reference for readers of *Sybase Developer's Guide*.

Regards,

Daniel J. Worden

1

Introduction to Sybase Client/Server

Introduction

THIS PART OF THE BOOK HAS BEEN INCLUDED FOR THOSE OF YOU who believe the best place to start something is at the beginning. Instead of getting right down to technical brass tacks, this section takes you through an introduction to Sybase the company: its products and its position in the marketplace. This section also describes the architecture of SQL Server itself. Finally, this section covers how client/server can be used in organizations and how it affects the methods with which you develop systems.

Consider this the high-level "context diagram" for the book as a whole. By reading this chapter you will be much more familiar with the overall Sybase culture and philosophy. You then can appreciate how this background has contributed to the development of SQL Server and other Sybase products.

Just as important, you should find yourself better able to assess your own experience and relate that to what it takes to build client/server systems using Sybase products.

For those of you who are focused on the technology alone, I recommend that you at least read Chapter 1.3 of this section. It is better still to take the time to read the material on systems development practices and techniques, as this will help you better understand how to use this new technology.

1.1

The Enterprise Client/Server Solution

Today Sybase is strategically positioned for providing integrated database systems across the entire organization. To understand how the vendor arrived at this point, it will help you to understand some background about the company itself.

Those of you more interested in getting right into the SQL Server product line and its features and benefits can skip to Chapter 1.2.

In the Beginning

In 1984, Mark B. Hoffman and Robert Epstein founded Sybase, Inc. At that time, Oracle had already been selling its relational database and tools for almost five years. Ingres and Informix were also already marketing commercial RDBMS products. DB2 was offered as the relational database management solution for IBM mainframes, and DEC supported RDB for its Vax product line. Sybase became the last new player in the relational database market.

The two men had a clear vision for the Sybase SQL Server: to create a truly open, high-performance, online, transaction-processing, relational database using client/server architecture. Whereas other relational database vendors were pushing tightly coupled databases and toolsets, Sybase saw the need to allow the database to be accessible to a vast array of programs and tools. This vision set the embryonic Sybase product distinctly apart from its competitors.

Less than 10 years later, Sybase has attained market acceptance and technical leadership, if not market dominance. This remarkable achievement is due primarily to the superior technical vision laid out by the company's founders and how well the product has delivered on that vision. Whereas some companies succeed on the strength of their marketing and self-promotion, Sybase has grown by delivering a solid product that meets needs its customers might not even know they had.

A New Approach to Relational Systems

Most relational databases were designed in an era when character-based terminals and batch programs operated on a single host. They were built for the host/slave model of computing. The Sybase vision saw past that architecture. Sybase may not have invented the client/server computing model, but it was the first to incorporate this architecture into a relational database, and the first to effectively promote the concept as an entirely new way to build systems.

To Sybase, client/server meant the exact opposite of the host/slave architecture, which made multiple applications run on one machine. Client/server allowed one application to run on multiple machines. It supported shared resources and balanced the use of processing power across many devices.

The real key to the client/server concept is the idea that a machine can be either a client of another system, a server to other machines, or both at the same time. This implies that the machine cooperates with other systems—that it provides some services and requests others. It also requires the machines to be interconnected over a local or wide area network. These prerequisites to a client/server database system simply did not exist in the era when most host/slave software products were developed.

Even when running on a single host, SQL Server was designed to operate in two separate and distinct components: the front- and back-end processes. Still today, the definition and implications of the client/server architecture escape most people who are just introduced to the technology. Perhaps this is due to a misunderstanding of just how tightly coupled most traditional RDBMS processes have been.

It is natural to think of the application running against the data as a separate and distinct process from the database engine. Before the Sybase implementation of client/server, however, this was not truly the case. The database server would run the application, and the user would simply use his or her application to view the results. In essence, the traditional approach gave users a way to view a single process, one that incorporated both the application and the database server. Sybase broke these processes apart and treated them as separate but equally important parts of an overall client/server equation.

The 1980's Market

The reality of most organizations looking for relational database solutions in the 1980s was a multicomputer environment. Much of the time, multiple computers meant multiple vendors. As intended, the client/server design concept allowed the SQL Server product to accommodate more than single-host environments. At Sybase, client/server meant that front-end processes could execute on one machine and connect over the network to a SQL Server back-end, splitting the workload across the two machines. This capability allowed database applications developers to fully exploit the various systems already in place in their organizations.

The SQL Server vision didn't end there.

Front-end processes did not have to be Sybase products running against SQL Server. When SQL Server was introduced, the other relational database companies did not provide access to their database other than through their own tightly coupled applications development tools, except through precompilers. These precompilers allowed a program written in another language, such as C, COBOL, or FORTRAN, to issue calls to the database and return the resulting rows to the program. This was the only way customers could build their own application or integrate their existing applications with the database. The value of this approach was still considerable, inasmuch as the database was relational. Throughout the 1980s, organizations moved applications wholesale from the hierarchical databases of the previous era, but not all relational databases incorporate the client/server architecture. Sybase, on the other hand, designed the SQL Server for the client/server architecture from the beginning.

Instead of simply offering precompilers like its competitors, Sybase published its Application Programming Interface, DB-LIB. Sybase opened up access to the SQL Server to anyone who wanted to write an application that talked to SQL Server by allowing them to interface with DB-LIB, which in turn talked to the SQL Server. This created an opportunity for third-party developers to write applications to do just that, enabling their programs to take advantage of the power of the SQL Server back-end. Because Open Client DB-Library used the same calls from one platform to the next, porting an application that talked to DB-LIB from one host environment to another was made significantly easier.

Through this, Sybase provided a truly open client/server database product.

Advantages of SQL Server

The client/server architecture offered significant, though subtle, advantages to those organizations that adopted SQL Server-based solutions. This was not the most significant attraction of the SQL Server product over others on the market, however. Systems designers and developers were interested in the client/server architecture and the different features offered by Sybase, but in the beginning that was not the basis for their buying decision. For most developers, the key difference between Sybase and its relational database competitors was performance. Sybase was, and is, a high-performance product.

To get that performance, Sybase had to not only write very efficient code but incorporate several features not available from competitive products. Specifically, stored procedures, triggers, and rules set the product apart from any other database.

The Programmable Database

By offering stored procedures, Sybase created a programmable database. Developers could decide to write an application that submitted SQL calls to the server, or they could write SQL routines on the database itself. Unlike SQL calls from an application, these routines were already compiled, making it unnecessary for the database to work out a query plan each time they were run. This allowed them to run significantly faster than other queries that had to first be optimized and then executed.

This programmable server allowed for the centralized control over data integrity after the database was programmed using stored procedures. Application developers could then develop applications without being overly concerned about data corruption, and the DBA did not have to worry about integrity issues posed by each individual front-end. Stored procedures also cut down on network traffic and allowed developers to be insulated from the underlying data structure.

Event-Driven Triggers

Triggers were defined as special stored procedures that fired automatically when any insert, delete, or update operation was performed on a table. In this way, developers could incorporate business rules into the database itself and ensure data integrity. By adding support across the network for SQL Servers to use remote procedure calls, triggers on one SQL Server could fire stored procedures on another. This allowed transparent, automatic, event-driven linkages between servers.

Multithreading

The other major innovation incorporated into the SQL Server architecture from the outset was multithreading. Other products relied on the operating system to manage connections to the database. This meant that performance degraded significantly as more users were added. Worse still, from a database user's viewpoint, every login session to the server took a bite out of the resources available for his or her database processes. On a production system, a print job or terminal session on a UNIX or Vax host, for example, counted against the database users for performance.

Sybase got around this by managing the database connections as part of the SQL Server, instead of allowing the operating system to manage the process. Sybase chose to fundamentally insulate the database engine from the rest of the computer. Most minicomputer or server operating systems are designed to be general purpose. They do everything as well as they can. Sybase knew it was in the database engine business, and it needed to optimize the server hardware to provide services specifically for database processing requirements. Sybase decided to take over the tasks of managing the hardware resources from the operating system.

It was a lot of work, but it paid off. Benchmarks comparing SQL Server performance when loaded with many users showed that SQL Server significantly outperformed any other similarly loaded product on the market.

By implementing a database product that conformed to the founders' vision of an open-architecture, client/server, high-performance, online, transaction-processing database, Sybase successfully created a powerful, competitive database engine truly distinct from its competitors.

Rounding Out the Product Line

In 1990, Sybase added to its product line by offering its SQL LifeCycle graphical tools for design, creation, testing, and maintenance of SQL-based applications. The tools strategy was twofold. From the outset, Sybase had wanted to encourage customers and third-party developers to write applications and even competitive tools as part of the open architecture. Second, Sybase recognized that customers wanted to maximize their investment in older technologies. To respond to this, Sybase wanted to offer development, query, and reporting tools that would span the client-side environment from character-based terminals to higher-end workstations with graphical user interfaces.

These tools—A Productivity Tool (APT) and DataWorkBench (DWB)—allowed user connections to the database from dumb terminals, UNIX workstations running Motif, or personal computers and Macintoshes. With the appropriate open-client software, applications developed with the products in one environment could be called up on any other platform and would operate without change. The key to the strategy was allowing organizations to continue using their existing character-based terminals, as well as the more expensive and less pervasive workstations. Of course, to support this, the tools tended to present screens with capabilities based on the lowest common denominator.

Open Server

As well as offering their SQL Server and later tools for client software development, Sybase acknowledged the need to incorporate other database products into its client/server vision. Enter the Open Server technology. To tie client applications back to other more proprietary databases, Sybase developed the Open Server toolkit to provide gateways to products such as IBM's DB2. In this way, Sybase began to move its product line and toolset into the role of pulling the customers' diverse database processes into a coherent whole. This was the beginning of the move to enterprise-wide systems thinking, which would later dominate the company's strategy.

DEFT CASE Tool

To strengthen the database development process through product offerings, in 1991 Sybase acquired DEFT, a Canadian CASE tool developer. DEFT provides database modelers with the capability to represent their data structures in entity-relationship diagrams and use the tools to produce tables, stored procedures, and triggers from the data model. DEFT even allows developers to reverse-engineer Oracle and DB2 databases by feeding the table descriptions into the CASE tool and generating appropriate SQL Server Data Description Language, for the creation of database objects.

More recently, Sybase has developed and announced connectivity products such as OmniSQL Gateway, a method of integrating DB2, Oracle, Ingres, and other relational and nonrelational databases with a SQL Server and its clients. By incorporating OmniSQL Gateway, an open client application may even transparently pass SQL calls against data contained in tables on a remote non-SQL Server database. This allows database architects and developers to connect the client once and then pass the client through to the other non-Sybase database resources, rather than having to interconnect every client with every server.

From the beginning, the Sybase vision for database applications revolved around multiple hosts from multiple vendors. Instead of the proprietary locked-in products of the past, the SQL Server was designed to offer a way of integrating and connecting a wide variety of computers and applications in true client/server fashion.

Rather than having to evaluate and correct the mistakes of yesterday to provide suitable products today, Sybase is in a position to reap the benefits of having been fundamentally on the right track from the beginning. This is quite an attractive feature to those developers who invested time and effort in learning the company's products and working with the new client/server paradigm.

The Present

With the announcement that Oracle 7 would include Sybase-initiated innovations such as stored procedures, triggers, and support for remote procedure calls, Sybase became the technical leader in the relational database marketplace. Sybase had designed these features into its database product from the outset, and now the competitor with the largest market share had to play catch-up.

This did not intimidate Sybase senior management. Sybase staff has stated in interviews that this move by Oracle acknowledges that the Sybase vision for client/server is a strong one. Continuing to define and refine that vision is the challenge to Sybase.

And characteristically, the company has not rested on its laurels. In 1993 alone, the company began delivery of several key new product offerings, including System 10, the newest Sybase product set including SQL Server 10, OmniSQL Gateway, the Replication Server, and Audit Server.

The introduction of third-party development tools such as PowerBuilder and Uniface for MS-Windows and X-Windows has also lent strength to any decision to go with SQL Server. The company is committed to continued open access to their servers through DB-LIB. Sybase recognizes that enabling clients to pick and choose among many modular products from Sybase and others strengthens its position in the marketplace. The open architecture is a key feature of the SQL Server and one of the reasons why the marketplace has rewarded Sybase.

Improving Support

The early 1990s has been a period of repositioning and restructuring for the company. Support policies and capabilities had been the source of frequent complaints over the first few years of the SQL Server and other products' lives. With the spread of SQL Server products to more mainstream IS shops as opposed to technology pioneers, the demands for support have increased dramatically. Coupled with the exponential growth in sales, the management of Sybase has been presented with a significant challenge.

Sybase has taken some time to address those issues within the context of an overall support program. By introducing new support facilities in Burlington, Massachusetts and dedicating federal government support centers in Bethesda, Maryland, Sybase has restructured to effectively accommodate the rapid and steady growth of the SQL Server install base.

As a provider of worldwide solutions to global companies, Sybase has recognized the need to offer support services that reflect the multinational makeup of the company's customers. Internationally, Sybase has opened support centers in Holland, Switzerland, and Japan.

New and Improved Tools

The company has also been active on the tool front. Not content to offer just SQL LifeCycle tools, in 1992 the company acquired Gain Technology and its Gain Momentum client/server tools. As a subsidiary of Sybase, Gain is now in the process of optimizing those tools to take better advantage of the SQL Server product. These object-oriented multimedia tools will enhance the capability of Sybase and related companies to provide customers with an integrated environment of development tools, servers, and connectivity options. The Gain products, however, have more of a market than simply as an adjunct to SQL Servers, so Sybase has decided to continue to market the products under the original Gain banner.

Developing New Server Products

Enterprise client/server solutions pose a great many issues of complexity, integration, and scale. Despite the growth enjoyed by Sybase to date, significant maturation is still on the horizon. The company is committed to becoming "the enterprise client/server company." It is presently in the throes of restructuring its product lines and internal organization to be able to reach this stated goal.

The SQL Server is at the heart of the Sybase product line. System 10 is the new name for the combined suite of client/server products, including the SQL Server database engine, Replication Server, and OmniSQL Gateway.

The System 10 Replication Server will be integral to customers who are looking for a practical and effective method of implementing distributed databases. Based on Sybase Open Server technology, the Replication Server shares data by distributing copies across the enterprise. The Replication Server handles the synchronization of the data through a number of control programs residing on the various database servers on the network. Data can be replicated as a function of a transaction or at designated time intervals. SQL Servers, Oracle and DB2 databases, and even nonrelational data sources can be integrated. The customer beta test began in June 1993 for SunOs and IBM RS/6000 platforms. Beta testing of Digital's Alpha OSF/1, the HP 9000, NCR 3000, and Solaris systems followed later in the year.

Future Developments

Anyone at Sybase will tell you that the future looks bright. And for Sybase customers, the future holds much more than watching the company post increased revenues from new installations as the popularity of its products grow. For Sybase developers, the future will require the company's continued technological trailblazing. Developers will be expecting Sybase to continue to offer new products that provide strategic and tactical capabilities. Sybase developers can then integrate these and other products into client/server solutions that benefit everyone.

Sybase has hinted at future involvement in areas such as electronic support systems (EPSS). This concept incorporates training and education components as well as services into the scope of applications. The multimedia capabilities of tools such as the Gain Momentum products could be used to develop applications that provide "as-you-use training" rather than the more limited online help screens offered by applications today. By involving themselves in such initiatives, Sybase is looking for ways to provide technological leadership, demonstrating and supporting whole new uses of technology that were not possible with the previous generation of systems products.

On the policy and directions level, Sybase has publicly announced the company's commitment to several developing technologies. The Distributed Computing Environment (DCE) from OSF provides a set of specifications to support directory, security, and timing services for distributed computing environments. The tangible form of Sybase's support is the demonstration of a prototype SQL Server 10 that incorporates the DCE technology. By supporting this facility, Sybase is clearly demonstrating its commitment to distributed computing and enterprise client/server. Ultimately, developing database applications under DCE will ensure that all server resources are utilized in a balanced and optimized fashion. Compute cycles will be transparently distributed across different servers, depending on availability and processing requirements.

On the language front, Sybase and Intermetrics have announced their codevelopment of a commercially available SQL Ada Module Description Language precompiler. This will make writing Ada client software less development-intensive, and allow Ada programmers to become more productive when writing applications that connect to SQL Servers.

Sybase products were originally intended to help integrate relational database technology with existing platforms and client software. As organizations continue to gain experience with client/server, however, it is becoming increasingly apparent that incorporating new technology onto a patchwork quilt of existing systems does not yield the biggest benefits to the user organization.

Robert Epstein has gone on record as saying the way to get the best return from your client/server investment is to reengineer the business processes that the system is supposed to support. Equally clear is the need to integrate workgroup and departmental client/server solutions into a fully functional enterprise solution.

What is just as important, but not quite as obvious, is the need to develop and define new development models to successfully implement and integrate client/server technology. The old methodologies were developed to build large systems using the traditional host/slave, character-based, closed-architecture products. These methods are no longer appropriate for dealing with the unique issues posed by enterprise client/server solutions; as yet, no new method has emerged as the dominant model to take the place of the mature, more traditional systems development methodologies.

By observing corporate directions and new products, you can begin to see the shape of the future as projected by Sybase. It falls to you, however, to develop systems for your organization that take advantage of the promise of these technologies and prove the validity of the Sybase vision.

The Emerging Client/Server Marketplace

Since the first version of SQL Server was made commercially available in 1987, Sybase sales have grown dramatically. Public and private sector organizations have enthusiastically adopted Sybase products, with the result that client/server has become a standard industry buzzword. Company revenues have grown from $103 million in 1990 to $160 million in 1991 and $250 million in 1992.

Multiplatform support for SQL Server has been a key objective for Sybase from the beginning, and although OS/2, VMS, and NetWare NLM versions of SQL Server have been sold and supported, UNIX-based servers account for 60 percent of the company's install base.

Early users of Sybase products tended to be more technical pioneers, people who knew what they wanted from technology and were prepared to work out the complications to get it. New Sybase customers seem to be from more mainstream systems environments. Economic trends, as well as executive and end-user pressure, have increasingly put corporate systems departments into downsizing mode. Sybase serves these customers by providing a high-performance database engine that is reaching maturity, and Sybase can point to successful installations of many configurations in any industry or sector. Third-party products for site-wide backup and automated administration are also beginning to address the concerns of organizations with large networks and rigid up-time requirements.

On the other end of the spectrum, many smaller organizations are in the process of outgrowing their flat-file dBASE and Paradox applications. These prospective customers are considering upsizing, or migrating to a more powerful client/server environment, to gain the benefits of relational technology. The scalability of SQL Server has brought this technology into the price range of PC LAN customers. Once again, the commitment to open architecture as part of the Sybase vision makes the product more attractive than the products of many competitors.

In both cases, the Sybase implementation of client/server technology offers the greatest benefits to a customer organization. For large organizations, the benefits include the ability to support SQL Servers on multiple platforms and integrate multiple, concurrent client applications on terminals, PCs, Macintoshes, or UNIX workstations.

For smaller outfits, the key advantage is the capability to seamlessly integrate SQL Server with the client software with which these organizations are already familiar.

No matter where in the customer continuum your development challenge falls, you can be sure that Sybase provides a strong feature set and proven products for your platform, and that the company will continue to enhance and upgrade its product offerings.

Third-Party Products

Many Sybase customers will tell you that one of the key strengths of the Sybase approach to the client/server arena is its open architecture. As I mentioned, the original vision of the product not only allowed but encouraged connection of third-party products and applications in the SQL Server environment. This has provided fertile ground for the development of application-specific programs and specialized application-development tools.

Sybase has remained consistent in its position that it is not a provider of end-user applications. If you are a third-party developer of Sybase solutions, you do not have to be concerned that your software will suddenly be competing with Sybase-developed applications. Sybase sells no products like Oracle Financials, for example, which is developed, sold, and supported by Oracle. The responsibility for development of application-specific software incorporating Sybase products falls strictly to third-party developers and end users.

This does not mean that the company has overlooked the need to provide and promote off-the-shelf solutions using its own technology. Far from it. The company has long recognized the need to provide an even greater combination of applications and support tools than it could develop and market on its own. Sybase knows that it wins only by providing the greatest possible range of options to its customers, who can, in turn, combine those options to form effective solutions to meet their organization's requirements.

Like systems manufacturers such as Sun and HP, Sybase provides marketing support to third-party developers through a published catalog of known products. For Sybase-specific solutions, this catalog is known as the Open Solutions Directory and is readily available from Sybase. Sybase customers can look for applications to solve business systems requirements that are based on SQL Server and written in either Sybase tools or third-party, application-development tools and languages.

Availability of third-party products is a strategic consideration and a critical success factor for any development environment, platform, or operating system. Sybase recognizes the importance of the contribution made by third-party developers, and the company has begun offering training and support to these developers, along with technical, sales, and marketing assistance.

Sybase has done more than simply use third-party developers as an opportunity to promote its own toolset. Sybase has encouraged its third-party partners to experiment with and learn new development models and object-oriented methodologies. The Sybase Developers' Conference, held in the fall of 1993, was one of the first conventions held by Sybase to be geared specifically for third-party developers.

Sybase understands that as its toolset grows in capability and complexity, developers must be exposed to ways to effectively exploit those capabilities. As the client/server model gains in acceptance, it is no longer appropriate to leave developers to "learn by doing." Third-party product excellence is not usually a result of trial and error, and Sybase has begun to address the support issues of this significant group of Sybase solutions providers by establishing third-party support structures and programs.

Through initiatives such as these, Sybase continues to demonstrate its commitment to being the enterprise client/server company and providing innovation in technology as well as its use.

Summary

Sybase started late and small in the relational database race, but offered a technically superior product that was soon accepted and endorsed by the marketplace. Over the past five years, the company has had to restructure and change, not only to handle its exponential growth rate but also to refine its corporate vision.

For most organizations, the question of moving to client/server systems has become a question of *when*, not *if*. Sybase's success has primarily been a result of providing highly effective departmental solutions. The company now sees the need to integrate all the various computing platforms. It also needs to bring all the various organizational data stores and computing platforms together, using Open Client and SQL Servers as the glue. Through its efforts to meet customer support requirements and to position itself as a provider of enterprise client/server solutions, Sybase has ensured that solutions developed using the SQL Server technology will remain relevant.

The Sybase client/server technology has matured along with the company and its customers. The products have gone from strong to stronger. Most importantly, those changes that needed to be made have been addressed with the development of System 10 products, as well as the creation of new support programs and policies.

Alongside these product-related issues, the company has identified the strategic directions that the industry as a whole will follow. Far from being an edict handed down from on high, this takes the form of compliance with industry-sponsored standards and initiatives such as DCE. These efforts ensure that Sybase solutions will continue to be useful and maintainable for the foreseeable future.

Sybase sees itself as a provider of technology that can be used to develop real solutions for organizations in the 1990s. The company emerged from the back of the pack in the 1980s because of its ability to provide this technology, and it has the momentum and commitment to continue in this vein.

Sybase developers are in an excellent position to benefit along with the company by taking advantage of the historical trends of the computing industry, which are driving the industry away from proprietary systems and toward open solutions. The Sybase product line has only begun to prove itself. Developers can continue to look forward to effective, high-performance products that will be useful tomorrow but can be put to work today.

1.2

The Benefits of Sybase Client/Server Computing

Many organizations have implemented SQL Server solutions using turnkey, third-party applications or custom software built with SQL LifeCycle or other tools. As any developer will tell you, every project has its own story—the official version, and what really happened. In this chapter, I look at a few examples of how Sybase developers have built appropriate systems solutions for their organizations. To make the examples applicable to your situation, I pay particular attention to what went wrong and what they did right.

Increasingly, you can see that information is the lifeblood of all organizations, and database applications are the most effective method of moving that information around. Database systems are the heart of the information circulatory system that pumps the information to where it is needed. No wonder so many organizations are using SQL Server-based solutions to bypass the rigid data management and reporting systems so often found in older systems.

Sybase has provided robust and feature-rich products for developers to assemble database solutions that meet the rapidly changing needs of organizations today. Successful Sybase developers have more in common than just the technology they use. Whether they have been building departmental client/server applications or pulling diverse systems together across the enterprise, Sybase success stories show how client/server technology is changing the applications development model. Also, the early adopters of the client/server model have built systems demonstrating the benefits to organizations, proving the value of migrating to the client/server architecture.

This book looks at a number of organizations, large and small, in both the public and private sector, which have made the decision in the past few years to move at least some applications to a SQL Server platform. These organizations have in common their decision to use Sybase client/server technology and, ultimately, the successful outcome of their various systems projects. In each case, the system developers have risen to the challenge of using new software development techniques, occasionally by inventing their own methods of solving the unique problems posed by client/server systems. In most cases, they have discovered problems and difficulties posed by this new technology and resolved them through trial and error. Their experiences may help you avoid some of the difficulties faced by early Sybase developers.

In the same way that client/server technology can most easily be described in layers, successful client/server systems are planned and implemented in layers. For an organization to truly benefit from its investment in a client/server system, the effort must be more than merely a technological experiment. Although grappling with the complexity of integrating client/server technology from a variety of vendors is a necessary part of the equation, equally important is the application's ability to meet the business needs of the system's users.

All new technology raises issues of how the organization works and why particular methods are employed. Questioning established methods and procedures for reasons of idle curiosity or academic interest is often unnecessary or undesirable. Many practical, action-oriented organizations dismiss this process as so much navel gazing, more applicable for theoreticians than for down-to-earth, achievement-oriented individuals.

As you will see, adopters of client/server technology soon realize that these systems bring with them capabilities that were previously unavailable. These systems also pose problems that previously did not exist. When successful organizations begin to grasp the power available to client/server developers, these organizations reevaluate their status quo and ask themselves what could be done differently. Client/server developers and implementors have a tremendous opportunity to use this technology to change the way their organization conducts business. It is both an opportunity and a challenge.

Meeting this challenge is the key to realizing the greatest benefits from your client/server system.

How to Identify the Benefits of Your Sybase Solution

When you talk about the benefits of a technology, you must be sure that you are describing the net effect of using the tools as opposed to discussing the tool itself. There is a tendency among technically oriented people to confuse the features of a technology with the benefits it brings. This generally springs from having a better understanding of the technology and automatically assuming that everyone can see the implicit relationship between what it does and why that is good.

In the examples of successful client/server projects covered later in this chapter, you see how each system provides some valuable service to all concerned parties. This includes providing new and powerful technology for the developers, flexible and enhanced business capabilities from a management perspective, and ease-of-use and increased data access for the users. Each organization derives specific benefits, such as a competitive edge or other strategic advantage. More nitty-gritty benefits like reduced costs can also be significant.

This chapter first evaluates the potential benefits of Sybase products in general terms. To ensure that I adequately cover the range of benefits that accrue to organizations implementing Sybase client/server solutions, I break out the features unique to their implementation of the client/server architecture and show the related benefits. Table

1.2.1 identifies the features of each Sybase product, describes the services provided by that feature, and outlines the associated benefits.

Table 1.2.1. Benefits table.

Product	Feature	Benefits
SQL Server	Open Architecture	Availability of integrated third-party products. Ease of integration of custom applications.
	Scalability	Ability to easily migrate database and objects from single user to multiprocessor-based h/w environments. Allows multiple SQL Servers to be integrated on the same network.
	Multiplatform Support	High degree of portability for database and objects from one server platform to another.
	Multithreading	Database server performance remains consistent as more users are added.
	Stored Procedures	Allows programming of the database itself. Multiple client programs can access one set of SPs, reducing maintenance requirements and increasing data integrity.
	Remote Procedure Calls	Allows SPs to activate SPs on another SQL Server. Effectively integrates multiple servers driven by events.
	Two Phase Commit	Ensures that an entire set of transactions must be completed or rolled back to point of origin. Increases data integrity for complex transactions.
Open Server	Interoperability	Mounts non-SQL Server database resources, allowing open clients to retrieve data from other vendors' databases as if talking to a SQL Server.

Product	Feature	Benefits
OmniSQL Gateway	Interoperability	Extends Open Server capabilities to support distributed joins, allowing applications to access data from distributed non-SQL Server resources, as if talking to one server.

As you can see from the table, the client/server architecture has several distinct benefits over previous-era alternatives. Many client/server products other than Sybase offer elements of these features; however, as discussed in the previous chapter, the SQL Server has incorporated and refined these features from the outset.

To make sure that you can readily identify the benefits of each of the Sybase products feature set, I need to go into a little more detail.

Open Architecture

SQL Server is built with published and readily available interface specifications. It is open to the extent that anyone can write a program that will connect to the server. This is unlike traditional proprietary database management systems, which could be accessed only with vendor-supplied tools or programs written with vendor-specific languages and compilers. More important, a great number of existing software applications have already been written to connect to SQL Servers as a result of this open architecture. The commitment to an open architecture is a reflection of the belief that there can be no "One-Vendor Solution" and that locked-in proprietary products that offer an all-or-nothing solution are not appropriate for building effective systems today. Sybase has recognized the importance to RDBMS customers of keeping their database engine open to all comers.

To a customer, this means that existing investments in software and skills do not necessarily have to be entirely replaced by the move to a Sybase client/server solution. End users who have spent time and energy mastering a particular PC environment or specific application can use their preferred tool to connect to the database server. Their view of the data will be familiar, and the methods they use to manipulate and report the data will also be the same. This reduces the learning curve with new applications, and allows users to quickly take advantage of the SQL Server's database services.

Scalability

All tables, SQL code, stored procedures, rules, and triggers work on SQL Servers regardless of which platform that server is deployed on. Applications developed on a single-user Sybase development environment can be scaled up to run on multiuser production platforms. Although the SQL Server has been scalable in design from the beginning, at the high end the System 10 Navigation Server provides transparent support for moving SQL Server capabilities to very large open-systems hardware environments that take advantage of parallel processing capabilties. More modest scaling can be accomplished simply by dumping the database from one environment and loading it into a SQL Server loaded on the new platform.

For developers, this means that prototype and proof-of-concept systems can be built on small-scale environments, which allows an organization to minimize the amount of investment required for these systems. When the smaller system is ready to be rolled out onto a large platform, only then does the organization have to make the larger investment.

An additional benefit is the segregation of risk. For a shop that is upsizing, for example, the prototype Sybase solution can be developed under the Novell NLM or OS/2 version of the product. When the organization is ready to proceed, the application might be moved to a UNIX server platform. This allows the organization to risk the RDBMS environment and client/server architecture first. When satisfied with the demonstrated results, the organization can choose to take on platform migration issues. Larger shops will be able to use the Navigation Server to migrate their already large SQL Server applications to even larger parallel processing platforms. These organizations can then support thousands of users and terabytes of data without rewriting their applications to take advantage of the new platform.

Interoperability

Starting with the Open Server toolset, Sybase has been committed to providing interoperability in its products for some time. With the introduction of System 10 products such as OmniSQL Gateway, this capability has been enhanced. *Interoperability* is the capability for Sybase client/server systems to transparently integrate with other vendors' products, such as DB2 and Oracle, or even older, proprietary hierarchical database products, such as IMS. This integration allows the users of an application to treat distributed data as if it were a local SQL Server database object.

By tying together diverse databases and systems, Sybase solutions allow the integration of business functions across the entire organization. Building client/server systems can now encompass the scope of the company as a whole, rather than isolated departmental or workgroup applications. Additionally, the organization can integrate the older or existing database solutions while providing consistent and more powerful user services. This provides the business with a powerful tool for prioritizing the systems and applications to migrate to the client/server architecture.

In a competitive economy in which resources are scarce, planning for the replacement of all of an organization's systems at once is impractical. By building transparent gateways to other servers and resources, the client software can be developed and proven first. When the business benefits of increased client-side capability are realized, the server-side data resources and platforms can be phased over to SQL Servers as appropriate. In many cases, the servers may never be targeted for migration. The key is to gain the benefits of integrating data resources in a multivendor, heterogeneous network. The OmniSQL Gateway product has been designed for precisely that purpose.

Distributed Database Support

Through the Replication Server, Sybase client/server solutions can be built to manage the duplication and distribution of data across a global network. Large organizations can begin to build applications that treat their networks of SQL Servers as a single, integrated resource. This differs from the OmniSQL Gateway product, which allows real-time integration, as replication involves copying data from one SQL Server to another.

Due to up-time requirements and bandwidth restrictions on wide area networks, tying globally distributed client programs back to a particular database server is not always feasible or desirable. By managing the distributed database process, Sybase System 10 Replication Server ensures that data integrity is maintained by refreshing local data stores with data from the officially designated primary tables. This replication is managed on a time or transaction basis. When key data is modified on the primary table, data can be replicated across the network. Additionally, transactions can be stored and forwarded or rerouted if network links to a particular server become inoperable.

Replication allows the coordination of timing and triggers for copying data from its designated primary database out to other databases that require access to that data. It involves controlling the distribution of ostensibly redundant data across the enterprise as a whole. This provides database solutions designers with several new options. Where data must be controlled in one location but used by others, designers can now set the frequency of the replication across the network. This means that the solution can make optimum use of communications links, keeping costs to the minimum required and ensuring the best performance for users who need local access to replicated data.

Systems Administration Tools

Sybase Control Server products allow remote monitoring and tuning of performance for client/server applications. Additional capabilities include backup and recovery services, and configuration and capacity monitoring and control.

As client/server solutions proliferate throughout an organization, use of these systems administration tools allow an organization to allocate accountability for these functions to a single person or group within one geographic area. This reduces the cost of systems administration, while at the same time ensuring the highest degree of backup as well as consistency in configuration and performance management.

The potential benefits offered by Sybase client/server products are attractive to many organizations for whom data is an important part of their business. I have identified and evaluated the features and benefits of the original SQL Server toolset as well as the new products brought by the company to the client/server marketplace. As you will see, the true value of the technology is not the potential benefits, but the benefits realized by an organization when putting the tools to work. Now that I have outlined the benefit set in general terms, I will describe the specific benefits gained by real organizations as they built Sybase client/server systems.

Some Real-World Examples

Following are a few real-world examples of Sybase client/server projects. The names have been kept confidential to protect the guilty.

Case 1: SQL Server Supports Global Consulting

An international human resources consulting firm with offices in 28 countries worldwide and annual revenues of $300 million found that it could not effectively keep up with the changing reporting requirements of its customers. The firm's practice was built on collecting, consolidating, and reporting worldwide salary data and assisting its clients in designing pay structures that would be competitive and effective. The company had a diverse collection of systems developed by the local countries using local products, languages, and architectures. As the company's clients looked for more flexible ways of paying various groups of employees, it required information that was shifted, filtered, and focused in ways that had never been required before. To meet that requirement, IS managers in various countries scrambled to deliver, using query tools, custom programs, and downloads to PC programs. The legacy systems were showing their age, and in some cases the delay in client service was simply unacceptable.

In one of the local offices, an IS manager had prepared a business case justifying a Sybase SQL Server solution. While the case was in the process of being approved, the company's Washington D.C. head office created the position of CIO. The CIO quickly unveiled a systems strategy predicated on a global move to client/server computing based on SQL Servers. The local office was told to wait to implement its system until the needs of the global business could be defined and a reusable solution could be developed.

As is frequently the case in such situations, the local office was under too much pressure to wait for a centrally developed solution. The IS staff went to its users and together begged for approval to proceed with the new system. The IS staff demonstrated the weaknesses of the existing 12-year-old COBOL-based system, and the users focused on the business benefits they would accrue if they were once again able to meet the client requests that they were currently unable to keep up with.

Faced with this unified message and armed with supporting facts, the local management carried the message back to the head office. It wanted its new system, and it wanted it right away.

The IS manager was invited to Washington to meet with the CIO and his steering committee. Ultimately, they negotiated a role for the local office to play in developing a pilot project using the client/server technologies they deemed strategic for the organization. The local office would take the point position on using the new technologies, identify the issues involved as they arose, and share that experience with other offices as they moved to the client/server model. Lastly, the pilot project developed would be considered an interim solution and would be replaced with the system developed for the organization as a whole. The project was approved to go ahead.

With the strategic role of the technology resolved, it was time to work on delivery. The negotiations during the approval process had cut into the development time allocated in the original project plan, and the users wanted the new system to handle the input, calculation, and production of their annual survey results in less than six months.

Fortunately, the local IS staff and the end users had spent the time awaiting approval in a joint application development exercise, documenting their expectations of the new system's services and building the data model. By the time the software and hardware arrived, the development team had a good idea where to start, and the more technical user representatives were beginning to understand the issues behind moving from a hierarchical to a relational database.

The first unexpected delay was technology related. The original plan called for development of the software in APT on X-terminals and the execution of the software on AT class PCs. As part of the company's technology infrastructure, however, the corporate IT group established Windows as the new standard environment for end-user stations. The development team reevaluated the end-user platform and after a little more than a month had worked out the interconnection of Windows 3.1 boxes back to its SQL Server. This exercise was complicated by the need to concurrently connect the PCs to a Novell Network and another UNIX workstation.

Significant components of the application had been targeted to be developed in Microsoft C. While this work continued, the central IS steering committee chose PowerBuilder as the company's Windows development environment. Copies of the product were promptly shipped to the local office for evaluation. In short order, prototypes of the key applications were developed by systems and reviewed by the users. Just as quickly, the users identified significant deficiencies and requested changes. This process continued as the deadline for processing the reports drew closer.

Due to a high degree of statistical calculation required in one of the application modules and to the belated start of the project, a customized, character-based plotting application had to be incorporated into the project. To accomplish this, the developer of the custom application was flown in from the company's operation in Paris. After a few late nights, the statistical application was integrated with Sybase and the other applications that had been developed thus far.

The date set for the "go/no go" decision arrived. After presenting the current version of the application to the users and management, the development team was given the go ahead. The team worked side by side with the users during the processing to resolve bugs and transfer skills. One of the key skills was the ability to work with programs in Microsoft Windows, which was new to the end users. As a result of the team's combined efforts, the annual reports were produced by the new system and shipped to the company's clients a week behind the original schedule.

While the local group was in the throes of implementing the new technology, the corporate systems group was holding design meetings, facilitated by a consulting firm specializing in joint application development. As well as identifying the menu structure and processing options for the corporate application, the team also developed a data model that incorporated the unique requirements of each country while ensuring that the application would still be useful for everyone. The reporting structures for the business unit being automated were changed to ensure that each of the local department managers was accountable to a central position for the operation of his or her unit. Additionally, new IS positions were created for Data Architecture, and a team was created specifically to standardize the nomenclature to use throughout the company's operation. This was used to standardize the names of the entities and attributes in the data model.

The expertise developed by the pilot team was transferred to the developers of the corporate system through several technical meetings and incorporated into the corporate implementation plan. This was fortunate, because many of the members of the development teams in both the local and head offices left the company to work for other companies as contractors and consultants.

Two years later, the company is well underway with the rollout of SQL Servers and Windows applications to its largest offices. The local operation is using the second version of its application, which was maintained and enhanced by a newly recruited technical team. Centrally, the company plans to phase out processing on its IBM mainframe by 1995, which will cut DP costs for the company in half. The company is confident that it will reach this goal and is quite satisfied with its investment in client/server technology.

Case 2: Sybase at the Stock Market

In 1989, a regional stock exchange evaluated its floor trading system and associated reporting and control applications. The question posed by senior management was to determine the suitability of the current platforms to sustain the exchange as it grew into the 1990s. The verdict was that the IBM System 38 was too slow and rigid and that the other systems running on a DEC Vax cluster would not easily accommodate changing needs. The report recommended a strategic move to client/server technology based on SQL Server and Sun microsystems.

Being a self-regulating, nonprofit organization, the stock exchange is funded by its member firms—stock broker companies with national and international affiliations. As well as a strategic move to client/server, the systems management at the exchange targeted the creation of a service to provide member firms with integrated reporting of the bidding and asking prices of all stocks listed on every major exchange. Until that point, each member firm had terminals or dedicated PCs that were tied through communications to each exchange. To determine the best price for a stock they wanted to trade, brokers had to consult many different terminal screens. The application developed at the exchange would retrieve the best price for any listed stock, regardless of where it traded, and present the result on a single workstation screen.

The member firms were presented with the concept, and work on a pilot system began. Within a year, the pilot was demonstrated and the members approved and decided to fund development of a full implementation of the project. The project uses X-Windows/Motif-based client software written in C to access data stored in SQL Servers running on Sun servers. The database is fed from online communications links that provide real-time trading information from the major North American stock exchanges.

As the project moved from development into the testing and acceptance phase, management saw a strategic opportunity. As an independent body responsible for regulating trading activity, the exchange has a mandate to collect and distribute information about public companies listed on it.

Based on the Exchange's experience with the Sybase implementation of client/server technology in its other project, an additional SQL Server database project for decision support was constituted.

The project mandate was twofold: store and report historical trading information about companies listed on the exchange, and replace an assortment of manual and PC LAN-based departmental applications within the administrative branches.

Given the existence of an extensive Novell LAN and user familiarity with Windows, PowerBuilder was selected as the development environment for the client-side software. Due to the lack of availability of exchange systems staff for developing GUI-based client/server systems, a team of consultants was hired with a mandate to develop the application.

The historical component of the database was estimated to require almost 15 gigabytes of data. The data model was developed in SilverRun to ensure a clear documentation trail and maintainability. At the same time, analysts worked with the users to model the reporting and control processes that would be automated using the new system. To accommodate users who wanted to be able to browse and review data in an ad hoc fashion, the Impromptu query tool was selected.

Lastly, the Exchange elected to use FrameMaker to format data retrieved from the database and print out the new reports.

At this time, the application is still in development and user-acceptance testing. The exchange sees itself positioned to use client/server technology to move away from its traditional floor trading system, and the database reporting project is well on the way to updating and automating the older manual control processes.

As far as this customer is concerned, adopting Sybase client/server products has allowed the organization to meet the needs of its internal users and external clients in more flexible and cost-effective ways.

Case 3: SQL Server and Risk Management

A major life insurance company decided to restructure its products and appeal to a more highly defined marketplace—in this case, professional women. To support this decision, a number of market research projects were undertaken to identify professional women's specific concerns and determine the most effective way to market products to this group.

One of the key points raised on numerous occasions was the credibility of the life insurance agent. A hot button for this group was the idea that a good insurance agent would have information at her or his fingertips. Professional women identified competence with automation.

Senior management had spun off a subsidiary company to address its new market and recruited a new IS director to build a new marketing support system from scratch.

He decided on Sybase SQL Server and PowerBuilder.

The first application to be developed was a prototype telemarketing application. As part of the marketing research, the company had identified several key differences from current practice to approaching, contacting, and following up with prospective customers. Mailing lists were fed into the database and the telemarketers made contact with the prospect and determined levels of interest. The system had to allow for future follow-up as well as obtaining and storing prospect-supplied data.

The prototype was developed and demonstrated to management. The ease of use and flexibility of the GUI-based client screens made a very favorable impact. The IS director was given funding to proceed.

After developing, testing, and deploying a full production version of the telemarketing application, the project moved into phase two—the client service and sales support applications.

The company's vision was clear. Send sales people out only on fully qualified leads and then arm them to the teeth with information.

The telemarketing module was developed for two shifts of in-house office staff. Although the client service module would be similar, the sales support application involved a completely different set of technologies. It had to be disconnectable from the database.

Client software running on portable notebook computers was supposed to be seamlessly integrated with the corporate database and mail services. However, the financial advisors were supposed to be able to disconnect from the network and still access the most recent data downloaded to their PCs, review it with the prospective clients, and upload the data on return to the company's offices.

To accomplish this, a transfer program that retrieved selected rows from the corporate database and populated a stand-alone PC database had to be developed. Because of the uploading of PC data back to the corporate database, security and data integrity were enforced through extensive triggers and stored procedures.

Within six months, a team of three developers had versions of both applications ready for user testing. As each major function was added during development, the work in progress was demonstrated to the users and management. The new business capabilities that the system provided generated enough excitement to invite senior managers from the parent company to see the systems.

Soon after, the parent company determined that client/server solutions would be developed within its organization, and funds would be allocated to the new subsidiary to create a reusable and portable version of the modules.

This organization has seen Sybase client/server technology move from a controlled experiment to a mainstay in the corporate systems arsenal.

Case 4: SQL Server and Health Care

A health care agency charged with the responsibility of providing tertiary care and specialized services for cancer patients had outgrown its 4381-based patient care system. The admission, discharge, and transfer modules were not integrated with the registry database, and treatment result records were kept manually. Appointments were handled through a combination of manual and automated processes, requiring significant amounts of manpower and allowing a high error rate. Laboratory and other investigative reports were kept in departmental subsystems, often indexed by a completely different patient number. Frequent complaints by the medical and nursing staff about the impact of the systems on patient care provided sufficient impetus for the agency to investigate alternatives.

After studying the database market carefully, the central systems group recommended building a customized patient care system to be based on Sun hardware and the SQL Server database. Off-the-shelf solutions were available, but the medical vertical market had been automated primarily by systems designed during the host/slave era. The IT staff of the agency felt that the emerging technologies coming on the market would be more appropriate to meet the agency's long-term requirements. Due to the need to provide online access and integration of departmental and regional satellite offices, the client/server architecture was determined to be ideal.

Whereas previously each treatment area was handled in a separate system and integration was not practical because of the structure of the data, the Sybase solution allowed the database to record each encounter with the patient, regardless of the department or the medical service involved.

The development efforts were split across two of the geographic centers for which the agency was responsible. From the outset it was made clear that each center would use components provided by the other. The development groups met frequently to work through technology issues and to keep abreast of developments in the other project.

Ultimately, the system was combined into a single application and rolled out for user testing. After incorporating the users' feedback into the application, the system was installed throughout the agency and the 4381 was phased out as the new system proved itself.

The client/server system provides greater flexibility and services to medical staff than the previous patient care system. Additionally, the new system has made passing treatment and outcome data to clinical researchers easier.

Case 5: SQL Server Helps Money Change Hands

An international foreign exchange company based in the U.K. researched and tested all the relational database products on the market in 1990, before determining that Sybase SQL Server would be the basis for its corporate systems.

Like many large organizations, a tenuous relationship exists between the head office and day-to-day practices in the operational units. Although there was some disagreement and lack of enthusiasm among the IT staff of the operational divisions, a corporate policy was established that all new systems would be developed in the SQL Server environment.

North American Operations had the most pressing requirement for replacement systems, so it was given permission to develop its new Point-of-Sale system using the corporate-sanctioned toolset.

Previously, all projects in North America had been developed for a Vax host/slave hierarchical architecture. For the IT staff of the division, the change meant not only a new database product, but an entirely new development environment—relational client/server. For the first system developed under this new model, the learning curve was steep indeed. Added to this, the hardware environment was deemed unable to meet the processing requirements, and Sun servers with NCD Open Look terminals were acquired and installed instead.

Consultants were hired to help with the development process. In order to deliver the prototype system within the time allocated, the consultants developed the application without requiring much of the company's IT staff's time. The staff had no complaints about this, as it was busy maintaining the existing applications and it wanted to see what kind of application could be developed using the new architecture.

Everyone loved the prototype. Users and management liked the interface. It was the first time they had seen a GUI-based front end. The IT staff was impressed with the speed and power. The consultants took the ball and ran with it.

By the time the application was in phase one rollout, in use by a dozen branches throughout North America, divisions from all over the world had come to see the new system. In spite of significant development efforts in head office IT, a global version of the Point of Sale application had not yet been developed. It was simply proving too difficult to get consensus on a unified business practice that would form the basis for systems specifications.

Eventually, the senior management of the other divisions pressed the head office to allow it to fund the modification and migration of the North American system for its use. In the face of a lack of viable alternatives, this was approved.

Management in North America was pleased that its initiatives would result in a reusable effort for other operating divisions. There was a catch, however.

The other divisions, especially Europe, could not justify the difference in price between the X-Windows terminals and MS-Windows applications running on PCs. Although the prices for X-Windows in North America were reasonably competitive with PCs, this was not true throughout the world. The other divisions wanted the client-side application ported to Windows.

The North American IT staff was less than enthusiastic. After investing considerable time and effort to learn the UNIX/X-Windows environment, the staff was quite satisfied with the service it provided. PCs were considered technically inferior and less desirable. Still, the SQL Server architecture supported multiple client environments, so the consensus was that the port should not be too difficult.

Further investigation turned up an unexpected problem. The consultants who developed the application had originally been more familiar with the X-Windows development environment than with the SQL Server architecture. Instead of incorporating business rules and referential integrity into the database with stored procedures, they had written everything into the client-side application. None of the work done with X-Windows would be portable to the MS-Windows environment.

Despite this setback, the company is proceeding with the port. The SQL Server environment provides a valuable service to the business, and the application software performs according to the original specifications. Because it was a deployment of a brand new technology, the company is treating it as a learning exercise. The bottom line is that the company considers its investment in Sybase technology to be a sound one, providing solid returns to the local division, yet still applicable to the organization as a whole.

Lessons Learned: Analyzing the Case Studies

For the case studies really useful to you as a Sybase developer, you need to look at a number of factors. Of course, your organization will pose unique problems, and even for similar problems you may not be able to use the same solutions for reasons specific to your environment. The case studies illustrate some key points that underline the reality of developing client/server solutions in organizations today. In the following sections, I discuss those points in the form of eight "rules" that can serve as a guide for your own projects.

Rules 1 and 2: Situation Normal...

1. We don't get to make the rules.
2. The rules keep changing.

Balancing the initiatives and directions taken by systems staff throughout the organization against the need for some level of overall coordination and control is a dilemma in many organizations today. When the definition of systems staff is expanded to include power users and PC application developers, the result may be chaotic.

Most developers do not enjoy the luxury of being able to "standardize" on a particular set of tools. For that matter, development priorities can change on a monthly, if not weekly or even daily, basis. This is a reality for most systems developers, and migrating to a client/server environment does not inherently change that. The larger the organization, the greater the conflict and competition among diverse groups of systems and user staff.

As the case studies illustrate, aspects of your projects can be affected by factors outside your control. Project deadlines, deliverables, even the tools used to create the applications can be selected one day and abandoned the next, as dictated by the powers that be. The Sybase toolset may not alleviate those pressures, but it can help deal with them.

The open architecture supported by DB-LIB and exploited by third-party developers ensures that you have a number of options from which to choose if you suddenly need to change client platforms. Power tools and application generators can save you time in developing prototypes, or even help you develop rough-and-ready production systems when the deadlines get really tight.

Hardware independence means that you can move your SQL Server and all the database objects you have labored over from one OS to another, if that becomes strategic or even necessary for price/performance reasons. You will see, however, that the developers must deliberately choose to design their software to exploit these features and to deliver on the promise of increased flexibility.

Rules 3 and 4: Never Mind How...

The case studies demonstrate two more useful points:

3. The users don't understand the server technology.
4. They don't really care about your technical problems.

This is a sad fact of life, as demonstrated by the stories of organizations that have successfully implemented client/server solutions. The users of database applications are more concerned with the data than with the technology used to deliver it to them. On the face of it, this may seem hard to understand. After all, developers find the technical aspects of these products fascinating and challenging. The users have some other reason for wanting to access and manipulate the data—something related to the business for which the organization was formed. This gives them a completely different view of the system than those charged with the responsibility of providing that data.

During the host/slave era, the users took an unflattering view of systems. People get used to new services very quickly and then want more: more fields, new reports, different layouts. Traditional systems were simply not able to keep up with the changing demands. This led, in turn, to demands for new systems and more and different technology. You have already seen how providing these services led end users and systems departments to quickly adopt Sybase client/server technology.

The Sybase toolset, augmented by third-party products, allows both systems developers and users to share the data. In many cases the users don't want permission to update or delete data. What they want is access, the ability to view, filter, and report data dynamically. They cannot provide rigid specifications because they simply don't know what data they need to see and how they intend to act on it. After all, the users live in the same rapidly changing world as you.

Each of the organizations that successfully developed client/server solutions approached the relationship with its users in the same way:

Rules 5 and 6: If You Can't Beat 'Em...

5. Give the users what they want.
6. Put the users to work.

As mentioned in regards to Rules 3 and 4, the client/server architecture is ideally suited to the appropriate separation of the user/client-side issues from the development/server side of an integrated systems solution. The features of the technology are less important to success in this area than how you go about implementing the technology. Successful implementation starts with a philosophy that it is good to give the users what they want. By committing to this, you can overcome the skepticism and lack of enthusiasm that decades of applications backlogs and broken delivery promises have engendered in users. Too often, experienced software developers have become jaded about user involvement and feedback. When asked what a user wants, they tell you that a user wants toasted ice or everything yesterday, or some other variation on a cynical theme.

Traditional software development has frequently devolved into repressed battles of Us versus Them, where the users were definitely not on the same side as the developers. Client/server technology can be used as a catalyst to change that thinking.

There is a catch, however. That is to make sure that the users define what data they want and focus on what they want to do with it, as opposed to encouraging the users to tell you how to build systems. Unfortunately, too often a vocal PC or Mac user does not understand the limitations of the platform and stridently insists that he or she could much more effectively develop the application in a single-user spreadsheet or similar product. This can test the patience of even the most ambassadorial developer.

Whatever the interpersonal dynamics, the new capabilities offered by client/server technology mean the potential for radical change in the way a department or even an entire organization does business. End users who are accustomed to waiting for IS to develop an application—only to criticize it unmercifully when it finally arrives—may be less than enthusiastic about allowing yet another new system to overhaul their entire organizational process. Not only that, but the end users generally see themselves as the only ones competent to redefine how their particular function relates to the business. Theoretically, they are accountable to a higher authority for their performance in the same way that a system is judged on the effectiveness of its deliverables. There is some merit to the users' view of themselves, and it usually helps smooth the process if the developer recognizes it.

You can get the users to willingly redefine their business practices as part of a client/server development effort. The way to achieve this is through Rule 6.

When you put the users to work, you effectively involve them in the process. Certainly some users seem to be telling you how to do your job. That is more a question of communication style than substance, because the users don't really care about how the system works. As soon as you involve them actively in the process of development, you can get them to give you the feedback you need to develop an acceptable client-side application for their use.

After all, if it's true that most users don't care about the system, surely the reverse is true as well. Most developers don't really care what the users do with the data. Everybody just wants to get on with their own job. By separating the client and server sides of the system in the development process as well as in the architecture, Sybase developers can ensure that their systems take advantage of the technology, while delivering real value to the organization.

Rules 7 and 8: Which Came First...

Last, the case studies show both the necessity and the pitfalls of having defined specifications for projects developed with client/server technology. This can be best described by the following two rules:

7. You must sufficiently define applications specifications.
8. You mustn't overly define applications specifications.

This is where developing systems using client/server technology becomes less than scientific. As demonstrated by the organizations that were successful in developing client/server systems, you must understand the application requirements you are going to build. Most software developers have been exposed to this concept to the point where it has become a mantra. Indeed, few developers would espouse taking 20 percent of the time to develop specifications and 80 percent of the time to code the application.

Yet this is the practice in many instances. To have a successful client/server application, the client software must provide valuable services to the users. Application specifications are not the data model, nor the business rules, nor any of the other server-side concerns. As demonstrated in Rules 3 and 4, these are not client-side issues. Application specifications deal entirely with the client side of the client/server equation. They define what the system will do with the data and outline the features the users will have access to with the new system.

More important, the application specifications set the users' expectations for what the client/server system will deliver to them. The specification becomes the commitment to a defined deliverable. Once promised, it is difficult to remove features or back away from target dates.

The single biggest problem posed by migrating to client/server is the complexity of the technology. Highly defined application specifications often rigidly outline what the system will look like, and if the specs are developed before the developers have experience with client/server, they can often be inappropriate.

The most successful cases of Sybase technology installed in organizations so far have been realized when developers worked closely with the users of the applications to be built. Understanding that the users are not terribly interested in the relational model or the marvelous server-side features that you are working feverishly to deliver, you can still define the client software to take advantage of the client/server model.

In some cases, practicality means opting for end-user query tools, instead of writing report and retrieval applications. Why write applications specs for software that can more quickly and easily be delegated to a readily available, shrink-wrapped product with existing training and support facilities?

In other cases, you will choose to develop your application using Rapid and Joint Application Development methodologies. Your users will watch the application grow in front of them, with changes incorporated in days and weeks, not months and years. This is why successful client/server systems have avoided over-defining their applications specifications.

The Benefits of Client/Server

Each of the organizations covered in the case studies had a unique business requirement, and each looked to Sybase to provide client/server solutions. The developers faced very different user groups and demands, yet similarities existed in the process employed by each system's effort. Successful client/server solutions tend to address similar issues, although not necessarily in a uniform fashion.

These case studies are representative of many organizations' experiences when they adopt client/server technology. These cases demonstrate the key elements of making client/server work for your organization, while also pointing to some of the many pitfalls and obstacles on the road to successful implementation.

The next section looks at some of the key factors these organizations addressed to gain the benefits of their investment in client/server technology.

Relevance to the Business

In each case, the technology was put to work to perform tasks that directly affected the business of the organization. Far from being limited to private sector firms, each organization had business that was its core reason for being. By applying client/server technology to this level, Sybase developers were able to ensure that their efforts were relevant, valuable, and appreciated. Even if you are not responsible for setting systems strategies within your organization or unit, you should still take the time to get a clear picture of what important business function your client/server system will support.

If you are in a position to affect which project is selected for a trial client/server implementation, look for an application that supports a strategic business initiative. As everyone experienced with organizational life knows, senior management rarely sees the backbiting and in-fighting that goes on further down the organizational ladder. The key ingredient for success in a new client/server system is collaboration among all concerned parties. Senior management-sponsored initiatives tend to encourage people to work together. This is a well-documented organizational phenomenon: observed behavior is changed behavior. By choosing a high visibility project, you optimize your chances for full cooperation across all organizational lines. Of course, you also run increased risks if your project fails, but that should only motivate you more.

The other major advantage to applying client/server technology to management-sponsored business initiatives and strategies is the implicit willingness of all parties to evaluate and redefine the business process itself. A new strategy generates new plans and procedures. This is precisely the environment in which Sybase client/server technology can shine.

Regardless of whether you choose a high- or low-profile project, the key to success is to bring all members of the project—developers, users, and management—into a functional team, and bring that talent to bear on identifying the changes you need to make.

Short-Term Payback and Long-Term Value

Even though many organizations opt to try their first client/server systems in small pilot or departmental applications, the full dividends from moving to client/server are realized over the long term. By investing in skills and experience and obtaining demonstrated results, the Sybase developers in the case studies found that they could solve local or immediate problems while gaining the expertise necessary to begin addressing the enterprise as a whole. The returns, even from a small beginning, can be compounded over time as more applications are identified as appropriate candidates for conversion to client/server.

Like any shift in culture, the big picture takes time to emerge. By breaking client/server systems into discrete projects, an organization can gain valuable experience with the technology. Although many of these projects generate significant returns right away, even ostensibly failed projects generate valuable experience. They identify weaknesses to be addressed in the management process or point out where there were unrealistic expectations. This may be difficult for people involved in those projects to accept, but it still provides a long-term value, because people learn from their mistakes.

The motivation to migrate to client/server does not have to be limited to a vision of small returns, however. As you have seen in the Sybase vision for the future and have also seen incorporated into the strategic vision of some of the case study organizations, the big returns from client/server systems come from their deployment across the enterprise as a whole.

By beginning to adopt the client/server architecture today, organizations put themselves on the path to ensuring an integrated, powerful, and flexible systems environment for tomorrow. The integration of all the business units and their data by implementing Sybase client/server products allows the organization to reap the benefits of the whole becoming far greater than the sum of its parts.

Integrating the Users

Inherent in the client/server architecture is the concept of the system's users. Contrast this to the underlying message found in the term *host/slave architecture.* What does this communicate as the relative importance of each component?

In each of the Sybase customer examples covered in this chapter, user involvement and service played a key role in making the project a success. The users were not bystanders, mildly curious to see how it would all turn out. Instead, they were integrated into the development team with a significant role to play and real value to add. They worked with the developers to produce the resulting system. It became their system, and they felt the pride of ownership that accompanies the successful conclusion of working hard to achieve something worthwhile.

Many people talk about empowerment and autonomy. Client/server technology provides organizations with a way to effectively build systems that incorporate these concepts without a corresponding lack of direction or control. From a database applications perspective, it is no longer a choice between centralized rigidity or decentralized anarchy.

One substantial benefit of the client/server architecture is the capability of users to access corporate data and to do so with whichever client applications they know and like. This is highly attractive to most end users, who generally do not enjoy having to learn new software tools.

The client/server architecture supports clients by providing them with flexibility and access. Successful Sybase developers take advantage of these features.

Leveraging Existing Systems

No matter how large the project budget or how supportive the senior management, there is always a limit to how much the older technology and methods can be replaced. Also, you are more likely to develop a successful client/server system if it doesn't have to do too much in too short a time. As you have seen in the examples, implementing client/server does not have to be an all-or-nothing exercise. In fact, it probably shouldn't be. Identifying and prioritizing the applications that can successfully transfer to client/server platforms makes more sense. At the same time, some older systems still provide solid value to their users and do not require either onerous maintenance or enhancement. In such situations the old adage still holds true: if you can't beat 'em, join 'em. Perhaps the updated version should be "if you can't replace it, integrate it." Whichever you choose to do, Sybase can be instrumental in the outcome.

Learning from Experience

Any dramatically different architecture places tremendous demands on both the staff who build the system and the people who use it. You have seen that the best results from a client/server system are reaped when the organization re-engineers its business processes to take full advantage of the technology. This has two prerequisites, however. One, the staff involved must know the technology well enough to know what it is capable of accomplishing. Two, the users must be willing to take a good look at their established business practices. Even if the user procedures are not established, at least they are familiar, and for many people this is important enough to fight for.

To successfully re-engineer the business, the system must become more than just the hardware and software working together; it has to be integrated with the daily activities of a group of users. They need to modify their habits to accommodate the system. This requires a great deal of trust and no small amount of faith, not only in the technology but in the software developers themselves. In many cases, it is a question not of facts, but of belief.

Successful Sybase developers start small and work their way up, building credibility with management and users. Gaining approval and cooperation to re-engineer the enterprise is much easier if you have already worked with management and staff to successfully remodel a single application to take advantage of the client/server technology. No doubt that application itself will need reworking soon after it is com-

pleted. Keep in mind that many Version Two client/server applications are as different from Version One as Version One was from the original system it replaced.

Experience is more than knowing the syntax and functions of the technology off the
top of your head. It is also knowing how best to address the concerns of the users and
where to balance the workload across various machines.

As the developer, you may choose to build your client/server application in a way
that does not provide the best response time to the users, in order to alleviate demands on the network, reduce disk access, or accommodate some other device. This
may be the optimum arrangement when you consider the way the user works with
the data.

Balancing these factors can come only from experience. It has been said that good
judgment comes from experience, and that experience comes from bad judgment.
You can gain the good judgment without the bad experience by not trying to accomplish too much too soon. To be successful as a Sybase developer, you probably need
to ensure that you have some time to put the technology to a practical and contained
test before trying to build an enterprise-wide client/server solution.

The organizations that have successfully incorporated client/server technology into
their operations have done so by doing more than simply acquiring new technology.
They integrated this technology into their corporate culture. Allowing a few key
developers to gain some experience with the technology and then look at wider applications for client/server systems was highly beneficial. More than this, however,
the organizations that gained the biggest return from their investment were the ones
that allowed the systems staff and the users to gain experience with each other, as
well as with the technology.

Return on Investment

During the early 1990s, tremendous pressures have been put on organizations
throughout the world. Cost-cutting and downsizing have been the rule for all but a
few organizations. Senior management has repeatedly come back to its organizations
looking for more effort, more performance, and more delivery for less cost. In spite
of the growth of many companies, including Sybase, during this period, IT shops all
over the world are being told to reduce the cost of managing information. Although
increased office productivity has been a goal of computerized systems since the first
commercial machines were shipped, too often this increase in productivity and effectiveness has not materialized.

You should not expect these tight budgets to be a temporary situation before a return to the hand-over-fist spending of yesteryear. Many CEOs are putting extreme

pressure on their senior IS managers to find ways to bring down the cost of systems and managing information while exponentially increasing data access and services.

System developers are fortunate to have products like the Sybase toolset to turn to.

Client/server systems can provide that measurable return on investment to an organization that successfully incorporates the technology while providing all the other benefits described.

Virtually all organizations have adopted systems technology to some extent, which means they have existing investments and ongoing systems expenses. Client/server is a new generation of software and hardware solutions. To be fair, the technology stands on the shoulders of the previous generation of systems and owes a tremendous intellectual debt to the work done by systems developers over the past few decades. The fact remains, however, that effective client/server solutions provide significantly more return for less investment than similarly powered, previous-era systems.

This has two implications: You can build systems that do more than the existing ones, and you can put a number on the costs of the existing systems. Older systems have real costs: hardware and software maintenance contracts, support salaries, supplies, and computer room expenses. Client/server solutions have hard dollar implications as well. Frequently, client/server projects cost more than was budgeted for, due to the unexpected costs of integrating "middleware" and integration utilities. The key point here is that pound for pound, a client/server solution provides more flexibility and costs less to build and maintain than many older systems.

Build, Buy, or Both?

Over the past several years, many systems architects have identified that the most cost-effective solution for most organizational systems is to buy something off the shelf if you can, modify it if you have to, and build it from scratch only if you must. With Sybase client/server systems, these options are built right into the architecture. First, many solid third-party applications written expressly for the Sybase client/server platform are readily available, complete with product maturity, training, and support. For many applications, building a new general ledger package, for example, is senseless. General Ledger functions do not differ greatly from one organization to the next, there is little opportunity for a competitive edge product to be developed, and other packages are already on the market. For applications such as these, the *Sybase Open Solutions Catalog* provides many options.

Effective database solutions are not always neat and tidy. Even if many aspects of your requirements can be dealt with by an off-the-shelf package, no doubt there are specific requirements unique to your organization. This is where the flexibility of the client/server architecture really makes itself apparent. Your complete application can easily be a combination of third-party products, shrink-wrapped query tools, applications generated from powertools, and handcrafted custom applications written in a 3GL. Because data integrity and security can be implemented at the SQL Server layer, there is no reason for these varied applications to inherently conflict with each other. This is the power of the Sybase client/server architecture, as you have seen successfully implemented at various customer sites.

Many organizations are just now seriously looking at the potential of client/server systems for their organizations. The early adopters and pioneers of this technology have taken the risks of the unknown and in many cases proven that this technology is more than smoke and mirrors. It can provide substantial qualitative and measurable business as well as financial results. Client/server technology is more than a fad—it is here to stay.

Pitfalls

Success is often not just a case of doing the right things but also of not doing the wrong things.

As you have seen demonstrated in the case studies, the path to client/server is not without its bumps and curves. Even though many organizations have already blazed a trail, it is far from a wide, smooth road.

The early adopters and pioneers of Sybase client/server technology took considerable risks by choosing to invest in new technology. These risks are often more organizational or managerial in nature than related to the technology itself. Whereas any new technology includes risks that the product will not work, the robustness of the SQL Server product and the choice provided by the open architecture has tended to mitigate this risk. The risks inherent in client/server technology have proven to be more along the lines of not taking advantage of the new features and finding that the technology could have been used more effectively.

The most dangerous risks are somewhat more subtle than straightforward. The following sections describe these risks.

Using Obsolete Development Models

Radically new and different tools such as client/server technology invariably require new techniques to gain their greatest benefits. It is possible to develop client/server applications that function exactly like host/slave programs, in the same way that people have written 3GL programs with 4GLs. It is not recommended, but it can be done.

Sybase SQL Server and its associated tools, whether from Sybase or elsewhere, can be incorporated into the same development models that have been enshrined in IT shops for years. The organizations that get the most value from their investment in client/server are the ones that recognize the need to adapt their management techniques and software development approaches to take advantage of features inherent in the architecture.

These products are not merely an evolutionary development of systems tools. They are as revolutionary for database applications as the introduction of the first mini-computers and PCs were to systems hardware environments.

Moving toward Sybase client/server applications begins with learning the features and functions of a new toolset.

The implications of client/server technology go far beyond merely learning a new syntax and vocabulary. Client/server brings with it an entirely new way to conduct the systems business. The expression "think global and act local" applies particularly well to this new technology. For example, client/server systems can be rolled out across the organization as a whole, even if they are developed first for local deployment. Small effective database applications might be developed by a single developer in a remote corner of the organization. If the application has merit, it can be scaled up for an entire multinational corporation to use.

In the past, corporate-wide applications have been developed according to a highly defined development model that incorporated such features as structured requirements analysis, applications specifications, integration, and user acceptance testing. By forcing Sybase solutions through the older structured, hierarchically oriented systems development methodologies, customers run the risk of finding that their Sybase solution did not incorporate the features that make it flexible. Of course, it is still possible to build rigid, static applications using client/server technology simply by creating rigid, static specifications. New technology requires a new way of approaching the building of systems and applications.

This chapter has established that aspects of the older development models may not be appropriate for development of successful Sybase solutions.

Developing in Isolation

In spite of the amount of attention that has been focused on the importance of user involvement, many IT professionals still develop their applications without adequate user input. The key word here is adequate. What the developer considers a suitable amount of user walkthroughs and co-development, the users may not see as adequate. Especially in larger, global organizations, it is sometimes too easy to assign development responsibilities to individuals who are not closely linked to the end users. In many cases, the developers may be physically or geographically removed from the users. These applications often tend to reflect the IS professionals' concern with data integrity and security, and focus less on the functions and benefits the user expects to get from the application.

Added to this is the nature of programming staff and software developers. Generally speaking, developers tend to be perfectionists, a handy trait when dealing with computers that don't forgive a missing comma or semicolon. This can translate to a reluctance to show work-in-progress and a tendency to put off showing what the application does right now, warts and all. Often developers tell themselves to wait until this feature or that function is added, then it will be ready. This leads to the developer spending time building the application without user feedback and input.

Another key factor that contributes to the isolated developer is the nature of offering work for criticism. End users are notoriously demanding and often ask for functions or features that would require months of effort or are simply not possible with the time or resources allocated. Also, an unfortunate fact of life is the lack of finesse that many people have when making observations about the work of others. A software developer, like anyone else, would rather have praise than criticism, no matter how constructive it may be. If this leads to a tendency for the developer to build the system in isolation, it is unlikely to result in an optimum application from the users' standpoint.

Human nature being what it is, software developers who work with like-minded professionals as part of a systems department or division are more likely to focus on the server-side issues of the client/server equation at the expense of the users' application.

With client/server technology, both concerns can be effectively addressed, but not by developing these systems in isolation.

Inadequate Specifications

Every experienced developer knows that application specifications change. If you wait for the specs to be completed, you will never even get started. The key word again is adequate. By keeping specifications and deliverables focused and contained, you increase the likelihood of developing an application that works and delivering it quickly. However, when dealing with strategic technology, it is important for developers to know what additional features and uses future releases of the software might address.

The purpose of custom-developed software in any architecture is to provide a specific and valuable set of services to some facet of the organization. As the sophistication of the software development process has grown, systems have increasingly become models of business processes. The programs reflect organizational activities and functions in the real world.

The best software developers begin by building an understanding of the business practice or process their software reflects. They work with the end users to ensure that they comprehend what their users actually do now and what they would like to use the system to do in the future. The documentation of this process is known as the application specification. In spite of the many structured development models that have emerged over the past few decades, there are still almost as many ways to write applications specs as there are developers to work with them.

Regardless of the format or style of the specifications, effective application specs have several key elements. Without these elements, the specifications are inadequate and the resulting application, without the intercession of a brilliant, mind-reading software developer, is inadequate as well.

Primarily, the application specifications must contain a complete understanding of what functions the users perform, what data they need to perform these functions, and what results they expect. Most importantly, the users have to agree that the specifications actually describe their operation. Secondly, the specs must detail which functions are to be automated or contained in the application, what data is required, and which results the application will generate.

By ensuring that all applications have documented at least this level of understanding of the user's functions and purpose in life, developers can be sure of what needs to be done. This positions them well to move over the technology and deal with the question of how it will be done. Lastly, this is an important device for bringing user expectations down to earth as the project wears on. When you have sufficiently documented application specifications, you have a blueprint for what you are going to build. When the occasional user imagines castles in the air and then expects you to build them, it can be very helpful to point to the blueprint as what you actually had agreed to build.

Insufficient Technology Transfer

Training existing staff and hiring external expertise in the form of consultants to assist in the development of a new client/server system has been proven to work. However, it is not automatically a beneficial process. The knowledge and expertise of consultants must be transferred to internal organizational resources in order for the application to be maintainable, let alone modifiable. Also, staff turnover affects all organizations. With the rapid deployment potential of client/server systems, sometimes an organization can overlook the need to take the time to learn—and document—the decisions and techniques as they are employed. This is a significant pitfall that can jeopardize the entire investment in client/server systems by leading to the creation of applications that are not maintainable or cannot be sufficiently enhanced.

Some of the problems that have plagued systems shops in past generations are not alleviated by client/server technology. Good help, for instance, is still hard to find, but with the popularity of client/server technology and the relative scarcity of experienced, capable staff, good help is even harder to keep.

Because of this, it is even more important when developing client/server applications to ensure that skills and expertise are transferred to others within the organization. With the elimination of indentured servitude as an employment option, most organizations have had to learn to deal with employee turnover. By committing to a process of technology transfer, you can ensure that your project avoids the pitfall of experts walking off the project to join another firm.

Underestimating the Complexity

Most of the delays and frustrations facing developers working with client/server technology for the first time are found in the tremendous increase in the number of factors that must be considered and balanced. It is possible to segregate your developers from the server-side and networking issues; however, this approach has proven time and time again to be problematic. Because so many diverse components are expected to work together in a client/server system, the developer can affect performance of the system without being aware of it. Entire human-years of effort can be wasted in the creation of applications that work in development and tests but don't work in production with multiple users and production-sized databases.

When you look at a completely functional production client/server application from a user's perspective, it is the tip of the iceberg. The system is easy to use: It is flexible, powerful, and responsive. If it's that easy to drive, how hard could it be to build? The difficulty of developing a client/server system is inversely proportional to its ease of use. If the client system transparently accesses multiple hosts using different protocols across a network, you can be sure that the installation and tuning of the integration of that system caused someone a few headaches. Often the task falls to developers to figure out.

Even if you work in an organization where you have the benefit of working side-by-side with competent, knowledgeable people who effectively look after every aspect of the installation, integration, and administration of the SQL Server network, as a developer you still need to know a great deal about the entire system. That's one of the greatest technical challenges facing a Sybase developer.

Summary

The early results are in: Sybase client/server technology can provide organizations with flexible, powerful, and strategic information systems applications. However, successful systems are not just a function of technology—they include the way the technology is used. Method is critical to success.

As a Sybase developer, you want to ensure that your work yields applications that provide the most value possible. No one enjoys working on a project that gets canned.

This chapter mentions several examples of sites where Sybase products have been used to develop strong information systems solutions. You have seen the benefits these organizations realized. The common approach taken by these companies included the following steps:

1. Strategic applications (though not necessarily mission critical apps first)
2. Keep deliverables small and timeframes short
3. Integrate with existing systems
4. Combine third-party and custom software
5. Give the users what they want

Today, the emphasis is on rapid deployment and flexibility. The name of the game is change, and client/server solutions can be ideally suited to meet this requirement. The key is how you view the software development approach, allowing for the new capabilities provided by client/server products.

There is no one right way to develop the best client/server systems. In fact, many new development models are emerging for client/server systems. Object-oriented approaches, for example, stress reusability, inheritance, polymorphism, and encapsulation. Regardless of what these terms mean in relation to your development project, there can be no question that developers are being bombarded with new tools, techniques, and philosophies. I explore many of these emerging development models and how they work.

Sybase products can be effectively incorporated into projects built with these new methodologies. You have seen that in many cases, the best results accrue to developers who give themselves time to grow with the technology, who go into partnership with their users (the client side of the client/server equation), and who take advantage of the architecture to build relevant solutions out of combined existing, third-party and custom applications.

I have also identified some of the pitfalls and obstacles that face client/server development projects. It is important to recognize that in many cases the organization itself is new to the technology. Far from being simply a bright new toy, client/server brings both subtle and profound implications to the way systems are built within a company.

By factoring these considerations into your client/server project, you can ensure that your development efforts have the best chance of success and the greatest payback to your organization.

For those organizations that have already successfully developed and deployed Sybase client/server systems, the full benefits of having decided to build applications with the Sybase product line are now making themselves apparent The company has been growing in power and sophistication along with its customers. As I identified in the Sybase vision section, the company sees the future as enterprise-wide client/server systems. The skills and applications that have been developed in over 5500 client sites worldwide using Sybase products can now be extended to integrate the company as a whole. This is one of the greatest benefits to having made the effort to develop client/server applications with Sybase.

As a developer, you can be confident that your investment in skills and learning will not only allow you to build effective systems today, but you are positioned to take advantage of new technology tomorrow.

1.3

An Overview of the SQL Server Environment

One thing all Sybase developers have in common is a SQL Server database engine somewhere in their environment. From this point, however, their various paths can diverge significantly, considering the many hardware, communications, and client software options available to Sybase solutions providers.

As you might expect, some small differences exist between SQL Servers depending on the platform and version in use, but generally speaking the engine has been consistently implemented across all server environments. This makes discussion of the architecture of the SQL Server possible, and makes that discussion relevant to Sybase developers regardless of their server platform.

This chapter touches on each of the software components that make up a typical SQL Server development environment. At the end, you should be familiar with each of these components and understand the role that they play in the operation of a client/server application. I describe the functions of the various separate products and parts that make up a typical Sybase application, and place them in context.

The treatment of the various constituent parts of the SQL Server is somewhat high-level and introductory. My goal is to briefly cover the architecture in its entirety and to clearly show the interrelationship of the components. More in-depth coverage of each part comes later in the book.

This section is most applicable for new Sybase developers and systems administrators, although it should also provide a valuable review for more experienced builders of SQL Server solutions. Although many developers and SQL programmers are not responsible for designing the architecture of the system with which they work, understanding the nature of the client/server environment as a whole can be extremely helpful. By being aware of the end-to-end process of a client/server application, you are in a much better position to design performance into your application from the outset and to understand where to begin analyzing performance problems when they do arise.

One of the criticisms about client/server systems is that they are very complex and difficult to understand. This chapter takes a step-by-step approach to clarify each aspect of a SQL Server solution. The objective is to break down each of the constituent parts of architecture and then show how they fit back together.

The SQL Server's Relationship to the Operating System

You have seen that Sybase intended SQL Server to be a high-performance Online Transaction Processing (OLTP) database engine from its inception. I have mentioned some of the features that enable the product to reach these performance objectives. Now, take a look at the internals of the database engine itself.

Sybase has gained a performance edge by developing a database engine that is insulated from the operating system of the server platform on which it is running. In fact, SQL Server takes over aspects of the computer that in other RDBMS implementations are left to the operating system. You can see the separation between operating systems and SQL Server functions in the diagram in Figure 1.3.1.

FIGURE 1.3.1.

SQL Server and OS.

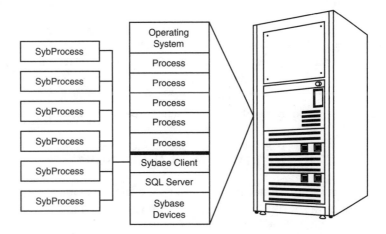

For most applications, an operating system spawns new processes as new users are logged in and start their programs. The operating system also manages memory allocation and disk access as well as the user accounts and permissions. The SQL Server architecture spawns one process for Sybase—the SQL Server engine called dataserver. Within that process, the SQL Server itself takes over the operating system's functions for all SQL Server processes running on that machine. The process by which Sybase takes over all SQL Server tasks and users is known as *multithreading*.

As indicated by the diagram above, SQL Server's multithreading makes more efficient use of the system's hardware resources and can support many more users and processes than the operating system itself. This is a result of the efficiency of the SQL Server kernel and how well that code was written and optimized for database activity by Sybase.

When the SQL Server is first installed, it is allocated certain resources: memory, disk storage, and query ports. The query ports are the SQL Server's network listening ports for clients across the network to be able to connect to Sybase. Whenever the SQL Server is started, the database takes over these resources, in essence relieving the operating system of that work for database connections and processes. The operating system merely knows that the SQL Server is running, and it looks like one process.

If a user process on the SQL Server needs to be killed, it is impossible to do this from the operating system, except by restarting the entire SQL Server process. This gives you an idea of just how isolated from the OS the SQL Server really is.

Although security benefits are derived from this architecture, database performance and portability were the real motivation for taking over the functions normally performed by the operating system. On each of the platforms supported by Sybase, the SQL Server has been written to work as closely as possible with the hardware, and to work more effectively than the general-purpose operating system with which it coexists.

After the Sybase software has been successfully installed and the SQL Server started, there is limited interaction between the operating system of the server platform and the SQL Server, and none at all from a user's standpoint. This is one of the ways by which the SQL Server architecture accomplishes the transparency of server access for clients working on other systems across the network.

Installation of the SQL Server

When you first install the Sybase software, the executables, utilities, and files required to run the SQL Server are installed into an operating system's subdirectory by the Sybase user. This means that to install and run a SQL Server, you need at least one operating system account and ownership of the directory where the SQL Server files are to reside.

SQL Server Software

Several components to the Sybase software are loaded from tape, including the following:

■ The dataserver executables

■ BCP, ISQL, and Syman utilities

   ISQL, the terminal monitor utility provided by Sybase, is necessary to run certain installation scripts and is useful afterwards for systems administration activities. BCP, or bulk copy, is a utility for copying data to and from tables in an ASCII file format. Syman provides online manual pages, similar to the UNIX manual pages utility.

■ Character sets

   Sybase provides the ability to sort data according to many conventions as well to display special characters, including accents. These character sets are installed as files. When first installing Sybase, you can choose which sort order and character set you want the SQL Server to use.

■ Termcap files

Sybase provides a number of termcap entries to support the ISQL utility on the SQL Server's host. These files allow ISQL and the other utilities to be used by a number of character-based terminal types and emulators.

This makes up the necessary files you must have installed in order to get your SQL Server up and running. The Sybase files and executables generally take around 20 to 30 megabytes of disk space.

The initial installation of Sybase runs scripts that perform the necessary functions to create the minimum devices and install the default version of the database.

To begin operation, the SQL Server must have access to at least one database device known as the master device, or master.dat by default. Sybase initially creates this device and then installs three system databases to reside on that device. The databases are called master, model, and tempdb.

To start Sybase, you generally log in as SYBASE and execute RUNSERVER or load SQLSRVR or, depending on your platform, run some other script that executes the dataserver program. The dataserver program starts up the SQL Server database engine, disk mirroring, and network services.

The only login ID that is set up as a default when you first install Sybase is SA (systems administrator). This ID is similar to the role played by root on a UNIX box or supervisor under Novell. SA can perform all the administration functions or drop and add all databases, tables, and users. Naturally, for security reasons, you want to be selective about granting access as SA.

Perhaps because they are both named master, developers and administrators new to Sybase sometimes have difficulty understanding the difference between the master device and the master database, as well as why each SQL Server should have disk devices specified before creating databases. I can clarify this by showing how devices and databases fit into the SQL Server architecture.

Sybase Devices

Because it takes over so many operating system functions, the SQL Server engine must have some way of allocating disk resources to various databases and other services, such as logs or database dumps. Within Sybase, these devices are known as logical devices. When first configured, the logical device name is mapped to the physical disk resource, which may be a raw disk partition or an operating system file, depending on your platform and configuration. You mount disk devices on OS files or partitions before you create your database on that device. When first installed, Sybase creates a master device and loads its required system databases on the device. It is left to you to configure the devices you need for your specific environment. For reasons I discuss in greater detail later, installing user databases and objects on the master device is not a good idea.

When you create a disk device with Sybase, Sybase claims all the disk resources allocated, even if you never create a database or other object on that device. The space is taken up by Sybase and can be reclaimed only by dropping the device. You may alter the size of databases upward, but devices must be dropped and re-created to change the size of the device.

As part of your performance and tuning considerations, you may create separate devices for user databases, transaction logs, and indexes. Frequently, a logical device maps to a separate physical disk, but you may create many logical devices on the same physical hard disk.

Dump devices are operating system files to which the contents of databases can be written when dumped, or restored from when the dump is reloaded onto the SQL Server. These dump devices are distinctly different from disk devices because they reside on the host, not the SQL Server, and they are created and used by different procedures. Tape drives and other storage devices also may be defined as dump devices.

Databases and Logs

All transactions performed against a database are kept in a log to allow roll-back or recovery in the event of a system failure. By default, a log is maintained on the same disk device where the database is created. However, this may not provide sufficient insurance against media failure or may negatively impact database performance.

For this reason, when you create your user database, you may choose to have the log written to a different device. Keep in mind that when you use a device for logging, you cannot use it for any other purpose. This is another reason why separating physical devices into smaller logical devices makes sense.

An additional reason for creating databases on logical devices is the capability to create databases across multiple logical devices. This allows you to create a single database that spans many physical disks.

The three databases created by Sybase when the SQL Server is first installed make up the minimum requirements to operate a SQL Server. You must have at least those three databases or your SQL Server will not run.

The master database contains all the information that the SQL Server needs to manage all databases, objects, and users in a set of system catalogs. These catalogs contain all database names, user logins, stored procedures, and devices by placing an associated entry in the appropriate system table on the master database. System procedures also reside on the master database, so they can be accessed by any user of any database as long as that user was granted permission to use the specific stored procedures. This catalog maintained in the master database is the equivalent of a data dictionary for all system database objects on that SQL Server. The data dictionary or data catalog for user objects, such as tables, indexes, and views are maintained on the system tables within the user database.

The model database is the template from which all user databases are created. It is modified to contain any user-defined datatypes, stored procedures, triggers, or other database objects that you would want in all databases in your environment. For example, you would add user names and grant permission to them for any users you wished to have access to all databases subsequently created on that SQL Server.

When a new database is created, the model database is essentially copied and renamed as specified in the create database command. For this reason, a database can never be smaller than the model database.

Tempdb is, as the name implies, a temporary or working database. Users who may not have write permissions on other databases can copy data into tempdb and work with it without restriction, because tempdb is cleared when the SQL Server is restarted. By encouraging developers to use tempdb, you can minimize the number of scratch or working tables, which take up valuable disk space.

Database Objects

From a Sybase perspective, a number of specific objects can be contained within any database. These are as follows:

- Tables
- Indexes
- Views
- User-defined datatypes
- Defaults
- Stored procedures
- Triggers

When a database is created, that database is owned by the user who created it. The database owner (DBO) is SA for that database. The DBO can, in turn, grant all or selected rights to other users in that database.

When tables are created, the DBO can set the indexes to run on a different device, effectively separating the table activity from the index searches when the different logical devices are also different physical devices.

Tables and other objects are named in three parts: the database in which they belong, the owner name of the object, and the object name selected when it was created. It is not necessary to explicitly name the three, as long as the chosen name does not already exist, because as a default Sybase appends the name of the current database and owner. For example, a table Test created by the DBO of userdata would have a full name of Userdata.dbo.Test.

User-defined data types are made up of regular Sybase data types that have additional default values or rules associated with them. They are useful for creating application- or customer-specific data types where consistent parameters or values are known in advance. By creating and incorporating a user-defined data type, rules and defaults that are consistently applied to a commonly used column (such as phone number) can be predefined and incorporated into any tables that are created. Not only does this save time, but the default values or rules can be modified for the data type and then effectively propagated throughout the entire database where that data type had been defined for a column in a table.

Data Dictionary

All relational databases provide some form of data dictionary—a method of describing the various database objects held by the system. Sybase provides a data dictionary in the form of system and database catalogs. The system catalog is a collection of system tables that are held in the master database and describe objects that are common across all subsequently created databases. As a convention, Sybase prefixes all system tables with *sys*. The system tables maintained in the master database are described in Table 1.3.1.

Table 1.3.1. System tables held only in the master database.

System Table	Description
sysconfigures	Lists the user-definable configuration options
syscurconfigs	Shows the current values set for those options
sysdatabases	Details all databases created on that SQL Server

System Table	Description
sysdevices	Holds the definitions for all database disk and dump devices (master.dat)
syslocks	Details any active locks
syslogins	Contains server login account information
sysmessages	Stores server error messages and nonfatal warnings
sysprocesses	Lists active Sybase processes
sysusages	Details disk resources assigned to databases

Although server-wide definitions are stored in master.dat, each database has additional catalogs to store database-specific option settings. These are known as the database catalog, and each database contains the following system tables.

Table 1.3.2. System tables maintained in each database.

System Table	Description
sysalternates	Maps server login names to database alias (d_worden to Daniel)
syscolumns	Stores table and view column details and stored procedure parameters
syscomments	Defines all defaults, triggers, rules, stored procedures, and views
sysdepends	Lists any dependency relationships between stored procedures, triggers, views, and other database objects
sysindexes	Details table indexes or lack thereof
syskeys	Contains primary and foreign key information for all database tables
syslogs	Holds the database transaction log information
sysobjects	Details database logs, rules, tables, triggers, stored procedures, and views
syssegments	Lists any defined disk segments
systypes	Details user-defined and system types
sysusers	Defines user's set up for the database

Between these two sets of system tables, every aspect of the databases held by the SQL Server is defined. To read any of the information contained in these tables, log on to the SQL Server, as any normal client would have to do. I mentioned earlier that ISQL is shipped with every SQL Server and provides a consistent method of accessing the contents of a SQL Server. Using ISQL or another query tool, you may select * from any of the tables to retrieve all the rows contained in the table. You may use the where clause with the select, just as you can in any other table. However, using ISQL or any other tool to directly delete, update, or insert rows into the system tables is inadvisable, because unpredictable (but predictably undesirable) results will occur. System tables are modified through the system-supplied stored procedures to ensure that the values are properly entered into the system tables. Additionally, you may run stored procedures simply to retrieve the result.

The SQL Server

After the data server starts the SQL Server kernel, Optimizer, Parser, and Compiler, it fires up the network handler, mirror, and checkpoint processes as well. This is the core of the SQL Server. No databases and no users—just processes listening and ready to go to work.

Similarly to UNIX, the SQL Server kernel starts and manages the other processes. It is the heart of the database engine. Rarely does the kernel make its presence known, as it is transparent to all users of the system, including the administrator. If the kernel does decide to appear, it is usually in the form of a complaint, and systems administrators may sometimes see kernel messages in the error log of a SQL Server that has gone down. This is actually quite rare, as the SQL Server kernel is a pretty robust piece of code.

The next three processes are more relevant to Sybase developers. They are the Parser, Optimizer, and Compiler. These three components of the SQL Server work together to process SQL calls that are made to a database.

The first step any systems administrator would take after installing Sybase is to create a user device to store user databases. Storing user objects in the master database is not a good idea because the master database gets completely overwritten if Sybase has to be reinstalled. The device is simply an area of disk where the database is held. The database can be smaller than the device but not larger.

Installation procedures, issues, and troubleshooting are handled in Section 3. For now, I am simply trying to give an overview of the SQL Server architecture as a whole.

At this point, assume that you have a running SQL Server and two devices, master.dat and user.dat. The user device has a database on it called userdata. Assume also that your database contains tables, data, and other necessary database objects.

Your SQL Server now looks like Figure 1.3.2.

FIGURE 1.3.2.

The various components of the SQL Server engine.

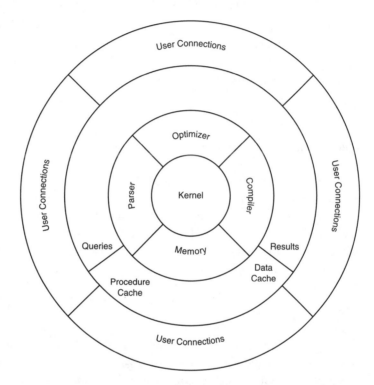

When a Sybase user attempts to log on to the SQL Server over a network, the packets are addressed to the SQL Server and picked up by the Network Handler. The TransAct SQL code is then passed to the Parser, where it is reviewed for validity, first checking that the key words and syntax are right, and next that the database objects referred to actually exist. Finally, the Parser checks to see that the user has the permissions necessary to complete the validated SQL request. After the request is validated, the Parser generates an intermediate or internal version of the SQL and passes it to the Optimizer.

Because SQL is a nonprocedural language, it deals with what to do with the data, not how to accomplish it. This function is performed by the Optimizer, which analyzes the query structure and selects the most appropriate index to use. It then determines the order of any joins specified in the query and computes the cost in terms of disk access and CPU usage. The Optimizer selects the lowest cost query plan and passes the query and the plan to the Compiler. Although this process is generally transparent to developers, some idea of how the Optimizer works can be helpful. For some queries, you have to trick or force the Optimizer into choosing particular query plans. This is covered in greater depth in Section 4.

As you might expect, the Compiler compiles the query using the execution plan and runs it. Query plans are filed in the cache, so they can be reused without performing the processes again. The query plans, data, and index pages get flushed from the cache, however, if enough diverse activity on the database causes the cache to fill up.

This is a high-level overview of the various components at work within the SQL Server. Now look at the client side of the equation.

Queries might be generated explicitly by a user on a client system but are more likely generated as part of an application with which the user is working. The DB-LIB API is an integral factor in this equation. DB-LIB contains all the function calls necessary to connect and pass TransAct SQL to a SQL Server. It was written to present the same interface to any client application or language. From a developer's perspective, the DB-LIB API allows you to build applications that talk directly to the SQL Server without requiring users to know SQL at all. In some cases, the user won't even be aware of being connected to a server. The entire program looks and acts like a local application.

Nothing could be further from reality, however. DB-LIB provides only the language interface to the SQL Server. That is, DB-LIB provides a way for the application program to make calls that Sybase can understand. A separate product manages the network connection and gets those DB-LIB-generated SQL calls from the client to the server. That product is called Open Client Net-Library and must be purchased for each PC, Macintosh, and OS/2-based workstation you wish to connect to a SQL Server.

As I mentioned, the Sybase vision for client/server computing incorporated heterogeneous networks. As a philosophical commitment, this was fine, but as a practical architecture, it posed certain problems. Not the least was how to connect any number of client configurations back to a SQL Server. The answer to this dilemma was to create Net-Libraries.

Net-Libraries

In the same way that DB-LIB provides a common interface for SQL Server to a great number of third-party languages and applications, Net-Libraries provide a common interface for DB-LIB to various networking and communications protocols. This process is probably one of the least understood by Sybase developers and very frequently the source of frustration and difficulty.

The physical configuration of local and wide area networks varies greatly, depending on the host environment with which you are working. The most well-known LANs are Ethernet, Token Ring, and Apple's Local Talk. The number of software companies that have written networking software to talk to the various communications hardware protocols is tremendous. In keeping with its philosophy of integration, Sybase chose to work with these vendors rather than try to duplicate their efforts. These products are known as transport software because the packages break up data into packets and transport it across a network.

Each transport layer software company supported by Sybase has its own Net-Library. There are several different versions for DOS and MS-Windows, Macintoshes, and OS/2. The combination of Net-Library and the communications software enables the client computer to connect to the SQL Server.

From a network architect's point of view, this provides several advantages. Applications can be written once to talk to DB-LIB and then DB-LIB talks to whichever Net-Library is acquired. In turn, Net-Library talks to the communications software, and it talks to the hardware. The various communications software companies support many different networking and communications hardware solutions. A single transport software package might support Ethernet, Token Ring, X.25, and PPP for local and wide area networking.

This enables a Sybase developer to build applications that are not network specific or even network aware. By incorporating DB-LIB and the Net-Library, Sybase has been able to make the entire client/server application entirely network independent as well as platform independent. The confusion surrounding Net-Libraries is partially because Sybase does not provide the transport software. As a result, many developers who are just starting with SQL Server discover that they are on their own to determine the most appropriate transport software solution, which is an area of expertise generally far removed from database application developers. What should be made clear to all new Sybase customers is the requirement to buy both transport software and Net-Library utilities for each PC, OS/2, or Mac client that the customer wants to connect to a SQL Server over a network. Depending on the size of your organization, this could be a significant cost.

DB-LIB for C and other languages, as well as Net-Library versions appropriate for your hardware and networking environment, are all available from Sybase.

A Sample Query

To illustrate how each of the components in the client/server process works, look at the complete path of a specific sample query. For this example, a PC client uses a local application to retrieve a phone number from a contacts table in the userdata database in a SQL Server across the network. At this time, I am concerned only with how the query flows through the Sybase architecture and interacts with each component it encounters—not with the specific functions of the user's application. Also, I take for granted that everything has been set up and properly configured already.

The user identifies the individual's name for the phone number to be retrieved. This is a function of how the local application incorporates the DB-LIB functions. These DB-Lib functions translate the contact name and set the parameters for the retrieve, identifying the database and table, as well as setting the user ID. These are then passed by DB-LIB to the Open Client Net-Library. The Net-Library manages the translation of the TransAct SQL code to the Communications layer, where it is broken into packets and addressed to the SQL Server's Query Port. The networking/communications software passes the packets through the physical network layer, managing the various handshaking and communication protocols used by that specific network.

On the SQL Server side, the Network Handler receives packets addressed to it and assembles them back into a TransAct SQL statement. This is passed to the Parser, where it is reviewed for valid syntax and structure. If the requested object exists and the user permissions match, the Parser generates an internal version of the request and passes it to the Optimizer. The Optimizer analyzes the query and picks the best execution plan. In this case, because you are looking for a phone number associated with a name, the Optimizer might choose to use the contact name index. The query plan is given to the Compiler, where it is compiled and executed. When the appropriate page containing the data is identified, a lock is placed on the page. For queries using select statements, the lock is shared, which means that another user also could read the page. The retrieved results are returned from the database and the Network Handler breaks up the resulting set and addresses the set back to the client.

The client PC picks up the packets, reassembles them, and passes them up through the chain until they are presented to the end user as the retrieved results, displayed in their spreadsheet of choice.

All selects, inserts, updates, or deletes are considered queries and are treated in much the same fashion. Functions such as updates or deletes require additional steps, such as locking the data pages being changed, but the end-to-end processing from an architectural standpoint is identical.

This is, of course, an extremely simplistic example. To convey a sense of the development issues and application design trade-offs involved, consider how this specific query might be designed for performance.

Because indexes on the basis of name are generally not unique, the application might have been set up to request a little more data from the server and to do a secondary sort itself. Working with the telephone number example, it might be faster for the overall retrieval to set up the server to retrieve a page from a telephone book and pass that back to the application. Once received, the application could use its local cycles to search the retrieved rows for an exact match or display all retrieved rows through which the user can browse. Someone looking for a telephone number frequently wants to scan a list of names close to the one specifically requested.

For example, someone might be listed only by his or her first initial and last name, or the user might have a slightly incorrect spelling. In cases like these, splitting the processing up would actually provide better application performance. Otherwise, in the event of an error, the request would have to be initiated again from scratch. As noted earlier, Sybase keeps data from recently executed query plans in cache; however, depending on how busy the SQL Server is and how long it takes the user to react to the retrieved results, there is no guarantee that the data will be available if the query must be run again.

A Sample Update

Structurally, an update is very similar to a query. A number of additional implications are involved, however, when an update or delete is performed.

The client connects to the SQL Server and initiates the T-SQL call in exactly the same fashion as the sample query described previously. However, after the specific data page containing the row to be updated or deleted is identified, it must be locked against access by another Sybase user with an exclusive lock. The exclusive lock means that that page is not available for either reads or writes until the current transaction is completed. In Sybase a page is 2K in size.

Additionally, assume that you had an update trigger on the table. After the user has successfully updated the row, the trigger initiates a stored procedure. For this example, a modification to the phone book might result in a new copy of the phone book to be replicated to another server somewhere on the network.

Summary

From this one simple example, you can see the inherent complexity of the client/ server architecture. The beauty of the architecture is how well protected the end user remains from all the underlying technology while enjoying the benefits of data access and security. As a developer, you may be somewhat isolated from it, but you will be much more concerned with the way the diverse components work together than the end users are. After all, end users must live with the development decisions and performance trade-offs that you make as you build the application.

Of course, a developer does not have to master every aspect of the client/server model in order to develop functional applications. Still, the better you understand the environment in which you are developing, the more elegant and effective your Sybase solutions are likely to be.

By effectively insulating the SQL Server from the operating systems of the platforms it runs on, Sybase has maximized the performance of the database engine along with increasing the potential for portability of client software. Along with providing a performance edge, there is also a security and data integrity benefit to having Sybase manage the system's functions. When Sybase uses raw disk partitions, it ensures that all changes are written to the disk before logging the transaction as closed, thereby ensuring data integrity. The operating system cannot declare the changes committed while leaving the data in cache or memory buffers. If this were allowed, a system failure at that moment would leave a discrepancy between the data and the transaction log. The result could be corrupted data.

Additionally, Sybase users do not need to have an operating system ID to use the SQL Server. Clients and servers can connect directly to the SQL Server and as long as they have permission, they can access whichever services they require. They cannot, however, access any operating system services. Conversely, users with operating system accounts are not automatically valid Sybase users. The user logins, accounts, and permissions are managed by Sybase as a completely separate process. This provides a licensing advantage as well. No matter how many Sybase users have logged on to the system, only one operating system process is counted. This means that 16 Sybase users could be logged in to the database on an 8-user server, with licenses for 7 logins left for the OS.

This chapter covered the entire SQL Server architecture from initial installation to creation of databases and connection of client applications at a very high level. The point is to ensure that you have a complete, albeit cursory, overview of the architecture within which you are developing client/server solutions. By now you should be familiar with all the terms used in the Sybase environment and be able to identify how that component relates to the others in the overall scheme of things.

You have seen how Sybase relates to the operating system of the platform on which it runs and how it manages devices. You also have looked at the functions performed by the Sybase-supplied databases, and how they relate to the databases you will create for your users. I covered the elements that make up a database and showed where system data is maintained in the system catalogs. From this high-level view of the overall Sybase client/server architecture, you can see how Sybase went about building an RDBMS product that lived up to the Sybase vision of an open architecture, high-performance, OLTP database environment.

From a Sybase developer's perspective, you can relate to the architecture in two fundamental ways. On one level, the ability to write applications that interface with Open Client DB-Library automates access to the SQL Server, allowing you to be somewhat removed from the database engine so that you can focus on the functionality and presentation of the screens and data from the end user's perspective.

On another level, you have seen the different aspects of the architecture and myriad ways the complexity of the client/server environment can affect performance and reliability. Depending on your role in the development process, you may be more or less concerned with these issues. As the book progresses, it goes into greater detail on each of the subject areas touched on in this chapter.

1.4

Integrating Sybase with Existing Resources

Previous chapters discussed how Sybase sees itself as performing the role of integrator or acting as the glue for tying existing systems and data resources together. As you move through the 1990s, you must recognize that models and cultures are shifting, aided and prodded as they are by new technologies such as client/server. At the same time, you must identify what is valuable and worth preserving in your past systems.

This might seem somewhat philosophical, but it can also be applied practically. Sybase acknowledges that it will never be the ultimate solution for an entire enterprise without providing hooks to various other third-party client and server platforms.

The original Open Server toolkit was the first step toward addressing this requirement. With the OmniSQL Gateway, Sybase has taken yet another step toward pulling all of an organization's systems together into an integrated client/server system. The reality of today's organizations is the requirement to move toward integrated systems, reflecting and supporting the operation of the enterprise as a whole. Sybase technology supported this concept from the beginning and has evolved rapidly to provide even more robust tools with their most recent product announcements.

The key to enterprise client/server computing is not simply integrating technology. Client/server developers must look for ways to integrate IS professional practices with the business practices of the system's users and internal clients. They must develop systems solutions that can be built and used by people who are not yet experts with the new technologies and their implications for how business may be conducted.

This chapter evaluates the differences between client/server systems development practices and those used to build more traditional systems. It exposes you to some of the newer methodologies that have been proving their worth in many organizations over the past several years and are particularly well-suited to building systems with Sybase. It also looks at what should be retained from your previous development methodologies, as well as what should no longer be emphasized in order to realize the best return from an investment in Sybase technology.

The resources that already exist in organizations today go well beyond hardware, software, and data. Organizations have a tremendous investment in people and their expertise.

Effective and successful Sybase developers must look for the best path to migrate these skills and gain as much advantage as possible from the wealth of experience of both systems and user staff.

By the end of this chapter, you should have a solid appreciation for how to develop Sybase solutions that appropriately and effectively incorporate existing resources.

Integrating Systems with SQL Server

The core technology available to Sybase developers is the SQL Server. As I mentioned in the overview of the SQL Server architecture, the database engine is designed to connect with a large variety of client systems and applications. The implication of this is that by virtue of acquiring a SQL Server, an organization has already taken a step in the direction of integrating its existing platforms.

Following is a specific example of how this integration can incorporate multiple platforms and existing systems.

Integration Opportunities Across Departmental Lines

Almost every organization goes through a flurry of activity at a point known as the budgeting process. Private and public sector, small agencies, microbusinesses, and multinational corporations all have a point during the year when all spending is projected and justified to the powers that be. My sample corporation, Amalgamated Monoliths, is about to embark on this particular endeavor.

A Departmental Solution with Enterprise Implications

In the past, the accounting department sent around paper forms for the company department heads to use to forecast capital and operating expenditures. These expenditures were reviewed and revised many times over several weeks. Recently, accounting developed a spreadsheet macro and distributed disks to the various departments requesting that the information be compiled on the disk and submitted, saving data entry problems and delays on the accounting staff side.

It was a good idea in theory. In practice, not all departments used the same spreadsheet, had compatible disk drives, or even worked on the same platform. Amalgamated Monoliths had Macintoshes in the marketing department, Sun workstations in engineering, and PCs using several different software products and versions sprinkled throughout the organization. Figure 1.4.1 shows the state of Amalgamated Monoliths systems integration prior to the introduction of SQL Server.

By the time the departments had transferred the disks, debugged the macros, and generally figured out what to do, they had spent more time working with the improved system than they had previously spent filling out forms.

This application was not without merit. Those departments working with 1-2-3 found the process much simplified, and the accounting department could get started on consolidating the budget data without having to wait for data entry. These are the kinds of benefits that many end-user departments and divisions are hoping to gain from information systems technology.

FIGURE 1.4.1.
Amalgamated Monoliths's computing environment.

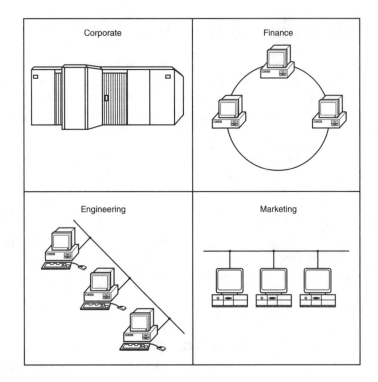

Centralized systems groups tend to want to deal with the company as a whole. In the case of Amalgamated Monoliths, accounting managed to get budget approval for a new system to handle the budgeting and reporting process.

The company's IT department took the opportunity to gain some practical experience with client/server technology and decided to put a SQL Server into the accounting department, connecting the various departments back to the Finance server through Open Client software and Net-Libraries.

The next year, when the accounting department needed budget forms completed, instead of distributing disks throughout the organization, each department updated a budget table using its own preferred client program. The department managers developed spreadsheet programs representing the columns and rows contained in the table as they built their own budgets. By using stored procedures and rules on the SQL Server, accounting could ensure that the submitted budgets were complete and accurate.

Additionally, as the information was refined and changed, each department head could see the numbers that accounting was using, without having to wait for printouts and interoffice mail. The accounting department not only realized the benefits for which they had originally hoped, but the organization as a whole gained more timely access to accounting and finance data. As demonstrated in Figure 1.4.2, SQL Server formed the basis for integrating previously diverse and isolated departmental systems.

FIGURE 1.4.2.

Integration of diverse clients through SQL Server.

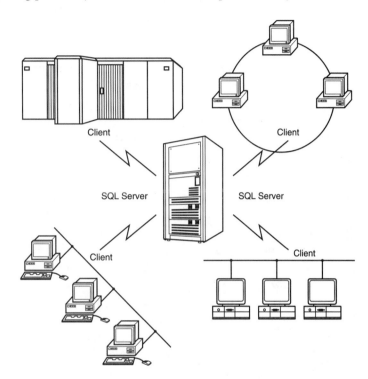

Through this approach, Amalgamated Monoliths was able to integrate diverse client systems for an important organizational function across all its departments and divisions.

SQL Server Dividends and Opportunities

With the success of the accounting system behind it, the IT department was ready to tackle a new challenge. For over a year, the senior management of the company had been expressing dissatisfaction with the reporting and monitoring capabilities of the systems with which it worked to manage the company as a whole. Either the reports were too sketchy, the information was not captured as part of a particular application, or the information was too detailed and bulky to wade through. Impressed with the feedback from its department managers and division heads, the senior management team decided to authorize the development of a client/server system to meet its reporting requirements.

As soon as the IT staff looked at the project in detail, it realized that it could not use the same approach it had used for the accounting system. Whereas the accounting system integrated many clients with one server, the decision-support system for senior management would be a single client and would have to be integrated with the many varied servers in departments throughout the company.

After looking at several products on the market, the company selected the OmniSQL Gateway solution from Sybase. Based on the Open Server technology developed by Sybase in the late 1980s, the OmniSQL Gateway allowed IT to treat the database resources as if they were running on a SQL Server. These database resources included an RDB server running on a Vax in marketing, an Oracle server on the Suns in engineering, and a DB2 database on the mainframe host that supported most of the corporate data processing applications.

By incorporating Open Server technology into its application, IT was able to build a system for management that was integrated and that accessed the data resources being used as the business systems for the various departments and divisions. Management could look at the same data as its operating managers, across the company as a whole. IT liked the solution because once the OmniSQL Gateway was set up for each of the servers, any Open Client could access that server. This meant a tremendous savings in time and reduction of complexity in the connectivity requirements for the decision-support system. Additionally, any other connections between the various clients now connected through Open Client and Net-Library to the Finance SQL Server could be much more easily connected to a non-SQL Server through OmniSQL Gateway.

Amalgamated Monoliths represents the current practice and state of the environment in many organizations. As a representative case study, you should see certain similiarities to your own situation. The Amalgamated Monoliths example shows how Sybase technology can help you move client/server systems from a localized solution. This technology provides a tool that allows you to integrate systems across your entire organization.

Traditional Systems Development Models

During the 1960s and 1970s, as software projects became larger and harder to implement and maintain, systems shops began to develop structured systems development methodologies. Originating in such organizations as Boeing and McDonnell Douglas, these methodologies were designed to build huge systems, incorporating literally hundreds of programmers, analysts, and designers. The development methodologies were one of the early applications of engineering methods to the development of commercial systems. Many of these methodologies were turned into systems products offered by consulting firms intended to help IS departments build maintainable, standardized systems. Most of these methodologies focused on the processes that should be used to build systems: which phases, functions, and roles needed to be addressed, in what order, and to what degree of specificity. They were, in essence, cookbooks for systems development.

The Top-Down Approach

One of the most prevalent approaches to developing systems became known as the top-down approach. When using the top-down method, a systems developer begins with the highest level of abstraction of the major components of the system. The developer begins at the top and works his way down to the nitty gritty. This was intended to assist developers in understanding the big picture before getting down to the level of writing code.

My intention is not to deal with any one particular systems development methodology (SDM). I simply want to identify what development models have been used in the past and how they worked.

The top-down approach was often combined with a management initiative or business direction. The need or objective for the system came from the top, and it too was directed downwards. An SDM is usually characterized by a great degree of detail and definition of the steps of the process. Most SDMs differ only in the names they give to the various phases and the level of detail they include in each one. Under an SDM, a top-down development model would first define the requirements. This consists of a systems analyst's review of the need for the system and the definition of exactly what those requirements are. Several people review the requirements report, and the next step is to conduct the analysis phase. Again, the exact definition of the term varies from one SDM to the next, and in some methodologies these functions would be combined. Once the requirement for the system is identified, however, the analysis phase recommends how those requirements might be met.

Although earlier methodologies expressed their reports in writing, this proved difficult to work with because the many people who needed to be involved in the process often arrived at different understandings of the same document—if they could comprehend the text at all. This gave rise to structured diagramming techniques, including data-flow diagrams and entity-relationship diagrams. The purpose of these diagramming techniques was to provide a picture of the system under discussion and to develop a standardized way of representing certain relationships, allowing staff to more readily grasp new systems. Other techniques defined ways of arriving at screen layouts and producing psuedo-code (readable, step-by-step instructions that could be given to a programmer).

This pseudo-coding was the next step for a traditionally developed system under the top-down model. After completion of the design phase, the system went into coding. Each of these phases had distinct starting and ending points. The system was coded in the language of choice, usually a 3GL, but later 4GLs were used, and the resulting code would be tested. After the tests identified changes to be made, the code would be evaluated for user acceptance and finally integrated with the other coded modules and the other systems. Each of these had their own testing specification. Once completely tested, the system was implemented and moved into maintenance, where 80 percent of the resources used by the project were consumed.

This was the traditional top-down development model as it was used in the 1960s and 1970s.

The Bottom-Up Approach

The introduction of the personal computer and its acceptance by business and government users began a trend away from the formal, hierarchical, and centralized information systems. As local area networks became increasingly popular, so-called "power users" were able to develop their own systems. They did this in response to their own perceived priorities and in reaction to the tremendous backlog of applications waiting to be developed by central IS resources. Often, they completely overlooked the documentation, design structures, and discipline necessary to develop maintainable systems. Perhaps ironically, the end users began to experience difficulties not unlike the central IS shops in the 1960s, and staff turnover meant that applications could not be maintained. There was a constant re-invention of the applications and approaches that had been developed elsewhere.

These end-user-driven solutions became more and more prevalent. There was one key reason why the grassroots systems continued to grow in popularity, even though they lacked the impressive features that occupied IS: These systems were owned by their users. They gave the users of the system the power to enter, access, manipulate, and report their own data in the formats they wanted.

In spite of a knowledge of how to develop systems, these users created applications. And they used them. As a result, the entire computing landscape changed.

The bottom-up method of developing systems yields a great many popular and centrally unsupported applications built with tools that are not part of the strategic technological direction for the organization—but they work. In many cases, they would be difficult to replace due to user resistance. What a bottom-up system lacks in conformity to standards, it makes up for with user acceptance. Often, IS departments discover that they need to support the system, even though the users were warned that if they developed an application on their own, they would have to live with the results. Management may be more concerned with the functioning of that department than with the turf wars over who chooses the technology and tools to be used.

This leads to another key point about bottom-up systems. Although they are generally not strategic and are often cobbled together with whatever tool was handy, they frequently contain the real data of the department. When end users create a system to help meet their daily accountabilities, they generally trust it. Part of that trust is a willingness to believe the data contained in the system. In some cases, this goes as far as having two systems in operation within a department—the home-grown one and the officially sanctioned corporate solution. When this is the case, the data is usually maintained and checked in the end-users' system and only later is the central system updated.

End users believe that their data belongs to them and should not be in the custody of a centralized support function, regardless of how many other departments are interested in their data. Bottom-up systems are usually a reflection of this belief.

The Results

Organizations in the 1990s have a blend of formal centralized legacy systems, departmental or branch office systems, and a myriad collection of end-user applications ranging from single users to complex networks. You can see from this that in terms of data and database applications, integrating new systems with existing resources is almost always required.

These resources are not merely hardware and software platforms and their associated applications. As with legacy systems, a cultural legacy must be integrated. Departments that were forced to run a gauntlet of IS objections and pressure tactics are likely to be less than enthusiastic about the prospect of being part of "the team." Previous insistence on rigid specifications and turgid technical documentation may lead some users to feel that working with corporate systems people is as much fun as a root canal. All these factors must be addressed in order to successfully integrate existing hardware, software, and wetware into a new client/server architecture.

The early adopters of client/server technology have done more than merely prove that the technology can be made to work. They have also been on the cutting edge of creating their own systems development models, ones that incorporate the best of what has been done before. Client/server systems do not replace older systems so much as they subsume those functions and add more features, while taking advantage of the price/performance of the various computing devices and software that have come on the market over the past decade.

Having selected the right technology and having a solid strategy and vision for the system is not enough. Those client/server pioneers who have made their systems work have also shown that you must go about it in the right way. Having the tools is not enough—you have to adapt your system's development practices to truly take advantages of them.

Lessons from the Past: What to Keep

I have mentioned in a number of chapters that client/server systems are not cure-alls or magic bullets to solve every problem previously posed by computer systems. Rather, developing a client/server system provides an opportunity to incorporate the most functional and effective aspects of past successful computing projects.

In the top-down approach, the single biggest factor is the focus on professional practice. Good process should be repeatable, and the structured approach to defining requirements, data flow, and process logic allows you to capture a permanent record behind the decisions. Also, through the structured process, an organization can develop a good sense of what works, which is a critical factor in developing successful systems.

Of course, standardization has its benefits. As people learn a structured approach, they begin to use the same terms and can decipher diagrams from one project to another. This makes it easier to assign new resources to a project team and increase productivity in as short a time as possible.

The top-down approach also gives the developer a structure to fit into. By ensuring that issues such as strategic goals and technical architecture are addressed as part of the structured methodology, developers don't need to worry that their project will not fit into the organization as a whole.

The bottom-up approach turns users into active participants—if not owners—of the system. With this ownership comes responsibility, and that translates into a system that gets used, even if it is not perfect (and what system is?). The bottom-up approach stresses applicability to the users' workflow, yields systems applications that perform functions, and provides services that users perceive as valuable. It deals with requirements at the operational level. This is important, because too many top-down systems projects deal more with theory than the practical aspects of getting the job done. The bottom-up approach effectively identifies tasks to be automated and can more easily accommodate quick changes in direction or features. Because of the unstructured nature of bottom-up approaches, users of systems developed with this model can identify changes during the processes and see those changes incorporated into the system. The very nature of the top-down approach makes this feedback more cumbersome and less likely. Bottom-up systems tend to change as the users learn more about the capability of the technology they are using. By incorporating the principles of local development, user involvement, practical relevance, and responsiveness to changes, developers can ensure that users will respond favorably to the system being developed.

As I discussed earlier, it is not only a question of doing the right things, but also of avoiding the wrong things. In terms of development models, you need to identify what to leave out of the traditional models in order to avoid making the same mistakes.

What *Not* to Keep

The emphasis on process rather than goals has led many top-down projects a long way down the wrong path. The implicit belief that copying previously successful motions will yield a valuable result is flawed at best. Understanding the objective to be reached by the system makes it easier to modify the system to reach that goal when the project gets off track. With a process orientation, people watch the wheels go 'round instead of watching the direction they are moving in. This makes it much harder to arrive at the desired destination.

Another avoidable component to the top-down approach is monolithic scale. Many structured development methodologies were created to coordinate huge teams of developers and programmers, each working on a miniscule portion of a huge project. These programmers often had no idea who would be using their code, let alone understand how the application was to function as a whole. This leads to dysfunctional team dynamics, where people working on the system become too narrowly focused on their particular deliverables and schedules, frequently at the expense of the application as a whole.

Last, many SDMs require a level of detail inappropriate to client/server systems. Building workable applications in the 1990s is more a question of hitting a moving target than creating something from detailed and fixed specifications. Because of the inherent reengineering in the business practices enabled by the client/server technology, users are not in a position to define their requirements in detail; and even if they do, those requirements can change dramatically over the project development period. Writing long, involved specifications and analyses do not help this process.

The biggest problem with the bottom-up approach to developing systems is the difficulty of integrating the resulting system into any kind of cohesive organizational framework. Even if Sybase technology can be used to integrate the various platforms and software of which these systems may be composed, the technology does not address issues such as nonstandard nomenclature. Field names and data structures may be fundamentally incompatible with the rest of the organization. Many departmental systems have their own coding schemes for customers or clients. Without naming conventions that specify the meaning of terms, integrating a bottom-up system can be technologically possible but practically impossible.

Additionally, bottom-up approaches to systems tend to lack a strategic vision or organizational issue with which to associate themselves. They generally work with the business unit as it currently operates. The old expression that if you automate a mess you get an automated mess still holds true, even if you automate it with client/server technology.

I have mentioned how organizations that reengineer their businesses, incorporating the new technologies, are the ones that realize the greatest gains from their investment in Sybase products. What needs to be left out of the bottom-up development model is the insularity that often accompanies these projects, and the resulting duplication of effort and investment. Last, because these two approaches are described here as on opposite extremes, it makes sense that the weakness of the one is the strength of the other. Bottom-up development tends to be more flexible; top-down is more strategic and disciplined. Bottom-up systems are quick and responsive to user needs; top-down systems are maintainable and standardized.

In summary, the main elements of the traditional approaches that are worth keeping are the following:

- Take a disciplined approach to systems development
- Stress the importance of user involvement
- Use formal reviews and feedback

The elements to avoid are as follows:

- Assembly-line thinking
- Building systems entirely on paper
- Balkanization of end users' systems

What you need for your client/server systems is an approach to systems development that incorporates these features while allowing for the unique new capabilities of the Sybase toolset.

Client/Server Development Models

Structured development techniques did not stagnate after the 1960s and 1970s. Even today, new twists on the structured theme are emerging, and many of them are applicable to Sybase products. My objective is not to attempt to give a detailed review of these new methods and techniques for developing systems. Instead, I look at these techniques and identify which aspects of them are particularly well-suited to client/server development.

Rapid Application Development

James Martin was one of the first to publish on the subject of Rapid Application Development (RAD), a set of management processes and techniques with which applications can be built very quickly. These techniques respond to a requirement that is particularly pressing in most client/server applications: the need to get the application developed and into production quickly. RAD has become more than simply a philosophical approach to developing software. In fact, Martin has expanded his idea to a formal commercial methodology complete with documentation and training, similar to a more traditional methodology.

The concepts underlying any approach to developing information systems quickly are readily perceived, with or without specific training. To allow rapid applications development, the scope must be narrow and highly defined, project team sizes must be small, and the time between reviews and modifications must be short.

With the increased pressures on organizations today, RAD is less likely to remain a methodology and more likely to become management's standard expectation for systems development in the near future. Not only is developing smaller, discrete applications quicker, it is also a good way to ensure that the application meets a real need and provides real value.

Joint Application Development

Joint Application Development (JAD) is a method of developing systems with the end users. The key elements are small, committed groups of technical staff and end users who review each phase of the system. As agreement and consensus is reached, a designated individual called a scribe writes it up in words or diagrams. The outcome of the meeting is readily available for group members to take away with them. This typically leads to less disagreement later, because people can review their decisions and think about the implications before moving on to the next step. Because users and systems people are involved, there is typically a growing mutual understanding between what the users want and what the systems people can build.

JAD is a highly useful approach for developing client/server applications, but it requires skillful management of the group meeting process, which is generally much harder than it seems. JAD sessions always run a risk of being dominated by one member, faction, or opinion, at the expense of the quality of the application. Although meeting with the users might seem like a straightforward way to define requirements, it is a subtle process that requires significant team-building and interpersonal communications skills to be successful.

Object-Oriented Programming and Design

One of the great buzzwords of the early 1990s, OOP (object-oriented programming) is a greatly misunderstood concept. Object orientation approaches the programming and design of systems from a completely different angle than the traditional approach. Whereas 3GL programmers might have function libraries and work on modules, an object-oriented approach to development uses objects and catalogs. Much of the confusion about the approach centers around the definition of terms such as *objects* and *functions*. The philosophical framework and definition of the concepts has been an ongoing result of the development of several languages, specifically Smalltalk and C++. My purpose in referring to object orientation is simply to describe a technological direction that has been increasingly making its presence felt. Far from taking the approach of a purist (who argues about whether C++ is object oriented or simply includes some object-oriented functions), I want to identify a few key concepts that may affect the way you see client/server systems.

These object-oriented terms are not simply updated buzzwords for things that have been around for years. Rather, they refer to a radically different way of seeing systems, one that is not as easily grasped by experienced systems people as it is by newcomers to the field. This phenomenon itself can irritate and alienate those developers who have worked hard and long to acquire skills and expertise in traditional systems. This chapter looks at OOP only from the point of view of how it relates to client/server technology on a philosophical level.

The philosophy underlying object-oriented programming is essentially expressed in the following four parts:

■ *Object encapsulation*

   Programs are a combination of data and methods. This combination is treated as a black box by an application that uses it; the data and methods are fully contained within the object, which provides services and responds to messages from other objects in the application.

■ *Object reusability*

   Objects should be reusable by a wide variety of applications. One-time code should be kept to an absolute minimum. The biggest challenge to reusability involves finding objects to reuse. Object orientation requires a commitment to coordinated control of programming objects that may run counter to a traditional programmer's mindset.

■ *Object inheritance*

Objects should inherit common characteristics from ancestors. These ancestors should allow changes to be propagated throughout the system, thereby decreasing maintenance coding. Where attributes have been modified by a descendant object, the changes are kept, while common elements are changed in accordance with the new attributes of the ancestor object.

■ *Object polymorphism*

Objects should be created to maximize their utility beyond the original functions. Attributes or properties belonging to an object can be changed, while retaining the original set of properties or characteristics that it encapsulated.

These techniques can be combined or incorporated into entirely new ways of constructing systems and project teams.

Side-by-Side Development Model

Both the top-down and bottom-up traditional models have something in common: they are hierarchical in orientation. This is a natural reflection of the computing architecture they were developed to support—the hierarchical host/slave environment. To get the greatest return from your client/server system, you need a development model that reflects this new environment. As you have seen, this model has to incorporate client- and server-side issues, while preserving the best elements of the more traditional development methodologies. I call this model the side-by-side development approach.

Organizations in the 1990s are flatter, leaner, and definitely faster. As organizational levels are reduced, there is a tendency for accountability to be pushed downwards. In some organizations, this is by design. Management wants to encourage everyone to take more responsibility. In others, as a result of having fewer people involved in the process, the remaining staff must take on increased responsibility to get the job done.

In client/server development methodology, everyone must work together for the application to be successful. The development teams should be made up of systems people and users working together in small groups (the management rule for span of control is fewer than six people) to develop contained and discrete applications quickly.

Although the client application is separate from the server database, both components receive equal emphasis in the development process. Responsibility for the definition and resolution of the business issues falls to the user contingent. This contingent defines what is to be done, and is accountable for identifying implications that the system might have to do business differently. Where this is identified, the users take that suggestion or problem back to their user departments and resolve the issue independently of the development team. From a developer's perspective, you should always be able to rely on your user team members to define what the application must do for them. It is simply up to you to deliver it.

Because the users are busy with the business and feature-definition process, the developers are accountable for identifying and resolving all technical server-side issues. This should be done in conjunction with the systems architect, project leader, or manager responsible for the system as a whole.

Functionality and ease of use of the client application are just as important as data integrity and security. During the design and development process, the development team must look for ways to accommodate both sets of concerns. Because the client and server components of the system are essentially two distinct halves of the application, this is usually possible to accomplish without compromising either side. The key is to acknowledge and understand that it is necessary to give both sides equal emphasis.

Developing client/server applications side-by-side with the users involves a mutual transfer of knowledge. To be a truly effective exercise, the developers must learn about the business and become vitally concerned with what the users are trying to achieve with the system. On the other side, the end users face a steep technological learning curve, with new terms and complex concepts to absorb and understand. By structuring the development process with a small group responsible for a contained application, you increase the likelihood that the group will work together to achieve the objective in as short a time as possible.

The Development Process

I have shown why the team has to be small and I have underscored the need for user and developer cooperation; to be effective, however, a development model must be more than philosophical. It must have a set of useful steps that take you toward your goal. The following section describes the steps for developing client/server applications side by side with your users.

Eight Steps Toward Successful Development

1. Model the existing process.

   Working together, the users and developers document their understanding of what is currently done. This can be achieved with written documents or diagrams, although usually the documentation is a combination of both. Some documentation of this process has to be reviewed and approved outside the development team to ensure completeness and accuracy of the model.

2. Model the improved process.

   The users' key responsibility is to identify how the system will change current practice from the model developed earlier. The developers need this model to understand where the application fits in with the users' business practices. Any suggested improved processes have to be reviewed and confirmed by the user department's management.

3. Model the database.

   The systems people's key responsibility is to ensure that they understand all the entities, attributes, and relationships of the database that will support the application under development. Using formal diagramming techniques such as ER diagrams and development tools has proven just as effective for client/ server development as any other systems project. The database model should be reviewed and confirmed with the systems architect or project leader to ensure conformity to standards. The developers, systems architect, or DBA also perform the initial physical design of the database at this time, including definition of defaults, rules, and triggers.

4. Map the database to the processes.

   The development team must ensure that it has accounted for all data to be used in the application. By reviewing the data model and the application model, the team can document its understanding of which aspects of the application use what data. This stage usually exposes misunderstandings within the team. Additionally, processes can easily be remodeled as the degree of specification becomes greater and a clearer picture of the application emerges.

5. Define screen specifications.

   By reducing the application to a set of screens with defined menus and functions, the application can be quickly described and documented. These screens identify what will be done with the data and in what form the data will be displayed.

6. Prototype the application.

   Once the screens are defined, a quick prototype of the application can be created with the screens and menu options. This prototype is reviewed for look and feel and also to ensure that all the intended functions are contained in the application. At this stage, a prototype does not actually contain any working functions—just menus and screens. It is essentially the frame of the application.

7. Build application features.

   The software developers add functionality to each of the menu options. At this stage, the developer must decide where to perform the work—in the application or at the database level. From a user's perspective, this is immaterial: an option is selected and a result is returned. From a developer's perspective, the question is highly material. If other applications are using the same data, stored procedures can be used to ensure data integrity. Developers will want to perform other functions on the client-side application, depending on the tool they have chosen to develop in.

8. Review and refine.

   As each new function is added, the users should see the application and work with it to ensure that it lives up to their expectations. Through this process, the users become familiar with the application as it is built, and the developers have an opportunity to change the application quickly. This process must occur frequently in order to convey to the users the confidence that their feedback will be reflected immediately in the application development process.

Developers who are already familiar with traditional methodologies and such events as user walkthroughs may ask themselves what the difference is between the traditional and proposed methodology. In the same way that these new tools can be used to develop applications in the traditional manner, new methodologies can be practiced identically to their predecessors. That is not, however, the point.

The key to success with the side-by-side or any other new methodology is the way the people work together and the frequency of the reviews.

When a developer comes back to the team at the end of each day with a little something new, two things occur. First, the focus on delivery is very short term: What have you accomplished today? Second, it is impossible to get too far off track. Immediate feedback translates into immediate correction. Interestingly, users who are involved in development teams of this nature generally become very strong proponents of the application to their own people. The user contingent within the development team works very hard to sell the system because they have a keen sense of ownership of it, along with the developers. This is because they worked side by side with the developers to create it.

Amalgamated Monoliths: A Case in Point

Go back and look at the budget-forecasting application that had been developed at Amalgamated Monoliths.

Having identified this application as one possessing both solid time-savings potential and high visibility and value added for all departments in the organization, IT selected three developers to spearhead the experiment with client/server technology. From the user side, two computer-literate financial analysts were selected for the team.

The first step was to ensure that the developers understood why budgets were necessary and how the process was conducted. The team used process bubble diagrams to show the flow of data through the organization and into accounting. Each diagram began on a white board and was modified until each member of the team understood what it represented. It was then drawn up using a PC-based drawing package, and printed out for both the systems and finance steering committees. These committees were rather low level, consisting of the department managers and the other analysts and staff who would eventually use the application but who were not directly part of the development effort.

Once the existing process was modeled from an overview of the processes to the detailed steps performed on the data, the development team began to identify which aspects of the project would be automated.

At the same time, one of the developers was assigned the task of identifying the technology associated with each department and determining the networking and connectivity requirements between them. This was made somewhat easier by the existence of a corporate office automation system that provided network services through Novell. To capitalize on this existing network, the systems department decided to use the Novell NLM version of SQL Server.

The additional software required, such as the appropriate Net-Libraries and SQL Server connection kits, were budgeted and acquired for each of the target client machines. During the development teams' modeling of the new process, the systems network manager worked out the specific requirements to connect the client programs.

Another developer was assigned accountability for developing the data model and ensuring referential integrity. When not involved with the development teams' modeling processes, this individual spent his time working out a detailed entity relationship diagram. When he had completed the draft and had it approved by the other developers, the server specialist presented the model to the two financial analysts. They had some difficulty understanding the relational model until the developer created a version of the data model that showed the data in views, which related much more readily to the analysts' understanding of the application. During this process, a number of the entities were redefined to more appropriately allocate the attributes. The development team decided that joins and data structures did not have to be understood to use the application.

By the end of the first month, the team had a model of the database and a set of specifications for the process logic of the application to be built. These were presented to the two steering committees without much reaction or comment.

During the second month, the development team spent much of its time mapping the process logic to a set of menu options and screens. Although the team had decided to develop the accounting system using a graphical user interface, it spent most of its time logically grouping functions together and determining the options that any given user would want to access at any particular point in the process.

While the team was working on this process, the other developer was given the responsibility of learning a new GUI development tool that worked with SQL Server. This tool was used to create mock-up screens with the features and menus the development team had worked out. After the screens were created using the windows development tool, the team arranged a demonstration for the two steering committees.

They were unprepared for the reaction. Even though the two steering committees had seen the data and process logic models, the committees offered considerably more feedback on the mock-ups. Some people were concerned that the menu options did not yet work, but most understood that they were simply looking at the way the application would be laid out. Generally, the remarks were positive, but they also identified a few key changes.

A week later, the development team again presented the prototype application, incorporating the feedback from the previous meeting. This time the reaction was highly positive, because the committee members had not expected such a quick turnaround from the last version. The financial analysts on the development team took the responsibility for explaining the screens and the functions of the application to their fellow users. At this point, the implication of the changes to their current procedures as reflected in the process diagrams began to sink in. The developers sat back and watched the sparks fly as the users on the team were called on to explain in great detail the rationale behind the business changes.

Over the next few weeks, two of the developers worked through the process of putting functionality behind the buttons and menu options on the screens. The end-user members of the development team spent their time testing the code as it was developed and reviewing the detailed requirements with the developers when they were stuck on how a particular function was supposed to operate.

At the same time, another developer who had more exposure to front-end software was working out the specific layout of the particular front ends that the departmental managers had requested their budget forms be displayed in. The time required to do this was considerably reduced, as all validations, calculations, and default values were performed on the database through stored procedures, rules, and defaults on the table columns. Testing was done by entering data from last year's submitted budget sheets and trying various legal and illegal values to see how the system would react.

As mentioned earlier in the chapter, the system was implemented in time, and it enjoyed rapid acceptance by the department heads and accounting users. By using a SQL Server to pull together various departmental systems, Amalgamated Monoliths was able to integrate its existing computing resources with client/server technology.

Summary

This chapter has covered the two ends of the spectrum for integrating existing resources with Sybase products. On the one end, a SQL Server can be used to provide data services to a large number of different client systems. On the other end, Open Server products such as OmniSQL Gateway can be used to connect an open client system to a large number of very different relational and nonrelational databases.

Also, you have seen that existing systems investments include more than hardware and software. It is vital to remember that the human factor is a significant contributor to complexity and has even more impact on the ultimate success or failure of your client/server project. Sybase products are designed to maximize your organization's investment in various software products and hardware platforms. To achieve this, you must be prepared to modify your software development techniques, grapple with the big picture, and work effectively with your users as a team.

Although this approach makes common sense, it is a far cry from the usual practice of many organizations today.

Dramatically different development techniques have emerged as well. Object orientation is only just beginning to demonstrate its effectiveness as a development methodology and has its own rich vocabulary and somewhat esoteric concepts. Rapid

Application Development focuses on getting results quickly, but it can seem at odds with the more methodical approach and emphasis on quality of traditional methodologies. Also, many IT developers find it difficult to adjust to the highly interpersonal nature of Joint Application Development. These radically different software development models are often the best way to effectively develop client/server solutions.

At the same time, past experience can provide valuable lessons. Formal documentation provides a record of intentions and agreements, and besides being useful for sorting out past promises, it can also serve as an effective tool for communicating the status of a project to a new member of the development team.

In this chapter, I covered the traditional approaches and recommended aspects that should be kept and identified others that are less helpful in developing a client/server application. I also briefly discussed the newer techniques and showed how some of these techniques have been used to get Sybase applications off the ground.

Ultimately, you need to pick and choose among the many options open to you and work with an approach that fits in effectively with your organization, users, and specific project. In this chapter, I have looked at some of the issues involved in integrating Sybase products into organizations with existing systems, staff, and processes. You have also been taken through an example of a process that shows step by step how to develop a client/server system. It is up to you to take these examples and determine what is relevant to your particular client/server application.

Section Summary

In the past four chapters, I have covered the startup of Sybase, Inc., the vision of its founders, and some of the company's history. I have also looked at the products that make up the Sybase toolset, and how and where they can be used. I have also covered some of the representative benefits realized by organizations that have built client/server systems with Sybase.

I have also outlined the key concepts and components of the SQL Server architecture in this section.

After reading this first section, you should be more comfortable with the client/server basics and the things that set this architecture apart from traditional systems. You should also have picked up a quick overview of the newer development methodologies that can be used to develop successful client/server applications.

The purpose of this section was to set the context for your particular Sybase client/server solution. By reading it, you should now have a solid grasp of the definition of

Sybase terms and how they relate to a generic client/server system. Also, you should have a better idea of what to expect during your own Sybase project—the pitfalls, process, and potential benefits your application can yield.

Finally, these chapters were intended to give you a sense of how to identify the existing systems resources and skills that you can integrate with your new technology to create an even stronger set of systems services for your organization.

2

Defining the Development Environment

Introduction

THE FIRST SECTION OF THIS BOOK COVERED SYBASE AND its vision and product line as well as client/server customers and the implications of this new technology for software development practices.

This section looks at how to define, structure, and customize your specific environment as you prepare for your client/server project. It deals with all aspects of the client/server development process in general. This includes outlining the roles and responsibilities for everyone involved in the project, logical and physical data modeling techniques, anticipating and designing queries, and estimating size and throughput implications for resource usage. You are also exposed to proven approaches for defining application specifications and translating those specifications into models to assist in the development of the database side of your client/server system.

When you complete this section, you should be able to identify who is responsible for each task necessary to develop a successful client/server solution. Also, you will see how the various modeling and diagramming techniques can be specifically applied to your Sybase client/server solution.

This should help you set the context in which to employ your SQL Server and its associated technology to develop a client/server system that provides valued services to your organization.

2.1

Roles and Responsibilities in a Client/Server Project

Every structured methodology for systems development incorporates a description of the functions that must be performed by various personnel in terms of staff roles, and defines the responsibilities associated with each of those roles. Whether you are a single developer working with Sybase products or are part of a large team, you should be aware of the various components of a client/server project. This will help you to determine where you fit in and to ensure that no important functions are overlooked.

This chapter identifies each of the roles in a typical client/server project and defines the responsibilities for those roles. You have already seen a few development models for client/server projects; now I cover specifically who works with that methodology, what tasks they perform, and the results they are expected to deliver. This provides an overview of all the contributors to a client/server development effort and helps you determine which of those roles you should play on your project.

The scope and scale of your particular development is less important to this process than identifying how each role will be fulfilled. As a lone developer, you would wear all the hats on your project. If this applies to you, this chapter gives you a better idea of just how thin you will have to spread yourself. Most often, even small projects have several developers involved. Previously, I mentioned the benefits of assigning a handful of developers to work together with the users in small teams. These teams can develop applications that, when integrated, address the requirements of a large organization or application.

The objective is to ensure that you have an adequate understanding of the specific roles that need to be addressed in order to develop a successful client/server application with the Sybase toolset.

Why Define Roles and Responsibilities?

In spite of an emphasis on flexibility and innovation, developers of client/server systems must remember that formal structures and process definitions can be instrumental in securing success. Speaking practically, a goal is more likely to be reached when it is defined and communicated among the people expected to achieve the goal. Even with the advances of computing and communications technologies in recent years, project management techniques as old as the pyramids can still offer valid approaches and help your project succeed. In this chapter, I try to incorporate and build on the software development techniques that were created and refined in previous generations of computing environments. I also identify newer techniques now emerging as a result of the introduction of client/server systems.

Not only is it helpful to a developer to know what must be achieved overall as part of a client/server project, it is vital to have some understanding of who is to do it. This is the essence of the definition of roles and responsibilities. I define them to ensure that there are no gaps, lapses, or overlaps in the assignment of staff to those functions that must be performed as part of your client/server project.

This becomes especially important when you have multiple developers working on various smaller applications. At some point, the various modules and components must be integrated into a cohesive, working whole. By defining the roles and assigning responsibilities, you can reduce wasted and duplicated efforts. Most important, you can ensure that everything that must get done actually gets done. These are the benefits of formal roles; I covered this in greater detail in the section titled "Lessons from the Past: What to Keep" in Chapter 1.4.

The roles are listed in Table 2.1.1.

Table 2.1.1. Roles and responsibilities in a client/server project.

Role	Responsibilities
Project Sponsor	The executive who approves and supports the system
Project Manager	The management-level individual with overall responsibility for the system
Project Leader	The technical team coordinator
Technical Specialists	All developers and technical staff assigned to the project
End Users	Those individuals who will operate the system as part of their job duties
End-User Developers	Non-systems people from the end-user group who work with the development team
Systems Architect	The overall technical designer
Applications Analyst	The individual who reviews the end-user requirements and defines the system specifications
Database Administrator	The manager of the database
Data Administrator	The person responsible for naming and controlling data element names and content

continues

Table 2.1.1. continued

Role	Responsibilities
Interface Designer	The technical specialist who determines optimum man-machine interface method and style
Network Architect	The technical specialist responsible for the integration of all systems components through data communication tools and protocols
Documentation Specialist	The technical specialist who develops user manuals, help programs, and technical descriptions of the system

Each of these roles is distinct from the others. In any given project, you may have partial or full responsibility for any or many of these roles. It is unlikely that any one person could effectively perform all these functions, except possibly in the case of a developer working on single-user systems of which he would be the sole user. That would hardly qualify as a typical client/server application. For my purposes, I consider a typical Sybase client/server development effort to involve a team of at least a half dozen individuals. In my coverage of various roles, I assume that the persons assigned certain responsibilities can perform those duties competently.

With that in mind, I take a more detailed look at the specific functions for which each of the roles is responsible.

Project Sponsor

In all successful client/server projects, someone higher up the organizational ladder has reasons for wanting the new system built. The sponsor is responsible for identifying the strategic value of the system and tying the technology back to a business initiative or service that benefits the organization as a whole. As well as ensuring that the right system gets built, the project sponsor is responsible for resolving issues and conflicts that arise across organizational lines. Generally the project sponsor operates at a senior level and can see the "big picture" as defined by the organization's senior management team. This still applies to departmental systems, although the project sponsor may restrict his or her vision to a departmental initiative.

The project sponsor sets the mandate and scope for the system. This role is generally filled by a member of senior management who is fully aware of the organization's strategy and has access to other senior departmental managers. The project sponsor can also leverage the success of the project into new systems applications using client/server technology.

Typically, the sponsor is involved most at the beginning and during the approval stages of the concept. However, the sponsor also attends milestone meetings and has significant deliverables demonstrated, which tends to focus the project team staff on their own commitment to results.

Project Manager

The project manager is accountable for managing the resources and staff involved in the project. Typically, the individual in this role is accountable for the delivery of the system within the time targets and financial resources that were budgeted and approved by the project sponsor. The project manager determines priorities and resolves any interpersonal, priority, or design conflicts that arise within the scope of the project.

The project manager translates the strategic value of the application into a definition of the core objectives the system must achieve. Because a project sponsor is generally a member of senior management, the project manager takes a more hands-on approach to the members of the project team.

The project manager is responsible primarily for the integration of the various project components and keeping the project focused on its value to the organization as it evolves through the design and development phases.

The project manager is heavily involved in the project during the start-up phase and remains aware of the status and difficulties as they arise.

Project Leader

The project leader assigns specific tasks to individuals and breaks down the overall project deliverables set by the project manager into discrete activities with defined starting and ending dates. The creation of a detailed project plan is usually the project leader's responsibility. The project leader should always be aware of exactly what each member of the team is working on and the nature of the technological challenges the team is facing at any given time. If a developer or other project team member falls behind on deliverables or runs into technical difficulty, he or she turns to the project leader first to help resolve the issue.

The project leader is responsible for ensuring coordination of the efforts of each team member. He or she is also accountable for the levels of quality in the work performed by all project staff. The project leader keeps the project manager informed of the status of development according to the plan and is also usually accountable for communicating with the end users who will be using the application.

Any re-engineering requirements with implications for the end users would be identified first to the project leader, who would have primary responsibility for communicating these issues to the users.

Technical Specialist

In any project, somebody has to be responsible for actually doing the work. In a client/server development effort, that responsibility falls to the technical specialist, who is usually a software developer. For each specific technical product in use as part of your client/server system, a primary technical specialist should be assigned within the development team. This ensures that one person is responsible for knowing the product and can transfer that knowledge to other members of the team when required. This especially applies when consultants are used to develop new systems. A staff member of the organization should be assigned to be the primary technical specialist for the products used and should stay on top of what the consultants are doing with the products. In this case, a technical specialist does not need to have much expertise with the technology to be the designated specialist.

Technical specialists become the in-house experts in an aspect of client/sever technology. This could include SQL syntax, systems integration, application software, design and development tools, or the SQL Server database management system. The complexity of features provided by client/server systems makes it vital to have a primary point of technical reference accountable for the proper usage of that technology. Without this focus, minor problems that could have been resolved if they had been identified can become exaggerated into serious threats to the project as a whole.

Because most successful client/server projects involve the use of smaller development teams focused on meeting tightly defined objectives, a single developer is likely to be the technical specialist for more than one technology. As a developer, you should be able to identify which technologies you are accountable for supporting, as well as being aware of who you can go to for assistance with other aspects of client/server technology. It is also helpful if your technologies are naturally related. For example, you might be a logical candidate for applications analyst, interface designer, and software developer, but you would likely not want to add database administrator to this list, as it is much more server-side in orientation. The most effective teams assign responsibility for technology for which the team members have a natural affinity.

End User

Everyone involved in your client/server project should have a clear idea of who the end users will be. The end user is responsible for actually taking over the application and making it do something worthwhile for the organization on an ongoing basis. This is not always as straightforward as it sounds. When they are not simply organizational experiments, information systems are intended to be a tool for someone, and effective tools perform best when properly used.

You incorporate this principle into your system by being aware of the end users and their requirements and objectives. It is pointless to develop a client/server system, release it to the end users, and then complain that they do not use it properly. The end users have their own organizational requirements that are supposed to drive the systems deliverables that must be achieved by your client/server system. There is an unfortunate tendency for systems analysts to believe that they understand the users' requirements better than the users themselves, and they lose sight of the end users by ignoring them.

Success is a function of how well your system identifies and meets the end users' requirements, not how well they understand and operate your system. They are your clients, and the success of your development efforts depends on how well they can put your system to work. It is your job to understand them, not their job to understand you. Only the end users working with the system can realize the benefits, no matter how well the system was designed and implemented.

End-User Developer

Most end users are too busy or just not interested in devoting much time to the systems development process. To be truly successful, however, your client/server project needs a sufficient amount of user input and feedback. When end users take on the additional role of developers, they become responsible for bridging the gap between the ultimate user of the finished product and those technical specialists who are responsible for building the application. The end-user developer is responsible first to convey an accurate sense of what the most useful features of a potential system would be and second to promote the system to the other end users as it is developed.

End-user developers serve as translators for both groups. The most effective client/server systems are developed using some form of iterative development, which occurs when improvements and enhancements are quickly incorporated from user feedback during the entire development process. End-user developers can provide a great deal of this feedback.

This process must also address two other functions, however. As you will see in your own client/server project, the system tends to change how the end users do business. New capabilities become new opportunities, which dictates a beneficial change in the status quo. The communication between the end users and the software developers is not simply one way. It is bidirectional, and the end-user developers serve a valuable function by making the end users aware of the new opportunities presented by the system.

Also, the sooner the end users become familiar with the look and feel of the new client/server application, the more likely they are to adopt it. The end-user developer takes responsibility for essentially pretraining the other users in the system while it is being developed, to make the system seem more familiar and less threatening. It is much more difficult for systems people to take on this responsibility because they are generally not regarded by the end users as really understanding them or being one of them. To be effective in this role, the end-user developers should be selected for their influence with the end-user group as a whole.

Systems Architect

The role of the systems architect goes beyond designing a single client/server application. A systems architect must take into account the organizational and computing environment as a whole. In this context, the systems architect defines how the elements of a client/server system fit together. Systems architecture encompasses hardware, software, and systems integration. For your client/server project, the systems architect is responsible for the overall technical design of the environment, the selection of tools for the various components, and the integration of the application with existing systems resources.

The systems architect typically works with the project manager and sponsor at the beginning of the project to ensure that it is strategic technically as well as operationally. The systems architect is expected to be highly aware of the technology itself and to ensure that the technology selected for the project has a strategic value. Technology has a strategic value in the sense that it can leverage existing resources, or that the investment in skills and expertise must be useful in the future as well as for the present. A strategic systems architecture is one that incorporates technology that will not become obsolete or esoteric. Because you are building your client/server systems with SQL Server, you can rest assured that at least one element of your architecture is based on a strategic technology.

The systems architect is also responsible for ensuring that the project is viable from a technical standpoint. Client/server technology is one of the more rapidly changing aspects of the computer industry. The systems architect is responsible for ensuring that the pieces that have been selected will actually provide the services needed and that they will integrate into an effective overall solution. No strategic value can be realized by a system that cannot be made to work.

Applications Analyst

On the opposite end of the spectrum from the systems architect, the applications analyst is accountable for developing specifications of what functions a specific client/server application will perform. The analyst is usually responsible for documenting the existing processes and systems as well as working with the users to determine what the new application will actually do. The applications analyst defines the application from a user or business standpoint, ensuring that the system performs the right functions and meets the users' business objectives rather than developing detailed programming specifications. The applications analyst, in conjunction with the users, identifies what impact the new system will have on current business practices.

The applications analyst investigates the user environment and allows the users to explain their operation in their own words. The analyst translates that description into specifications for other people to read, including members of the development team, who will gain an understanding of the users' requirements from that document. That understanding will in turn be translated into programming specifications for the creation of the software application itself.

Applications analysis has been an integral part of the software development process from the first generation of computers. There are many useful techniques for documenting application specifications, and the applications analyst is responsible for using those techniques to document your specific client/server system.

Database Administrator

The DBA is responsible for developing first the logical and then the physical data models. These data models detail each database object that must be created to support the application, including all tables, views, stored procedures, rules, defaults, indexes, and triggers. The DBA generally has the final word on how the database will be constructed and has primary accountability to ensure not only that all the database objects are created, but that the database supports the application under development. Due to the inherently separate nature of the server and client aspects of a database application, it is quite possible to develop a database structure that does not support the application, even while incorporating all the rules of proper database design. The database administrator works with the development team to ensure that the database design will support the application through an iterative logical and physical data model.

After the physical data model is implemented, the DBA typically reviews system performance with the development team and modifies the database in order to speed up data retrievals based on the query's actual performance requirements.

In most organizations, the database administrator is a centralized position accountable for managing many database applications. In such cases, the database administrator is responsible for ensuring that database objects such as stored procedures are tested and documented, and that they conform to organization-wide standards. The database administrator would be aware of existing stored procedures or other database objects that could be used or modified by the development team.

The DBA usually has the SA account in your SQL Server and is responsible for the setup of all users, accounts, and permissions, as well as for designing the physical data model to take advantage of the hardware platform on which your SQL Server runs. There are a great many technical areas in the SQL Server architecture that a software developer never sees but that nonetheless affect application performance. The DBA has primary accountability for this, as well as for database security and data integrity.

Data Administrator

Data administration is a distinctly different responsibility from database administration. The data administrator is much more concerned with the corporate standards for definition of datatypes and the nomenclature used in columns and tables than is the database administrator. A data administrator ensures that standard coding practices are used, often importing work done elsewhere in the organization or using approved code tables from appropriate standards bodies like IEEE, OSF, CCITT, and Good Housekeeping. The coding conventions used within your organization are highly dependent on the nature of your business. The data administrator is responsible for knowing which standards to use for your development effort.

It is the data administrator's responsibility to ensure that databases can be mapped together and that like terms have identical meaning across many databases. The definition conventions used by data dictionaries or data catalogs are the responsibility of the data administrator, even if creating the data dictionary is assigned as a database administration task.

In many projects, no distinct responsibility is assigned for data administration—everything falls to the database administrator. This may or may not be appropriate, considering the level of understanding of the data itself that is required. Certainly for smaller shops, where the DBA is likely also a developer, it is possible for one person to understand both the technology and the data. For larger projects or even smaller projects within large organizations, however, data administration is a unique task that should be specifically assigned.

For client/server systems that are expected to roll into an enterprise-wide solution, the issues of data administration are central to the success of that integration effort. Anyone who has worked with integrating multiple departmental systems or applications spanning several subsidiaries will tell you that often these initiatives fail not because they were technologically impossible, but because the data simply could not be matched. Application-specific code tables without an external reference or key are often the culprit in such cases.

Successfully accommodating these issues falls into the province of the data administrator. If you are intending to take on this role along with other responsibilities, it is important to be fully aware of just how this function can affect your client/server application's future and address these issues accordingly.

Interface Designer

As application programs move to a graphical user interface, the requirement for the new role of interface designer is emerging. Although even traditional applications could have benefited from an emphasis on the design and development of effective user-machine interfaces, meeting this responsibility has become vital with the increase of PC-Windows, Mac, and UNIX workstation client software. The user interface designer determines which screens are presented to the user and ensures that the rules of visual layout and design are incorporated into those screens. As multimedia applications become a more prevalent part of client/server systems, responsibility for appropriate use of sound, color, graphics, and forms falls to the user interface designer. As well as defining the face of the application, the user interface designer determines which of the many interface options is most appropriate given the task the user wants the application to perform.

Menu layout and structures, task options and features, and application conventions such as keyboard shortcuts and quick keys are all responsibilities of the user interface designer. It is important not to overlook or underestimate the impact of this role on the success of your Sybase solution. Many mediocre technical solutions have been enthusiastically accepted and endorsed by end users who fell in love with the systems interface. Conversely, many technically excellent projects have bitten the dust because the users would not work with them. Although beauty may be in the eye of the beholder, this is ultimately an important success factor for your development effort. The user interface designer is responsible for ensuring that your technically sound system looks good and fits well with the way the system's end users work.

Network Architect

Client/server systems treat the communications and networking services in your environment as a key element of an integrated solution. To ensure that the communications design can support the data throughput requirements, a network architect must be assigned accountability for layout and design of the end-to-end network topology. The architect is responsible for identifying all software and hardware required to link the clients and servers, thereby allowing the application to perform transparently on a complex arrangement of communications devices and protocols.

As you have seen, with flexibility comes complexity, and nowhere is the complexity inherent in a client/server system more apparent than in the networking of client applications to SQL Servers over a network. In some cases, the network architecture may be considered a subset of the overall systems architecture; however, communications technology is comprehensive and quite distinct from computing architectures. For this reason, I have identified the network specialist as a distinct role with specific accountabilities. Whereas the systems architect sees the entire technology set involved in the development, the network specialist is responsible for the implementation as well as the design. Many client/server projects begin development late because the planners and developers underestimated the degree of difficulty in simply integrating the clients with the server. When these systems integration issues are resolved, however, they tend to stay resolved until new operating systems and software versions are upgraded at the site or network hardware is changed.

In any event, you definitely want to know who is accountable for integrating the client and server software, hardware, and communications services before you can begin developing even the smallest client/server application. As more Sybase client/server solutions incorporate OmniSQL Gateway technology, integrating diverse host platforms and connectivity standards, the network specialist is becoming a key player in the development of enterprise-wide client/server systems.

Documentation Specialist

Although the development of comprehensive software documentation has long been considered an important part of a professionally developed system, the reality of software development has often pushed documentation to the background. As client/server systems become more prevalent, online help documentation has emerged as a standard requirement of any GUI-based client application. Responsibility for the creation of this documentation falls into the realm of a documentation specialist. This person is accountable for the creation of clear and comprehensible instructions for the operation of the system by its end users. As the documentation processes gain sophistication, this specialist is responsible for organizing the documentation and creating hypertext documents that allow the user to retrieve applicable instructions in the context of the activities they were having trouble performing.

Advances in training and communications technology such as multimedia also have an impact on your definition of documentation. Whereas a simple handbook or binder of instructions may have sufficed a few years ago, context-sensitive online help has become the rule, not the exception, for top-flight client/server applications. Soon, new applications will need to incorporate more than simple text instructions. They will take advantage of desktop computing power to train users as they go, while offering enhanced systems services as part of newly developed software applications.

In the same way that technology has created new roles such as interface designers, a documentation specialist will soon be required as a distinct role for any well-developed client/server application.

Documentation is not just for end users and operators of the systems you build. To improve maintainability and to enable quick incorporation and release of new features, documentation of the software development process itself can be highly useful.

The documentation specialist is more than merely someone who got stuck with the responsibility for writing up the system. These specialists need to understand how people learn, and structure what is known about the application to make its users and future developers more effective.

Each of these roles is unique and distinct from each other. Whether you are responsible for one or many of these functions, you should now have a clear idea of what specific responsibilities you must address as part of your client/server development effort. The responsibilities associated with each role can be grouped into four basic categories: server and systems issues, management level, development team, and end-user issues. The project leader plays a pivotal role in coordinating the various players in each of these areas. Figure 2.1.1 illustrates which roles fall into these categories.

In many cases, applications bog down or don't live up to their potential because a development team has overlooked or underestimated the importance of a key role and responsibility set. From this chapter you should now be able to identify what accountabilities should be assigned to the members of your project team and know how you fit into the development effort as a whole.

You can see in Figure 2.1.2 how and where each role and responsibility set contributes to a client/server system.

FIGURE 2.1.1.

Project roles and their interrelationships.

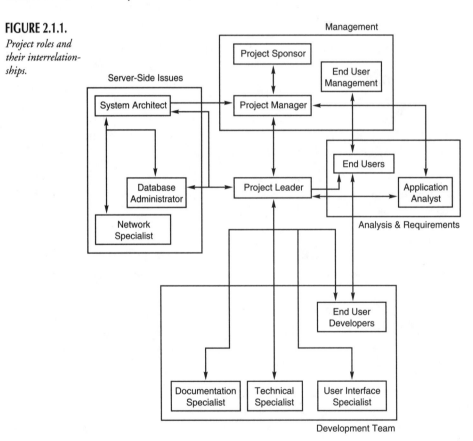

FIGURE 2.1.2.

Roles and their relationships and impact on the development process.

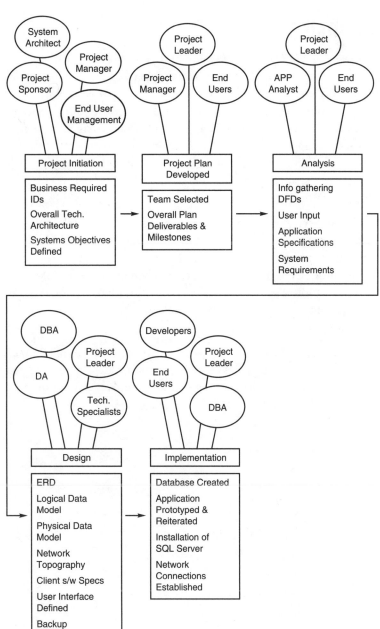

Summary

By reviewing your project and comparing it to the roles defined in this chapter, you should now be able to determine whether any key areas have been overlooked or are unassigned. As explained in this chapter, it is not necessary for any one role to be a full-time job. The key is to ensure that the responsibilities associated with the role are assigned and actually met. From a project management perspective, being a client/server applications developer involves much more than mastering the features and syntax of the Sybase product. Identifying and incorporating each and every contributor to the application into the development process is critical to the success of any systems project.

Your SQL Server offers a tremendous amount of technical power and capability. By ensuring that the development process is properly staffed and managed, you greatly increase the likelihood that this technology will be put to work effectively for your organization. Even if you are not personally responsible for making these decisions, by understanding your role fully, as well as gaining an understanding of the contributions made by others, you can much more easily create functional client/server applications.

The very nature of client/server systems is to integrate. In this chapter, you have been introduced to the "people" side of the equation. Integrating these people, in the context of their project roles, into an overall client/server solution encompassing you, them, and the technology is critical to success.

2.2

Developing Application Specifications

This chapter looks at the first few steps you would take to develop a typical client/server system. It shows how the role of the applications analyst is critical to the success of all further development efforts. As well as covering the process, it introduces you to several methods of creating application specifications that are specifically tailored for building client/server systems. Last, it takes you through a sample application using the application specification approaches recommended in this chapter.

Experienced software developers commonly feel they already have sufficient familiarity with the application development process. That experience may work as effectively for client/server systems as it has done for them in more traditional software development efforts. Whether you choose to use your own established approach or learn a new methodology specifically oriented to client/server applications, this chapter identifies the critical elements that must be defined as part of the application specification process. The objective of this chapter is to fully explain how and why an applications analyst must define the system's requirements to allow other members of the development team to use those specifications. Unlike other, more mature industries, the client/server world does not yet have standard specifications or blueprints that can be read by architects, engineers, and those constructing the system. There are many methodologies for building systems and just as many (if not more) methods for describing the requirements and objectives the system is expected to meet.

At the end of this chapter, you are exposed to a proven process for creating specifications for client/server applications, and you are shown how that process could be used to build a sample system. This is not the only way to write application specifications; I am merely proposing a method that has worked, outlining its components in sufficient detail to allow you to check your own processes and ensure that those aspects required for client/server systems are covered. If you are not responsible for the creation of the application specifications for your project, this chapter gives you a better understanding of what those specifications should contain and how to relate them to your role in building a Sybase solution.

Application Specifications: Form Follows Function

There is a very old adage in architecture and design that applies just as well to building systems: Form follows function. Usually this is taken to mean that the appearance and shape of the design must support the use of the thing being designed and built. Think of your own experience. Have you ever bought something, an electrical appliance for example, that just didn't fit right? Often, these things may look interesting or appealing, but if the design innovation does not assist the user of the product, the design detracts from the value of the product. In these cases, form does not follow function, with predictable results.

On the other hand, think of a product you have come to depend on. I am willing to bet that this object has design innovations that make it more useful to you than any other similar items you may have tried. If the form works to advance the function or the use, then it is superior to other products that do not incorporate those features. To build a better mouse trap, you don't just add racing stripes. It has to catch more mice.

Perhaps the clearest example of form following function is the current trend toward incorporating aerodynamic styling in automotive designs. The function of the automobile is to move, and streamlining the shape of cars accomplishes this movement more efficiently. The form itself is pleasing, but ornamentation is not the primary motivation—it is secondary to reducing wind drag.

This principle applies particularly well to client/server systems. If the form or the design of the application effectively supports the purposes for which it is intended to be used, it will be a more successful system than one that does not.

This is all very well, you may say, but haven't you already established that client/server systems are not static, that the requirements change rapidly and the systems designers and developers struggle to keep up with those changes? True, one of the key benefits of client/server technology is enhanced flexibility in meeting changing requirements. It is also true that users new to the technology will learn to expect things that they did not specify in the beginning. This is exactly why the application specification process is so critical to the success of your client/server project.

Good application specs identify the key business functions and core delivery objectives to be met by the system, without locking you into a set of features that your users will outgrow. In fact, to be fully effective, application specifications should work to describe the users' functions more than the system's functions. The specifications should describe what the users need to achieve, not how they will achieve it. Unless the very nature of their business changes (in which case, all bets are off), the specifications provide meaningful direction for successive versions of the system.

The process you see in this chapter shows you how application specifications lay the groundwork or foundation for developing your client/server system. It provides you with a way of describing the system to the users before you build it and ensures that your understanding of the job to be done is complete and accurate. Just as importantly, these specifications provide a means of communicating that understanding to the many members of the development team from the outset, as well as during the development and maintenance phases of the application's life.

Very few software development professionals will tell you that you should not have effective application specifications. However, the practice is often that systems are built with inadequate specifications, or that the process used to create the specs is focused on the wrong elements of the application.

To be effective, application specifications must achieve what the term itself implies: They must specify or detail exactly how the technology will be applied to the organization, not how the technology will work. The specification process deals with what the system will achieve, not how it will achieve it. The specification is less a description of the technology and more a way of defining the use to which the technology will be put.

My point may seem to be unnecessarily repeated. This focus on the users runs contrary to the nature of many in the systems world. Frequently, software developers want to work immediately with the software products with which the application is to be built. They want to get to work immediately and create something. To build effective client/server systems, this temptation must be resisted.

Good application specifications ensure that the system to be created will provide relevant and valuable services to the organization. They serve as a bridge in the understanding of what the system will do, and as the functions and services are defined, they drive the form the system will take. As you will see, the application specifications are quite distinct from the data model or any other server-side design document. Application specs deal exclusively with the use of the system and the context within which it will operate. By spending the time to develop good application specs, you can be sure that your client/server project delivers the right information to the right people at the right time. On the other end of the spectrum, by skipping or minimizing the application specs, you run the risk that your system will be a state-of-the-art, whiz-bang white elephant, of no use to anyone. Who wants to spend their time creating one of those?

An Application Specification Model

At the most simplistic level, the application specification process takes user input and turns it into a requirements document that is handed off to the systems development team, where it is used to direct the creation of the system. The difficulty facing most software developers is defining what that document should contain and the process they should follow to arrive at it.

The flow chart in Figure 2.2.1 demonstrates the high-level steps involved in specifying a new application.

FIGURE 2.2.1.
*A high-level view of
the application
specification process.*

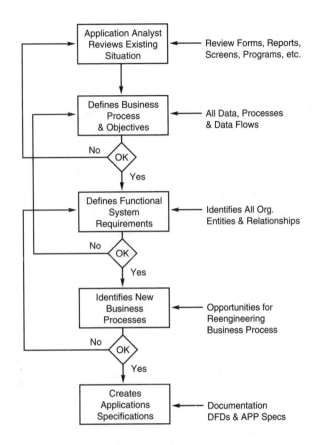

The process to be used by an applications analyst requires significant involvement with the users. Effective application specifications cannot be created in isolation because they are a reflection not only of the prospective systems users' current business practices, but also of what they would like to do differently. These specifications are a map of the users' business functions and a definition of the existing systems supporting that function.

The first step in this process is information gathering. The analyst must determine not only what data is used but what is done with that data. Most important, the analyst must define what purpose the original system was intended to serve and whether that requirement still exists or has been modified. The applications analyst uses this process to translate user-speak into a language that can be understood by the software development team from the outset and as the project continues.

As the application specification process defines the requirements and objectives for the system, it also results in a definition of the real-world events to be recorded and supported by the system. The technology is supposed to be applied to a real-world requirement, and the application specification process is the description of how this is to take place. These real-world persons, places, or things are referred to as entities, and each entity has a series of attributes or descriptions associated with it. As these entities interact with each other, they are considered to have relationships describing how each entity affects the others. Another important consideration is the rules governing these relationships. These become the business rules that place constraints on how the entities can interact.

The terms I use to describe these objects and events are metaphors for things existing and occurring in the real world. The application specification process only identifies these things—it does not create them. The entities, their attributes and relationships, as well as the rules defined by the organization, all exist outside the system. The extent to which your application specifications accurately and completely reflect these elements determines how successful your client/server system can be.

Most members of the software development team never encounter the real-world events their system is designed to support. The application specification process is where their future work becomes grounded in the reality that their system's users have to face every day.

I can go into more detail now that you can see how the application specification process works as a whole.

Information-Gathering Techniques

There are three main methods of gathering information about the users' operations and business practices:

- Observation
- Interviews
- Questionnaires

Of these, observation is the most powerful technique for arriving at a solid understanding of how the users work and what the system should do to support them. By working through the users' processes with them, the applications analyst can see firsthand what functions are performed and how. At some point, however, the analyst needs an idea of the history of how the current practices evolved and why they were set up that way to begin with. Understanding the purpose of user activities is central to defining how any new system will support them. By fully comprehending what the organizational unit is expected to achieve, the applications analyst can be sure to correctly identify the features and functions the new system must address to be successful.

This understanding is generally reached by interviewing members of the user group and their management team.

The single biggest drawback of the interview process is the requirement that the individual being interviewed know what he or she talking about. Frequently, ineffectual systems solutions are created because the people specifying the system at the beginning did not fully understand what really needed to be done by the new system. Also, many times the end users (and systems staff too, for that matter) with the strongest opinions and the loudest voices are not the ones who best understand the business processes to be supported. The applications analyst must be careful to check the results of the interviews for accuracy and completeness. An error or omission at this stage will become magnified during the systems development process and result in a great deal of wasted effort.

Questionnaires are the weakest method of information gathering; however, they can be useful when a user population is large or spread over a wide geographic area. Questionnaires can be used to confirm findings of interviews or observations and are also an effective way of balancing development priorities, at least as perceived by the group responding to the questionnaires. Questionnaires can be an effective way of uncovering problems that are known by a group of employees but for various reasons (often political) are not discussed openly.

By distributing questionnaires and preserving anonymity, the applications analyst can gain a good idea of the areas that are seen by a large group as needing change or improvement. With the relatively recent widespread distribution of e-mail and other electronic communications vehicles, questionnaires have been used as an effective way to create an open forum for discussion and broadcast the findings of the analysis.

Applications analysts most commonly use the interview technique to gain an understanding of the current business practice and definition of what needs to be done. To ensure that your client/server application is properly defined, there are a number of key aspects to successfully deriving application specifications from interviews.

FIGURE 2.2.2.

A sample questionnaire illustrating several methods of obtaining user feedback.

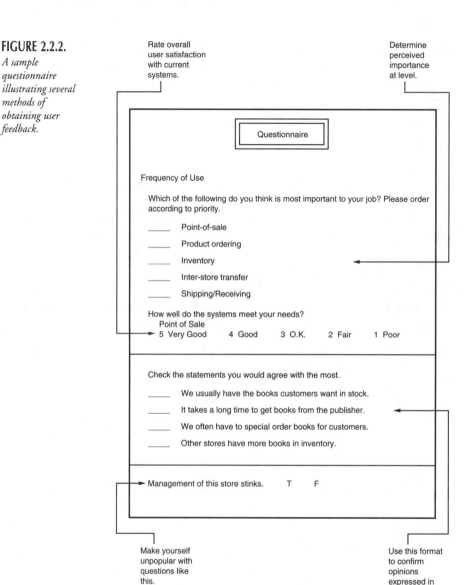

Rate overall user satisfaction with current systems.

Determine perceived importance at level.

Questionnaire

Frequency of Use

Which of the following do you think is most important to your job? Please order according to priority.

_____ Point-of-sale

_____ Product ordering

_____ Inventory

_____ Inter-store transfer

_____ Shipping/Receiving

How well do the systems meet your needs?
Point of Sale
5 Very Good   4 Good   3 O.K.   2 Fair   1 Poor

Check the statements you would agree with the most.

_____ We usually have the books customers want in stock.

_____ It takes a long time to get books from the publisher.

_____ We often have to special order books for customers.

_____ Other stores have more books in inventory.

Management of this store stinks.   T   F

Make yourself unpopular with questions like this.

Use this format to confirm opinions expressed in interview.

Defining the Business Practice versus the Existing System

The key responsibility of the applications analyst is to get beyond the description of the existing processes and identify the core functions of a business unit or applications area. People often tend to describe their responsibilities in light of what they currently do, as opposed to what they should be doing. If your application specifications deal only with existing processes and not the underlying objectives of the unit, you run the risk of simply migrating the current system with all its weaknesses and problems to a new systems environment. The trick is to identify the key business activities that the existing system was created to support and to document those to allow the new system to address those as effectively as the old system, if not better.

The perspective of the management team heading the area to be affected by the new application can often shed a great deal of light on the function that the unit is expected to provide to the organization as a whole. With this information, the applications analyst is in a better position to interpret the information gained by interviewing the staff members involved in performing the daily tasks of the unit. Additionally, you might remember from the previous section that the greatest benefits of implementing a Sybase client/server solution are gained from reengineering the business processes to take advantage of these new technologies.

The applications analyst can represent this by depicting the role of the applications area relative to the other key business functions with which the area interacts. This gives the analyst the opportunity to set the context for the system at the highest possible level, ensuring that the new system's specifications do not overlook any key interrelationship or affect any department or process existing outside the area being investigated.

By focusing on the business functions of the organizational area as a whole, as opposed to simply analyzing its existing systems, you can create application specifications that take a fresh view of what services the system should provide. Your client/server system, beginning with the analysis of the requirements, can serve as a powerful catalyst for changing the status quo. When you include all aspects of the area's functions, operations, and mandate in your specifications, you ensure that any system you build to meet those specifications will be a relevant and effective solution to real organizational requirements.

The Interview Process

As discussed earlier in the chapter, the key element to success with the interview process is selecting the right people to interview. If you use the Joint Application Development process referred to in Chapter 1.4, you can ensure, if not the right people, then at the very least an opportunity to balance opinions and viewpoints across the members of the group. The elements of the interview process are the same whether you conduct your interviews one-on-one or as part of a series of JAD sessions.

Ultimately, as you conduct your interviews you want to establish the answer to one question: Who does what to whom with which? Additionally, you may want to know when, where, and why these things are done. By answering these questions for a particular application area, you can establish the real-world entities and their interrelationships. You also identify the actions that are taken and who (or what) is affected by that action. Also, by defining the business practices in the context of this question, you can identify the rules governing each action.

I use this approach to define a set of application specifications for a store as part of the example of the technique. However, to make the previous general statement clear, consider a typical activity using the Who Does What methodology as "A customer buys a product from a store."

This is obviously a real-world event, one that everyone participates in regularly. One key to developing good application specifications is identifying the central entity at the beginning of the statement. In this case, it is the customer. Of course, using the Who Does What methodology, you could just as easily state the same event as "A store sells a product to a customer."

However, this puts the store as the primary element, and any store owner will tell you that this is not an optimum selling strategy. If possible, you want your application specifications to express the events in a manner that conveys their relative importance. In this case, a store may offer products for sale, but the sale does not take place unless a customer buys a product. This is the primary transaction, without which nothing else takes place. Frequently, when interviewing users you will find that they express the entities and relationships in the way that affects them personally: "I sell a product to a customer," as opposed to "The customer buys a product from me." As the applications analyst, you should look for ways to describe the business activities so that the description does not overly stress the role of any one participant in the process. Again, this is part of managing the interview or JAD processs.

In any case, regardless of whether you express the relative importance of the various entities in all their subtlety, the fact remains that by defining Who Does What (in whichever order), you still end up identifying the entities and the actions relating them. The key to success is to identify all the entities and situations in which they are involved.

Optionally, you also have the opportunity to express other factors that affect the relationship. For example, the date of the sale may be a significant piece of information for some other process. As the applications analyst, you investigate the area and its practices from a number of perspectives. In many cases the applications analyst ends up with a clearer understanding of the operation of the unit as a whole than most of the staff who work within the unit. However, this occurs only when a great deal of investigation has been done and confirmed as correct.

At this point in the process, the application specification is simply a description of what activities a business unit performs and what is involved in those activities. There is nothing specifically applicable to either client/server technology or even relational database management systems in general. The application specifications should stand on their own as a description of the functions performed by the business unit.

You should keep in mind that by developing application specifications first, you are both defining the process logic of the application (what the client software has to do) and identifying the data necessary to support that application.

As part of the interview process, you need to ask questions. Usually, the key questions to be resolved by an applications analyst are as follows:

1. Who is involved in the functions of this unit?
2. How do they perform these functions?
3. What are the rules governing what they do?
4. What are the exceptions to the rules?
5. When do they do it?
6. Why do they do it?
7. Where do they do it?

No doubt this seems like common sense to most of you, but developers frequently assume that they already know the answers and go off to begin work. These questions are deceptively simplistic. I do not believe I can stress enough the importance of thoroughly investigating the user requirements and deriving detailed answers to these simple questions. To ensure that the applications analysis is a useful design document, assign the applications analysis function to someone who will later be involved in the implementation of the system.

Of course, any applications analyst can ask these questions, listen to the answers, and go back to the office and write a lengthy narrative report detailing their findings. In some cases, a report of this nature is very helpful, providing background and explanations to anyone unfamiliar with the operation of the applications area. All too frequently, however, such a report is not only hard to write but even harder to read. For many people, creating a mental model of a system from a text description is difficult at best and impossible or erroneous at worst. Although people trained in a particular traditional systems development methodology may be able to quickly comprehend a system under discussion from a functional requirements document, end users generally cannot.

However, the analyst can turn the findings of the interview process into diagrams that can be reviewed with the users and quickly grasped by any systems development staff who view them later. This is one area where a picture is truly worth a thousand words. This was identified years ago by the pioneers of the structured analysis methodologies, and the techniques discussed here are based on their work. Much of the groundwork for data flow diagrams was developed by Yourdon and Demarco as part of their Structured Analysis approach to building systems. When combined with entity relationship diagrams (Peter P. Chen is considered the original inventor of this diagramming technique), these approaches to depicting systems are particularly applicable to client/server applications.

Over the past decade, many effective diagramming techniques and variations have been used for systems analysis and specifications. It is not my intention to recommend a particular methodology or technique, only to demonstrate representative samples of how these methodologies can be used. This chapter introduces you to several of the most common and effective structured analysis approaches and diagramming techniques for client/server software development.

Data Flow Diagrams

Typically, data flow diagrams (DFDs) deal with the people, places, and things encompassed by the application and the interrelationships of these things from the perspective of the data that is passed among them. As implied by the name, a DFD shows the origination of an activity as a process and expresses the flow of data from that point to the next process. These processes may be automated or manual; they may involve existing computer programs, paper, or even verbal orders.

The simplest data flow diagrams are simply a collection of circles or bubbles with processes concisely described inside them. The processes are then linked by arrows showing the flow of data from one process to another. Although at first glance this may seem too simplistic, these diagrams can be a highly effective way of depicting your understanding of the unit's main functions and how they interrelate. One advantage that simple diagramming techniques have over more complex forms is the readiness with which they can be read and interpreted by end users.

More complex DFDs can illustrate which work center or function is involved and the form number or program used to collect data, as well as identify where it is stored. As a rule, the more detail you try to capture and represent in your diagrams, the more difficult interpreting them becomes.

The purpose of the DFD is to explain the complete flow of the data at a uniform level of detail. For this reason, DFDs are usually nested so that a process represented by a single bubble in a high-level DFD is broken down into constituent parts at a lower level of detail. This is consistent with many other aspects of the client/server approach, allowing you to treat highly detailed processes as black boxes, where you understand the inputs and outputs connected to the black box without necessarily understanding how those services are provided.

By creating your diagrams in multiple levels of abstraction or specificity, the diagrams can be read and reviewed by appropriate people who will not get lost in details they are not expected to understand or deal with. Just as important, using this approach allows the analyst to start with the big picture and ensure that it is complete and correct before embarking on the next layer of detail. If you are the analyst, this means that you can provide a picture of your understanding and have it confirmed or corrected, as it develops.

FIGURE 2.2.3.
Nested levels of detail expressed in a simple data flow diagram.

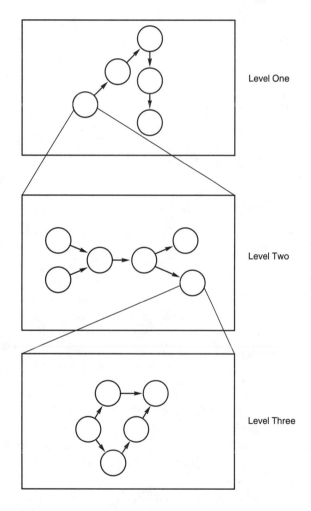

As you can see in Figure 2.2.3, charts and diagrams can have a nested structure much like an outline in written documents. Overly detailed diagrams have the same effect on comprehension as attempting to read the Income Tax Act. All the information may be there, but it is difficult to access the relevant information. By organizing your diagrams into layers of related levels of detail, it is much easier to convey and comprehend the points being made.

By using this process as the investigation proceeds, the applications analyst can demonstrate an increasingly greater understanding of the end users' work environment, which is expressed as new sets of lower-level data flow diagrams. This frequently has the effect of gaining the users' trust in the software development process and building credibility for the development team. Good DFDs often help the users themselves better understand how their business unit functions.

DFDs are generally used to depict the system from a user's viewpoint and are somewhat less useful for modeling the database itself. For data modeling, a different diagramming technique, called *entity relationship modeling*, can be used. Through DFDs you can show how the data will be retrieved, updated, and deleted, tying those data functions to specific business activities. This is especially useful for developers of client-side software programs that will use the database. Additionally, those developers working with the database server can use the DFDs to identify how the client programs will use and affect the data.

Entity Relationship Diagrams

As useful as DFDs are for depicting how the users work with the data, they are not really an effective way of demonstrating how data should be structured in the database itself. Whereas DFDs illustrate how the data is processed, the database needs a more static perspective. The data inside the database changes frequently (depending on the application), but the database objects must be more stable in order to be available to a number of programs and users. Frequent changes to the data model can require rewriting applications programs that referred to the modified tables or columns. Arbitrary changes to the database structure can dramatically and negatively affect work in progress by developers of client software.

This is not to say that the database or data model will not or should not change during the course of your development. At some point virtually all client/server projects involve refining and redesigning the way the database is structured. The closer you can get to defining a workable, stable database structure, however, the sooner you can work on supporting the areas that change most frequently, such as how the data is used and manipulated as opposed to how it is stored. Given the nature of client/server applications, where frequently the database is transparent to the users, all work spent on the server side of the equation is not seen by the users as adding much value to their application. It does, of course, add significant value to the overall client/server system, but it is rarely perceived as progress by the system's users.

The objective is to arrive at a stable and sustainable database structure as quickly as possible. This structure is referred to as the data model and it comes in two flavors: the logical data model and the physical data model. The *logical data model* depicts the entities and their attributes and may be normalized (designed to eliminate the storage of redundant data). This process is a cornerstone of any relational database application, whether client/server in nature or not. Whether normalization occurs in the logical or physical data model for your development exercise, your logical model must at least identify all entities, attributes, and relationships.

The *physical data model* relates to exactly which tables, views, indexes, and other database objects are to be created on the SQL Server and typically involves some level of denormalization (storage of redundant data) for performance reasons. The logical data model is defined and approved first, and the physical data model is created subsequently. The physical data model is refined after the application is tested and actual performance is measured.

Before you can define the logical data model, you must first know what database entities and attributes are required. These entities were identified in the application specifications process, and they generally map to real-world people, places, or things. The logical data model entities were identified as part of the Who Does What investigation performed by the applications analyst.

To assist in creating a database structure that will support your application, you first must describe the entities and their interrelationships. You describe this through an entity relationship diagram.

The first step is to identify all the distinct entities involved in your application and link them by relationship. For the store analogy, a first-level E-R diagram might look like Figure 2.2.4.

FIGURE 2.2.4.

High-level entity relationship diagram depicting the store, product, customer, and sales transactions.

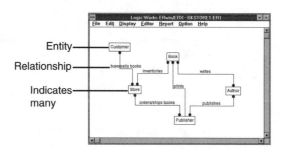

After you have identified the entities, you are in a position to describe their attributes, which are the discrete data elements that will be contained by the entities. As you can see, these entities will translate into tables and columns during the definition of the physical data model. By creating your entity relationship diagram in phases, you can be sure that you have identified all the data required by the application. As you gain a greater understanding of the application, you will be able to specify the datatypes for the columns, the length of the field, any default values, and whether null values should be allowed. These specifications are not recorded as part of an entity relationship diagram but are required before you create any tables in the SQL Server.

To get back to the E-R diagramming process, the relationships between tables are expressed as one to one, one to many, or many to many, and these relationships may be optional or mandatory. (Each table either depends on another table or has optional links to it.) A table that can exist on its own is called a parent table, and any dependent tables are called child tables.

Identification of these relationships is a key server-side consideration because of the need to ensure data integrity. In the database structure, this is referred to as referential integrity. By properly identifying parent and child relationships between tables, the database administrator can ensure that it is not possible to delete a row in a parent table without first deleting any child table rows that depend on the parent. An example of this would be to ensure that you could not delete a store in the store table without first ensuring that all products held in inventory in that store were reassigned or otherwise deleted. Referential integrity is described in greater detail in both this chapter and Section 4, Chapter 5.

FIGURE 2.2.5.

Detailed E-R diagram, including attributes.

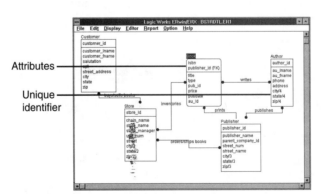

In the same way that DFDs allow the analyst to create documentation to reflect the system in varying degrees of detail, so too can the entity relationship diagram be developed and refined in an ongoing process. You begin with the big picture and fill in the details as the analysis continues.

Computer Assisted Software Engineering (CASE) tools typically represent the system being designed in some form of entity relationship diagrams. The notation conventions change from one CASE tool to another. For purposes of clarity in using the ERDs, many of these CASE tools support the use of aliasing or code names. This allows you to represent the data with readable names, including spaces within the column names or table titles, for example. Spaces and other special characters are not generally allowed in database object names. Because many CASE tools allow you to automatically generate table create scripts in the form of DDL (Data Definition Language), these code names allow you to have one set of names that are meaningful to the users and another that results in legal database object names. The drawback to multiple naming conventions is the increased number of terms used to describe essentially the same entities. If you choose not to use aliasing, you should always use system valid names, such as first_name, or fname.

Object-Oriented Diagramming Techniques

As object-oriented software development techniques are making their presence known, new ways of representing applications are being promoted. One of these is called CRC Cards, where CRC stands for Class, Responsibility, and Collaborator. The card in this case can literally be a 3" x 5" file card or some equivalent computer-based screenform. Using this approach, the applications analyst reviews the business unit to establish the scope or domain of the problem to be solved by the system. The CRC approach is predicated on the assumption that the system is a solution to a real-world problem and requires clear and concise methods of defining the problem to be solved.

The first step in the analysis phase using this technique is to identify the classes of objects encompassed by the problem domain or application area. These classes can be defined as the distinct set or template of characteristics and structures that contain an object. For the bookstore, Products would be a class and Books would be objects within that class. The characteristics of the class Products would include unit price and supplier. Additional attributes might include volume discount levels for the product. Any object or instance of the product class would include these characteristics. Objects and classes are typically defined with the vocabulary in use as part of the application area where the new system is to be deployed. In other words, you use their terms rather than inventing your own.

When translating these attributes to the CRC Cards, you can capture more detail by simply writing the attributes and description of the classes of objects on the back of the card itself.

When using CRC Cards to analyze system requirements, you would define each class as presented in Figure 2.2.6.

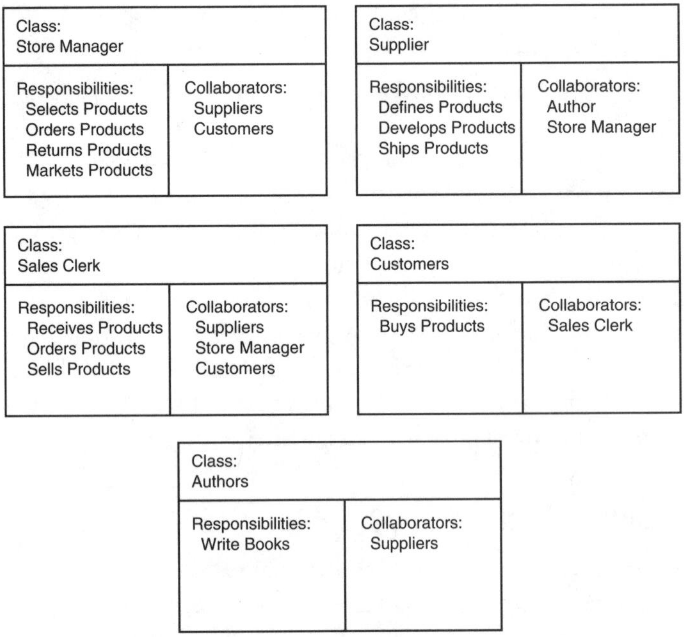

FIGURE 2.2.6.

The CRC Card represents an application as classes of objects with responsibilities and collaborators.

Class: Store Manager	

Responsibilities:
  Selects Products
  Orders Products
  Returns Products
  Markets Products
	Collaborators:
	  Suppliers
	  Customers

Class: Supplier	

Responsibilities:
  Defines Products
  Develops Products
  Ships Products
	Collaborators:
	  Author
	  Store Manager

Class: Sales Clerk	

Responsibilities:
  Receives Products
  Orders Products
  Sells Products
	Collaborators:
	  Suppliers
	  Store Manager
	  Customers

Class: Customers	

Responsibilities:
  Buys Products
	Collaborators:
	  Sales Clerk

Class: Authors	

Responsibilities:
  Write Books
	Collaborators:
	  Suppliers

As part of the analysis, you should determine not only what the classes contain but also how they behave and what knowledge or information is contained within that class. Each class must discharge its responsibilities through its behavior with the collaborators. This becomes the basis for the messages that are sent from one object to another. Messaging is a key distinction of object-oriented applications from more traditional function-oriented languages.

As you can see, the principal elements uncovered through the design process remain fundamentally the same. Through the development of the application specifications, you describe the data and the processes affecting that data as well as the relationships between the processes. The key to success is not necessarily to use a particular methodology, but rather to identify these elements during the analysis phase so that they can be used as the basis for the design of your client/server solution. In any case, whichever analysis technique you use, you must still create a data model as a separate process. There is as yet no complete end-to-end methodology for building client/server systems, and it is unlikely that there will ever be one flexible enough to deal with all the client platforms and requirements that exist in the real world.

Object-oriented analysis and design is quite different from traditional approaches but is becoming increasingly popular as an approach to building applications software in a client/server system. There are, of course, many other approaches to object-oriented analysis and design than the CRC Card methodology. The purpose of including a brief description of object-oriented analysis and design is only to demonstrate that your SQL Server solution can be built using any design methodology, including the newer object-oriented approaches.

A Sample Application

In this chapter, you have been inundated with general descriptions of analysis and design methods, techniques, and practices. At this point, you should have some idea of how the different approaches could be made to fit together to create application specifications that can serve as the foundation for your design documentation.

To make the different approaches as clear as possible, look at a real-world example of how these techniques could be used to analyze a system's requirements and express that analysis as a set of specifications and data models.

You have been assigned responsibility for the development of the first client/server application for a regional chain of bookstores. Your job is to work with the users to define their requirements, design the system, and oversee development with two other client/server technical specialists. On this project, you will perform many roles, including applications analyst, designer, developer, and project leader.

Your first step is to select a few user representatives to work with you in developing the application. Having found two or three keen, computer-literate and business-knowledgeable candidates, you interview them to investigate the nature and relationship of the store's business processes.

Your written documentation might look something like this:

Objective	To create a client/server system to support the sale, inventory, and ordering of books for the selected bookstore.
Terms of Reference	We will use Sybase SQL Server as the database.
	We will provide for the functions already automated with the existing system.
	We will allow for more active customer contact and direct marketing with the new system.
Existing Situation	Currently, the bookstore receives lists of titles offered by various publishers. The marketing manager for each store is responsible for determining which titles will be sold through the store and what quantity should be ordered.

Books are ordered from the publishers and placed on the bookshelves. Books that do not sell within six months are returned to the suppliers for credit. Customers may special order titles. Customers are notified when special orders are ready to be picked up.

The existing system provides for tracking all product orders and sales; however, it does not provide for tracking customer data, including repeat buyers.

System Requirements
The new system must maintain data on all sales, products, customers, suppliers, and transactions for a period of one year on a rolling-date basis. The system will allow tracking of any given product from order to sale as well as provide reports on activity. Customer data must be maintained to support targeting promotions based on the customer's buying practices.

To describe the functions to be automated by the new system, you might choose to list each of the activities in the Who Does What format. Using this format, the bookstore activities could be quickly described in this way:

The customer buys a book from the store.

The customer orders a book from the store.

The store orders books from a supplier.

The supplier ships the books to the store.

The store receives the books as inventory.

The store sends a payment to the publisher.

The store returns books to the publisher.

The salesclerk takes a payment from the customer.

The store sends promotional material to the customer.

The customer returns a product to the store.

Using process bubbles, you would represent the bookstore application in the following manner: The highest-level diagram would be the context diagram showing how the bookstore interacts with the various other entities involved in selling books. ·

Additionally, the analyst would record any rules that govern the transactions covered by the application specifications. A practical example of a rule might be a policy on returned products. If the store has a business rule that returns for refund may be made only within one week, this rule must be tied to the return process. Identifying such rules as part of the application specifications makes it much easier for software developers or database administrators to incorporate these rules into the system, rather than relying on staff training and knowledge to properly handle the event externally from the system.

FIGURE 2.2.7.
Bubble diagram of Bookstore, Publisher, Author, Book, and Customer.

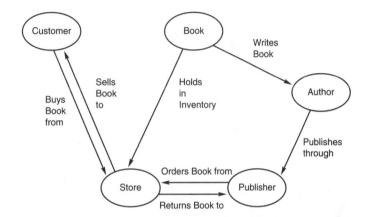

After you have established a complete diagram describing the entire process to be affected by the application and identifying all the entities involved in the process, you can move into a more detailed layer of description. This level may not identify any new entities or relationships, but it could define a greater degree of detail about the data and how it is used within the process.

At the lowest level of depiction, this diagramming technique can be used to show the step-by-step workflow for a particular process, including all entities involved, the data required or generated, and the order in which the data flows from subprocess to subprocess.

Figure 2.2.9 is based on modeling a sales transaction where the salesclerk might use a bar code reader to obtain product information and a register to capture customer credit information, such as name and card number.

FIGURE 2.2.8.

Bubble diagram of the product ordering process.

FIGURE 2.2.9.

Detailed bubble diagram of bookstore clerk selling a product to a customer.

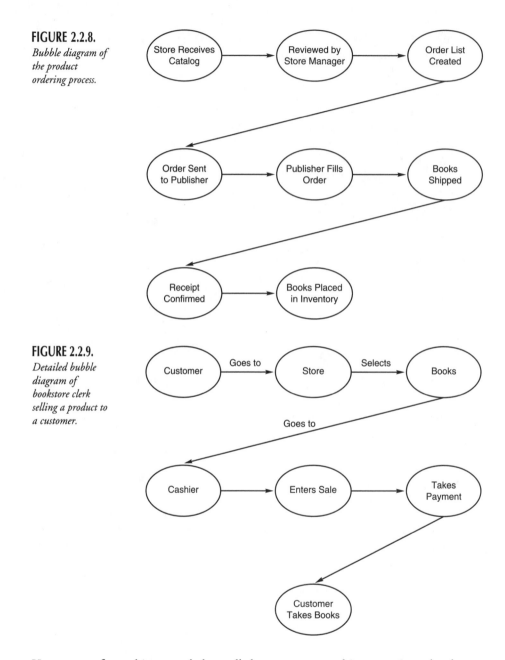

You can see from this example how all the processes used in operating a bookstore can be represented from the highest level of overview down to the single-step activities taken by a store clerk when selling the product to the customer. More detailed DFDs can be created to explain these same processes containing more information about the data involved.

As you can also see, although the detailed data flow diagram contains more information, it may not be as readily apparent to an end user or future software developer exactly how the business processes fit together. The details can become more confusing than useful.

You may want to develop several versions of a DFD for a particular level, depending on to whom it will be shown. Operational staff typically wants to see every step represented before feeling comfortable that the analyst understands their workflow, whereas management is generally more concerned with the flow of data and integration of each process with other aspects of the business. They can live without the detail.

You could also choose to represent the application using a methodology different from DFDs.

Using CRC Cards, the diagrams would look quite different but contain much of the same information. As the applications analyst, you would define the bookstore application as presented in Figures 2.2.10 and 2.2.11.

FIGURE 2.2.10.
This figure illustrates how each of the classes would work with each other.

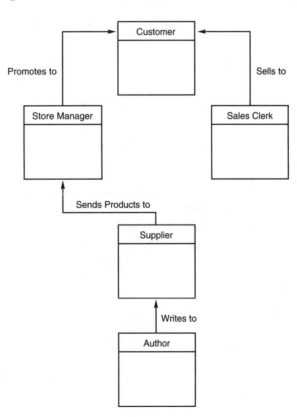

FIGURE 2.2.11.

More detailed steps of each object and how the steps relate to the bookstore processes overall.

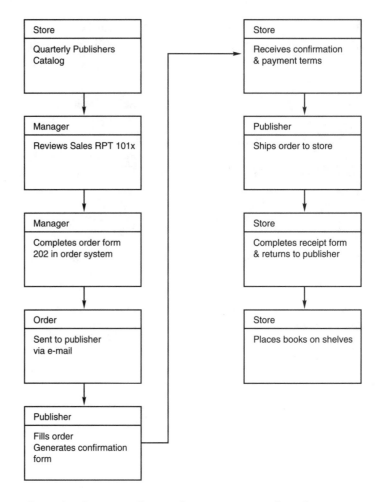

This method of specifying the elements of an application maps well to the creation of objects in the client software. Like the DFDs and process bubbles, these methodologies work to define the business processes and data flow within the business. None of these approaches alone lends itself easily, however, to the creation of application specifications that address all aspects of a client/server project.

To provide the details you need to begin building a logical data model, you need to abstract the findings of the application specifications into an entity relationship model. The entity relationship diagram for the bookstore database would look like Figures 2.2.4. and 2.2.5.

In the same way that DFDs can be used to depict the business or application processes in varying degrees of detail, the ERD can be used to describe the data at the most conceptual levels or at the lowest levels. The next chapter goes into more depth on how data is modeled and expressed in entity relationship diagrams.

Summary

In this chapter you have been exposed to several approaches that an applications analyst might take to define the nature and scope of a client/server solution. Although I have only touched on the rudiments of these approaches, you should nonetheless have a good grasp of the importance of the application specifications and how the users' input may be obtained and structured.

This chapter has emphasized the role of the users in defining where the application will fit into the overall business practice and what services the system will provide. It should be apparent how the applications analyst can use these methodologies to prepare the users for the reengineering of their applications to better take advantage of client/server technology. The objective is to understand the users' business requirements and to build a certain level of trust that the new system will effectively support those requirements. When users believe that, they become much more open to discussing potential changes to the way they do business.

You have also seen demonstrated how traditional structured analysis techniques, such as data flow diagrams and entity relationship diagrams, work to define the shape of both the client software and server database structure. At this point it should be clear how the application specifications translate an understanding of the system from the end users to the software developers in a documented fashion. This documentation not only serves as a road map for the development process, but also as a stated commitment to what functions the new system will provide. It becomes a delivery contract between the users and the software development team. This contract works both ways, in as much as the developers must commit to providing the features and services identified in the specifications, and the end users' expectations must be confined to what is in the specs, rather than growing into an impossible dream.

You cannot overestimate the importance of the contribution made by the front-end analysis and the extent to which the resulting application specifications drive the development effort (unless you thought you did not have to do any actual work after analysis). By fully understanding and clearly documenting the roles and services of the system from the practical perspective of the end users, you can ensure that your client/server application delivers valued services that live up to the expectations of both users and management.

2.3

Developing a Data Model

This chapter introduces you to the how and why of building data models to support your SQL Server environment. The importance of the logical and physical data models is demonstrated, and you see how each data model relates to the client software and the responsibilities of the members of the development team.

Data models generally fall within the jurisdiction of the database administrator, who may or may not be involved in the analysis of the user requirements. In this chapter, you see how someone who had not been involved with the definition of the application specifications can use entity relationship and data flow diagrams to identify appropriate database objects. Data models can be seen as existing on a continuum of design. Definitions of where the ER diagram ends and the logical data model begins can be somewhat arbitrary and vary from site to site. The specific division of steps between the logical data model and physical data model is also open to interpretation. My intention is to take you through the end-to-end process to identify all the steps that should generally be performed. I use the expression "end to end" in place of top to bottom because the latter expression has connotations of priority and hierarchy that I want to avoid. In any case, you may want to spend more or less time and effort on any one step, depending on your unique requirements.

Also in this chapter, I begin to focus on the way Sybase specifically deals with database objects, and how the data model can be shared among many applications independent of the platforms on which they run. I explain the distinctions between the logical and physical data models as well as introduce the considerations that affect both stages of the database environment's development. I discuss how the roles and responsibilities of each of the members of the development team relate to the modeling process. You are also exposed to the pros and cons of allowing stored procedures to be created by developers, and situations where stored procedures can be used to provide access to developers for which they do not have permission.

Last, you are taken through the step-by-step creation of a logical data model for the bookstore application for which specifications were created in the preceding chapter. From this example, you should be able to see how to apply the concepts and approaches for the creation of data models to your particular database requirements.

How the Data Model Supports the Application

One of the difficulties in working with database servers is a tendency for database administrators and server-side developers to lose sight of how "their" database relates to the outside world. As a repository or warehouse for data, the database can take on an almost exaggerated significance in the development of client/server applications. There is a danger that it will become the main focal point for development efforts.

The database becomes the center of their universe. I have been warned that this observation will not endear me to veteran database administrators. The point remains that as a Sybase developer, you must keep the role played by any aspect of client/server technology in perspective. This includes the database itself.

As I mentioned earlier, one of the key reasons for the success of the client/server architecture is implicit in the meaning of the term client/server. The database exists only to provide useful and reliable data to a multitude of client applications that use the data. You have already seen that the success of your client/server application is directly proportional to the value and utility of the data provided to the users of the system. To achieve any real value and utility, however, the database must ensure the integrity of its data and the stability of the database structure. Data integrity is ensured by applying stringent rules to who is granted permission to modify, update, and delete data, which weighs against the freewheeling access that many end users want to "their" data.

In terms of the database structure, end users cannot get useful information from a database that changes so frequently that they don't know how to find the data they need. Even the developers themselves must have some assurance that the database objects called in their application programs will not change abruptly, returning nasty "not found" messages to the user of the application when it executes.

From these requirements, you may be getting a sense that the flexibility and responsiveness to change that form key benefits of the Sybase client/server architecture do not apply to the data model. Although the database administrator has powerful system-supplied stored procedures for creating, manipulating, and deleting database objects, it is not generally desirable to have too much of this activity in the development process. For this reason, the logical data model should be developed, refined, and approved very early in the design process, and then translated into a sustainable physical data model. In other words, it is important to do the design first.

The logical data model identifies all the entities in the database, including their attributes and keys. From the logical data model, the developers can tell which entities contain the data elements that the applications need. The physical data model is the real database, and it defines exactly where the data is stored and accessed. The physical data model provides for all the database objects you will use as a Sybase developer. Without a logical data model defined from the outset, however, you run the risk of being forced to radically redesign your physical data model on a number of occasions (few of which will be pleasant).

The purpose of the logical data model is to identify all the required data and to show the grouping and the interrelationships of the groups. The reason you model the data logically is to identify the complete set of entities, attributes, and relationships to be required by your application and contained in your database. This is the main reason you express your database through the creation of a logical data model in the first place. The logical data model is derived from the application specifications, and the physical data model is based on the logical data model. The physical data model provides the database objects—the tables, views, and indexes—that are used by the developer in the creation of client/server applications.

FIGURE 2.3.1.

The process by which application specifications are developed.

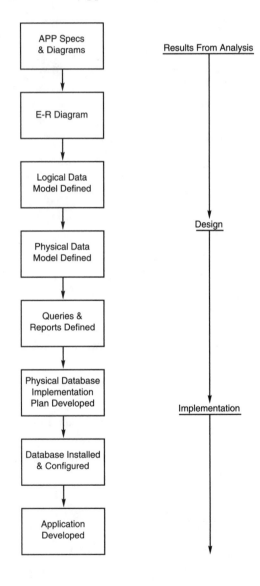

The data models are developed as a direct reflection of the application requirements and must be created before the application software that uses the data held in the database is developed.

Integrating Multiple Applications with the Data Models

A CASE tool is often used in the development of client/server systems. The role of the CASE tool is to define and manage the logical data model, in order to keep a master copy of the model. The model is manipulated, modified, reviewed, and approved in the CASE tool before implementing any real changes to the database. Data model changes are not necessarily a result of mistakes in the analysis and design phases. Frequently, the reason for modifications to the data model is a result of changing requirements or new applications that have an impact on existing data and relationships. Also, re-engineering business processes can roll back design work to incorporate improvements into the application as it is being designed and developed.

In more traditional, nonrelational applications, each system might have its own self-contained dataset, requiring data to be copied or otherwise updated across applications. No doubt you have seen the result of such approaches: the databases end up being incomplete and inaccurate. Although Sybase is addressing some of these concerns through the introduction of the Replication Server product, my purpose is to understand how to minimize duplication of data through the creation of data models dealing with a single database.

If you accept that one of the key benefits of using a SQL Server is the ability to provide a uniform database back-end to a variety of front-end clients, you must also accept the requirement to modify the database to accommodate the different needs of the distinct applications being added and integrated.

As you develop your data model, you should first determine whether the data your application requires is already stored in the database. A new application may use some existing data but most likely requires the incorporation of its own unique data as well. To accommodate this, you must first review your data model to determine where this new data will fit. This process is especially common during the development of the first few client/server applications. The data model is not so much concerned with what applications are being served by the database; it is more focused on ensuring that all data is stored in as normalized a fashion as possible and that all business relationships are identified. New applications often create the need for new tables, and the greatest impact on the data model is determining how the new tables will relate to the existing data model.

As you identify new data requirements, you need to determine the degree to which the applications deal with related data. There are performance and security implications in segregating users across databases. When you are designing multiple client/server applications, you should ask yourself whether it is necessary for each application to use the same database. If the amount of common data is negligible or low, you will want to create a separate database and data model for that application or set of applications.

The Logical Data Model Defined

The logical data model is built on the work that was done in the process of creating the first entity relationship diagrams. These ERDs identify real-world objects and show their interrelationships. This can be considered to be the logical data model at the highest conceptual level. The next level of abstraction requires the logical data model to reflect the unique attributes for each entity and to determine which attributes might be shared or duplicated across a number of entities. As you define the real-world entities that make up the logical data model, you may also choose to address the issue of cardinality. Cardinality is the term describing whether the relationships between tables have any restrictions. Through this process, you identify whether a particular table must have at least one entry before making an entry in another. Or you may delineate a specific number of entries that govern the relationship (minimum or maximum). For example, you would express the relationship between books and sales as one-to-one or one to many, not one-to-zero. You cannot sell zero books. (Although some authors might lament that it is all too possible to sell zero books, for purposes of your transaction table, you must sell at least one book.)

Typically, notation is used to express the cardinality between entities. Although there are many conventions for this expression, the legend of the ERD should identify which figures represent one-to-zero, one-to-one, one to many, and specific numbers if known. Using one convention, the cardinality between entities can be represented as shown in Figure 2.3.2.

Your users should be able to identify any of the cardinality rules governing the relationships between the entities that stem from defined business rules or practices.

The last level of detail to be identified as part of the logical data model is the data domains. Domains for columns are the valid and legitimate values that may be contained in a column. This is definitely something that your users will know about their data and that should be incorporated into the definition of the column attributes to provide for the integrity of the data. Book prices, for example, must always be positive numbers, and the users might identify that no book can have a price greater than

$200.00. By specifying the domain of the price column as $0.01 to $200.00, the logical data model conveys the range of values or domain of the data allowed in the database.

FIGURE 2.3.2.

The cardinality of relationships between the entities.

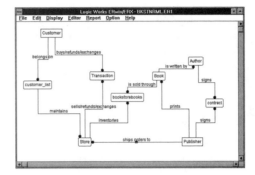

As mentioned in the last chapter, it is important to identify these constraints and implement them as part of the database, as opposed to placing the validation logic in the application, especially in a client/server environment. Although on some occasions you may choose to implement validation in an application for performance reasons, SQL Server provides many excellent features to make it easier and more straightforward to handle this consistently on the database server side of the client/server equation.

User Walkthroughs of the Data Models

I have been involved in a number of client/server implementations for which well-meaning consultants have made understanding the data model a requirement for end-user access to data. I have also observed how difficult this task is for many intelligent, hard-working end users who simply don't have the time or interest to invest in learning systems structures or terminology.

The number of users of client/server systems who actually generate their own SQL code has been estimated at as low as 2–5 percent. This implies that an overwhelming majority of users will be accessing a SQL Server or other SQL database without having any idea of how this access is achieved. You have already seen that one of the chief benefits of the Sybase implementation of the client/server architecture is the capability to support just this transparent application access to centralized data.

This creates a problem when it concerns ad hoc queries and other user data-retrieval activities on the data. The lack of appreciation about server-side issues on the part of the users can also create misunderstandings about the nature of the data that become enshrined in the data model, only later to emerge as tremendous pains in the neck. In other words, you must have your data model reviewed by users who understand the data and can relate to the data model. This is one of the responsibilities of the user members of your development team.

You should not make understanding the data model a prerequisite, however, to having access to the data for all end users. Certainly the ability to create views appropriate to predefined tasks meets a large number of the data access requirements. For those users whose requirements fall somewhere between ad hoc queries and standard predefined data pulls, a number of data access tools go against SQL Servers without requiring the user to understand table structures and join strategies. The point is that although a rationalized data model is a requirement of a successful client/server application, most of your end users have no idea about the structure of either the data model or the database itself.

The logical data model serves as a clear representation of the database structure only to users technical enough to understand the rudiments of the relational model. By having your model reviewed by experts on the data, you increase the likelihood that any errors or omissions are caught. It is important to keep in mind that the user view of the data model is almost always from the perspective of data access as opposed to data integrity. Integrity and security issues should be identified and dealt with in the physical data model, which is generally used more by the software developers than the end users, with the possible exception of the end users who serve on the development team.

The key point is that the logical data model serves as a bridge between the users' understanding of their data and the structure of the database in which it is to be stored.

Risks and Costs Associated with Modifying the Data Model

Earlier in this book, you were told that the best client/server applications develop in an iterative manner. That is to say that successive versions of the system contain an increasing number of refined functions and services and reflect the increased understanding of the technology gained through the developer's experience with the application and the technology.

This does not apply quite as well to the structure of the database. Although the client applications will and should develop and grow through reiterative development, you will want to anchor your applications to a stable database structure as soon as this becomes practically achievable.

In many cases, the progressive identification of application requirements, often completely valid and unavoidable, also creates a requirement to modify the data model. Several significant risks and costs are associated with this.

The first is the potential for wasted development time and effort. When an application has been designed to call for specific tables and generate complex SQL code, this code has to be reviewed and modified to reflect the changes to the database structure. This has similar implications to maintaining code in more traditional 3GL environments. The difference in a client/server environment is that you may not be aware of all the end-user query applications created to go against a specific data model. From this, you can see that modification and stabilization of the physical data model should occur as early in the design and development process as possible.

I have discussed the difficulties inherent in training users in the specifics of the data model, relational concepts in general, and SQL in particular. When you significantly alter the database structure beyond adding or deleting a few columns, you create a retraining requirement that can generate a significant end user backlash. The way to avoid this is to think through the logical database design very carefully and methodically from the beginning.

The second major implication is the difficulty in actually manipulating the database itself. Depending on your data volumes, it can be a time-consuming effort to move data out of tables, create new tables, and repopulate the new tables with the old data. Additionally, there are a few rules specific to Sybase that govern the way tables can be created with null, not null, and default values. I cover these in more detail later, but for now you should be aware that modifying tables already populated with data is not as easy as it looks, or at the very least, it can be a time-consuming and annoying exercise.

Please do not get the impression that you must set your data model in stone and that it cannot, or even should not, ever be changed. You can expect to go through a few iterations of the database structure, especially if your development team is new to the SQL Server product. The main point here is that time invested in designing and modeling the database structure pays off handsomely as your client/server application develops. The creation of logical and physical data models is no place to scrimp on effort or cut corners, and doing so will come back to haunt you.

Description of the Physical Data Model

If the logical data model simply ensures that you have accurately and completely identified all the data entities, attributes, rules, and relationships to be contained in your database, the physical data model is the blueprint of exactly how those elements will be implemented. The physical data model is the complete specification for the database structure, and it not only includes the data but incorporates how the database will be configured to use the SQL Server's host hardware. The physical data model not only details the tables and their column attributes but encompasses the views, indexes, triggers, and rules that will make up the database. Also, the physical data model may be denormalized for performance and include summary or high-access tables consisting of partial sets of duplicate data. The physical data model is where you document everything that exists in the database itself.

Whereas the ERD for the logical data model identifies the attributes associated with each entity, the physical data model goes beyond this to define the common keys used to link the entities. Entities exist in the physical data model as tables, and the keys are expressed as primary or foreign keys. A primary key is defined in the data model as belonging to the row of that table. You would be able to find that attribute identified as a column associated with the entity in the ERD. A foreign key is a duplication of a primary key that is used to link tables. In other words, the primary key belongs to the table, and foreign keys are duplicates used to link related tables together.

You may be able to see the relationship of primary and foreign keys more clearly in Figure 2.3.3.

FIGURE 2.3.3.

Diagram depicting bookstore application.

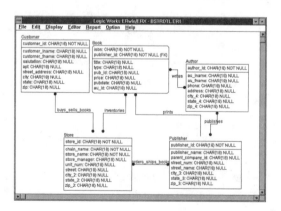

As you can see, the tables are defined, including primary key (isbn) associated with a book listed in the book table and associated foreign key entries in the transaction and inventory tables.

Unlike some other relational database management systems, the Sybase SQL Server prior to Release 10.0 did not provide for automatic creation and management of foreign keys. The database administrator must ensure that no rows with foreign-key entries can remain stored in the database if the matching row with a primary key is deleted. This process is known as maintaining referential integrity. The table with the primary key is known as the parent table, and all tables with that column as a foreign key are considered child tables. If a parent row is deleted and its child rows are not, those child rows become, appropriately enough, orphans. When rows are orphaned, the data stored in those rows is incomplete because the parent table contains information relevant to that child row. For example, if a book entry is deleted from the product table but an entry remains in the inventory table, it is no longer possible to identify the book title. The default within the SQL Server environment is to allow the database owner or anyone with delete permissions to delete parent rows without first deleting child rows and tables. This can cause quite a problem if it is not provided for in the logical data model and managed correctly from the outset.

The logical data model gives the database designer an opportunity to identify these parent-child relationships and determine how referential integrity will be handled within the database. In some cases, restrictions are placed on delete and drop permissions within the applications accessing the database, as opposed to the database itself. If you are accommodating multiple applications, however, this defeats one of the purposes of implementing a client/server environment. Most often, the database administrator ensures referential integrity through the definition of triggers and the creation of stored procedures. The requirement for these items is identified through the definition of the logical data model.

Each entity must have a unique identifier in the data model. This unique identifier is sometimes a combination of attributes, called a concatenated key. The need for concatenated keys can best be demonstrated by using the bookstore model once again. In this case, you see that the transaction table is made up of columns that exist elsewhere in the database. To make this record unique, the product_id, customer_id, date_time, and transaction_type fields must be treated as one long key, in order to make the row unique.

As you work through the process of creating the logical data model, you may come across situations where you have several levels of dependent tables. As a rule of thumb, you would not create a table that required more than four or five columns to make up a unique key. In a case where that number of columns was required to arrive at a unique combination, you would instead create an artificial attribute in the tables to be linked, which would be used as an alternate key. This alternate key would be used to link tables that had a number of foreign keys in common. In the case of the transaction table, you could create an artificial key that would be made up of a sequential or arbitrary transaction number.

FIGURE 2.3.4.

The book, customer, and transaction tables demonstrate how concatenated fields can be used to make a row unique.

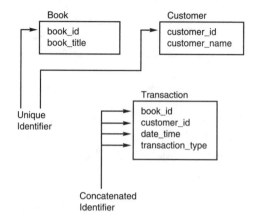

For example, Figure 2.3.5 demonstrates how the addition of an arbitrary sequential number provides a workable method of making each row unique.

FIGURE 2.3.5.

The creation of an arbitrary transaction number makes the transaction row unique.

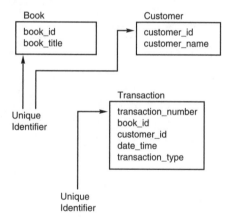

In most organizations, the physical data model is the responsibility of the database administrator. It is in the database administrator's best interests to ensure that the model is maintained in a complete and up-to-date fashion to be of assistance in managing the database environment.

As a developer, you will refer to the physical data model extensively, although if you are building client applications you will be more interested in the actual database objects available to you than information about how the system handles them. Your applications will use the views, tables, indexes, and stored procedures defined in the physical data model. It is in this model that the developer finds the correct table and column names as well as choosing which database objects will best accomplish the goals of the application work under development. From a developer's perspective, working with a well-maintained and complete physical data model is imperative.

Determining Permissions for Creating Database Objects

I have touched on the importance of maintaining the physical data model and also said that this is typically the database administrator's responsibility. This implies that only the database administrator is empowered to create the database objects, which would then be reflected in the data model. You could, of course, structure your development environment so that the physical data model may be maintained or modified by developers who also modify the database structure according to their application's requirements. Either approach has several important implications.

If the database administrator has sole responsibility for the creation of database objects, that individual can become bombarded with work requests. Views should be no problem for developers to create themselves, because the views relate more to applications requiring the data than the underlying database structure. In fact, there is an additional benefit to allowing the developers to create views. By using views for all retrievals, the developers can insulate themselves from changes to the database tables that make up the views, as long as the new or modified tables use the same names as those tables used to create the view to begin with. If a table is re-created with a new table, all views that incorporated the table previously still work exactly as they did before. For obvious reasons, if you delete a column, this statement no longer applies.

Depending on how your SQL Server environment is structured, creating tables and indexes may be more complex than you would want the members of your development team to have to deal with. Remember that every developer with a SQL Server account can create tables in tempdb and use those to work through application development issues. This may be preferable to allowing developers the permissions to create tables on the database used by the application. If the developers are not granted CREATE permissions, after they have identified what objects are required, they must still get the database administrator to create the objects for them.

Although this may be a manageable approach when you limit the database objects to tables, indexes, and views, it becomes a completely different issue when you include stored procedures.

As you might remember, stored procedures have several advantages, not the least being increased execution speed over a SQL statement issued from a client application. The capability to create stored procedures carries with it a greater requirement to understand how Sybase works. Nested stored procedures can quite easily get their creator into a series of dangerous loops, modifying other tables or initiating activities and triggers of which the developer had no knowledge. Some other undesirable results could occur, depending on what the stored procedures were intended to achieve, how well they were written, tested, and debugged, and whether the affected tables had any triggers. The key point here is that an in-depth understanding of how stored procedures work and the exact layout of the database is required to develop good stored procedures.

Stored procedures can also be created by the database administrator to perform tasks that the developers themselves do not have permission to execute. A stored procedure to create tables, for example, could be written to ensure that the appropriate log device was specified. Developers are often unaware of the internal structure of the database environment. You may choose to provide them with the ability to execute the create table stored procedure, while restricting their ability to create tables through straightforward SQL commands. This ensures that the server-side work performed by the developers is consistent with the requirements of the architecture. At the same time, it provides the developers with a method of meeting their own requirements without relying on the DBA to do the work for them.

On the other hand, depending on the nature of your development environment, the number of people involved, and their levels of expertise, you may want to allow developers to create stored procedures themselves to return results to be used in applications, as opposed to creating stored procedures used to manage the database itself. The key to being able to maintain and support the database is in how well you manage the inclusion of any stored procedures and their operation in the physical data model. Allowing stored procedures to be created and used without properly documenting them is a recipe for disaster. By creating a physical data model that contains all the elements of the database, however, you can ensure that predictable results are achieved from any given action in the database.

The optimum balancing of responsibilities across the members of your development team depends on the expertise of the people involved. It is best to define the specific responsibilities of each member of the team and then reflect those in the database permissions granted to each person. To encourage the development of reusable stored procedures, you need to assign accountability for managing their use. This usually falls within the domain of the database administrator.

Defining Database Objects as Part of the Physical Data Model

You now have an overview of the physical data model, as well as some idea about the implications of who manages the creation and documentation of the model that reflects those objects. Now consider how you map your logical data model and application specifications into a physical model of the data. I first look at the complete specification for the database objects and then go into how those objects are mapped to the SQL Server disk resources.

As part of the entity relationship diagramming process, and as you would have further refined in the logical data model, you should have a pretty clear idea of which tables must be created to support your application, as well as what column attributes, datatype, length, and default values the column should have. You can also identify what the primary unique key is for each table you intend to create. This serves as the basis for your first index. To identify any other indexes that must be created, you need to understand how the data will be accessed by the applications. Before doing this, you want to ensure that you have identified all the tables your database will contain.

The logical data model may identify entities with a many-to-many relationship between row values held in those tables. For example, a bookstore may have many books, and a book may be sold in many bookstores. These many-to-many relationships must be resolved in the data model to allow developers to retrieve desired results from joining the tables together as part of a SQL routine. You cannot determine whether a bookstore has a particular book in a data model that allows many-to-many relationships. To overcome this problem, you need to develop intersection tables to provide for one-to-zero, one-to-one, or one-to-many relationships for all the tables in your database. An intersection table is a child table of two parent tables. The intersection of the parents makes for one big happy family.

For the books and bookstore example, you have two entities, (books and bookstores). To create an intersection entity for these two, you would create something called bookstorebooks, which would represent all the books in a particular bookstore.

In this case, the real-world entities books and bookstores do not have a clean relationship between them. For example, any given book may or may not be in any bookstore, or it could be in many bookstores or all the bookstores. Conversely, a bookstore has many books. By creating a database object (table) that contains a unique bookstore ID and a unique book ID, a developer can easily identify all books for any bookstore or all bookstores for any book. The unique key for this table is the concatenation of `bookstore_id` and `book_id`. You can also see from this example how important maintaining referential integrity becomes. If a developer or an application is permitted to delete a book without deleting the corresponding entry in the bookstorebooks table, the data in that table becomes meaningless. The physical data model not only identifies all intersection tables that must be created to support the applications but also demonstrates how referential integrity will be maintained through stored procedures and table triggers. The alternative to identifying these in the physical data model is to simply implement uncommented triggers and stored procedures, which would result in some very interesting investigations for someone as part of the debugging and maintenance of the database.

Mapping the Physical Data Model to the Server Environment

As you remember from the overview of the SQL Server environment, Sybase extends to you a great deal of flexibility in how the database takes advantage of the hardware resources of the server. This is the lowest layer of the data model and should be managed by the database administrator.

At this point you would identify any segregation of logs, indexes, and tables as part of this process, determining their exact placement on separate disks. This kind of resource balancing is usually done later in the development process as part of the tuning and optimization of the application. However, allowing for some of it as part of the initial database design can save a great deal of time and effort.

The database administrator needs to create a model for the SQL Server environment identifying the specific resources available and how the database objects relate to those resources. Sybase uses logical disk devices to name physical hard disks and allows the system administrator to create segments that span multiple disks. In this way, a database can be defined to hold tables on one set of disks, log transactions to another, and hold the table indexes on a third. For a generic SQL Server environment, this structure might be defined as shown in Figure 2.3.6.

As developers, you don't need to be concerned with the physical allocation of the database objects used in their client/server applications. These activities are handled transparently to you. All these items should be modeled, mapped, and named, however, by the database administrator before any of the database objects are physically created. If you are wearing many hats as part of a small SQL Server development team, you may need to look after each of the steps yourself. However, given the complexity of the task, you can no doubt see why it is recommended to assign distinct server- and client-side accountabilities within even a small development team. It is precisely this level of complexity and the problems posed by "too many cooks" that make it necessary to restrict permissions for the creation of some database objects such as tables, indexes, and stored procedures.

FIGURE 2.3.6.

Hard disks, logical device names, segment names, and allocation of tables, indexes, and logs to hardware resources.

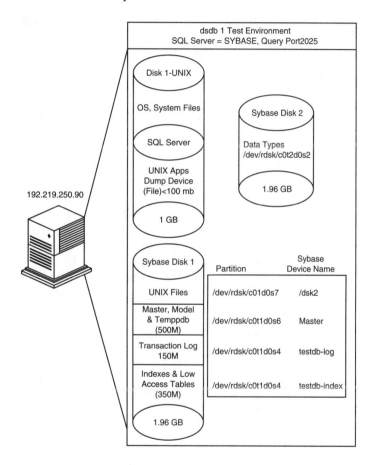

dsdb 1 Test Environment
SQL Server = SYBASE, Query Port2025

192.219.250.90

Disk 1-UNIX

OS, System Files

SQL Server

UNIX Apps
Dump Device
(File)<100 mb

1 GB

Sybase Disk 2

Data Types
/dev/rdsk/c0t2d0s2

1.96 GB

Sybase Disk 1

UNIX Files

Master, Model
& Temppdb
(500M)

Transaction Log
150M

Indexes & Low
Access Tables
(350M)

1.96 GB

	Partition	Sybase Device Name
UNIX Files	/dev/rdsk/c01d0s7	/dsk2
Master, Model & Temppdb (500M)	/dev/rdsk/c0t1d0s6	Master
Transaction Log 150M	/dev/rdsk/c0t1d0s4	testdb-log
Indexes & Low Access Tables (350M)	/dev/rdsk/c0t1d0s4	testdb-index

Summary

At this point, you should be able to see how each of the roles identified in Chapter 2.2 relate in the end-to-end process of creating a client/server application using SQL Server technology. A great many data modeling techniques and approaches can be used successfully to build client/server systems. The objective of this chapter was to introduce you to a step-by-step approach to identify applications requirements, model the data that would be used, translate that data into SQL Server database objects, and map those objects into a physical SQL Server environment. Also, you now have a better idea about the implications of restrictions on the permissions given to each developer on the project. Believe it or not, some first-time SQL Server development teams allow everyone to log in as SA!

You should also now see the reasons why the specification and modeling process is so instrumental to the successful building of client/server applications. You should also have a clear idea of how to model your application.

It is important to remember that documented models do more than simply help you plan your work. They form a vital communication link in relating the users' data requirements to the structure of the supporting database. And just as important, they serve as a road map to those new contributors to the application who will someday inherit the system from you. By paying close attention to the modeling process, you can identify applications requirements that were not previously considered, and you can ensure that your SQL Server database environment is complete and accurate. Not only that, but you can save yourself a lot of headaches by walking through your models with every member of the development team and ensuring that everyone else has a clear picture of how it all hangs together.

All the models and techniques discussed in this chapter are rooted in past systems practices and are in the process of evolving through implementation of client/server projects in organizations like your own. Those of you who are downsizing from more traditional systems architectures have already been well grounded in the benefits that accrue to a disciplined development approach. For developers who are migrating their systems up to the client/server architecture, this chapter should have provided you with some insight on how to structure your design process to successfully specify exactly what you should build.

In either case, there is no guaranteed recipe for success. It is up to you to take the essentials of the approaches recommended here and apply them to your own organization and situation. By doing so, you can assure yourself of a maintainable, workable client/server system that delivers what the users want while maintaining data integrity and system security.

2.4

Modeling Queries

So far in this section, you have been taken through the application specification and data modeling processes. At this point, you are ready to begin working on the definition of queries to retrieve and manipulate the data. This chapter introduces you to a process for translating user requests for data into SQL queries and determining how the database should be structured to support these queries.

This chapter covers how more complex queries can use various table join strategies. This chapter also looks at how these strategies affect your SQL Server database. Additionally, you will see how indexes and views can be used to provide faster and more simplified access to desired data. The implications of large queries and batch reports are discussed.

By the end of this chapter, you should have a clear picture of how the application drives the query specification process and how that creates its own demands for database objects to be used to support the identified queries.

Last, I look at the application specifications and database structure for the bookstore application. From this you can see how the query definition process works, and you should be able to apply that approach to your own client/server application design.

The Role of Queries in the Application

You have already been introduced to the application specification and data modeling processes. From this exposure you should have a good sense of the application as the driver of the technology and the database as the raw material for meeting the user demands for data. What you need at this point is a means of meeting the users' requirements for data from the database structure you have created. You need queries.

For these purposes, queries consist of all SQL statements that retrieve, update, insert, or delete data. The common denominator is that all those SQL calls must be written in TransAct SQL, the Sybase implementation of SQL, and they will access data modeled through the process identified in the previous chapter.

At this point, you should be able to see why the application is designed as shown in Figure 2.4.1.

Without fully understanding the users' requirements, you could not identify all the data required; and without a comprehensive data model, you would have no idea how to best structure your SQL statements to retrieve that data. I will proceed from here under the assumption that you are fully convinced of the need to spend time and effort defining comprehensive application specifications and modeling your data. Now you are ready to define your common queries.

FIGURE 2.4.1.

Application specifications flow to data models through query definition, and database objects are created.

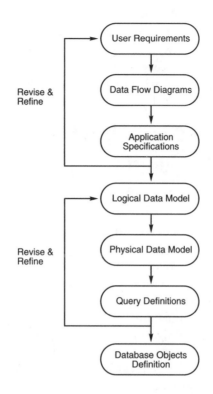

One of the selling features of a SQL Server solution is the flexibility in providing ad hoc access to data. For obvious reasons, predicting the extent and nature of ongoing user requests for data is difficult. At the same time, you can provide access only to data that has been identified and modeled as part of the design process. For this reason, ad hoc queries can be treated as simple sorts, filters, and reports based on production reports and predefined queries, which are required on an ongoing basis as part of the application. In other words, you should identify most or all of the query requirements in advance, even if they are implemented as ad hoc queries rather than programmed as part of an application. What you want to avoid is uncovering an ad hoc query that would require redefinition of the database. The query definition process becomes central to the success of meeting your users' requirements in the building of your client/server system.

It also serves as an excellent test of your database model. Rest assured that as you define the regular queries the application is expected to generate, you will identify changes or improvements to your data model. After all, the queries define how the data will be used, and the database structure exists primarily to support this process.

At this point, you should not be terribly concerned with the client application software that will generate the SQL for the queries. The query specification process should first be treated as part of the database design, and as such the queries can be written as vanilla-flavored SQL statements. Only after the queries have been specified and the database structure validated do you have to address the issue of exactly how your application programs will generate the SQL for the queries.

Translating User Data Requests into SQL Queries

As you review your application specifications, particularly the lower-level DFDs, you can identify where reports or screens are required by the users. From the specs, you should be able to put the use of the data into the context of the work the users will be performing. This helps you define a query that pulls all the data necessary from the database to support that function. At this point, the end-user members of the development team contribute most. No matter how much time you have invested in understanding the user requirements, when you get to the detailed level of exactly which fields will be required by a particular job function, your users will know more. One of the most straightforward and quickest ways to specify queries is to review the DFDs with your end-user development team members, and create query specifications for each data retrieval identified in those DFDs. If you don't have the luxury of working this closely with your end users, you may have to identify the required queries yourself and ask the users to review the query definition for completeness.

To model queries, you need to know which data elements the users must have to support the job functions within the application area. One effective method of ensuring that you have a solid grasp of the users' requirements for data is through a forms review. You can probably safely assume that you are not building the business function from scratch and that some existing manual or automated processes are available. Even if you want to completely reengineer these processes, the forms, whether paper- or screen-based, will be useful in determining what data needs to be displayed together.

Determining SQL Query Types

Before you can map your requirements into actual SQL queries, you should be aware of the query types supported by SQL Servers through TransAct SQL. Each of these types has implications for the database, not the least of which are performance considerations. Still, you should be aware of the nature and features of each type of query in order to identify the query strategy appropriate to meeting your users' data requirements. The issues that arise from designing simple retrieval queries can be expanded when dealing with changes to the database tables using insert, update, and delete commands. You should first address simple database queries to retrieve data.

The SELECT Command

Although many of you are already very familiar with SQL queries, I will still hit the highlights of the command in review before covering how modeling queries relates to the overall design process. Those not yet familiar with SQL will find the following a brief overview of the capabilities of SQL queries, not a tutorial in creating SQL syntax. T-SQL is covered in more depth in Section 4, Chapter 3, "TransAct SQL."

The SELECT command allows you to retrieve rows of data from tables held in your database. To retrieve all rows from a table, you need only create a query using the SELECT statement, such as

```
SELECT * FROM Table_name
```

This returns everything contained in the table.

The SELECT command supports several qualifications, including WHERE.

This allows you to specify values to retrieve subsets of the table matching the condition identified in the WHERE clause. This clause supports all comparison operators, including greater than, less than, equal to, and not equal to, as well as the logical operators AND, OR, and NOT. This allows you to create queries with compound WHERE clauses. Using this syntax, you can construct queries that allow you to retrieve any number of columns where data meets the specified conditions. For example,

```
SELECT * FROM table_name WHERE column1 = xyz AND column2 < 10 OR column3
> 100
```

This simple SQL statement retrieves all rows with xyz in column1 and with either column2 values less than 10 or column3 values greater than 100. Through combinations of conditions, your queries can narrow the results retrieved from a table or tables to the exact requirements of the application.

Additionally, you may use range conditions with the WHERE clause, such as between, not between, like, not like, in, not in, is null, or is not null.

WHERE clauses may also contain subqueries, which are select statements nested within another select, insert, update, or delete statement. The outer query operates on the data returned first by the subquery nested within it. Subqueries may contain subqueries themselves.

The resulting output can then be managed with the following modifiers:

■ GROUP BY: This allows the returned rows to be sorted according to the value of the column named. For example, `SELECT * FROM table_name GROUP BY column1` displays the returned rows with each row sorted by the values in `column1`. This is useful when you would like to see the retrieved output displayed in order of city or department number, for example.

■ ORDER BY: This sorts the data in alphabetic or numeric ascending or descending order. This is useful to display data differently than the default sort order of the database. Rows are generally returned in the order in which they are stored in the database. The ORDER BY clause ensures that they are sorted as the query requires. For example, `SELECT * FROM table_name ORDER BY column1 asc, column2 desc` sorts the returned rows first by `column1` in ascending order and within that by `column2` in descending order.

As mentioned earlier, the specific syntax and modifiers for Sybase are addressed in greater detail in "TransAct SQL," Section 4, Chapter 3. Here you will find only a brief description of each of the query types supported within a SQL Server environment.

The SELECT command may be used with several additional options, such as DISTINCT to suppress duplicate rows, or INTO to populate a new table with results retrieved from an existing table.

As you can see, the SELECT command provides a great deal of power to retrieve data according to many criteria and format that output in a manner that is most useful for the application.

Using SELECT with Multiple Tables

For all its power, you will find that retrieving data from a single table using the SELECT statement will not meet all your query requirements. SELECT statements can be used to retrieve data from multiple tables by either using the UNION operator or joining tables.

The UNION operator combines the results of two or more SELECT statements into one result set, suppressing duplicates as a default. The SQL statement `SELECT * from table1 union SELECT * from table2` provides a result set of all the unique rows from the two tables. Several rules govern the use of the UNION operator, which I cover later in the T-SQL chapter in Section 4. During the course of this chapter you are only introduced to the various query options open to you, in order to better understand how to structure your database to retrieve data from it.

SELECT statements may be written to allow you to retrieve rows from multiple tables by specifying the column on which the tables are to be joined. This join is expressed as a WHERE statement. For example,

```
SELECT * from table1, table2 WHERE table1.column9 = table2.column8.
```

This query retrieves all the rows from `table1` and `table2` that have the same value in `table1.column9` and `table2.column8`. Conceptually, you use the SELECT statement to create a single table from which you retrieve all the rows you require. These joins are at the heart of the relational model and are one of the reasons you have to spend so much time modeling the data. Without columns with which to link tables, you cannot retrieve the results you want. If you duplicate columns willy-nilly, the performance of your database will be so poor as to make it unusable. The query definition process allows you to determine which tables will be linked in queries to support the application.

Selection criteria such as <>= , as well as AND, OR, and NOT can be used to affect the join to retrieve the exact data set desired. As you might anticipate, several rules and qualifications govern this process. These are covered in the TransAct SQL chapter. For these purposes, it is sufficient to say that by using WHERE clauses incorporating multiple search conditions, you can define queries that retrieve exactly the data your application requires, with the caveat that the database structure must support the linking of the tables you wish to access.

Both using UNIONS and creating table joins as part of the SQL query require you to have a good grasp of the data and the data model. As I mentioned earlier, this is not generally expected of end users, even those who are technical enough to use SQL to retrieve their data.

Another method of representing data from multiple tables is through views. After defining the view, subsets of the data may be retrieved using a SELECT statement where the view name is used in place of the table name. The same qualifier and operand options may be used against the views as can be used to retrieve data from tables. Views are especially useful for defining complex table joins, which require a great deal of familiarity with relational database concepts and SQL syntax rules. The views are set up in advance by a developer or the database administrator and can then be accessed as if the rows were contained in a single table.

The JOIN Command

You saw in Chapter 2.3 on data modeling that the relational model for databases calls for normalization or the absolute elimination of duplicate data. Also, denormalization may occur for performance enhancement and system optimization.

Because the relational model insists on data normalization, it must also provide a method of retrieving related data contained in many tables. This feature is known as the JOIN command and is a central distinction between a relational database management system and any other type of database.

Because joins are an important concept in any relational system, let alone a client/server RDBMS, it is important to have some understanding of how they work in order to design an application that uses them properly. A misused join statement does not necessarily result in the return of an error code. Instead, a bad join can yield misleading or invalid results without a complaint. This is another reason that joins are important to developers and often are kept transparent to end users of an application.

The first step performed by a query that contains a JOIN statement is to form the Cartesian Product of the tables identified in the query. For a join of two tables, the Cartesian Product is the result of multiplying the number of rows in one table with the number of rows in the other to identify all possible relationships between the rows. This has significant performance implications for even moderate or small tables. The Cartesian Product of two tables with 1,000 rows in each is 1,000,000.

Once the Cartesian Product has been formed, all rows not matching the conditions defined in the WHERE clause are eliminated. Because many of the relationships that are mathematically possible between two tables are neither valid nor meaningful, all queries incorporating joins must have a WHERE clause defined. This yields a result set of a manageable size, even if all the rows in each table are retrieved.

Sybase has incorporated methods of reducing the overhead required by this process into the query optimizer. For this reason, in which order you specify the tables or columns to be retrieved is not important because the query optimizer determines the most effective strategy for retrieving the data from the tables. Even the query optimizer cannot help you, however, if you do not at least provide a simple WHERE clause condition to return a result set smaller than the Cartesian Product.

Join Strategies and Options

Whether you define your join as part of an ad hoc query or as part of the create view syntax, several options and restrictions affect the join. The most common form of a table join is the equi-join, or a straightforward linking of two tables based on a matching column. In the physical data model, you identified foreign keys. These keys are used to create equi-joins between two tables, allowing you to retrieve the desired result set from both in one select statement. The results retrieved eliminate the duplicate column by default. This is known as a natural join.

Several other joins can also be used, including the following:

- Self-joins: This is the joining of a table to itself. You would use a self-join to obtain rows that compared values in different columns that could not be simply expressed with Boolean operands greater than, less than, or equal to. For example, you may wish to retrieve a subset of rows with one column in common. A self-join is one method of getting exactly the rows desired from the database; more straightforward retrieves will not suffice.

- Not-equal joins: This is a variation of the equi-join and uses the same syntax as an equi-join except it contains a greater than, less than, or not equal to symbol in place of the equal sign. This type of join yields results that contain implicit comparisons other than equality.

- Outer joins: These joins are used when you wish to retrieve all the rows from one table in addition to selected rows from another table. An equi-join would give you only the rows that matched, whereas an outer join can give you additional information that matches rows where it exists. For example, you would use an outer join to retrieve all employees from a department, and if they had a parking space, retrieve information about their cars as well. An equi-join will not suffice for this example because the results retrieved would simply be all employees who had parking spaces and cars, not all employees, plus car information if applicable.

Using Views in Place of Joins

After you have identified the appropriate tables, columns, and conditions for a query, you may wish to streamline the retrieval by creating a view. The view presents a logical table to a user or application and has already defined the join columns and conditions to be satisfied. A single `SELECT * from view` statement returns the same results as the more complicated `SELECT * from table1, table2 where <several conditions>` statement. For more technical end users, this is a far more convenient method of providing data access. Views can be customized to provide different presentations of the same data, filtering out data that is not germane or of interest. Lastly, views can be used by a variety of individuals with a diverse range of expertise or familiarity with systems.

From the database administrator's perspective, having control over the definition of joins reduces the chances that someone will execute a SELECT statement that yields inappropriate results or consumes horrendous system resources. Additionally, views allow for security because users can query and modify only data presented through the view. Other table columns not defined in the view are neither visible nor accessible.

At this point, you should review your application specifications, DFDs, and data models and be able to determine exactly what retrievals your application will require. When you identify those queries, review your data model to ensure that you have all the foreign key relationships you need to retrieve the data.

Having modeled your database for data retrievals and queries, now look at some of the implications of modifying the tables in the database.

The INSERT Command

The INSERT command is used to add rows to tables in the database. You can use INSERT to explicitly identify the values to populate the columns, or you can use a SELECT statement to pull values already in another table. An INSERT statement identifying the specific values to add to a table might look like this:

```
INSERT into table_name
values ("xyz", "ABC", $9.99, 12345)
```

To use this syntax, you must have a correctly specified value that maps directly to each of the columns in the table. In this example, the table has four columns, the first two being character, varchar, or text, each of which requires that the values be placed in quotation marks when dealing with values in columns of these types. The next value is a dollar figure stored in a money column, and the last an integer.

You may change the order or insert values into a subset of columns by listing the columns after the table name.

```
INSERT into table_name (column1, column3)
values ("xyz", $9.99)
```

An error will occur, however, unless the table allows nulls or has specified defaults for the columns where specific values have not been provided.

The INSERT statement can be combined with a SELECT to retrieve data from other tables. This could be expressed as follows:

```
INSERT into table_name
    SELECT * from other_table
```

This statement operates similar to a subquery, which is a query within a query. The SELECT statement is executed first and the results are passed up to the INSERT statement. Naturally, the values from the other_table must be compatible with the number of columns and the defined datatypes or an error will occur.

Also working within the same restrictions regarding nulls and defaults as applied in the previous examples, the INSERT with a SELECT can be used to retrieve a subset of another table's columns.

```
INSERT into table_name (column1, column3)
   SELECT (column1, column3) from other_table_name
   WHERE <expression>
```

Sample Queries

If you review the data flow diagrams for the bookstore application, you can see that several input forms, retrieval screens, and printed reports have been identified. To complete the specification process for the sample application, you must also define exactly how these queries will select data from the physical data model and determine whether you need any additional database objects.

Looking at the physical data model, you can see that all product information is in books. Because the unique key for a particular book is the ISBN, your first query will determine that number from the known subject, author, title, and publisher data.

To accomplish this, your query can be expressed as follows:

```
select isbn from books where subject = <expression>
or author = <expression> or title = <expression>
or publisher = <expression>
```

This query would be awkward to implement because you would likely not know all the values to supply to the WHERE clause. You could either create dummy values (such as "xxxx") for the unknowns or restrict the WHERE clause to include only the knowns. For purposes of modeling the query, however, I have identified all the possible qualifiers, the data to be retrieved, and the table from which to retrieve it. Although the actual implementation of the query would yield syntax that was somewhat different, as a query definition it serves to identify whether you have the right database objects to support the query.

Following the DFD, you can now determine whether the book is in stock through the following query:

```
select * from bookstorebooks where isbn = <previously_retrieved_value>
```

The result of this query tells you which bookstores have the book. To determine whether a particular bookstore has the book in stock, you might use the following query:

```
select * from bookstorebooks where isbn = <value> and bookstore =
<value>
```

This may not give you enough data if the reason for the retrieve is to fill a multiple order. Although you could establish whether a book was in stock at a particular store, the application needs to know how many books are in inventory at that store. From this you might choose to modify your database structure to store the value quantity in bookstorebooks. While you are undergoing this process, you might also identify that you want to include a number of other columns, such as department, under bookstorebooks to make it easier to send the customer to the right place to find the desired book.

As you can see, the query process identifies whether you have all the data you need. Modeling the queries before finalizing the database structure is a vital component to avoiding duplication and wasted effort in the client/server development process.

After modeling the previous query, you identified that a table needed to contain more information. In some cases, the data may already be in the database, just held in a different table. Moving to the next query flagged as required in the DFD, you can see specifically how this might be defined for your application.

To sell the book to a customer, you need to retrieve the book's price and title information, then update the quantity column in bookstorebooks to reflect the sold book. Through this modeling process, you can see how the database objects defined in your physical data model will be used by your application.

Summary

In this chapter, you have been given an overview of the various types of SELECT statements and options by which data can be retrieved from one or more tables. You should have a better appreciation of why it is necessary to model your application's queries in advance of building your application itself, and be aware of some of the implications for performance that these queries may present.

It may seem that most of the work in building your client/server system is up front and does not require physical access to a SQL Server. As discussed in the client/server application development models, the importance of design and specification of the application before building it cannot be overstated. The more familiar you are with the business process, database structure, and query definitions, the better chance you have of quickly implementing a successful client/server system that takes full advantage of the SQL Server's open and relational architecture.

Gaining a full understanding of the results returned by various queries allows you to demonstrate to your users that your client/server application will effectively meet their requirements. The alternative to modeling the queries is to learn by doing. This can result in wrong or incomplete data being returned by the query and can negatively affect the users' confidence in the system. By modeling the queries, you can ensure that you define the joins, views, and qualifications for the SELECT statements according to sound relational database principles, and also that the returned results are valid for the application.

As soon as you know exactly which queries will be run against the data, you can begin the process of determining whether the queries should be generated by the application or be executed as stored procedures. The implications for performance and potentially wasted effort do not encourage a trial-and-error experimental approach.

By modeling your queries as discussed in this chapter, you can now prepare to build the application itself. To clarify the query-definition process, look at how you would apply what you have learned to the bookstore client/server application.

2.5

Defining Report Requirements

Systems built with the traditional host/slave architecture introduced batch reporting to organizations many years ago. Organizations found themselves covered in a blanket of printed reports, many of which were of questionable timeliness, accuracy, and validity. These useless reams of paper are a common complaint of traditional systems users.

When introducing a client/server system to an organization, there is a natural tendency to stress the online query capabilities of the new application. This plays to one of the strengths of the new systems architecture. Batch reporting is far from dead, however. In fact, your SQL Server may find many of its most vocal supporters in end users who never get close to working directly with the system.

There is no reason why a client application running against a SQL Server database cannot generate and print batch reports. Online capabilities are so powerful and appealing that developers tend to want to build applications that emphasize those capabilities.

As part of your design, you must identify those data query and reporting requirements that will be handled as part of a batch process. Like your online queries, modeling these reports may identify database objects or entity relationships that are not at first apparent. Additionally, many front-end tools are intrinsically oriented to online display and do not support the necessary formatting and document management capabilities that more mature report-writer applications support. Your design needs to identify how these requirements will be addressed.

Batch Reports versus User-Generated Reports

Even with the most powerful SQL Server environment built on top of the most capable hardware environment money can buy, lease, or rent, you can still find ways to build queries that take eons to execute. Of course, query optimization and database tuning alleviate some of this. You saw in Chapter 2.4 that using a SELECT without a WHERE clause yields a Cartesian Product (a table that contains a total number of rows equal to the rows in each table multiplied together). A table of this nature is as effective and elegant as a pig on stilts.

You can probably safely assume that you will soon be familiar enough with the syntax to avoid these sorts of mistakes (if you're not already). Of course, it is still possible to develop the "query from Hell."

Provided that you must run the query, this is the sort of retrieve that is a natural candidate for a batch report. Batch reports were introduced as a way of compensating for host performance, and even with the inherent power of the client/server architecture, you may still need to resort to this technique.

Of course, you must also design the end use of the report into the query definition. Not everyone working with the data will have (or want) access to a computer. There is always a requirement to print reports that can be taken away, and these reports are not always merely extensions of online queries. Additionally, the introduction of GUI-based client software has made it possible to relate batch reports to the online process in new and interesting ways.

Questionnaires

Many database applications incorporate data from sources outside the organization. Although strides have been made to integrate communications electronically, the medium of the day is still primarily paper, at least as a backup. Questionnaire applications using client/server technology allow batch reports to be built that output data in the database in the format in which they would normally be entered. For a census application, for example, this means that instead of circulating a blank form every time, a report could be written that would pull the data and preprint the questionnaire. The targeted recipient could then change only the data that was not current or relevant. How many times have you complained of being required to repeatedly write down the same data on a single set of forms or questionnaires?

Forms

Information exchange between individuals and organizations has become standardized through the use of forms. True, some of these forms are online and interactive, but a great many forms are still printed on paper and distributed. Client/server applications lend themselves well to retrieving data and presenting the results in a screen form. It is a small step from there to print that form. This may seem to be part of an online process in which the application user brings up the form and then, as one of the application's options, prints the form. This works for a low volume of a few forms, but many form-based applications involve the distribution of hundreds or thousands of such precompleted forms. This is definitely a candidate for a batch-reporting process.

Database Publishing

One of the most interesting batch-reporting applications that has been enabled by client/server technology is database publishing. Manufacturers, for example, often offer their products in the form of catalogs in which the object offered for sale has corresponding data, such as a part number, price, and quantity, which must be maintained in a database. Even for the bookstore application, you can easily see how a particular bookstore or even publisher might use database publishing to retrieve data held in the database and output it to paper for subsequent printing and distribution.

Database publishing is a more interesting form of reporting than traditional batch reports due to the capability of storing graphic data in the form of TIFF images and other binary large objects (BLOBS). In this sort of application, the catalog creation and publishing process itself becomes an end user of the database application. This is the sort of requirement and capability that you want to identify in advance of implementing your client/server database application. Creating camera-ready art from data held on a database places extensive and unique demands on an application. The benefits often greatly outweigh the risk and costs involved, however.

Retrieving Data for Reports

As discussed earlier, T-SQL statements in the form of stored procedures can retrieve data from tables for any application. However, batch reports often require summary, subtotal columns that may or may not be held on the database. In some cases, you may want to store such data in tables so that it can be calculated and used by many applications. Summary data is redundant data, however, because if you store the original values, you can always compute the summaries, subtotals, and averages as you need them. The considerations here are the trade-offs between storing redundant data and the time it takes to calculate these columns. Additionally, you need to determine whether you should arrive at these calculations in your application. If the data is required by more than one application, you may want to calculate it using a stored procedure to eliminate duplication of effort.

Summary

In short, new client/server systems tend to stress online, interactive queries and reporting. Certainly the emphasis on graphical user interfaces (GUIs) strictly apply to users sitting in front of a computer.

In spite of this focus on the online aspects of client/server systems, batch reports and data publishing will continue to be important components of new systems. Delivering the right information to the right person using batched and printed reports may still be timely. This is especially true when the computing resources consumed to satisfy a query simply cannot be reasonably performed online.

The key point to take away from this chapter is that even if you can provide every user with online access to data, there will still be times when batch processing is the most appropriate option.

2.6

Data Integrity and Recovery

You are now ready to address the last step of the database design phase. Having completed the applications analysis, logical and physical data models, and the query definition process, you can address the issues of security and data integrity.

Like every other aspect of good client/server systems development practice, security and integrity must be designed into your application. This chapter introduces you to the considerations and implications of database security, including identifying appropriate access permissions and determining the most effective backup strategies for your application. Additionally, you are taken through a step-by-step process for determining the data integrity requirements for your application.

This chapter also covers protecting your database from the perspective of defined perils. You need to determine what could go wrong, consider the risks and costs associated with that threat, and identify an appropriate method of protecting your system accordingly.

Issues of data integrity and security can range from restricting specific columns from view or modification by particular users all the way to establishing "hot sites" that can immediately take over all the processing of your entire server in the event of a disaster.

Enterprise-wide, mission-critical applications require comprehensive and effective backup plans. Even the smallest, prototypical client/server applications have some security and integrity requirements. In this chapter, you see how to incorporate those requirements into your design and use SQL Server options to accommodate them.

Threats and Perils

Like any type of insurance, data security and integrity issues revolve around the identification of the worst-case scenario. You must play a game of "what if" and work through the scenarios until you arrive at a conclusion. This may seem somewhat morbid, as if your system were cursed or in some way doomed. As a software developer, you are no doubt more used to building and creating things than being fascinated by the multitude of ways they could be damaged or destroyed.

This is a very useful exercise to undergo because identifying the specific threats your application may face can help you bolt the barn door before the horse is stolen. Of course, if the door is bolted really well and a fire breaks out...

The point is this: By identifying specific potential threats or perils, you also can identify effective steps to either protect your database applications or recover from disasters if they do occur. Inherent in the client/server design is the opportunity to provide centralized services, such as backup, transparently for data that might have previously been maintained in a department without the discipline of a professional IS shop. This is one more of the ways that your organization can benefit from integration of your database applications with SQL Server.

In general, the risks of compromise or loss of data are consistent for most organizations. Risks of floods, earthquakes, or falling meteors are statistically the same for nearly everyone. What differs is the degree of impact that loss might have on the organization. Some of the more common and realistic threats to system security include unauthorized access and systems failure.

Unauthorized Access

A recent Supreme Court ruling handed down the decision that confidentiality was not a right; it was something a person or an organization enjoyed. The implication of this decision is that it is entirely your responsibility to protect your data against unauthorized access, if you wish to "enjoy" confidentiality.

Protecting against unauthorized access includes some distinct variations:

- **Breach of Confidentiality**: Some data is more sensitive than other. Almost all organizations want payroll information to be kept confidential, for example. Even the capability to retrieve certain data may be undesirable. As part of your design process, you must identify what data should have restricted access and to whom access should be provided.

- **Willful or Accidental Deletion**: Whether motivated by malice or merely an accidental slip, unrecoverable deletions of data can be costly. In many organizations, data is considered an organizational asset, and appropriate precautions should be taken to protect that asset against destruction or loss.

Systems Failure

This is one of the more familiar and somehow less threatening perils. All systems fail at some point or another. As part of the design process, you must identify what the costs and implications of systems failure would be. Several aspects of systems failure can be considered separately:

- **Media Failure**: In the unlikely event of a forced landing of your disk heads, what happens to your data? Certainly not all disk failures result in catastrophic data loss, but what if one does? You must be prepared to recover your data and determine how much loss in terms of time and/or effort your application can withstand. What is the cost of losing a week's worth of data or transactions? A day's? An hour's? These are the specific issues that must be addressed as part of the security and integrity phase of your client/server systems design.

■ **Systems Failure**: Even if the data is not lost, what are the costs and implications of not being able to operate the application for a period of time? For decision-support applications, the up-time requirements may not be that stringent. However, mission-critical applications are just that—critical—and the ability to provide guaranteed access to the database can be a key requirement. You need to establish the exact up-time requirements for your particular application.

■ **Network Failure**: Considering that the link between client applications and the SQL Server database is most often a network, this distinct type of threat should be considered separately. There is no point to ensuring 100 percent up-time for your database server without also considering how the client applications will gain access to that server. The underlying network is a critical component of the entire client/server system and, as anyone who has worked with networks knows, they can and do go down.

These are the areas that typically threaten data security or negatively affect the system. Whether the applications analyst has identified these requirements as part of the specification process or you must initiate the evaluation yourself, you do not want to find out about security and integrity requirements after the fact. How you structure your SQL Server environment is directly affected by these factors and, once again, you can save yourself time and effort by identifying them in advance.

Threats to Data Integrity

Securing your system is still no guarantee that the data within the database is valid, accurate, and up to date. In previous chapters, you were introduced to the role of the database as a metaphor for real-world events. Data integrity defines the extent to which the database reflects that reality. Depending on the nature of your application, your database can be out of synch with the entities and events it is supposed to track. Usually, these problems arise as a result of subtle errors or omissions in the design of the application or in the database structure.

One of the key aspects of data integrity in a relational database like SQL Server is referential integrity. You were introduced to this concept briefly as part of the discussion on parent and child tables in Chapter 2.3, "Developing a Data Model." What I cover here is how the lack of referential integrity can affect a database. You will also see methods for ensuring data integrity within your SQL Server environment.

One of the difficulties of working on a large software development project (and, conversely, one of the benefits of being part of a smaller team) is the challenge of understanding the various interrelationships of the data within an application. To ensure data integrity, you must explicitly guarantee that any change to a table affects all other tables appropriately.

From a higher perspective, this has been one of the greatest difficulties in developing applications using duplicate data sets. Managing the update and synchronization process across multiple files, tables, or databases—let alone servers—is a problem.

Even within the more contained context of a single, normalized database, the problem remains. To understand how changes affect the database, you must first understand the application and the nature of the data itself. This is usually a somewhat weaker area for developers and database administrators, who are also wrestling with the specifics of client/server technology.

Everyone agrees that an application that cannot assure the integrity of the data it provides is useless. Worse, decisions may be made on misleading or incorrect data. Ensuring data integrity is absolutely vital to the value of the application and the success of your client/server project. To address this requirement, look at some of the main aspects of data integrity within a SQL Server database.

Column-Level Data Integrity

The most simplistic level of integrity is based on getting the right type of data into any given column or even ensuring that a column has a value entered to add the row to the database. This is handled through the specification of NULL or NOT NULL for each column when the table is created. You may also provide for some rudimentary level of data integrity at the column level by establishing default values for columns. If data in a table is date sensitive, you could require each row to have an entry in the date column. By using the date as the default, you reduce the possibility of errors because the value is system-supplied. You could use the system-supplied timestamp datatype to accommodate the time-identification requirement.

A somewhat more powerful method of ensuring data integrity for any given column incorporates the column's datatype. When you define a column as having a specific datatype, you are limiting the kinds of data that can be successfully inserted into that column, thereby ensuring at least some level of data integrity. Subtle performance considerations exist for datatypes as well, but at this point I assume that you are selecting datatypes to ensure that column data meets your integrity requirements.

At the column level, this approach to ensuring data integrity can be greatly enhanced by creating rules and binding those rules to columns in the database. Rules can be bound to one, some, or all columns in a table. They may also be incorporated into a user-defined datatype, which can be used to propagate the rule across newly created tables.

Rules can include almost any valid TransAct SQL expression, including all Boolean comparisons, logical operators, and the between and like string-matching functions. Rules can be used to ensure that inserted data not only conforms to the correct datatype definitions but is also formatted in specific ways. Any application such as reservation confirmation numbers, which include alphabetic characters in specific places, could have a datatype confirmation_number created to validate any inserted numbers. 111XXX222YYY would be an accepted number, and 11XXX222YYY would be rejected.

Incorporating rules into column definitions and then creating and using user_defined datatypes is a very powerful method of ensuring data integrity at the column level. It supports extensive validation of data type and format at the database level.

Table-Level Data Integrity

One of the key requirements for maintaining data integrity at the table level is providing for referential integrity. As I mentioned in Chapter 2.3, rows in child tables are dependent on values stored in rows in their parent table. If a parent row is deleted while child rows still exist within the database, those child rows become orphans. I established earlier that deleting a book from the product table while a store maintained that ISBN in inventory would make it impossible to retrieve the book's title from the database. Ensuring that this cannot happen is what is meant by ensuring referential integrity.

In essence, referential integrity means that you cannot delete a row in a table with a primary key if that value is held in another table as a foreign key. The row with the foreign key must be deleted first.

Some RDBMS systems build this into their database automatically. Sybase does not. In SQL Server, as long as you have drop-table permissions, you cannot delete an entire table if it has other tables dependent on it. The client/server developer is responsible for explicitly building referential integrity into the database. Typically, this is achieved using triggers and stored procedures, although their usefulness is not limited to ensuring referential integrity. You may use triggers and stored procedures to ensure that the data is valid for the application or that complex operations involving multiple modifications are completed as a set or rejected. Triggers and stored procedures are powerful features and their use should be designed into your database from the outset.

Although you can establish only one trigger each for insert, delete, and update operation taken on a table, there are no restrictions on the number of stored procedures that can be defined. Triggers are actually stored procedures but they operate in a slightly different manner. Triggers are not executed like stored procedures; they become effective as soon as they are defined, and when an insert, delete, or update operation is performed on the table, the defined trigger is invoked. Unlike stored procedures, triggers are self-contained and cannot be passed parameters. Triggers may be nested up to 16 levels. A trigger does not call itself recursively, however. For example, if you specify an update trigger on a column and it updates another column in the table, the trigger is not called a second time.

Using stored procedures to ensure data integrity must be handled somewhat differently because stored procedures are not automatically invoked when a table has an operation performed on it. Instead, you may choose to allow modification to tables only through stored procedures, passing the parameters to the stored procedure either from an application or directly from the user. In this way, you could ensure that an entire set of modifications was completed successfully or the transaction would be rolled back to its starting point, leaving the data as the transaction found it.

Database-Level Integrity

The entire set of database objects that make up the database must also be fully recoverable. As discussed earlier, database integrity is maintained through regular dumps of the database to disk and tape devices. To ensure that changes are not lost in the event of a systems failure, the database dump is augmented by ongoing transaction logs that reflect every table operation since the database dump was performed.

If restoration speed is an issue for your application, you should carefully evaluate the device options available to you for storing database dumps. Dumps to disks may be restored the most quickly, and the various tape device options offer widely varying restoration speed rates. Eight-millimeter tape drives are generally faster than Digital Audio Tape (DAT) devices, which in turn are significantly faster than streaming tape devices. Data might be restored at a much slower rate than the data is written to tape. You should identify what restoration times are supportable by your application and select dump devices accordingly.

Transaction Logs

To support rollback transaction and other database recovery options, you log every transaction that modifies data in your database. This log is a systems table (syslogs), and a separate transaction log is maintained for each database. As I mentioned in the chapter discussing SQL Server architecture, the log device can be mapped to a separate physical disk for performance reasons. Doing this also allows you to dump only the transaction log to disk or tape (as opposed to the whole database), and you can more closely manage the systems resources consumed by the transaction log. As a general rule, transaction logs should be allocated between 10 and 25 percent of the space allocated to the database itself.

When changes are requested to a database, the changes are recorded first in the transaction log in the order in which the changes occur. The transaction log works on a write-ahead basis. If the system goes down in the midst of an operation, the log is checked on restart. All incomplete transactions are rolled back, completed transactions are rolled forward, and the changes are reflected in the database. A successfully completed transaction might not result in immediate physical changes to the database due to the internal caching and I/O processes managed by the SQL Server engine. The transaction log ensures that these changes do not get lost.

In the event of a catastrophic systems failure, you use the transaction logs in conjunction with the database dump to restore the database. The transaction logs reflect all changes made to the database subsequent to the last database dump. To restore the database, first load the database dump, then load each incremental transaction log to play through all changes to the database. The database dump is a static picture of your data at a particular point in time, whereas the transaction log is a record of the operations performed on it from the time of the dump through to the time of the systems failure. By recreating the transactions maintained in the transaction log, you can ensure that your database is restored with complete integrity after even the most severe systems failures.

Incomplete Transactions

I have identified systems failure as a key peril to protect against, and one of the undesired results of a badly timed failure could be incomplete transactions. In such a case, valid modifications may have been made to the tables but those modifications may have been part of a set that should only be allowed completely or not at all. This can be handled through transactions on a single server, but when dealing with applications that involve complex transactions across distributed SQL Servers, you need to ensure that the rollback of a transaction can occur if a second transaction on a different server has not been successfully completed. As part of its design for a true distributed mission-critical OLTP database, Sybase has built two-phase commit into the SQL Server product from the beginning.

Two-phase commit involves declaring transactions to be dependent on successful completion across a distributed system. These transactions take the all-or-nothing approach to execution where multiple SQL Servers are involved. As part of your design, you want to identify any database operations that should be structured to take advantage of the two-phase commit capability.

Perhaps the most widely used example of two-phase commit is the banking transaction using an automated teller machine. A transfer between accounts requires that the withdrawal from one account and the deposit to the other be made as a set. If the system fails while the transaction is pending, it would be rolled back to the point of origin. Without structuring this transaction as a two-phase commit, the withdrawal could be successfully completed and the money left in limbo. Although this may have some potentially attractive aspects for the systems people involved, it is undesirable from a business standpoint.

Two-phase commit requires that even when one SQL Server has successfully completed a transaction, that transaction can be rolled back if the second phase of the transaction on another server is not successfully completed. This requires that each SQL Server is aware of the status of the entire transaction. This is handled in the two-phase commit protocol by the appointment of a Commit Server for the transaction. In the first phase of the transaction, each server affected by the transaction prepares to commit. The second phase involves the actual commitment of the changes, based on directions from the Commit Server. This server maintains the status of the transaction as a whole, and if any of the participating servers fail in their operation, the Commit Server instructs the other servers to roll back the transaction, in spite of their own successful completion. You need to incorporate two-phase commit transactions only in applications involving more than one SQL Server. Transactions involving multiple databases on the same SQL Server can be handled using regular transaction statements.

Transactions are written using the TransAct SQL extension to SQL provided by Sybase. Transactions may be written without incorporating two-phase commit because the nature of the transactions is entirely dependent on the requirements of your application and how you decide to handle them. (This is one more reason that I stress the importance of the design process and introduce these features at this time!)

Application Logic Bugs

Even after having defined insert, update, and delete triggers for all tables in the database, data integrity can still be compromised by faulty application logic. In the same way that queries define the relationship of the data in the database, the application-generated updates can greatly affect the validity of the data. True, you can protect against out-of-range values being added to the database through rules, but application logic errors sometimes yield reasonable or valid but inaccurate results. As a developer, you must understand the relationship of the data and recognize when a modification to one column necessitates an update to a column elsewhere in the database. You must also design tests for your applications that determine whether the data being produced or input is correct. This is entirely driven by the requirements of your application and demonstrates once again the importance of applications analysis and database modeling.

Addressing System Security with Sybase

As covered in the architectural overview of the SQL Server environment, the database environment is completely isolated from the operating system. This means that user logins, accounts, and permissions can be established specifically for each database. Other than SA and the database owner, each user must be granted permission explicitly in each database. The default permissions granted to a newly created user include the following:

- Begin Transaction
- Commit Transaction
- Create Table
- Print
- Roll Back Transaction
- Save Transaction
- Set

By default, a new user who is not the database owner does not have permission to do much in the database. The user may create his or her own tables, however. For these tables, the user has the following additional privileges:

- Alter Table
- Create Index
- Create Trigger

- Delete
- Insert
- Select
- Truncate Table
- Update
- Update Statistics

Optionally, the systems administrator or database owner can assign these permissions to any given user for tables and objects of which he or she is not the owner. Additionally, the following permissions could be granted (or revoked):

- Create Database
- Create Default
- Create Procedure
- Create Rule
- Create View
- Dump Database
- Dump Transaction
- Execute (stored procedures)

The systems administrator may specifically grant or revoke privileges for any given user for each database. It is often easier for purposes of administration to place users with similar profiles into groups and then manage the assignment of privileges on a group basis. Individuals can have more privileges within the database than the group to which they belong if the additional permissions are explicitly granted. By default, all users belong to the group Public and have the permissions identified in the first list.

You may wish to restrict the privileges of a group of users to exclude modification or deletion of data but need to provide that capability as part of an application. In this case, you can use stored procedures to provide this capability without compromising the security of your database.

Stored Procedures as a Security Mechanism

Users may execute stored procedures that perform operations that the users themselves do not have permission to execute. The developer or database administrator can create a stored procedure that performs the necessary validation and ensures that all aspects of the modification are addressed as part of its execution. This also ensures that the right SQL syntax is used rather than running the risk of a user initiating a modification with valid but incorrect SQL code that performs undesired operations on the database.

This method of securing the database can also be an effective way to ensure that applications do not access the data in an unauthorized or unwanted fashion. Whether the user issues direct SQL calls to the server or these are generated transparently as part of an application, you can use stored procedures as a method of ensuring that your database is secure.

Security Through Backups

If prevention of data loss is the best medicine, being able to restore your data to good health is a close second. As with any systems backup strategy, the key is how frequently the database should be backed up. Sybase offers an advantage over many other database vendors because databases can be dumped while they are in use. It is not necessary to have all users log off in order to dump the database to a dump device.

In fact, stored procedures and/or triggers can be used so that a database dump is performed after (or before) operations that affect the database. This is particularly recommended for operations that affect the master device. This offers significantly greater protection than the incremental and full backup strategies that were a common way of backing up databases in traditional systems environments.

Sybase offers the ability to dump databases to either disk or tape devices. The amount of time required to back up your database depends on the dump device you choose and the size of your database. This is likely to affect when you choose to perform a database dump before executing a particular stored procedure.

Disk Mirroring

For some applications, the up-time requirements are so stringent that recovering database data from tapes is an unacceptable alternative. Time is money, or perhaps your application supports real-life situations involving life and death. Sybase has provided a means of accommodating these requirements.

As part of your systems architecture, you can choose to mirror your database across multiple disk drives. This effectively insulates your database application from a media failure on the hard disk. The disk mirror maintains a complete and exact image of the mirrored database device. If a media failure occurs, the mirror immediately takes over. Newer multiprocessor server platforms extend this kind of protection to insulation from processor failure. Whereas multiprocessor support is a function of the hardware environment on which you run your SQL Server, disk mirroring is a software option that can be handled through Sybase independent of your hardware platform, provided that you have installed sufficient disks.

Summary

This chapter identified specific threats to the security and integrity of your database. It also evaluated several strategies for using Sybase features to reduce the potential damage that might be caused. It looked at several reasons why the security and integrity requirements of your application should be identified in advance of actually building database objects. Several strategies for backup, data validation, and assigning privileges to users were also covered.

The use of triggers and stored procedures as methods of ensuring referential and application data integrity was introduced. Also, the privileges and permissions to be allocated to database users were considered.

Design of your client/server system begins with a thorough analysis of the application and extends through the structure of the database and the definition of standard queries. Perhaps the most important contributors to the ongoing health and value of your system are the back-up and security considerations covered in this chapter. At this point, you have been taken through all the major aspects of the design phase and are now ready to begin moving into the implementation phase.

Section Summary

In this section, you have been taken through all the steps that should be performed before actually installing your SQL Server and setting up your database. The roles and responsibilities of everyone involved in client/server projects have been covered. You should be able to identify the tasks associated with your own role as well as ensure that all other aspects of the development effort have been assigned to a specific person.

You have also seen how the development methodologies discussed in the first section can be applied to the development of your own application. The process by which you develop your own application specifications may be quite different, but I covered the elements that must be incorporated by any application-specification process.

This section also looked at the relationship between the specifications and development of logical and physical database models and the query-definition process. New forms of batch reporting enabled by client/server technology were also considered. The requirements for data security and integrity rounded out the section.

The purpose of covering these topics is to ensure that, as a Sybase developer, you have a clear definition of all the terms used in a client/server application design process. For experienced client/server developers, this should serve as a good review of the major elements of design for a relational database application. For experienced systems people who are new to either Sybase specifically or the relational database environment generally, my objective was to encompass the entire application specification and design process in a few short chapters.

Obviously, this treatment is necessarily high-level and introductory. If this is your first application development exercise as a Sybase developer, however, you now should have a clear idea of how to begin designing your client/server solution. At the very least, the meaning and relationship of design elements such as logical data modeling and referential integrity should be clear. For those developers who want more in-depth coverage on the specification and design process, several excellent books are available.

I also hope that the emphasis on the importance of the design process has not gone unnoticed.

Everyone talks about the importance of design, but how that talk translates into action is what counts. In this section you have been introduced to the major elements of client/server design. The specification of the application-programming process itself was minimized because it depends very much on your specific requirements and the tools you intend to use as front-ends. In terms of the database design, I challenge you to review your own design documentation. Corporate America is littered with the corpses of failed client/server projects. These projects almost always fail as a direct result of insufficient design: people have tried to build the wrong thing. There are also some inspiring examples of how Sybase client/server applications have given departments and organizations a new lease on life. I am willing to bet that these systems were built on top of a solid design effort.

In this section, I covered how you could go about designing your client/server system. From here, I work from the premise that you have performed those steps and are ready to get down to the work of actually building your SQL Server solution.

3

Installing and Configuring SQL Server

Introduction

NOW THAT YOU HAVE COMPLETED THE ANALYSIS AND design phases of your Sybase development effort, you can finally get down to work. Hands-on installation and configuration of any SQL Server differs from platform to platform and site to site. This section covers all the common elements of any SQL Server installation and identifies platform-specific considerations and constraints.

This section is aimed primarily at database administrators and developers responsible for installing the SQL Server and getting it set up out of the box. It covers the installation procedures and picks up where the Sybase product documentation leaves off. I cover known bugs for each release and explain procedures that commonly cause confusion among new installers. I consulted experienced developers and administrators on each platform and they have contributed their two cents' worth to help make this section relevant to your development effort, independent of the platform and version you will be working with.

Physical resource allocation considerations and procedures are identified and you are taken step-by-step through a sample installation. Disk and memory rules of thumb will help you relate the sample configuration to the requirements of your specific site.

No installation is complete until the system can be used. This section shows you how to add users and groups, as well as grant rights and permissions. Lastly, you will see how dump devices are defined and used through dump and load database and log procedures.

As befits a hands-on section, from this point forward the book is considerably more technical in nature, with examples of syntax and results from SQL Server. You will find copies of these scripts contained on the disk that comes with this book.

The objective of this section is not only to explain the installation procedures and configuration options for SQL Server but to save you time and effort in setting up your own Sybase engine. This section should cover everything you need to know about SQL Server installation and configuration, from taking the tape out of the box through creating your first database tables, indexes, and logs. However, you will still need to thoroughly read your Sybase product documentation as well!

3.1

Installing Your SQL Server

This chapter addresses the initial installation and setup of a SQL Server. You are exposed to the general procedures followed when installing a SQL Server regardless of the server's platform. Because a great many SQL Servers are installed on UNIX servers, the examples used in this chapter are most consistent with that platform. Specific differences and requirements of the various platforms on which SQL Servers can run are covered in Chapter 3.2, "Platform-Specific Issues."

Whatever your platform, if you are preparing for your first SQL Server installation, you should read this chapter first.

Getting Started

A few key requirements must be met before you can install your SQL Server. These are as follows:

1. Before you do anything else, read the release notes that were shipped with your copy of Sybase for your specific platform.

2. A Sybase user must be set up on your system and given ownership of the directory where you wish to install the SQL Server executables, utilities, and other files. (Sybase requires about 55M for these files.) The Sybase environment variable must be set to that directory.

3. You must determine a valid network address and query port for your SQL Server.

   (Most SQL Servers use IP numbers that look like 192.9.200.1. The default query port number for SQL Servers is 2025. Default networking for Novell is IPX/SPX and for OS/2 is named pipes.)

4. You must determine the character set and sort order you wish to install.

   (You really don't want to change your mind later!)

5. You must give the Sybase user ownership of the physical disks or operating system files where you wish to install your database devices.

6. You must check and/or set any shared system memory variables to allocate system memory to SQL Server.

This sounds simple enough, doesn't it? It is actually pretty straightforward, but you might want to know a few of the reasons why these things are required, to help you decide how best to configure your particular SQL Server.

The Release Notes

These notes have all the up-to-date information you need to successfully perform the Sybase installation for your platform. You must read them over carefully and be sure that you have covered every item flagged in the notes. Because SQL Server works so closely with the server computer, you must be sure that your operating system version is explicitly mentioned in the release notes. If not, call Sybase customer support for clarification. (Maybe I shouldn't admit this here, but I once installed SQL Server for Solaris 2.1 on a Sun with Solaris 2.2, and it was highly problematic until I received the correct SQL Server version.) Even minor OS upgrades can make a big difference to the SQL Server software.

The Sybase User

Almost all multiuser systems have a standard super-user identity. In the UNIX world, this user is known as root, and it is the only user installed on bootup; root can do anything it pleases to the system. Once SQL Server is installed, it has an equivalent entity, known as SA, for systems administrator. Sybase still requires, however, a super-user from the standpoint of installing and configuring the SQL Server from the operating system. That is the user ID sybase.

You cannot successfully install SQL Server as root or any other user. You must first set up a user called "sybase," establish a home directory for it, and grant it all ownership rights and permissions. This is consistent for SQL Servers across all platforms. You also need to create a Sybase environment variable and set it to the full path name of the directory in which you intend to install the Sybase files. Additionally, the DSLISTEN environment variable must be set to the server name to allow the Sybase user to start the SQL Server. Platform-specific environment variables are covered in the following platform-by-platform review of SQL Server requirements.

The SQL Server Address

Although many servers have their own native networking support, platforms such as Novell and OS/2 still allow you to set an IP address for your SQL Server. This is especially useful for establishing consistent network addressing and access regardless of the platform on which you run your SQL Server. Each SQL Server on your network must have a unique name. Sybase is the default name, which gets a little confusing when you have a user named sybase installing a server named sybase. When several people are involved, the conversation can become quite convoluted until someone finally asks which sybase you are talking about. In any event, you cannot have two servers named sybase (or any other duplicate name) on the same network, nor can you give them the same IP address. You must ensure that each SQL Server name is distinct from any other host name on the network as well. You can, however, use the same query port number for any number of SQL Servers, as long as they are on physically separate host or server platforms. If you know you will have only a single SQL Server to deal with, you might want to keep the default name as sybase because many of the client software packages and utilities that work with SQL Server look for a server named sybase as the default. Keeping the defaults can sometimes save you a little time down the road. In most cases you will want to name your SQL Server something meaningful to you, like Dick, Jane, or maybe Spot.

The use of IP numbers is related to the historical trend of having the largest percentage of SQL Servers installed in a UNIX environment. UNIX servers tend to use Ethernet and support Internet addresses as a means of differentiating servers and workstations. It allows different machines on the network and subnetworks to communicate with each other easily. Usually the SQL Server uses the same IP address as the host, unless the platform on which it is running does not require or support IP addresses, in which case the IP address is assigned to the SQL Server alone. The actual network address of the SQL Server, however, is a combination of both the IP address and the query port—192.9.200.1,2025, for example. The four groups of numbers separated by the periods are the IP address (in this case the default IP numbers for Sun circa 1986) and the number after the comma is the query port. You should get valid IP numbers from your network specialist or administrator. (Unless you are the network administrator, in which case you would have selected the IP addresses when you installed the OS on the server machine.)

These network addresses are associated with the server name in the interfaces file in the Sybase home directory. The interfaces file allows the server to find the network address and query port for any particular server name. This is especially important for integrating multiple servers on the same network. The interfaces file specifies an additional port, which is usually one number greater than the query port (i.e., 2026). This is used for debugging purposes.

Character Set and Sort Order

When you first install SQL Server, you have an opportunity to establish which character set and sort order you want to have as the standard for all databases created for that server. The character set offered as a default depends on the platform on which you are installing the SQL Server. Each platform has a native character set, and these differ from vendor to vendor.

There are several important considerations for choosing a character set. First, if you have more than one SQL Server, you should be aware that if the character set and sort order are not identical, the database dumps from one server cannot be read by the other. This could be a severe nuisance if you need to transfer database contents from one to the other (for instance, from a development server to a production server).

Second, if you require special characters in your databases, you may have to choose a different character set from the default. Multilingual databases, for example, commonly have special characters over vowels or other characters such as the German umlaut. If you expect to have to store these characters without stripping off accents, you will also likely want to have the data naturally sorted with the accented vowels sorted next to their unaccented relatives. Again, this is an option you choose when first installing your SQL Server.

Last, even if you don't have any unusual character set or sorting requirements, you may have an opinion about whether you want to support case sensitivity. By selecting a case-insensitive sort order, you can ensure that a database object name or value in a unique row can be entered only once. For example, TABLE_NAME and table_name would be the same. If you select a case-sensitive sort order, upper- and lowercase names become separate and unique entities, which can cause naming convention difficulties for the developers if someone generates duplicate table and column names in a different case than the existing ones.

Sort orders come in two main flavors: binary and dictionary. Binary sorts according to the byte value of the character; an uppercase *Z* would be listed before a lowercase *a*, for example. Dictionary sort orders allow language conventions to be used in the sort order. This can be important for applications where you will be working extensively with list data with foreign characters. Sort orders affect all indexes, results from selects on char and varchar data with GROUP BY and ORDER BY qualifiers, and all operations involving comparisons.

All character sets support 128 ASCII characters, but additional characters are supported depending on the set selected. To display additional characters beyond 128, any client or other server accessing your SQL Server must be configured to use the same extended character set.

Default Language

SQL Server has several international features that allow you to configure language, time, date, and money formats appropriately for your site. U.S. English is the default language and many of you have no reason to change it. If you want to see message text expressed in a different language, however, such as German, French, or Japanese, you can specify your server's default language as such on installation. Your server can support many languages at once, for specific applications or users, but the server is limited to one default language. You may also choose to modify the server's default language at a later time, using the `sp_configure` command. You can acquire additional languages and load them onto your SQL Server after installation. These languages simply allow a user or application to see systems messages in their language of choice. If for some reason a translation or message is missing, the U.S. English message is displayed instead.

Ownership of Physical Resources

As you saw in the overview of the SQL Server architecture, Sybase designed their database engine to relieve the operating system of a great many responsibilities. Although yielding a significant performance advantage, this does require you to set a few additional permissions and settings when installing the SQL Server software.

Because the networking addresses have already been covered, the remaining physical resources to be managed by your SQL Server include systems memory and disk storage. If you need to set the shared memory parameter for your environment (it is sometimes necessary for UNIX versions, but not in Novell or OS/2), you need to establish how much RAM is available for allocation to your SQL Server. Obviously, you want to ensure that you have sufficient RAM for your operating system and other applications, but you should keep in mind that RAM has a significant impact on SQL Server performance. The specific requirements and syntax for setting this parameter are covered in the platform-specific instructions for installing SQL Server. Memory can also be allocated as part of the `sp_configure` procedure.

Storage is a somewhat different issue. By nature, database applications are disk and I/O intensive, as opposed to being processor or cycle hogs. As I stated previously, Sybase offers performance advantages through bypassing the middleman or operating system. For many installations, this means that Sybase needs to own the disk partitions to be used for your databases. Whereas the operating system partitions a hard disk and mounts that partition to use the disk, SQL Server can see the partitions directly without their being declared to the operating system. These are referred to as "raw" partitions.

Sybase accomplishes performance increases through the use of asynchronous I/0 compared to block or character I/O to these raw partitions. To use a raw partition with your SQL Server, you may have to make a few changes to your operating system kernel, in order to support asynchronous I/O. Where possible, you should use asynchronous I/0 and raw partitions to get the best possible performance from your SQL Server.

These are the information you must obtain and the decisions you must make prior to actually loading your SQL Server files from the distribution media. The installation process can be depicted as shown in Figure 3.1.1.

FIGURE 3.1.1.

The steps to take before loading Sybase SQL Server files from the distribution media.

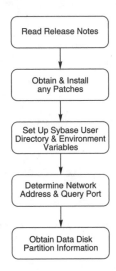

You are now ready to install Sybase!

Installing Sybase from the Distribution Media

Except for Novell and OS/2 installation, which are covered separately, Sybase products are installed from tape. Sybase provides a utility called sybload for loading the software from non-rewinding tape drives. This utility manages the extraction and copying of the files from the tape to your Sybase directory. It also verifies your installation with your Customer Authorization String. This string should be on a piece of the documentation that came with the tape. You can use sybload from a local tape drive or from across a network.

You can extract sybload using either a rewinding or non-rewinding tape device. When you run sybload, however, you should use the non-rewinding device.

To extract sybload, log in as sybase, and then be sure you are in the directory where you wish to install the SQL Server files. This should be the home directory of the user sybase. (Upgrading versions is slightly different, because you would need to create an upgrade directory and update the Sybase environment variable to that directory.) Check your documentation to get the specific syntax for your specific device name. For a UNIX tape drive, the command is similar to the following:

```
tar -xvbf 20 /dev/rmt0 sybload
```

Loading from a remote system, you might use this syntax:

```
rsh <remote_tape_server_name> dd if=<tape_device_name> ibs= 10k ¦ tar
xvbf 20 - sybload
```

You should then have the sybload utility extracted to the Sybase home directory. If not, you are going to have to figure out the exact names and syntax required for the particular machines at your site. Assuming that sybload itself loaded correctly, you can now load the files.

The following shows you a sample successful sybload session across the network:

```
./sybload
Sybase (c) 1992
Is this the correct directory for installation?
Current directory is /usr/sybase/491
If so, please enter 'y' or 'Y' to continue:
>y
Is this a Local or Remote installation, as defined in your Installation
Guide? Please enter L for Local and R for Remote.
>r
Please enter the name of the machine with the tape drive:
>guido
You specified guido as the name for the machine with the tape drive. Is
this correct?
Please enter 'y' or 'Y' to continue:
>y
Please enter the name of the device where your media is mounted:
>/dev/rmt0
You specified /dev/rmt0 as the name for the media device. Is this
correct?
Please enter 'y' or 'Y' to continue:
>y
Please enter your Customer Authorization String, letters only
>abcdef ghijkl mnopqr stuvwx yzabcd efgh
Sybase Products available for installation:
Product No. 1: SQL Server
Product No. 2: French Language Module
Product No. 3: German Language Module
Product No. 4: Japanese Language Module
Please enter the Product Numbers that you wish to install, one per line.
Terminate your entries with a blank line.
>1
>
The following products were chosen for installation:
Choice No. 1:  SQL Server
If this list is correct as shown,
please enter 'y' or 'Y' to continue,
'q' or 'Q' to quit,
```

```
or any other character to make another set of choices:
>y
Tape will now be positioned for loading.
x ./locales/us_English/common.loc, 208207 bytes, 407 tape blocks
/* more file listings */
666+1 records in
12345+0 records out
The following products have been distributed from tape:
SQL Server
This concludes the tape distribution portion of the Sybase installation.
Please consult your Installation Guide for further instructions.
```

Your files have now been loaded from tape onto the server where you will install the SQL Server. So much for the easy part!

At this point, you can begin installation of the SQL Server itself. This is accomplished by running sybconfig on UNIX platforms or sybinst on Novell. To help you understand the installation process, I cover the major activities performed by these utilities.

When successfully executed, sybconfig performs the following:

- Initializes the software by setting the correct permissions on the files you loaded from tape
- Creates a completed interfaces file in the Sybase home directory
- Runs the buildmaster utility to create a master disk device
- Creates a SQL Server startup command called RUNSERVER
- Sets up all systems tables, objects, and stored procedures by running the installmaster script
- Installs the specified default language for your SQL Server
- Installs the specified default character set and sort order

Sybconfig takes you through each of these steps in the appropriate order. You are given ample opportunity to change any settings you want before final execution. Sybconfig takes varying times to complete, depending on whether you have elected to load any additional languages or character sets. Upon successful completion, sybconfig will have built the three system databases—master, model, and tempdb—on the master device and started your SQL Server. This is the basic SQL Server configuration, and you are now ready to begin customizing for your specific requirements.

Error Logs and Messages

When you first start SQL Server, the command line specifies the name of the errorlog file with the -e option. Each time your SQL Server starts, information on the status of the server and the activities taken during the boot process are written to the errorlog. To read the errorlog while the SQL Server is running, you must use the cperrlog utility to write a copy of the error log to a text file. The startup file looks something like this:

```
93/11/11 15:14:40.00 kernel  DBMS task stack area range:  %xcb892c to
%xda512c
93/11/11 15:14:42.00 kernel  initializing virtual device 0, "SYS:/
SYBASE/MASTER.DAT"
93/11/11 15:14:42.00 kernel  virtual device 0 started using ASYNCHRONOUS
I/O
93/11/11 15:14:43.00 kernel  ninit: transport provider: T_COTS
93/11/11 15:14:43.00 kernel  Using asynchronous disk I/O for 'SYS:/
SYBASE/MASTER.DAT'
93/11/11 15:14:43.00 server  Number of buffers in buffer cache: 1358.
93/11/11 15:14:43.00 server  Number of proc buffers allocated: 339.
93/11/11 15:14:43.00 server  Number of blocks left for proc headers:
436.
93/11/11 15:14:43.00 server  Opening Master Database ...
93/11/11 15:14:44.00 server  Loading SQL Server's default sort order and
character set
93/11/11 15:14:44.00 kernel  network name /dev/tcp, port
\x02001000c009c8450000000000000000
93/11/11 15:14:44.00 kernel  ninit: transport provider: T_COTS_ORD
93/11/11 15:14:44.00 kernel  ninit: transport provider: T_COTS
93/11/11 15:14:44.00 server  Recovering database 'master'
93/11/11 15:14:45.00 server  Recovery dbid 1 ckpt (1841,20)
93/11/11 15:14:45.00 server  server is unnamed
93/11/11 15:14:45.00 server  Activating disk 'db_dev1'
93/11/11 15:14:46.00 server  Activating disk 'testdb'
93/11/11 15:14:46.00 kernel  initializing virtual device 7, "sys:/
SYBASE/db.dat"
93/11/11 15:14:46.00 kernel  virtual device 7 started using ASYNCHRONOUS
I/O
93/11/11 15:14:46.00 kernel  initializing virtual device 9,
"\sybase\testdb.dat"
93/11/11 15:14:46.00 kernel  virtual device 9 started using ASYNCHRONOUS
I/O
93/11/11 15:14:46.00 kernel  Using asynchronous disk I/O for 'sys:/
SYBASE/db.dat'
93/11/11 15:14:46.00 kernel  Using asynchronous disk I/O for
'\sybase\testdb.dat'
93/11/11 15:14:47.00 server  Recovering database 'model'
93/11/11 15:14:47.00 server  Recovery dbid 3 ckpt (45,29)
93/11/11 15:14:47.00 server  Clearing temp db
93/11/11 15:14:52.00 server  Recovering database 'target'
```

```
93/11/11 15:14:52.00 server  Recovery dbid 4 ckpt (473,7)
93/11/11 15:14:53.00 server  Recovering database 'johnsdb'
93/11/11 15:14:53.00 server  Recovery dbid 5 ckpt (270,3)
93/11/11 15:14:54.00 server  Recovering database 'pubs'
93/11/11 15:14:54.00 server  Recovery dbid 6 ckpt (451,4)
93/11/11 15:14:54.00 server  Recovery complete.
93/11/11 15:14:54.00 server  SQL Server's default sort order is:
93/11/11 15:14:55.00 server  'bin_cp850' (ID = 40)
93/11/11 15:14:55.00 server  on top of default character set:
93/11/11 15:14:55.00 server  'cp850' (ID = 2).
```

From this file, you can see what disk devices were initialized by the server, whether they are using asynchronous I/O, and the character set, server name, and status of the automatic recovery of databases run by SQL Server on startup. Any kernel error messages are written to this file when they occur during operation of the server. The "server is unnamed" message is not an error and does not indicate that the server's networking services are not operating. You can run your server without problem with this message; however, if it bothers you, you can change it by naming your server through the sp_addserver command. Generally, this must be run if you wish to have multiple servers connected to each other. For a single SQL Server on a network with clients, it has no effect, other than the message reflected in the initial startup error log. You can name your server anything you want, but adding a server name consistent with the name in the interfaces file makes the most sense. To run this command, you would use the following syntax as SA:

```
use master
go
sp_addserver SYBASE, local
go
```

You must then shut down your SQL Server and reboot for the change to take effect. On bootup, the error log reads "The Server name is SYBASE."

This command sets the value of the server name to the name SYBASE. It could, of course, be set to any legal name you choose. The local option tells the SQL Server that the server name entered with the sp_addserver command is the local machine and not a remote machine. You must set the local server name with this procedure if you wish to allow communication between your SQL Server and any remote SQL Servers.

Enabling Remote Server Communications

As you saw in the discussion on SQL Server architecture in Section 1, the capability to allow transparent communication between SQL Servers on a network is a highly attractive feature of Sybase. This communication could take the form of remote execution of triggers, two-phase commit applications, or simply passing through a local user to log on to a remote SQL Server. To enable these servers to communicate, however, a few parameters must be configured first. You already learned that you could use `sp_addserver` to name your local server, thereby eliminating the annoying "server is unnamed" message in the errorlog. You must do this as part of the server-to-server communications process. You must also add the names of any remote servers (without the local parameter) and ensure that they are listed in the interfaces file so that your SQL Server knows what network and query port address to use in contacting the remote server. Both the local and the remote servers must have corresponding entries. Additionally, you must change the default configuration value of the remote access and remote login parameters for your SQL Server. The default is set to not allow remote access or logins. You must add specific remote users through the `sp_addlong` and `sp_addremotelogin` procedures, and finally you must add the remote user as a user of each specific database you want them to be able to access.

Files versus Raw Partitions

For platforms such as VMS, Novell, and OS/2, the Sybase disk resources are treated as operating system files. That is, although you cannot use the database directly from the operating system, you can see it as a filename in a directory listing. UNIX provides an additional method of managing disk resources, known as raw partitions. These partitions are formatted disks that are not mounted as a file system by the operating system. Using raw partitions has several advantages over operating system files in the UNIX environment, not the least being assurance of data integrity. Operating system file writes are buffered, and in the event of a server crash when a transaction has been successfully completed from a SQL Server perspective but the operating system file has not written the cache to disk, those changes to the physical database are not made and cannot be rolled back. The data would then be lost.

For initial installations of training, development, or experimental databases, however, using OS files is somewhat more straightforward than using raw partitions. In Chapter 3.3, "Configuring Your SQL Server," you see the syntax and results of using both approaches to create Sybase logical disk devices.

Physical Database Implementation Plan

From your physical data model, you should be able to document a physical database implementation plan. This plan will help you identify all the precise names and sizes of the hard disk partitions to which you will allocate your Sybase logical disk devices.

Through the implementation plan, you will be able to identify how you will spread the data, logs, and indexes across multiple disks and controllers. In Figure 2.3.7 you can see how distinct disk partitions have been allocated for these purposes. As part of your plan, you will want to follow a few rules of thumb to allocate an appropriate amount of space to the various functions.

It is difficult indeed to properly configure a SQL Server without having some idea of how big the database objects will be. Whereas you can always make your databases bigger (but not smaller), the logical disk devices themselves are defined once and cannot be made smaller or larger without dropping and re-creating the device. Partitioning and repartitioning the hard disks themselves (in the UNIX environment) is not something you want to do repeatedly, either. A functional estimate of your database size requirements is necessary to configure your SQL Server properly.

Estimating Resource Requirements

In Chapter 2.2, "Developing Application Specifications," you were exposed to the various processes involved in analyzing and designing your database, including cardinality. During the design phase of your project, you will arrive at some idea of how many occurrences there will be for particular entities. As part of the physical data modeling process, you can estimate the number of rows that will be held in each table. Multiply the ballpark number of rows by the length of each column, and you have an estimate for the full size of each table. Once you have arrived at a general idea of your table sizes, you can treat 15–25 percent as a rule-of-thumb estimate for the transaction log and an additional 20–25 percent for indexes.

Estimating the appropriate size for tempdb is another issue. Tempdb is used for sorting data and as workspace for your developers. You don't want to restrict access to tempdb by allocating insufficient space to it when configuring your server. Your tempdb size should be at least the size of your largest table.

Another important resource component is the amount of memory available to SQL Server. The theoretical minimum to run SQL Server is 2M, but the default is set for 6M. As well as requiring memory for the SQL Server kernel itself, memory is also allocated to data and procedure cache and user connections. The data and procedure cache are percentages of unused or available memory allocated between data pages recently retrieved and procedure compile and executions. In both cases, if a user can access data or a procedure already in cache, execution speed is increased because SQL Server no longer has to retrieve the data or procedure from the hard disk. This can result in a considerable performance enhancement. For purposes of calculating memory requirements, you should be aware that each user connection requires between 32K and 48K, depending on your platform. You should set the number of users only as high as it needs to be; otherwise you will be taking memory away from the data and procedure cache for unused connections.

Summary

In this chapter, you have been introduced to the initial considerations when installing your SQL Server. Issues such as case sensitivity and disk partitioning are best dealt with from the outset. Whereas you have a great deal of flexibility when working with SQL Server, case sensitivity, character set, and sort order can require significant effort to change. This is especially true when you have created databases and objects that you want to keep.

The purpose of this chapter has been to identify the general issues you will want to tackle before installation of the software itself. Perhaps the single biggest nuisance I have encountered when installing SQL Servers is the tendency for the installer to opt for the SQL Server defaults (specifically the case sensitive option), and then have to deal with a team of PC developers who do not want it.

3.2

Platform-Specific Issues

SQL Server operates on a wide array of operating systems and hardware vendors. The preceding chapter looked at the general installation procedures for the SQL Server product. This chapter evaluates the different platforms on which SQL Server runs and identifies the characteristics and requirements unique to each.

There are considerable differences between the releases supported on each platform, with associated restrictions. For example, Windows NT supports the 4.2 and System 10 versions of SQL Server, whereas the OS/2 and Novell versions have remained at 4.2, and Sun Solaris supports up to 4.9.1.

This chapter will be of interest to those who are installing SQL Server for the first time on their platform; it also provides a reference for those looking at SQL Server solutions based on a variety of vendors' platforms. As well as detailing the unique requirements of each SQL Server flavor, this chapter identifies any known problem areas during configuration and setup. By reviewing the section relevant to your site, you should be able to quickly identify any prerequisites and action steps for making your installation a smooth one.

UNIX

SQL Server for UNIX represents over 60 percent of the installed servers. However, several variations exist within the UNIX version. You have already seen that SQL Server is designed to work very closely with the target server platform and operating system. Even within the UNIX family, several distinct versions of the product exist, each with their own requirements.

SunOS 4.1.3

The SunOS 4.x operating system supports all releases of the SQL Server, including System 10, as of November 1993. Typically, new products and versions are developed and released for the SunOS platform ahead of any others. Asynchronous I/O is enabled as a default.

SQL Server Versions Supported	*System 10, 4.9.1 to 3.9.1*
Kernel modifications required	options SHMSIZE=0X20000
	options SHMMNS=640
	options SHMMNI=256
Asynchronous I/O	options LWP
	options ASYNCHIOl
O/S patches required	Refer to Release Bulletins

Sun Solaris 2.x

The other major operating system offered by Sun, the Solaris OS is also supported by SQL Server. However, first releases of new products are not typically for this platform.

IBM Risc System/6000 AIX

Like many of the UNIX versions of SQL Server other than SunOS and HP-UX, the IBM Risc System/6000 is in the second tier of release levels for SQL Server versions. At this point, AIX 3.2 supports SQL Server versions 4.9.1 and lower.

The defaults for the IBM AIX environment are as follows:

character set	cp850
Asynchronous I/O	not enabled
Memory setting	8M
Storage required	45M

The steps for loading Sybase are identical to the general procedures outlined earlier. You use sybload to load the files from tape and sybconfig to set up the initial SQL Server installation. As root, you must first set Enable Asynchronous I/O and establish a user sybase and home directory. However, there are a few distinctions in the AIX environment. Specifically, AIX deals with logical volumes as opposed to raw partitions. Logical volumes have two files associated with them—a character device and a block device. You should use the character device to take advantage of asynchronous I/O, which provides the fastest and most reliable method of writing data to disk using SQL Server. As with raw partitions, the user sybase must be made the owner of the logical volumes, which are to be used for database devices. In all other respects, the procedure for loading and installing SQL Server on AIX is identical to any other UNIX platform.

SQL Server on an HP-UX Version 9.0 Platform

For those of you who will be running your SQL Server on the HP-UX platform or will be upgrading an existing Sybase database engine to version 9.0 of the HP variant of the UNIX operating system, you will find a very new and significant disk feature. Logical volumes are now incorporated into the HP platform, as well as on the IBM RS 6000 series host.

Logical volumes take a dramatically different approach to physical disk resources compared to previous UNIX hosts. Until the introduction of logical volumes, installing SQL Server using raw partitions of the disk was necessary (or at least recommended). To manage the assignment and placement of database objects such as tables, indexes, dumps, and logs, you created segments and used stored procedures within Sybase to effect the storage of these objects.

Logical volumes treat physical disks in much the same way as the more traditional concept of raw partitions. When you opt to use logical volumes on the HP, you still gain the significant performance and integrity advantages of raw partitions. However, you also gain the ability to dynamically allocate and deallocate disk space to various volumes. For many systems administrators, this is a significant advantage over previous versions of HP UX, which did not incorporate this feature.

As an HP-authorized consultant, I was quite familiar with the HP-UX versions 7 and 8 and knew them to be highly stable and reliable platforms on which to run SQL Server. The systems administration interface is much uglier than Sun's, but it has proven to be nonetheless serviceable for me. I was recently asked by a new SQL Server site to review their environment, make recommendations, and reconfigure their HP and SQL Server for their development team. That setting was where I discovered the new logical volume features offered by HP. I assume that many of you are in the same position I was when exploring this new capability, so I will take you through it in a step-by-step fashion.

Imagine that you are considering installing SQL Server on an HP 9000/840 running HP-UX 9.0. It is configured with 256M RAM and five 2-gigabyte SCSI drives. To see the drives, you can simply look at the contents of /dev/dsk, where the OS references to the drives and their partitions are kept. The file listing of this subdirectory would look something like this:

```
# cd /dev/dsk
# ls
c0d0s0     c0d0s6     c1d0s2     c2d0s12    c3d0s0     c3d0s6     c4d0s2     c5d0s12
c0d0s1     c0d0s7     c1d0s3     c2d0s13    c3d0s1     c3d0s7     c4d0s3     c5d0s13
c0d0s10    c0d0s8     c1d0s4     c2d0s14    c3d0s10    c3d0s8     c4d0s4     c5d0s14
c0d0s11    c0d0s9     c1d0s5     c2d0s15    c3d0s11    c3d0s9     c4d0s5     c5d0s15
c0d0s12    c1d0s0     c1d0s6     c2d0s2     c3d0s12    c4d0s0     c4d0s6     c5d0s2
c0d0s13    c1d0s1     c1d0s7     c2d0s3     c3d0s13    c4d0s1     c4d0s7     c5d0s3
c0d0s14    c1d0s10    c1d0s8     c2d0s4     c3d0s14    c4d0s10    c4d0s8     c5d0s4
c0d0s15    c1d0s11    c1d0s9     c2d0s5     c3d0s15    c4d0s11    c4d0s9     c5d0s5
c0d0s2     c1d0s12    c2d0s0     c2d0s6     c3d0s2     c4d0s12    c5d0s0     c5d0s6
c0d0s3     c1d0s13    c2d0s1     c2d0s7     c3d0s3     c4d0s13    c5d0s1     c5d0s7
c0d0s4     c1d0s14    c2d0s10    c2d0s8     c3d0s4     c4d0s14    c5d0s10    c5d0s8
c0d0s5     c1d0s15    c2d0s11    c2d0s9     c3d0s5     c4d0s15    c5d0s11    c5d0s9
```

In previous versions of HP-UX, you would have simply identified which partitions you wanted to initialize as disk devices to Sybase and used the logical names of the partitions accordingly for defining your databases and segments. However, with the new version, you use SAM (or see the documentation for performing these tasks manually) to create a logical volume group. The logical volume group looks to the operating system as though it were a physical device. There is an entry in the /dev/dsk directory for your logical volume group. In this case, imagine that you have created two logical volume groups: vg00 and vg01.

HP-UX allows you to define as many physical disks or disk partitions to the volume group as you deem appropriate. This provides you with the biggest single advantage of using logical volumes: You can shrink or grow them at will without affecting SQL Server.

Of course, this does not mean that you can shrink a logical volume to a size that is less than the databases and logs allocated to your SQL Server. Rather, you can add, reallocate, or remove disks from the logical volume group if they are not being used. From a systems administrator's standpoint, this means that you can use the logical volume groups to manage the assignment of database objects such as tables and indexes, as well as logs and databases themselves, rather than performing these functions entirely within SQL Server. The benefit of this is that you can now wait to allocate space to database objects until it is required and more flexible. You can unmount, move, and mount regular UNIX file systems and swap space. Rather than simply being an advantage for SQL Server or for the UNIX systems administrator, the logical volumes have benefits in ease of administration for both.

Allowing the operating system to manage these raw partitions also involves risks and other implications. If you do not watch carefully how you create your logical volume groups, you might discover that the volume group manager defeats the purpose of assigning database objects across different drives and partitions.

```
vgdisplay -v
-- Volume groups --
VG Name              /dev/vg00
VG Status            available
Max LV               255
Cur LV               17
Open LV              17
Max PV               16
Cur PV               3
Act PV               3
Max PE per PV        1016
VGDA                 6
PE Size (Mbytes)     4
Total PE             1430
Alloc PE             645
Free PE              785
Total PVG            0
```

```
-- Logical volumes --
LV Name                /dev/vg00/lvol1
LV Status              available/syncd
LV Size (Mbytes)       104
Current LE             26
Allocated PE           26
Used PV                1

LV Name                /dev/vg00/lvol2
LV Status              available/syncd
LV Size (Mbytes)       48
Current LE             12
Allocated PE           12
Used PV                1

LV Name                /dev/vg00/lvol3
LV Status              available/syncd
LV Size (Mbytes)       136
Current LE             34
Allocated PE           34
Used PV                1

LV Name                /dev/vg00/lvol4
LV Status              available/syncd
LV Size (Mbytes)       1312
Current LE             328
Allocated PE           328
Used PV                1

LV Name                /dev/vg00/lvol5
LV Status              available/syncd
LV Size (Mbytes)       200
Current LE             50
Allocated PE           50
Used PV                1

LV Name                /dev/vg00/lvol6
LV Status              available/syncd
LV Size (Mbytes)       100
Current LE             25
Allocated PE           25
Used PV                1

LV Name                /dev/vg00/sybmast
LV Status              available/syncd
LV Size (Mbytes)       48
Current LE             12
Allocated PE           12
Used PV                2

LV Name                /dev/vg00/DSSlog
LV Status              available/syncd
```

```
LV Size (Mbytes)        100
Current LE              25
Allocated PE            25
Used PV                 1

LV Name                 /dev/vg00/DSSdb
LV Status               available/syncd
LV Size (Mbytes)        200
Current LE              50
Allocated PE            50
Used PV                 1

LV Name                 /dev/vg00/sybmastdmp
LV Status               available/syncd
LV Size (Mbytes)        48
Current LE              12
Allocated PE            12
Used PV                 1

LV Name                 /dev/vg00/dssCOMMdmp
LV Status               available/syncd
LV Size (Mbytes)        20
Current LE              5
Allocated PE            5
Used PV                 1

LV Name                 /dev/vg00/dssctlgdmp
LV Status               available/syncd
LV Size (Mbytes)        20
Current LE              5
Allocated PE            5
Used PV                 1

LV Name                 /dev/vg00/dssosstdmp
LV Status               available/syncd
LV Size (Mbytes)        32
Current LE              8
Allocated PE            8
Used PV                 1

LV Name                 /dev/vg00/dsspiqddmp
LV Status               available/syncd
LV Size (Mbytes)        20
Current LE              5
Allocated PE            5
Used PV                 1

LV Name                 /dev/vg00/dsspscbdmp
LV Status               available/syncd
LV Size (Mbytes)        32
Current LE              8
Allocated PE            8
```

```
           Used PV                   1

           LV Name                   /dev/vg00/dsswactdmp
           LV Status                 available/syncd
           LV Size (Mbytes)          60
           Current LE                15
           Allocated PE              15
           Used PV                   1

           LV Name                   /dev/vg00/lvol7
           LV Status                 available/syncd
           LV Size (Mbytes)          100
           Current LE                25
           Allocated PE              25
           Used PV                   1


           -- Physical volumes --
           PV Name                   /dev/dsk/c0d0s2
           PV Status                 available
           Total PE                  476
           Free PE                   0

           PV Name                   /dev/dsk/c3d0s2
           PV Status                 available
           Total PE                  477
           Free PE                   308

           PV Name                   /dev/dsk/c1d0s2
           PV Status                 available
           Total PE                  477
           Free PE                   477


    VG Name                   /dev/vg01
    VG Status                 available
    Max LV                    255
    Cur LV                    3
    Open LV                   3
    Max PV                    16
    Cur PV                    2
    Act PV                    2
    Max PE per PV             1016
    VGDA                      4
    PE Size (Mbytes)          4
    Total PE                  954
    Alloc PE                  550
    Free PE                   404
    Total PVG                 0

       -- Logical volumes --
       LV Name                   /dev/vg01/lvol1
```

```
LV Status              available/syncd
LV Size (Mbytes)       100
Current LE             25
Allocated PE           25
Used PV                1

LV Name                /dev/vg01/lvol2
LV Status              available/syncd
LV Size (Mbytes)       2000
Current LE             500
Allocated PE           500
Used PV                2

LV Name                /dev/vg01/lvol3
LV Status              available/syncd
LV Size (Mbytes)       100
Current LE             25
Allocated PE           25
Used PV                1


-- Physical volumes --
PV Name                /dev/dsk/c4d0s2
PV Status              available
Total PE               477
Free PE                0

PV Name                /dev/dsk/c5d0s2
PV Status              available
Total PE               477
Free PE                404
```

From the listing above, you can see how the new logical volume groups are reported. The logical volume name translates to the raw partition name you would use with either an older version of HP-UX, or when mounting drives on a Sun platform. Additionally, the listing reports the logical volume status and the total physical extents or size and amount available.

```
# //ll /dev/vg010
total 0
brw-r----   1 sybase   sybase      64 0x000009 Nov 26 15:59 DSSdb
brw-r----   1 sybase   sybase      64 0x000008 Nov 26 16:33 DSSlog
brw-r----   1 sybase   sybase      64 0x00000b Nov 26 12:47 dssCOMMdmp
brw-r----   1 sybase   sybase      64 0x00000c Nov 26 12:48 dssctlgdmp
brw-r----   1 sybase   sybase      64 0x00000d Nov 26 12:48 dssosstdmp
brw-r----   1 sybase   sybase      64 0x00000e Nov 26 12:49 dsspiqddmp
brw-r----   1 sybase   sybase      64 0x00000f Nov 26 12:50 dsspscbdmp
brw-r----   1 sybase   sybase      64 0x000010 Nov 26 12:51 dsswactdmp
crw-r--r--  1 root     sys         64 0x000000 Nov 10 13:28 group
```

```
brw-r----  1 root     sys       64 0x000001 Nov 10 13:31 lvol1
brw-r----  1 root     sys       64 0x000002 Nov 10 13:31 lvol2
brw-r----  1 root     sys       64 0x000003 Nov 10 13:31 lvol3
brw-r----  1 root     sys       64 0x000004 Nov 10 13:31 lvol4
brw-r----  1 root     sys       64 0x000005 Nov 10 13:28 lvol5
brw-r----  1 root     sys       64 0x000006 Nov 10 13:32 lvol6
brw-r----  1 root     sys       64 0x000011 Nov 26 12:52 lvol7
crw-r----  1 sybase   sybase    64 0x000009 Jan  5 14:07 rDSSdb
crw-r----  1 sybase   sybase    64 0x000008 Jan  5 14:07 rDSSlog
crw-r----  1 sybase   sybase    64 0x00000b Dec  6 11:16 rdssCOMMdmp
crw-r----  1 sybase   sybase    64 0x00000c Dec  6 11:17 rdssctlgdmp
crw-r----  1 sybase   sybase    64 0x00000d Jan  5 10:07 rdssosstdmp
crw-r----  1 sybase   sybase    64 0x00000e Dec  6 11:20 rdsspiqddmp
crw-r----  1 sybase   sybase    64 0x00000f Dec  6 11:21 rdsspscbdmp
crw-r----  1 sybase   sybase    64 0x000010 Jan  5 10:05 rdsswactdmp
crw-r----  1 root     sys       64 0x000001 Nov 10 13:28 rlvol1
crw-r----  1 root     sys       64 0x000002 Nov 10 13:28 rlvol2
crw-r----  1 root     sys       64 0x000003 Nov 29 14:20 rlvol3
crw-r----  1 root     sys       64 0x000004 Nov 29 14:21 rlvol4
crw-r----  1 root     sys       64 0x000005 Nov 29 14:19 rlvol5
crw-r----  1 root     sys       64 0x000006 Nov 10 13:28 rlvol6
crw-r----  1 root     sys       64 0x000011 Nov 26 12:52 rlvol7
crw-r----  1 sybase   sybase    64 0x000007 Jan  5 14:07 rsybmast
crw-r----  1 sybase   sybase    64 0x00000a Dec  6 11:15 rsybmastdmp
brw-r----  1 sybase   sybase    64 0x000007 Nov 26 16:50 sybmast
brw-r----  1 sybase   sybase    64 0x00000a Nov 26 12:46 sybmastdmp
# ll /dev/vg01
total 0
crw-r--r--  1 root     sys       64 0x010000 Nov 26 12:42 group
brw-r----  1 root     sys       64 0x010001 Nov 26 12:53 lvol1
brw-r----  1 root     sys       64 0x010002 Nov 26 12:54 lvol2
brw-r----  1 root     sys       64 0x010003 Nov 26 12:54 lvol3
crw-r----  1 root     sys       64 0x010001 Nov 26 12:53 rlvol1
crw-r----  1 root     sys       64 0x010002 Nov 29 14:21 rlvol2
crw-r----  1 root     sys       64 0x010003 Nov 26 12:54 rlvol3
```

The listing above shows you the ownership and create information on each of the logical volumes. You may use the 0x000000 to determine to which physical volume the logical volume was actually allocated. The third digit from the left indicates the physical volume.

To see the logical volumes used to mount UNIX file systems under HP-UX, look at the /etc/checklist file:

```
# more /etc/checklist
/dev/vg00/lvol1    /        hfs defaults 0 1 # root volume
/dev/vg00/lvol2    swap     ignore sw    0 0 # pri swap 48 MB
/dev/vg00/lvol3    /usr     hfs defaults 0 2 #
/dev/vg00/lvol4    /users   hfs defaults 0 2 #
/dev/vg00/lvol5    /tmp     hfs defaults 0 2 #
```

```
/dev/vg00/lvol6     swap    swap sw    0 0 # sec swap 100 MB
/dev/vg00/lvol7 .... swap pri=0 0 0 16409
/dev/vg01/lvol1 .... swap pri=0 0 0 16409
/dev/vg01/lvol3 .... swap pri=0 0 0 16410
/dev/vg01/lvol2 /disk2 hfs rw,suid 0 3 16410
#
```

From these reports, you see how the physical disk partitions are turned into logical volumes and then grouped. HP-UX gives you even more flexibility in moving your SQL Server raw disk partitions around than Sybase does. Additionally, you benefit from being able to use the same approach to manage not only your SQL Server databases and disk resources but those of the regular UNIX file systems as well.

The installation of the SQL Server software for the HP platform is handled in the same fashion as the other UNIX hosts. For best performance you will need to install the Asynch80 patch to enable asynchronous IO. Also, check your release bulletins to determine if any other patches or system upgrades must be acquired.

Novell NLM

In summary form, the SQL Server offering for the Novell operating system is expressed in the list below.

Component	Required
OS version	3.11
SQL server version	4.22
RAM required	16M
Patches required	SNLMINST (supplied by Sybase)

Installation Procedures

The SQL Server NLM first installs the Novell IPX/SPX networking protocol. On installation you are asked to define the network number and query port for the SQL Server. The network number is the same number specified in the autoexec.ncf as the IPX internal net number.

Sybinst is the name of the installation utility in Novell rather than sybconfig, but it performs the same functions. To choose a different sort order than binary, you must elect to run the buildmaster script manually after completing sybinst, so answer N for no to the "Master Device Install?" prompt. You must also build the master device manually if you wish to load a database from SQL Server running on OS/2.

TCP/IP connectivity must be added manually to both the SQL Server and the NetWare server on which it is installed. However, TCP/IP services are included as part of the NetWare 3.11 NOS. The following is a sample autoexec.ncf to successfully start up TCP/IP services to be used by a SQL Server NLM:

```
file server name Princess
ipx internal net 1
load c:\wdplussv port=280 frame=ethernet_II name=ipnet
load tcpip
bind ip to ipnet addr = 192.9.200.69
bind ipx to wdplussv net=00000999
set maximum packet receive buffers = 200
search add sys:/sybase/nlms
search add sys:/sybase/ncfs
mount all
```

SQL Server NLM uses asynchronous I/O on operating system files. You do not have the option of mounting raw partitions with this version of SQL Server.

Known Problems

Netx versions prior to 3.10 do not allow you to connect users to the SQL Server NLM.

OS/2 SQL Server

OS/2 SQL Server version 4.2 is supplied by Microsoft and supported for operation under Microsoft OS/2 version 1.3, which is bundled with the SQL Server. The Microsoft versions of SQL Server are intended for access by clients over LAN Manager, Banyan VINES, and other networks with named pipes support. They do not support a TCP/IP network address as all other SQL Servers do.

Due to Microsoft's decision to move away from OS/2 development, Microsoft does not recommend operation of SQL Server under OS/2 versions 2.0 and 2.1. However, some have ignored Microsoft's position on this and discovered that SQL Server can be successfully installed and run under the other versions, especially OS/2 2.1.

Several utility programs are shipped with SQL Server for OS/2. ISQL is a PC client-based executable and can be run from across the network. Additionally, the Systems Administration Facility is provided with SQL Server to assist in setup and configuration.

SQL Server for OS/2 is designed to work either as a LAN Manager server-based application or as a NetWare Requester Application on a network and is accessed through named pipes. The NetWare Requester software manages the communication between OS/2 and the SQL Server passing through any named pipe requests and responses. A Novell network is not necessary to use the NetWare requester, but it does support OS/2 clients connecting to both SQL Server (OS/2) and Novell NetWare servers. PCs and other clients connect by loading Novell's IPX for network communications and then loading a named pipe program and a Net-Library Dynamic Link Library (DLL) into the client PC's memory. You should note that the SQL Server is a database server that usually co-exists on the Novell network, not on the Novell file server. Generally, you would dedicate an OS/2 machine to this SQL Server function.

Installation Procedures

To install the OS/2 version of SQL Server, you must have a working OS/2 machine with networking software installed. (The stand-alone version of OS/2 SQL Server is covered later in this chapter.)

Insert the first setup diskette and enter Setup. The installation program is menu-driven and prompts you for the information it needs to successfully install and start up SQL Server. There are two main streams taken, depending on the networking environment in which you are installing your SQL Server.

LAN Manager

The key difference between the LAN Manager installation and other OS/2 SQL Servers is the ability to place SQL Server directly on a LAN Manager file server. Other networks use an OS/2 client machine to function as an application server rather than a file server process.

When installing SQL Server for OS/2 to work in a LAN Manager or compatible network environment, the setup program checks that named pipe interprocess communication (IPC) is installed on the server machine and writes the files from the diskettes to the hard disk of the server. It updates the server startup files to accommodate SQL Server, creates the master device, starts the SQL Server, and runs seven SQL files through ISQL. These files are as follows:

INSTMSTR.SQL	Installs the full version of the master database, including systems procedures
INSTMODL.SQL	Installs the model database
INSTPUBS.SQL	Install the pubs database (optional)
CONFIG.SQL	Sets the initial sp_configure values based on information supplied by the menu prompts
HELPSQL.SQL	Creates the sp_helpsql procedure
INSTCAL.SQL	Sets up the stored procedures for systems catalogs
INSTGUI2.SQL	Sets up the SQL Administrator stored procedures

The approach for loading OS/2 SQL Server for Novell and Banyan networks is similar. The setup program checks that the named pipe IPC has been installed and is functioning on the OS/2 machine intended as the SQL Server. The files are transferred from the diskettes to the system's hard disk. C:\SQL\BINP is added to the path, and C:\SQL\DLL is added to the libpath in the config.sys file. The master device is created, the SQL Server is started, and the same seven SQL batch files run through ISQL.

SQL Server 4.2 Manual Installation

The following script was passed to me from CompuServe, where it was posted for public consumption. It is quite detailed, and I saw no reason to change it. Thank you for the contribution! (Who was that masked man?)

4.2 manual installation is currently required for customers running OS/2 2.0 with a boot partition other than drive C:. 4.2 manual installation is also currently required on Windows NT, including the October Beta version of Windows NT. There are updated Windows NT OS/2 subsystem DLLs that will allow 4.2 to install successfully on the October Beta version of NT. These are available from MS Product Support Services.

Before starting, verify the following items:

1. Check that the disk partition on which OS/2 swap file SWAPPER.DAT or Windows NT PAGEFILE.SYS resides has at least 10M free space. The location of SWAPPER.DAT can be found in CONFIG.SYS, on the line starting with "SWAPPATH". On Windows NT, you can search for the filename PAGEFILE.SYS, or check the Windows Control Panel "System" applet.

2. Verify that SQL Server is not running by doing a "PSTAT /c | MORE" from the OS/2 prompt. The Windows 32 SDK has an equivalent utility, PSTAT.EXE.

3. Verify that no SQL Server or DB-LIB program is running on the SQL Server machine. This includes SAF, ISQL, Q+E, etc. You may want to use the OS/2 file manager or equivalent to search all disk partitions for the files PDBLIB.DLL and DBNMPP.DLL. On Windows NT, just use the DIR /S command. No older versions of these files should be present on the machine.

Then begin the manual installation:

Comments:

a. Drive d:\ is used in the following example.

b. Capitalization used for clarity only. DOS, OS/2, and Windows NT are not case-sensitive.

NOTE

In the following example, the SQL Server version 1.X strict compatibility code page and sort order are installed. You may select a different code page and sort order if you do not require compatibility with version 1.X. In this case, just change the names CP850 and NOCASE34.850 to the desired code page and sort order.

---

1. Create necessary directories:

   a. md d:\sql   (make \sql directory)

   b. md d:\sql\data   (make \sql\data subdirectory)

   c. md d:\sql\binp   (make \sql\binp subdirectory)

   d. md d:\sql\dll   (make \sql\dll subdirectory)

   e. md d:\sql\charsets   (make \sql\charsets subdirectory)

   f. md d:\sql\charsets\cp850   (make \sql\charsets\cp850 subdirectory)

   g. md d:\sql\install   (make \sql\install subdirectory)

2. Unpack files. Execute the UNPACK program from the A: drive.

   a. Copy unpack.exe program from the SQL Server OS/2 Setup Disk to someplace on your local hard drive that is on the searchpath

   b. Unpack sqlservr.ex@ d:\sql\binp\sqlservr.exe (executed from the A: drive)

   c. Unpack instmstr.sq@ d:\sql\install\instmstr.sql

   d. Insert the SQL Server OS/2 Disk 2

   e. Unpack bldmastr.ex@ d:\sql\binp\bldmastr.exe

   f. Unpack isql.ex@ d:\sql\binp\isql.exe

   g. Unpack charset.ex@ d:\sql\binp\charset.exe

   h. Unpack nocase34.85@ d:\sql\charsets\cp850\nocase34.850

   i. Unpack pdblib.dl@ d:\sql\dll\pdblib.dll

      j. Unpack dbnmpp.dl@ d:\sql\dll\dbnmpp.dll

      k. Unpack instcat.sq@ d:\sql\install\instcat.sql

      l. Unpack instmodl.sq@ d:\sql\install\instmodl.sql

      m. Unpack helpsql.sq@ d:\sql\install\helpsql.sql

3. Edit the CONFIG.SYS file of the machine and add d:\sql\dll to the LIBPATH setting and d:\sql\binp to the PATH setting. Shut down and reboot the machine.

4. Create MASTER database:

```
bldmastr /dd:\sql\data\master.dat /c /s 7680
```

5. Start SQL Server (preferably with the following syntax):

SQLSERVR (executed from the \sql\data directory)

You will see the SQL Server errorlog begin scrolling past the screen as SQL Server starts. It will not return to a command prompt but continues displaying the errorlog screen. This is normal.

6. Switch to another OS/2 screen group and run the CHARSET program with the following syntax:

```
CHARSET -P -Ld:\sql\charsets\cp850 nocase34.850
```

The CHARSET program will acknowledge its successful completion.

NOTE

It is not mandatory to create the \sql\charsets\cp850 directory and copy the NOCASE34.850 file there. You could optionally place the file elsewhere (even on a different drive letter) and use a different syntax to invoke the CHARSET program. Following is an example of this.

---

      a. MD d:\tempdir

      b. Copy NOCASE34.850 d:\tempdir

      c. CHARSET -P -Ld:\tempdir nocase34.850

7. Using ISQL, log in to SQL Server and run the following query. (See 4.2 Language Reference, page 482, for details on how to run ISQL.) The following command syntax is case sensitive:

```
update sysconfigures set value=49 where config=123
```

In this example, the value 49 represents the "strict compatibility" sort order. If you loaded another character set, you should use the corresponding sort ID for that character set. Following is a list of character set/sort order files and their corresponding sort IDs:

```
Charset/Sort file      ID
altdict.850            55
altnoacc.850           57
altnocs.850            61
altnocsp.850           56
cp850bin.850           40
diction.850            41
noaccent.850           44
nocase.850             42
nocase34.850           49
nocasepr.850           43
diction.iso            51
iso_1bin.iso           50
noaccent.iso           54
nocase.iso             52
nocasepr.iso           53
cp437bin.437           30
diction.437            31
noaccent.437           34
nocase.437             32
nocasepr.437           33
```

8. Then run this query:

   ```
   reconfigure with override
   ```

9. Use the SHUTDOWN command to shut down the server.

10. Start SQL Server (preferably with the following syntax):

    SQLSERVR (executed from the \sql\data directory)

    SQL Server should indicate that the Default Sort Order has been success-
    fully changed, and that SQL Server is shutting down after verifying System
    Indexes.

11. Start SQL Server (preferably with the following syntax):

    SQLSERVR (executed from the \sql\data directory)

12. Run the following scripts in the indicated order to complete 4.2 installation:

    ```
    INSTMSTR.SQL
    INSTCAT.SQL
    INSTMODL.SQL
    ```

```
HELPSQL.SQL
```

And optionally

```
INSTPUBS.SQL
```

```
ADMIN2.SQL
```

Typical script running times on 386/33:

```
INSTMSTR.SQL   7 min.
INSTCAT.SQL    1 min.
INSTMODL.SQL   1 min.
HELPSQL.SQL    3 min.
INSTPUBS.SQL   2 min.
ADMIN2.SQL     2 min.
```

Example of how to run a script on the server machine with ISQL:

```
isql /Usa /P /iINSTMSTR.SQL > INSTMSTR.OUT
```

This should complete a manual installation of a 4.2 SQL Server.

Summary

In this chapter you have been taken through the steps necessary to successfully install SQL Server for specific platforms. Where possible, I have included tips and tricks relating to particular versions of these specific platforms. This chapter is intended to help those of you preparing for your first SQL Server installation. Like many other chapters in this book, my intention has been to pull together the significant pieces of information relating to the preparation and steps you will take when installing your SQL Server. There is no substitute for thoroughly reading the release bulletins and installation instructions for your machine, however. This chapter should serve to provide you with a concise list of all the steps necessary to achieve your desired aim—the successful installation of your SQL Server database engine.

3.3

Configuring Your SQL Server

As you remember from the section on the SQL Server architecture, the master device is the Sybase name for the disk allocated to the three system databases. The master database, which resides on the master disk, holds all stored procedures (for versions earlier than Release 10) and information on user databases. The pubs database is also installed on the master database by default. Model is used as the template database to allow you to ensure propagation of selected user-defined datatypes, rules, or users in all subsequently created databases. Tempdb is a working database used for sorts and temporary tables. Tempdb is re-created each time SQL Server is booted.

As the first step in configuring SQL Server for your site, you must create logical disk devices, on which you will place all subsequent databases, logs, and indexes. You should do this even if you have only one hard disk for your entire server, to better support transaction logging, and also to allow you to more easily alter your database structure when you add disk resources in the future.

Configuration Rules

SQL Server has a few caveats, provisos, and quid pro quos that must be taken into account when determining how you should configure your database environment. First, note that you do not want to install any user objects on the master database. Any modifications you make to the master database (including adding new stored procedures) are completely overwritten if you have to run the BUILDMASTER utility again. To avoid this, you must create devices and databases for your users that are held separate and apart from the master database/device.

Logs should be maintained on a separate disk from the database. If you log to the same logical device as the database, you cannot successfully execute the dump trans command. Instead you should dump the entire database. Also, a log device is dedicated to the logging process. You cannot create a device and use it for both logs and indexes, for example.

Optimum performance is gained by sharing the work across multiple devices. Although you need to tune and optimize your particular SQL Server according to your workload, several configuration options are available to you from the outset. I have noted that tables and indexes should be kept on separate logical devices and where possible on separate hard disks handled by separate controllers. Even if you have little idea of how often your users and applications will use indexes, you should opt for this segregated configuration from the outset.

NOTE

As part of the dumping and restoring of user databases, SQL Server requires that you have an identical disk/database structure. To ensure this, and to save time, you should modify the provided administration scripts (or create your own) and back them up. This allows you to duplicate your environment exactly, if you have to create it from scratch or bring up an additional server on which you want to restore a database dumped from another server. Using the scripts also saves time and aggravation. Running the following scripts will result in a SQL Server configured as shown in Figure 3.3.1.

FIGURE 3.3.1.

Sample logical disk configuration for operating system files.

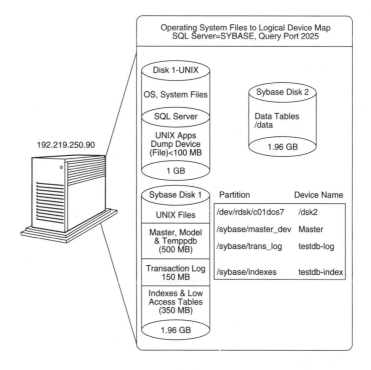

Working from your physical implementation plan, you can run the following script to create a logical disk device called database1_device:

```
/* DISK INIT to build a 20 MB physical device in the physical
   directory */
/* /sybase/databases.  This device will be used for building a
   database */
/* called database1. */
```

```
use master
go
disk init
 name = "database1_device",
 physname = "/sybase/databases/database1_device",
 vdevno = 1,
 size = 10240
go

/* DISK INIT to build a 5 MB physical device in the physical
    directory  */
/* /sybase/logfiles.  This device will be used for the
    logfiles for     */
/* database database1.       */

disk init
 name = "database1_log_device",
 physname = "/sybase/logfiles/database1_log_device",
 vdevno = 2,
 size = 2560
go

/* DISK INIT to build a 10 MB physical device in the physical
    directory */
/* /physdisk3/indexes.  This device will be used for some of
    the          */
/* indexes for database database1.       */

disk init
 name = "database1_index_device1",
 physname = "/sybase/indexes/database1_index_device1",
 vdevno = 3,
 size = 5120
go

/* DISK INIT to build a 5 MB physical device in the physical
    directory  */
/* /physdisk4/indexes.  This device will be used for the
    logfiles for   */
/* database1.       */

disk init
 name = "database1_index_device2",
 physname = "/sybase/indexes/database1_index_device2",
 vdevno = 4,
 size = 2560
go
```

For SQL Server, the size parameter is given in 2K blocks. To arrive at the correct size parameter for your requirements, you can use this formula: blocks = ((#M * 1,024,000)/2048)). For example, if you want to create a disk device of 15M, you would specify the number of blocks as 7500. (15*1024000) = 15,360,000, which, divided by 2048, results in 7500, the correct 2K block specification for 15M.

Using raw partitions rather than operating system files for logical disk devices requires a few additional steps. First, the disks must be partitioned to the sizes you wish. Your disk device can be only as large as the partition, but you can have databases that straddle multiple disk devices. An example of this is demonstrated later in the chapter. If you intend to dedicate the entire hard disk for SQL Server use, beware! You must not include cylinder 0 in your available partition map, because this causes the disk information to be overwritten by SQL Server. You can do this and the system will not complain; however, when you reboot, your machine will no longer see the hard disk and everything will have to be configured again from scratch. To avoid this, start with cylinder 1, not 0. The partitioning command syntax and options vary for each UNIX operating system version. For the purpose of an example, however, I will continue to work with the sample database environment established in Figure 2.3.7, which appeared in Chapter 2.3. The disk partitions were established as shown in Figure 3.3.2.

FIGURE 3.3.2.

Raw partition information for sample database application.

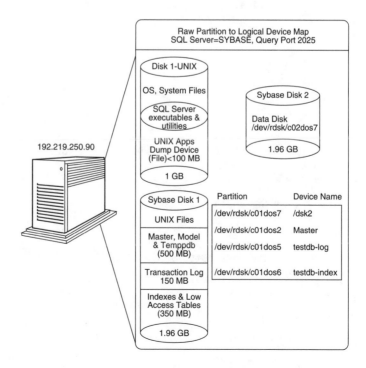

To ensure that you are working with a raw disk, check the file systems table (typically /etc/fstab) and ensure that the partitions to be used are either not listed or commented out. To set partitions for your hard disks, check your UNIX system's documentation under format.

To create identical disk devices to the ones resulting from the previous scripts, modify the scripts as follows:

```
/* DISK INIT to build a 20 MB physical device in the physical
   directory */
/* /sybase/databases.  This device will be used for building a
   database */
/* called database1. */
use master
go
disk init
 name = "database1_device",
 physname = "/dev/rdsk/c1t1d0s2",
 vdevno = 1,
 size = 10240
go

/* DISK INIT to build a 5 MB physical device in the physical
   directory */
/* /sybase/logfiles.  This device will be used for the
   logfiles for      */
/* database database1.     */

disk init
 name = "database1_log_device",
 physname = "/dev/rdsk/c0t1d0s5",
 vdevno = 2,
 size = 2560
go

/* DISK INIT to build a 10 MB physical device in the physical
   directory */
/* /physdisk3/indexes.  This device will be used for some of
   the          */
/* indexes for database database1.      */

disk init
 name = "database1_index_device1",
 physname = "/dev/rdsk/c0t1d0s6",
 vdevno = 3,
 size = 5120
go
```

```
/* DISK INIT to build a 5 MB physical device in the physical
   directory */
/* /physdisk4/indexes.  This device will be used for the
   logfiles for  */
/* database1. */

disk init
 name = "database1_index_device2",
 physname = "/dev/rdsk/c0t1d0s6",
 vdevno = 4,
 size = 2560
go
```

At this point, you can see how I have exactly the same Sybase logical device names. In this case, however, these devices reside on raw disk partitions; they are not mounted on operating system files. You can now create databases on your logical device drives.

The create database syntax is very straightforward:

```
/* CREATE DATABASE database1 using up all 20 MB of the database device*/
/* database1_device, all 10 MB of database1_index_device1 and all 5 MB*/
/* of database1_index_device2, with logfile on separate log device.   */
use master
go
create database database1
on database1_device = 20,
database1_index_device1 = 10,
database1_index_device2 = 5
log on database1_log_device
go
```

By specifying the logical database devices on which the database is to be created, you can create a database that straddles multiple physical disk drives. If there is not enough room on any of the devices specified in the command, the command still executes, but you are granted only as much room as was available on the device.

If you need to allocate more space to your database after you create it, use the alter database command. The syntax for this command works identically to the create database statement. You can use the alter database command to extend your database across new physical disks that have been installed and initialized with the disk init command.

As you can no doubt tell, your options for expanding your database sizes are significant. What you cannot do is reduce the size of a database or disk device, without first dropping it and then re-creating it with the new size.

Segments

Each logical database device can be broken into as many as 32 segments. A single segment can also be configured to straddle multiple database devices. By using segments, the systems administrator or database owner can exercise increased control over placement and usage of specific database objects. This makes the system more flexible to administer and often results in performance increases. Flexibility is gained by the capability to extend segments across new devices if you find your existing storage capacity insufficient. Improved performance comes from being able to segregate tables, indexes, and even text and image columns from other, more highly active data within the table.

Segments are added to existing databases through the use of the `sp_addsegment` stored procedure. The syntax is

```
use master
go
sp_addsegment segment_name, database_device1
go
```

where the `database_device` is any logical device name already initialized with DISK INIT. To map multiple segment names to a database, you must declare each `segment_name` with an explicit `sp_addsegment` command.

You can define segments any time prior to creating your database objects, after you have installed and configured your SQL Server. You can then create your database objects to take optimum advantage of the devices and segments you have defined. If you have already created a table and wish to take advantage of segments, you can use `sp_placeobject` to allocate any future data in the table or index to a newly defined segment. You cannot reallocate existing table or index data, however, without copying the data out and dropping and recreating the table with the segment specified.

As you can see in Figure 3.3.3, the database objects are created or moved to reside on segments. These in turn reference logical disk names, which are internal Sybase names for physical disk resources.

FIGURE 3.3.3.

The relationships between database objects, segments, logical devices, and physical disk drives in a SQL Server.

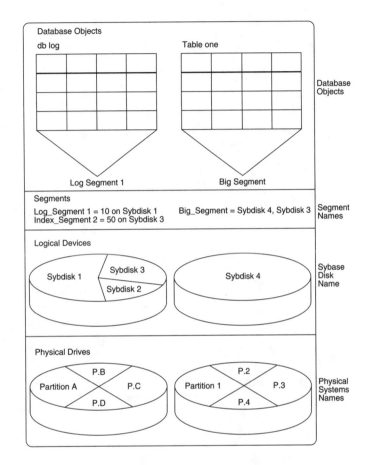

Summary

This chapter has shown you the structure of how Sybase database objects sit on top of the underlying hardware of the platform on which your SQL Server has been installed. As you can see, the level of abstraction in the naming conventions increases as you move away from the hardware and toward the view of the database taken by a developer. By using segments as the base on which the developer sees the database objects, only the Sybase systems administrator and the platform's administrator (often the same person) need to be concerned with the actual disk partitions. Through segments and logical disk devices, Sybase allows you to create, alter, and drop tables and objects according to the physical disk resources you have available. You should now be in a good position to determine how to best structure your hard drives and partitions for logs, indexes, and other database objects.

3.4

Memory and Configuration Options

This chapter covers the basic settings that can be affected by using the `sp_configure` stored procedure. In the previous chapter, you saw how the sybload and sybconfig utilities installed and configured a SQL Server as the default. Here you see how you can modify those settings and the impact of various configurations on performance and resources.

SQL Server is nothing if not flexible and, as you have seen already, flexibility has its price in terms of complexity. It is possible to set values with `sp_configure` that do not allow you to start your SQL Server. This chapter covers exactly what those parameters are, as well as how to recover from a bad configuration. By the end of this chapter, you should be comfortable with the list of the parameter settings that can be set for a SQL Server and be well on your way to planning the configuration that will best fit your specific site.

sp_configure

The settings that affect the configuration of your SQL Server on bootup are displayed and set through the `sp_configure` stored procedure. For any changed settings take effect, however, the systems administrator must issue the RECONFIGURE command. To make effective changes that would not normally be considered optimum, the systems administrator must issue the RECONFIGURE WITH OVERRIDE command.

RECONFIGURE privileges default to the systems administrator and cannot be transferred. If you make changes through `sp_configure` and do not issue the RECONFIGURE command, the SQL Server abandons the changes and starts up with the configuration values that had been set previously.

To obtain the current SQL Server configuration variables, enter the `sp_configure` command with no options after it. Your SQL Server will look like Listing 3.4.1.

Listing 3.4.1. `sp_configure` **output.**

```
1> 2>  name               minimum   maximum  config_value  run_value
       ----------------   -------   -------  ------------  ---------
       recovery interval        1     32767             0          5
       allow updates            0         1             0          1
       user connections         5         5            10          5
       memory                1000     32000          3200       3200
       open databases           5       100             0         10
       locks                 5000    500000             0       5000
       open objects           100     10000             0        500
       procedure cache          1        99             0         20
       fill factor              0       100             0          0
```

```
time slice                        50      1000           0        100
database size                      2     10000           0          2
tape retention                     0       365           0          0
recovery flags                     0         1           0          0
serial number                      1    999999           0          0
nested triggers                    0         1           1          1
devices                            4       256          10         10
remote access                      0         1           0          0
remote logins                      0      4096           0          0
remote sites                       0       256           0          0
remote connections                 0      4096           0          0
pre-read packets                   0       256           0          0
upgrade version                    0 2147483647         420        420
default sortorder id               0       255          40         40
default language                   0      9999           2          0
language in cache                  3       100           3          3
(25 rows affected, return status = 0)
```

As you might expect, the minimum and maximum values indicate the acceptable range of values that you can set with this command. The `config_value` indicates the values you have set with sp_configure. You could choose to set a number of configuration variables with sp_configure and check the `config_value` column to ensure that they are the settings you wanted before restarting the SQL Server to make the changes take effect. The `run_value` column indicates the parameters that were set the last time the SQL Server booted. They are the values that were in effect when the sp_configure command was run with no options to get the listing.

To change a SQL Server configuration variable, enter the sp_configure command followed by the name of the configuration variable to be changed and the new value to which you want it set. For example, to change the number of nested triggers configured for a specific SQL Server, you would enter the following command:

```
use master
sp_configure "nested triggers", 16
go
```

The values in the `config_values` column would change to read 16. (Please note that SQL Server versions 4.2 and earlier did not support nested triggers and this value would not be legal for those servers.)

To have the new settings take effect, you must restart the SQL Server. This is true for all the configuration variables, with the exception of recovery interval and allow updates. These are dynamic and take effect as soon as you have successfully executed reconfigure after making the changes through sp_configure. The recovery interval sets the maximum time a database should take to recover after a systems failure. The SQL Server evaluates the activity on each database and factors in the recovery interval to determine how often to checkpoint each database. The recovery interval is set in minutes per database. The allow updates variable determines whether the systems administrator can have direct access to make changes to the systems tables. Because this is generally not something you want to do, the default is 0 for off. When it is set to 0, the only way to change the systems tables is through the systems procedures.

The other values set through `sp_configure` include the following:

- **User connections**: This sets the maximum number of user connections that can be concurrently connected to your SQL Server. This should not be confused with the maximum number of processes. The maximum number of user connections is a function of the operating system and varies from platform to platform. (SQL Server itself is limited by the number of file descriptors supported by the host. The effective number for your platform will most likely be lower.) You can obtain the number of the maximum number of connections supported by your SQL Server platform by issuing a `select @@max_connections` command. To determine the number of maximum user connections, you must subtract the number of connections that will be required by your server for such functions as network handler, checkpoint, disk, and dump devices. Any SQL Server will need a minimum of six for the master device and another connection for each additional database device initialized. Remote server connections are required for each remote server while they are executing a remote procedure call; disk and tape dumps need a connection while in operation. Each ISQL and DB-LIB connection counts as a user connection. The number of user connections plus systems connections must not total more than the `max_connections` limit for your platform. Like any multiuser system, it is possible to have more login IDs generated than connections due to the transient nature of user connections in general. Typical office applications do not require a dedicated, full-time connection to the server. If a user connection fails because sufficient user connections are not available, they will receive an error message to that effect.

- **Memory:** This variable sets the amount of SQL Server memory expressed in 2K pages. In some platforms the SQL Server simply seizes the physical RAM needed when it boots; others require a shared memory variable to be set to reserve that much memory for Sybase. For those platforms (check your release notes), you must ensure that the memory variable set through `sp_configure` is less than the amount specified in your OS kernel configuration file or your SQL Server will not be able to start. The same is true on systems without an OS kernel entry where the amount of RAM specified through `sp_configure` exceeds the amount of memory available after the OS is loaded. Theoretically, SQL Server can operate with 2M of RAM, (as seen in the minimum values column of `sp_configure`), but even a small working system generally needs a minimum of 8M (16M is more realistic). This memory is used for the SQL Server kernel, user connections, and data and procedure cache. For applications with a great deal of query activity, increasing the amount of memory available to SQL Server can really pay off.

■ **Open databases**: The default is 10 but there is little impact on performance or storage if the value is set higher, so if you need more, hike the value up.

■ **Locks**: The number of available shared and exclusive locks is indicated by this variable. If you need more locks, increment the number until your insufficient locks error messages go away. Like the open databases parameter, setting this number higher has little impact on the system (other than a small amount of memory reserved for each lock).

■ **Open objects**: This refers to the maximum number of database objects, tables, indexes, `stored_procedures`, and so on that can be in use at any one time. Once again, there is little impact on resources if you declare a number higher than the default (300).

■ **Procedure cache**: After SQL Server takes the memory allocated to it and divides it up for the necessary number of locks, user connections, and the kernel itself, the remaining memory is split between the procedure cache and the data cache. The number set here refers to the percentage of the remaining memory to be allocated to stored procedures. If you use stored procedures intensively, you may find a real performance improvement from adjusting this percentage upward for the procedure cache. As a general rule, development systems use stored procedures more often and a default of 50 percent would be more appropriate.

■ **Fill factor:** As your SQL Server fills up data and index pages, it must split the data into new pages. The default of 0 indicates that the pages will be filled 100 percent, with a reasonable allowance made for expansion of the index B-tree. You will most likely not need to change this setting, but if you do, the optional fill factor parameter when creating indexes will override the default value set here.

■ **Time slice:** This variable indicates the number of milliseconds any given user process is allowed to run. The default is 100 milliseconds.

■ **Database size:** This sets the default size of new databases created without an explicit size indicated in the create database command. If your model database is expanded to beyond the default 2M and you wish to create databases with a default size, you must change this value using `sp_configure`, because a new database cannot be smaller than the model.

■ **Tape retention:** As discussed in the section on dumping and restoring databases, you may want to ensure that SQL Server checks the date on tapes to be used to hold dumps and gives a warning if the dump on the tape is within a certain number of days—for example, seven days. The default is to allow you to write on anything without complaint.

■ **Recovery flags:** This variable determines whether SQL Server displays only minimal information about a database when it is being recovered. The default of 0 yields a database name and message indicating that a recovery is in progress. A setting of 1 tells you information about each and every transaction and whether it was aborted or committed during the recovery.

■ **Serial number:** This is the only place that the serial number entered when you first installed SQL Server shows.

■ **Nested triggers:** As discussed earlier, nested triggers are supported; however, you must set the number of nested triggers with `sp_configure`. The default is to allow nested triggers.

■ **Devices:** SQL Server is provided with a default number of disk and dump devices of 10. You can change it through `sp_configure`.

■ **Remote access:** To allow other SQL Servers and their users to connect, log in, and issue remote procedure calls, you must change this setting from the default 0 to 1, which allows remote access.

■ **Remote logins:** This parameter allows a maximum number of users from remote servers to connect to your SQL Server.

The remaining four variables are simply displayed for information. You do not change character sets, sort orders, and default languages through `sp_configure`. If you have a number of languages in use by applications on your SQL Server, however, you may want to change the number of languages in cache with `sp_configure`.

SQL Server evaluates the changes to determine whether the new values set with the `sp_configure` command are valid and reasonable. If they are not considered to be either of the two, an error message is returned. If you have some reason to want to force your SQL Server to accept the values anyway, you must use the RECONFIGURE WITH OVERRIDE. As mentioned earlier, it is possible to set configuration values that make it impossible for the SQL Server to run. For example, if you set the memory setting higher than the amount of physical memory or the amount of shared memory allocated in the operating system (depending on whether your platform supports this), your SQL Server will not be able to claim all the memory set through sp_configure and will fail to start. In the event that sp_configure values become really out of whack, you can reinstall the master database with the default settings. This will allow you to begin setting your configuration variables again from scratch. In the process, however, it will usually overwrite your users, groups, and stored procedures contained in the master database. Check the installation guidelines for your SQL Server platform to determine whether you can load the default sp_configure settings without overwriting the rest of the master database.

To avoid this rather undesirable situation, Sybase has provided the -r flag for the BUILDMASTER utility, which will restore your SQL Server to the default configuration values, without affecting previously defined devices and databases.

Summary

As you can see from this chapter, each SQL Server takes its configuration from the sysconfigures systems table, which you read and modify through sp_configure.

Access and manipulation of these values can greatly affect the performance and behavior of your SQL Server, so you should carefully think through any changes before you make them effective.

If you are not the administrator for your SQL Server, you may still find it interesting and useful to be aware of the settings for your particular environment. Reading this chapter will have provided you with a basis for interpreting the output from running the sp_configure systems procedure.

3.5

Creating Tables, Views, and Indexes

Database objects are really your SQL Server's reason for existence. The data itself is held in tables, and a number of database objects assist in the access and manipulation of that data. This chapter looks at some of the considerations and the precise syntax for creating tables, views, and indexes.

Additionally, you will gain a good sense of the performance implications of your original table create specifications, how indexes can speed frequent access to data, and how views can be used as a convenience for end-user data access as well as a method of increasing data security. This chapter uses examples to proceed step by step through the initialization of disks, segments, and tables for particular examples, as well as the creation of views and indexes.

This chapter introduces the key concepts underlying these database objects and puts you in a position to begin implementing your physical data model implementation plan, thereby creating your own database objects. I have already looked at how user permissions affect access to tables and other database objects. In this chapter, you see exactly how to restrict retrieval and updating of tables and views and are introduced to the various indexing methods that could be established for your tables. These three database objects form the greatest number of server-side elements that you as a developer will have to deal with in the creation of your SQL Server solution. The following material covers how you can structure these objects in the best fashion to support your particular requirements.

Tables

In the relational model, a good database structure calls for a high degree of normalization in the design process prior to implementing your model by creating actual database objects. In the real world, things are not always so straightforward. The table creation process is not simply one of ensuring that you have the right data elements contained in your database. You must also be aware of the implications of the physical environment for performance.

As is the case with many aspects of SQL Server, you have a great deal of choice and flexibility in structuring your tables. Not only are there many distinct datatypes, including support for datatypes you create yourself, but you have complete discretion over how your tables reside on your physical disk drives.

From a developer's perspective, depending on your particular project and responsibilities, you may be concerned only with the specification of the table's contents: the columns, datatypes, and keys. From an administrator's perspective, you will be much more concerned with distribution of the table across devices, type of access and frequency, and integrity constraints that need to be reflected in the creation of the table.

I established earlier in this section that databases could be created on multiple devices, and that segments could be created allowing you to spread your database across those devices. As your tables and other database objects increase in size, you can extend these segments to allow the objects to grow. You will find it awkward, however, to move the table from one device to another without dropping it and re-creating it on the desired devices. The point is simply that you should give some thought to allocation of tables to segments and devices from the outset, rather than deferring it until you have populated the table with data and have an idea of the real-world requirements. This is advisable partially because you can always copy the data out of the table, drop the table, drop the indexes, re-create them as you want them, and then copy the data back into the new table. By considering exactly how you want to balance your tables, indexes, and other objects across segments from the outset, however, you can often save yourself time and effort.

You may be nodding and agreeing and wondering exactly how you are going to achieve this lofty and desirable goal. You can see from the following statement exactly how a table called books could be created to span the segments and devices outlined in Figure 2.3.7. For purposes of this example, the table is expected to be very large and needs to be spread across two devices, known as data_disk1 and data_disk2. As identified in the section dealing with database creation (Chapter 3.3) you could specify that the database itself should be split across the two disks. This does not provide any guarantee that the table itself will be shared across the disks, however. For example, if the table is half the size of one of the disks, it could easily fit on one disk, which would defeat the purpose of sharing the table access across two physical disks. You can ensure that a particular table is striped, or split across multiple devices, by declaring segments.

The basic table create statement is as follows:

```
use database1
go
create table newtable(column1 char(20) not null, column2 tinyint not
➡null, column3 varchar(255) null)
go
```

This statement creates a table called newtable with three columns on the default segment for database1. You remember that database1 was created on database9_device. Imagine for a moment that you have discovered that this table will be large and frequently accessed. Or that the database9_device is utilized at close to storage capacity and you do not want to risk filling the device as you populate your new table. First, you must alter the database to project database1 across the new Sybase disk device. To accomplish this, you could choose to use the following script:

```
use master
go
disk init
 name = "database10_device",
 physname = "/dev/rdsk/c1t1d0s2",
 vdevno = 4,
 size = 2560
go
```

Remember that you can have only one logical device initialized for each physical hard disk partition. If you are running SQL Server on a platform that forces you to use operating system files, remember to ensure that each file you specify is mounted on a different disk device, if possible.

To create a table that you force to be held on two disk devices, you would then alter the database as follows:

```
use master
ALTER DATABASE database1 on database10_device = 100
go
```

This extends database1 to include the new logical device, making the size of the database 100M larger while maintaining the existing allocations for data, indexes, and logs that were defined as part of the initial create database command (see Chapter 2.3, "Developing a Data Model").

At this point you can create a segment that exists on both database9_device and database10_device using the following commands:

```
use database1
go
sp_addsegment two_device_seg database9_device, database10_device
go
```

After running this script (or modifying it to suit your exact purposes), you should get a message from SQL Server indicating

```
DBCC execution completed. If DBCC printed error messages, see your
System Administrator.
Segment created
(return status = 0)
```

This indicates that you now have a segment within the database1 database. The last step finally involves the creation of a table. To create a table placed on a specified segment rather than the default segment (the logical database device the database was created on), use the following syntax:

```
use database1
go
```

```
create table newtable(column1 char(20) not null, column2 tinyint not
➥null, column3 varchar(255) null) on two_device_seg
go
```

This results in a table called newtable, which will be stored on both devices defined during the creation of the two_device_seg segment. You should note that anyone with create table permissions granted in the database can create the table on the segment. You may want to define segments for each database and allow developers to create their own tables, or you may choose to assign accountability for creating these objects to an administrator or other centralized body.

Altering Tables

You can add columns to a table at any time using the alter table command. The syntax for this command is as follows:

```
use database1
go
alter table newtable
add column9 char(20) null, column10 int(8) null
go
```

This adds column9 and column10 to the table newtable. When using the alter table command, you must specify all columns being added as null. The command does not execute if you specify any of the columns as not null, because the column has no values in it when you issue the alter table command, which violates the not null requirement for that column.

To drop columns, or to alter a table so that it contains not null columns, you must first create a new table with the specifications you require, modify your existing table to contain the new column (or create a new table that contains the column and values for the new not null column), select into your new table from your existing table, drop the old table, and rename the new table to the old table name.

For a table where you wished to drop a column, you could use the following syntax:

```
use database1
go
create table newertable(column1 char(20) not null, column2 tinyint not
➥null, on two_device_seg
go
select into newertable column1, column2
from newtable column1, column2
where column2 > 0
go
drop newtable
go
sp_rename newertable newtable
go
```

This, in essence, drops column3 from newtable. Any indexes that were created on newtable must be re-created, and any stored procedures, views, or other database objects that referenced column3 must also be modified and recompiled to function properly.

If you add columns to a table with the alter table command, you must re-create any stored procedures that retrieved all from the table to reference the newly created column. Without re-creating these sp_ procedures, you will get only the columns that existed in the table when the stored procedure was created. Recompiling the stored procedure is insufficient; you must drop and re-create it to get it to see the added column.

Datatypes

It is difficult to consider the full implications of creating and altering tables without some understanding of the datatypes supported by SQL Server. The datatypes form the most basic element of the table. They are the fundamental definition of the type of values that will be stored. By selecting appropriate datatypes, you can build a level of integrity into your database at the ground level. Specifying all columns as character would allow someone to enter a last name into a date field. By choosing datetime as the datatype for the column, you ensure that some level of integrity checking is performed even without triggers, rules, or validation efforts.

An additional benefit to selecting appropriate datatypes is the operations supported on the data. Each datatype has some level of overhead and access services built into it. Here you see a treatment of each datatype, where it is generally used, and any restrictions, requirements, or rules governing that use. Each of the SQL Server datatypes has been developed to meet a specific need for database developers.

You may choose to create your own datatypes if you have requirements that are not met by the supplied datatypes. The default SQL Server datatypes are as follows:

Table 3.7.1. SQL Server dataypes.

Datatype	Description
int	Integer datatype holds whole numbers between –2,147,483,647 and +2,147,483,647
smallint	Small integer datatype holds whole numbers between –32,767 and +32,767
tinyint	Tiny integer datatype holds whole numbers between 0 and 255

Datatype	*Description*
`float`	Floating-point datatype holds decimal and whole numbers
`real`	Real datatype holds floating-point data, but only to 4 bytes long
`char(n)`	Character datatype holds up to 255 characters, letters, numbers, and symbols
`varchar(n)`	Variable-length character datatype holds character data varying widely between 0 and 255
`text`	Text datatype holds printable character data up to 2,147,483,647 bytes
`binary(n)`	Binary datatype holds up to 255 binary characters in fixed length
`varbinary(n)`	Varbinary datatype holds varying amounts of binary data up to 255 characters in length
`image`	Image datatype holds between 0 and 2,147,483,647 bytes of binary graphic data
`bit`	Bit datatype holds 0 or 1
`money`	Money datatype stores between −922,337,203,685,477.5807 and +922,337,203,685,477.5808
`smallmoney`	Smallmoney datatype stores between +214,748.3647 and −214,748.3648
`datetime`	Datetime datatype holds date/time to precision of 3.33 milliseconds
`smalldatetime`	Smalldatetime datatype holds date/time to precision of 1 minute
`timestamp`	Timestamp datatype is used to automatically record time of insert or delete operations

As you can see from this quick coverage of the various datatypes, in some situations your choice of datatype is driven by the nature of your application and the desire to economize on storage space consumed. `smallmoney` is half the size of the `money` datatype, for example. It consumes four bytes as opposed to eight. The price of a book in either pubs or the bookstore database will never exceed $214,748.36 (although I can dream). If the book table contained 100,000 rows, the difference between choosing the `smallmoney` datatype over the `money` datatype is almost half a megabyte.

Other datatypes have performance implications, such as char and varchar. Although the varchar datatype conserves storage space, the char datatype is accessed somewhat more quickly by SQL Server during retrieves. For large tables, where the data held in the column does not significantly vary in length, (such as zip or postal codes), you would likely choose the char datatype over varchar.

Still other datatypes, such as text and image, have retrieval restrictions you need to take into account. You cannot perform string matching functions within a text datatype except with the LIKE keyword in a WHERE clause. text datatypes are also restricted from being used as parameters to stored procedures, local variables, contained in indexes, subqueries, and joins. If you want to be able to manipulate the data held in a text column, you should consider a char or varchar datatype instead. This does, however, mean that you are restricted to the 255-character upper limit of the char and varchar datatypes. In some applications, this might mean you would define an abstract of the text column with the char datatype and retrieve the text on the basis of searches of the abstract.

Each of the datatypes you can choose for various column storage requirements is covered in more detail in the sections that follow.

Integers

int	Storage size for the int datatype is 4 bytes, and the range of values that can be stored within a column defined as int is any whole number between 2,147,483,647 and –2,147,483,648.
smallint	This datatype takes up half as much storage space as int, with 2 bytes per value. Acceptable values range from 32,767 to –32,768. (Are you wondering why it stores a higher negative number than positive? Don't forget that 0 counts as a value.)
tinyint	With a storage size of 1 byte, tinyint can hold values ranging from 0 to 255 inclusive.

Floating-Point Datatypes

float	Storage size for floating-point values is 8 bytes. This datatype is used to hold decimal positive or negative numbers. The precision of the floating-point datatype and the number of significant digits is a function of the platform on which your SQL Server runs. You can also store exponents in a column created as a float by entering a

number followed by an E. The E indicates exponent and can be upper- or lowercase. The number can be positive or negative and can include a decimal point.

real
This datatype operates identically to `float` except the storage size is 4 bytes, which reduces the number of digits that can be held in the column to that of the `int` datatype.

Money Datatypes

money
The `money` datatype provides the facility to store values from +922,337,203,685,477.5807 to –922,337,203,685,477.5808 as double-precision floating-point values. The storage size for this datatype is 8 bytes. To have values accepted as money, the input must be preceded by a $ symbol. If this symbol is not supplied, the value is treated as a `float`, possibly losing some of the value's precision or even being rejected. This is necessary even if the money being tracked in the column is not U.S. dollars. SQL Server provides no currency conversion features. When money values are displayed, they are rounded off to two places.

smallmoney
This is like the `money` datatype, but the range of values is limited to between +214,748.3647 and –214,748.3648 and the storage size is 4 bytes.

Character Datatypes

char(*n*)
The character datatype can be used to store up to 255 letters, symbols, and numbers. The specific letters, symbols, and numbers depend on the character set you specified when you first loaded SQL Server. When using the `char(n)` datatype specification, you indicate how long the column should be by replacing the n with a number between 0 and 255. Input longer than the number of characters specified for the column length is truncated; shorter entries are padded with blanks. You can use wildcards and LIKE to retrieve values from character columns; trailing blanks are ignored.

varchar(*n*)
This datatype is structured the same way as the `char` datatype. Its distinction is that entries are not padded with blanks and the storage space required is somewhat reduced.

	varchar columns are accessed a little more slowly than char columns, however.
text	Text columns are of variable length and can contain up to 2,147,483,647 characters. You can retrieve data from text columns using LIKE and wildcard characters; however, you cannot use the text datatype for variables or parameters in stored procedures. SQL Server provides facilities that allow text columns to be stored separately from the rest of their table for performance reasons.
binary(n)	Binary columns are used to store up to 255 binary (not hexadecimal) characters, such as programming code and image data. Space consumed within the database is always equal to the length of the column as defined, independent of whether any data values are held in the column. Because input to binary columns is in hexadecimal form (the hex values are translated to binary values when stored), the space consumed by binary columns is twice that of the number used in the create statement. For example, a binary (255) column actually stores 510 characters.
varbinary(n)	The variable length binary datatype operates like the binary datatype and is subject to the same considerations. Like its variable character cousin, varbinary saves storage by storing the actual length of data entered, but there is some performance penalty.
image	This is similar to the text datatype, in that it can store between 0 and 2,147,483,647 bytes, although the image datatype stores binary data, not text characters, and the image datatype cannot be used for variables or as parameters in stored procedures.

Date/Time Datatypes

datetime	This datatype is used to hold either or both date and time information in two 4-byte integers, one for date and one for time. datetime datatypes store time values accurate to 3.33 milliseconds. It is not necessary to enter both date and time information to a column that has been defined as datetime; either may be left out. The datetime datatype provides for many formatting styles and can be manipulated with built-in functions.

smalldatetime   Like `datetime`, this datatype holds compound dates and time values. However, it requires only 4 bytes for storage because the dates that can be accommodated range from Jan 1, 1900 to June 6, 2079, with time values stored in hours and minutes.

Other Datatypes

bit   The `bit` datatype stores one bit of data expressed as 0 or 1. If values other than 1 are entered, they are treated as 1. The `bit` datatype is generally used for true or false, yes or no questions. Nulls are not permitted, and you cannot create and index on bit columns.

Built-In Functions

SQL Server comes with a number of built-in functions that operate on data within the databases. The built-in functions include certain functions to assist you in manipulating various datatypes, such as text and image data and mathematical, date, and string functions. A convert function allows you to compare and manipulate values maintained in completely unlike datatypes, such as character and integer. Look at each type of built-in function to determine how you could use it. Your ability to manipulate datatypes through these functions could determine which datatype you wanted for a particular column within your database.

String Functions

SQL Server allows you to perform several functions on character strings. These functions include the following:

- Putting values and expressions in front of retrieved values
- Assembling a series of retrieved values into one apparent statement
- Comparing names through the soundex algorithm
- Stuffing one string of characters into the middle of another
- Retrieving and displaying subsets of strings
- Converting integers, money, and dates to character strings

A string in this case is considered to be a group of characters. The string functions manipulate these character groups or expressions, allowing you to structure the data being retrieved as part of the SELECT statement.

The simplest example of how and where you can use string functions is through a retrieval of first and last names. Putting different expressions together into what seems to be one whole unit is known as concatenation. For example:

```
use pubs
go
select (au_lname + "," + au_fname)
from authors
order by au_lname
go
```

This example retrieves the first and last name from the authors table and displays them separated by a comma and sorted by last name. The string function allows you to insert a character or symbol between values being retrieved as part of the SELECT statement. Generally, string functions operate on character data, although a few of the functions can be used on binary data as well. It is also possible to put both binary and character strings together and treat them as one expression using string functions. These strings allow you to retrieve results, which are surrounded by words describing the values being retrieved. You would use a string function to display a description in front of a retrieved set of values from a column. For instance, to display Total Sold Year to Date in front of the year-to-date sales value from the ytd_sales column, you could use the following string function:

```
use pubs
go
select * ("Total Sold Year to Date" + Convert char(10) + ytd_sales
from titles
go
```

The character expression Total Sold Year to Date is displayed immediately ahead of the values retrieved from ytd_sales. To perform this function (adding a character string in front of a number), the number first had to be converted to a character string. The convert char(10) expression executes the built-in convert function and treats the retrieved values from ytd_sales as a 10-digit character string. Using varchar rather than char gives you a slightly different format of the retrieved values, especially if you are retrieving multiple values in the same statement. You could also use a similar approach to insert the appropriate currency symbol for values retrieved from a money field.

Substrings

This function allows you to retrieve and display parts of a character string or expression. You could, for example, retrieve only the first 20 characters of a title with the following syntax:

```
use pubs
go
select title = (substring(title,1,20))
from titles
where type = "psychology"
go
```

This select retrieves a list of five titles (unless you have added some) from the pubs database and displays the first 20 characters of the title. This is especially useful if you are not certain of the contents of the entire character string.

Converting Datatypes

As part of your retrieve statements when manipulating the data, you may need to ensure that columns being joined or compared are explicitly converted to compatible datatypes. This is different than simply converting the output of a column to character for purposes of concatenating strings and expressions to the output. SQL Server takes care of this datatype conversion automatically in many situations, which is referred to as an implicit conversion. For example, if you had defined a column as character and stored date information in it, you can successfully execute statements that compare that column to a datetime column, because SQL Server performs an implicit conversion. You cannot execute a statement that takes a number from a column defined as character and compares it to a column defined with the int, smallint, or tinyint datatype, however, without explicitly stating the conversion. Here is an example straight out of the Sybase manual:

```
use pubs
go
select title, convert(char(12), ytd_sales)
from titles
go
```

In this example, ytd_sales (which is an int datatype) is being converted to a 12-character column during the retrieve. Convert statements are useful for formatting changes, such as changing the datetime display to yy/mm/dd. Convert statements are required, however, to compare values of incompatible datatypes.

You can also lose the benefits of a datatype when you convert it to another. For example, the money datatype is very precise and is kept to one ten-thousandth of a dollar (or whatever currency you are using). When you use bulk copy to write out table contents to a host file and convert a money datatype to character, the character format values are recorded only to the nearest two places.

Creating Views

In the context of data access permissions, views provide a great deal of built-in security for any SQL Server installation. If you provide access to developers or even some end users, it is always possible (however unlikely) that they will find a way to gain authorized access to table data that you have set permissions to protect. Views are one bulletproof method of ensuring that only the columns you wish to be seen are, in fact, seen.

As a relational rule of thumb, views are not updated. It is possible, however, to define a view in such a way that one of the underlying tables that make up the view can be updated. As you might expect, several conditions govern this. First, you should become familiar with the data retrieval aspects of using views.

Using Views

A view is a database object that retrieves and displays data from one or more tables. You create your view with a list of columns and tables, as well as by supplying a select statement to provide conditions for retrieved data. In this way you can not only restrict the columns displayed but also set conditions that filter the rows being retrieved for the view. To a user, views look exactly like tables. Because of the ability to create views incorporating SQL syntax, however, a view allows you to create a complex product of joins, retrieved columns matching values, derived columns, and many other SQL functions that your application might require. At the same time, users are able to use less sophisticated data access tools, such as PC spreadsheets, to manipulate the data in the view as if they were accessing the underlying tables.

Views can be highly useful during a development effort because the structure of underlying tables that form the view can be modified and the view will still operate, as long as none of the columns specified as part of the view were dropped or renamed. You can even drop and re-create a table and application using views that will function as soon as the replacement table is available.

Views are created and managed with syntax similar to the table commands; create view and drop view are used to both establish a view in the current database and delete an existing one. The select statement associated with a view can be almost any combination of the SQL features normally provided for selects, with a few restrictions. Views cannot be defined to incorporate the Select DISTINCT keyword, nor can INTO, ORDER BY, or COMPUTE be performed by a view's select. Views must reference tables that exist in a user database or even the master database but cannot be created on temporary tables in tempdb.

If you look at the 10 tables provided as part of the pubs database, you notice that although author, title, and publisher information is held in the tables, the tables themselves do not hold the titles of the books written by each author. To see this you must select the data from three tables with the following select statement:

```
use pubs
go
select title, au_ord, au_lname, price, ytd_sales, pub_id
from authors, titles, titleauthor
where authors.au_id = titleauthor.au_id
and titles.title_id = titleauthor.title.id
```

This statement yields the title of each book, the author's last name, the orders per title, the price, year to date sales, and the publisher's ID. The information is obtained through this simple select statement that joins three normalized tables in the pubs database. You have already seen that only a small percentage of SQL Server application users will be comfortable generating their own SQL statements. You could put the select statement into an application to pull the data and then present it to the users, or you could choose to use a view. In fact, this particular example is the one view supplied by Sybase with the pubs database. It is called titleview, and the syntax for creating it is as follows:

```
create view titleview
as
select title, au_ord, au_lname, price, ytd_sales, pub_id
from authors, titles, titleauthor
where authors.au_id = titleauthor.au_id
and titles.title_id = titleauthor.title_id
```

By issuing the following statement

```
select * from titleview
```

you retrieve exactly the same results as the three-table join select statement used in the previous example. This is not surprising, as the join was performed by the create view statement; however, you can see how views can be used to hide more complex SQL code from users or even application developers.

Say that you wanted to create a view that showed each author, the number of books published by the authors, and the titles. Because the number of books per author is not a column stored in any of the pubs tables, it must be computed:

```
create view authorbooks (au_fname, au_lname, title, numbooks)
as
select au_fname, au_lname,  title, (count(*))
from authors, titles, titleauthor
where authors.au_id = titleauthor.au_id
and titles_title_id = titleauthor.title_id
```

Control over the data represented in the view is limited only by your imagination, command of the SQL select statement, and the minor restrictions mentioned earlier. No COMPUTE BY, GROUP BY, or distinct qualifiers are allowed.

Views are not static. Once defined, each time you use one the view undergoes a view resolution. Through this process, your SQL Server validates each database object referenced in the view, ensuring that it exists and that the datatypes are compatible, and checking for violation of any view restrictions, such as data modification rules. Additionally, views containing computed columns or derived information are recalculated each time the view is referenced. This ensures the currency of data expressed in the view.

Modifying Data Through Views

Views can support insert, update, and delete operations on data, as long as certain preconditions are met.

Update and insert can take place only on a single underlying table, even if a number of tables are joined in the definition of the view. Put another way, if you choose to update data in a view, the columns being affected must all belong to a single table, or the update will fail.

The not null requirements of columns in the underlying table affect your update or insert operation. For example, if your view does not contain all the columns for which not null is the default, you cannot update the table through your view. Attempting to insert rows to the underlying table would fail because you have not supplied a value for a not null (required) column. As long as all columns not contained in the view allow nulls, your insert operation will succeed.

Modifications to tables containing columns that have been derived or computed with built-in functions are not supported.

Views created with aggregate functions or including the GROUP BY clause do not support updates, inserts, or deletes to underlying tables.

These are the types of data modification restrictions evaluated in the view resolution process. If you submit an operation that attempts to make a modification through a view that violates one of these restrictions, the operation will fail. At that point, you may have to make the modification to appropriate tables directly rather than by using the view.

Indexes

Indexes are used to improve the speed of data retrieval from tables. Because many different requirements for data retrieval exist, creating indexes on your SQL Server tables is an effective way to ensure that your users and applications get the data they want in the least amount of time. If you do not create an index, SQL Server reviews every row in the table to determine whether it matches the SQL criteria identified in the operation. This is referred to as a table scan. The creation of indexes can alleviate the need to perform a table scan by pointing SQL Server directly at the desired rows from known values contained in the index.

SQL Server supports two main types of indexes: clustered and nonclustered.

Clustered Indexes

A clustered index is essentially the ordering of data on the disk according to one of the columns. In the pubs database, for example, you might choose to store the titles information clustered by publisher. This would allow you to quickly retrieve all the rows for a particular publisher, as they would all be kept together. Another example of a clustered index is the yellow pages phone book. Each telephone number is grouped according to the service description of the subscriber (Rental Cars, Restaurants, etc.). An important feature that applies to clustered indexes can be found at the top of each page of the phone book. Listed are the first and last names of the services contained on that page. This allows you to skim through, looking for the upper and lower range values bracketing the specific data you wish to retrieve. A SQL Server clustered index is structured in a similar fashion.

As implied, a clustered index involves the sorting of the data rows in the table itself. You cannot hold a clustered index on a different disk than the data. Because you can have different levels of clustered indexes, sorting by author within publisher (to extend the pubs example), these higher levels are maintained as separate index pages. Still, they must also be held on the disk device. For example, the following syntax could be used to create a clustered index on publishers:

```
use pubs
go
create clustered index pub_index
on publishers (pub_id)
go
```

Because you can have only one clustered index per table and the publisher table already has a clustered index on it when installed, if you ran this script you would be told to drop the existing clustered index before creating another. It demonstrates the syntax you use when creating a clustered index, however.

When you create a clustered index, it accepts the ON segment argument, but the table is then moved to the segment specified in the create clustered index on segment statement. Unless you want to move your table to a different segment, do not use the ON parameter when specifying a clustered index.

Other software switches that can be used when creating a clustered index include the fillfactor, ignore_dup_key, and ignore_dup_row/allow_dup_row parameters.

The syntax to create a unique clustered index on authors with the ignore duplicate key parameter set would be as follows:

```
use pubs
go
create unique clustered index authors_ndx
on authors(au_id)
with ignore_dup_row
go
```

The unique parameter sets the index so that duplicate values in the au_id would be prohibited. You might choose this if you wanted to know all the numbers assigned to authors as au_id, possibly to determine a new unique value and assign it to a new author. Actually, I am not sure why you would ever want to create a unique clustered index on authors.au_id, but the preceding script would accomplish it.

In any case, the fillfactor refers to a percentage representing how full you want each page when creating a new index on existing data. As data is added, the fillfactor does not affect the amount of data held in each index page. The default is 0, which actually yields completely full pages when the index is created, and there will likely be very few situations where you choose another value.

ignore_dup_key applies to either clustered or nonclustered indexes and allows transactions with updates that attempt to write rows into a table, which would result in the creation of a duplicate key. The particular row that would have resulted in the duplicate key is ignored and the rest of the transaction proceeds, with an appropriate error message at the end. This is useful for selecting into a table where you require a unique index but suspect that some values may not, in fact, be distinct. For example, multiple null values in key columns would be treated as duplicate keys and identified at the end of your transaction.

Allow/ignore duplicate rows applies only to clustered indexes. If you choose to allow duplicate rows, you can insert or update rows that duplicate other rows within the table. If any other indexes specify that columns must be unique, however, you cannot create the clustered index with the allow duplicate rows parameter. On the other hand, the ignore duplicate row setting allows you to eliminate duplicates from a batch of data. Like the allow duplicate row option, this parameter is not accepted if a unique index exists on any column in the table.

If a table has duplicate rows and you simply enter the create clustered index command without any duplicate row or key parameters, the command does not execute. If you create a clustered index with ignore duplicate rows, the command completes, but duplicate rows are rejected and you see an error message identifying this. If you create the clustered index with allow duplicate rows, the command successfully creates a non-unique clustered index.

Overall, a clustered index yields the best data retrieval time over any other indexing method. You need to make sure that each of your tables has a clustered index that supports your most frequently used data retrievals. You should be aware that indexes slow down performance for updating data, because the new data must not only be added to the table but indexed as well. The index also takes up additional room on the disk. Allow approximately another 20 percent for index storage when you define a clustered index.

You should create your clustered indexes before nonclustered indexes, because any existing nonclustered indexes have to be rebuilt after creating a clustered index. This makes sense if you consider that the clustered index is the arrangement of the actual data in the tables and any other indexes need to point to the proper location of the data in the tables. Because adding a new clustered index changes this location, the nonclustered indexes would need to be verified or updated.

Nonclustered Indexes

The syntax to create a nonclustered index is the same as you use to create a clustered index, except that you don't need to explicitly state nonclustered in the create statement. The default for the create index command is to create a nonclustered index. Additionally, the ON segment_name option actually creates the indexes on a separate segment without affecting the table containing your data. This is one of the most effective tuning steps you can take when first establishing your tables and indexes. To create a nonclustered index on titles, which would allow you to quickly retrieve a row on the basis of title_id or the actual title of the book, you could use the following syntax:

```
use pubs
go
create unique index title_id_ndx
on titles(title_id, title)
on index_segment
go
```

For this example, you can assume that there should not be duplicate titles or IDs in the database, and therefore you would specify a unique index. To place the index on a discrete segment (which as you were shown earlier in the chapter would have to undergo the disk init and alter database sequence), you simply specify the segment name at the end of the create index statement.

If you wanted to be able to quickly retrieve all titles published by a particular publisher, knowing that the pub_id column of the titles table will have duplicate values, you could create this index:

```
use pubs
go
create index pub_id_ndx
on titles(pub_id)
on index_segment
go
```

This would allow you to obtain speedy results from a query such as `select * from titles where pub_id = "1234"`.

In your data modeling process, you should have identified a unique key for each table. Whether you choose to create a clustered or nonclustered index for this key, you can ensure data integrity by not allowing duplicate rows. In some cases you may have to use several columns to arrive at a unique key for the column. Prior to placing a transaction or sales number on the sales entity in the bookstore application, you saw that it was necessary to create a concatenated key of more than four columns to make each transaction unique. The following syntax demonstrates how you could create a unique nonclustered index on these columns:

```
use bookstore
go
create unique index transact_ndx
on transaction(book_id,store_id,customer_no,datetime)
go
```

By creating this index, you ensure that each row in the transaction table is unique, unless the same customer buys the same book, in the same store, at the same date and time. You can also see, however, that it is probably quicker and easier to simply assign an arbitrary unique transaction number to each row. (No wonder travel people always want you to keep your confirmation number!)

A few rules govern the creation of indexes. You cannot create an index on a view, although you can index temporary tables created in tempdb. You cannot exceed 250 indexes per table, and you can define a maximum of 249 nonclustered indexes, even if you do not define a clustered index. As a matter of course, you should index columns that are used frequently in join statements. In fact, any column frequently accessed in where clauses is a good candidate for an index. The usefulness of the index is directly proportional to the frequency of access and the number of values in the column.

A column with only two or three possible values (male, female, or other, for example) will not benefit from indexing. Additionally, columns that are rarely accessed should not have indexes, because indexes do take up additional storage space on your system and add time to update, insert, and delete operations on the data. Clustered indexes are best for unique key columns on a table, where retrievals are frequently on a range of values (`select * from table where key_column > 10 and key_column < 100`). Indexes should be created when they can help you identify a subset of your data as part of a retrieve statement.

As a general rule, SQL Server will elect to perform a table scan rather than use an index if more than 20 percent of the table will be retrieved by the command. Your indexes will be used by the server when they help you retrieve less than 20 percent of the overall table data. Retrieving on the basis of male or female, for example, would result in a scan of the table, even if you set up an index on that column. Creating an index on gender and date of birth could be useful, however, if you wanted to identify all females born on a particular day. This retrieve would likely yield less than 20 percent of your table and as such the index would be used rather than the table scan.

As you can see, SQL Server provides you with an ample amount of flexibility not only in the kind of indexes you create, but also in how you allocate your disk resources to those indexes. Appropriate indexing is one of the keys (pun intended) to the fastest data retrieval from your SQL Server tables.

Summary

You should now be familiar with the syntax and options of SQL Server tables, views, and indexes. You saw how indexes can be highly useful in speeding data retrieval and ensuring unique column values within your tables. You were also taken through the various options and parameters for the creation of the index types supported by SQL Server. In the coverage of views, you were exposed to how views can isolate users from complex SQL syntax and how to perform joins to view their data. Just as importantly, you saw how views can perform a unique security service, providing access to specific columns and rows of selected ranges and ensuring that updates, deletes, or modifications were handled properly (mostly by disallowing them through views). The methods by which tables reside on disk devices and table segments was also explored.

From an administrator's perspective, these three database objects and the way they relate to the SQL Server architecture are the key areas for system optimization and performance. As a developer, you should be aware of the structure of your database, the characteristics of the objects within it, and the various ways they can help you address your application requirements. This chapter was intended to provide you with the conceptual framework and syntactic structure to do just that.

3.6

Adding Groups and Setting Permissions

As part of the installation and setup for your SQL Server, you will want to setup users and groups and grant permissions appropriate for your development effort. I have already established that SA and DBO have ownership of the system and database, respectively. You now learn how you can selectively award rights and permissions to other users of the database. Additionally, you will see how to create groups and use aliasing for ease of administration.

Only a few commands cannot be granted to specific users. These include disk initialization and modification commands, as well as reconfigure, shutdown, and kill process commands, which are the responsibility of the systems administrator. Also, certain tasks fall to the database owner that cannot be granted, including checkpoint, DBCC checkdb, grant or revoke permissions, and setuser. These commands are restricted to those who should be given sole responsibility for administration of either a database or the SQL Server as a whole. You may have more than one person who is aware of the passwords and login IDs for these users, but as a general rule these users should be of a highly confidential nature.

All other commands may be granted or revoked as you see fit, and this provides the potential for a great range of activities to be performed within the database. These restrictions should hardly affect anyone operating in a development or user role for the database.

In this chapter, you see how specific logins and users are established and how permissions are granted and revoked. You also see the operations that may be performed within those constraints. By the end of this chapter, you will be able to modify the user setup scripts provided to the requirements of your specific site.

Adding Logins to the SQL Server

Allowing users to access data held in a SQL Server database table is a two-step process. First, you must create a login identity for them in the master database. This allows them to log in to begin with. Next, you add them as users to specific databases. This allows them to connect to a database and perform some useful work after logging in.

To add a user to your SQL Server, you can run the following script:

```
/* Create SQL Server Logins */
use master
go
sp_addlogin testdev, password, database1
go
```

This simple script creates a login record for the login name testdev and sets the password for testdev to the word password. The default database for the testdev login is database1. If you do not specify a default database in the sp_addlogin statement, the default database is master.

> **TIP**
>
> Make life easier for yourself—specify default databases for users other than master. This ensures that users do not create objects in the master database.

Creating a login ID means that anyone wishing to log in to the SQL Server can now go to any client program (such as ISQL) and log in as testdev with the password password and get connected to the SQL Server. If you would prefer not to set passwords but allow the users to define their own, enter null rather than the word password, which allows the user to log in and press Return instead of having to enter a preset password.

In any case, at this point, the users cannot accomplish anything meaningful in their default database (with or without a password) until you add them as users. This must be performed for each database for which the login requires access. Keep in mind that the same user may have varying permissions set on the same SQL Server, depending on how his or her permissions were granted for any given database.

To add a user to a database, you can run the following script:

```
/*create users for database1 database */
use database1
go
sp_adduser testdev
```

Several optional parameters can be set at this time, including specifying a name by which the user will be known in this particular database and a group to which you want the user to belong. The name_in_db option is useful for setting a more personal tone for a user who may have a name similar to others on the SQL Server but does not wish to have the system refer to her as JQSmith in her own database. By modifying the sp_adduser string to read sp_adduser jq_smith, joan, the user jq_smith would be referred to as joan. To make testdev a member of the group developers without having to specify a name_in_db, you would modify the sp_adduser string to read

```
sp_adduser testdev, null, developers
```

This adds the user testdev to the database, known as testdev, and keeps testdev in the group developers. The null is required to tell the adduser command that the name_in_db will not be changed. If you do not include the null, but simply add testdev, developers, this does not put testdev in the group developers; it sets the name_in_db for testdev as developers.

When you have a number of users who will belong to a database and who have similar profiles, you can make administration of user rights and permissions somewhat easier in one of two ways.

First, you can create distinct groups of users and grant rights to the group. For example, if you set up a group of training logins on the training database without knowing the names of the students, you could run the following scripts:

```
/* Create SQL Server Logins for training students*/
use master
go
sp_addlogin, student1, student1, Training
go
sp_addlogin, student2, student2, Training
go
sp_addlogin, student3, student3, Training
go
```

This has created three user logins for students 1, 2 and 3 whose password is identical to their login name and whose default database is Training. To add these users to the training database, type the following:

```
/*add users to Training database */
use Training
go
sp_adduser student1,null,students
go
sp_adduser student2,null,students
go
sp_adduser student3,null,students
go
```

To create a group called students and set permissions for all these students at once, you would run the following script:

```
/* Create user groups for the training database */
use training
go
sp_addgroup students
go
sp_addgroup trainers
go
sp_addgroup advanced_students
go
```

As you can see, I took advantage of the opportunity presented by this script to create two other groups as well. Whenever you add users to a SQL Server database, they automatically have public permissions. These include the following:

```
Create table (temporary)
BEGIN TRANsaction
COMMIT TRANsaction
RAISERROR
ROLLBACK TRANsaction
SAVE TRANsaction
SET
```

Because transactions can be considered to consist of insert, update, or delete operations against database objects, the default permissions for newly added users do not allow them to accomplish much. The create table command works only for the creation of temporary tables. To do any useful work within the database, appropriate privileges must be specifically granted to new users. As mentioned earlier, the approach taken to permissions by SQL Server is to allocate privileges according to ID. The systems administrator always has all privileges, the database owner has most of them, and the object owner has some. Other users within the database are explicitly granted permissions as appropriate. The grouping of privileges that accrue to each of these IDs is depicted in Figure 3.6.1.

Of course, you may use the grant statement (provided that you have permission to grant permissions) to explicitly grant permissions to each and every user. By default, all newly created users belong to the group Public. You may want, however, to create groups that allow you to refine the assignment of permissions.

You can see an example of how permissions can be allocated more easily through the use of groups by running this script as SA:

```
use training
go
grant all to trainers
go
grant create proc, create rule, create table, create view,
dump database, dump tran,
to advanced_students
go
grant select, insert, update, delete on table1 to students
go
```

FIGURE 3.6.1.

Sets of privileges for SA, DBO, and users, shown in nested circles.

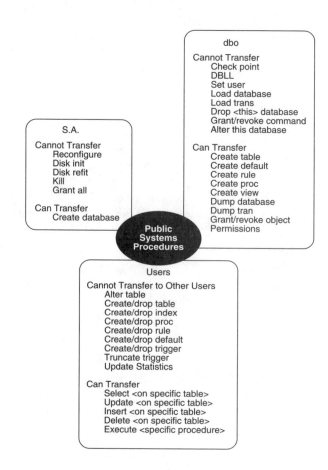

In this example, SA has granted all rights to those users belonging to the trainers group. Advanced students were given all but the create database and create default command. With this permission set, they would be able to create their own objects, such as tables and views. Finally, students were granted only the ability to retrieve and modify rows within `table1`. To give permission for the execution of a specific stored procedure, you would use the following syntax:

```
use training
go
grant exec on sp_test to student1
go
```

In addition to using `grant`, you may choose to revoke permissions from groups or users. After having granted all permissions to every user in the group `Students`, if you wanted to ensure that `student1` could only retrieve data, for example, you would execute the following commands:

```
use training
go
revoke all from student1
go
grant select to student1
go
```

By using a combination of grant and revoke with all and specific permissions for both groups and individual users, you can provide exactly the permissions you want each user to have.

This may be somewhat awkward if you have a number of users, groups, and permission sets. Setting permissions can also be handled in ways other than granting all rights to a user or explicitly setting permissions for each user object, user, or group.

Aliasing

Through aliasing, you can create a user with a profile of permissions and then have your users take on that profile when they log in to the database. Because the DBO has all permissions within the database they own, you may want to simply alias new users to the DBO user name when setting up your users and permissions. For example, say that the user trainer1 is the database owner for the training database. If you wanted to provide all trainers with the same permissions as trainer1, you could alias all trainers to the trainer1 ID. You could accomplish this by running the following script as SA:

```
use master
go
sp_addlogin trainer2,trainer2,training
go
use training
go
sp_addalias trainer2, trainer1
go
```

At this point, when trainer2 logs on to the training database, all the permissions of the database owner trainer1 will be set. Systems procedures such as sp_who identify that trainer2 is logged on to the database; however, using sp_helprotect to determine which permissions have been set for trainer2 will yield the message "No such object or user exists in the database." Using aliases allows you to create template users or permission sets and then simply alias your users' IDs to that permission profile instead of setting them explicitly for each user.

setuser

Another method of changing permissions is through the use of the `setuser` command. This command can be run by the database owner and cannot be transferred to other users. This means that the database owner can set his own user ID to mimic that of another user, thereby gaining access to user objects created by others within that database. For example, if `advanced_student1` has been granted create table permissions within the training database, in order to access this table, the DBO (trainer1) must run the `setuser` command to take on the identity of `advanced_student1`.

If the DBO tries to access the table without running the `setuser` command, SQL Server will return the message `SELECT permission denied on object table2, database training, owner advanced_student1`. To select (or perform any other operation), the DBO would issue the following command:

```
setuser "advanced_student1"
```

When executed by the DBO within their database, the return code should be 0, indicating a successful impersonation of user `advanced_student1`. Any operations taken on the database while the `setuser` command is active are treated exactly as if that user were logged in. The DBO might choose to use the set user command to assist a user in the creation of tables, views, or other objects, which would be owned by the user rather than the DBO. The `setuser` command functions in much the same way as the su (switch user) command in UNIX. Like root in UNIX, the DBO does not need to know the password of the user being impersonated.

Summary

From this chapter you should be able to clearly see the hierarchy of permissions within a SQL Server database, and your options for setting them. At the lowest level, a user who has been given object create permissions is the only one able to access those objects, with the exception of the DBO, who must impersonate that user, or the systems administrator, who can do anything he or she wants (including dropping the table by issuing a drop table ownername.tablename statement). To allow every user in the database, you can choose to simply grant all to either specific users, groups, or a combination. You have seen that unless you specify otherwise, everyone is a member of the group Public, and you can easily set every user in your database with all transferable permissions.

Your options are hardly all or nothing. For databases with a number of users with distinct access profiles, you can define permissions on a per command basis down to the table and even the column level. For administration purposes this can be a little irritating, because you must explicitly state which operations (select, insert, update, and delete, for example) you wish to be granted for specific tables, views, and columns. If you add an object, you must explicitly grant the permissions to the users in your database.

Although it would be convenient, perhaps, to grant select on all for users and groups, SQL Server forces you to either grant all or explicitly state which objects the select will be granted on.

For development databases, you may decide to simply create developer IDs and give them all privileges on the database. Keep in mind that there are administrative advantages to being able to identify exactly who is logged on to the SQL Server when diagnosing sleeping processes or deadlock situations. If possible, make your user names meaningful to allow you to track users down, should the need arise. For production databases, security and integrity are key considerations. You do not usually leave your car unlocked downtown, and it is advisable to take appropriate precautions with your database as well. The security of appropriate permissions is well worth the increased administration.

3.7

Defining and Using Dump Devices

The capability to back up and recover data and database objects is a vital component of any useful database system. In this chapter you will see how Sybase has implemented these features and procedures in SQL Server.

As with many of the other aspects of the SQL Server architecture, because Sybase has insulated its database engine from the operating system, it is necessary to provide SQL Server-specific procedures for backup and restoration of data.

Although this may be a duplication of effort vis-á-vis operating systems utilities for the same purpose, one advantage is that the procedures remain the same as you move from one SQL Server platform to another.

This chapter deals with the concepts and syntax for database backup and restore, for all SQL Server versions except SQL Server Release 10, which is discussed in Chapter 7.1.

Defining Your Dump Device

SQL Server uses dump devices to back up databases and transaction logs. These dumps are integral to ensuring recoverability of data in the event of a system crash or an unexpected or undesired operation on the data by a user. All databases except tempdb should be dumped. Because changes to the SQL Server such as adding new databases and users or configuration parameters are stored in the master database, the master device should be dumped after any such operation. The model database should be dumped after being changed if you want to be able to recover those changes rather than re-creating them in the event of corruption or loss of the database. User databases must also be dumped regularly to ensure recoverability. Databases and transaction logs can be dumped while the system is in use, though you should be aware that there are some implications on database performance, because SQL Servers earlier than System 10 slow down when dumps are performed.

Having established that everything should be backed up, you need to know exactly how to accomplish this. Valid SQL Server dump devices include diskettes, hard disks, or tape units. To add a dump device during system installation and configuration, you must use sp_addumpdevice, as the following script illustrates:

```
/* ADD DUMP DEVICE (sp_addumpdevice).  Add 1.2 GB tape device. */

sp_addumpdevice "tape", tape_backup, "/dev/tape1", 3, skip, 1200
go
```

In this example, you would specify the type of dump device (either tape or disk), the name it will be referred to by SQL Server (tape_backup), and the exact device name your system uses for your tape drive. The next value is the control type; for tape drives it may be types 3 through 8. (The exception is Sun SCSI tape drives, which are treated as controller type 2 but cannot be used with the console utility.) A control type in this range allows you to use the console program to perform the dump, which prompts the operator when a new tape must be loaded. If you have multiple tape devices that you wish to use concurrently, make sure to specify unique control type numbers for each tape device.

The skip or no-skip is optional depending on whether you want to automatically overwrite the tape even if there are existing labels on it. To ensure that any existing tape labels (existing files on the tape) are respected, specify no-skip. The next value is the size of the tape unit, in this case 1200M. You must explicitly express this value, because there is no default for size.

Dumping to tape is often significantly slower than dumping to disk, given the nature of the different devices. If making quick backups of the data is important, you will likely prefer to create a disk-based dump device. This can be a file on the operating system, as long as there is sufficient room to dump the device. You should, however, copy the dump from disk to tape in order to protect against systems failure on the dump disk as well.

To create a disk-based dump device, you would modify the dump device script to read as follows:

```
/* ADD DUMP DEVICE (sp_addumpdevice).  Add disk dump device.        */

sp_addumpdevice "disk", disk_backup, "/sybase/dump", 2,
go
```

For this device, you must specify the exact path and file name rather than the device name. Always use control type 2 for disk dump devices. The control type 2 indicates that the data should be dumped through a byte stream. The file created as a result of a dump to disk should be copied to tape or another device, because subsequent dumps will overwrite the contents of the dump device file. You should also be aware that the device name diskdump sends your data off to "Never Never Land," so call it something else. Use the diskdump device only if you want to dump a database or transaction log out to the ether rather than save it for posterity.

As you might remember from Section 2, in which I discussed data recovery requirements, it is important to know exactly how often you must back up your data. The SQL Server approach to backups is to dump the database first, as a snapshot of the database, and then record subsequent changes in the transaction log. If you did not create a separate transaction log device for your database, you cannot back up the transaction log and must dump the entire database each time to be able to recover it. This is not recommended for databases larger than 4M. All operations that change the data (such as insert, delete, or update) are considered transactions and are recorded in the transaction log defined in the logon clause of the create database command. Additionally, SQL Server records transactions in a systems table called syslogs; however, this transaction log is used only for automatic recovery in the event of the SQL Server going down or being restarted. You cannot retrieve any of your data from the syslog table, and making efforts to do so can cause serious problems. The way to retrieve your data is to use your dump devices to make periodic backups of your databases and transaction logs.

If the size of your database and logs varies significantly from one dump to another, and if you are concerned about storage space on the dump device, you should be aware that a SQL Server dump does not reclaim space on the dump device. For example, if the existing disk dump device had a database dump file of 100M and you overwrite that dump with a smaller dump, the file size will remain 100M. If saving space is a concern, delete the dump file before dumping the database or transaction log. As implied by this statement, you can delete the dump file from the disk without affecting your ability to dump new databases or logs. You may choose to copy disk dumps to tape and then delete the file as part of your ongoing backup strategy. Maintaining ongoing copies of dumps has several advantages because, in some cases, inappropriate modifications may be made to the data that are not caught or corrected between dumps. In such a case, you would want to have database dumps (and all subsequent transaction logs) in order to restore the database to its proper state. Transaction logs must be kept in their sequence because they essentially replay all operations that were taken on the data. If you miss one in the series, you cannot restore your database past the missing transaction log. The entire collection of transaction logs must be maintained as a complete set to restore the database contents.

Backing Up Your Data

Once you have defined your dump device, you can then dump your databases and transaction logs at will. To accomplish this, issue the appropriate commands from ISQL or run this script:

```
/* DUMP DATABASE database1 to tape_backup. */

dump database database1 to tape_backup
go
```

That's it. To dump your database to the disk dump device specified earlier, the syntax is almost identical:

```
/* DUMP DATABASE database1 to disk_backup. */

dump database database1 to disk_backup
go
```

What could be easier? Dumping transactions are handled in an identical manner:

```
/* DUMP TRANSACTION log of database1 to tape_backup. */

dump trans database1 to tape_backup
go
```

If you like to type, you can also issue the command as DUMP TRANSACTION. However you choose to enter it, this command removes any committed transactions successfully written to the database from the log after the log is dumped. This has the net effect of shrinking the size of the log to contain only transactions uncommitted at the time of the dump.

You can add a few additional clauses to the DUMP TRANS command: WITH TRUNCATE_ONLY and WITH NO_LOG.

If your database device fills up because of the transaction log, you may have to dump trans WITH NO_LOG to clear out the inactive transactions to make room. The WITH TRUNCATE_ONLY achieves the same objective, but it also logs the DUMP TRANS command. This is the command most commonly used for the master and small databases to free up space in the transaction log. Assuming that you dump your databases and transaction logs frequently enough, not only should you not run out of disk space, but you will also be in position to recover a database completely if the need arises.

Another important data integrity feature included with SQL Server is the database consistency checker (DBCC). Because not all database losses are catastrophic events complete with smoke and flames, you can use DBCC to check on your database and its objects to determine whether they have become corrupted in some way. You can run DBCC periodically as the systems administrator or the database owner. If you are not the DBO or SA, but you own tables in the database, you can use DBCC to check the consistency of any tables you own. The options available for DBCC are as follows:

- DBCC CHECKTABLE TABLENAME: This command is used to establish pointer consistency and to determine whether index and data pages are properly sorted and linked. If there is a problem with the table, an error message is returned.

- DBCC CHECKDB: This command performs the same function as the preceding one, except on all tables.

- DBCC CHECKALLOC: This command checks for correct allocation and use of pages within the database. Again, the command returns error messages to tell you whether you need to do anything about the database.

■ DBCC CHECKCATALOG: This option reviews each of the systems tables for a specified database and ensures that consistency has been maintained throughout.

If the DBCC commands confirm your suspicions that your database has been corrupted, you must load the database and transaction dumps you have made to recreate it. If DBCC confirms that a database has been damaged, you must run DBCC DREPAIR to drop the damaged database before you can proceed with reloading it from the dump.

Reloading a Database from a Dump Device

The worst has happened and you need to use the database and transaction dumps you have so prudently made. For purposes of this example, you can assume that the database that needs to be restored was merely a user's database and not something more serious, such as the master database.

One of the advantages of keeping the transaction log on a separate device is the capability to dump the transaction log even after the database has become inaccessible, such as in the case of a hard disk crash. This allows you to fully restore the database to its condition at the moment it went down. To accomplish this, use the WITH NO_TRUNCATE option of the DUMP TRAN command. This allows you to dump all the transactions that were processed since the last DUMP TRAN, including transactions that had been successfully committed.

To make the operation and syntax clear, assume that the database has been corrupted but the disk device itself is functional. In this case, to recover your database you would follow these steps:

1. Drop the database.
2. Exactly recreate the database using the appropriate scripts.
3. Load the database from the dump device.
4. Load the transaction log from the log device.

As noted earlier, to reload from the dump device you must first duplicate the database, including specification of the database devices.

If you have actually lost a disk, obviously you cannot successfully run the original DISKINIT script. To successfully reload the data at that point, you must first establish how the database was structured. Reviewing the original DISKINIT script, you can see the following:

```
use master
go
create database database1
on database1_device = 20,
database1_index_device1 = 10,
database1_index_device2 = 5
log on database1_log_device
go
```

The database has been allocated across four devices. It is not necessary to map the database to the exact logical database device names; you must only ensure that it has been constructed anew with the same allocations. The following script would result in the creation of a database named database1, to which the database and transaction logs could be loaded.

```
use master
go
create database database1
on database9_device = 20,
database1_index_device1 = 10,
database1_index_device2 = 5
log on database1_log_device
go
```

The scenario here is that the database1_device (otherwise known as physical device named /dev/rdsk/c1t0d2) has failed, making your database1 database inaccessible. Because you cleverly distributed your indexes and logs across other physical devices, the space on the functioning disks was made available when the database was dropped. Provided that you first ran a DISKINIT to create a Sybase disk device called database9_device, this script would execute successfully.

Because an identically configured database named database1 exists, you can load your database from the dump device. The syntax to accomplish this is as follows:

```
/* LOAD DATABASE database1 from tape_backup.        */
/* This will overwrite the                                    */
/* database database1 with the version from the tape.    */

load database database1 from tape_backup
go
```

To bring the database up to the state it was in when the hard disk failed, you then load your transaction log. This syntax is as follows:

```
/* LOAD TRANSACTIONS from disk_backup.  This will bring the    */
/* database database1 up to date                               */

load trans database1 from disk_backup
go
```

While the database and transaction logs are being reloaded, the database cannot be accessed by users. All other activity using other databases can take place as normal, however.

Dump and load commands can also be used to transfer databases from one SQL Server to another; however, they would have to be of the same platform (the dump format is machine dependent), and the target databases must be configured identically (as described earlier). Also, the two SQL Servers must have matching sort orders and character sets. To move data between SQL Servers when these conditions are not met, use the bulk copy utility.

Restoring the Master Device

The master database should be dumped as soon as you have successfully installed your SQL Server and again after every operation that modifies the master database. Typical commands that affect the master database are as follows:

```
DISK INIT
sp_adddumpdevice
sp_dropdevice
CREATE DATABASE
ALTER DATABASE
sp_addlogin
sp_droplogin
sp_configure
```

The alternative to restoring the master device from a dump is to reinstall it to factory defaults and perform again from scratch any work using these commands. Once again, you can see how useful keeping administration scripts for your site could turn out to be.

To restore your master device from a dump, the systems administrator must perform the following operations:

1. Run the buildmaster -m script to build a new master database.
2. Run the installmaster script to load the systems procedures.
3. Run sp_adddumpdevice to configure the dump device from which you wish to load.
4. Restart SQL Server in single-user mode (add the -m flag to the dataserver startup string in the RUNSERVER command).
5. Load the most recent master database dump.

6. Restart the SQL Server in single-user mode.

7. Run DBCC CHECKALLOC.

8. When everything checks out, restart SQL Server in multiuser mode.

Summary

As you can see, the actual dumping and loading of SQL Server databases is not that involved. It may be somewhat time consuming, depending on your data volumes and whether you are running a dynamic dump while users have active sessions or are performing the dump during down-time. The key to successfully recreating a database is having an appropriate strategy for the database and transactions. This section covers this point because so many of your future options are affected by your initial installation and configuration options. Although SQL Server does provide for flexibility in reconfiguring databases and devices as needed, it is always best if you can properly anticipate your requirements at the beginning. Certainly you have seen in this chapter the necessity of creating several logical devices and spread your database across them. This can yield not only improved performance, but safety and security returns as well. After all, even with improvements being made to systems hardware all the time, devices can and do fail. By anticipating that eventuality and configuring your SQL Server environment accordingly, you can minimize the impact of any such failure.

4

Using SQL Server Features

Introduction

THE PAST SECTIONS HAVE TAKEN YOU THROUGH MANY ASPECTS of the client/server development process from the perspective of various roles. Until this point, the approach was to assume that you had not yet worked with a SQL Server or were relatively new to the technology. This section gives more of the details from an applications developer's point of view. Starting with the Sybase-supplied stored procedures, moving through an in-depth look at the TransAct SQL facilities, and finishing with detailed descriptions of how to develop transactions, stored procedures, and triggers, this section takes you through the server-side tools you can use to develop highly effective client/server solutions.

Once you have finished this section, you should be familiar with the database options available to you when dividing the application processing between your client applications and your SQL Server. You should also be fully aware of the language facilities and capabilities provided to you on the server side. Most important, you will have many functioning examples of T-SQL statements and output to clearly illustrate the points covered in this section. You will also see how the SQL Server triggers and stored procedures can be used to build referential and data integrity into your tables on the server side. This is a vital element of any client/server system, even if you plan to devote a great deal of effort to validation and error-checking on the client side. Without server-side integrity, you cannot guarantee that the data is valid. In this section you will see exactly how these goals can be achieved using Sybase-supplied commands and features.

4.1

Sybase-Supplied
Stored Procedures

The previous section introduced the steps involved in the installation and configuration of your SQL Server. Many of these steps require the use of stored procedures; these were covered in some detail. This chapter introduces the most commonly used and useful Sybase-supplied stored procedures. Although creating disk and dump devices are important and significant activities, they are most often performed by the systems administrator and are hardly daily occurrences. This chapter covers all the stored procedures used by developers and power users who might have direct access to their SQL Server through ISQL or some other command-line query tool for ad hoc queries.

In spite of the proliferation of GUI-based products, the basic interface to a SQL Server right out of the box is through a character-based command-line client program that issues T-SQL commands directly or calls stored procedures These are especially useful to those of you who must deal with the SQL Server while developing the GUI-based client software referred to earlier. Often it is necessary to use systems procedures to determine how your program is behaving, to test and debug portions of T-SQL code, or to experiment with indexes.

This chapter provides an outline of the commands provided by Sybase, their syntax, and practical examples of what they do when run, including sample output. This should serve as a guide for those of you who are new to SQL Server and a useful reference for experienced Sybase developers.

Getting Around SQL Server

In any new computing environment, probably the first thing you want to know is how to figure out where you are, and the next is to get a listing of the files or other objects available to you. Unfortunately, this is somewhat less than intuitive in SQL Server. There are no commands for whoami, ls, or dir. Instead, Sybase has supplied stored procedures for determining this information, and when you get used to them, they work pretty much the same as similar navigational commands in any development environment. Additional stored procedures are available to help you get detailed information on database users and objects, as well as to help you manage users and permissions in your database.

These commands are as follows:

```
sp_who
sp_helpuser
sp_helpprotect
sp_addalias
sp_defaultdb
sp_changedbowner
```

```
sp_adduser
sp_help

sp_addgroup
sp_defaultlanguage
sp_dropalias
sp_dropgroup
sp_dropuser
sp_helpgroup
```

As you can see from this list, the convention in SQL Server for all stored procedures is to begin with sp_. There are three major types of sp_ procedures—add, help, and drop—as well as meaningful terms that define the work of the command. Look at the use of the commands in more detail:

COMMAND:	sp_who
SYNTAX:	sp_who
USED BY:	Any user
USED FOR:	Determining who is logged on, what they are doing, and which database they are using
EXAMPLE:	sp_who
	go
SAMPLE:	

```
sp_who
go
spid   status      loginame      hostname    blk dbname    cmd
====== =========== ============= =========== === ========================
1      runnable    sa                        0   master    SELECT
2      sleeping    sa                        0   master    NETWORK HANDLER
3      sleeping    sa                        0   master    NETWORK HANDLER
4      sleeping    sa                        0   master    MIRROR HANDLER
5      sleeping    sa                        0   master    CHECKPOINT
6      runnable    reader        PC Client   0   master    EXECUTE
```

You use this command to see your login name, the database you are using, and the status of any command you have issued, as well as any other logged-on users. In the preceding listing, you can see that you are logged on to the master database with the username reader and that you are executing a stored procedure. The spid is the Sybase process ID and is needed to kill processes without shutting down the entire SQL Server.

COMMAND:	sp_helpuser
SYNTAX:	sp_helpuser [username]
USED BY:	Anyone

USED FOR: Obtaining information on a specified user of the
               current database or all users if no name is supplied

EXAMPLE: `sp_helpuser reader`

SAMPLE:

```
use pubs
go
sp_helpuser
go

Users_name          ID_in_db Group_name          Login_name       Default_db
================== ======== ================== ================ ===========
dbo                1        public              sa               master
guest              2        public
reader             3        public              reader           master
```

From this you can see that three users are set up in the pubs database: the DBO (SA), guest, and reader. The user reader has been accidently set up with the master database as the default_db. The next command would correct this:

COMMAND: `sp_defaultdb`

SYNTAX: `sp_defaultdb user, default_database`

USED BY: Systems administrator or any user to set their own
               default database

USED FOR: To set a user's (or your own) default database on login
               to the SQL Server

EXAMPLE: `sp_defaultdb reader, pubs`

SAMPLE:

```
sp_defaultdb reader, pubs
go
Default database changed
1 row affected
```

From this point forward, whenever a reader logs onto this SQL Server, the database used will be pubs. This makes it unnecessary to issue the use pubs command prior to executing any T-SQL statement or stored procedure; it also ensures that reader will not accidently create user objects on the master device. You can also change other default options for users, such as the language default they use when they log on to the SQL Server. You would accomplish this as SA with the sp_defaultlanguage procedure, or you can use the procedure to change your own default language:

COMMAND: sp_defaultlanguage

SYNTAX: sp_defaultlanguage [, language]

USED BY: Systems administrator or anyone to set his or her own personal language preference

USED FOR: Setting the language and format of months and days displayed to a user when he or she retrieves date data

EXAMPLE: sp_defaultlanguage, new_reader, french

SAMPLE:

```
use master
sp_defaultlanguage new_reader, french
go
new_readers default language is changed to french
(return status = 0)
```

To determine what languages are available on your server, use the sp_helplanguage procedure.

The DBO for pubs was set for SA. Because you would likely want to make another user the database owner for the pubs database, look at how you change the owner of a database:

COMMAND: sp_changedbowner

SYNTAX: sp_changedbowner login_name [,true]

USED BY: Systems administrator, database owner

USED FOR: Changing the owner of the current database to a new user

EXAMPLE: sp_changedbowner reader, true

SAMPLE:

```
sp_changedbowner reader
go
The proposed new db owner already is a user in the database
(return status = 1)
```

That didn't work. To successfully execute the sp_changedbowner command, the user specified must have a valid login (created through the sp_addlogin command) but cannot already be a user in the database. Generally, the systems administrator would create a database and add a login, then execute the sp_changedbowner command to give the new user ownership of the new database and allow the user to use the database. You should note that the name of the database owner is not the name you set using the sp_changedbowner command. To grant permissions or use any other stored procedures dealing with users inside a database, the database owner will be known literally as DBO after you use the `changedbowner` command. To give a user of another database temporary access to a database as a user currently set up in that database (including the DBO), you would run the following command:

COMMAND:	`sp_addalias`
SYNTAX:	`sp_addalias login_name, name_to_use`
USED BY:	Systems administrator, DBO
USED FOR:	Granting access to a database without adding a user to that database
EXAMPLE:	`sp_addalias reader, dbo`
SAMPLE:	

```
use pubs
go
sp_addalias new_reader, reader
go
Alias user added
(return status = 0)
```

If you run an `sp_who` after an alias user has been added, they will display their true login name, such as `new_reader`, not the name to which they have been aliased. The addalias command simply sets the database access and permissions to the equivalent of the database user. `new_reader` can have all the permissions and access of the user reader in the pubs database, but `new_reader` does not masquerade as reader. All activities are still traceable to the `new_reader` login ID. As discussed in the previous section, to change the permissions profile of an existing user, you would use the grant command. To add a new user to your database who already has a valid login set up by the systems administrator, you would use the `sp_adduser` command:

COMMAND:	`sp_adduser`
SYNTAX:	`sp_adduser login_name [, name_in_database [, group_name]]`
USED BY:	Systems administrator, database owner
USED FOR:	Adding new users to the database, establishing a name by which they will be known while in that database, and making them members of existing groups
EXAMPLE:	`sp_adduser new_reader, Dave, readers`
SAMPLE:	

```
use pubs
go
sp_adduser new_reader, Dave, readers
go
```

```
New user added.
(return status = 0)
```

This procedure added the user with the login name of new_reader to the pubs data-base as user Dave and made Dave a member of the group readers. To log on to the SQL Server, the user must use the new_reader login name. However, while within the pubs database, new_reader is not a valid user. For all activities where you specify a user name within pubs, new_reader becomes Dave and can be accessed only by using that name.

Because it is easier to administer users when they are part of groups, you need to know how to determine what groups are already on a database when deciding where a new user should belong.

To find information on what groups are available, use the sp_helpgroup procedure:

COMMAND:	sp_helpgroup
SYNTAX:	sp_helpgroup [group_name]
USED BY:	Anyone
USED FOR:	Determining what groups are already on a database and who belongs to those groups
EXAMPLE:	sp_helpgroup or sp_helpgroup readers
SAMPLE:	

```
use pubs
go
sp_helpgroup
go


Group_name                       Group_id
==============================   ========
public                           0
readers                          16384
```

After you know the name of a group, you can display more information about it by passing the group name as a parameter to the sp_helpgroup stored procedure.

```
use pubs
go
sp_helpgroup readers
go


Group_name                Group_id Users_in_group            Userid
========================  ======== ========================  ======
readers                   16384    Dave                      4
```

If you decide that it is time to add a new group to your database you would use the sp_addgroup systems procedure.

COMMAND:	sp_addgroup
SYNTAX:	sp_addgroup group_name
USED BY:	Database Owner
USED FOR:	Creating specific groups to which you wish to assign users
EXAMPLE:	sp_addgroup readers
SAMPLE:	

```
use pubs
go
sp_addgroup readers
go
result = 0
```

To determine what permissions are set for a particular user or database object, you would use the sp_helprotect procedure. This procedure also treats groups as users and as such gives you any permissions that have been defined for a group.

COMMAND:	sp_helprotect
SYNTAX:	sp_helprotect name [, name_in_database]
USED BY:	Anyone
USED FOR:	Determining the permissions associated with an object or user. Use the object name plus the user name to determine what a specific user's permissions are for a specific database object.
EXAMPLE:	sp_helprotect reader
SAMPLE:	

```
use pubs
go
sp_helprotect reader
go
type    action               object           column
======  ===================  ===============  ==========
Grant   Create Database                       All
Grant   Create Default                        All
Grant   Create Procedure                      All
Grant   Create Rule                           All
Grant   Create Table                          All
Grant   Create View                           All
```

```
Grant  Dump Database                    All
Grant  Dump Transaction                 All
```

These results are displayed for a user who has been granted all permissions within a particular database. Any specific restrictions or other permissions that have been revoked would be displayed at the end of the `sp_helprotect` listing or in an `sp_helprotect` listing for the object on which the permission was revoked. `sp_helprotect` displays permissions in the form of GRANT/REVOKE actions that have been taken within the database. Otherwise default permissions are assumed. If no one has been explicitly prohibited from any operation on the titles table, for example, running `sp_helprotect` will not yield any results. However, if the user reader has delete permissions revoked for the titles table, the `sp_helprotect` output on titles would be as follows:

```
type     action                user              column
=======  ====================  ================  ==========
Revoke   Delete                reader            All
```

This is the format of `sp_helprotect` results for database objects. The actions explicitly granted or revoked for specific users are displayed to the column level. There are other methods of obtaining information about database objects, as opposed to the users in the database. The general `sp_help` command is one method of getting a list of all the objects held in a particular database:

COMMAND:	`sp_help`
SYNTAX:	`sp_help [object_name]`
USED BY:	Anyone
USED FOR:	Obtaining a list of all objects, owner, type for the current database, including user-defined datatypes
EXAMPLE:	`sp_help titles`
SAMPLE:	

```
Name               Owner            Object_type
===============    ===============  ======================
titleview          dbo              view
authors            dbo              user table
discounts          dbo              user table
publishers         dbo              user table
roysched           dbo              user table
sales              dbo              user table
stores             dbo              user table
titleauthor        dbo              user table
titles             dbo              user table
deltitle           dbo              trigger
sysalternates      dbo              system table
syscolumns         dbo              system table
```

```
syscomments      dbo              system table
sysdepends       dbo              system table
sysindexes       dbo              system table
syskeys          dbo              system table
syslogs          dbo              system table
sysobjects       dbo              system table
sysprocedures    dbo              system table
sysprotects      dbo              system table
syssegments      dbo              system table
systypes         dbo              system table
sysusers         dbo              system table
byroyalty        dbo              stored procedure
reptq1           dbo              stored procedure
reptq2           dbo              stored procedure
reptq3           dbo              stored procedure
pub_idrule       dbo              rule
ziprule          dbo              rule
datedflt         dbo              default
phonedflt        dbo              default
typedflt         dbo              default
```

User_type	Storage_type	Length	Nulls	Default_name	Rule_name
===========	==============	========	=======	==============	===========
id	varchar	11	0		
tid	varchar	6	0		

This output represents a complete listing of all the objects in the pubs database, including tables, indexes, views, stored procedures, rules, defaults, and user-defined datatypes complete with their underlying type, length, and null/not null acceptance status.

To eliminate users, groups, or aliases, you use a variation on the stored procedure used to add them in the first place. sp_dropuser, sp_dropgroup, and sp_dropalias all function in a similar fashion. However, some rules apply. sp_dropalias allows the systems administrator or database owner to drop an alias at any time, even if that user has created database objects. The database objects created by someone under an alias belong to the user they were impersonating. Similarly, you can drop a group using sp_dropgroup without affecting the users who make up that group. (Other than their permissions, users default to Public unless they belong to a group with different rights or have rights explicitly granted to them.) You execute sp_dropuser, however, if there are still database objects that belong to that user. These must be deleted or transferred to another user before the sp_dropuser procedure will execute.

Sometimes you may find that you need to know (or remind yourself) about certain features and settings of your SQL Server, even if it is not in your power to change them. For example, you might want to know exactly what sort order your SQL Server

uses to determine the ordering of rows. To accomplish this, you would use the
sp_helpsort system procedure:

COMMAND:	sp_helpsort
SYNTAX:	sp_helpsort
USED BY:	Anyone
USED FOR:	Displaying your SQL Server's installed character set and sort order
EXAMPLE:	sp_helpsort
SAMPLE:	

```
Sort Order Description
======================================================================
Character Set = 2, cp850
    Code Page 850 (Multilingual) character set.
Sort Order = 40, bin_cp850
    Binary Sort Order for the CodePage 850 Character Set


Characters, in Order
======================================================================
 !  "  #  $  %  &  '  (  )  *  +  ,  -  .  /  0  1  2  3  4  5  6  7  8  9  :  ;  <  =  >  ?
 @  A  B  C  D  E  F  G  H  I  J  K  L  M  N  O  P  Q  R  S  T  U  V  W  X  Y  Z  [  \  ]  ^  _
 `  a  b  c  d  e  f  g  h  i  j  k  l  m  n  o  p  q  r  s  t  u  v  w  x  y  z  {  |  }  ~  ·
 ·  ·  ,  ƒ  „  …  †  ‡  ·  ‰  Š  ‹  Œ  ·  ·  ·  ·  '  '  "  "  ·  —  —  ·  ™  š  ›  œ  ·  ·  Ÿ
 ·  ¡  ¢  £  ¤  ¥  |  §  ¨  ©  ª  «  ¬  -  ®  ¯  °  ±  ²  ³  ´  µ  ¶  ·  ¸  ¹  º  »  ¼  ½  ¾  ¿
 À  Á  Â  Ã  Ä  Å  Æ  Ç  È  É  Ê  Ë  Ì  Í  Î  Ï  Ð  Ñ  Ò  Ó  Ô  Õ  Ö  ×  Ø  Ù  Ú  Û  Ü  Ý  Þ  ß
 à  á  â  ã  ä  å  æ  ç  è  é  ê  ë  ì  í  î  ï  ð  ñ  ò  ó  ô  õ  ö  ÷  ø  ù  ú  û  ü  ý  þ  ÿ
```

If you have any questions about the characters supported by your SQL Server,
sp_helpsort displays the entire character set as specified during the installation.

Manipulating Database Objects

Along with navigating through SQL Server databases, setting up user and group
permissions, and determining what database objects are available, you need to know
how to manipulate database objects. You will also want to know how to obtain more
detailed information about the database objects you will use. A number of systems
procedures are supplied to assist you in accomplishing just that. These include the
following:

```
sp_depends
sp_helpindex
sp_helpjoins
sp_helptext
sp_rename
```

As you saw earlier in this chapter, `sp_help` gives you a listing of all the objects within a database. When you pass an object name to the procedure, you get more detail on the construction and ownership of the object. As you work with database objects, you will see that each object often references another or, in the case of views and stored procedures, it depends on the existence of an object in a certain form to be able to execute successfully. As you become more familiar with your database environment in SQL Server, you will want to see at a glance if any other database objects will be affected by dropping or modifying an object. To accomplish this, you use the `sp_depends` system procedure:

COMMAND:	`sp_depends`
SYNTAX:	`sp_depends object_name`
USED BY:	Anyone
USED FOR:	Determining which objects contain references or depend on a specified database object
EXAMPLE:	`sp_depends pub_titles`
SAMPLE:	

```
Things the object references in the current database.
object                                   type            updated selected
======================================== =============== ======= ========
dbo.titles                               user table      no      no
dbo.publishers                           user table      no      no
```

From this output you can tell that the view `pub_titles` references or depends on the existence of the titles and publishers tables. You can also tell that no other stored procedures, views, or triggers depend on `pub_titles`. If any objects that referenced `pub_titles` had existed, an additional list entitled "Things inside the database that reference the object" would have been displayed. From the output of `sp_depends`, you can establish that you can modify or drop an object without affecting any other object in the database.

In this case, say that you are considering modifying the view `pub_titles`. As you have already seen, it is safe to modify the view, but before you do that you might want to look at exactly how the view is currently constructed. To look at the definitions of views, stored procedures, and triggers within a database, you use the `sp_helptext` command:

COMMAND:	`sp_helptext`
SYNTAX:	`sp_helptext object_name`
USED BY:	Anyone

USED FOR:	Reviewing the exact text used to create the object
EXAMPLE:	`sp_helptext pub_titles`
SAMPLE:	

```
<col 01>
===========
1
```

```
text: create view pub_titles as
select pub_name, title, price, ytd_sales
from publishers p, titles t
where p.pub_id = t.pub_id
```

All views, stored procedures, and triggers are stored as text descriptions as well as database objects. Through the `sp_helptext` systems procedure you can determine exactly what syntax has been used to create the object.

As discussed earlier, you can obtain information on any database object through the `sp_help` command. However, in some cases you may want to limit the output retrieved to deal strictly with the indexes on a given table. To accomplish this, you can use the `sp_helpindex` systems procedure:

COMMAND:	`sp_helpindex`
SYNTAX:	`sp_helpindex table_name`
USED BY:	Anyone
USED FOR:	Obtaining index information on a table
EXAMPLE:	`sp_helpindex publishers`
SAMPLE:	

```
index_name       : pub_index
index_description: clustered located on default
index_keys       : pub_id
```

The output from the `sp_helpindex` systems procedure provides you with a quick look at all the indexes on a table, the type of index, and the index key. This is useful for determining whether a clustered index already exists for a table, or for evaluating the nonclustered indexes as part of your query performance analysis.

As you work with your initial database configuration, you will no doubt do a great deal of experimentation not only with indexes and performance considerations but also with the ways you can structure your retrieve statements using SQL. Later in this section you will be taken through the entire T-SQL language structure, enhancements, and options, but while you are looking at systems procedures you should be

aware that there are ways to help determine your join strategy. The systems procedure `sp_helpjoins` provides information on exactly what columns between tables
(or views) are likely candidates for a join.

COMMAND:	`sp_helpjoins`
SYNTAX:	`sp_helpjoins table1_name, table2_name`
USED BY:	Anyone
USED FOR:	Determining which columns could be reasonably expected to join to tables together
EXAMPLE:	`sp_helpjoins publishers, titles`
SAMPLE:	

```
publishers      titles
==========      =========
a1: pub_id      a2:pub_id
b1              b2
c1              c2
d1              d2
e1              e2
f1              f2
g1              g2
h1              h2
```

Out of all the possible columns between the two tables that could be matched, only
one was identified by `sp_helpjoins`. You can see through this the importance of naming conventions when dealing with multiple developers who are creating their own
tables and other database objects. `sp_helpjoins` looks for any columns with matching datatypes first and then for identical column names with matching datatypes.

In some cases, you will want to change the name of an object you have created. To
perform this task, SQL Server uses the `sp_rename` system procedure. You must be
the owner of an object to rename it. This is true even for the database owner and the
systems administrator. To rename objects that belong to a database user, the DBO
must impersonate that user with the set user command. However, here you can assume that all you want to do is rename a table to conform with your organization's
naming conventions.

COMMAND:	`sp_rename`
SYNTAX:	`sp_rename old_object_name, new_object_name`
USED BY:	Anyone
USED FOR:	Renaming your own database objects

EXAMPLE: `sp_rename pub_titles, publishers_titles`

SAMPLE:

```
Object name has been changed
1 row affected
```

This systems procedure simply moves an object from one name to another. You can also use `sp_rename` to change the names of columns within tables and views, simply by specifying the object name as table.column. `sp_rename` executes successfully only for objects within a current database that you own. If you ran `sp_depends` on an object and discovered that other database objects referenced the name you changed, remember that you must change the view, trigger, or stored procedure that looks for that name. These database objects work even after the name has been changed until they are recompiled, which can happen at any time without notice. You should always run `sp_depends` on an object you intend to rename, and change any dependent references immediately.

A number of systems procedures are useful for administering a SQL Server and its databases. These include the following:

```
sp_checknames
sp_helplog
sp_helpsegment
sp_dboption
sp_diskdefault
```

These procedures give the systems administrator, or any interested party, the ability to check and in some cases set database and server options. If you, as a database owner, need to set single or multiuser mode, DBO use only, checkpoint options, and truncate log settings, you would use the `sp_dboption` systems procedure. To rename an entire database, you use the `sp_renamedb` option. These database housekeeping tasks will likely be infrequently used, but you may be called on to use them at any point. Look first at the database rename procedure:

COMMAND: `sp_renamedb`

SYNTAX   `sp_renamedb old_database_name,`
                 `new_database_name`

USED BY: Systems administrator

USED FOR: Renaming a database

EXAMPLE: `sp_renamedb pubs, publications`

SAMPLE:

```
Database name changed.
```

However, the systems administrator cannot just waltz around changing database names at will. Like changing the name of any database object, any views, triggers, stored procedures, or rules that reference the database name have to be updated and recompiled to ensure that they will work in the future. Procedurally, the systems administrator must also set the database to single-user mode prior to running `sp_renamedb`. This is just one example of when you would need to use `sp_dboption`:

COMMAND:	`sp_dboption`
SYNTAX:	`sp_dboption [database_name, option,` `{true¦false}]`
USED BY:	Only systems administrator and database owner can change settings
USED FOR:	Setting single/multiuser access, DBO-only access, select into/bulkcopy enable/disable, and truncate logs on checkpoint operation
EXAMPLE:	`sp_dboption pubs, bulkcopy, true`
SAMPLE:	

```
Run the CHECKPOINT command in the database that was changed.
(Return status = 0)
```

This somewhat cryptic message is really trying to tell you that you successfully changed the database option to allow bulkcopy and select into. However, you must first run the checkpoint command to have the new settings take effect. To successfully execute `sp_dboption`, you must first be in the master database. To determine what the current settings for your database are, execute the `sp_helpdb` procedure. The settings allow you to lock everyone out of the database but the DBO, through the `sp_dboption`, `database_name`, `dbo`, `true` option. The read, true option allows users to continue to retrieve data, but the database will not be writable.

When single user is true (`sp_dboption database_name, "single", true`), only one login at a time is supported. The truncate log on checkpoint option means that the transaction log is cleaned of all committed transactions each time the checkpoint process takes place. You can turn this feature on while doing development on your system, to keep the transaction log from growing.

The select into/bulkcopy option allows you to create new tables and populate them without logging the transactions. This speeds up the table creation process, but it does not allow you to recover your transactions if the operation is interrupted. In that case, you have to begin again from scratch. A bulkcopy or a select into could fail if the target database became full before the data was successfully copied into the new table. At that point, the systems administrator or database owner would have to increase the space available for the target table. The first step in accomplishing this would be to identify which segment should be used to extend the table onto.

COMMAND: `sp_helpsegment`

SYNTAX: `sp_helpsegment [ segment_name]`

USED BY: Anyone

USED FOR: Determining information about segments in the current database for tables, indexes, and logs

EXAMPLE: `sp_helpsegment seggie`

SAMPLE:

```
segment name                            status
======= ============================== ======
0       system                         0
1       default                        1
2       logsegment                     0
3       index_seg                      0
4       index_seg1                     0
5       seggie                         0

segment name                            status
======= ============================== ======
5       seggie                         0

device                        size
============================= =======================
db_dev1                       1MB

table_name                    index_name                  indid
============================= =========================== ======
newtable                      newtable                    0
table1                        test_index                  1
```

Here you see first the results of running `helpsegment` without a segment name. This yields a list of all segments for the current database, followed by a detailed listing for the segment seggie, which you can see resides on database device `db_dev1`, has a size of 1M, and holds two tables and indexes. If you work with the assumption that you were trying to bulkcopy or select into newtable, which ran out of room, you can see that the database device size is too small. To increase the space available to a table that has been defined on segments, you can use the `sp_extendsegment` system procedure. First you need to know what devices are available for you to extend your segment onto. You can accomplish this through the `sp_helpdevice` system procedure:

COMMAND: `sp_helpdevice`

SYNTAX: `sp_helpdevice [device_name]`

USED BY: Anyone

USED FOR: Obtaining information about devices available or
                  details on a particular Sybase device

EXAMPLE: `sp_helpdevice`

SAMPLE:

```
device_name  : db_dev1
physical_name: sys:/SYBASE/db.dat
description  : special, physical disk, 2 MB
status       : 2
cntrltype    : 0
device_number: 0
low          : 117440512
high         : 117441535

device_name  : diskdump
physical_name: nul
description  : disk, dump device
status       : 16
cntrltype    : 2
device_number: 0
low          : 0
high         : 20000

device_name  : floppydump
physical_name: A:DUMPDATA.DAT
description  : tape, 1 MB, dump device
status       : 16
cntrltype    : 3
device_number: 0
low          : 0
high         : 32

device_name  : floppydumpb
physical_name: B:DUMPDATA.DAT
description  : tape, 1 MB, dump device
status       : 16
cntrltype    : 3
device_number: 0
low          : 0
high         : 32

device_name  : master
physical_name: the_master_device
description  : special, default disk, physical disk, 16 MB
status       : 3
cntrltype    : 0
```

```
device_number: 0
low          : 0
high         : 8191

device_name  : scsitape
physical_name: NOVADIBI
description  : tape, 40 MB, dump device, skip header
status       : 24
cntrltype    : 5
device_number: 0
low          : 0
high         : 1280

device_name  : sysdump
physical_name: SYS:\DUMPDATA.DAT
description  : disk, dump device
status       : 16
cntrltype    : 2
device_number: 0
low          : 0
high         : 0

device_name  : tapedump
physical_name: WANGTEK
description  : tape, 40 MB, dump device, skip header
status       : 24
cntrltype    : 4
device_number: 0
low          : 0
high         : 1280

device_name  : testdb
physical_name: \sybase\testdb.dat
description  : special, physical disk, 4 MB
status       : 2
cntrltype    : 0
device_number: 0
low          : 150994944
high         : 150996991
```

This is a listing of all devices defined on this SQL Server. To restrict the listing to just one device, you simply pass the name of the device to the sp_helpdevice procedure on the command line. The information retrieved is the same. In this case, you might decide that you wish to extend the segment seggie to include testdb, as well as db_dev1. To achieve this, you can now execute the sp_extendsegment command:

COMMAND: sp_extendsegment

SYNTAX: sp_extendsegment segment_name, device_name

USED BY: Database owner

USED FOR:	Extending a segment's size within the current database device or across multiple devices
EXAMPLE:	`sp_extendsegment seggie, testdb`
SAMPLE:	

```
DBCC execution completed. If DBCC printed error messages, see your
Systems Administrator.
Segment extended.
1 row affected.
```

From this message you can tell that rows written to table newtable, which was created on segment seggie, will now be written to the testdb device. Other systems procedures allow you to move logs as well as tables around devices. To get information about a transaction log, use the `sp_helplog` systems procedure:

COMMAND:	`sp_helplog`
SYNTAX:	`sp_helplog`
USED BY:	Anyone
USED FOR:	Determining what device the log starts on
EXAMPLE:	`sp_helplog`
SAMPLE:	

```
In database "pubs", the log starts on device "testdb"
(return status 0)
```

Logs can be split across a number of devices. This procedure tells you which device holds the first page of the log. You might use this procedure to check that the transaction log for a particular database was, in fact, being written to a separate database device. This is important, because the transaction log can be dumped separately from the database itself only when they are maintained on separate devices. The `sp_helplog` system procedure can be used to check that anyone who has created a database has used the log on option of the create database command to separate the log and the database.

If your transaction log is on a separate database device and you need to allocate more room for it, you would use the `sp_extendsegment` systems procedure. If you were working with a small, noncritical database (in development, for instance) and you did not use the log on option of the database create command, and you still needed to allocate more space to a transaction log, you would use the `sp_logdevice` systems procedure:

COMMAND: `sp_logdevice`

SYNTAX: `sp_logdevice database_name, device_name`

USED BY: Database owner

USED FOR: Increasing the amount of space allocated to a log by moving new log pages to a different device

EXAMPLE: `sp_logdevice pubs, testdb`

SAMPLE:

```
Syslogs moved.
```

This systems procedure is one you will not use much if you have created your databases in the manner recommended in Section 2, "Defining the Development Environment." You should keep in mind that you must have already declared the database device when you created it or you must execute the alter database command prior to executing the `sp_logdevice` systems procedure. You cannot allocate tables, logs, or any other database object to a device that has not been specified as usable by that database.

Assume that you have set up your database in that fashion. You have chosen to create segments and created your tables to reside on those segments. As covered in Section 3, "Installing and Configuring SQL Server," you can specify exactly what disk resources are used by a specific table or index in your database. To do this you use the `sp_placeobject` systems procedure:

COMMAND: `sp_placeobject`

SYNTAX: `sp_placeobject segment_name, object_name`

USED BY: Systems administrator, database owner, and table owners

USED FOR: Specifying a particular segment to hold all new data written to a table or index

EXAMPLE: `sp_placeobject new_data_segment, students`

SAMPLE:

```
DBCC execution completed. If DBCC printed error messages, see your
System Administrator.
'students' is now on segment 'new_data_segment'.
(return status = 0)
```

In cases where you are splitting a table or index across multiple disk fragments, you will get DBCC error messages, which you can ignore. The `sp_placeobject` systems procedure gives you a great deal of flexibility in allocating table and index storage requirements to specific segments and therefore physical disks. You should keep in mind that `sp_placeobject` refers only to new rows written to the database; it does not move existing data from its current segment. To move the contents of a table from one segment to another, try creating a table on a device and selecting into it all the rows from the existing table.

Systems Procedures for Documenting Key Relationships

A number of systems procedures do not actually modify the database but allow you to document your tables according to your specifications in the data modeling process. These include:

```
sp_commonkey

sp_primarykey

sp_foreignkey

sp_helpkey
```

These are specifically related to the keys that are held in the various tables within the database. As you saw earlier, a table might have a primary key, which is owned by that table, and a number of foreign and common keys used to join tables together. I discuss how to ensure referential integrity throughout your database later in this section. These systems procedures do not perform this function; however, they do set up a useful documentation trail for any developer who is working with the various tables. SQL Server System 10 does provide for declarative referential integrity, meaning that it can be built automatically into the tables within the database. However, earlier versions did not. The systems procedures discussed here have been available since the earliest versions of SQL Server were released.

COMMAND:	`sp_primarykey`
SYNTAX:	`sp_primarykey table_name, column1 [, column2, column3 ]`
USED BY:	Table owners
USED FOR:	Explicitly declaring the unique key of a table
EXAMPLE:	`sp_primarykey publishers, pub_id`
SAMPLE:	

```
New primary key added.
```

Only one primary key can be declared for each table by the owner of the table. However, the key can be concatenated or combined from up to eight columns within the table, as long as that key is then unique. By explicitly declaring the primary key for a table, you make it possible for an application program to retrieve that information from the database, rather than requiring the application (or user) to know it in advance. The primary key information is listed at the bottom of the output from the `sp_help table_name` system procedure or by executing the system procedure `sp_helpkey`:

COMMAND:	`sp_helpkey`
SYNTAX:	`sp_helpkey [object_name]`
USED BY:	Anyone
USED FOR:	Obtaining information on primary, foreign, and common keys declared for tables and views
EXAMPLE:	`sp_helpkey`
SAMPLE:	

```
keytype        : primary
object         : authors
related_object:  — none —
object_keys    : au_id, *, *, *, *, *, *, *
related_keys   : *, *, *, *, *, *, *, *

keytype        : foreign
object         : titleauthor
related_object: authors
object_keys    : au_id, *, *, *, *, *, *, *
related_keys   : au_id, *, *, *, *, *, *, *
```

Executing the `sp_helpkey` command without a view or tablename yields a report on all keys defined in the database—otherwise you will get the keys declared for the specified object. Again, it should be noted that this report is useful only if you have taken the time to document your keys with the stored procedures discussed here. It is not derived automatically by the system. To define explicit foreign key relationships for child tables, you would use the `sp_foreignkey` system procedure:

COMMAND:	`sp_foreignkey`
SYNTAX:	`sp_foreignkey child_table, parent_table,` `foreignkey`
USED BY:	Table owners
USED FOR:	Documenting the foreign key relationships between two tables in the database
EXAMPLE:	`sp_foreignkey children, family,` `unique_family_number`
SAMPLE:	

```
Foreign key added.
```

When you add a foreign key relationship using the `sp_foreignkey` system procedure, you automatically add an entry for commonkey, used to indicate that two tables could be joined on these columns. The purpose of defining a foreign key is to declare exactly what columns the table depends on for other information. In the mythical child table, for instance, to arrive at the children's address you would join the parents' table with the children's table on the unique_family_number. Since you can have a family without children, the primary key on the family table is the unique_family_number. You would store the family address in this table. To find the address for any children, you would have to join the child table to the family table on the family number. Because the family number is unique in the family table, it is the primary key, and because you need it to get information about the children, it is a foreign key for that table. Because you can join the two tables on that column, it is a common key for those tables.

The definition of the foreign key must include all the columns in the same order as they are declared for the primary key. As you saw in the `sp_primarykey` notes, this could be a single or a concatenated key. In any case, the foreign key must be specified in the same way as the primary key it depends on for the system procedure to execute successfully.

COMMAND:	`sp_commonkey`
SYNTAX:	`sp_commonkey tableA, tableB, columnA1, columnB1 [,columnA2, columnB2]`
USED BY:	Table owner
USED FOR:	Documenting columns used to join two tables
EXAMPLE:	`sp_commonkey tickets, drivers, license_no, license_no`
SAMPLE:	

```
New common key added.
```

In this example, you are documenting that the tickets table contains a license_no column, which is used to join to the drivers table that also has a license_no. `sp_commonkey` allows you to document non-foreign key relationships used for joins. If the two tables have a primary/foreign key relationship, use the `sp_foreignkey` procedure, which will update commonkeys automatically. You can specify up to eight column names to join over as the commonkey definition.

Summary

This chapter took you through the most commonly used systems procedures provided with your SQL Server. Other special purpose systems procedures are covered in the context of achieving particular results. From this chapter, you should have a sense of the administrative and navigational uses of the Sybase-supplied stored procedures. These `sp_` procedures provide the basis for your interaction with SQL Server, and—like other server-based utilities such as `vi` or `edit`—can be highly useful if you must deal with a number of different SQL Server sites.

The SQL Server systems procedures provide a valuable service in the way they manage the updating of systems tables, ensuring that any operation on the server, database, or database object is completed properly. The alternative to using stored procedures in this fashion would be to update the systems tables directly. This can result in many undesirable and unanticipated complications. An entry to the syslogs table, for instance, is itself logged to the syslogs table, resulting in an endless loop and filling up your database. By using the systems procedures provided with your SQL Server, you can protect yourself from these unwanted complications, especially if you are new to the SQL Server environment.

After completing this chapter, you should have a clear idea of which systems procedures are commonly used, by whom, and for what. Also, samples of the actual syntax and output generated should help you when running these stored procedures at your own site.

4.2

Database Integrity

In Chapter 2.6, "Data Integrity and Recovery," you were exposed to some of the considerations surrounding the issue of data integrity. You were shown how the architecture of the SQL Server lent itself to ensuring data integrity on the server side. Many application designers feel quite strongly that there should be validation and error handling on the application side, and there are many reasons to support this. One reason is the more immediate response to the user when an error is made. Another is the ability to provide error messages that are meaningful in the context of the operation being performed. However, if data integrity is not fully implemented on the server side, the integrity of the data in the database can never be assured. You can access data in a SQL Server in many ways, which is the benefit of the open client/server architecture. To allow anyone connecting through a query tool that supported updates or even ISQL to have access to data without server-side integrity would compromise integrity. The bottom line is that you will likely need to ensure data integrity on both the client and server sides of the application, but you must definitely have it on the server side.

This chapter covers the use of rules and defaults in ensuring data integrity. You will see how user datatypes can be set up to incorporate many integrity features and how these can easily be used and re-used by developers. This chapter covers the concepts and the syntax for creating, manipulating, and dropping these database functions. By the end of this chapter you should know exactly why and how to create your own datatypes that build in rules governing the data appropriate to your business. You will also see how to use the systems procedures provided for working with rules and default values for table columns. The aspects of data integrity dealt with in this chapter are limited to the data to be contained in the tables themselves and do not extend to referential integrity, which is covered in Chapter 4.5, "Triggers and Referential Integrity."

Ensuring Data Integrity through Rules and Defaults

The previous section talked about the various levels of database integrity on the server side: column-level, table-level, and database-level integrity. Rules and defaults are two means of ensuring that the values written to a column fall within approved parameters. As you remember from Chapter 3.5 on creating tables, you can set a column's values to null or not null when you create the table. By forcing the value to not null, you ensure that there will be a value in that column for a row to be successfully inserted or updated in the table. By using rules and defaults, you can further define the values that are added to those or any columns. A default value substitutes the default instead of a null when a table is inserted or updated, and no value is explicitly set for a column with a default. A rule is a way of enforcing basic integrity constraints, such as formatting or domains (allowable ranges) to be set for the column. Defaults are single values that get written into the column, whereas rules are formulated with expressions. The domain for the column is the set of all possible values that could be stored within that column.

Both rules and columns are developed in a two-stage process. First you define the rule or default, then you bind it to the column to make the rule or default active. Rules and defaults can be bound to one, many, or all columns within a table. To drop a rule or default, you must first ensure that it is not bound to any columns in the database. Additionally, rules and defaults can be incorporated into user-defined datatypes, which are then used by developers when they create their tables. When rules or defaults are defined as part of a user-defined datatype, you do not need to define or bind them when creating a new table. They are automatically contained in any use of the datatype in which they have been bound.

Defining Defaults

Defaults are often simply values, such as character strings, numbers, or dates, to be stored in a row in place of a null. However, defaults can also be constructed out of expressions and functions, though you cannot reference a database object within the expression. In fact, when creating a default you can use any constant expression, though you must be careful to follow the usual rules governing the base datatype of the column. For instance, you must enclose character and date values in the expression within quotation marks. Money, integer, and floating point constants do not need quotation marks. Binary data is always preceded with a 0x, and money data with a dollar sign to ensure precision. To create a default, use the following syntax:

```
Create default default_name
as <expression>
```

A more useful example of this syntax could be illustrated as follows:

```
Create default home_state
as "New York"
```

A default of this type might be useful for a table that contained addresses of a local population. You could override the default by providing an explicit value for anyone who was to be added to the database and whose home state was not New York. For everyone else, having the default set as New York would simply mean you didn't have to enter it to have it stored in the table.

From this example you can see that defaults of this nature can be quite useful in reducing the amount and/or scope of the data that has to be captured and written to the database.

After you have defined the default, you must bind it to the column using the sp_bindefault system procedure.

COMMAND:	`sp_bindefault`
SYNTAX:	`sp_bindefault default_name, object_name [,` `futureonly]`
USED BY:	Table owner, database owner, systems administrator
USED FOR:	Making default values for columns effective
EXAMPLE:	`sp_bindefault home_state, customers.state`
SAMPLE OUTPUT:	Default bound to column

At this point, any null values entered into the state column of the customers table are translated to the state specified in the create default expression. The futureonly parameter is to allow you to bind defaults to a user-defined datatype without affecting existing occurrences of that datatype. When you specify futureonly, the default takes effect on new uses of the datatype in create or alter table commands. To unbind a default from a column, you must use the sp_unbindefault systems procedure, which uses the same syntax as the sp_bindefault procedure, or you can simply run sp_bindefault again on the same column with a new default. The futureonly flag works on both systems procedures. If you do not specify futureonly on the sp_bindefault, the default will still be active for any existing tables containing the user-defined datatype that had the default bound to it.

You can have only one default per column, and binding a default overwrites any existing default that might have been on the column. Defining and binding a default does not supply a value to a column defined as not null where a null was supplied by the insert statement. However, if no value is defined to be inserted into a column that has a default and does not allow nulls, the default value will be written into the column. If you do not have an explicit value to write into a not null column with a default bound to it, don't try to insert a null. Just leave it alone and the default will take care of it. If the column has been defined as allowing nulls, the nulls are written as the value declared in the default for that column.

Rules

Rules are handled in a similar manner to column defaults. They are first defined, then they are bound. They must be unbound before they can be dropped. However, rules contribute a great deal more to data integrity than default values do. A rule is a way of translating business requirements into your database. By themselves rules are a method of ensuring that all data in the database is reasonable, if not exactly accurate. Rules are flexible and can be changed with the business. Rules restrict the range of legal values for a column, depending on the definition of legal at the time the rule is bound or unbound. Rules are not retroactive and do not affect data already held in the columns; they simply affect new insert or update operations. Like defaults, you use a create rule command to define the rule first:

```
Create rule rule_name as
<expression>
```

Take a practical example. Say your company had developed an extensive database for U.S. customers that was used for mailing catalogs. You would define a rule for ensuring zip codes as follows:

```
create rule zipcode_rule as
@zip like '[0-9][0-9][0-9][0-9][0-9]'
```

This would ensure that any legal values for zip codes would fall between 00000 and 99999. In fact, if you execute an `sp_help` on the authors table in the pubs database, you will see that there is a column for zip codes and that a rule has been bound to it. Using the command `sp_helptext ziprule`, you will find that the syntax in the rule matches this example. The @ sign precedes the symbolic name for the value to be evaluated by the expression. In this case, the @zip says "the value to be inserted into the column must be." It does not have to exactly match the column name, because the rule identifies which column to apply to when it is bound. However, the symbolic name must be formed using the same rules and naming conventions that apply to any SQL Server object name. The expression in this case is contained inside quotes or double quotes because the underlying datatype is character.

A rule of this nature would have been fine before the recent expansion of the zip codes. To accommodate the newer formats as well, you could modify the rule to read as follows:

```
create rule zipcode_rule as
@zip like '[0-9][0-9][0-9][0-9][0-9]'
or @zip like '[0-9][0-9][0-9][0-9][0-9]-[0-9][0-9][0-9][0-9]'
```

The OR operator links the two parts of the expression; the AND as well as the NOT operator are also supported in the rule expression. You might note that as far as the zip column in the authors table goes, the table would have to be modified to allow for a column with more than five characters, so the expanded zip codes would not fit. This would mean that you would have to engage in the somewhat awkward process of creating a new table with the column definitions you wanted, selecting the authors data into the new table, deleting the authors table, and renaming the new table. Dropping or modifying columns is more of a nuisance than adding columns.

I will make the example more interesting. Say that your organization has expanded its operations to take advantage of recent Free Trade agreements and now you are required to enter customer addresses containing Canadian postal codes, which use a combination of letters and numbers in a fixed order. To allow insertion of rows with these values in the zip code column, the rule would have to be modified to look like this:

```
create rule zipcode_rule as
@zip like '[0-9][0-9][0-9][0-9][0-9]'
or @zip like '[0-9][0-9][0-9][0-9][0-9]-[0-9][0-9][0-9][0-9]'
or @zip like '[a-z][0-9][a-z][0-9][a-z][0-9]'
```

The zip code column will now accept regular or expanded U.S. zip codes or Canadian postal codes.

As I touched on earlier, you can construct expressions using any legal T-SQL WHERE clause code that does not reference database objects; the expressions must be entirely self-contained. You can also use built-in string, mathematical, aggregate, and date functions within your rule's expression. The uses and syntax of these functions are covered in more detail in Chapter 4.3, "TransAct SQL"; however, it may be appropriate to give you some idea of how they can be specifically incorporated into rule expressions.

If you wanted to ensure that any inserted value fell within a predefined range of acceptable values, you would use the IN qualifier. For instance, to ensure that only predefined values could be entered into the column type in the titles table of the pubs database, you could create a rule like this:

```
use pubs
go
create rule type_rule as
@type IN ("trad_cook", "business", "psychology", "popular_comp",
"UNDECIDED")
go
sp_bindrule type_rule, "titles.type"
go
```

This means that any future inserts to the type column of the titles table must include an entry from this list. As you can imagine, this is a highly effective way of ensuring that users cannot simply make up their own types and that if they do not know, the only legal value allowed is UNDECIDED. At any time, an expansion to the rule could add new types to the list.

You might want to use a mathematical function for a rule for price checking. In the analysis and design of the bookstore application, I determined that a book should sell for between 0 and 200 dollars. You would enforce this with a rule structured like this:

```
use pubs
go
create rule price_rule as
@price between $0 and $200
go
sp_bindrule price rule, "titles.price"
go
```

You might need a date function to ensure the validity of a value being entered. For example, if you wanted to ensure that any date entered into the pubdate column of the titles table fell within an acceptable range of dates, you could create the following rule:

```
use pubs
go
create rule date_rule as
@pubdate <getdate() and @pubdate >"1/1/55"
go
sp_bindrule daterule, "title.pubdate"
go
```

In this case the rule allows only publications with pubdates between the current date and the first of January, 1955. For purposes of this example, the 1/1/55 date could be the date the publishing firm began printing books, so any dates prior to that could not be valid. You can see how rules can be used to build data integrity into your database.

You must ensure that the expression in the rule is compatible with the column's datatype. Beyond requiring quotation marks for character datatypes, this means that you cannot use string functions on numeric columns or date functions on columns defined with the character datatype.

If you create a rule that will not execute, it will allow you to create and bind the rule and generate an error message only when you attempt to write a value into the column bound with the bad rule. You should get in the habit of thoroughly testing your rules for actual performance as you develop them, because you cannot rely on the SQL Server to check the reasonability or validity of the construction of a particular rule.

Incorporating Rules and Defaults into User-Defined Datatypes

The process of creating user-defined datatypes was introduced in Chapter 3.5. One of the key reasons for creating a user-defined datatype is to easily propagate rules and defaults through your databases. You can create the user-defined datatype in the model database, and all subsequently created databases will contain that user-defined datatype. In this way, you can create and bind a default and/or a rule to a column and ensure that it is used throughout your SQL Server environment. Because user-defined datatypes are based on and subject to the same considerations as SQL Server datatypes, defaults and rules are the key reasons for providing user-defined datatypes.

To create a user-defined datatype, you could use the following procedure:

```
use model
go
sp_addtype intl_phone_type, "char(20)", null
go
create rule intl_phone_rule as
@phone [0-9][0-9][0-9]-[0-9][0-9][0-9]-[0-9][0-9][0-9]-[0-9]
[0-9][0-9][0-9]
go
sp_bindrule intl_phone_rule, intl_phone_type
go
```

This procedure could not be combined as part of a single script, because the create rule command must always be issued as the first line in a session. However, using ISQL or another command-line facility for connecting to your SQL Server would do fine. In any case, this procedure would result in a new datatype being added to the model database that would provide for a country code in all international phone numbers. Of course, in real life it might be easier to simply create a new column for country code and populate it only for customers or contacts with international addresses, but the approach to defining the datatype and rule would be quite similar.

User-defined datatypes are always created in the current directory. If you had an existing database in which you wanted to use intl_phone_number or any other user-defined datatype, you must create it within that database. There is no facility for copying database objects across databases, except where they exist in the model database prior to the creation of a user database.

When you are binding rules to columns and datatypes, the order in which you perform the binding is important. Although you can override rules that are bound to columns or datatypes by binding a new rule to that column or datatype, the rule bound to the column overrides the rule bound to the datatype. This can be useful when you have chosen to use a user-defined datatype but wish to modify the rule and bind that rule to the column. This works fine without affecting any of the other columns defined with the datatype. However, if you bind a new rule to the datatype, any rules bound to columns will not affect columns defined with that datatype if they already have rules specifically bound to them. It will, however, affect columns that were defined with the datatype and were not bound with any overriding rule.

Summary

This chapter has taken you through the concept, syntax, and examples of creating column defaults and rules. These are two of the powerful SQL Server features for building data integrity into the database server. No matter what client tool is used, data that does not conform to the column rule will not be inserted into the column unless someone explicitly drops the rule. From the examples, you can see how any business rule can be incorporated into SQL Server. The only restriction on the use of T-SQL statements as expressions in rules is the inability to refer to a database object. This means that you cannot make a rule contingent on the result of some other column's contents. As explained in this chapter, defaults and rules deal with column-level data integrity. Referring to other columns falls in the domain of table-level data integrity, and this would be handled primarily through triggers.

Defaults can greatly reduce the requirement for data input, where the values in a column are usually but not always of a particular result. Defaults allow you to require the entry of only the exceptions and not the rule when it comes to values in the table. Setting up temporary defaults when loading data into tables as part of a data migration or creation effort is often extremely useful. After all, when you are working late nights, anything that saves a few minutes is helpful.

Rules are an extremely powerful method of ensuring that the values inserted into the database conform to the business expectations. Those of you who have built systems already—client/server or otherwise—know that you cannot always expect users to be sensible and to check the data they are entering. Rules allow you to ensure that the values entered are reasonable, if not completely accurate.

You can really see the advantages of defaults and rules when they are bound to a user-defined datatype that is then rolled out to developers. By using this approach, only a a core group of people responsible for data integrity (such as the data administrator and the database administrator) can define datatypes that contain checks and balances for data entered without requiring each developer to build their own datatypes. Conversely, if a developer has a great deal of experience with a particular application or database, that developer might create the datatype, defining and binding defaults and rules as appropriate. How you choose to roll out responsibility for these functions depends on your client/server environment. However, you can be sure that by incorporating defaults and rules into your tables, you and your users will gain a great deal of confidence in the integrity of your database.

At this point, you would move to integrity issues at the table and database levels. Multicolumn and referential integrity are vital in a relational database management system, and you will likely find them just as important for your applications. However, writing triggers and stored procedures that deal with such integrity issues usually incorporate a good deal of T-SQL code. At this point you have to go through the TransAct SQL language provided with your SQL Server and then move on to incorporating that code in triggers, stored procedures, and transactions.

4.3

TransAct SQL

TransAct SQL is the Sybase implementation of the ANSI standard Structured Query Language for manipulating data in relational databases. Although the standard approach to SQL does deal with join syntax and operations, it does not provide enough functions to write applications for a relational database environment. In the ANSI standard version of SQL, IF statements are not supported, for example. T-SQL addresses these deficiencies with extensions to SQL to ensure that you have all the functions, operators, and qualifiers you need to build robust SQL Server applications.

You have already been introduced to some of the features of TransAct SQL, including the create tables, views, rules, defaults, and some examples of how WHERE clauses can be structured. Additionally, commands such as DISK INIT and DUMP DATABASE are T-SQL extensions.

This chapter takes you through the rest of the T-SQL command set. Through TransAct SQL statements you can create the transactions you want to retrieve, insert, delete, and manipulate the data in your database. As earlier chapters mentioned, T-SQL syntax is used in the creation of triggers and stored procedures, as well as in the definition of expressions for rules.

By the end of this chapter, you will be fully familiar with the range of commands and syntax used for TransAct SQL statements. At that point, you should have a grasp of the building blocks used to write triggers and stored procedures for your database applications.

What Is TransAct SQL?

TransAct SQL is the specific implementation of the Structured Query Language designed to work with SQL Server. SQL was developed by IBM in the 1970s to be a standard method of retrieving data from relational databases. The power of relational databases is in the ability to join tables together, and SQL was developed to support that power. SQL is offered by almost all relational database management systems. However, the command set is too restrictive to provide support for all the operations you would require in a typical relational database management application. To get around these restrictions, RDBMS vendors have developed their own versions of SQL, and Sybase is no exception to this process.

T-SQL is a feature-rich SQL implementation and contains many enhancements and extensions intended to provide you, as a developer, with greater control over your data. SQL operates by structuring a statement with a keyword, object name, and optional clause. A keyword might be SELECT, INSERT, UPDATE, or even CREATE. The object name refers to the database, table, view, or column on which the keyword is to operate. The clause specifies the conditions that must be fulfilled before the keyword can successfully operate. A typical SQL statement might read as follows:

```
Select * from readers
where title = "Sybase Developer's Guide"
```

From this straightforward structure, complex activities can be performed on data through SQL. When a select operation is performed, results meeting the criteria specified are displayed. For other operations, such as insert, update, and delete, a return code or status message is issued at the end of the operation to indicate success or failure. A result code of 0 indicates that the operation was a success. Depending on the nature of the problem and the operation being performed, other result codes could point to a problem that must be resolved prior to the successful execution of the command.

SQL supports the specification of data in multiple tables, as long as columns that are shared between the tables are identified to support the joining of these two tables. Different join strategies yield different result sets, even if the selection criteria remain the same. Selection criteria can be defined to greater or lesser degrees of detail. Each datatype has its own unique features on which it can be selected or manipulated. The operators (equal to, not equal to, greater than, and less than) can be combined to achieve radically different results from a simple modification to a short SQL statement. The purpose of this chapter is to take you through the various statement structures and options open to you using T-SQL. How you incorporate these options into statements that meet your own data retrieval requirements is entirely up to you.

T-SQL Extensions and Enhancements

Taken as a whole, several major areas make up TransAct SQL. These are as follows:

■ Control-of-flow language

This component of T-SQL allows you to write transactions or build batches of SQL statements which, as the name implies, control the flow of the statements and data like a programming language. These extensions include constructs such as BEGIN-END, BREAK, CONTINUE, DECLARE, GOTO <LABEL>, IF-ELSE, PRINT, RAISERROR, RETURN, WAITFOR, and WHILE. Local variables can be declared and assigned values within the transaction or statement batch using Declare. By providing these features, T-SQL allows you to build applications that run on the server. While in a client/server system, you would naturally not want to use this capability exclusively. Many applications are best executed server side, including stored procedures and triggers.

■ Stored procedures

Through this extension to SQL, T-SQL gives you the ability to combine the power of SQL statements with the control-of-flow constructs listed earlier, precompile them, and run them on the server, thus making the server itself programmable. Through the communications capabilities built into SQL Server, it is possible to execute stored procedures on remote servers. This aspect of T-SQL gives you the ability to create transactions that transcend a single application program or even a single SQL Server.

■ Triggers

A trigger is a dedicated stored procedure with a few differences. Triggers are fired when specific operations are taken on tables, such as insert, delete, and update. They are not executed like stored procedures; once bound to a table, a trigger is fired whenever the key operation is performed. Triggers are most often used to ensure the integrity of data that refers to other tables. This is known as referential integrity.

■ Rules and defaults

T-SQL allows you to define values to be inserted into rows when a different value is not explicitly provided. You can also use T-SQL to develop rules governing the acceptable ranges and format of data that can be successfully appended to the database. These two extensions to SQL are very powerful means of ensuring data integrity at the column level and through defaults, restricting the need to specify data to exceptions to the norm, rather than each and every case.

■ Compute clause

T-SQL allows you to derive summary values from rows in conjunction with aggregate values. Compute allows you to create and display column subtotals, which allow you to essentially build reports within the T-SQL statements, rather than being forced to use an external query tool or report generator. Compute displays these summary values as new rows rather than columns, making the returned results appear more like a report.

■ Error handling and SET

T-SQL allows you to create your own error messages as part of your server-side application. In a client/server environment, this can save having to develop error-handling routines for a large number of different client systems and environments. Through the RAISERROR and PRINT statements, you can direct the error message of your choice back to the user. Through SET, you can activate diagnostic tools, show processing statistics, and rearrange the returned results to meet your own requirements.

■ Systems administration features

T-SQL provides several unique capabilities to assist you in the administration of your system. These include the database mirroring capability to ensure up-time as well as the commands allowing you as systems administrator to determine exactly what physical devices you want indexes, logs, databases, and even tables to reside on.

Other unique features of T-SQL include the following:

■ Update data through views

■ Greater control over GROUP BY and ORDER BY clauses

■ User-defined datatypes allowed

■ Nested queries

■ Temporary tables and database objects

■ Greater control over moving data between and within tables

■ Large text and image storage with unique datatypes

■ Built-in functions

Each of these is covered in the context of how they can be used to help you meet your data retrieval and manipulation requirements.

You have already seen how T-SQL handles joins in Section 2, "Defining the Development Environment." Look now at how you can restrict the results to the rows that match certain conditions set in your WHERE clause. You can use T-SQL extensions for data retrieval and manipulation through the use of the following:

■ Wildcards with LIKE

■ String manipulation

■ Converting data

■ Date functions

■ Mathematical functions

■ Aggregate functions

By incorporating the extension into your WHERE clause, you can dramatically affect the results you receive from the SQL statement.

Wildcards

LIKE is an ANSI standard qualifier that enables you to retrieve results that match the condition on one or more characters rather than matching exactly. If you wanted all the last names that started with B, for example, you would use the LIKE predicate in your WHERE clause. You can use LIKE with % to match any or all characters, or _ to match a single character.

The % symbol is used to enable you to pull out any rows where the characters can be found in the column. For example, to retrieve all titles for all cookbooks in the pubs database, you could use the following query:

```
use pubs
go
select title
from titles
where type like "%cook%"
go
```

The pubs database has five books in the general category cookbooks. However, you would use LIKE in the preceding statement because the pubs database has two distinct types of cookbooks: trad_cook and mod_cook. By using the LIKE "%cook%" construct, you avoid having to specify your query with type = "mod_cook" or type = "trad_cook". In this example, you can retrieve the data you want using either approach; however, in some cases you must use LIKE to get the rows you need.

For example, to get information on a book with a particular word in the title, you could use the following query:

```
use pubs
go
select * from titles
where title like "%Sushi%"
go
```

This query retrieves information on the book "Sushi, Anyone?". What if your SQL Server has been set up to be case sensitive? You can retrieve a row based on the occurrence of a word in a column, whether it is upper- or lowercase, with the following structure:

```
use pubs
go
select * from titles
where title like "%[Ss]ushi%"
go
```

In this query, the square brackets surrounding the Ss indicate that the word can start with either an upper- or lowercase S.

You could also retrieve rows based on the specification of a single character. The query can be structured so that any of a set, a character matching, or all characters not matching the specified character will be used when evaluating the column.

For example, to retrieve information on all authors whose last names start with *S*, you could use this query:

```
use pubs
go
select * from authors
where au_lname like S%
go
```

This query gives you the three authors whose last names start with S.

The placement and selection of the wildcard options are important not just for matching character strings in queries, but for structuring any string-matching clause for retrieving data from char, varchar, and date_time data. The wildcard options are as follows:

%	Matches any and all characters in the string
_	Matches a single character in that position
[]	Matches any of the characters within the brackets
[^]	Matches any character but the ones specified in the brackets

You can use all these options in a single WHERE clause. To retrieve all titles published with a PC, TC, or MC at the beginning of the title_id, where the type is not equal to trad_cook and the title starts with S, you could use the following query:

```
select * from titles
where title_id like "_C%" and type like "[^t]%" and title like "[S]%"
go
```

This query yields the two books that have a C as the second character in the pub_id, whose titles start with an S, and whose type does not start with the character t. This is, of course, a goofy little query that you would probably structure completely differently if you actually wanted to find these two books. It does, however, demonstrate all the methods you can use to screen out or select string patterns within a table's columns.

String Operations and Manipulation

A string is simply a bunch of characters. Because of the implicit conversion of certain datatypes within SQL Server, you can treat datetime data in the same fashion as char and varchar data. You can use T-SQL string functions to achieve many other things besides the select operations listed earlier. You can use string functions to concatenate multiple characters together, extract a substring from within a large string of characters, and convert a character string to all upper- or lowercase. The list of functions follows:

Table 4.3.1. The built-in functions of T-SQL for manipulating strings.

Function	Description
substring	Allows you to retrieve a subset of a string
right	Places the character string a specified number of characters from the right
upper	Converts the string to all uppercase characters
lower	Converts the string to all lowercase characters
charindex	Used to determine the starting position of the literal char or varchar columns specified
patindex	Used to determine the starting position of the char, varchar, or text columns and allows wildcards
ASCII	Gives the ASCII code value of the first character in the string
char	Allows you to enter a character by the ASCII code definition (useful for special characters such as umlauts and accented characters, which do not have dedicated keys on a U.S. English keyboard)
ltrim	Removes leading blanks
rtrim	Removes trailing blanks
replicate	Repeats a character expression a number of times
space	Inserts a string of spaces
str	Converts numbers to characters
stuff	Moves a number of characters from one string and stuffs them into another string
soundex	Converts character strings to codes for purposes of matching and comparing similar sounds with different spellings (used for name matches where spellings vary widely: Chris Christophersen and Kris Kristofferson, for example)
difference	Compares the soundex values to determine the difference between them
+	Adds two or more character or binary strings, column names, or a combination of these

String functions are often used for retrieving data from a number of columns and representing the returned rows as a single data element. A simple example of this is retrieving a list of authors consisting of the authors' last names and first initials. To accomplish this, you might use the following query:

```
select (au_lname + ","  + substring(au_fname,1,1) + "."
from authors
go
```

This query returns a list of authors' last names and first initials in the format Lastname, I (for example, Worden, D). As you can see, the string functions are used to qualify the target select columns and in this example retrieve part of the column and surround the results with formatting characters before concatenating them together.

These functions can be used to place brackets around area codes when retrieving phone numbers or placing dashes or other separators in numbers, as opposed to storing those characters in the database itself.

You can also use the string functions to force the case of the retrieved row. For example, select upper(title) from titles or select lower(title) from titles, if you wanted to make the title appear entirely in upper- or lowercase. When dealing with varchar data when you want to ensure that each column is a certain length, you might choose to use a substring defined to the exact maximum length you want the column. When retrieving character data, you could choose to truncate trailing spaces.

Datetime Functions

Although SQL Server implicitly converts datetime column values to characters for purposes of string functions, a few datetime functions provide some useful services to you as a developer. Sybase has implemented a single datetime datatype, while many other RDBMS vendors have both a date and a time datatype. The SQL Server datetime datatype is precise to 3.3 milliseconds. However, you can leave out aspects of the date or time if you do not know them. In other words, regardless of how precise the datetime datatype is itself, it can still be used to store a simple date or a time without a date. SQL Server places default values into the column if you choose to store only part of the entire datetime value. It is because of these defaults, and the fact that you can choose to store parts, that SQL Server provides datetime functions specific to this datatype. They are as follows:

Table 4.3.2. The T-SQL built-in functions for dates and time.

Function	Description
getdate()	Gets the current date from the system
datename	Returns the specified datepart value for a given date

continues

Table 4.3.2. continued

Function	Description
datepart	Returns the integer value of a datepart for a given date
dateadd	Adds the number of dateparts to the date
datediff	Determines the number of dateparts between two dates

SQL Server uses dateparts to determine which aspect of the entire datetime value you wish to operate on. The dateparts are based on incremental numbers from a defined point. The dateparts for days are values 1 through 7, with 1 being Sunday. To determine what the datepart value is for a given date, you would use the datepart function. To determine the datepart value for the day of the week that December 31, 1999 falls on, you could use the following statement:

```
select datepart (weekday, "Dec 31, 1999")
go
```

The result returned is the datepart value for day of the week; in this case it equals 6. Because you know that datepart 1 for weekday is Sunday, you can figure out what day 6 is, but there is another, perhaps easier way:

```
select datename (weekday, "Dec 31, 1999")
go
```

The result returned tells you that New Year's Eve for the turn of the millennium will be a Friday night. (Excellent news for you party people.)

The datepart function returns the system values, and the datename function tells you what they are in English (unless you have changed your default language, in which case it tells you in the language you set up for your own default). The datediff function allows you to calculate the number of dateparts separating two given dates. For example, if you were calculating the Olympic swim meet records, you could use the datediff function to determine exactly how much faster the gold medal winner was than the silver medal winner.

```
select datediff(millisecond, "12:10:45.345", "12:10:47.232")
go
```

The result returned is 1886, meaning there is exactly 1 second, 886 milliseconds between the two times. As you can see, the date values themselves are always placed within quotes, and in the previous example the hour number had to be supplied for the function to execute properly. The first set of digits before the colon are taken to mean the hour. If you do not have an hour and minute specified, you can use the SQL Server defaults for time, which are 12:30. In this example, the times being compared were actually 10 minutes, 45 seconds, and 10 minutes, 47 seconds. Keep in mind that while milliseconds can easily be calculated manually, the datediff function calculates the time differences in base 60, which is a little harder to figure out with pen and paper. In any event, how you use the date functions depends on the nature of your requirements, and I am sure you do not need to be convinced of the advantages SQL Server offers over manual manipulation of data.

The last date function is the `dateadd` function, which allows you to arrive at a new date by adding dateparts to a date. For example, if you wanted to determine the exact date of 100 days from now, you could use the following expression:

```
select dateadd(day, 100, getdate())
go
```

The returned result is the datetime of the current systems date plus 100 days (convenient if you can't remember "30 days has September, April, June, and November").

The names used to specify dateparts are as follows:

year	yy
quarter	qq
month	mm
dayofyear	dy
day	dd
week	wk
weekday	dw
hour	hh
minute	mi
second	ss
millisecond	ms

Retrieving Data from Datetime Columns

You can use a straightforward WHERE datetime = dd/mi/yyhh:mm:ss, if you happen to know all those items. Because values in datetime fields always have defaults inserted, you might find using LIKE rather than equals to be more effective for many of your query needs. For example, if you simply wish to retrieve time values from a bus schedule, you can structure the query like this:

```
select arrival_time
from schedule
where time like %22:00%
```

All the guidelines for the LIKE statement apply here. The major benefit to using LIKE over equals is that to use equals you must provide the default date of 1-1-1900, which is automatically appended to any datetime entry. There are a few additional points to remember about using LIKE to retrieve from datetime columns. When using the LIKE keyword, SQL Server first converts the dates in the expression into datetime and then into varchar as part of the implicit conversion of the datatype. The display format then consists of the three characters used as short form for the months (Jan, Feb, Mar), two characters for the day, and four characters for the year, with the time expressed in hour and minutes with the suffix AM or PM.

The more flexible input formats for datetimes are not supported when using LIKE. You can incorporate explicit convert parameters into your SQL Statement to work with the format that is most useful for you. For instance, to retrieve the full times for Olympic medal winners while using a LIKE keyword, you would have to structure the query in a manner similar to this:

```
Select name, country, sport, medal, time from medal_winners
where convert(varchar(20), time, 109) like %3:__.___%
```

Using the convert at this point in the query allows you to display the seconds and milliseconds, even though you are using the LIKE keyword for the selection criterion.

Aggregate Functions

Instead of manipulating character strings and the display of the results returned from your query, you may want to know some things about the number of rows that conform to your query's select criteria. You may simply want to count how many occurrences of a particular item there are, or you may want to sum or average the values. These are accomplished through the use of aggregate functions.

The aggregate functions include the following.

Table 4.3.3. T-SQL built-in functions for determining aggregate values.

Function	Description
count (*)	Counts the number of rows retrieved by the select statement
count (*column_name*)	Counts all values in a column, (excluding nulls)
sum (*column_name*)	Adds the values in a column and returns the sum
avg (*column_name*)	Returns the average value in the column
max (*column_name*)	Finds the highest value in the column
min (*column_name*)	Finds the lowest value in the column

For instance, to determine the book with the highest number of sales for the year to date, you could use an aggregate:

```
select max(ytd_sales)
from titles
```

This returns the number that represents the highest number in the `ytd_sales` column of the `titles` table. This number does not tell you much, although this procedure could be useful if you wanted to know what the maximum value in a table was in order to determine appropriate ranges for defining rules or something similar. When using aggregate functions as a qualifier while wanting to retrieve other values as well, you must be careful about the way you structure your query. To use aggregate functions in a WHERE clause, you must contain the aggregate operation in a subquery. For example,

```
select title, ytd_sales
from titles
where titles.ytd_sales =
(select max(ytd_sales) from titles)
go
```

In this case, the subquery performs the select to retrieve the value of the highest `ytd_sales` in `titles`, then retrieves the title and the `ytd_sales` value for the row where `ytd_sales` match. To simply have written the query as

```
select title, max(ytd_sales)
from titles
go
```

would yield a list of every title in the table and the highest value of the `ytd_sales` column along with it. The query would have run, but the results would not have been what you had wanted to retrieve.

Aggregate functions are most often used as part of the GROUP BY and HAVING clauses. These clauses affect the results returned by a select statement. The GROUP BY clause puts the results into groups as specified, and the HAVING clause restricts the groups being returned. Continuing with the title and year to date sales example, assume you wanted to know how much each type of book had sold in the year to date while also displaying the ytd_sales for each book. To achieve this, you would use the GROUP BY clause and an aggregate function as follows:

```
use pubs
go
select type, title, TypeTotal = sum(ytd_sales)
from titles
group by type
go
```

The resulting output looks like this:

```
type    : business
title   : The Busy Executive's Database Guide
ytd_sales: 4095
TypeTotal: 30788

type    : business
title   : Cooking with Computers: Surreptitious Balance Sheets
ytd_sales: 3876
TypeTotal: 30788

type    : business
title   : You Can Combat Computer Stress!
ytd_sales: 18722
TypeTotal: 30788

type    : business
title   : Straight Talk About Computers
ytd_sales: 4095
TypeTotal: 30788
```

By incorporating a HAVING clause into your SQL statement, you can apply search conditions instead of using a WHERE clause. The biggest advantage to using the HAVING clause to accomplish this is your ability to include aggregate functions. As you have seen, WHERE clauses do not allow the incorporation of aggregate functions. To retrieve the same data as before, but restricting the results to only those types whose books have sold more than 10,000 units, you could use the following syntax:

```
use pubs
go
select type, title, ytd_sales, sum1 = sum(ytd_sales)
from titles
group by type
having sum(ytd_sales) > 10000
go
```

This returns output in the same format as the previous listing, but the psychology type has been excluded as a result of the requirement to have year to date sales in excess of 10,000. Through the GROUP BY and HAVING clauses, you can retrieve any rows you require filtered directly through an aggregate function.

Mathematical Functions

As well as the aggregate functions covered earlier, SQL Server provides a number of complex mathematical functions that can be performed during a select statement. These operations include the following.

Table 4.3.4. T-SQL built-in functions for mathematical operations.

Function	Description
abs	Absolute value of the specified expression
acos	Angle in radians whose cosine is the floating point value
asin	Angle in radians whose sine is the floating point value
atan	Angle in radians whose tangent is the floating point value
atn2	Angle in radians whose tangent is expression1/expression2
ceiling	Smallest integer > or = to the numeric expression
cos	Cosine of the angle in radians
cot	Cotangent of the angle in radians
degrees	Degrees converted from radians
exp	Exponent of the defined value
floor	Largest integer < or = to the specified value
log	Natural logarithm of the defined value
log10	Base ten logarithm of the defined value
pi	Constant value of pi
power	Value of the numeric expression to the power specified in the statement
radians	Radians converted from degrees
rand	Random float number using the integer expression as an optional seed
round	Numeric expression rounded off to the precision defined in the integer expression
sign	Pos +1 Zero 0 Neg -1
sin	Sine of the angle in radians
sqrt	Square root of the defined value
tan	Tangent of the angle in radians

Look at an example of how you can use the mathematical functions in a select statement. Assume that you wanted to find the discounts provided for every store in the pubs database and round that number off to the nearest whole number. You could use the following query to achieve this:

```
use pubs
go
select stor_id, round(discount, 0)
from discounts
go
```

As it turns out, the discounts table does not have `stor_id` as a not null field, so when you actually execute this query you get some discounts that do not have associated `stor_ids`, but, hey, this is just an example, right? The point is that the returned discounts are expressed as numbers that have been rounded to the nearest whole number. In this example, the whole number was specified with the 0, indicating that the rounding should take place to 0 decimal points. By specifying the number 2 instead of 0, each discount would have been rounded to the nearest hundredth.

The same structure is used to invoke mathematical functions on any value retrieved from a column or provided as part of the select statement itself.

Systems Functions

Another set of built-in functions returns information about the SQL Server environment in which you are working. You can use these built-in functions to obtain information about the SQL Server, its databases, logins, and contents of the systems tables. The built-in systems functions included with Sybase are as follows:

Table 4.3.5. Built-in systems functions in T-SQL.

Function	Example	Results
DB_NAME	db_name()	The name of the current database
HOST_NAME	host_name()	The name of the computer hosting SQL Server
SUSER_NAME	suser_name()	SQL Server login ID
USER_NAME	user_name()	Your current user name
COL_NAME	col_name(1,1)	The column name of the object ID and the col_id
COL_LENGTH	col_length(table, column)	The length of the column specified
ISNULL	isnull(columnname, "nothing")	Substitutes the string or value expressed when nulls are retrieved from specified column

Function	Example	Results
DB_ID	db_id(pubs)	Returns the database ID for specified database
SUSER_ID	suser_id(sa)	Returns server login ID
USER_ID	user_id(sa)	Returns the database user ID

As well as being useful to determine who and where an application or user are within the SQL Server, systems functions such as ISNULL can be used to translate null values into a returned result that is more meaningful in the context of your current application. The ISNULL systems function could be used to report nothing found, instead of an empty column with the following syntax:

```
select title_id, isnull(notes, "not yet defined")
from titles
```

This returns all the rows of the titles table and inserts the string "not yet defined" in place of the empty space of the records where the value of the notes column is null.

Changing the Order of the Output

T-SQL also provides extensions that give you greater control of the sorting of the results from your queries. The ORDER BY clause in a select statement allows you to rearrange the order of the retrieved rows according to whatever criteria you determine. If you have a clustered index on a table and you wish to see the retrieved results in that order, you would not need to use an ORDER BY clause. However, if you do not have a clustered index, you will get the output in the order that the rows were added to the table.

The default for a query is to return the rows according to how they are physically stored in the table. To override this, you would use the ORDER BY clause. ORDER BY always follows a GROUP BY clause (if there is one in the query), which allows you to sort the order within the groups defined in the select statement. Combining these clauses with the ability to sort in ascending or descending order based on columns or even defined expressions gives you a great deal of control over the display of output from your query. The default sort order when using the ORDER BY clause is ascending, and you can sort more than one column. For example, this query retrieves all titles and publishers and sorts the resulting output first by publisher and then by publication date.

```
use pubs
go
select title, pub_id, pubdate from titles
order by pub_id, pubdate
```

The resulting output looks like this:

```
title  : Emotional Security: A New Algorithm
pub_id : 0736
pubdate: Jun 12 1985 12:00AM

title  : Prolonged Data Deprivation: Four Case Studies
pub_id : 0736
pubdate: Jun 12 1985 12:00AM

title  : Is Anger the Enemy?
pub_id : 0736
pubdate: Jun 15 1985 12:00AM

title  : You Can Combat Computer Stress!
pub_id : 0736
pubdate: Jun 30 1985 12:00AM

title  : Life Without Fear
pub_id : 0736
pubdate: Oct 5 1985 12:00AM

title  : Silicon Valley Gastronomic Treats
pub_id : 0877
pubdate: Jun 9 1985 12:00AM

title  : Sushi, Anyone?
pub_id : 0877
pubdate: Jun 12 1985 12:00AM
```

As you can see, the resulting list displays the title first, then the pub_id, and for multiple publ_ids the date published is used as the sort criteria. You can also sort by relationships defined in expressions associated with the ORDER BY clause. For example, to determine which books contribute the most to a publisher financially, starting with the big sellers and working down, you could use this query:

```
use pubs
go
select titles.title_id, price, qty, price*qty
from titles, sales
where titles.title_id = sales.title_id
order by price*qty desc
```

The results look like this:

title_id	price	qty	contribution
==========	=======================	======	========================
PC8888	20.00	50	1,000.00
TC3218	20.95	40	838.00
PS2091	10.95	75	821.25
PC1035	22.95	30	688.50
PS1372	21.59	20	431.80
BU7832	19.99	15	299.85
PS3333	19.99	15	299.85
TC7777	14.99	20	299.80
BU1111	11.95	25	298.75
TC4203	11.95	20	239.00
PS2091	10.95	20	219.00
BU1032	19.99	10	199.90
MC2222	19.99	10	199.90
PS7777	7.99	25	199.75
PS2106	7.00	25	175.00
PS2091	10.95	10	109.50
BU2075	2.99	35	104.65
BU1032	19.99	5	99.95
MC3021	2.99	25	74.75
MC3021	2.99	15	44.85
PS2091	10.95	3	32.85

It is not necessary to retrieve a column to sort the results by that column. You can order by any value contained in the table or tables used to retrieve rows with your query. However, you cannot specify more than 16 columns in the ORDER BY clause. ORDER BY can be used on all columns except text and image datatypes, and when using an ORDER BY, null values will come before any others.

There is another significant method of organizing the output from a select statement using an ORDER BY clause—the COMPUTE BY T-SQL extension.

Using COMPUTE BY in a SELECT Statement

First, you must always precede a COMPUTE BY clause with the ORDER BY statement. The columns to be manipulated in the COMPUTE BY clause must be listed in the ORDER BY clause, and they must be in the same left-to-right order, start with the same expression, and contain all the expressions in the ORDER BY clause.

The only exception to this rule is for calculating subtotals on columns. In that case, you can use the compute statement without a corresponding ORDER BY clause.

You would use a COMPUTE BY statement to calculate subtotals and to provide control-break summaries of sorted results. To give you a better idea of what this means, look at the results of the sales by type for the publishers in the pubs database:

```
use pubs
go
select titles_type, price, price*qty
from titles, sales
where titles_title_id = sales.title_id
order by type,pub_id,qty desc
compute sum(qty) by type, pub_id
go
```

Summary

This chapter has taken you through the syntax and structure for writing statements with T-SQL. This language is used not only for selects, inserts, and updates, but for using expressions in rules, triggers, and stored procedures. T-SQL forms the building blocks with which you create all the other objects that make SQL Server uniquely powerful and flexible.

You saw how and when to use string, aggregate, and mathematical functions, as well as display options for returned rows using ORDER BY, GROUP BY, and COMPUTE BY clauses.

Many of the administrative features supported by T-SQL extensions have been covered in other chapters. This structure allows you to see the syntax of how something is done at the same time as you are exposed to the implications and trade-offs inherent in the operation. This chapter was intended to provide you with a more in-depth look at how you can manipulate your data and structure statements to allow you a great deal of freedom in retrieving exactly the data you require. By reading this chapter, you should not only have a better idea of exactly how to use TransAct SQL to select and update data but also how you can use the powerful T-SQL extensions to perform sophisticated calculation, formatting, and sort functions.

4.4

Writing Stored Procedures

As previously discussed, stored procedures are a powerful extension to your SQL Server RDBMS. Stored procedures make your server programmable, which gives you a great deal more control over the server side of the client/server equation. Like rules and triggers, stored procedures are written in T-SQL. All the operations supported in a regular interactive query can be incorporated into a stored procedure. Additionally, stored procedures can accommodate batches of SQL statements, incorporating the control-of-flow features of T-SQL. They can even allow you to pass parameters to them as well as develop specialized error handling and messaging routines as part of the stored procedure.

This chapter takes you through the use and structure of customized SQL Server stored procedures. By the end of this chapter, you should have a good idea of what you can use stored procedures to accomplish and exactly how to incorporate T-SQL statements into a stored procedure.

Stored Procedures Defined

A stored procedure is a collection of T-SQL statements that reside on the SQL Server and can be executed by any user who has been granted execute permission. Stored procedures can accept parameters and return parameters, values, and messages, as well as call additional stored procedures. Stored procedures execute faster than commands with identical syntax issued from an interactive or applications session. Stored procedures are parsed and stored with the query plan that was developed the first time the stored procedure was compiled and executed. Other queries must be parsed, compiled, and have a query plan developed for them each time the query is run. Stored procedures are sometimes automatically recompiled, depending on whether certain operations were performed on the database. For example, if a referenced table or index was dropped and re-created, the stored procedure would recompile to ensure that all the required objects were available. After successfully recompiling, the stored procedure would once again be executed as stored, until another such major database activity takes place. It is possible to define procedures that must be recompiled each time they are run, by using the `with recompile` flag.

The Benefits of Stored Procedures

Throughout this book you have been exposed to the argument that your SQL Server operates as a hub around which various client programs and data access methods are supported. By allowing you to place your queries into stored procedures, you not only increase execution time of the query, but reduce network traffic. Because the query is already stored on the server, the client must transfer only the stored procedure name and any parameters that are to be passed to it prior to execution. Although this might not seem a significant savings in a high-speed LAN environment, it can certainly improve user perception of systems performance in a WAN or even a dial-up communications setting.

Another important benefit of using stored procedures is the ability to isolate the permissions necessary to execute the procedure from granting access to the underlying database objects referenced by the stored procedure. In other words, users who are able to execute a stored procedure might not have access to the table being operated on by the stored procedure. Like the concept of using views to ensure that users can see only the data you want, you can use stored procedures to ensure that the data is retrieved, manipulated, or deleted in a predetermined fashion.

Of course, it is not necessary to develop stored procedures as part of your Sybase client/server solution. They are provided only as one more method to meet your client/server application requirements. No strict rules exist regarding when to use stored procedures. Some developers use them extensively and merely set up the client programs to pass parameters and accept results returned from the procedures. Other applications minimize the use of stored procedures to perform as much work as possible on the processor of the client machine. Whatever you choose to do, you should be aware that incorporating stored procedures has many performance and architectural benefits and that you will likely find a few key uses for them on your site.

Writing Stored Procedures

The syntax to create a simple stored procedure is as follows:

```
use pubs
go
Create proc sp_getitle as
select * from titles
```

To run the procedure you simply enter

```
sp_getitle
go
```

The results from this procedure are identical to entering the select statement from ISQL or another client program that supports interactive SQL to the server.

In and of itself, a stored procedure of this nature hardly seems impressive. However, consider that if you revoked select on titles from Public, no member of the group Public would be able to retrieve data in the titles table in the pubs database. However, if you (as the DBO or SA) granted exec on sp_getitle to Public, even though members of the Public group could not select data out of the titles table directly, they could still get a listing of the titles by executing the sp_getitle stored procedure. From this you can see that even the simplest stored procedures have something to offer in terms of increased security.

However, you might not want to restrict your users to always retrieving everything from a table. To get around this, you can structure your stored procedure to accept parameters. For example, if you wanted to create a stored procedure like the preceding one, but wanted to restrict the returned result set to titles with a pubdate that fell between two dates, you could use the following syntax:

```
create proc sp_getitlebydate
(@first_date datetime, @last_date datetime)
as
select * from titles
where pubdate > @first_date and pubdate < @last_date
```

When executing this stored procedure, you would use this command:

```
sp_getitlebydate "Nov 1 1984", "Nov 1 1990"
```

The results returned would consist of the 17 titles whose pubdates fall within that range.

It is also possible to define defaults for the parameters when you create the stored procedure. By using defaults, the user of the procedure would need to enter only the parameters unique to their query; otherwise they could simply execute the procedure and the defaults would operate. To create a procedure that used an arbitrary date as the default for the first_date parameter in the sp_getitlebydate procedure, you could use the following syntax:

```
create proc sp_getitlebydate
(@first_date datetime = "Nov 1 1985")
as
select * from titles
where pubdate >@first_date and pubdate <getdate()
```

Unfortunately, there are no facilities for editing an existing stored procedure. To modify your procedure, you must first drop it and then re-create it using the new syntax. This is yet another reason why you should use scripts extensively to create your database objects, including stored procedures. The syntax for dropping a procedure is very similar to any of the other drop commands:

```
drop proc sp_getitlebydate
```

This drops the sp_getitlebydate procedure and allows you to create a new one.

Returning Values and Status Messages from Stored Procedures

Whenever you execute a stored procedure, a result code is returned, indicating the status of your procedure. If the procedure executes successfully, the result code is 0. If it fails, it returns a result code ranging from -1 to -99, depending on the nature of the failure. You can test for return status within your stored procedure and take appropriate action, depending on the status result returned. You can also define your own status codes and error messages within your stored procedure definition; however, the -1 through -99 result codes are reserved by Sybase. You can use positive numbers or -100, -101, and so on.

To write a stored procedure that defines a return status, you would use the following syntax:

```
/*      Procedure to detect status code and print customized error
     ➡ message */
create proc get_publisher_proc
(@pubid char(4))
as
if @pubid = null
    begin
    print "Must supply a publisher id number"
    end
    return 13
if not exists (select * from publishers where pub_id = @pubid)
    begin
    print "No such publisher id number"
    end
    return -666
select * from publishers
where pubid = @pubid
```

This procedure simply takes the returned result code and checks to see if it is something other than zero, because SQL Server returns a 0 for success. If the procedure was executed successfully, the row from the publishers table is returned, giving the user a pretty good indication that the procedure worked. However, if the pub_id is not in the table or if a null value instead of the pub_id was entered on the command line, an error message is printed.

Through working and experimenting with stored procedures, you will become familiar with the syntax and how flexible you can make your procedures. As a general rule, you should anticipate the error conditions that will likely result when someone executes your stored procedures and incorporate meaningful error messages into them. Like any form of programming, plentiful comments make maintaining and debugging stored procedures easier.

As you can see, stored procedures provide a very powerful and flexible method of programming your SQL Server to allow and restrict access to data as well as building methods of modifying data in complete sets or blocks of statements, or not at all.

Stored Procedure Restrictions

There are some restrictions to what you can do with stored procedures. Stored procedures cannot contain the following statements:

```
Create View
Create Default
Create Rule
Create Trigger
Create Procedure
```

You can issue the create table statement, but the create table portion of the statement must come first in the procedure, before any reference to it. You cannot create, drop, then re-create a table with the same name as part of one procedure.

Remote Procedures

One of the facilities provided by SQL Server is the ability to execute stored procedures on a remote SQL Server. In this case, all the rules for establishing remote communications between servers apply—you must have the remote server listed through sp_addserver, and you must have the appropriate logins and entry in both machines' interfaces file. However, assuming that two (or more) SQL Servers can talk to one another, to execute a stored procedure remotely you only have to specify the name of the procedure, including the remote server name.

For example,

```
execute remoteserver.pubs.dbo.sp_storedprocedure
```

In this case, the stored procedure sp_storedprocedure owned by the DBO of the pubs database would be executed on the remoteserver. You can incorporate remote stored procedures into local stored procedures and triggers.

Summary

With the exceptions noted, primarily create database objects commands, you can incorporate the full range of T-SQL commands into a stored procedure. These stored procedures can be executed by triggers, other stored procedures, and by applications and users both on the local SQL Server and indirectly through remote SQL Servers.

You use stored procedures to automate difficult or complex database activities, improve security and restrict access to data, or to ensure the integrity of your database. You can also improve application response time, depending on the nature of your query and the demands on the resources of your particular environment.

You have seen examples of stored procedures that demonstrate how flexible and powerful these database objects can be. You can write your own stored procedures that take input parameters, have conditions and branches, and provide customized error messages. Stored procedures can also retrieve values that are passed as parameters themselves to other procedures.

As you work with stored procedures, you should take care to ensure that your database environment restricts the dropping of objects on which stored procedures depend. Like any other form of programming, it is possible to create user-unfriendly code, which always proves difficult to maintain. By employing the good programming habits you have already developed, you can ensure that the power and flexibility of your stored procedures are not offset by complexity and turgidity.

4.5

Triggers and Referential Integrity

You were introduced to the concept of primary, foreign and common keys for SQL Server tables in the chapter dealing with data modeling in Section 2. It should be noted that SQL Server versions prior to System 10 do not support declarative referential integrity. That is to say that you cannot simply specify a child table with foreign keys when it is created and ensure that updates, deletes, or insertions to the child tables will correspondingly reflect the changes in the parent table. How these declarative referential integrity features are implemented in System 10 is covered in the chapter that covers the unique features of SQL Server Release 10. But wait! Even if you are intending to use SQL Server 10, you should still read through this chapter. Triggers are the means used to enforce referential integrity in pre-Release 10 versions of SQL Server, but they also allow you to accomplish much more.

In this chapter, you will see how you can define triggers and stored procedures to allow you to explicitly incorporate referential integrity into your database. Both of these techniques build on the understanding of the data you would have developed during the data modeling process. Additionally, you can incorporate your understanding of T-SQL and stored procedure capabilities into the definition of triggers for your database. By combining these into your triggers, you can enforce any business rules that can be expressed using T-SQL as well as ensuring the integrity of the data held by your database tables.

Referential Integrity

When you first create your tables in a SQL Server database, you may drop any or all of them as you wish, provided that you have appropriate permissions. As the database owner, for example, you are free to drop whichever database objects you see fit. In some cases, however, this would not be an appropriate action because there may be data in other tables that depend on the table you just dropped. As you know, a normalized data model will be structured with tables containing primary and foreign keys. A table containing employee benefits, for example, might have a foreign key consisting of the employee number. The employee number would be the primary key of the employee table. To retrieve an employee record complete with benefits, you perform a join of the two tables on the employee number column. That's fine, but we just established that the database or table owner could drop any database object he or she chooses. This means the employee record could be dropped without deleting the corresponding row in the benefits table. The result is that the values in the benefits table can become suspect or meaningless.

By ensuring that any table having a primary key cannot be dropped when another table contains that column, you are ensuring referential integrity. Actually, this process goes beyond the wholesale dropping of tables. To truly maintain referential integrity, you must ensure that no row on the table with a primary key can be deleted without first modifying the row in any tables that contain that value as a foreign key. When the primary key of a table is changed or deleted, where another table maintains that column as a foreign key, the data must be changed accordingly or deleted in the second table. If the foreign key is changed or deleted, some method of validating this change against the table holding the primary key should be enforced. The main point here is that when you can blow away an entire table with data that other tables depend on to be meaningful, let alone delete or modify a single row, you have a potential data-integrity problem that should be addressed.

In SQL Server, this problem is addressed through triggers.

Using Triggers

Triggers are defined for update, insert, and delete operations on tables. You may have only one of each for any given table. When an insert, delete, or update takes place on a table for which a trigger has been defined, that trigger will fire once. If the trigger calls for a modification to another table for which a trigger has been defined, that trigger will fire. Triggers can fire up to 16 levels of nesting. To allow more than this would be to potentially allow circular referencing of tables so that the triggers never completed their operations. In the event that more than 16 triggers are fired as a result of a single operation, the whole shebang is aborted and rolled back.

Triggers can evaluate defined conditions, and if the conditions are not met, the batch of statements that fired the trigger are cancelled and the data returned to its original condition. Triggers have two special tables: the inserted and deleted tables. Any rows affected by an operation for which a trigger has been defined will be written to these tables. Any values to be added will be written to the inserted table, and any values to be deleted will be added to the deleted table. If the trigger comes across a condition that forces it to cancel the statement, the values are read back from the deleted table. Update transactions are treated as a combination of the two, as the old data is deleted and the new data is inserted. In all cases, the original data values are held in the trigger's deleted table. This is how the trigger is able to roll back the changes once they have been completed, but the trigger requires a subsequent operation to successfully execute before the changes become final.

Trigger Syntax

You may use virtually all of the T-SQL statements available to you when create a stored procedure. A trigger does not take parameters, however, nor can a trigger create database objects. Within the trigger, Sybase supports an additional feature, the

IF UPDATE function, to determine whether a specific column has been updated for an update trigger. This allows you to refine your trigger operations to execute depending on which column has been updated.

To create a trigger, you could use the following syntax:

```
CREATE TRIGGER new_trigger
ON table_name
FOR {insert/update/delete}
AS
SQL Statement batch...
IF UPDATE (column_name) [AND/OR UPDATE (column_name)]
SQL Statement batch...
```

It is not necessary to include an IF UPDATE statement, nor are you limited to one IF UPDATE per trigger as implied in the example above. IF UPDATE tests may be combined with Boolean AND and OR operators.

Cascading Deletes

The term *cascading delete* refers to the deletion of all occurences of a key value across a number of tables. For example, if a book title were to be deleted in the pubs database, it would have to be removed not only from the titles table but also from titlesauthor and sales. Leaving a title value in those tables without a corresponding row in the titles table would make the row in titlesauthor and sales meaningless. To delete a title then, you must establish a cascading delete and you would do this in the form of a trigger.

The syntax to accomplish this could be as follows:

```
create trigger cascade_delete_titles
on titles
for delete
as
delete sales
from sales, deleted
where sales.title_id = deleted.title_id
delete titleauthor
from titleauthor, deleted
where titleauthor.title_id =deleted.title_id
delete roysched
from roysched, deleted
where roysched.title_id = deleted.title_id
```

This trigger will fire whenever you attempt to delete a title from titles, and ensure that any of the tables in the pubs database that could contain a reference to that title_id will delete the value from the tables if they find it. Another example of a good time to employ triggers is in updating tables with foreign keys. You can define a trigger on insert, which will ensure that there are rows in the tables corresponding to its foreign keys. For instance, you would want to ensure that you had a book stored in the titles row before you could update the sales table. This would explicitly enforce the business rule that you have to have a book to sell a book. A trigger of this type could look like this:

```
Create trigger foreign_key_sales_trg
on sales
for insert, update
as
declare @num_rows int
select @num_rows=@@rowcount
if @num_rows = 0
return
if (select count (*)
from titles, inserted
where titles.title_id=inserted.title_id) !=@num_rows
begin
raiserror 999 "No valid title_id exists for this sale - Denied"
rollback transaction
return
end
if (select count (*)
from stores, inserted
where stores.stor_id= inserted.stor_id) !=@num_rows
begin
raiserror 888 "No valid stor_id exists for this sale - Denied"
rollback transaction
end

return
```

This trigger looks first to determine how many rows were modified by the operation. If there were no rows affected, it quits. If one or more rows were affected, the trigger counts first the number of `title_ids` in the special inserted table to ensure that there are matching `title_ids` in the titles table for each book inserted or updated in the sales table. The titles table holds `title_id` as a primary key, whereas it is a foreign key for the sales table. If the count does not match, the transaction is rolled back. However, if the titles match, the trigger then counts the number of `stor_ids` in both the inserted and the stores tables for the same reason explained previously. If the count matches, the trigger completes, leaving the insert operation as performed. However, if there is a discrepancy between the two, the transaction is rolled back and an error message raised for the user or application to deal with.

Trigger Behavior

You cannot run triggers as you can stored procedures. Triggers are activated only when the operation for which they have been defined is performed. That is to say, they are fired only when an update, insert, or delete is performed. Triggers fire only once per SQL statement, so there may be cases in which multiple rows are affected by the statement. To determine this in the body of your trigger, you can retrieve or refer to the value of @@rowcount, which stores the number of rows affected by a SQL statement when it has been executed. You can use this value to operate on summary values by the number of rows affected by the statement that fired the trigger. You should ensure, however, that your test of @@rowcount occurs toward the beginning of the statement, as an IF statement, or any other statement that does not return rows will reset @@rowcount to zero.

You should avoid incorporating SELECT statements into your triggers. This is especially true for those that return results from the select and display them to the user, as you would have to trap and manage these results within every application that fired the trigger. Also keep in mind that if you rename any of the objects that are referenced by the trigger, you must drop and recreate the trigger to have it reference the new object name. Like stored procedures, there is no editing facility for triggers.

Again, the same TransAct-SQL syntax is used to create the trigger as for stored procedures and statement batches. Triggers cannot create database objects, however. Triggers are useful for inserte, update, and delete operations on primary and foreign keys, as well as for ensuring that derived data is recalculated when the values in the base tables have changed.

You may view the syntax of a trigger through sp_helptext trigger_name, and you can rename the trigger with sp_rename. Using sp_depends, however, will not list the triggers that are defined on a table. To see the object references of a trigger, you must use sp_depends trigger_name. You should use naming conventions that make it easy to determine the table and operation for which your trigger has been defined. You may define triggers only on tables; you may not define triggers on views or temporary tables. Any insert, update, or delete operation on a table with a defined trigger will fire it; however, fast bulk copy and truncate table do not activate triggers.

The active trigger is always the last one defined for a table, and the permission to create triggers for a table always accrues to the table owner. Permission may not be transferred.

Trigger overhead is generally quite low, as the inserted and deleted tables are maintained in memory, rather than written to disk. Triggers may involve, however, some time to execute when referencing many tables that may have to be loaded into memory from disk.

Nested triggers can create a deadlock. For example, say that you attempt an operation for which a trigger is defined—an update, perhaps—and a trigger fires, making a change to another table also containing a trigger. If that trigger causes a change to the original table, the transaction could end up deadlocked. This is because the transaction cannot be committed until the triggers have fired and completed successfully. The first transaction would be holding an exclusive lock on the data pages affected by the SQL operation. If a subsequently fired trigger required access to a page locked by the initial operation, it would neither complete nor fail. It would wait for access to the data pages until the SQL Server detects the deadlock and kills the transaction. It is important to follow through the trail of nested triggers to ensure that the firing of nested triggers makes sense within the context of the application as well as from a database integrity standpoint.

Finally, it is not possible to get caught in an endless loop of firing triggers. Well, it would be possible, but triggers can only be nested to a finite level; that is, they can call up to only 15 other triggers for a total of 16 triggers. If trigger a modifies table b, which fires trigger b, which modifies trigger a, well, this kind of loop can only execute to a total of 16 triggers before it aborts and the transactions are rolled back. The support for nested triggers is set for the SQL Server as a whole by the systems administrator. The rollback of the entire transaction will preserve your data, but you will want to use comments, messages and other error-handling methods in your triggers to preserve your sanity, should one of these loops happen to you.

Summary

The capability to define triggers rounds out the SQL Server toolset for incorporating rules, ensuring data integrity and supporting maximum recoverability. Although you may choose to develop triggers only to ensure referential integrity, your ability to create complex checks and balances on your database is greatly enhanced through the triggers facility. Through calling stored procedures and remote stored procedures, you can ensure that your data is synchronized with other databases resident on other SQL Servers.

You can use triggers to compare the values of the table, before and after the defined operation has been performed. For example, if you have a legislated requirement to keep rent increases below a certain percent, the trigger can calculate the percent value of a change to the base rent if your table contained rented apartments. If the rent increase submitted for an update violated the percentage defined in the trigger, the transaction would be aborted. You can write your trigger in such a way as to compare the new values with the values in the old version of the table, which is maintained in the deleted table. By providng you with these two tables, SQL Server gives you a much greater range of potential values to compare before finalizing a transaction.

Additionally, triggers allow you to determine why a transaction should be rejected and return an error message that allows the user to diagnose the problem and take corrective measures before trying again. By defining triggers within a transaction, you can ensure that the entire block of SQL statements will be rolled back. Triggers are an excellent means of ensuring an all-or-nothing approach to involved update, insert, or delete operations across mulitple tables. Even though many rows or columns are being updated by your transaction, the trigger fires only once for the entire transaction.

4.6

Writing Transactions
in SQL Server

Many of the examples you have seen used to demonstrate the T-SQL syntax have been structured as simple *ad hoc* queries. This is somewhat due to the provisions of ISQL as the standard means of accessing a SQL Server. ISQL lends itself to an interactive process of querying and manipulating database objects. However, most organizations that have acquired SQL Server will want to structure some kind of application to manipulate their data. In this chapter you learn about the structure and implications of transactions in the SQL Server environment. This includes a discussion on how SQL Server handles committing or rolling back changes to the database made by a transaction. As an online transaction processing (OLTP) RDBMS, Sybase has provided many controls over writing changes to the database with transactions. In this chapter you learn about the structure of SQL statements within transactions and how various conditions affect the rollback of data for partially executed transactions. Additionally, you will see how stored procedures and triggers can be defined to include transactions and the implications of executing sp's and triggers containing those transactions.

Rollback is a key attribute of transaction processing within SQL Server. By treating a series of SQL statements as a single, indivisible unit, Sybase can guarantee that all the changes in a transaction are actually made to the database or else the data is returned to its original condition. Toward the end of this chapter, you are given a high-level overview of how distributed transactions are handled across multiple SQL Servers using the two-phase commit protocol. By the end of this chapter, you should have a solid idea as to how and why you would use transactions in developing your SQL Server applications.

Statement Blocks, Batches, and Transactions Defined

If a select is considered a single SQL statement, a block can be seen as a discrete group of one or more SQL statements. A block of select, insert, update, or delete statements can be manipulated with the control-of-flow extensions provided by T-SQL. To create discrete blocks, use the BEGIN and END statements. These blocks can themselves be manipulated with such T-SQL extensions as IF, ELSE, WHILE, RETURN, and WAITFOR. Taken together, these blocks are put into a batch of statements. A batch contains the blocks of statements and the batch delimiter. For SQL Server, the default delimiter for a batch of statements is the word go.

As you saw in Chapter 4.3, "TransAct SQL," many useful programming constructs and functions within T-SQL allow you to build batches that support messaging, condition testing, and all the other features you would expect from a programming environment.

Special Batches

Several commands, such as use, create, and some set commands, require that each command be contained in a discrete batch. These commands are as follows:

```
use database

set showplan

create procedure

create rule

create default

create trigger

create view
```

You may directly call a stored procedure only on the first line of a batch of statements; otherwise you must precede it with the exec command. For example, the following batch would work:

```
sp_help
select * from tablename
go
```

To have a stored procedure execute on any other line, you must use a syntax similar to this:

```
select * from tablename
exec sp_help
go
```

To incorporate comments into a batch, for improved readability and decreased maintenance effort, you must precede the comment with the /* symbols and end the line with the */ symbols. For example:

```
/*   Comments are within these symbols.                    */
/*   You must have them on every line to be commented.      */
/*   There must be closing comment symbols for every open set.  */
```

Usually, a batch is sent to the SQL Server for execution as the result of an application using OPEN CLIENT interface or as a text file from an ISQL-like interface. SQL Server evaluates the entire batch for valid syntax, compliance with rules, and existence of referenced database objects. The batch of statements is then executed and the results or error messages returned. The entire batch must execute successfully or it is aborted. This may not be the behavior you want, however. SQL Server treats batches as atomic units—the entire batch, regardless of the number of SQL statements within it, must complete entirely or not at all.

Containing Batches within Transactions

You can selectively determine changes to be committed or rolled back in the event of an error or failure. To control exactly when and how far to roll back database changes made as a result of a batch of statements, you would write a transaction. Through the use of transactions, you as a developer can determine when to commit database changes and how far a series of statements will be rolled back for an error or systems failure. Transactions are a series of statements that the SQL Server treats as a single event. These transactions dictate which changes to a database will be logged and also which locks will be placed on the data pages of tables affected by the transaction. The locking of data pages can have a significant impact on the user's experience of the application's response time. The way locks work and their impact on performance is covered in later in this section. For now, look at the way transactions are structured.

Transactions

By default, each insert, update, and delete statement issued against tables in a SQL Server database is treated as a transaction. SQL Server has four main transaction control statements:

BEGIN TRANSACTION [name]   This initiates a transaction and optionally names it.

SAVE TRANSACTION other_name   This specifies a point in the transaction for partial rollback.

ROLLBACK TRANSACTION [name or savepoint name]   This reverses the changes to the savepoint named or to the beginning of the transaction if no name is provided.

COMMIT TRANSACTION   This writes the changes made within the transaction to disk, making the changes permanent.

You don't need to enter the word transaction as part of the transaction syntax; you can use tran as the short form with begin, save, rollback, and commit.

The main characteristic of a transaction is that until it has completed successfully, the database changes specified in the transaction can be rolled back. These changes are written first to the transaction log and secondly to the database. The process of making the changes to the affected tables themselves is known as the commit. This process is most useful when making a series of changes to multiple tables in a database. For example, here is how you would write a transaction that adds a new book and author to the pubs database:

```
use pubs
go
begin tran new_book

insert titles
     values ("PC8088","Sybase Developers Guide",
"business","null",null,null, null, null, "null",
     "May 1, 1994")
insert titleauthor
     values ("403-275-6180", "PC8088")
insert authors
     values ("403-275-6180","Worden", "Daniel", "416-597-
9258","null","null","null","null",1)
commit tran
```

In this example, all the insert statements must be executed successfully or the entire set is rolled back. However, if you wanted to ensure that the first two statements executed even if the last one failed (which it would if the author already existed in pubs), you could structure the transactions like this:

```
use pubs
go
begin tran new_book

insert titles
     values ("PC8088","Sybase Developers Guide",
"business","null", null, null, null, null, "null",
     "May 1, 1994")
insert titleauthor
     values ("403-275-6180", "PC8088")

save tran newbooktran
if not exists (select * from authors where au_id = "403-275-6180")
insert authors
     values ("403-275-6180","Worden", "Daniel", "416-597-
9258","null","null","null","null",1)
else
rollback newbooktran
commit tran
```

With this modification, the title and titleauthor values are still inserted, even if the insert authors statement fails. You would generally incorporate condition testing to determine whether to roll back your changes. In this example, you are looking for the existence of an author in the table already. If not found, the values are inserted;

if a row with that value for author ID already exists, the insert statement is rolled back to the savepoint. Without the save tran tran_name statement, the entire transaction would have been rolled back.

You can write your transaction with multiple begin and commit statements; however, SQL Server ignores additional begin and commit tran commands and operates only on the first and last ones. Placing additional begin and commit tran statements in a transaction can serve as documentation of the levels of transaction nesting, but the transaction is still treated as a single block for rollback purposes. To manage the commit and rollback of changes made within a transaction, you must use the save tran feature. You can have multiple save tran names within a transaction, and you can name your rollback to effect a rollback to the named savepoint. Although you use names for each save tran command, you do not name the transactions with the begin tran statement. You can name the tran at the first begin tran statement (and only the first), but using transaction names in stored procedures or triggers can cause errors. For this reason, you should restrict using names within a transaction to your save tran <arbitrary name> operation. A rollback tran command without a savepoint name refers to the entire transaction.

Incorporating Stored Procedures and Remote Procedure Calls within Transactions

You can incorporate rollback commands into the stored procedures you write for your SQL Server. However, unlike its behavior within a transaction, the rollback command in a stored procedure rolls back only changes made before the stored procedure; it does not abort the entire transaction. This is useful for ensuring that some of the changes you want a transaction to make are actually committed regardless of whether another part successfully executes. By calling a stored procedure within your transaction, you essentially segregate the two transactions from the standpoint of the rollback. The rollback statement is contained within the stored procedure. In the event of a failure, the stored procedure rolls back the changes made by the transaction but continues to execute the remaining statements within the transaction. A rollback within the transaction aborts the transaction as a whole. If you know you want database changes made as part of your transaction regardless of the successful execution of other operations, you would place the changes you want done last in the transaction and call stored procedures containing rollbacks for the conditional operations.

If you execute a remote procedure call as part of a transaction that is subsequently aborted, the rollback does not affect or undo the operations performed by the remote procedure call. To incorporate multiple servers into one transaction that can be rolled back, you must use two-phase commitment. System 10 products such as Replication Server and Omni Server Gateway have been developed to assist you in achieving this capability more easily. However, the default behavior of rollback is not to roll back changes performed through a remote procedure call if the transaction is aborted or rolled back.

Rollbacks and Triggers

If a transaction attempts to modify a table with a trigger containing a rollback that gets fired, the rollback in the trigger aborts the entire transaction, unlike stored procedure operation. By defining your trigger with a rollback statement, the trigger not only refuses to allow the changes to the table but does not allow any of the changes made by the transaction that fired the trigger. This presupposes, of course, that the transaction did not pass all the criteria defined in the trigger and was unsuccessful. Transactions that perform operations successfully passing the trigger's conditions move on to the next statement defined until the transaction is completed and the database changes are committed.

Any additional transactions or operations performed by the trigger are also rolled back if the transaction that caused the trigger to fire is aborted and rolled back. If you contain a transaction within a trigger, you can use the save to tran savepoint name to keep the batch or other procedures from being affected if a rollback occurs.

Nesting Transactions

As mentioned earlier, you can nest multiple begin and commit transaction statements within a single transaction. Although they do not actually affect rollbacks, they can be used to keep track of the level of nesting being performed. This is useful for displaying messages to help in debugging a transaction. Transactions use a global variable to track the nesting level. Each begin tran statement within a batch increments @@trancount by one, and each nested commit tran decrements @@trancount by one. The entire transaction is not committed until the value of @@trancount equals 0. Every use of a begin tran statement requires a matching commit tran for the transaction to execute.

Error Handling within Transactions

Failure of a transaction yields an error message indicating the reason that the transaction did not execute, if it involves a missing or invalid database object name. The returned error message is the same as a simple select using the same statement. However, when a transaction is rolled back, the message is a little more cryptic, typically looking something like this:

```
MSG 513, Level 16 State 1:
Server 'SYBASE' Procedure 'newproc', Line 4:
A column insert or update conflicts with a rule imposed by a previous
create rule command. The command was aborted. The conflict occurred in
database 'pubs', table 'titles', column 'pubdate'.
Command has been aborted.
```

In this case the stored procedure newproc, which contained a transaction that would have entered a new book title in the titles table, has violated a business rule bound to the table. The transaction was rolled back. You can write your stored procedures and triggers to test for an error level with the @@error global variable. Depending on the value of @@error, you might decide that you wanted the transaction to commit anyway rather than automatically abort. On the other hand, by making the transaction roll back, you can protect yourself against poorly constructed queries and applications. You can test the errorlevel within your transaction by selecting the value of the errorlevel and branching to an appropriate condition. Listing 4.6.1 shows an example.

Listing 4.6.1. The use of error handling and messaging within a stored procedure.

```
/*
** This procedure will delete from the titleauthor, sales, and title
** tables. After each delete, @@error is stored, to be printed in case
** something is wrong. If all 3 deletes worked, the transaction will
** be committed. Otherwise, any errors from the 3 tables will be
** reported and the transaction rolled back.
*/

use pubs
go

drop proc delete_title
go

create proc delete_title @title_id tid
as

declare @save_err_titleauthor int, @save_err_sales int
declare @save_err_titles int
declare @err_msg char(70)

begin transaction

delete titleauthor
from titleauthor
where title_id = @title_id
```

```
select @save_err_titleauthor = @@error

delete sales
from sales
where title_id = @title_id

select @save_err_sales = @@error

delete titles
from titles
where title_id = @title_id

select @save_err_titles = @@error

if (@save_err_titleauthor = 0 and @save_err_sales = 0 and
    @save_err_titles = 0)
  begin
    print 'No errors'
    commit transaction
    return(0)
  end
else
  begin
    if (@save_err_titleauthor != 0)
      begin
        select @err_msg = 'Error # ' +
          convert(char(5),@save_err_titleauthor) +
          ' occurred while attempting to delete from titleauthor'
        print @err_msg
      end

    if (@save_err_sales != 0)
      begin
        select @err_msg = 'Error # ' +
          convert(char(5),@save_err_sales) +
          ' occurred while attempting to delete from sales'
        print @err_msg
      end

    if (@save_err_titles != 0)
      begin
        select @err_msg = 'Error # ' +
          convert(char(5),@save_err_titleauthor) +
          ' occurred while attempting to delete from titles'
        print @err_msg
      end
    rollback transaction
    return(1)
  end

go
```

By testing for errors, the transaction containing an if statement similar to the preceding one could determine that the error was of sufficient severity to abort the transaction. Other errors would result in the commitment of the database changes, in spite of an error. This example also demonstrates how you can map error messages to output what you want the transaction to generate.

Transaction Restrictions

Several rules govern the use of transactions and what operations can be performed within them. You cannot perform any of the following functions as part of a transaction statement:

- Create a database
- Create a table
- Create an index
- Alter a database
- Alter a table
- Truncate a table
- Drop an object
- Select into
- Grant permissions
- Revoke permissions
- Load a database
- Load transaction log
- Disk init
- Execute a stored procedure that creates temporary tables

Additionally, the number of active transactions per user on a SQL Server at any given time is restricted to one. You cannot execute multiple concurrent transactions as a single user.

Two-Phase Commit

Many people new to SQL Server have misconceptions about two-phase commit. This SQL Server feature is an extension of the transaction function allowing transactions to be executed across multiple SQL Servers. You must write applications that incorporate special functions provided as part of a special library contained in the Open Client DB-Library software you get from Sybase. Interestingly, you will not find references to two-phase commit in the indexes provided with the Sybase SQL Server documentation. The two-phase commit process is initiated and managed by an application or client program, even though it is essentially an extended transaction. There is no way to use two-phase commit inside a stored procedure or batch of T-SQL statements that execute on the server through ISQL. You have to write an application to take advantage of the two-phase commit services.

The key to two-phase commit is the ability to roll back changes on all servers if an error arises and the rollback is initiated on one of the servers involved in the transaction. If you intend to write applications incorporating two-phase commit, you will need more information than is included here. For those developers who simply want an idea of what it is and when you might use it, this high-level overview should suffice.

Two-phase commit manages the distributed update process across multiple SQL Servers. Through the Open Server technology, one or more of the distributed servers might not be a SQL Server. However, provided they were set up under Open Server technology, their participation in the two-phase commit would work as if they were SQL Servers.

Distributed transactions affect multiple servers, databases, disks, and logs and are linked through communications. As a result of the number of components, many points of potential failure exist. The objective of the two-phase commit protocol is to ensure that a transaction involving these multiple servers can still be treated as an atomic unit—one that can be completely rolled back at any time prior to successful commitment. As noted earlier, even though a regular SQL Server transaction can issue a remote procedure call, it cannot roll back the changes made by that RPC if the transaction is aborted. Two-phase commit addresses this issue by requiring the application that initiates the two-phase commit to create a commit services process, which essentially manages the distributed transaction. I call this facility the Commit Manager. This Commit Manager can run on a SQL Server involved in the transaction, or it might be another SQL Server not affected directly by any of the operations defined within the transaction. You define the name of the server to process the commit services in the same way you specify the SQL Servers you intend to affect with your transaction. You open a login record for the commit service and affect servers through the application program as well. The Commit Manager monitors the global transaction status of all the SQL Servers directly involved in the transaction.

Once initiated by an application, incorporated within the process normally used by any client application, a distributed transaction has two distinct stages: the prepare phase and the commit phase. As implied by the terms, the first step involves the preparation of all the involved servers to make the commit, then the commit is actually performed. If there is a failure during the prepare phase, all servers roll back their transactions. If there is a failure in the commit phase, the global status maintained by the Commit Manager is used to roll back or commit the individual server database changes. The steps taken in the two-phase commit process are described in Figure 4.6.1.

FIGURE 4.6.1.

Two-phase commit process depicted with a single transaction across two servers.

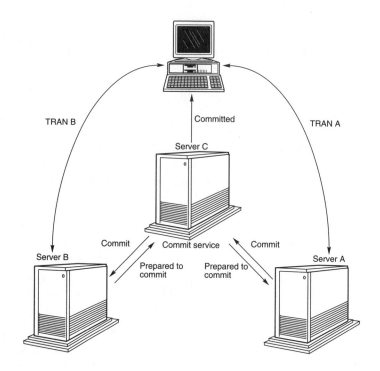

When a single SQL Server manages transactions that cross a number of databases, the two-phase commit protocol is used, albeit transparently to the developer or user of the transaction. This is necessary to ensure that the various multiple logs and recovery capabilities are maintained consistently. In the event of a systems failure where one database had already committed the changes, the SQL Server would not be able to roll back those changes without using some two-phase commit process.

To write a user-defined transaction involving two-phase commit across multiple SQL Servers (whether through Open Server, Omni SQL Gateway, or actual Sybase products), a developer must explicitly write the transaction to accommodate the various servers and their processes. Using Open Client software, the developer writes a program that sends the correct two-phase commit protocol messages to the participating servers and provides the commit server function. The application deals with each server independently, except that the application must inform all servers about the status of the prepare and commit phase for the transaction as a whole. This is handled through the `open_commit()` and `close_xact()` functions to connect and disconnect from each server. The transaction is started, committed, and aborted with the `start_xact()`, `commit_xact()`, and `abort_xact()` functions respectively.

The transaction identifier used across the distributed system must be unique to allow referencing of the log records specific to that transaction for each server. The prepare transaction statement must be issued for each participating server prior to the commit, and the commit server must be aware of the status of each `rollback/commit tran` through the `remove_xact` function. This allows the commit server to decrement its counter for each distributed transaction participant until all are accounted for. If one of the SQL Servers (or the communications link between them) fails during the transaction, the process that initiated the two-phase commit waits to reestablish communication with the other servers. The local commit might have been performed, even though the remote system or the Commit Manager has not indicated that the transaction as a whole was committed. If the systems administrator on a local system kills the process, on restoring communications to the Commit Manager, there would be no way to roll back the commit on the local server. To avoid database inconsistency, you should avoid killing two-phase commit processes until communication is reestablished or the other servers are brought back up, thereby allowing the transaction to commit or roll back on its own.

Refer to your *Programmer's Reference for C* manual to obtain more information about the functions and how they are used to build distributed transactions. For more information on Sybase products for managing distributed databases, check into the Replication Server, which is part of the System 10 product suite.

Summary

Transactions are at the heart of SQL Server applications. Through transactions you have a great deal of control over how data is changed, the conditions under which sets of changes are made, and the extent to which changes are rolled back in the event of an error or failure. By using transactions, you can ensure that multiple operations affecting your database are performed as a set or the data is restored to the condition it was in at the beginning of the transaction. This allows you to ensure data integrity on the server side, independent of your applications through including transactions within triggers and stored procedures. You can structure your SQL operations to incorporate transactions as part of a client application. The syntax and the operation of transactions within your SQL Server are the same in either case.

Although any simple SQL operation entered from a command line interface to a SQL Server such as ISQL is seen by the server as a simple transaction, you can build robust and complex applications using the control-of-flow extensions provided by T-SQL. Transactions can take input from users during their execution, provide error and status messaging, and handle condition testing and branching. Transactions can manage the updating, insertion, and deletion of data across multiple tables and even multiple databases, when properly structured. Most importantly, transactions provide you with an effective means of ensuring that all these operations occur in the right order and completely, before making any permanent changes to the data.

You also learned about some of the aspects of two-phase commit and how distributed transactions work. The chapter in Section 5 that covers Open Client DB-Library includes more discussion on the functions and techniques used to perform two-phase commit transactions.

4.7

Table Locks in SQL Server

Up to this point you have been only briefly exposed to the function and purpose of table locking. Like any RDBMS, some method of concurrency controls must be implemented to support concurrent access to data. SQL Server accomplishes this through page locking. This chapter takes you through the locking process and explains the implications of various SQL operations on multiuser access to the tables in your database.

The Need for Concurrency Controls in SQL Server

In any system where multiple users and applications can access the same data, you must implement some form of concurrency control. In a more primitive system, the entire data file itself might be locked. That is, one user has already marked the file as open and reserves the right to make changes to it. In that case, no one else can gain access to the data in that file. Strictly speaking, data accessed under this structure is accessed not concurrently but serially. For your client/server applications, you must be able to support multiple users accessing the data at the same time, but you need a process to manage this access.

If user A changes the same table at the same time as user B, which set of changes ultimately gets written to the database? If user C is reading data that user A has changed while user C is reading it, how are the changes made by user A reflected in the data being reviewed by user C? Without concurrency controls, a database could lose transactions, retrieve and display data that was in the process of being changed, and mangle transactions so that the database becomes inconsistent and corrupt. Obviously, a multiuser database cannot operate on the basis of a free-for-all, nor can the entire database be locked off when a single user chooses to work with it.

SQL Server Locks

The locking mechanism developed for SQL Server is similar to that used by many other RDBMS vendors. As a developer, you need to be aware of two basic types of locks: shared and exclusive locks. In both cases, when SQL Server declares a lock, a piece of the table consisting of 2K of contiguous disk space is marked as locked. This is referred to as a data page, and SQL Server uses what is often referred to as page locking. Conceptually, this works as row-level locking, considering that in many tables 2K is a reasonable row size. Sybase has selected this 2K page size for locking as the best balance between performance and overhead for management of locks.

You can lock an entire table, but that is discussed later in the chapter. You should also note that indexes are locked in the same ways and for the same reasons as tables; they contain data that is read and in some cases modified. Locks are used to manage the various concurrent operations that can be taken on either indexes or tables.

Shared Locks

These locks are also known as read locks, since they are activated by any select statement. Anyone wishing to select and display data from a table needs to be sure that no one else can change the data until after they have executed their SQL statement and relinquished their lock. Of course, retrieving data in no way affects anyone else wishing to simply execute a select, which is why the read locks are known as shared locks—any number of concurrent users can select data from a table. Shared locks are relinquished as soon as the data page has been read.

Update Locks

These locks allow a user to update data but also permit other transactions to read the data pages. Other update or exclusive locks are blocked until the transaction issuing the initial update lock is committed or rolled back.

Exclusive Locks

For any operation that causes a change to the data—such as an operation containing an insert, delete, or update—the transaction must acquire an exclusive lock. These locks are also known as write locks, and they are not shared. By granting an exclusive lock to any transaction that changes the data, SQL Server ensures that the transaction can be rolled back at any time prior to the commit. Once the commit or rollback is completed, the exclusive lock is relinquished and any other transaction can place its own shared or exclusive lock on that data page.

How the Locks Interact

During regular operation of your SQL Server environment, you will likely have a mix of read and write activities being performed on your database. This concurrency dramatically affects performance. As a developer, you need to be mindful of the way your users and their applications can affect database performance. For instance, you may have a blistering fast hardware environment, high-bandwidth networking, and all the latest and greatest front-end software, but if your users have to wait for a lengthy process to finish updating a table, the system can look very slow indeed. The reason for this is that SQL Server must wait for the locks to clear prior to granting new ones of a different type.

This is true in principle, but it is not how things actually work in practice. Because shared locks can be granted to multiple users, and because these multiple users can initiate selects just before another user's select has completed, a group of people performing selects on a database could keep someone else from ever gaining clear access for an insert, delete, or update operation. As you have seen, those operations require that the pages be exclusively locked. You could conceivably grant write operations a higher priority than read operations so that the users performing selects would be bumped in favor of the write user, but that is not how SQL Server handles this contentious issue.

Instead, each new database operation registers with the SQL Server what sort of lock this operation requires (transparently to you as either a user or a developer). This is known as the intent lock, and the intent is to set either an exclusive or a shared lock on a page (or pages) within the table. As you can imagine, complex multi-table operations require SQL Server to manage locks for each page affected within every table specified. The intent lock prevents another transaction from acquiring an exclusive lock on the table containing a page needed by the transaction registering the intent. In essence, it is a way of reserving access to a particular kind of lock.

This is reinforced with demand locks. Demand locks prevent any further shared locks from being set and designate a transaction as next to issue a lock on a page. These demand locks are granted to a transaction with a requirement for an exclusive lock and ensure that no more than four shared locks are issued to other transactions before the write operation is given the lock it needs. In this way, SQL Server manages the interaction of transactions requiring read and write access to the same data concurrently.

You can gain information about locks using the sp_locks systems procedure supplied with your SQL Server. It is used in the following manner:

COMMAND:	sp_lock
SYNTAX:	sp_lock [spid, spid]
USED BY:	Anyone
USED FOR:	Determining the status and nature of locks on a SQL Server
EXAMPLE:	sp_lock 6

SAMPLE OUTPUT:

```
spid    locktype                table_id    page        dbname
======  ====================    ==========  ==========  ================
6       Sh_intent               685245496   0           master
6       Ex_extent               0           128         tempdb
```

The `spid` can be obtained by executing `sp_who`.

This output shows that `spid 6` has an intent to place a shared lock on the master database and an extent lock on `tempdb`. An extent lock is issued on a set of eight database pages while they are being allocated or deallocated. These locks are set as part of `Create` or `Drop` commands and also `insert` statements that result in a requirement for new data or index pages.

To determine the table name using the table ID, you can use one of the systems functions described in an earlier section: the `object_name()` function. For example, you could use the following syntax to determine the table name:

```
use master
go
select object_name(685245494)
go
```

This statement yields the table name of `spt_values`. This process is somewhat more useful when identifying locks that are being declared on user databases and their tables.

Deadlocks

If you extrapolate the process of page-level locking, you can see how in some cases two transactions could be running, each one with an exclusive lock on a page that the other needs to complete. In these cases, each of the two transactions sit and wait for the other to relinquish the lock it needs. Since it cannot do that until the transaction commits, meaning that it has been completely and successfully executed, the two transactions are deadlocked. Keep in mind that this also means that no further shared locks can be issued on those pages. In other words, those pages are inaccessible. Your SQL Server is designed to detect and break up deadlocks. To do this, it must choose one transaction to commit at the expense of the other. By killing one of the transactions, it can then be rolled back, relinquishing its locks and allowing the other transaction to proceed normally.

The application cannot determine which transaction to kill in the event of a deadlock. This is managed by SQL Server. As a general rule, you can minimize the potential occurrence of deadlocks by keeping your transactions short and by writing your transactions so they always access tables in the same order.

Table versus Page Locking

Sometimes it makes more sense to lock the entire table for performance reasons. For instance, any transaction that performs an operation on every row in the table is a good candidate for this. Also, there is a certain amount of overhead in the lock allocation process. The intents must be declared, the lock granted, the operation performed, and the lock removed. Doing this for every data page in a table might require more resources than simply locking the entire table. Your SQL Server itself can decide to lock an entire table when too many single pages will be locked to be effective. In this case, the SQL Server escalates the lock by trading in each of the page locks for an entire table lock. Naturally, no other transaction can access the table while it is locked. However, in some cases the subsequent write operations are completed more quickly than if page locking was used, and the performance perception of any waiting users is enhanced.

Holdlocks

When writing your transactions, you may choose to keep a shared lock on a table until the entire transaction has completed. You would do this if your transaction required a read from the table prior to updating values. By declaring a holdlock, you ensure that no one else can lock the table for writing before your transaction commits. The holdlock keyword is used with the following syntax:

```
begin tran
declare @max money
select @max =max(advance)
from titles holdlock,
     publishers holdlock
where [blah, blah,blah]
if @max >25000
update titles [blah, blah, blah]
commit tran
```

As you can see, the `holdlock` keyword is specified immediately after the table where the lock will be declared.

Browse Mode

You don't always need to place locks on the table simply to view the contents. Much of the requirement for locks depends on your specific requirements. Up-to-the-minute data for month end and period reporting and decision support is not always necessary, for example. In such cases, once the data has been deemed stable and is not subject to further inserts, deletions, or updates (at least on a particular subset of the data), you can access this data without locks by using the browse mode of the select statement.

When you issue a select statement in browse mode, the data is copied into temporary tables in `tempdb`. Because the database tables themselves are not being accessed, locking the data pages to prevent anyone else from gaining an exclusive lock isn't necessary. You might choose to use this approach when you have a retrieval requirement on older data held in tables where new records are actively being added. In that case, the new records would not affect the results you had retrieved, whereas placing a shared lock on the table as a result of your select would adversely affect those applications requiring write access. You can even update the rows you have selected in browse mode (provided you have the necessary permissions). The browse mode opts for optimistic concurrency control, which holds no locks while you are accessing data. Conversely, pessimistic concurrency control locks everybody except you out of the database, even if you are just looking. Naturally, pessimistic concurrency control is the most effective means of ensuring that you can insert, update, or delete data from the tables if you choose to.

On the other hand, the browse mode allows other users to access the data while you are working with your copy. In a high-demand, multiuser database, extensive use of arbitrary exclusive locks for an application can really draw attention to your software—and not the kind you want! When you use the select statement in browse mode, you must have created a timestamp column in your table. SQL Server will automatically update the timestamp values on any inserts and/or updates. Through this, if another user changes data in the source tables while you work with the data, when you go to write your changes, the timestamp will not match. Of course, if they do match, you know that your copy of the data is still valid and you can safely overwrite your new rows on the database tables without affecting some other user's write operation.

To use browse mode in an application, you would follow this approach:

1. Submit a `SELECT FOR BROWSE` statement.
2. Fetch the result rows into application variables.
3. Determine changes, if any, to be made to the values.
4. Build and submit appropriate `UPDATE` statements with `where` equal to `timestamp`.
5. Repeat for each row to be affected.

Alternately, you can take advantage of optimistic concurrency control by retrieving the timestamp into your application and appending the `tsequal()` system function to the UPPDATES WHERE clause.

Summary

Although locks occur in the background, their effects on application performance can be very noticeable to your users. SQL Server looks after locks automatically, but in some cases you may wish to intervene or write your applications and transactions with the implications of locks in mind. This chapter has given you an overview of the locking process used by SQL Server, how to obtain information about it, and options for dealing with locks in your transactions. You also learned about managing locks using browse mode for data retrieval and even updates. From this discussion, you should have a better appreciation for the role played by tempdb in a busy database environment.

Because each 2K page read by SQL Server as part of a select statement is granted a lock, you can see why the number of locks set by sp_config is so high. Certainly, sites do run out of sufficient locks and must reset this number to accommodate the number of users performing higher than the numbers of read operations allowed by the defaults.

From this chapter you should have a good idea how multiple users, applications, and transactions manage concurrent access to your SQL Server database.

4.8

The SQL Server Systems Tables

This chapter takes you through the various systems tables maintained within your SQL Server environment and explains the purpose and content of each table. By the end of the chapter, you should have a good idea of where SQL Server stores the various values used during regular database operations, as well as what they are.

Like many powerful development environments, SQL Server has its own quirks and idiosyncrasies when it comes to the commands used to list and manipulate database objects. Many of these values are stored in the systems tables, and Sybase provides stored procedures to retrieve these values for various purposes. However, many of these stored procedures are a real nuisance to use, especially when you are interfacing to the SQL Server over a character-based ISQL session. As a developer, you often want to know who you are logged in as this time, or what the exact view, table, or index names are in a particular database. In this chapter, you will see how you can query the systems tables to gain this information. That being said, memorizing the systems tables' contents may not be your number one learning priority when it comes to your first (or even third or fourth) SQL Server.

For those who would like to be able to gain quick and easy answers to questions like whoami (Who am I), and what database am I currently using, I have provided a few stored procedures you can use to learn this information quickly and directly. The names of these procedures currently correspond to their UNIX equivalents: `whoami`, `pwd` (print working directory, or in this case, database), and `ls` for list. If you are more comfortable with DOS or another environment (except for the Mac—in that case you're out of luck!), simply use `sp_rename` to move the procedures from `ls_table` to `dir_table`, for example. There are scripts for creating these stored procedures on the attached diskette; they are also listed in this chapter for purposes of illustrating the contents of the systems tables.

SQL Server Systems Tables

All information about SQL Server database objects is maintained in systems tables, known as the systems catalogs. One catalog in the master database maintains server-wide information such as logins and remote servers. Each database has a catalog. These catalogs are directly analogous to what other relational databases refer to as the data dictionary. From a developer's perspective, the biggest advantage to maintaining database descriptions and operational statistics is the ability to query those tables directly using any command-line interface or application that can pass T-SQL retrieve statements through to those systems tables. I am going to restrict my remarks to retrieving data, because modifying systems tables directly is not at all a good idea unless you are very, very good and very, very careful. Sybase provides stored procedures to ensure that all tables that require updating are updated, and in the appropriate order. Hey, it's a free country, and at times you may decide to get in and modify the systems tables directly. In any case, you should understand what information is available to you.

Perhaps the most interesting and useful systems tables are the following:

Sysobjects   This catalog table contains a row for each object in the database, including tables, views, stored procedures, triggers, defaults, and the transaction log. The row consists of the object name, the user ID of its creator and owner, the type of object, an object ID, and other information about the object.

Syscolumns   This catalog table contains a row for every column of every table or view, and each parameter defined for all stored procedures in the database. The row consists of the column (or parameter) name, the object ID, the datatype, and length of the column, among other things.

Sysindexes   This catalog table contains a row for each index, as well as a row for every table without a clustered index, and also a row for all tables containing text or image data. These rows hold the name of the index or table, the table ID, and a flag to identify the type of object. A table is value 0, a clustered index is 1, and the remaining values identify nonclustered indexes. This table is used to maintain location data in the form of physical addresses as well as the index statistics.

Sysusers   This catalog maintains one row for each user allowed in each database. Groups defined within the database are also stored in this table with one row per group. All newly created databases have two users recorded in the database's sysusers table: one for the database owner and one for the group Public.

Sysprotects   This catalog contains all user permissions, with a row for each grant and revoke statement issued within that database.

Additional systems tables that you may use to look up information about your database include the following:

Sysalternates   For every SQL Server user aliased to a user in another database, a row is maintained in this systems catalog.

Sysprocedures   This catalog contains entries for all views, defaults, rules, and triggers, as well as every stored procedure defined for the database. The sysprocedures catalog differs from the sysobjects catalog because it stores the execution plan or sequence tree for each object. This is generally not used by developers.

Sysdepends   All the references for each view, procedure, and trigger defined on the database are held in the sysdepends table for each database. The systems procedure sp_depends accesses and reports references and dependencies from the sysdepends table.

Syskeys   As discussed in the chapter dealing with referential integrity (Chapter 4.5), keys can be explicitly documented in each SQL Server database. All foreign, primary, and common key relationships between tables so defined are stored in the syskeys systems table.

Systypes   All Sybase-supplied and user-defined data types are recorded in this systems catalog.

Syssegments   One row for each defined segment is stored in this catalog.

FIGURE 4.8.1.

The relationship among the tables that make up the systems catalogs.

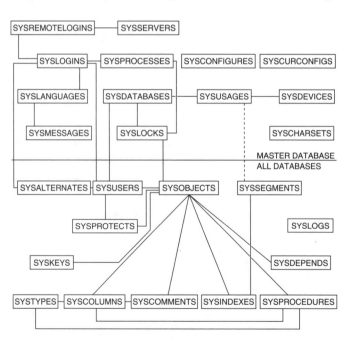

Accessing Systems Tables with Stored Procedures

To augment the systems procedures supplied with your SQL Server, and to illustrate how you could directly query the systems tables to identify information meaningful to you, the following stored procedures have been provided:

ls_table	This procedure identifies all tables in the current database.
ls_view	This procedure identifies all views in the current database.
ls_proc	This procedure identifies all stored procedures in the current database.
ls_trig	This procedure identifies all triggers in the current database.
ls_rule	This procedure identifies all rules in the current database.
whoami	This procedure tells you who you are.
pwd	This procedure prints the working database.

```
/* ls_table - list all tables in working database */

create procedure ls_table
as

select Table_Name = a.name, Owner = b.name
from sysobjects a, sysusers b
where   a.uid = b.uid and
        a.type = "U"

go
```

This procedure retrieves the name and user ID of all tables in sysobjects and selects the owner's name from the sysusers table after joining the two tables on the uid or user id column for the type U, which is the flag used to identify tables in sysobjects (don't ask me why).

```
/* ls_trig - list all triggers in working database */

create procedure ls_trig
as

select Trigger_Name = a.name, Owner = b.name
from sysobjects a, sysusers b
where   a.uid = b.uid and
        a.type = "TR"

go
```

This procedure retrieves the name and user ID of all triggers in sysobjects and selects the owner's name from the sysusers table after joining the two tables on the uid or user id column for the type TR, which is the flag used to identify triggers in sysobjects.

```
/* ls_proc - list all procedures in working database */

create procedure ls_proc
as

select Procedure_Name = a.name, Owner = b.name
from sysobjects a, sysusers b
where  a.uid = b.uid and
       a.type = "P"

go
```

Here you retrieve the name and user ID of all procedures in sysobjects and select the owner's name from the sysusers table after joining the two tables on the uid or user id column for the type P, which is the flag used to identify procedures in sysobjects. (This one I think you can tell why.)

```
/* pwd - print working database */

create procedure pwd
as

select working_database = b.name
from master.dbo.sysprocesses a, master.dbo.sysdatabases b
where  a.dbid = b.dbid and
       a.status = "runnable"

go
```

This procedure selects the name of the current database from the sysprocesses table in the master database by joining with sysdatabases table and retrieving the name matching the ID of the database where the procedure is stored.

```
/* whoami - reports current user */

create procedure whoami
as

select whoami = name
from master.dbo.sysprocesses a, master.dbo.syslogins b
where  a.suid = b.suid and
       a.status = "runnable"

go
```

This procedure does much the same thing as the pwd procedure except the user ID is matched to the names held in the syslogins table. The results retrieved display the name of the user logged in to the database. If you are logged in to a database under an alias, this procedure tells you your real login name, not who you are impersonating.

```
/* listrule - list all rules in working database */

create procedure ls_rule
as

select Rule_Name = a.name, Owner = b.name
from sysobjects a, sysusers b
where   a.uid = b.uid and
        a.type = "R"

go
```

This procedure retrieves the name and user ID of all rules in sysobjects and selects the owner's name from the sysusers table after joining the two tables on the uid or user id column for the type R, which is the flag used to identify rules in sysobjects.

```
/* listview - list all views in working database */

create procedure ls_view
as

select View_Name = a.name, Owner = b.name
from sysobjects a, sysusers b
where   a.uid = b.uid and
        a.type = "V"

go
```

This procedure retrieves the name and user ID of all views in sysobjects and selects the owner's name from the sysusers table after joining the two tables on the uid or user id column for the type V, which is the flag used to identify views in sysobjects.

Master Database Systems Tables

Most of the data you require as a developer is maintained in sysobjects or sysusers, as you can see from these stored procedures. The purpose of these procedures is not so much to pull new or previously unavailable data from the systems tables but more to restrict the retrieved data to just what is required. Anyone working with ISQL will soon be frustrated by the program's unfortunate habit of scrolling off the screen. Granted, some terminals allow you to change your scroll settings so this problem is minimized, but in most cases it is more desirable to simply view the exact set of results you want rather than to try picking them out of a larger list of superfluous objects.

As you can see in the whoami and pwd procedures, not all of the useful systems tables are stored as part of your working database—some are maintained in the master database. The master systems catalogs are listed in Table 4.8.1.

Table 4.8.1. Systems tables contained only in the master database.

Table Name	Description
Sysconfigures	Stores the values of the user-definable configuration options
Syscurconfigs	Displays the current values in use by the SQL Server
Sysdatabases	Maintains one row for each database defined on the server
Sysdevices	Contains all dump devices, disk devices, and partition data for the server
Syslocks	Holds values describing all locks active at the time
Syslogins	Maintains one row for each valid login ID on the server
Sysmessages	Holds all systems error and warning messages
Sysprocesses	Contains status for all server processes
Sysremotelogins	Identifies each valid remote SQL Server user login ID
Sysservers	Identifies each valid remote SQL Server
Sysusages	Holds one row for each disk partition or OS file allocated to a database

Using the systems procedures to modify these tables affects the operation of your SQL Server as a whole. In case you were wondering, the difference between sysconfigures and syscurconfigs is primarily that you can change your SQL Server's configuration options through sp_configure and the changes will not take effect until the system is restarted (with two exceptions, allow updates and recovery interval). The values the server is currently operating under (the values that were set at last boot) allow you to compare your new values with the original settings. This is very handy if you want to reset some to original settings and still make changes to other parameters without aborting the whole change.

Some of the rationale for the various systems tables was discussed implicitly in the section that covered the architecture of the SQL Server. By storing all SQL Server messages in the sysmessages table, for example, it is easier for SQL Server to operate identically even if all the messages are in a language other than U.S. English. Architecturally, SQL Server still operates the same way, as all messages are called from the sysmessages table.

As a developer, you may be most interested in the processes, users, and logins set up on your server. These tables contain the precise names and IDs you need to define and debug some of your more complex transactions, stored procedures, and applications.

Summary

In this chapter, you have gained a better idea of how SQL Server manages what in many systems would be called the data dictionary. The Sybase approach to this differs from many other vendors, in as much as you use the same SQL syntax to retrieve and manipulate the data stored in the catalogs. Many other products have distinctly different syntax, menus, and procedures for retrieving data about the databases.

Separating database information out from the master database also has a recoverability advantage. If the master database becomes corrupted or fails and must be reinstalled, it is much easier with SQL Server to reinstall the master database and inform it of the existence of user databases.

You could argue that the systems procedures typically used to retrieve and affect data within these systems catalogs are much like the data dictionary programs mentioned earlier. However, the fact remains that you can create your own "systems" procedures by creating stored procedures that perform the retrieval functions according to your own exact requirements. This is what this chapter has done in providing you with the navigation and reporting utilities used as examples of what information can be obtained from the systems tables. Conceivably, you could write your own customized stored procedures for modifying the systems tables—if you really feel you must. However, under no circumstances should you modify or rename the Sybase-supplied systems procedures; this can make recovering from errors a truly daunting exercise. Sybase has supplied tested and proven stored procedures for writing to the systems tables, and it is unlikely that you will not be able to accomplish your aims with those.

At the same time, much of the reporting of systems users, processes, and objects depends on your unique requirements. By all means use the procedures provided here and create your own to report the systems table data you want and need.

4.9

The Use of Cursors in SQL Server

Cursor support has long been provided as part of the SQL Server feature set, at least for programs that accessed SQL Server databases through embedded SQL. More recently, Microsoft has extended cursor support for interactive SQL through extensions to the functions provided with Open Client DB-Library. In this chapter, you will see how and why cursors are used, as well as the syntax for declaring and populating them with data. Cursors provide a flexible means of manipulating the retrieved rows from a table, including the ability to manipulate the kind of locks defined on the table's data pages while the cursor is open.

A cursor allows you to treat the rows in a table similarly to the way a traditional program reads a flat file—line by line. (Or in this case, row by row.) This chapter addresses the use of cursors to meet specific applications development requirements.

Cursors Defined

Like a view, a cursor is a symbolic way of looking at and manipulating data in underlying tables. A cursor is declared in association with a T-SQL select statement. The cursor itself consists of the result set (which is the zero, one, or many rows retrieved by the associated select statement) and the cursor position, which points to a specific row within the result set. Cursors can be defined as read-only, or they can allow updates to the underlying database tables that make up the cursor. Cursors were originally used strictly with programs that accessed SQL Server databases. The cursor served as a means of representing table data to a program as if it were a flat file. Because relational database management systems are essentially set-oriented, SQL Server does not have an explicit method of representing a single row within a table. In other words, in any RDBMS, you are able to perform an operation on a single column but not process one row or record at a time. The only way to deal with a single row is to retrieve it with a where clause so restrictive that no other rows are selected. Cursors are used to select, update, and delete rows within a table; you cannot use cursors to insert new rows.

Look at this from the point of view of the telephone book analogy used in Section 1 of this book. Within SQL Server you can easily retrieve name or number, because these are individual columns. You could retrieve a single row by selecting all the columns where one of the columns equaled a unique identifier. But what if you want to retrieve a subset of the table, such as all the rows where the last name equaled smith, and you wanted to display one row at a time until a particular row was selected? This one-row-at-a-time processing is very common to more traditional programming approaches, but it is not an integral component of a relational database. Enter cursors, which serve to bridge this gap.

There are three main types of cursors:

Static Cursor: The result set retrieved by the `select` associated with this cursor cannot be changed while it is open. The values in the set, their order, and membership are fixed until the cursor is closed. Essentially, this cursor takes a snapshot of the results by creating a temporary table using `select into`; however, you could choose to place a lock on the entire results set on the actual table instead.

Keyset-Driven Cursor: This is like a static cursor in that the membership of rows and their order within the result set are fixed; the keyset-driven cursor differs in that changes made by the cursor owner can be displayed. Updates that change row order and membership are allowed; however, changes to affected rows are not displayed until the cursor is closed and reopened. Keyset-driven cursors allow changes to the data contained in the cursor but fix membership and ordering by requiring a unique identifier for each row and maintaining a buffer of this keyset. To supply these keys, the table from which the results will be selected must have a unique index.

Dynamic Cursor: Using this cursor, the changes committed by anyone and uncommitted changes made by the cursor owner are displayed as soon as the user scrolls through the displayed results. In this case, changes include inserts and deletes as well as changes in membership and order. The cursor requires a single unique key index on the table from which the results will be selected.

Positioning within Cursors

There are two methods of positioning the current row of the cursor: relative and absolute. When the cursor is opened, the current row is just before the first row of the result set. You can move to the next row, which is an example of relative positioning, or you can choose to move to a row number. The absolute position is the number of a particular row in the result set. Every cursor operation is performed in relation to the current cursor position.

Cursors and Concurrency

As touched on earlier, these cursors may be defined as read-only to allow other users to select data on the tables underneath the cursor. Additionally, the cursors may be defined as updatable, in which case all the rows in the buffer lock when the rows are affected by a transaction. The rows (actually the data pages containing the rows) are locked as soon as the transaction issues a `begin tran` command, and they remain locked until the `commit tran` command is issued.

Additionally, SQL Server has implemented a form of managing multiuser access to the same data, known as optimistic concurrency control. This allows the application to detect conflicting updates between those performed by the owner of the cursor and those performed by other SQL Server users and applications. Any rows that were changed by a user subsequent to opening the cursor return an error when the cursor is closed and the updated rows are written to the database. Another method of optimistic concurrency control used by a cursor is defining a timestamp on the rows contained in the cursor. By appending a timestamp value to the rows in the cursor, SQL Server allows the application to refresh the cursor buffer and retry updates that have failed because of conflict with other users. This is optimistic in the sense that the application proceeds as if no conflicts will take place and takes steps to resolve them only if and when they occur.

How Cursors Work

Several distinct steps are performed whenever a cursor is used within an application:

1. The cursor is declared.
2. The cursor is opened.
3. The cursor's current row is set through a fetched operation.
4. The fetched row is processed by the application.
5. The cursor is closed.

For versions of SQL Server prior to System 10, cursor support is provided as part of the Open Client function library (DB-Library). Provided with the library are extensions that allow cursor support to be defined and used through an application program. However, System 10 supports the declaration and use of cursors directly with T-SQL. They can be entered interactively as part of an ISQL session, for example, or they can be incorporated into stored procedures and triggers.

Cursors themselves do not invoke transactions. They do not initiate the `begin` and `commit tran` commands. These are performed as part of the locking method selected when the cursor is declared and opened using the `dbcursoropen` function supplied with DB-Library. To best illustrate how a cursor works, start at the conceptual level with a straightforward read-only example.

To declare and use a cursor against a snapshot of data, choose the locking method you wish to employ with the cursor. If you select read-only, the cursor operation first creates a temporary table and populates it using the SELECT INTO T-SQL command. By opening the cursor on the temporary table, any requirement for a shared lock on the source table is eliminated, freeing the table for update and read access by other users.

Because the cursor is associated with a select statement, the results set available to a cursor is defined by that statement. The select represents the total number of rows that the cursor can address. However, because the point of the cursor is to allow you to deal with one row at a time, there has to be a method of identifying that subset row or rows of the result set. This is accomplished through the use of a fetch function. The fetch does exactly that—it gets the row at the current cursor position and returns it to the application. By coding operations to be taken on the data (for this example you use derived column calculations), the application could show the values retrieved from the row as well as displaying an additional column containing the subtotal of the rows displayed so far. Within DB-Library, you are provided with many functions for manipulating the rows in the result set, including

```
FETCH_NEXT
FETCH_PREVIOUS
FETCH_RANDOM
FETCH_RELATIVE
```

Once the application is exited, or the connection to the SQL Server broken, the cursor is discontinued and closed. In situations where the cursor had been declared and opened on real database tables, tables and locks held are relinquished as soon as this occurs.

Restrictions on Cursors

As you define the cursor and its associated select statement, you cannot use the FOR BROWSE, INTO, COMPUTE, or UNION keywords. Nor can you use more than one view, and you cannot define joins. Additionally, dynamic cursors restrict the use of order by, group by, and having clauses in the select statement.

Incorporating Cursors into Open Client Applications

Cursor support is available on all SQL Server versions through the Open Client functions. With the incorporation of cursor support into the database itself with System 10, Sybase developers will likely see more of them. The specific features found in the System 10 cursor support are covered in the chapter addressing the unique features of SQL Server 10.

For those of you who do not yet have access to a System 10 server, the *Programmer's Reference for C* manual supplied with your Sybase documentation (the book that says "Microsoft SQL Server" in big letters on the cover) indicates how a cursor can be incorporated into an application using Open Client functions.

Summary

This chapter has introduced a completely different method of managing the output from a `select` statement through the use of a cursor. Perhaps in the past this would have been seen as applying only to those developers who wanted to write their own C language applications to go against SQL Server. Although many of you may fit that description, throughout this book you have seen that using a Sybase database engine as the hub of your client/server solution will allow you to address the needs of a wide variety of users and developers.

The reason for including this description about cursors was to get you thinking about where you might use them and how they could help you meet your application requirements. Since cursor support is now available in System 10, you can expect to see more stored procedures and triggers that return data rows using cursors. From this chapter, you should have a better understanding of what they are and where they fit among the other functions, features, and services provided as part of your SQL Server developer's toolset.

4.10

Opportunities for Optimization

Not all approaches to optimizing SQL Server performance yield the same degree of improvement. Many aspects of your SQL Server's configuration can be tweaked to provide a small performance increase. Some of these are time-consuming and even risky. On the other hand, a number of areas can be evaluated and modified that have been proven in many SQL Server installations to provide significant performance enhancement. This chapter introduces these areas and covers a prioritized checklist of SQL Server elements that you should evaluate when attempting to improve the performance of your client/server system. This chapter deals exclusively with the SQL Server database and applications that run against it, rather than discussing ways to balance SQL Server resource requirements and other applications running on the host platform.

By the end of this chapter, you should have an action plan for reviewing your own SQL Server applications and have a solid understanding of how to approach your first pass at server optimization. As you saw in the overview of the SQL Server architecture, Sybase has developed a cost-based query optimizer. The optimizer determines the best access method of retrieving data, selecting which index, if any, will be used, and the best order in which to join the tables. Cost is expressed in terms of page I/Os from the disk. A page is the smallest unit manipulated by SQL Server—the fewer pages read from disk, the faster the query result is obtained. It is possible to determine what the cost optimizer chooses for any given query through the T-SQL command SHOWPLAN. I cover SHOWPLAN more specifically in Section 4 chapter 10. The objective here is for you to be able to see the interrelationship of table, index, and query structures.

The Importance of Good Design

Experience in many SQL Server sites has shown that logical database design, index availability, and query structure have the greatest impact, positive and negative, on SQL Server application performance. These three areas almost always yield the best return on time and effort when you want to optimize access and manipulation of data through a client/server application. Of course, it is always possible to write a truly bad client application that performs unnecessary tasks, retrieves spurious data, or simply does not work. For purposes of this discussion, I assume that you have a functional grasp of the client environment in which you have chosen to develop. Your focus here is on the implications of SQL Server object structure as the chief factor in performance.

This brings me back to your database. When evaluating query performance as part of an application, you should take care to identify all triggers that may be fired as a result of an insert, delete, or update operation. In some cases, the trigger slows down the application, not the SQL statement that fires it. Having identified cases such as these, you are in a better position to address the performance of the trigger, thereby speeding up the application as a whole. Although queries can be incorporated into views and stored procedures, you should run the queries separately, and then insert them into the views or stored procedures after you have determined which indexes should be built and the optimum structure for the query. This approach should also provide pointers to problems with the size or structure of the tables within the database. Where such problems occur, you can address the issue with a review of the data models and the extent of database normalization.

Generally speaking, a balanced approach to normalization provides the single greatest boost to application performance when using any RDBMS, and SQL Server is no exception. To bring the concept of normalization down to a practical level, look at your database tables. Do you have a large number of tables with a few columns or a few tables with many columns? The normalization process involves breaking tables down into the smallest number of related columns. (Put aside purist debates about normalization being a logical data modeling task restricted to entities and attributes. Here you are dealing with the "down and in" aspects of your SQL Server, and this translates into tables, columns, and rows.) That being said, however, the highest degree of normalization means that you are constantly performing complex table joins to retrieve the rows you want, and this can adversely affect performance as well.

The key to success here is in taking a balanced approach to normalization. You definitely do not want to store all your data in one large table, because this defeats the benefits of using the relational database features of your SQL Server. On the other hand, you want to be able to retrieve the data required by your application with as few operations as possible. As a general rule, you should not have to join more than five tables together to obtain the desired rows, because a greater number of joins would result in performance degradation and increased complexity, which is more difficult to manage. Where your normalization effort has made it necessary to perform transactions of this type, you should consider denormalizing your database by reducing the number of tables and increasing the columns held in each.

On the whole, the benefits of normalization far outweigh the drawbacks. These benefits include the following:

- Narrow tables support faster sorts and index creates because less data is involved.
- The more tables you have, the more clustered indexes are allowed.
- Tables can each be allocated to specific segments, giving you better control over disk usage.
- Fewer nonclustered indexes per table speeds update operations.

If, after reviewing your database, you determine that increased normalization would yield performance increases, keep in mind that these changes can be implemented in several ways. You can hide the breakup of one table into a number of smaller ones by creating a view that presents the data as if it were one unified table. With the few exceptions covered in the chapter on views, you can treat a view like a table without having to rewrite the applications code that is looking for a particular table name. Or you could use stored procedures to access the database tables and provide the retrieved results to the application. In any case, by normalizing your database you will most likely gain the greatest performance return possible with the least expenditure of time and effort.

Indexing Options

Nonclustered indexes exist as completely distinct objects from the tables in the database. They may be created, modified, or dropped as your needs warrant without affecting the table structures or application logic in any way.

Clustered indexes can affect the table structure in two ways. First, the lowest level of a clustered index is the physical sorted order of the rows held in the table. Second, it is possible to specify which segment the clustered index is held in, which causes the table to move or migrate to the hard disk on which the segment was defined.

In both cases, the provision of indexes greatly boosts data retrieval performance. Especially with nonclustered indexes, you should experiment with many different index designs to determine which ones are most useful for your specific applications. The SQL Server query optimizer is a reliable and effective part of the database engine. You can rely on it to make the best choice of indexing when determining an execution plan for query. In fact, you have no choice but to trust it, because you cannot force the optimizer to use a specific index. You can, however, provide the optimizer with a number of indexes from which to choose in order to avoid time-consuming table scans.

When evaluating your queries to determine the best indexing strategy, first examine the WHERE clause of your SQL statements, because this is key to how the optimizer will choose to execute the statement. Naturally, you are most interested in your most frequent queries, or those queries perceived as slow. Ideally, you will evaluate every query in your application, but this may not be practical given time and human-resource constraints.

Identify the columns specified in the WHERE clauses. Do you have indexes for them? How are these indexes structured? Indexes of a few columns are generally more effective than multicolumn, compound indexes. You should also keep in mind that the query optimizer keeps statistics only on the most significant column in the index. If this column is not useful for a particular query, the optimizer may not choose to use that index. Providing a larger number of narrower indexes increases the likelihood that the query optimizer will find an index to use. Even considering that having a large number of indexes may slow update operations, you should still try new indexes on an ongoing basis. If you notice that update, insert, and delete operations are becoming slow, you can always drop the indexes you don't use. Even update operations must read through the table, however, to determine which rows to modify, and these reads use indexes as well.

Clustered indexes are especially useful because they are the fastest form of index available. You can have only one clustered index per table, so you should make sure it is appropriate for either a wide variety or frequently executed query set. As a rule of thumb, clustered indexes are best suited for queries that are retrieving a large number of rows or selecting rows according to a range of values.

Nonclustered indexes are most appropriate when you wish to retrieve a small number of rows. You can use nonclustered indexes to quickly pinpoint the exact row or rows to retrieve from within a large table. Because the optimizer sets the cost of using a nonclustered index at one page I/O for each returned row, however, it becomes more efficient to simply scan the entire table if the returned rows total more than 20 percent of the table. In that case, a nonclustered index is not used.

Clustered indexes, on the other hand, are used even if the entire table is returned as the result of a query.

Query Structure

For your SQL Server solution, results from SQL queries determine how effective your system is in meeting your application requirements. Because the nature and structure of queries can vary widely from site to site, it is very difficult to develop cast-iron rules regarding the structure of SQL queries. You will be introduced, however, to the elements of a methodology for evaluating queries and determining their cost in terms of systems resource utilization. From this you will be in a better position to structure your queries appropriately from the outset as well as to identify and modify problem queries already in operation.

In spite of the fastest hardware, most efficient database engine, normalized database design, and profusion of indexes, you can still create monster queries. These are queries that are inherently resource intensive. There is no way to build an optimizer that will eliminate them; as the developer, it falls to you to ensure that they are generated only when absolutely necessary to meet the needs of your application.

Resource-intensive queries are usually built with the following characteristics:

- Large result sets
- IN/OR queries
- Very inclusive WHERE clauses
- Not equal to operations
- Expressions and datatype conversions in the WHERE clause
- Declaring local variables as part of the WHERE clause
- Group By and Order By parameters in complex views

Obviously, you do not want to eliminate these options from your SQL Server statements; they provide valuable and effective methods of manipulating data. You can, however, structure these functions to allow the optimizer to restrict the result set before applying the clause containing the resource-consuming statement. You should be able to reduce the size of the result set for most of your queries. By making your query as specific as possible, you reduce the size of the retrieved rows. This not only takes less time to execute (due to index usage) but also has a significant impact on the networking and local processing requirements for a client/server system. Finally, long queries can place locks on the table, keeping other users from updating or modifying data and leading them to complain about system performance. The bottom line is keep your retrieved result sets to the smallest possible size.

Nesting your queries and incorporating subqueries can be one of the most effective methods of achieving this. The inner query returns the retrieved results to the outer query, which operates on those results. By nesting a subquery within your resource-intensive query, you can dramatically reduce execution time.

```
use pubs
go
select sum(ytd_sales) from titles
```

This query performs a table scan because it must go through the table row by row in order to sum the year-to-date sales. If you can restrict the operation by specifying a publisher, however, you can optimize the query considerably. For example,

```
use pubs
go
select sum(ytd_sales) from titles
where pub_id = "1389"
go
```

This query first selects all publishers with the pub_id 1389, then sums the year-to-date sales column and returns the dollar value requested. In cases in which the retrieve is being issued against a large table, it makes more sense to reissue the select for each publisher you wish to sum year-to-date sales for and perform the sum operation on that subset back at the server. For larger tables, the total time spent in retrieving the specific pub_ids and then performing the sum operation is less than the time it would take to sum the column row by row. Of course, for those situations in which what you wish to know is the total ytd_sales, you may have to live with the performance provided by a table scan. The key is to be fully cognizant of the exact results your application and users require and structure the queries accordingly.

From this treatment of the role of tables, indexes, and query structure in determining the performance of your SQL Server applications, you should be in a better position to review your own queries and database objects. As discussed in the configuration options for your SQL Server, other methods of impacting performance are available, such as increasing memory, percentages allocated to procedure cache, or the use of stored procedures for database access. The greatest impact on performance, however, is almost always found in the three main areas covered earlier: the normalization of the tables, availability of effective indexes, and optimized query structure. Although there are ways of improving your SQL Server performance through hardware, you can't go wrong by paying close attention to the guidelines addressed here when you set up your SQL Server environment from the beginning.

Defining and Monitoring Performance

One of the great joys of working with complex things is determining what performance measures to use. Certainly, one can choose to focus on one aspect of the equation—the server hardware, for example. By ensuring that the database server environment has 256M of RAM, a series of SMP RISC processors, and a vast, fast array of disks, many people would feel confident that they had equipped their environment with the greatest possible horsepower for getting phenomenal performance.

Unfortunately, it doesn't work that way.

In the late 1970s, buying and selling component, high-fidelity stereos was almost an art form. The array of choices ranged from QUAD four-corner speakers to amplifiers that boasted enough wattage to make your ears bleed. (Don't worry, I have a relevant point to make, and I promise, I will eventually get to it.) The vendors of such equipment had a favorite benchmark that they liked to use (and may still use today, I suppose), something they called Total Harmonic Distortion. In fact, as I remember moving from one stereo manufacturer to another, with the distortion rates moving into ever smaller numbers, someone finally informed me that ALL of these distortion rates were below the threshold of discernment for the human ear. The benchmarks measured something that it was impossible for the listener to perceive, and by extension, could not benefit from.

So what? you may say; this proves only that I was old enough to buy stereos when SuperTramp was releasing new albums. The point is that, like any component system, the performance is only as good as the weakest link. Having an extremely powerful hardware platform offset by slow client machines will result in the overall system having poor performance. You must look at the system as a whole.

In this part of this chapter, you will be taken through the various elements of the client/server equation from a performance perspective and introduced to various methods to assess their relative contribution to overall performance. The following sections of this chapter also will show you how to monitor and evaluate client/server performance as an isolated component.

Keep in mind at all times that the end result can be like playing a poor quality cassette tape on a very high quality system. The flaws are faithfully reproduced by the technology but it's difficult to enjoy the music.

Areas of Performance Impact

A number of factors can be seen as primary when addressing performance issues. The relative priority of these factors will depend entirely on your requirements, environment, and the teeth your users show. These factors include the following:

Response Time	The system's performance in processing ad hoc queries for end users.
Throughput	The volume of work handled within a specified period of time.
Cost	The financial implications of the system (especially ongoing operating costs).
Integrity	The level of assurance that the system yields correct results.
Security	The degree to which unauthorized activities are prohibited.
Availability	The percentage of down-time experienced by systems users.

As you can appreciate from this list, it will be impossible to satisfy everyone. Frequently, systems designers are asked to give the users everything they want for a buck and a half and deliver it by next Tuesday. This is just not possible.

So, now that your expectations have been set as low as I possibly can persuade you to set them, what can you do to make the best of a bad job? Actually, quite a lot.

The first step is to be aware of the real priorities. All of you who have done this once or twice before know that no matter what kind of system you are developing, client/server or otherwise, different players in the organization have different priorities. This places you squarely in the middle of conflicting interests. So, you optimize the system by balancing these competing pressures. To accomplish this, you have to follow a few general rules.

Rule #1: Give the User What He or She Wants

Performance isn't about right or wrong. It's a perception, and that perception is first and foremost held by the user. A client/server system has to put a very strong emphasis on the client. Remember, you are no longer developing in a host/slave environment!

There is a practical reason for this as well. Users who like the system will forgive it a few little idiosyncrasies. Usually, they will even forgive a great many not-so-little idiosyncrasies (read bugs, not features). If they don't like it, they will hate it no matter how well you can make it perform. It pays to work with (not against) human nature.

Rule #2: Give the User Something to Do

Ideally, you can structure your system to provide a little thought-provoking information directly relevant to the applications user. But hey, even if you can't do that, at least let the user know that something is happening. (Elevators have mirrors because people believe the ride is faster when they can look at themselves—I'm not making this up!)

Rule #3: Explain Everything as a Benefit (But Don't Lie)

Often, performance problems are perceived because the user has no idea what is going on behind the scenes. Make sure that your users hear that it isn't that the system is slow when they log in, but rather that it has great security features to protect their data against unauthorized access.

Rule #4: Take Advantage of the Environment

As part of your client/server systems architecture, you have a great many ways to skin the performance cat (apologies to all feline aficionados). When designing and optimizing your system's performance, look at the way the components are being used together and try to place the biggest load on the most powerful, under-utilized participants. Remember to include the user in that equation!

Rule #5: Second-Guess Your Assumptions

Client/server systems are inherently unstable. There are performance implications to elements of the overall system that will fall outside your control. When you are faced with performance issues, you must be willing to "go back to the drawing board" and rework, refine, and revise your system. Like leaving work at rush hour, the shortest route is not always the fastest way home.

Performance of the Technology

This chapter is still, of course, primarily about tweaking performance by addressing technical issues of the SQL Server, the data model, the query structures, communications channel throughput and client display and processing environment.

As you work with your client/server environment, you will come to gain an almost intuitive grasp of how the various components work together. In some situations, this is about the most you can hope for, particularly in areas such as intermittent bugs or days of extraordinary demands on the system. Performance tuning means balancing the demands for the most common workloads, not necessarily continually optimizing the system to accommodate an unpredictable range of peaks and valleys.

In most systems, conflicts for systems resources will fall into the following areas:

I/O Bound	The application spends a great percentage of time in disk read/write operations.
CPU Bound	The application waits while it consumes or shares central processing unit cycles.
Network Bound	The transmission of data between the client and server takes a significant percentage of time.
Screen Delay	Painting returned results on the client's workstation screen can make systems performance painful for users.

Generally, there are a few tools to help you evaluate and assess these areas of resource contention. I describe these tools in the sections that follow.

Host Performance

One of the first things you will want to know is how busy your SQL Server platform is being kept. Many sites require their SQL Server database engine to run on a host platform, which must provide other services as well. In some cases, your client/server application may not be the culprit at all, and in fact another process or application may be hogging resources. I have found this most frequently in environments in which the SQL Server host was also providing X-Terminal support. When SQL Server first starts up in the UNIX environment, it tries to acquire as much memory as specified through sp_configure. However, if it cannot grab that much it will sometimes settle for less, which can affect systems performance. In any case, from a hardware perspective, you should check to ensure that the performance of the host platform as a whole is not being compromised.

In the UNIX environment, you can obtain statistics on host performance through a number of utilities. (These may vary from flavor to flavor.)

ps -ef   This command lists the processes and their accumulated CPU time for a particular server. At the very least, it will give you an at-a-glance view of who is doing what on the system, which is helpful when trying to identify resource hogs.

sar   This command evaluates the absolute and relative percentage of I/O for each disk and controller. This is helpful for identifying disks that may be overworked relative to others on the system, which can provide a clue for identifying frequently accessed database objects that might be better spread across multiple devices.

vmstat   This command reports the usage of the host's virtual memory. In cases in which the system is configured with insufficient RAM to meet paging demands on it, the swapping rates of pages from disk to memory will be high.

time   This command will return the user, system and real-time resources used by an application.

You also may want to look at and evaluate the performance of other applications running on your server. Remember, it is how the systems components operate as a whole that affects performance. This means you will need to monitor and measure performance across your entire system, rather than focusing on detailed reports on one or two areas. In terms of tools, anything that points you to bottlenecks and trouble areas will help you optimize your system.

SQL Server Performance

When I covered the SQL Server architecture at the beginning of this book, I told you that the database engine maintains an almost self-contained system within its host, and this is largely true. Although applications running outside the SQL Server on a host machine could conceivably affect the resources available to and the performance of the database engine, it is also true that Sybase itself could be bottlenecked on an otherwise underutilized machine.

Perhaps the single most common contributor to poor performance is database design. You were exposed to an overview of the costs and benefits of normalization in Section 2 of this book. Here you will be taken through the steps and utilities that you can use to diagnose poorly performing queries and identify opportunities for changing your data model.

SQL Server processes all queries through an effective cost-based optimizer that calculates the best method for accessing data, including join order and selecting indexes. The optimizer evaluates every possible join order and calculates the cost of using every index. From these calculations, the optimizer selects the query plan that involves the least amount of I/O from the disk, which is the most constrained resource in a database management environment.

Using SHOWPLAN

You cannot make SQL Server select one query plan over another. However, there are ways to monitor how your queries are being processed that will allow you to determine whether you should modify your query or create a new index to increase performance. The way to monitor the actions of the optimizer is through the SET SHOWPLAN ON command in T-SQL.

The syntax for using SHOWPLAN with ISQL is demonstrated below:

```
1> set showplan on
2> select title, title_id
3> from titles
4> where price >19.99
5> go
```

The resulting output looks like this:

```
STEP 1
The type of query is SETON
STEP 1
The type of query is SELECT
FROM TABLE
```

```
titles
Nested iteration
Table Scan
0 rows affected.
title Computer Phobic and Non-Phobic Individuals: Behavior Variations
title_id PS1372
title Onions, Leeks, and Garlic: Cooking Secrets of the Mediterranean
title_id TC3218
```

The SHOWPLAN command breaks the query into discrete steps, each step representing the unique group of activities that must be taken on the data in order to provide results to the query. In the preceding simple query example, you can see that the results were achieved in one step. The first STEP 1, "type of query is SETON," refers to the processing of the SET SHOWPLAN ON statement itself. Once SET SHOWPLAN has been set on, it will remain active for the remainder of your ISQL or other connected session.

The second STEP 1 refers to the select title query. In other examples, you will see that showplan will specifically identify other different activities beyond the select, insert, and delete range.

In this case, the next line of output from SHOWPLAN indicates that the query type is a nested iteration. The term nested iteration does not actually tell you much, because even a select * from table with no qualifiers is also a nested iteration, as are all the other query types using select, insert, or update. Actually, a nested iteration is, as the term implies, a series of steps taken one within the other as part of the larger task. In other words, it has to do more than one thing to achieve the result.

The Table Scan statement is much more significant. In the case of a table scan, the query has elected not to use an index and instead read the entire table row by row to satisfy the query. For the pubs database this may not be significant in terms of performance; however, for large databases, table scans can take much longer to complete. Generally, the optimizer will choose to perform a table scan if more than 20 percent of the entire table's data will be retrieved by the query. Of course, the query optimizer has no choice but to perform a table scan if a useful index has not been defined on the table. *Useful* in this context can be defined as an index on the column specified in the WHERE clause. The biggest difficulty is that the optimizer will not always choose to work with the index, just because one has been defined. The trick is to define one that is appropriate for the query. The SET SHOWPLAN option can be used by you as a developer or administrator to determine whether your indexes are in fact being used by your queries.

As part of this process, you may be interested in determining the query plan without necessarily wanting to execute the query itself. After all, if you are working to determine the best form for the query, the last thing you would want to do is issue the least efficient form you could devise!

To support this, Sybase supports the NO EXEC option. An example of syntax for determining the query plan without executing it follows:

```
1> set showplan on
2> go
0 return
1> set noexec on
2> go
STEP 1
The type of query is SETON
0 return
1> select * from titles
2> where title_id != "0"
3> go
STEP 1
The type of query is SELECT
FROM TABLE
titles
Nested iteration
Table Scan
0 return
```

Now you could work with indexing the titles table until the cows come home and still never get an index to be used. This is because not equal to (!=) operations always result in table scans. If you think about it for a moment, how else could not equal to be implemented? Anything that falls outside a sorted range of unique values would necessarily be not equal to the value specified. An index could, at best, allow the query to identify the records the value was equal to and then select the remaining records. But it doesn't work that way. Queries with != operators always result in table scans.

Let's assume that you have created a unique clustered index on the `titles.title_id` column. (pubs is shipped with one!) You want to build a query that will actually use that index.

Because the title_id column is a user-defined datatype, tid, you must first determine the base datatype of the title_id column. (Hint: `sp_help tid`.) Because the user-defined data type is built out of the `varchar` definition, you use the like and other character operators. (Right? We did cover this stuff!)

To use the clustered index to obtain all of the rows from the title table where the title_id begins with 1, you could use the following syntax:

```
1> select * from titles
2> where title_id like "BU%"
3> go
STEP 1
The type of query is SELECT
FROM TABLE
titles
Nested iteration
Using Clustered Index
title_id BU2075
title You Can Combat Computer Stress!
...
```

In some cases, this may not select the complete set of results you require. By using showplan, you can try different variations of the query until you have the exact results you want and have determined that SQL Server is in fact using an index. If you wanted to retrieve the same title, but wanted others on either side of its title id, you could use the following syntax:

```
1> select * from titles
2> where title_id between "BT%" and "BV%"
3> go
```

The resulting output from showplan indicates that the clustered index was used in the retrieve.

```
STEP 1
The type of query is SELECT
FROM TABLE
titles
Nested iteration
Using Clustered Index
title_id: BU2075
title: You Can Combat Computer Stress!
...
```

Using FORCEPLAN

Earlier you were told that there is no way to force SQL Server to use a particular index. Actually, this is not true, strictly speaking. You may specify which index is to be used within the query itself. Also, you can make the optimizer select the join order of the tables to be taken from the FROM clause with an undocumented feature called FORCEPLAN.

Forcing the use of particular indexes is entirely up to the user; the risk stems from the possibility that the indexes may have been dropped and re-created, resulting in different index numbers. In a development database, however, you may find it useful to determine whether response time would be improved by the use of a particular index instead of trying to dance around with the syntax to get the optimizer to select that index of its own accord.

To demonstrate the use of both FORCEPLAN and dictating specific indexes, look at the following query:

```
1> set showplan on
2> set forceplan on
3> go
1> select * from titles(1)
2> WHERE title_id != "BZ%"
```

The resulting output is the output from showplan, indicating that the clustered index was used, followed by all the rows from the titles table.

The number surrounded by the parentheses indicates to FORCEPLAN which index is to be used. If that index cannot be used (that is, it is the wrong number), the query will terminate, indicating that the index specified in the FROM clause does not exist.

FORCEPLAN might be most useful for forcing the use of an index for a query on a large table, where the optimizer otherwise insists on a table scan.

Rules of Thumb

Remember from the coverage of indexes that there are implications and overhead to each type of index. For this reason you should not simply throw an index on all primary keys, just because they are keys. Also, depending on the nature of your queries, clustered indexes may not necessarily be the best choice. If you take the time to evaluate your queries and use showplan to determine whether SQL Server is using the indexes, you can optimize application performance. The best rule of thumb is to experiment for your own environment. There are no hard and fast rules about optimization, as too much depends on the specifics involved.

However, at the risk of incurring arguments about exceptions, the following guidelines may be able to help you in this process:

1. Structure Your Queries to Use Indexes: If you run your queries with the set showplan on option, you can see which, if any, index is being used by your query. Unless the table is very small (<100 rows), or you will be retrieving a large part of it (>25%), using indexes will speed up your query.

2. Watch the Join Order: For queries where you must join many tables together, pay particular attention to the first four in the from statement. Place those tables with defined indexes at the beginning of the statement.

3. Watch the Where Clause: While you can have as many where clause conditions as you like, you can affect whether your query uses an index by the order of those conditions. To ensure an index is used, your where clause should list the columns in the order they are indexed.

4. Use Clustered Indexes for Selects: If you have a great requirement for selecting ranges of data on a column or set of columns, using a clustered index is frequently the fastest means of retrieval.

5. Use Indexes when the Search Condition Matches the First Field Specified in the Index: The highest level of the index determines whether it will be used or not. It is not sufficient to simply create an index containing five of the keys you might want to query the table on.

6. Use Fast to Insert Data on Multiple Tables: Drop table triggers and indexes in order to get the best `bulkcopy` performance. Remember that re-indexing takes additional temporary space, as well as time. However, the time to re-index will most often be less than inserting data through `bulkcopy` in slow mode.

7. Retrieve Small Datasets from the Indexes Themselves: Remember that if your query contains only the rows maintained by the index, the optimizer will provide the result set from the index itself without going back to the table for data. This may help you identify which columns to include in the index, where you might include a column in the index not so much because it is searched on, but because it must be returned by frequent queries.

8. Keep Your Transactions Short: Locks are not relinquished until the commit or rollback takes place. If you are updating many tables and those tables have triggers, there may be performance implications for other users. Inserts and updates especially can prove irritating in this context, as the locks that are acquired are exclusive and select queries cannot complete until the change operation is finished. To a user, this looks like a long wait.

9. Index All Columns Used in Joins: The fastest queries involve two tables joined on a primary and foreign key, both of which are indexed.

10. Update Statistics: Run the update statistics command after making volume delete, update or insert operations. This will ensure your indexes perform optimally.

    Experiment for Yourself: work with your indexes and query structures until you get the performance you want. No one will argue with results!

11. Avoid the NOT EQUAL TO operator, as it does not use indexes but will perform a table scan.

Query Examples

Because you have the option of building your queries in many different ways, why not select the method most likely to yield higher performance? For instance, the following query

```
SELECT au_id, au_lname,au_fname
FROM authors
WHERE au_id = "172-32-1176" or au_id= "274-80-9391 "
```

will yield two rows after performing a table scan. However, this query

```
SELECT au_id, au_lname,au_fname
FROM authors
WHERE au_id = "172-32-1176"
UNION
select au_id, au_lname, au_fname
from authors
where au_id= "274-80-9391 "
```

will yield the same result while using the clustered unique index that is provided with the pubs database. (Try it!)

Storing Redundant Data

Relational databases are built on their own math and have their own rules for structuring data. As you might remember from the section on data modelling, normalization is a key concept in any relational database, and SQL Server is no exception. Normalization also has an impact on performance.

To save you from skipping back and rereading previous material, we can define normalization as follows:

First Normal Form	This form ensures that every row and column in a table has a single discrete value. Repeating groups are not supported within a normalized rdbms.
Second Normal Form	This form ensures that every nonkey column value depends on a primary key. In cases in which the primary key is a composite of multiple columns, all other column values must be identifiable by the entire primary key and not a subset of it.
Third Normal Form	A nonkey column value never depends on another nonkey column.

These rules are applied to data as they are organized through the data modelling process. Often, you will hear people describe their relational data model as highly normalized. In that case, not only are all the columns appropriately keyed, but redundant data is virtually eliminated from its tables.

The biggest benefits of normalization are as follows:

> Reduced redundancy translates into less overall data held in the database, and smaller databases mean faster I/O.

> With smaller tables and smaller rows, more rows fit on each data page, which results in less logical I/O. More rows are processed per I/O operation, which is more efficient; and more rows are kept in cache, which requires less physical I/O.

Costs and Implications of Normalization

Joins are necessary to obtain data across multiple tables. Joins can be costly in both CPU resources and I/O activity.

Although it may be a theoretical heresy to recommend that a relational database contain redundant data, this is one of the most widely practiced approaches to tuning performance for database servers. There are several situations in which you will want to "de-normalize" the database for performance reasons. These include the following:

1. Summary values—Where queries are run that consistently summarize data already in the database, but the response time is problematic, it is easier to store the summarized values in a table and retrieve from that table than to perform the calculations for each query.

2. Active data—Where a database table is highly active with inserts, yet a select requirement exists that will not be affected by the new data, it may make more sense to create a stable, read-only copy of the table. This is especially useful for providing select access to data that was for a historical time period. Anyone concerned with the numbers for last month will not be affected by inserts of today's values to the table. However, contending for locks with the updating operations may provide performance problems. Keep a redundant copy of the data instead.

3. Temporary tables—In many cases, you will find it faster to create a temporary table on the database and then retrieve all values held by the temporary table into your client application. For as long as the temporary table is active, the data is redundant. Perhaps the two biggest advantages of this approach

are that all the work is done on the server, and the locks placed on the original tables can be relinquished more quickly than if the query involves complicated joins to retrieve the result set.

Denormalization through Redundancy

Once you have gone through the exercise of normalizing your database, you can identify performance problems and denormalize the datamodel. If you have not undergone the effort of normalization, don't kid yourself into thinking that you simply have a denormalized database. The *de* in denormalization assumes that you know what it would look like when normalized and have made decisions about where to hold redundant data for performance reasons.

To successfully denormalize your database, you must have some real experience with how the data is used and how queries are being structured. It is not generally useful to forecast and predict how the queries will be structured and denormalize prior to testing for performance with a fully loaded database as part of the development process.

Denormalization necessarily tunes a database for a particular application or set of queries. Where you have data that is required as part of a wide variety of applications and ad-hoc queries, denormalization may "rob Peter to pay Paul."

Assuming that you have made the decision to denormalize by adding duplicate data, however, pay particular attention to consistency. You will need to add triggers to the designated master tables that update the denormalized tables. The triggers themselves may have a performance penalty. But not implementing such a mechanism creates the risk of the data becoming different between the two tables. This will create problems of its own for those users who retrieve results from the tables and potentially make decisions based on that data. The best candidates for denormalization are nonvolatile data, such as finance data for a period that has already been closed. Copying such rows off into a separate query table has no real impact on the validity of the data for those users who retrieve it, and it ensures that applications that must update the master tables do not have to contend with multiple shared locks placed by select statements.

Denormalization through Table Segmentation

As you become more familiar with the queries issued against your database in practice, you may frequently find that a specific subset of a larger table is required. For instance, in a financial database, last month's results may be selected frequently from a database containing annual information. For performance reasons, you may want to segment or split your tables into multiple tables on the basis of columns or rows.

For example, for the finance database above, you might choose to segment your tables by time, in order to separate the most active data from the largest collection of data. For instance, you could choose to break your data into 12 tables one for each of the last 12 months. Keep in mind that this segmentation is much different than simply maintaining a duplicate data set. Segmentation separates the data through naming multiple tables to contain subsets of what in a normalized database design would normally be held in a single table.

Additionally, you can split the tables out across columns, duplicating the primary key for each of the new tables and turning them into foreign keys. In this way, the columns per table would be smaller, yielding all the performance benefits referred to earlier in this chapter. The cost is in duplicating the indexed column, but this may prove to be a more desirable duplication than an entire table.

Remember that the more active the data, the less attractive duplicate data becomes as the likelihood of database inconsistency increases.

Contrived Columns

Another method of denormalizing your database is to add contrived or arbitrary columns to your tables. By placing sequential row numbers that have no real meaning of their own other than to identify a row, you can reduce long composite primary and foreign keys. An example of this would be to place arbitrary numbers on the titles table for each unique book title IF there had not already been a title_id column. If the data is not provided by the application or business unit, there may be performance benefits to creating such columns for use by the database. These benefits are derived by using these columns in indexes to replace larger composite keys. Creating contrived sequential keys on tables can be awkward in SQL Server prior to System 10, in which this feature is supported explicitly. You can use the global variable @@DBTS, however, which is the database timestamp to supply you with a unique value.

Database Objects and Performance

You will affect performance through your choice of columns and tables, and you will inherit performance implications from your selection of datatypes and table structure. I have discussed how data pages are locked and form the basis for I/O operations. At this point, you should become more familiar with the structure of a data page itself and how it affects performance.

In SQL Server, all data pages are 2048 bytes (except Stratus-based systems, which are 4096). Of these 2048 bytes, 32 bytes are used for the page header and an additional 32 bytes are allocated to contain the row id offset to allow rows to move on the page. Remember that clustered indexes involve a physical sorting of the data. Inserts then have the implication of requiring the reordering of rows held on any given page.

SQL Server manages these data pages by linking them within the table and allocating new pages in extents, or 8-page groupings. As such, when a new row is added, requiring an additional page of storage for the table, 16K is allocated. This ensures that rows can be added without requiring an allocation operation for each new row.

When you define your columns in a table, 4 bytes of overhead are allocated in addition to the row size, which is the cumulative size of the columns. However, this is only the case for rows that do not contain variable length columns such as varchar and varbinary. In cases in which columns are defined with variable lengths, an additional 5 bytes are allocated for the first variable length column, plus 1 byte more for each additional variable length column in the row. But here's the kicker: Any column that allows nulls is automatically stored as if it were a variable length column. Depending on the number of rows in your table, this can amount to a sizeable storage cost for allowing nulls.

Calculating Table Size and Data Pages

Because you now know how to determine the exact number of bytes required per row, including SQL Server allocated overhead, and it has been established that the net data per page is equal to 1984 bytes, you can use this calculation:

```
TS=(CL+OH)*R
```

where TS is table size, CL is column length, OH is overhead, and R is equal to the number of rows. For a million-row table, with 10 columns each with a length of 12 and 6 allowing nulls, this calculation would be as follows:

```
TS=(120+14)*1,000,000 or 134,000,000 bytes or 130.85 Mb
```

However, for performance-monitoring purposes, SQL Server expresses everything in pages of I/O. To determine how many data pages this represents, you must divide the column length and overhead into the amount of storage space available per page.

Sybase generally uses an average of 75 percent full for each data page to allow for random updates and deletes. As such, the calculation would be as follows:

```
RPP=DP/(CL+OH)
```

where RPP equals rows per page, DP is the amount of data storage actually available on a data page (1984 bytes), and the column length and overhead for the row is represented by CL and OH respectively. For the preceding example, the calculation would be as follows:

```
RPP=1984/134
```

or 14 rows per page, rounding to the nearest complete row. To determine the total number of data pages contained in this table (TDP), you must divide the number of rows (R) by the number of rows per page (RPP) times the percentage of data pages full (75 percent). This can be represented as follows:

```
TDP=R/(RPP*F%)
```

Once again working with our million-row example, this would be expressed as

```
TDP=1,000,000/(14 *.75) or 95,238 data pages.
```

The number of data pages for a table becomes a useful measure when you use the set statistics IO on option. This will tell you how many data pages are read as part of a query operation. When trying to predict performance, you can use a baseline estimate of 50 data pages per second read, but you should be aware that every system will be somewhat different based on CPU and RAM resources available.

Another method you might use to calculate space requirements within a given database is through some Sybase-supplied stored procedures—specifically, sp_estspace and sp_spaceused.

sp_spaceused is a Sybase-supplied stored procedure used to determine the amount of space allocated for a specified table, the amount used for data and indexes, and the amount available or unused. This stored procedure computes the number of rows, data pages, and space used by an object or objects in the current database. However, users of it have found it less than completely accurate and/or useful. As a result, an UNSUPPORTED stored procedure has been making the rounds. I have included it here for those who wish to review it (or use it) and have kept it intact including the credits for authorship. This sp was downloaded from CompuServe, where I assume it has been placed for public consumption. I do not know the authors, but would like to say thanks on behalf of all the people who use sp_estspace. (This procedure has been accepted, formalized and included with SQL Server Release 10.0.)

The sp_estspace procedure is as follows:

```
create procedure sp_estspace
    /*  A procedure to estimate the disk space requirements of a table
    **  and its associated indexes.
    **  November 21, 1991
    **  Written by Malcolm Colton with assistance from Hal Spitz
    **  Modified by Jim Panttaja November 25, 1991
    */
        (@table_name varchar(30)=null,  /* name of table to estimate */
         @no_of_rows float = 1,          /* number of rows in the table */
         @fill_factor float = 0,       /* the fill factor */
         @cols_to_max varchar(255) =null  /* variable length columns for
which
                        to use the maximum rather than 50% of
                        the maximum length  */
        )
    as

    declare @msg    varchar(120)

    /*  Give usage statement if @table_name is null */

    if @table_name = null or @no_of_rows = 1
    begin
        print 'Usage is:'
        print ' estspace table_name, no_of_rows, fill_factor,
        ➥cols_to_max'
        print 'where table_name is the name of the table,'
        print ' no_of_rows is the number of rows in the table,'
        print ' fill_factor is the index fill factor (default = 0) '
        print ' cols_to_max is a list of the variable length columns'
        print ' for which to use the maximum length instead of the
        ➥average'
        print '                          (default = null)'
        print 'Examples: estspace titles, 10000, 50, "title, notes"'
        print ' estspace titles, 50000'
        print ' estspace titles, 50000, 0, null, 40'
        return
    end

    declare  @sum_fixed     int,
        @sum_var   int,
        @sum_avgvar     int,
        @table_id int,
        @num_var   int,
        @data_pages     float,
        @sysstat   tinyint,
        @temp           float,
        @index_id int,
        @last_id   int,
        @i         int,
```

```
        @level_pages   float,
        @key          varchar(30),
        @usertype tinyint,
        @type           tinyint,
        @level          tinyint,
        @vartype   smallint,
        @more           bit,
        @next_level    float,
        @rows_per_page smallint,
        @row_len   smallint,
        @length         tinyint,
        @index_name    varchar(30),
        @page_size      smallint,
        @page_K         tinyint,
        @index_type    varchar(20),
        @factor         float

select   @sum_fixed=0,
    @sum_var=0,
    @sum_avgvar=0,
    @table_id=0,
    @num_var=0,
    @data_pages=0,
    @row_len=0,
    @sysstat=0

set nocount on

/* Make sure table exists */

select @sysstat = sysstat,
    @table_id = id
        from sysobjects where name = @table_name
        and uid = user_id()

if @sysstat & 7 not in (1,3)
begin
    select @msg = "I can't find the table "+@table_name
    print @msg
    return
end

/* Get machine page size */

select   @page_size = low - 32
    from master.dbo.spt_values
        where type = 'E'
        and number = 1

select @page_K = (@page_size +32) /1024
```

```
    if @fill_factor !=0
        select @fill_factor = @fill_factor / 100.0

/* Create tables for results */

create table #results
    (name      varchar(30),
     type      varchar(12),
     level     tinyint,
     pages     float,
     Kbytes float)

create table #times
    (name           varchar(30),
     type           varchar(12) null,
     tot_pages      float,
     time_mins      float      null)

/* Create table of column info for the table to be estimated */

select length, type, name, offset
    into #col_table
        from syscolumns
            where id = @table_id

/* Look up the important values from this table */

select @sum_fixed = isnull(sum(length),0)
    from #col_table
        where offset !< 0

select @num_var = isnull(count(*),0),
        @sum_var = isnull(sum(length),0)
    from #col_table
        where offset < 0
            and charindex(name, @cols_to_max) > 0

select @num_var = @num_var + isnull(count(*),0),
  @sum_avgvar = isnull(sum(length / 2),0)
    from #col_table
        where offset < 0
            and charindex(name, @cols_to_max) = 0

/* Calculate the data page requirements */

if @num_var = 0
    select @row_len = 4.0 + @sum_fixed
else
    select @row_len = 8.0 + @sum_fixed + @sum_var +@sum_avgvar
+ @num_var + (@sum_var +@sum_avgvar) / 256.0
```

```
    /* Allow for fill-factor if set to other than zero */

    if @fill_factor = 0
        select @temp = convert(float, @no_of_rows) *
            ( convert(float, @row_len) / convert(float, @page_size) )
    else
    begin
        select @temp = convert(float, @no_of_rows) /
            (convert(float, @page_size) * convert(float, @fill_factor)
)
        select @temp = convert(float, @row_len) * @temp
    end

    /* Now add in allocation pages */
    select @temp = @temp +(@temp / 256.0)
    select @data_pages = @temp + 1.0
    if @data_pages < 8.0
        select @data_pages = 8.0

    insert #results values
        (@table_name, 'data', 0, @data_pages, @data_pages * @page_K)

    /* See if the table has any indexes */

    select @index_id = min(indid)
        from sysindexes
            where id = @table_id
                and indid > 0

    if @index_id = null /* We've finished if there are no indexes */
    begin
        select @msg = @table_name + ' has no indexes'
        print @msg
        select name, type, level,
            Pages = str(pages,12,0), Kbytes = str(Kbytes,12,0)
            from #results

        select Total_Mbytes = str(sum(Kbytes)/1000.0,15,0)
            from #results

        drop table #results
        return
    end

    select    @sum_fixed = 0,
        @sum_var = 0,
        @num_var = 0,
        @temp = 0

    /* For each index, calculate the important variables
    ** use them to calculate the index size, and print it */
```

```
while @index_id != null
begin
    select @index_name = name
        from sysindexes
            where id = @table_id
            and indid = @index_id

    if @index_id = 1
        select @index_type = 'clustered'
    else
        select @index_type = 'nonclustered'

    select    @num_var = 0,
        @sum_var = 0,
        @sum_fixed = 0

    select @i = 1

    /* Look up each of the key fields for the index */

    while @i <= 16
    begin
        select @key = index_col(@table_name, @index_id, @i)

        if @key = null
            break
        else            /* Process one key field */
        begin
            select @type = type, @length = length, @vartype =
            ➥offset
                from syscolumns
                    where id = @table_id
                    and name = @key

            if @vartype < 0
                select @num_var = @num_var + 1
            else
                select @sum_fixed = @sum_fixed + @length

            if @vartype < 0
            /* variable:check if in @cols_to_max */
            begin
                if charindex(@key, @cols_to_max) = 0
                  select @sum_var = @sum_var + (@length / 2)
                else
                  select @sum_var = @sum_var + @length
            end
        end

        select @i = @i + 1
        /* Get next key field in this index */
    end
```

```
/* Calculate the space used by this index */

if @num_var = 0
    select @row_len = 5 + @sum_fixed
else
    select @row_len = @sum_fixed + @sum_var + @num_var + 8

if @index_id != 1   /* add row id for nc indexes */
    select @row_len = @row_len + 4

select @level = 0

/* Allow for fill-factor if set to other than zero */

if @fill_factor = 0
    select @rows_per_page = @page_size / @row_len - 2
else
    select @rows_per_page = @page_size /
            @row_len * @fill_factor

if @rows_per_page > 256
    select @rows_per_page = 256

/* For clustered indexes, the first level of index
** is based on the number of data pages.
** For nonclustered, it is the number of data rows      */

if @index_id = 1
    select @next_level = @data_pages
else
    select @next_level = @no_of_rows

select @more = 1     /* Flag for end of index levels */
while @more = 1
begin

    /* calculate the number of pages at a single index level */

    select @temp = @next_level / convert(float, @rows_per_page)

    /* Add in a factor for allocation pages */
    if @temp > 200.0
        select @temp = @temp + (@temp /256.0) + 1.0

    select @level_pages = @temp

    insert #results values
        (@index_name, @index_type, @level, @level_pages,
            @level_pages * @page_K)

    if @index_id != 1 and @level = 0 /*adjust NC non-leaf rows */
```

```
                        begin
                        select @row_len = @row_len + 4

                        /* Allow for fill-factor if set to other than zero */

                        if @fill_factor = 0
                            select @rows_per_page = @page_size/@row_len - 2
                        else
                            select @rows_per_page = @page_size/@row_
                                    len*@fill_factor
                        end

                if @rows_per_page > 256
                    select @rows_per_page = 256

                select @next_level = @level_pages
                select @level = @level + 1

                /* see if we can fit the next level in 1 page */
                if @rows_per_page >= @next_level
                    select @more = 0
            end

        /* Account for single root page */
        if @level_pages > 1
            insert #results values
                (@index_name, @index_type, @level, 1, @page_K)

        /* Now look for next index id for this table */

        select @last_id = @index_id
        select @index_id = null
        select @index_id = min(indid)
            from sysindexes
                where id = @table_id
                and indid > @last_id

    end

select name, type, level, Pages = str(pages,12,0),
    Kbytes = str(Kbytes,12,0)
from #results

select Total_Mbytes = str(sum(Kbytes)/1000.0,15,0)
from #results

drop table #results
drop table #col_table

return
```

The `sp_estspace` procedure is more reliable and accurate than the Sybase-supplied `sp_spaceused`. As with any unsupported software, no one will guarantee that it will work for your particular environment and Sybase version. But, hey, give it a try. It probably beats calculating everything with a pencil and paper!

Hardware Impact on Performance

If you strap a jet engine to a brick, you can make it fly. Frequently, performance bottlenecks can be a function of hardware, whether in the amount and configuration of disk, RAM resources, CPU, or network. Hardware has a significant impact on performance. Let's look at a few of the considerations you might want to take into account when evaluating your SQL Server hardware environment.

DISK   As you have seen before, database applications are almost always I/O constrained. This is where the bulk of the bottlenecks occur. The following is a checklist for evaluating disk configurations for your Sybase client/server solution:

■ Many smaller disks
■ Fastest possible access time
■ High throughput rate
■ Enable asynchronous I/O on the host
■ Use raw disk partitions

There are a number of reasons why you should take this checklist into account. Sybase recommends asynchronous disk I/O and raw disk partitions for the optimum performance consideration. Raw disk partitions have added data integrity services as well, in as much as the operating system cannot buffer any committed transactions.

However, you should take into account the type and configuration of the hard disks themselves. Part of this relates to the operation of hard disks generically. To make clear the impact of disk types on your SQL Server's performance, you will be shown a little of how a hard disk functions. For software people, including DBAs, this is frequently a revelation. If you already know all this, sorry, but I think it's important, so why not look it over for review.

When ordering a system to be a dedicated SQL Server, often much discussion takes place about how much disk will be required, and this discussion is justified. Management never likes to approve expansions and extensions after having invested serious dollars in such esoteric gear as SQL Servers and such. But an equally important consideration is the type of disks and their configuration.

The checklist recommends many smaller disks over one or two big disks. As I review how hard disks work, the reasons for this should become more evident.

A hard disk is an electromechanical device. Unlike integrated circuits, it has moving parts and is limited to the speed of those parts. The disk heads must range over the platters where the data is stored in order to perform read and write operations. The speed with which these heads move is called the ACCESS TIME. A fast hard disk will have an access time <10 milliseconds. However, access time on its own does not give you a true picture of how well your disk subsystem will perform. You must also evaluate the TRANSFER RATE of your hard disk. This refers to the amount of data that can be picked up by the disk and passed through for processing. A typical hard disk has a transfer rate of approximately 1.5 megabytes per second. The transfer rate will determine how fast the data can be read or written once the heads have been positioned on the appropriate section of the disk.

The reason for choosing many disks over one or two is simply the manner in which SQL Server operates. Because of the write ahead log, SQL Server is always performing database changes at least twice: once to log the change, and then once again to actually perform it on the database. By allocating logs, indexes, and data onto separate physical hard disks, the work is split among the various disk devices. When these disks are also managed by separate controllers, considerable speed increases can be achieved. Reads and writes can occur in parallel rather than in sequential order. This is where the hard disk configuration for your system can place a tremendous physical restriction on the performance of your SQL Server. As you can appreciate, where a limitation or bottleneck is physical in nature, you can evaluate queries, change strategies, denormalize the database, and generally run around like a chicken with its head cut off and nothing will improve performance past that point.

RAM   There is no substitute for physical memory. Virtual memory has been a great boon for systems since it was developed and incorporated by a big blue company that shall remain nameless. However, for your database application, you must ever keep uppermost in mind that your system is likely to be I/O bound. And that means that you do not really want the system to have to go out to get pages from disk, swapping them in and out of RAM. It is much better for everything to be loaded in RAM, as it will execute much more quickly.

Remember that Sybase must compete with other applications for RAM on the server platform. If you are running other applications, review the situation carefully— Sybase will not always complain that it could not grab all the RAM for which it was configured on boot up. Especially watch X-Term sessions, if you are running in a UNIX Motif environment. The server must allocate approximately 1M of RAM for every X-Term session it supports.

Although Sybase will run on as little as 8M, remember too that the data and procedure cache are important contributors to performance. When a query has been executed and the data is held in RAM (in the data cache), subsequent queries against that data execute much more quickly. The same is true of stored procedures. If you repeatedly execute an sp and it remains in the cache, you will find that there is a real performance increase. Cache is important and it is a function of the amount of RAM that has been installed on your server. Ensure that you have sufficient RAM and you can eliminate a bottleneck almost as important as the disk.

Network Performance

Perhaps by now you are getting tired of constantly being reminded that the network is an integral part of the client/server equation. Well, too bad. Sorry if that seems harsh, but the more awareness you have of the role played by your communications channel, the more likely you are to be able to design and develop high-performance applications.

First, let's consider what the network does. The primary purpose of the network is to relay queries from the application running on the client back to the server and return the resulting data to the application for display and further manipulation. Sounds simple enough. But as I have discussed elsewhere in the book, million-row tables are hardly out of the question for many SQL Server sites. To simply bring all of those rows down to a PC or workstation client will definitely choke a network. The key is to tailor the solution to fit the requirements and the environment.

A local area network, such as Ethernet, has a theoretical throughput of 10 megabits per second, or 1.25 megabytes per second. This translates to the equivalent throughput of a hard drive. However, in reality an ethernet network never achieves the theoretical maximum throughput for a number of reasons. Network traffic, collisions, and delays all add overhead and deduct time available to effect a transfer, thus reducing the speed. The speed of the Ethernet cards between the server and the client may be mismatched or busy with additional requests for data from other servers.

Additionally, as you have seen in the chapter on Net-Lib, many PC's and other workstations are dedicated to supporting more than one protocol. All of this takes away from the processing power devoted to transferring SQL Server data from client to server and back again. The net result? Much slower transfer rates than a hard drive. In fact, the average throughput for Ethernet in many circumstances is approximately 300-400 kilobytes per second.

Consider, then, that almost half a megabyte per second is still a lot of data; networks, however, require addressing and control characters in the packets, so of that 400 Kbps, a considerable percentage is not data, but rather addressing and packet overhead. Once you take all of this into account, the effective throughput seems more like the transfer rate of a floppy diskette drive rather than that of a local hard drive.

The key to optimizing network performance is to ensure that the traffic is minimized. However, where you have a result set that an application will not require refreshed data for, it is frequently worthwhile to load the data into the PC at the beginning of the session. From then on the user works with the application and processes the data locally, enjoying the response time of a dedicated machine without the worries of network traffic or high server utilization.

Wide-Area Networks

This requirement applies especially to users who are connected over a serial asynchronous link or some kind of packet-switching network. The bandwidth or throughput rates for these communications channels are highly limited. Even with data compression and fast modems, a remote link to a SQL Server will yield a throughput rate of only 2kpbs (based on a 14.4k modem). Faster modems will, of course, increase the rate, but look at the base number—twice as fast is still not very fast.

Does this mean that you should not look to incorporate WAN users into your SQL Server solution? Not at all. It means simply that you may find yourself reworking your applications in order to compensate for the restricted communications channel. For example, stored procedures are called by name and can take parameters. From that standpoint, a remote client can issue a call to the SQL Server that is very short and quite practical for a remote link. On the server side, the server performs all the work specified in the stored procedure and returns the result. For links such as these, you would not want to have many raw rows returned to the end user or client machine for further processing. Instead, you perform as much work as possible on the server and return the minimum number of rows to the application across the communications channel.

Balancing the Load

Evaluate each component of the client/server equation. How powerful is the server? What utilization rate does it have? Is there excess capacity? Is the client workstation new and fast or old and pokey? Is the network busy with multiple servers and little segmentation? Are collisions frequent? Do any users expect to log in remotely?

With a powerful dedicated server, a solid network, and an older PC, you will want to perform as much work as you can on the server. If your server, on the other hand, is used for many things, and the workstations are new and fast, with a reliable network connection, structure your queries to bring the results down to the local machine. If you have good client workstations, a high-speed fiber network, and a powerful dedicated server, do whatever you want. But review the results. Performance can bottleneck in any number of places. Use the troubleshooting methodology not just to solve connection problems, but to systematically review your actual Sybase client/server solution's performance, and look for ways to improve it. Don't be afraid to experiment and evaluate. This is the key to optimizing your SQL Server system.

Summary

I have often said that you can often use hardware to overcome systems performance deficiencies—for example, with a powerful enough jet engine you can make something with the aerodynamics of a brick actually fly. The real performance payback comes, however, from investing in good database design, and watching how your queries take advantage of indexes.

By paying attention to these factors, you might just be able to save yourself a little money on hardware. More important, as a developer, these are things over which you may have more influence than issues such as Server platform, configuration, and competing applications.

Performance is difficult to design for. Even with the hardware side of the equation, frequently a client/server systems architect ends up overestimating requirements and hopes the configuration will be sufficient. And even with a thorough data-modeling process, you will be hard-pressed to identify which database objects are going to give you response-time headaches. Instead, you must have some idea of how your database is being used, and you must monitor actual performance to identify problem areas. There are a number of ways to deal with performance problems, ranging from more hardware to denormalization and storing redundant data. Keeping the considerations covered in this chapter in mind, you should be in a better position to address some of the poor performing areas of your Sybase client/server solution.

Performance and tuning of a SQL Server environment is a subject for an entire book. I would like to be able to cover the subject in more detail, but the purpose here is to introduce you to the general performance and tuning considerations. From here you should have the basis to be able to review and evaluate your own environment, and determine which of the potential bottlenecks is likely to be the culprit. Then you can proceed to get the more in-depth information you will need to be able to make a difference for your site.

The Open Client Architecture

Introduction

UNTIL NOW, YOU HAVE BEEN TREATED TO A VIEW OF YOUR SQL Server as a self-contained environment running on the host platform. Although some discussion of the commitment to open architecture through the application programming interface was included, most of the focus has been on internals, such as T-SQL, datatypes, and database performance.

This section addresses the SQL Server as one component of an integrated client/ server solution. Integration of existing applications and other third party software is the single biggest reason for moving to Sybase. As a developer of client/server solutions, it is vital that you understand the principles of the Sybase approach to open architecture.

This section introduces all the various software components that make up an end-to-end client/server application. Sybase-supplied products such as the Open Client Net-Library, which allows your applications to connect to your Sybase database engine over a number of networks, are covered in detail.

The DB-Library API is also covered in some detail. Although those of you who are using off-the-shelf development environments will be using products that already incorporate DB-Library, anyone wishing to build applications in C (or other languages) will need to know how to incorporate the DB-Library functions into their applications. This section introduces each of the required components and takes you through several detailed examples of the steps you must take to build a client\server application of your own.

The first chapter is a generic introduction to the Open Client DB-Library product offered by Sybase for a number of environments. This chapter introduces the typical methods in which it is used and shows functional examples of the DB-Library syntax.

Later chapters have increasing amounts of detail, including demonstrations of how you can manage connections to multiple servers, and methods to split the processing requirements for a given query across the client and server machines.

By the end of this section, you as a software developer should have a solid grip on the functions and services available to you when you create custom programs. The role of each software product is also discussed, as this is frequently a source of confusion among developers new to the SQL Server development environment.

5.1

The Open Client DB-Library

As you remember from the history of Sybase, there has been a commitment to connection to third-party products from the earliest implementation of the SQL Server product. Unlike other relational database products on the market that enable you only to build applications with their tools or to use embedded SQL to write in your language of choice, SQL Server was one of the first RDBMS products to support an API. This application programming interface was known as DB-Library.

Although T-SQL can be used to access the data in your SQL Server interactively through ISQL or through a stored procedure, the Open Client software provides even more functions and features for accessing the database through an applications program.

This chapter introduces the Open Client DB-Library functions and explains how they can be used generically. By the end of this chapter, you should have a good grasp of what people mean when they throw around the terms Open Client and DB-Library, and more importantly, you will know whether these products will play a role in your SQL Server environment. If you are a Sybase Developer, it is more than likely that at some point they will.

What Is Open Client DB-Library?

I thought you'd never ask! Open Client is the term used by Sybase to refer to a set of prewritten and compiled functions that are supplied to a programmer for use in developing applications that access the database. Open Client is the way Sybase sends ISQL queries and statements to a SQL Server through a program rather than interactively.

You have to buy the Open Client libraries from Sybase separately (in some cases they come with your SQL Server but on a separate diskette). Like the Net-Libraries, there are different products that you can choose between to best meet your needs. There are versions of Open Client DB-Library for C, FORTRAN, Pascal, Ada, and CO-BOL programming languages. The most widely used approach is to write application programs in C.

For writing applications in the C language running on Microsoft-based personal computers, you would use the Open Client DB-Library for PC/DOS. Provided with this version are the libraries necessary to successfully include and compile DB-Lib calls into your C programs. The documentation with this package indicates that Microsoft C compiler version 6.0 and higher are supported. To determine whether your particular programming language and target environment is supported by an Open Client offering, call Sybase customer service or sales support at 1-800-8SYBASE.

These functions include compiled 3GL functions, source files, and macros. You don't need to understand exactly how these Sybase-supplied functions have been implemented—in fact, Sybase does not recommend modifying the DB-Lib header files. To write applications, you need to know only what syntax to use, the parameters the functions require, and how to handle the returned results. The functions included in Open Client DB-Library have been specifically written by Sybase to take advantage of the distributed architecture inherent in client/server applications. By using them, you ensure that you are creating client/server applications without necessarily having to understand how to manage the client/server calls from the ground up.

The process used when creating applications using Open Client DB-Library is as follows:

1. Establish a connection with your SQL Server.
2. Assemble a batch of SQL statements in the buffer.
3. Submit the statement batch to the SQL Server.
4. Sequentially process the statements and retrieve the results.
5. Close the connection.

You use the Open Client DB-Library functions to manage the login and database connection process, as well as the submission of the statements, returned results, and handling of any errors. The SQL Server behavior during transactions also applies to statements submitted through DB-Library, including all server locks, rollback, and commit tran activities.

The Open Client DB-Library works with Net-Library to establish a connection to the SQL Server, submit a query, and pass data back to the application. The specific requirements of the network software and hardware are entirely handled by Net-Library. Because of this, any successfully compiled program that incorporates DB-Library functions can execute on any network or communications channel for which Net-Library access has been installed. This enables you to develop applications that are portable across the many different connectivity schemes supported by SQL Server.

Note that the Open Client DB-Lib calls are handled according to the same principles regardless of the programming language you use them in.

Establishing a Connection

The first step when building a DB-Lib application is to provide for the SQL Server login. This involves several steps. Within the client application, each login is handled as a distinct process and is identified at the beginning of the program with the dbproc.

You can have multiple open logins within the application as long as you establish each with a unique dbprocess name, such as dbproc1 or dbproc2. To complete the login sequence, you must set the user name, password, and application name and send them to the SQL Server with the dbopen function. As such, a valid block of code for establishing a connection with a SQL Server could be as follows:

```
DBPROCESS *dbproc;
LOGINREC  *loginrec;

loginrec = dblogin();
DBSETLUSER(loginrec, "sa");
DBSETLPWD(loginrec, "esoteric_password");
DBSETLAPP(loginrec, "application_name");
dbproc = dbopen(loginrec, "dsquery");
```

This demonstrates the elements of the Open Client DB-Lib commands necessary to initiate communications between the client application and the SQL Server. As stated already, this presupposes that the necessary Net-Library programs and environment variables have been set up as well as the network software and hardware.

The definitions of the functions are as follows:

> dblogin()   This function allocates space for and returns a pointer to a LOGINREC structure for use by the dbopen() function. If the structure cannot be allocated, a NULL is returned. As well as user name, application name, and password, the login structure can incorporate a workstation name and national language (DBSETLHOST and DBSETNATLANG respectively).

> dbopen()   This function allocates and initializes a DBPROCESS structure, which is used until the session is closed or the application is exited. The dbopen() function passes the login record defined through dblogin and sends it to the target SQL Server. You can use any valid Server Name or, in the event of a defined local SQL Server such as DSQUERY, you can use a null pointer and the local server is assumed by default.

> In the event of error, a NULL is returned. Errors include unavailable SQL Server, incorrect login, and insufficient memory for process.

After the application has been established, but before T-SQL commands can be built into the program buffer, you must tell your application which database to use. To accomplish this, you use the dbuse() function, passing to it the name of the dbprocess and the database to use. To use the pubs database with the login established here, you would add the following:

```
DBPROCESS *dbproc;
LOGINREC  *loginrec;

loginrec = dblogin();
DBSETLUSER(loginrec, "sa");
DBSETLPWD(loginrec, "esoteric_password");
DBSETLAPP(loginrec, "application_name");
dbproc = dbopen(loginrec, "dsquery");
dbuse(dbproc,"pubs")
```

dbuse()   This returns one of two values: SUCCEED or FAIL. You can process your error handling based on either of those values. More on error handling is included later in the chapter, but for now you will see only the most straightforward examples of DB-Lib syntax and structure.

Having successfully issued a dbuse, you can begin building your query in the command buffer.

Assembling the Command Batch

The dbcmd() function places text in the command buffer of the dbprocess. As you issue successive dbcmd functions, the text is appended in the buffer until sent to the server.

dbcmd(dbproc, string)   This function moves the enclosed literal string into the command buffer of the dbprocess structure identified. The returned values are either SUCCEED or FAIL. Subsequent dbcmd calls are concatenated; you must include a space at the beginning and end of the strings if you wish them to be separated. For example, dbcmd(dbproc, this is a li) dbcmd(dbproc, ne of text) would be treated in the buffer as a string consisting of "this is a line of text". When you are issuing separate statements, you must ensure appropriate spacing or the strings assembled in the buffer will be garbled. Sending the buffer to the SQL Server clears the buffer, so you don't need to worry about appending new commands to the previous ones in the buffer after the batch has been sent.

dbfcmd(dbproc, string)   This supports the appending of commands to the DBPROCESS buffer with the C run-time library sprintf style formatting options. The function is used to interpret a format string and pass program data to the command buffer, avoiding the need to rebuild or recode the query. To work with this feature, you specify a % symbol followed by c for character. The sprintf program variable types are as follows:

%c	char
%d	int
%e	double
%f	double
%g	double
%s	null-terminated string
%u	unsigned decimal
%x	unsigned hexadecimal string
%%	none

You might choose to build your command buffer using dbfcmd to retrieve a name with the following syntax:

```
dbcmd(dbproc, "select * from authors")
dbfcmd(" where au_id = %s", get_id)
```

In this case, the %s formats the value get_id as a null-terminated string and places it in the command buffer appended to the select statement as one complete T-SQL expression.

As you can see from this example, you can use dbcmd and dbfcmd interchangeably to build commands in your buffer according to the variable formatting and handling requirements of your application.

Sending the Commands to the SQL Server

Once you have built a valid command or set of commands in the buffer, you send them to the SQL Server through the dbsqlexec() function.

dbsqlexec(dbproc)   This function sends all the commands in the buffer to the SQL Server for processing, flushing the buffer for any new commands. Optionally, you can set the DBNOAUTOFREE option, which requires you to specifically issue a dbfreebuf command to flush the command buffer. However, the default is to free all space in the command buffer on issuing a dbsqlexec() call. The returned result from calling dbsqlexec is either SUCCEED or FAIL. The entire batch must be syntactically correct or none of the commands will execute. Additionally, the command batch might fail due to incorrect permissions or wrong database object names. If it fails for any reason, the returned code is simply FAIL.

In the following sample, you can see that using DB-Library functions to declare a login structure, build a query in the command buffer, and send the commands to the SQL Server could be written in a manner similar to this:

```
DBPROCESS *dbproc;
LOGINREC  *loginrec;

loginrec = dblogin();
DBSETLUSER(loginrec, "sa");
DBSETLPWD(loginrec, "esoteric_password");
DBSETLAPP(loginrec, "application_name");
dbproc = dbopen(loginrec, "dsquery");
dbuse(dbproc,"pubs")
dbcmd (dbproc, "select * from authors");
dbcomd (dbproc, " where au_lname = worden");
dbsqlexec(dbproc)
```

However, at this point, you still need to handle the results returned from the query.

Managing the Returned Results

For purposes of this example, you can assume that you are managing the statements sent to the SQL Server with discrete dbsqlexec calls. Depending on the nature of your application and environment, you could choose to log out of the SQL Server altogether or exit the application. It is generally good practice to treat each discrete set of queries as a separate batch. This allows you to more easily handle the returned rows or messages from the SQL Server. You use dbbind to manipulate the returned rows. However, to know whether or not the query was in fact successful, you must first look at the value returned for dbresults().

dbresults()   This function returns one of three values: SUCCEED, FAIL, or NO_MORE_ROWS. FAIL usually indicates a syntax error in the command buffer sent or a dead/inactive dbproc. However, it is also possible to trap the exact error if you have installed error and message handlers in your application. The dbresults() function is commonly used for processing subsequent commands in the command buffer. For example, if dbresults() = SUCCEED, then your program moves on to the next set of functions you wish it to perform.

The dbresults() function does not return control to your application until it receives a response from the SQL Server. In some cases, this is not desirable. You can call the dbdataready() function prior to dbresults() and set the Open Client DB-Library timeout value to allow you to regain control after a set period.

Assuming you have obtained results from your query, you must now bind the results into program variables, using dbbind().

```
dbbind(dbproc, column_number, variable_type, variable_length,
variable_address)
```

Starting with the first column (column1), the dbbind command binds the value retrieved from the SQL Server into a declared program variable. One call to dbbind is required for each column specified in the command buffer that was sent by dbsqlexec. For the select * from authors command that you saw a little earlier, the results might be handled in this fashion:

```
DBPROCESS *dbproc;
LOGINREC  *loginrec;

loginrec = dblogin();
DBSETLUSER(loginrec, "sa");
DBSETLPWD(loginrec, "esoteric_password");
DBSETLAPP(loginrec, "application_name");
dbproc = dbopen(loginrec, "dsquery");
dbuse(dbproc,"pubs")
dbcmd (dbproc, "select * from authors");
dbcomd (dbproc, " where au_lname = worden");
dbsqlexec(dbproc)
dbresults(dbproc)
dbbind(dbproc,1, NTBSTRINGBIND, (DBCHAR) 0, au_id);
dbbind(dbproc,1, NTBSTRINGBIND, (DBCHAR) 0, au_lname);
dbbind(dbproc,1, NTBSTRINGBIND, (DBCHAR) 0, au_fname);
dbbind(dbproc,1, NTBSTRINGBIND, (DBCHAR) 0, au_phone);
dbbind(dbproc,1, NTBSTRINGBIND, (DBCHAR) 0, au_address);
dbbind(dbproc,1, NTBSTRINGBIND, (DBCHAR) 0, au_city);
dbbind(dbproc,1, NTBSTRINGBIND, (DBCHAR) 0, au_state);
dbbind(dbproc,1, NTBSTRINGBIND, (DBCHAR) 0, au_zip);
dbbind(dbproc,1, NTBSTRINGBIND, (DBCHAR) 0, au_contract);
```

Of course, each of the program variables must be defined in the application prior to attempting to bind the retrieved column values. A full example of a valid C program that integrates all the sample DB-Lib functions covered so far is included towards the end of this chapter. To this point, however, you should be gaining a better grasp of how Open Client DB-Library functions process data from the application, user, and SQL Server to form a truly client/server application. You can see from the preceding example that the retrieved column values are copied into program variables using `dbbind`. Once they are held in program variables, you can select and manipulate them in any way you choose through your application program. Also, to get more utility from the `dbresults()` function, you could test for the `NO_MORE_ROWS` condition. To achieve this, you might use the following syntax:

```
while ((result_code = dbresults(dbproc) ) != NO_MORE_ROWS)
{    if (result_code ==SUCCEED)
     {
     dbbind(dbproc,1, NTBSTRINGBIND, (DBCHAR) 0, au_id);
     etc.
```

This would allow `dbbind` to continue to copy the column values for each retrieved row until all the retrieved rows had been written into program variables within the application. To bind values retrieved as part of a COMPUTE clause, you must use a slightly different implementation of `dbbind`.

> `dbaltbind(dbproc, computeid, column, vartype, varlen, varaddr)`
>
> This function allows you to bind computed column values to program variables that were retrieved as part of the successful completion of the `dbsqlexec`. Because computed columns are not table columns, `dbbind` specifying a column number is not used. Instead, each of the computed columns is numbered sequentially, beginning with computeid 1.
>
> Using `dbbind` to map retrieved column values into program variables is not mandatory—you can also use the `dbdata()` function.
>
> `dbdata()`   This function returns a pointer to the data for a returned column. It is different than `dbbind` because it does not actually copy the column values into program variables. Instead, `dbdata` automatically binds data to your program variables. For example,

```
DBPROCESS *dbproc;
DBINT          row_number = 0
DBCHAR      au_lname
```

```
dbcmd(dbproc, "select au_lname from authors");
dbsqlexec(dbproc);
dbresults(dbproc);
while ((result_code = dbresults(dbproc) ) != NO_MORE_ROWS)
{    if (result_code ==SUCCEED)
    {
    row_number++;
    au_lname = *((DBCHAR *)dbdata(dbproc, 1));
    }
}
```

In this example, you can see how dbdata treats the variable au_lname as the column values retrieved from the dbsqlexec without having to copy them explicitly to program variables, as is the case with dbbind.

Closing the Connection

Once you have copied your retrieved data or automatically bound it to program variables, you can close DBPROCESS, otherwise known as your connection to the SQL Server. There are two methods of closing the applications connection to SQL Server:

dbclose()	This closes and deallocates a single named DBPROCESS structure (dbproc in the preceding examples). dbclose() is the counterpart to dbopen(). It closes the network connection to a specific SQL Server and frees the memory previously allocated through dbopen(). You must ensure that dbclose() is issued with a DBPROCESS structure name that was defined with a dbopen. Never issue a dbclose() for a name that was not returned by dbopen().
dbexit()	This function first issues a dbclose() for all DBPROCESSES that had been established through dbopen() calls, closing network connections and freeing memory space. dbexit() simply closes all the sessions with one command.

Your application might still be running, even though you have closed the connections to any SQL Servers to which you had previously been connected. Neither dbbind nor dbdata are affected by closing the connections; when your retrieved data has been bound into program variables, they remain local to your application. You can manipulate the variables and then open new DBPROCESSES to return modified, updated, or new rows to the SQL Server from whence they came. It is good programming practice to call dbexit() prior to exiting your application to free any memory allocated by the DB-Library functions. However, you don't need to issue an explicit dbclose() if you call dbexit().

Error Handling

Without a user-defined error and message handling routine declared in your Open Client DB-Library application, when your application fails, it does so with no explanation. To circumvent this behavior in your programs, you must install error and message handlers. Sybase provides basic routines in the sample subdirectory of the Open Client DB-Library software. You can develop and enhance these routines to meet the requirements of your applications and environment. For purposes of illustration, the basic error and message handlers supplied with Sybase look like this:

```
/* Forward declarations of the error handler and message handler.*/
int     err_handler();
int     msg_handler();
```

At the bottom of the source code listing, you will find the following:

```
}

int err_handler(dbproc, severity, dberr, oserr, dberrstr, oserrstr)
    DBPROCESS *dbproc;
    int  severity;
    int  dberr;
    int  oserr;
    char *dberrstr;
    char *oserrstr;
{
    if ((dbproc == NULL) || (DBDEAD(dbproc)))
        return(INT_EXIT);
    else
    {
        printf("DB-LIBRARY error:\n\t%s\n", dberrstr);

    if (oserr != DBNOERR)
        printf("Operating-system error:\n\t%s\n", oserrstr);

    return(INT_CANCEL);
    }
}

int msg_handler(dbproc, msgno, msgstate, severity, msgtext)
    DBPROCESS *dbproc;
    DBINT      msgno;
    int  msgstate;
    int  severity;
    char *msgtext;
```

```
{
    printf
    ("SQL Server message %ld, state %d, severity %d:\n\t%s\n",
    msgno, msgstate, severity, msgtext);
    return(0);
}
```

These default error and message handling routines report any SQL Server messages that are not 0, which avoids filling the error log with reports of successful database context changes (a return status zero is not an error). All other errors are reported to the client program as returned from the SQL Server.

Programming Functions Available with Open Client DB-Library

Those of you who have already acquired a SQL Server might have noticed a *Microsoft SQL Server Programmers Reference for C* included with the documentation. The purpose of this book might not be readily apparent, especially if you ordered a version of SQL Server directly from Sybase rather than from Microsoft. However, Sybase includes the book with each of their SQL Servers shipped, because it provides a thorough treatment of all the DB-Library functions available for building client applications that directly access a SQL Server. For purposes of illustration and quick reference, a summary of each DB-Library function has been culled from that book.

Although the functions covered so far in this chapter introduce you to the minimum number of commands necessary to establish a successful SQL Server access and manipulate the returned results, the following functions can be used to perform other useful actions in your applications program. The full set of DB-Library functions is as follows in Table 5.1.1.

Table 5.1.1. The DB-Library commands.

Command	*Description*
dbadata()	Returns a pointer for a computed column
dbadlen()	Returns the actual length of the data for a compute column
dbaltbind()	Binds computed column results to a program variable
dbaltcolid()	Returns the operand column ID for a compute column

Command	Description
dbaltlen()	Returns the maximum length of the data for a compute column
dbaltop()	Returns the type of aggregate function for a compute column
dbalttype()	Returns the datatype for a compute column
dbaltutype()	Returns the user-defined datatype for a compute column
dbanullbind()	Associates an indicator variable with a compute-row column
dbbind()	Binds a returned table column to a program variable
dbbylist()	Returns the bylist for a compute row
dbcancel()	Cancels the current command batch
dbcanquery()	Cancels pending rows from most recent query
dbchange()	Informs application of change of current database
dbclose()	Closes and frees memory allocated to a single DBPROCESS structure
dbclrbuf()	Clears rows from the row buffer
dbclropt()	Clears an option set by the dbsetopt() function
dbcmd	Adds text to the DBPROCESS command buffer
DBCMDROW	Determines whether the current command can return rows
dbcolbrowse	Determines whether the source of a result column can be updated with DB-Library browse mode facilities
dbcollen	Returns the maximum length of the data for a given column (in bytes)
dbcolname	Returns a pointer to the null-terminated name of a particular result column
dbcolsource	Returns a pointer to the name of the database column from which the specified result column was derived
dbcoltype	Returns the datatype for a regular result column

continues

Table 5.1.1. continued

Command	*Description*
dbcolutype	Returns the user-defined datatype for a regular result column
dbconvert	Converts data from one type to another
DBCOUNT	Returns the number of rows affected by a T-SQL statement
DBCURCMD	Returns the number of the current command
DBCURROW	Returns the number of the row currently being read
dbcursor	Inserts, updates, deletes, locks, or refreshes a particular row in the fetch buffer
dbcursorbind	Registers the binding information on the cursor columns
dbcursorclose	Closes the cursor associated with the given handle and releases all contained data
dbcursorcolinfo	Returns column information for the specified column number in the open cursor
dbcursorfetch	Fetches a block of rows into the program variables declared by the user in dbcursorbind()
dbcursorinfo	Returns the number of columns and rows in the keyset at the end of the results set
dbcursoropen	Opens a cursor, specifies scroll and concurrency options, and determines the number of rows to be retrieved with a single fetch
dbdata	Returns a pointer to the data for a result column
dbdataready	Determines whether database command processing has been completed
dbdatecrack	Converts a machine-readable DBDATETIME value into user-decipherable format
dbdatlen	Returns the actual length (in bytes) of the data for a specified column
DBDEAD	Determines whether a particular DBPROCESS is inactive
dberrhandle	Supplies a user function to handle DB-Library errors

Command	*Description*
dbexit	Closes and frees memory for all DBPROCESS structures in an application
dbfcmd	Adds text to the DBPROCESS command buffer using C run-time library sprintf-type formatting
DBFIRSTROW	Returns the number of the first row in the row buffer
dbfreebuf	Sets the command buffer in a DBPROCESS structure to NULL
dbfreelogin	Frees a login record
dbfreequal	Frees memory allocated by the dbqual() function
dbgetchar	Returns a pointer to a character in the command buffer
dbgetnaxprocs	Determines the current maximum number of simultaneously open DBPROCESS structures
dbgetoff	Checks for the existence of T-SQL statements in the command buffer
dbgetrow	Reads the specified row in the row buffer
DBGETTIME	Returns the number of seconds that DB-Library waits for SQL Server to respond to a T-SQL statement
dbgetuserdata	Returns a pointer to user-allocated data from a DBPROCESS structure
dbhasretstatus	Determines whether the current T-SQL command or remote stored procedure generated a return status number
dbinit	Initializes DB-Library
DBISAVAIL	Determines whether a DBPROCESS is available for general use
dbiscount	Indicates whether the count returned by DBCOUNT is real or not
dbisopt	Checks the status of a SQL Server or DB-Library option

continues

Table 5.1.1. continued

Command	Description
DBLASTROW	Returns the number of the last row in the row buffer
DBLOCKLIB	Locks DB-Library segments for the Windows environment only
dblogin	Allocates a LOGINREC for use by dbopen()
DBMORECMDS	Indicates whether there are more commands to be processed
dbmoretext	Sends part of a text or image value to the SQL Server attached as part of DBPROCESS
dbmsghandle	Installs a user function to handle messages from SQL Server
dbname	Returns the name of the current database
dbnextrow	Reads the next row of the results set
dbnullbind	Associates an indicator variable with a regular result row column
dbnumalts	Returns the number of columns in a compute row
dbnumcols	Determines the number of columns for the current results set
dbnumcompute	Returns the number of COMPUTE clauses in the current results set
DBNUMORDERS	Returns the number of columns specified in the ORDER BY clause of a T-SQL select statement
dbnumrets	Calculates the number of returned parameter values generated by a stored procedure
dbopen	Allocates and initializes a DBPROCESS structure
dbordercol	Returns the ID of a column found in the most recent query's ORDER BY clause
dbprhead	Prints the column headings for returned rows
dbprrow	Prints all returned rows
dbprtype	Converts a SQL Server token value to a readable string
dbqual	Returns a pointer to a WHERE clause to update the current row in a browsable table

Command	*Description*
DBRBUF	Determines whether the command processing has been completed
dbreadtext	Reads part of a text or image value from SQL Server
dbresults	Sets up the results of the next query
dbretdata	Returns a pointer to a value generated by a stored procedure
dbretlen	Determines the length of a return-parameter value generated by a stored procedure
dbretname	Determines the name of the stored procedure parameter associated with a particular return-parameter value
dbretstatus	Determines the stored procedure status number returned by the current command or remote stored procedure
dbrettype	Determines the datatype of a return-parameter generated by a stored procedure
DBROWS	Indicates whether the current statement returned rows
DBROWTYPE	Returns the type of the current row
dbrpcinit	Initializes a remote stored procedure
dbrpcparam	Adds a parameter to a remote stored procedure
dbrpcsend	Signals the end of a parameter list for a remote stored procedure and sends it to be executed
dbrpwclr	Clears all remote passwords from the LOGINREC structure
dbrpwset	Adds a remote password to the LOGINREC structure
dbsetavail	Marks a DBPROCESS as available for general use
DBSETLAPP	Sets the application name in the LOGINREC structure
DBSETLHOST	Sets the workstation name in the LOGINREC structure
DBSETLNATLANG	Sets the name of the national language in the LOGINREC structure

continues

Table 5.1.1. continued

Command	Description
dbsetlogintime	Sets the number of seconds that DB-Library waits for a SQL Server to respond after a request for a DBPROCESS connection
DBSETLWP	Sets the user SQL Server password in the LOGINREC structure
DBSETLUSER	Sets the username in the LOGINREC structure
dbsetmaxprocs	Sets the maximum number of simultaneously open DBPROCESS structures
dbsetnull	Defines substitution values to be used when binding null values
dbsetopt	Sets a SQL Server or DB-Library option
dbsettime	Sets the number of seconds that DB-Library waits for SQL Server to respond to a T-SQL statement
dbsetuserdata	Saves a pointer to user-allocated data within a DBPROCESS structure
dbsqlexec	Sends a command batch to SQL Server
dbsqlok	Verifies that a command batch is correct
dbsqlsend	Sends a command batch to a SQL Server without waiting for a response
dbstrcpy	Copies a portion of the command buffer in the DBPROCESS structure to a specified memory location
dbstrlen	Returns the length (in characters) of the command buffer
dbtabbrowse	Determines whether the specified table can be updated with the DB-Library browse-mode facilities
dbtabcount	Returns the number of tables involved in the current SELECT statement
dbtabname	Returns the name of a table based on its number
dbtabsource	Returns the name and number of the table from which a particular result column was derived
dbtsnewlen	Returns the length of the new value of the timestamp column after a browse-mode update

Command	Description
dbtsnewval	Returns the new value of the timestamp column after a browse-mode update
dbtsput	Puts the new value of the timestamp column into the given table's current row in the DBPROCESS
dbtxptr	Returns the value of the text pointer for a column in the current row
dbtxtimestamp	Returns the value of the text timestamp for a column in the current row
dbtxtnewval	Returns the new value of a text timestamp after a call to dbwritetext
dbtxtsput	Puts the new value of a text timestamp into the specified column of the current row in the DBPROCESS
DBUNLOCKLIB	Unlocks DB-Library segments in the Windows environment only
dbuse	Specifies a database to be used by the DBPROCESS
dbvarylen	Determines whether the specified data in a regular result column can vary in length
dbwillconvert	Determines whether a specific datatype conversion is available within DB-Library
dbwinexit	Informs DB-Library that the Windows application is about to exit (for Windows environment only)
dbwritetext	Sends a text or image value to SQL Server

This represents the complete set of DB-Library functions for version 4.2. Many of these functions are seldom if ever used for most application requirements. However, all the DB-Library functions have been included here to give you a clear picture of how feature-rich DB-Library is. For the convenience of those of you new to applications development using DB-Library, the most commonly used functions have been printed in bold. As you can see, the subset of functions you need to know to be able to create working DB-Library applications is approximately a dozen of the possible 160.

Sample DB-Library Program

To demonstrate the use of the Open Client DB-Library functions in a useful fashion, the following program in Listing 5.1.1 contains all the declarations necessary to actually compile and execute some of the DB-Library calls discussed in this chapter.

Listing 5.1.1. A sample DB-Library program.

```
#include  <stdio.h>  /* Found in c:\msvc\mfc\include */
#include  <sqlfront.h> /* Found in c:\sql\include */
#include  <sqldb.h>  /* Found in c:\sql\include */


/* Forward declarations of the error handler and message handler. */
int  err_handler();
int  msg_handler();

/*   Establish the Connection to the SQL Server */
DBPROCESS *dbproc;
LOGINREC  *loginrec;
loginrec = dblogin();
DBSETLUSER(loginrec, "sa");
DBSETLPWD(loginrec, "esoteric_password");
DBSETLAPP(loginrec, "application_name");
dbproc = dbopen(loginrec, "dsquery");

/*   Declare the Program Variables */
DBCHAR    au_id;
DBCHAR    au_lname;
DBCHAR    au_fname;
DBCHAR    au_phone;
DBCHAR    au_address;
DBCHAR    au_city;
DBCHAR    au_state;
DBCHAR    au_zip;
DBCHAR    au_contract;

/*   PREPARE THE COMMAND BUFFER */
dbuse(dbproc,"pubs")
dbcmd (dbproc, "select * from authors");
dbcomd (dbproc, " where au_lname = worden");

/*   SUBMIT THE QUERY */
dbsqlexec(dbproc)

/*   PROCESS THE RESULTS */
dbresults(dbproc)
dbbind(dbproc,1, NTBSTRINGBIND, (DBCHAR) 0, au_id);
dbbind(dbproc,2, NTBSTRINGBIND, (DBCHAR) 0, au_lname);
dbbind(dbproc,3, NTBSTRINGBIND, (DBCHAR) 0, au_fname);
```

```
dbbind(dbproc,4, NTBSTRINGBIND, (DBCHAR) 0, au_phone);
dbbind(dbproc,5, NTBSTRINGBIND, (DBCHAR) 0, au_address);
dbbind(dbproc,6, NTBSTRINGBIND, (DBCHAR) 0, au_city);
dbbind(dbproc,7, NTBSTRINGBIND, (DBCHAR) 0, au_state);
dbbind(dbproc,8, NTBSTRINGBIND, (DBCHAR) 0, au_zip);
dbbind(dbproc,9, NTBSTRINGBIND, (DBCHAR) 0, au_contract);

/*   CLOSE THE CONNECTION */
dbclose (dbproc);

}

int err_handler(dbproc, severity, dberr, oserr, dberrstr, oserrstr)
    DBPROCESS *dbproc;
    int   severity;
    int   dberr;
    int   oserr;
    char *dberrstr;
    char *oserrstr;
{
if ((dbproc == NULL) ¦¦ (DBDEAD(dbproc)))
    return(INT_EXIT);
else
{
    printf("DB-LIBRARY error:\n\t%s\n", dberrstr);

if (oserr != DBNOERR)
    printf("Operating-system error:\n\t%s\n", oserrstr);

return(INT_CANCEL);
}

int msg_handler(dbproc, msgno, msgstate, severity, msgtext)
    DBPROCESS *dbproc;
    DBINT     msgno;
    int   msgstate;
    int   severity;
    char *msgtext;
{
printf
    ("SQL Server message %ld, state %d, severity %d:\n\t%s\n",
    msgno, msgstate, severity, msgtext);
    return(0);
}
```

This example has been written, compiled, and executed as a C program. However, the C code has been restricted to a minimum to incorporate only the Open Client DB-Library calls, as much as possible. This enables those of you who will be writing applications in Ada or COBOL to see roughly how the Open Client DB-Library functions are implemented, without getting too involved with C coding conventions and practices. For those of you who will be building DB-Library applications in C (and statistics indicate that this includes most of you), the next chapter deals exclusively with incorporating DB-Library functions in C/C++ application programs. The intent here was to demonstrate a DB-Library application that was as generic as possible.

Summary

The purpose of this chapter was primarily to introduce to you the Sybase Application Programming Interface, marketed by Sybase and Microsoft as Open Client DB-Library. There are many performance advantages to using function calls over embedding SQL into a programming language, and there are flexibility advantages for those of you who want to get closer to the code as well as the data. As you saw earlier in this chapter, there are DB-Library products for a number of languages, so those of you who are committed to a great deal of existing COBOL code or are aficionados of Pascal or Ada can take heart; you can use many of the functions and techniques discussed in this chapter to incorporate SQL Server access into your client programs. It is not strictly limited to C programmers, although admittedly there is a bias toward that programming environment due to sheer weight of numbers.

Whatever your environment, you should at this point have a better appreciation for the role of the Net-Libraries in making your SQL Server accessible. No matter what your communications and networking people put between you and the server, chances are that your (debugged) Open Client DB-Library applications will work without modification.

Naturally there are many subtle variations, limitations, restrictions, twists, and curves of using a product like DB-Library. My intention was never to teach you how to program using DB-Library, but merely to introduce you to yet one more arrow in your Sybase client/server quiver. Target practice is up to you.

The Open Client DB-Library products have proven their usefulness in the hands of application programmers who have created solid business systems solutions with shared processing between the users' local machine and a relational database server on the back-end. By reviewing the DB-Library open client functions, you should now have a better idea of exactly what it takes to achieve this kind of functionality for yourself. The next chapter goes into considerably more detail on the choices you face when structuring Open Client DB-Library applications using the C/C++ programming environment.

5.2

Using DB-Library Calls in the C/C++ Programming Environment

The preceding chapter took you through a discussion of the functions and process of how Open Client DB-Library calls connected a client application to a SQL Server, issued commands, and processed the returned results. In this chapter, you will see specifically how you can include Open Client DB-Library functions in C programs and what steps are necessary to use these functions with C and C++ programs. To make this treatment as practical as possible, you will be taken through the steps necessary to create both MS-DOS and Windows programs using the Visual C/C++ 1.0 compiler from Microsoft.

As with the other discussions of technology related to SQL Server installations, it is not my intention to recommend this product over any of its competitors. Again, this product has been chosen foremost because it is the product I use and have available as I write this text, and also because it is a very popular and common product suite with high visibility in the marketplace. As such, I hope the examples in this chapter will be directly relevant and applicable to you as you explore developing client/server applications with C/C++ and Open Client DB-Library function calls.

For those of you who are zealously committed to other development environments, thank you for bearing with me. You will find the discussion of the approaches and options for application processing to be relevant regardless of the programming language.

By the end of this chapter, you will have a solid introduction to the steps necessary for installing and using Open Client DB-Library functions for both the MS-DOS and Windows environments. Wherever possible, you will be shown specific examples that use the files shipped with the product. If you have acquired these products yourself, you'll benefit as this chapter walks you through the installation, configuration, and testing process.

Additionally, this chapter will cover how to break out the processing to whichever machine is most appropriate, splitting the workload between the SQL Server and the client PC. The implications of calling remote stored procedures and using cursors will also be covered. The special libraries for two-phase commit and bulkcopy will be addressed as well. Finally, you will find several examples of how to write effective C programs incorporating DB-Library calls.

This chapter is intended for those of you who are expected to begin developing C language client/server solutions for PCs. By the end of the chapter, you should be familiar with the first steps and should be well on your way to planning and developing Open Client solutions appropriate for your specific environment and requirements. Those of you who will not be programming your own applications right away will still find this chapter a useful overview of the processing options and implications facing a client/server developer regardless of the tool chosen to create the client program.

Installing Open Client DB-Library

First, take note: you must have the Open Client DB-Library for your specific language and deployment environment. For writing C programs for the PC/DOS environment, you need Open Client DB-Library for PC/DOS (part #10910-10-0420-41). To develop Windows applications, you need Open Client DB-Library for PC/Windows (part #10930-10-0420-41). Also, you must have acquired and installed the relevant Net-Library for PC/DOS or Net-Library for PC/Windows and have installed and configured the appropriate transport software (for example, Lan Work Place for DOS) and network hardware. Sounds like a lot, doesn't it?

Actually, a lot of software *is* required. You might not be surprised to learn that many sites and developers new to the SQL Server version of client/server computing neglect to acquire or even budget for these components for their development and user environments. I sincerely hope that this is not the first place you have come across a complete list of requirements.

From here I will assume that you have all the necessities, that you have already installed your Net-Libraries and all (confirmed with a `dbping` or `wdbping`), and that you are now moving into the installation of C/C++ and the Open Client DB-Library software.

In the interests of simplicity, I will deal first with installing and testing the DB-Library functions for C under PC/DOS and then move into the Windows environment.

Open Client DB-Library for PC/DOS

From the diskette, you install these programs and files with the install routine shipped with the product. As with the Net-Library products, several prompting screens ask for the target drive and directory, source drive, and serial number of the product from the diskette. You also are prompted for the default SQL Server name you will use for your applications (for example, DSQUERY) and your choice of editor. The installation utility for version 4.2 shows its age by defaulting to EDLIN (which doesn't even ship with newer versions of MS-DOS).

Idiosyncrasies such as these aside, following the screen prompts takes you through the installation of the files, including the isql, bcp and defncopy utilities. If you previously installed the Open Client files to get these utilities, you have already installed the dblib, include, and lib subdirectories containing the necessary DB-Library files. These are the files you need:

> \sql\include\sqlfront.h
>
> \sql\include\sqldb.h
>
> \sql\lib\rmdblib.lib
>
> \sql\lib\rldblib.lib
>
> \sql\sample\dblib\sqltestr.c
>
> \sql\sample\dblib\example1.c

There are other example C programs, which you might or might not choose to use. In any case, the first four files listed are mandatory, and they will have been copied into whichever directory you specified as the home directory for DB-Library. The default is SQL, but many sites use SYBASE or such. The point is that within that directory, you will find the lib, include, and sample\dblib subdirectories containing the required files.

If you opted for the full installation of the Open Client DB-Library software, you find several other programs in the sample\dblib subdirectory, including a sqltestr.exe. This compiled version of the sqltestr.c program assumes that your SQL Server is fresh out of the box and has no password on SA. Because earlier it was established that the first thing you do on installing the SQL Server is set the password for SA, the program as it is supplied is not going to work. (Hey, many of you won't even know what SA's password is. But it's for your own protection, right?!) So, I'll modify the testing program to work in a specific environment.

Listing 5.2.1. The SQLTESTR.C program supplied with Open Client DB-Library.

```
/*************************************************************************

      PROGRAM: SQLTESTR - SQL  Data Server sample program for MS-DOS
            Copyright (c),    1988-1990 by Microsoft Corp.


*************************************************************************/
#define   DBMSDOS         /* must identify operating system environment */
#include <sqlfront.h>
#include <sqldb.h>  /* DB-LIB header file (should always be included) */

#define     NULL    0

main ()
```

```
{
    DBPROCESS    *dbproc;   /* allocate a DB-LIB process structure    */
    LOGINREC     *login;    /* allocate a DB-LIB login structure      */
    int          errno;     /* variable to store DB-LIB error number in */
    char         *msg;      /* used to receive DB-LIB error message pointer*/

    /* Variables used to store the returning data */
    char         au_lname[41];
    char         au_fname[20];
    char         id[12];
    char         phone[13];
    char         address[41];
    char         city[21];
    char         state[3];
    char         zip[6];
    char         getname[41];
    char         Servername[25];
    RETCODE      result_code;

    /* Forward declarations of the error handler and message handler */
    int          err_handler();
    int          msg_handler();

    /* Install the user-supplied error-handling and message-handling
     * routines. They are defined at the bottom of this source file.
     */
    dberrhandle(err_handler);
    dbmsghandle(msg_handler);

    /* Get server's computer name */
    Servername[0] = NULL;
    printf ("\nEnter LAN Manager Network Computer Name of SQL SERVER: ");
    gets (Servername);

    login = dblogin();                   /* get login record from DB-LIB */
    DBSETLUSER (login, "YOU");           /* set the username            */
    DBSETLAPP (login, "example1");  /* set the application name     */
    DBSETLPWD (login, "YOUR PASSWORD"); /* set the SQL Server password */

    /* Now attempt to create and initialize a DBPROCESS structure */
    if(   (dbproc   = dbopen (login, Servername)) == NULL)
      {
      printf ("dbopen failed\n");
      return (1); /* exit program */
      }

    dbuse (dbproc, "pubs");  /* use the "pubs" database    */

    while (TRUE)
      {
```

continues

Listing 5.2.1. continued

```
printf ("\nEnter author's last name to retrieve (return to exit): ");
gets (getname);

if (getname[0] == NULL)  break;   /* if only a return was entered */

/* construct command buffer to be sent to the SQL Server */
dbcmd (dbproc, "select au_id, au_lname, au_fname, phone,");
dbcmd (dbproc, " address, city, state, zip");
dbcmd (dbproc, " from authors");
dbfcmd (dbproc,      " where au_lname = '%s'",getname);

dbsqlexec (dbproc);  /* send command buffer to SQL Server */

/* now check the results from the SQL Server */
while ((result_code = dbresults(dbproc)) != NO_MORE_RESULTS)
    {
    if (result_code == SUCCEED)
      {
      dbbind (dbproc,      1, NTBSTRINGBIND, (DBINT) 0, id);
      dbbind (dbproc,      2, NTBSTRINGBIND, (DBINT) 0, au_lname);
      dbbind (dbproc,      3, NTBSTRINGBIND, (DBINT) 0, au_fname);
      dbbind (dbproc,      4, NTBSTRINGBIND, (DBINT) 0, phone);
      dbbind (dbproc,      5, NTBSTRINGBIND, (DBINT) 0, address);
      dbbind (dbproc,      6, NTBSTRINGBIND, (DBINT) 0, city);
      dbbind (dbproc,      7, NTBSTRINGBIND, (DBINT) 0, state);
      dbbind (dbproc,      8, NTBSTRINGBIND, (DBINT) 0, zip);

      /* now process the rows */
      while (dbnextrow(dbproc) != NO_MORE_ROWS)
          {
          printf ("Author ID:  %s\n",   id);
          printf ("Last Name:  %s\n",   au_lname);
          printf ("First Name: %s\n",   au_fname);
          printf ("Address:    %s\n",   address);
          printf ("City:       %s\n",   city);
          printf ("State:      %s\n",   state);
          printf ("Zip Code:   %s\n",   zip);
          printf ("Telephone:  %s\n",   phone);
          printf ("\n");
          }
      }
    else
      {
      printf ("Results Failed\n");
      break;
      }
    }
} /* while (TRUE) */

/* Close the connection and exit */
```

```
      dbexit();
}

int err_handler(dbproc, severity, dberr, oserr, dberrstr, oserrstr)
DBPROCESS *dbproc;
int       severity;
int       dberr;
int       oserr;
char      *dberrstr;
char      *oserrstr;
{
      if ((dbproc == NULL) ¦¦  (DBDEAD(dbproc)))
            return(INT_EXIT);
      else
      {
            printf("DB-LIBRARY error:\n\t%s\n", dberrstr);

            if (oserr != DBNOERR)
                  printf("Operating-system error:\n\t%s\n", oserrstr);

            return(INT_CANCEL);
      }
}

int msg_handler(dbproc, msgno, msgstate, severity, msgtext)
DBPROCESS    *dbproc;
DBINT         msgno;
int          msgstate;
int          severity;
char         *msgtext;
{
      printf
            ("SQL Server message %ld, state %d, severity %d:\n\t%s\n",
            msgno, msgstate, severity, msgtext);
      return(0);
}
```

Based on the coverage of DB-Library functions in the preceding chapter, the sample program included with the Open Client DB-Library for PC/DOS diskette should be relatively easy to interpret. The first 16 lines or so establish the files to be included and set up the DBPROCESS and login record structure. The next section of code establishes program variables for the column values of the author table from the generic pubs database. (Of course, this program works only if you have been granted select permission on the pubs database.)

Next is the forward declaration and installation of the user-defined error and message handling routines that are defined at the bottom of the program. As touched on in the preceding chapter, the user-defined routines shipped with the sample work fine. These have been provided to meet most general requirements and should work for you if you do not have a requirement for more complex message and error handling.

Then the login record values themselves are defined. Note that this is where you must modify the code to include your user ID and password. It is not necessary to change the application name. If you wanted to name your workstation and change the national language used by the application, you would do it in this block of code (see DBSETLHOST and DBSETNATLANG). Most of you will not need to change the language used by the application, but I promised to include a little something relevant for my buddies in Montreal, so there it is!

As you work through the rest of the program, you will see that it simply prompts you for an author's last name or names. Finish entering the names by pressing Enter with no name displayed. The application then builds a query in the command buffer to retrieve the columns from the author table and binds them to the declared program variables. Finally, the program prints the program variables to the screen.

Compiling the Test Program

Included with the sample C code is a file called sql\sample\dblib\sqltestr. This file consists of the command and switches to compile the sqltestr.c program. Specifically, it reads:

```
SQLTESTR.exe: SQLTESTR.c
    Cl /Lr /AM SQLTESTR.C RMDBLIB.LIB
    Del SQLTESTR.obj
```

When you try running the cl command with these options under Microsoft C/C++ version 8.0, you might get the following message:

```
sqltestr.c
sqltestr.c(8) : fatal error C1083 : cannot open include file
➡'sqlfront.h' : No such file or directory
```

If you do get this message, copy the two header files sqlfront.h and sqldb.h into the msvc\include directory. Now when you run the command listed in the sqltestr file, you will get a different error message (at least I did):

```
sqltestr.c
sqltestr.c(40) : warning C4113: function parameter lists differed
sqltestr.c(41) : warning C4113: function parameter lists differed

Microsoft (R)  Segmented Executable Linker Version 5.50
Copyright (C)  Microsoft Corp 1984 - 1993 All rights reserved.
```

```
Object Modules [.obj]: sqltestr.obj
Run File [sqltestr.exe]: "sqltestr.exe: /noi
LIst File [nul.map] : NUL
Libraries [.lib]: rmdblibl.lib /NOD:SLIBCE SLIBCER.LIB
Definitions File [nul.def] : ;
LINK : warning L4051 : SLIBCER.LIB : cannot find library
Enter new file spec:
```

There is no SLIBCER.LIB library installed with Microsoft C/C++ Version 8.0; however, you can specify the SLIBCE.LIB (the *R* is used to indicate real or PC/DOS mode libraries). But, hey, when you try this you get a really nasty-looking set of error messages that scroll off your screen that will intimidate all but the most intrepid and experienced.

This is a result of the ignored memory model switch when using the suggested command line to compile sqltestr.c. If you instead use the command line

```
cl /Lr /Mm sqltestr.c rmdblib.lib
```

you should see the following output:

```
sqltestr.c
sqltestr.c(40) : warning C4113: function parameter lists differed
sqltestr.c(41) : warning C4113: function parameter lists differed

Microsoft (R)  Segmented Executable Linker Version 5.50
Copyright (C)  Microsoft Corp 1984 - 1993 All rights reserved.

Object Modules [.obj]: sqltestr.obj
Run File [sqltestr.exe]: "sqltestr.exe: /noi
LIst File [nul.map] : NUL
Libraries [.lib]: rmdblib.lib /NOD:MLIBCE MLIBCER.LIB
Definitions File [nul.def] : ;
LINK : warning L4051 : MLIBCER.LIB : cannot find library
Enter new file spec:
```

Enter MLIBCE.LIB here and press Enter. You should get a returned prompt and see a new sqltestr.exe file in your directory. Provided that you are connected to a SQL Server with pubs installed, when you run the program, you will see the following prompt:

```
Enter your LAN MANAGER  computer name of SQL Server: [            ]
```

Enter DSQUERY, or if you have specified another name, use it. The next prompt should be this:

```
Enter Author's last name to retrieve : [            ]
```

You can try my last name, but because I am not one of the lucky few recorded for posterity in the pubs database and shipped over the planet with every SQL Server, not much will happen. Try Smith instead.

You should have the author table data for Laurence Smith flash across your display. I know, I know, Holy Scrolling Screens, Batman, now what?

Well, even though the retrieved data won't affect the security of the Western world, by successfully compiling and executing the sqltestr.exe program, at least you know that your environment works. Before consigning you to many happy (sic) hours slaving over your own Open Client DB-Library for PC/DOS applications, you might want to make a couple of quick changes to the sqltestr program so that you don't end up leaving your password lying around in text files. While you're at it, change the prompt from the Lan Manager Network thing. I don't know about you, but after installing DB-Library for IPX/SPX and TCP/IP, I was a little misled by the references to LAN Manger and named pipes.

To accomplish these changes, modify the sqltestr.c program to that shown in Listing 5.2.2.

Listing 5.2.2. The modified sqltestr.c program.

```c
#define    DBMSDOS            /* must identify operating system environment*/
#include <sqlfront.h>
#include <sqldb.h>  /* DB-LIB header file (should always be included) */

#define    NULL    0

main ()
{
    DBPROCESS     *dbproc;  /* allocate a DB-LIB process structure  */
    LOGINREC      *login;   /* allocate a DB-LIB login structure    */
    int           errno;    /* variable to store DB-LIB error number in */
    char    *msg;       /* used to receive DB-LIB error message pointer */

    /* Variables used to store the returning data */
    char     au_lname[41];
    char     au_fname[20];
    char     id[12];
    char     phone[13];
    char     address[41];
    char     city[21];
    char     state[3];
    char     zip[6];
    char     getname[41];
    char     Servername[25];
    RETCODE  result_code;

    /* Forward declarations of the error handler and message handler */
    int         err_handler();
```

```
int           msg_handler();

/* Install the user-supplied error-handling and message-handling
 * routines. They are defined at the bottom of this source file.
 */
dberrhandle(err_handler);
dbmsghandle(msg_handler);

/* Get server's computer name */
Servername[0] = NULL;
printf ("\nEnter the name of your SQL SERVER: ");
gets (Servername);

 /*Get login name and password from user */
 Username[0] = NULL;
 printf ("\nEnter your User name: ");
 gets (Username);
 Password[0] = NULL;
 printf ("\nEnter your Password: )
 gets (Password)
login = dblogin();             /* get login record  from DB-LIB */
DBSETLUSER (login, Username);       /* set the username        */
DBSETLAPP (login, "example1");  /* set the application name    */
DBSETLPWD (login, Password);       /* set the SQL Server password */

/* Now attempt to create and initialize a DBPROCESS structure */
if(    (dbproc = dbopen (login, Servername)) == NULL)
 {
 printf ("dbopen failed\n");
 return (1); /* exit program */
 }

dbuse (dbproc, "pubs");  /* use the "pubs" database     */

while (TRUE)
 {
 printf ("\nEnter author's last name to retrieve (return to exit): ");
 gets (getname);

 if (getname[0] == NULL)  break;   /* if only a return was entered */

 /* construct command buffer to be sent to the SQL Server */
 dbcmd (dbproc, "select au_id, au_lname, au_fname, phone,");
 dbcmd (dbproc, " address, city, state, zip");
 dbcmd (dbproc, " from authors");
 dbfcmd (dbproc,     " where au_lname = '%s'",getname);

 dbsqlexec (dbproc); /* send command buffer to SQL Server */
```

continues

Listing 5.2.2. continued

```
/* now check the results from the SQL Server */
while ((result_code = dbresults(dbproc)) != NO_MORE_RESULTS)
    {
    if (result_code == SUCCEED)
        {
        dbbind (dbproc,    1, NTBSTRINGBIND, (DBINT) 0, id);
        dbbind (dbproc,    2, NTBSTRINGBIND, (DBINT) 0, au_lname);
        dbbind (dbproc,    3, NTBSTRINGBIND, (DBINT) 0, au_fname);
        dbbind (dbproc,    4, NTBSTRINGBIND, (DBINT) 0, phone);
        dbbind (dbproc,    5, NTBSTRINGBIND, (DBINT) 0, address);
        dbbind (dbproc,    6, NTBSTRINGBIND, (DBINT) 0, city);
        dbbind (dbproc,    7, NTBSTRINGBIND, (DBINT) 0, state);
        dbbind (dbproc,    8, NTBSTRINGBIND, (DBINT) 0, zip);

        /* now process the rows */
        while (dbnextrow(dbproc) != NO_MORE_ROWS)
            {
            printf ("Author ID:   %s\n",    id);
            printf ("Last Name:   %s\n",    au_lname);
            printf ("First Name: %s\n",     au_fname);
            printf ("Address:     %s\n",    address);
            printf ("City:        %s\n",     city);
            printf ("State:       %s\n",     state);
            printf ("Zip Code:    %s\n",     zip);
            printf ("Telephone:  %s\n",     phone);
            printf ("\n");
            }
        }
    else
        {
        printf ("Results Failed\n");
        break;
        }
    }
    }   /* while (TRUE) */

/* Close the connection and exit */
dbexit();
}

int err_handler(dbproc,   severity, dberr, oserr,   dberrstr, oserrstr)
DBPROCESS *dbproc;
int       severity;
int       dberr;
int       oserr;
char      *dberrstr;
char      *oserrstr;
{
    if ((dbproc == NULL) || (DBDEAD(dbproc)))
        return(INT_EXIT);
```

```
    else
    {
        printf("DB-LIBRARY error:\n\t%s\n", dberrstr);

        if (oserr != DBNOERR)
            printf("Operating-system error:\n\t%s\n", oserrstr);

        return(INT_CANCEL);
    }
}

int msg_handler(dbproc,  msgno, msgstate, severity, msgtext)
DBPROCESS      *dbproc;
DBINT           msgno;
int            msgstate;
int            severity;
char           *msgtext;
{
    printf
        ("SQL Server message %ld, state %d, severity %d:\n\t%s\n",
         msgno,   msgstate, severity, msgtext);
    return(0);
}
```

When running this program after successfully building it, you can enter the user name and password you want into the program.

From these examples and the discussion of compiling Open Client DB-Library function calls in your PC/DOS programs, you should be ready to experiment with your own creations!

Incorporating Open Client DB-Library Calls into Windows Programs

Although there is still a vast army of DOS machines and users out there, the growth area is unquestionably Windows. No doubt many of you signed up for the Sybase client/server solution to develop applications that could actually do Windows. This section will introduce you to the development of C/C++ applications using the Microsoft C/C++ Visual C compiler and Visual Workbench. Again, this discussion is primarily to get you oriented to the environment and not a tutorial in C programming. However, by walking through the sample Windows programs provided with your Open Client DB-Library for PC/Windows, you will be in a much better position to appreciate the power (and complexity) of the product. By the end of this section of the chapter, you should have a clear idea of how the components work together and just what it will take to begin development of your own C/C++ SQL Server client applications for Windows.

Installing Open Client DB-Library for PC/Windows

As with the Net-Library offerings, Sybase expects you to buy a specific version of the DB-Library for Windows. If you develop both Windows and DOS applications, you must buy both. The Open Client DB-Library for Windows part number is 10930-10-0420-41.

The version shipped to me for Sybase did not take advantage of the Windows setup features that most Windows developers and users are familiar with. Instead, you must install the files from the DOS prompt. The installation procedures are virtually identical to Open Client DB-Library for PC/DOS, complete with edlin default editor and annoying "are you ready y/n" default-to-n menu options. However, no doubt Sybase will upgrade the interface soon, if it hasn't already. The point is that the necessary DB-Library files are copied from the distribution diskette to your development workstation or network drive.

These are the files installed:

    \sql\binr\sqlsetup.exe
    \sql\binr\sqlver.exe
    \sql\dll\w3dblib.dll
    \sql\include\slqfront.h
    \sql\include\sqldb.h
    \sql\install\w3dblib.cpr
    \sql\install\w3dblib.spr
    \sql\lib\w3dblib.lib
    \sql\sample\dblib\example1.c
    \sql\sample\dblib\sqlcursw
    \sql\sample\dblib\sqlcursw.rc
    \sql\sample\sqltest3.c
    \sql\sample\sqltest3.def

\sql\sample\sqltest3.h

\sql\sample\sqltest3.ico

\sql\sample\sqltest3.rc

These files represent the complete set of Open Client DB-Library for PC/Windows files, libraries, and executables necessary to create MS-Windows applications under C that access SQL Server. Two of these files, SQLSETUP.EXE AND SQLVER.EXE, can be run from within Windows. SQLSETUP.EXE enables you to enter the name of a sqlserver and profile connect string into your WIN.INI, and SQLVER.EXE shows you a nice banner page with a lot of legalistic-looking text complete with intimidating terms such as *DEFENSE DEPARTMENT* and the version number of the DB-Library installed. It's all very nice, but you should have installed the WIN.INI connect string as part of your installation of Net-Library for Windows. To determine whether this has been done, or to double-check the names of the servers available on your system, open your WIN.INI file and search for the [SQLSERVER] section. For more information, refer to the chapter on Net-Library.

OK, so you now have your various and sundry files loaded, and you can assume from this point forward that your Microsoft Visual C programs along with the Net-Library and networking software/hardware for your system are installed and working.

Compiling the Windows Test Program Under Microsoft Visual C/C++ 1.0 (MSVC)

When you first start the Visual Workbench under Microsoft Visual C/C++, you see a screen like the Microsoft Visual C/C++ Workbench opening screen.

Under this development tool, the first step is to create a new project—in this case, dbwintst. MSVC appends the extension .MAK to the project name. The next step is to associate various resources, libraries, and source code with the project. The workbench needs these associations to find all the various headers, definitions, and resources required during the compilation and build of the application.

Ensure that the executable type is Windows.exe or QuickWin.exe. There are several other options as well, such as MS-DOS.EXE or various DLL target options. And it is not necessary to use the Microsoft foundation libraries.

When you close the project definition dialog box, you will see MSVC flash through the dependencies associated with the code and resources for the project. (At least on a 486/66, it pretty much flashes at the "blink or you'll miss it" level.)

At this point you are ready to compile and build your application. However, as with the PC/DOS version of the DB-Library sample application, the login record is set up as SA with no password. To add a password, you must insert the DBSETLPWD statement. To do this within the workbench, select File Open and use the file browser dialog box to specify C:\SQL\SAMPLE\DBLIB\sqltest3.c. (If you installed the Open Client DB-Library files on some strange drive or subdirectory, naturally you'll have to hunt around until you find it!)

You can now edit the source code and insert the password. After saving the modified source code, or skipping this step if you are still working with a wide-open SQL Server (which nobody recommends), you are ready to compile, build, and execute the application. Under the Project menu option, you have the options to compile, build, or rebuild dbwintst. If you are feeling lucky, go right for the rebuild, which compiles and links the source code into an executable application. Provided there are no syntax errors inserted into the code, you should see two warnings, but no errors. You can now execute the sample program.

By entering the name of your SQL Server as specified in the win.ini (that is, dsquery or sybase), you can then click Select and enter an author's last name. Those of you who actually read through the DOS material earlier will remember that there is no point in looking for me in the pubs database, so I suggest that you try Smith instead. The sample program behaves a bit primitively: if the author's last name is not found, the screen simply remains white (or whatever), allowing you to believe that the program didn't actually work. When I tried it the first time, it took a minute for me to remember that the SQL Server I was connected to was case-sensitive and I had typed *smith* rather than *Smith*.

At this point, you might be wondering exactly what the program looks like and why it was structured that way. As with the section on Open Client DB-Library for PC/DOS, I fully intend to walk you through the application itself so that you can decipher the requirements for yourself. However, I thought that it might be a good idea to get a clear picture of what the thing does before looking at how it is constructed.

The SQLTEST3.C Application

Listing 5.2.3 is the source code listing supplied with Open Client DB-Library for PC/Windows from Sybase.

Listing 5.2.3. A sample DB-Library application for Windows.

```
/***********************************************************************

    PROGRAM: SqlTest3.c
            Copyright (C) 1988-1990 Microsoft Corp.

    PURPOSE: SqlTest sample Windows applications

    FUNCTIONS:

     WinMain() - calls initialization function, processes message loop
     SqlTestInit() - initializes window data and registers window
     SqlTestWndProc() - processes messages
     AboutSQL() - processes messages for "About" dialog box
     SelectSQL() - processes input of author name
     ConnectSQL() - processes input of server name and connects to server

    COMMENTS:

     Windows can have several copies of your application running at the
     same time. The variable hInst keeps track of which instance this
     application is so that processing will be to the correct window.

     You need to initialize the application only once. After it is
     initialized, all other copies of the application will use the same
     window class, and do not need to be separately initialized.

    ***********************************************************************/

#include "windows.h"            /* required for all Windows applications*/
#define DBMSWIN                 /* needed to define environment        */
#include "stdio.h"
#include "string.h"
#include "sqlfront.h"           /* standard dblib include file         */
#include "sqldb.h"              /* standard dblib include file         */
#include "sqltest3.h"           /* specific to this program            */

DBPROCESS *dbproc = (DBPROCESS *)NULL;
                        /* dbprocess pointer for dblib connection*/
HANDLE hInst;                   /* current instance                    */
HWND ghWnd;                     /* global window handle for handlers    */
HWND errhWnd;                   /* global window handle for current error */


/***********************************************************************

    FUNCTION: WinMain(HANDLE, HANDLE, LPSTR, int)

    PURPOSE: Calls initialization function, processes message loop
```

continues

Listing 5.2.3. continued

```
COMMENTS:

    This will initialize the window class if it is the first time this
    application is run. It then creates the window and processes the
    message loop until a PostQuitMessage is received. It exits the
    application by returning the value passed by the PostQuitMessage.

************************************************************************/

int PASCAL WinMain(hInstance, hPrevInstance, lpCmdLine, nCmdShow)
HANDLE hInstance;                    /* current instance          */
HANDLE hPrevInstance;                /* previous instance         */
LPSTR lpCmdLine;                     /* command line              */
int nCmdShow;                        /* show-window type (open/icon) */
{
    HWND hWnd;                       /* window handle             */
    MSG msg;                         /* message                   */


    if (!hPrevInstance)              /* Has application been initialized? */
        if (!SqlTestInit(hInstance))
            return (NULL);           /* Exits if unable to initialize   */

    hInst = hInstance;               /* Saves the current instance      */

    hWnd = CreateWindow("SQL Test",            /* window class    */
     "SQL Server Sample Windows Application",  /* window name     */
     WS_OVERLAPPEDWINDOW,                      /* window style    */
     CW_USEDEFAULT,                  /* x position        */
     CW_USEDEFAULT,                  /* y position        */
     CW_USEDEFAULT,                  /* width             */
     CW_USEDEFAULT,                  /* height            */
     NULL,                           /* parent handle     */
     NULL,                           /* menu or child ID  */
     hInstance,                      /* instance          */
     NULL);                          /* additional info   */

    if (!hWnd)                       /* Was the window created? */
        return (NULL);

    ghWnd = hWnd;                    /* set global handle       */
    errhWnd = hWnd;

    ShowWindow(hWnd, nCmdShow);              /* Shows the window        */
    UpdateWindow(hWnd);                      /* Sends WM_PAINT message  */

    while (GetMessage(&msg,          /* message structure              */
        NULL,                /* handle of window receiving the message */
        NULL,                /* lowest message to examine              */
```

```
        NULL))                    /* highest message to examine        */
    {
    TranslateMessage(&msg);       /* Translates virtual key codes      */
    DispatchMessage(&msg);        /* Dispatches message to window      */
    }
    return (msg.wParam);    /* Returns the value from PostQuitMessage */
}

/**********************************************************************

    FUNCTION: SqlTestInit(HANDLE)

    PURPOSE: Initializes window data and registers window class

    COMMENTS:

    Sets up a structure to register the window class. Structure includes
    such information as what function will process messages, what cursor
    and icon to use, etc.

**********************************************************************/
BOOL SqlTestInit(hInstance)
HANDLE hInstance;                     /* current instance            */
{
    HANDLE hMemory;                   /* handle to allocated memory */
    PWNDCLASS pWndClass;              /* structure pointer          */
    BOOL bSuccess;                    /* RegisterClass() result     */

    hMemory = LocalAlloc(LPTR, sizeof(WNDCLASS));
    pWndClass = (PWNDCLASS) LocalLock(hMemory);

    pWndClass->style = NULL; /*CS_HREDRAW | CS_VREDRAW; */
    pWndClass->lpfnWndProc = SqlTestWndProc;
    pWndClass->hInstance = hInstance;
    pWndClass->hIcon = LoadIcon(hInstance, "SQLITEST");
    pWndClass->hCursor = LoadCursor(NULL, IDC_ARROW);
    pWndClass->hbrBackground = GetStockObject(WHITE_BRUSH);
    pWndClass->lpszMenuName = (LPSTR)"SQLTest";
    pWndClass->lpszClassName = (LPSTR)"SQL Test";

    bSuccess = RegisterClass(pWndClass);


    LocalUnlock(hMemory);                   /* Unlocks the memory    */
    LocalFree(hMemory);                     /* Returns it to Windows */
    return (bSuccess);     /* Returns result of registering the window */
}


/**********************************************************************
```

continues

Listing 5.2.3. continued

```
 FUNCTION: SqlTestWndProc(HWND, unsigned, WORD, LONG)

 PURPOSE:  Processes messages

 MESSAGES:

   WM_SYSCOMMAND - system menu (About dialog box)
   WM_CREATE     - create window
   WM_DESTROY    - destroy window
   WM_COMMAND    - application menus (Connect and Select dialog boxes

 COMMENTS:

   To process the ID_ABOUTSQL message, call MakeProcInstance() to get
   the current instance address of the About() function. Then call
   Dialog box, which will create the box according to the information
   in your SqlTest.rc file and turn control over to the About()
   function. When it returns, free the instance address.
   This same action will take place for the two menu items Connect and
   Select.

 *************************************************************************/

long FAR PASCAL SqlTestWndProc(hWnd, message, wParam, lParam)
HWND hWnd;                         /* window handle            */
unsigned message;                  /* type of message          */
WORD wParam;                       /* additional information   */
LONG lParam;                       /* additional information   */
{
    FARPROC lpProcAbout;           /* pointer to the "About" function */
    FARPROC lpProcSQL;             /* pointer to the Select/Connect   */
                                   /* functions                       */
    HMENU hMenu;                   /* handle to the System menu       */
    static FARPROC lpdbwinMessageHandler; /* pointer to message handler */
    static FARPROC lpdbwinErrorHandler;   /* pointer to error handler */

    switch (message) {
     case WM_SYSCOMMAND:      /* message: command from system menu */
         if (wParam == ID_ABOUTSQL) {
          lpProcAbout = MakeProcInstance(AboutSQL, hInst);

          DialogBox(hInst,           /* current instance        */
              "ABOUTSQL",            /* resource to use         */
              hWnd,                  /* parent handle           */
              lpProcAbout);          /* About() instance address */

         FreeProcInstance(lpProcAbout);
          break;
         }
```

```
            else                 /* Lets Windows process it        */
              return (DefWindowProc(hWnd, message, wParam, lParam));

     case WM_CREATE:                    /* message: window being created */

         /* Get the handle of the System menu */

         hMenu = GetSystemMenu(hWnd, FALSE);

         /* Add a separator to the menu */

         ChangeMenu(hMenu,               /* menu handle         */
          NULL,                          /* menu item to change */
          NULL,                          /* new menu item       */
          NULL,                          /* menu identifier     */
          MF_APPEND ¦ MF_SEPARATOR);     /* type of change      */

         /* Add new menu item to the System menu */

         ChangeMenu(hMenu,               /* menu handle         */
          NULL,                          /* menu item to change */
          "A&bout SQL Test...",          /* new menu item       */
          ID_ABOUTSQL,                   /* menu identifier     */
          MF_APPEND ¦ MF_STRING);        /* type of change      */

                      /* Now make the message and error   */
                      /* handler instances                */
            dbinit();
         lpdbwinMessageHandler =
             MakeProcInstance((FARPROC)dbwinMessageHandler, hInst);
         lpdbwinErrorHandler =
          MakeProcInstance((FARPROC)dbwinErrorHandler, hInst);
                      /* Install the instances into dblib */
         dbmsghandle(lpdbwinMessageHandler);
         dberrhandle(lpdbwinErrorHandler);
         break;

     case WM_COMMAND :              /* menu selections generate */
                                    /* the WM_COMMAND message    */
         switch(wParam)             /* menu in WORD parameter    */
         {
          case IDM_CONNECT :        /* connect to server         */
             lpProcSQL = MakeProcInstance(ConnectSQL, hInst);

             DialogBox(hInst,    /* current instance                 */
              "CONNECT",         /* resource to use                  */
              hWnd,              /* parent handle                    */
              lpProcSQL);        /* ConnectSQL() instance address */

             FreeProcInstance(lpProcSQL);
             break;
```

continues

Listing 5.2.3. continued

```
          case IDM_SELECT :         /* select an author        */
              lpProcSQL = MakeProcInstance(SelectSQL, hInst);

              DialogBox(hInst,      /* current instance        */
                "SELECT",           /* resource to use         */
                hWnd,               /* parent handle           */
                lpProcSQL);         /* About() instance address */

              FreeProcInstance(lpProcSQL);
              break;
          }
          break;

      case WM_DBRESULTS :                   /* a select has been issued */
          SqlTestProcessResults(hWnd);      /* process results          */
          break;

      case WM_DESTROY:                 /* message: window being destroyed */
          dbexit();                    /* free any active dbprocesses     */
          FreeProcInstance(lpdbwinMessageHandler); /* release handlers */
          FreeProcInstance(lpdbwinErrorHandler);
             dbwinexit();
          PostQuitMessage(0);
          break;

      default:                 /* Passes it on if unproccessed    */
          return (DefWindowProc(hWnd, message, wParam, lParam));
      }
      return (NULL);
}

/**********************************************************************

    FUNCTION: AboutSQL(HWND, unsigned, WORD, LONG)

    PURPOSE:  Processes messages for "AboutSQL" dialog box

    MESSAGES:

     WM_INITDIALOG - initialize dialog box
     WM_COMMAND    - input received

    COMMENTS:

     No initialization is needed for this particular dialog box, but TRUE
     must be returned to Windows.

     Wait for user to click "Ok" button, then close the dialog box.

 **********************************************************************/
```

```
BOOL FAR PASCAL AboutSQL(hDlg, message, wParam, lParam)
HWND hDlg;
unsigned message;
WORD wParam;
LONG lParam;
{
    switch (message) {
      case WM_INITDIALOG:              /* message: initialize dialog box */
          return (TRUE);

      case WM_COMMAND:                 /* message: received a command */
          if (wParam == IDOK) {             /* "OK" box selected?      */
            EndDialog(hDlg, NULL);          /* Exits the dialog box    */
            return (TRUE);
          }
          break;
    }
    return (FALSE);                    /* Didn't process a message    */
}


/**************************************************************************

    FUNCTION: SelectSQL(HWND, unsigned, WORD, LONG)

    PURPOSE:  Processes messages for "SelectSQL" dialog box

    MESSAGES:

    WM_INITDIALOG - initialize dialog box
    WM_COMMAND    - input received

    COMMENTS:

    No initialization is needed for this particular dialog box, but TRUE
    must be returned to Windows.

    Let user input into edit control the name of an author (the select
    IS case sensitive). When user presses OK, format the select
statement
    then send it to the server and execute it via dbsqlexec(). If the
    dbsqlexec() SUCCEEDs, post a WM_DBRESULTS message so the results
    may be retrieved and processed.

    Wait for user to click "Ok" button, then close the dialog box.

    **************************************************************************/

BOOL FAR PASCAL SelectSQL(hDlg, message, wParam, lParam)
HWND hDlg;
```

continues

Listing 5.2.3. continued

```
unsigned message;
WORD wParam;
LONG lParam;
{
    char szSelectAuthor[41];          /* string for authors name     */
    char szServerMess[45];            /* string for server response  */
    char szAName[40];                 /* format string for author    */
    switch (message) {
     case WM_INITDIALOG:              /* message: initialize dialog box */
         SendDlgItemMessage(hDlg,     /* limit input to 40 characters  */
          AUTHORNAME,EM_LIMITTEXT,40,0L);
         return (TRUE);

      case WM_COMMAND:                /* message: received a command   */
         errhWnd = hDlg;
         switch(wParam)
         {
          case IDOK :                 /* "OK" box selected?       */
             *szSelectAuthor = NULL;  /* Null author              */

             GetDlgItemText(hDlg,AUTHORNAME, /* get input name    */
              (LPSTR)szSelectAuthor,
                 MAX_ANAME);
             if(dbproc == (DBPROCESS *)NULL) /* if not a valid process */
             {
                     /* No server to query        */
              MessageBox(hDlg,
                  "No SQL Server Connected to Query",
                   "SQL Test",M_ICONHAND | M_OK);
             }
             else if(*szSelectAuthor != NULL) /* if a name exists */
             {
              DBLOCKLIB();            /* lock down the library  */
                         /* format the select statement */
              dbcmd(dbproc,
                  (LPSTR)"select au_id, au_lname,"
                  "au_fname, phone, address, city, state, zip");
              dbcmd(dbproc, (LPSTR)" from authors");
              dbcmd(dbproc, (LPSTR)" where au_lname = ");
              sprintf(szAName,"'%s'",szSelectAuthor);
              dbcmd(dbproc,(LPSTR)szAName);
              if(dbsqlexec(dbproc) == FAIL)
              {
                  sprintf(szServerMess,      /* error, not in db */
                   "%s not found in database pubs",
                       szSelectAuthor);
                  MessageBox(hDlg,
                      (LPSTR)szServerMess,(LPSTR)"SQL Test",
                       M_ICONHAND | M_OK);
              }
```

```
                else /* query SUCCEEDed so               */
                {    /* post message to process results  */
                    PostMessage(GetParent(hDlg),WM_DBRESULTS,0,0L);
                }
                DBUNLOCKLIB();      /* unlock library  */
            }
            EndDialog(hDlg, NULL);             /* Exits the dialog box */
            return (TRUE);
            break;
          case IDCANCEL :
            EndDialog(hDlg, NULL);             /* cancelled select */
            return(TRUE);
            break;

        }
        break;
    }
    return (FALSE);                      /* Didn't process a message  */
}

/***********************************************************************

    FUNCTION: ConnectSQL(HWND, unsigned, WORD, LONG)

    PURPOSE:  Processes messages for "Connect" dialog box

    MESSAGES:

     WM_INITDIALOG - initialize dialog box
     WM_COMMAND    - input received

    COMMENTS:

     No initialization is needed for this particular dialog box, but TRUE
     must be returned to Windows.

     Wait for user to click "Ok" button, then close the dialog box.

    ***********************************************************************/

BOOL FAR PASCAL ConnectSQL(hDlg, message, wParam, lParam)
HWND hDlg;
unsigned message;
WORD wParam;
LONG lParam;
{
    char szSQLServer[31];
    char szServerMess[81];
    static LOGINREC *LoginRec;
```

continues

Listing 5.2.3. continued

```
*szSQLServer = NULL;
switch (message) {
 case WM_INITDIALOG:            /* message: initialize dialog box    */
     SendDlgItemMessage(hDlg,     /* limit input to 30 characters */
      SQL_SERVER,EM_LIMITTEXT,30,0L);
     return (TRUE);

 case WM_COMMAND:                      /* message: received a command   */
     errhWnd = hDlg;
     switch(wParam)
     {
      case IDOK :                    /* "OK" box selected?      */
          GetDlgItemText(hDlg,SQL_SERVER,
           (LPSTR)szSQLServer,
             MAX_SERVERNAME);   /* get Server name */
          if(*szSQLServer != NULL) /* was something input    */
          {
           DBLOCKLIB();            /* lock down library      */
           if(dbproc != (DBPROCESS *)NULL) /* if an active   */
                                   /* process close it       */
               dbclose(dbproc);
           if((LoginRec = dblogin()) != (LOGINREC *)NULL)
                                             /* get loginrec */
           {
               DBSETLUSER(LoginRec,(char far *)"sa"); /* set user */
                          /* now open the connection to server */
               if((dbproc = dbopen(LoginRec,(LPSTR)szSQLServer))
                     == (DBPROCESS *)NULL)
               {
                    /* if NULL couldn't connect */
                dbfreelogin(LoginRec);
               }
               else /* got connect so use the pubs database */
               {
                dbuse(dbproc,(LPSTR)"pubs");
                dbfreelogin(LoginRec);
               }
           }
           else /* memory allocation problem */
               MessageBox(hDlg, "Could not allocate Login Record",
               ➥"System Error", MB_ICONHAND | MB_OK);
           DBUNLOCKLIB(); /* done unlock library    */
          }
          EndDialog(hDlg, NULL);           /* Exits the dialog box */
          return (TRUE);
          break;
      case IDCANCEL :
          EndDialog(hDlg, NULL);
          return(TRUE);
          break;
```

```
            }
        break;
    }
    return (FALSE);                    /* Didn't process a message */
}


/***************************************************************************

    FUNCTION: CheckForScroll(HWND, int, int, int)

    PURPOSE:  Check if next output line will be out of client area

    PARAMETERS: hWnd - Handle to the window.
        CurrentPosition - Current y coordinate for the line of
            text just written to the client area.
        Spacing - The height of the line (including the space
            separating lines) of the text just written.
        Length - The length of the line just written in device
            units.

    RETURN:   Returns the y coordinate for the next line of text.

    COMMENTS:

    Will determine if the next line of text will be out of the client
    area. If so will scroll the window for the next line. Also validates
    the current line of text so that a WM_PAINT will not clear it.

***************************************************************************/

int CheckForScroll(hWnd,CurrentPosition,Spacing, Length)
HWND hWnd;
int CurrentPosition;
int Spacing;
int Length;
{
    RECT rect;                     /* RECT structure for validation */
    rect.top = CurrentPosition;      /* top of last line of text   */
    rect.bottom = CurrentPosition+Spacing+1; /* bottom of last line    */
    rect.left = 1;                   /* left-most column of line   */
    rect.right = Length+1;           /* right-most column of line  */
    ValidateRect(hWnd,(LPRECT)&rect);  /* validate line so that it is */
                                       /* not blanked on next paint   */

    GetClientRect(hWnd,(LPRECT)&rect); /* get rect for current client */
    if(CurrentPosition + (Spacing*2) > rect.bottom) /* will line fit  */
    {
                        /* if not scroll window and   */
                        /* update client window       */
      ScrollWindow(hWnd,0,-(Spacing+1),NULL,NULL);
```

continues

Listing 5.2.3. continued

```
        UpdateWindow(hWnd);
        return(CurrentPosition);
    }
    return(CurrentPosition+Spacing);
}


/***************************************************************************

    FUNCTION: SQLTestProcessResults(HWND)

    PURPOSE:  If a valid dbprocess is present, process all results from
              pending select statement, output each field to client area.
              Whenever a new line is written to client area, it is checked
              to see if the client area needs to be scrolled.

    PARAMETERS: hWnd - Handle to the window.

    RETURN:   Returns the y coordinate for the next line of text.

    COMMENTS:

    This function will bind the fields in the select statement to
    local variables, format an output string, then write that string
    to the client area via TextOut. It is called by the main message
    processing loop SQLTestWndProc via the message WM_DBRESULTS.

***************************************************************************/

BOOL SqlTestProcessResults(hWnd)
HWND hWnd;
{
    HDC hDC;                    /* display context          */
    TEXTMETRIC tm;             /* text metric structure    */
    char szId[12];             /* Author ID for binding    */
    char szLastName[41];       /* Author last name for binding    */
    char szFirstName[21];         /* Author first name for binding */
    char szPhone[13];             /* Author phone for binding    */
    char szAddress[41];           /* Author address for binding    */
    char szCity[21];              /* Author city for binding    */
    char szState[3];              /* Author state for binding    */
    char szZip[6];                /* Author ZIP code for binding    */
    char szOutputString[81];      /* general output string    */
    RETCODE result_code;       /* results code from dbresults    */
    int Y;                     /* y coordinate for text output */
    int Spacing;               /* Spacing between lines      */
    errhWnd = hWnd;

    hDC = GetDC(hWnd);              /* get display context       */
    GetTextMetrics(hDC, (LPTEXTMETRIC)&tm); /* get font info       */
    Spacing = tm.tmExternalLeading + tm.tmHeight; /* set up spacing */
```

```
Y = 1;                            /* start at line 1            */
if(dbproc == (DBPROCESS *)NULL)    /* if process null, no results */
{
 ReleaseDC(hWnd,hDC);                     /* free resources and return    */
 return(TRUE);
}
SendMessage(hWnd,WM_ERASEBKGND,hDC,0L); /* always erase background */
UpdateWindow(hWnd);                  /* force painting of window    */
DBLOCKLIB();                         /* lock down library           */

                        /* get all results from the query*/
while(((result_code = dbresults(dbproc)) != NO_MORE_RESULTS) &&
➥result_code != FAIL)
{
 if(result_code == SUCCEED)    /* if results ready     */
 {
                        /* Bind all data of interest   */
     dbbind(dbproc,1,NTBSTRINGBIND, 12L, (LPSTR)szId);
     dbbind(dbproc,2,NTBSTRINGBIND, 41L, (LPSTR)szLastName);
     dbbind(dbproc,3,NTBSTRINGBIND, 21L, (LPSTR)szFirstName);
     dbbind(dbproc,4,NTBSTRINGBIND, 13L, (LPSTR)szPhone);
     dbbind(dbproc,5,NTBSTRINGBIND, 41L, (LPSTR)szAddress);
     dbbind(dbproc,6,NTBSTRINGBIND, 21L, (LPSTR)szCity);
     dbbind(dbproc,7,NTBSTRINGBIND, 3L, (LPSTR)szState);
     dbbind(dbproc,8,NTBSTRINGBIND, 6L, (LPSTR)szZip);
     while(dbnextrow(dbproc) != NO_MORE_ROWS) /* get all rows  */
     {
            /* here we format each field and write it to client */
            /* area checking to see if the client area needs to */
            /* be scrolled after each line is written           */
        sprintf(szOutputString,"Author ID: %s",szId);
        TextOut(hDC,1,Y,szOutputString,strlen(szOutputString));
        Y = CheckForScroll(hWnd,Y,Spacing,strlen(szOutputString) *
        ➥tm.tmMaxCharWidth);

        sprintf(szOutputString,"Last Name: %s",szLastName);
        TextOut(hDC,1,Y,szOutputString,strlen(szOutputString));
        Y = CheckForScroll(hWnd,Y,Spacing,strlen(szOutputString) *
        ➥tm.tmMaxCharWidth);

        sprintf(szOutputString,"Address:   %s",szAddress);
        TextOut(hDC,1,Y,szOutputString,strlen(szOutputString));
        Y = CheckForScroll(hWnd,Y,Spacing,strlen(szOutputString) *
        ➥tm.tmMaxCharWidth);

        sprintf(szOutputString,"City:      %s",szCity);
        TextOut(hDC,1,Y,szOutputString,strlen(szOutputString));
        Y = CheckForScroll(hWnd,Y,Spacing,strlen(szOutputString) *
        ➥tm.tmMaxCharWidth);
```

continues

Listing 5.2.3. continued

```
            sprintf(szOutputString,"State:     %s",szState);
            TextOut(hDC,1,Y,szOutputString,strlen(szOutputString));
            Y = CheckForScroll(hWnd,Y,Spacing,strlen(szOutputString) *
            ➥tm.tmMaxCharWidth);

            sprintf(szOutputString,"ZipCode:    %s",szZip);
            TextOut(hDC,1,Y,szOutputString,strlen(szOutputString));
            Y = CheckForScroll(hWnd,Y,Spacing,strlen(szOutputString) *
            ➥tm.tmMaxCharWidth);

            sprintf(szOutputString,"Telephone: %s",szPhone);
            TextOut(hDC,1,Y,szOutputString,strlen(szOutputString));
            Y = CheckForScroll(hWnd,Y,Spacing,strlen(szOutputString) *
            ➥tm.tmMaxCharWidth);

            Y = CheckForScroll(hWnd,Y,Spacing,0); /* add extra line    */
                                                  /* after each results */
        }
    }
    }

    DBUNLOCKLIB();                    /* unlock library    */
    ReleaseDC(hWnd,hDC);              /* free resource     */
    return(TRUE);
}

/***********************************************************************

    FUNCTION: dbwinMessageHandler(DBPROCESS *, DBINT, DBSMALLINT,
             DBSMALLINT, LPSTR)

    PURPOSE:  When the Data Server returns a message to dblib this
             function will be called to process that message. This function
             is installed into dblib via MakeProcInstance. It must be
             declared as a FAR cdecl function, not as a FAR PASCAL function,
             unlike other call-back routines, as dblib conducts all of its
             calls in the cdecl fashion. You must return 0 to dblib.

    RETURN:   Returns 0

    COMMENTS:

***********************************************************************/

int FAR dbwinMessageHandler(dbproc, msgno, msgstate, severity, msgtext)
DBPROCESS       *dbproc;
DBINT           msgno;
DBSMALLINT      msgstate;
DBSMALLINT      severity;
LPSTR           msgtext;
```

```
{
    MessageBox(errhWnd,msgtext,(LPSTR)"SQL DataServer Message",MB_OK);
    return(0);
}

/*************************************************************************

    FUNCTION: dbwinErrorHandler(DBPROCESS *, int, int, int, LPSTR, LPSTR)

    PURPOSE:  When dblib returns an error message to the application,
              this function will be called to process that error. This
              function is installed into dblib via MakeProcInstance. It must
              be declared as a FAR cdecl function, not as a FAR PASCAL
              function, unlike other call-back routines, as dblib conducts
              all of its calls in the cdecl fashion. You must return
              INT_CANCEL, INT_CONTINUE, or INT_EXIT to dblib.

    RETURN:   Returns continuation code.

    COMMENTS:

*************************************************************************/

int FAR dbwinErrorHandler(dbproc, severity, errno, oserr, dberrstr,
➥oserrstr)
DBPROCESS *dbproc;
int severity;
int errno;
int oserr;
LPSTR dberrstr;
LPSTR oserrstr;
{
    MessageBox(errhWnd,dberrstr,(LPSTR)"DB-LIBRARY error",
    ➥MB_ICONHAND ¦ MB_OK);

    if (oserr != DBNOERR)      /* os error    */
    {
     MessageBox(errhWnd,oserrstr,(LPSTR)"Operating-System error",
     ➥MB_ICONHAND ¦ MB_OK);
    }

    return(INT_CANCEL);  /* cancel command */
}
```

Interpreting the Sample Program

As you can see, there is a significant difference in the size and complexity of the Windows test application versus its DOS-based counterpart. Additionally, very little of the code is dedicated to DB-Library functions. One of the reasons for reviewing the functionality of this application first was to demonstrate graphically how much code goes into even a small application.

Generally speaking, you should keep the following information in mind when developing DB-Library applications for Microsoft Windows.

Windows Templates

To help those who are planning to use DB-Library with C/C++, I am including several examples of Windows/DB-Library programs for you to use as templates. This should give you a good idea of how a programmer in the real world (as opposed to Microsoft's demo team) actually builds programs. The templates are shown next.

The Windows C/C++ program in Listing 5.2.4 can be used as a generic template for developing your own DB-Lib applications for Windows.

Listing 5.2.4. A template for DB-Lib applications.

```
/*************************************************************************

    PROGRAM: SQLGEN.c

    PURPOSE: Generic template for Windows 3.1 applications using DBLibrary

    FUNCTIONS:

      WinMain() - calls initialization function, processes message loop
      InitApplication() - initializes window data and registers window
      InitInstance() - saves instance handle and creates main window
      MainWndProc() - processes messages
      About() - processes messages for "About" dialog box

    COMMENTS:

      Windows can have several copies of your application running at the
      same time. The variable hInst keeps track of which instance this
      application is so that processing will be to the correct window.


*************************************************************************/
```

```
#include "windows.h"           /* required for all Windows applications */

#define DBMSWIN               /* SQL: Needed for sql includes */
#include "SQLFRONT.H"          /* SQL: Standard dblib include file */
#include "SQLDB.H"             /* SQL: Standard dblib include file */

#include "SQLGEN.h"            /* specific to this program         */
#include "SQLUTILS.C"          /* SQL: Utility Functions */

DBPROCESS *dbproc = (DBPROCESS *)NULL; /* SQL: Initialize global  */
                                       /* dbprocess                */
HWND errhWnd;                 /* SQL: Global dblib handle         */


/* Forward Declarations */

int PASCAL WinMain(HANDLE, HANDLE, LPSTR, int);
BOOL InitApplication(HANDLE);
BOOL InitInstance(HANDLE, int);
long CALLBACK __export MainWndProc(HWND, UINT, WPARAM, LPARAM);
BOOL __export CALLBACK About(HWND, unsigned, WORD, LONG);


HANDLE hInst;                 /* current instance                 */

/***********************************************************************

    FUNCTION: WinMain(HANDLE, HANDLE, LPSTR, int)

    PURPOSE:  Calls initialization function, processes message loop

    COMMENTS:

    Windows recognizes this function by name as the initial entry point
    for the program. This function calls the application initialization
    routine, if no other instance of the program is running, and always
    calls the instance initialization routine. It then executes a message
    retrieval and dispatch loop that is the top-level control structure
    for the remainder of execution. The loop is terminated when a WM_QUIT
    message is received, at which time this function exits the
    application instance by returning the value passed by
    PostQuitMessage().

    If this function must abort before entering the message loop, it
    returns the conventional value NULL.

    **********************************************************************/

int PASCAL WinMain(hInstance, hPrevInstance, lpCmdLine, nCmdShow)
HANDLE hInstance;                 /* current instance          */
HANDLE hPrevInstance;             /* previous instance         */
```

continues

Listing 5.2.4. continued

```
LPSTR lpCmdLine;                    /* command line          */
int nCmdShow;                       /* show-window type (open/icon) */
{
    MSG msg;                        /* message               */

    if (!hPrevInstance)             /* Other instances of app running? */
    if (!InitApplication(hInstance)) /* Initialize shared things  */
        return (FALSE);             /* Exits if unable to initialize    */

    /* Perform initializations that apply to a specific instance */

    if (!InitInstance(hInstance, nCmdShow))
        return (FALSE);

    /* Acquire and dispatch messages until WM_QUIT message is received */

    while (GetMessage(&msg,     /* message structure            */
        NULL,           /* handle of window receiving the message */
        NULL,           /* lowest message to examine        */
        NULL))          /* highest message to examine       */
    {
    TranslateMessage(&msg);  /* Translates virtual key codes    */
    DispatchMessage(&msg);   /* Dispatches message to window    */
    }
    return (msg.wParam);     /* Returns the value from PostQuitMessage */
}

/***********************************************************************

    FUNCTION: InitApplication(HANDLE)

    PURPOSE: Initializes window data and registers window class

    COMMENTS:

    This function is called at initialization time only if no other
    instances of the application are running. This function performs
    initialization tasks that can be done once for any number of running
    instances.

    In this case, we initialize a window class by filling out a data
    structure of type WNDCLASS and calling the Windows RegisterClass()
    function. Since all instances of this application use the same window
    class, we need to do this only when the first instance is
    initialized.

***********************************************************************/
```

```
BOOL InitApplication(hInstance)
HANDLE hInstance;                      /* current instance      */
{
    WNDCLASS  wc;

    /* Fill in window class structure with parameters that describe */
    /* the main window                                              */

    wc.style = NULL;                 /* Class style(s)                    */
    wc.lpfnWndProc = MainWndProc;    /* Function to retrieve messages     */
                                     /* for windows of this class         */
    wc.cbClsExtra = 0;               /* No per-class extra data           */
    wc.cbWndExtra = 0;               /* No per-window extra data          */
    wc.hInstance = hInstance;        /* Application that owns the class    */
    wc.hIcon = LoadIcon(NULL, IDI_APPLICATION);
    wc.hCursor = LoadCursor(NULL, IDC_ARROW);
    wc.hbrBackground = GetStockObject(WHITE_BRUSH);
    wc.lpszMenuName =  "SQLGENMenu";   /* Name of menu resource in .RC
                                      ➥ file */
    wc.lpszClassName = "SQLGENWClass"; /* Name used in call to
                                      ➥ CreateWindow */

    /* Register the window class and return success/failure code */

    return (RegisterClass(&wc));

}

/********************************************************************

    FUNCTION: InitInstance(HANDLE, int)

    PURPOSE:  Saves instance handle and creates main window

    COMMENTS:

    This function is called at initialization time for every instance of
    this application. This function performs initialization tasks that
    cannot be shared by multiple instances.

    In this case, we save the instance handle in a static variable and
    create and display the main program window.

    ********************************************************************/

BOOL InitInstance(hInstance, nCmdShow)
    HANDLE          hInstance;   /* Current instance identifier       */
    int             nCmdShow;    /* Param for first ShowWindow() call */
```

continues

Listing 5.2.4. continued

```
{
    HWND            hWnd;           /* Main window handle                  */

    /* Save the instance handle in static variable, which will be used */
    /* in many subsequence calls from this application to Windows      */

    hInst = hInstance;

    /* Create a main window for this application instance */

    hWnd = CreateWindow(
        "SQLGENWClass",                 /* See RegisterClass() call      */
        "SQLGEN Sample Application",     /* Text for window title bar     */
        WS_OVERLAPPEDWINDOW,            /* Window style                  */
        CW_USEDEFAULT,                  /* Default horizontal position   */
        CW_USEDEFAULT,                  /* Default vertical position     */
        CW_USEDEFAULT,                  /* Default width                 */
        CW_USEDEFAULT,                  /* Default height                */
        NULL,                           /* Overlapped windows have no parent */
        NULL,                           /* Use the window class menu     */
        hInstance,                      /* This instance owns this window */
        NULL                            /* Pointer not needed            */
    );

    /* If window could not be created, return "failure" */

    if (!hWnd)
        return (FALSE);

    /* Make the window visible; update its client area; and return */
    /* "success"                                                   */

    ShowWindow(hWnd, nCmdShow);  /* Show the window                    */
    UpdateWindow(hWnd);          /* Sends WM_PAINT message             */
    return (TRUE);               /* Returns the value from PostQuitMessage */

}

/***********************************************************************

    FUNCTION: MainWndProc(HWND, UINT, WPARAM, LPARAM)

    PURPOSE:  Processes messages

    MESSAGES:

    WM_COMMAND    - application menu (About dialog box)
    WM_DESTROY    - destroy window
```

COMMENTS:

To process the IDM_ABOUT message, call MakeProcInstance() to get the
current instance address of the About() function. Then call Dialog
box, which will create the box according to the information in your
SQLGEN.rc file and turn control over to the About() function. When
it returns, free the intance address.

```c
*************************************************************************/

long CALLBACK __export MainWndProc(hWnd, message, wParam, lParam)
HWND hWnd;                        /* window handle        */
UINT message;                     /* type of message      */
WPARAM wParam;                    /* additional information    */
LPARAM lParam;                    /* additional information    */
{
    static FARPROC lpdbwinMessageHandler; /* SQL: pointer to message handler*/
    static FARPROC lpdbwinErrorHandler;   /* SQL: pointer to error handler*/

    switch (message)
    {
        case WM_CREATE:
            /* SQL: Initiate the dblibrary environment */
            dbinit();

            /* SQL: Make instances of the message handlers */
            lpdbwinMessageHandler =
                MakeProcInstance((FARPROC)dbwinMessageHandler, hInst);
            lpdbwinErrorHandler =
                MakeProcInstance((FARPROC)dbwinErrorHandler, hInst);

            /* SQL: Install message and error handlers into dblib */
            dbmsghandle(lpdbwinMessageHandler);
            dberrhandle(lpdbwinErrorHandler);

            break;

        case WM_COMMAND:      /* message: command from application menu */
            if (wParam == IDM_ABOUT)
            {

                DialogBox(hInst,          /* current instance         */
                    "AboutBox",           /* resource to use          */
                    hWnd,                 /* parent handle            */
                    About);               /* About() instance address */

                break;
            }
            else                          /* Lets Windows process it  */
                return (DefWindowProc(hWnd, message, wParam, lParam));
```

continues

Listing 5.2.4. continued

```
        case WM_DESTROY:              /* message: window being destroyed */

            dbexit();                /* SQL: close any active dbprocesses  */
            FreeProcInstance(lpdbwinMessageHandler); /*Free Msg handler */
            FreeProcInstance(lpdbwinErrorHandler); /*Free Error handler */

            PostQuitMessage(0);
            break;

        default:                     /* Passes it on if unprocessed    */
            return (DefWindowProc(hWnd, message, wParam, lParam));
    }
    return (NULL);
}


/***********************************************************************

    FUNCTION: About(HWND, unsigned, WORD, LONG)

    PURPOSE:  Processes messages for "About" dialog box

    MESSAGES:

    WM_INITDIALOG - initialize dialog box
    WM_COMMAND    - input received

    COMMENTS:

    No initialization is needed for this particular dialog box, but TRUE
    must be returned to Windows.

    Wait for user to click "Ok" button, then close the dialog box.

***********************************************************************/

BOOL __export CALLBACK About(hDlg, message, wParam, lParam)
HWND hDlg;                 /* window handle of the dialog box */
unsigned message;          /* type of message                */
WORD wParam;               /* message-specific information    */
LONG lParam;
{
    switch (message)
    {
        case WM_INITDIALOG:          /* message: initialize dialog box */
            return (TRUE);

        case WM_COMMAND:                 /* message: received a command */
            if (wParam == IDOK          /* "OK" box selected?          */
```

```
            ¦¦ wParam == IDCANCEL) /* System menu close command?  */
        {
            EndDialog(hDlg, TRUE); /* Exits the dialog box          */
            return (TRUE);
        }
        break;
    }
    return (FALSE);                    /* Didn't process a message   */
}
```

The following program in Listing 5.2.5 can be used, too.

Listing 5.2.5. A second sample template for DB-Lib applications.

```
/***********************************************************************
**      Copyright (c) 1994 Munro Systems
**
**      Filename:    SQLUtils.C     - Generic SQL Server utilities
**
**      Functions:   dbwinMessageHandler()
**                      -SQL Server Message Handling function
**                   dbwinErrorHandler()
**                      -DBLibrary Error handler
**                   dbConnect()
**                      -Generic Server connection function
**                   SQLNoReturn()
**                      -Function to execute SQL with no results
**                   SQLTranCount()
**                      -Function to check if a transaction has
**                       been rolled back
**
***********************************************************************/
/***********************************************************************

    FUNCTION: dbwinMessageHandler(DBPROCESS *, DBINT, DBSMALLINT,
              DBSMALLINT, LPSTR)

    PURPOSE:  When the Data Server returns a message to dblib, this
              function will be called to process that message. This function
              is installed into dblib via MakeProcInstance. It must be
              declared as a FAR cdecl function, not as a FAR PASCAL function,
              unlike other call-back routines, as dblib conducts all of its
              calls in the cdecl fashion. You must return 0 to dblib.

    RETURN:   Returns 0
```

continues

Listing 5.2.5. continued

```
*************************************************************************/

int FAR dbwinMessageHandler(dbproc, msgno, msgstate, severity, msgtext)
DBPROCESS       *dbproc;
DBINT           msgno;
DBSMALLINT      msgstate;
DBSMALLINT      severity;
LPSTR           msgtext;
{
    MessageBox(errhWnd,                      /* Display the message   */
            msgtext,                         /* in a message box      */
            (LPSTR)"SQL DataServer Message",
            MB_OK);

    return(0);
}


/************************************************************************

    FUNCTION: dbwinErrorHandler(DBPROCESS *, int, int, int, LPSTR, LPSTR)

    PURPOSE:  When dblib returns an error message to the application, this
            function will be called to process that error. This function is
            installed into dblib via MakeProcInstance. It must be declared
            as a FAR cdecl function, not as a FAR PASCAL function, unlike
            other call-back routines, as dblib conducts all of its calls
            in the cdecl fashion. You must return INT_CANCEL,
            INT_CONTINUE, or INT_EXIT to dblib.

    RETURN:   Returns continuation code.


*************************************************************************/

int FAR dbwinErrorHandler(dbproc, severity, errno, oserr, dberrstr,
➥oserrstr)
DBPROCESS *dbproc;
int severity;
int errno;
int oserr;
LPSTR dberrstr;
LPSTR oserrstr;
{
    MessageBox(errhWnd,                         /* Display the error in  */
            dberrstr,                           /* a message box         */
            (LPSTR)"DB-LIBRARY error",
            MB_ICONHAND | MB_OK);

    if (oserr != DBNOERR)      /* os error    */
    {
```

```
            MessageBox(errhWnd,
                       oserrstr,
                       (LPSTR)"Operating-System error",
                       MB_ICONHAND ¦ MB_OK);
    }

    return(INT_CANCEL);   /* cancel command */
}

/*************************************************************************

    FUNCTION: RETCODE dbConnect(  connect_proc, server_name,
                                     login_name, password )


    PURPOSE:  Generic server connection routine

    RETURN:   Returns SUCCEED or FAIL

    COMMENTS:

*************************************************************************/

RETCODE dbConnect( connect_proc, server_name, login_name, password)
DBPROCESS **connect_proc;
char *server_name;
char *login_name;
char *password;
{
    static LOGINREC *LoginRec;
      RETCODE return_code;
       DBLOCKLIB();   /* lock down library, needed for all dblib calls */
                      /* to ensure libraries are not moved in memory   */

    if(connect_proc != (DBPROCESS *)NULL) /* if an active    */
            dbclose(connect_proc);         /* process close it */



    if((LoginRec = dblogin()) != (LOGINREC *)NULL) /* get loginrec */
    {
            /* Set Login information */
            DBSETLUSER(LoginRec,(char far *)login_name); /* set user */
            DBSETLPWD(LoginRec,(char far *)password); /* set password*/
            DBSETLHOST(LoginRec,(char far *)server_name);
                                                /* set server name */

            /* now open the connection to server */
```

continues

Listing 5.2.5. continued

```
                if((connect_proc = dbopen(LoginRec,(LPSTR)server_name))
                        == (DBPROCESS *)NULL)
                {
                        /* if NULL couldn't connect */
                    dbfreelogin(LoginRec);
                    return_code = FAIL;
                }
                else /* got connect so use the pubs database */
                    return_code = SUCCEED;        /* Success! */
        }
        else /* memory allocation problem */
                return_code = FAIL;


    DBUNLOCKLIB(); /* unlock library */


    return (return_code);      /* Return status of operation */
}

/**************************************************************************

    FUNCTION: RETCODE SQLNoReturn


    PURPOSE:  Generic server connection routine

    RETURN:   Returns SUCCEED or FAIL

    COMMENTS:

     This routine is convenient for executing any SQL that has no
     result sets (stored procedures, environment settings, etc.)

**************************************************************************/

RETCODE SQLNoReturn( sqlproc, SQLText )
DBPROCESS *sqlproc;
char *SQLText;
{

    RETCODE return_code;

    return_code = SUCCEED;

    if (sqlproc == (DBPROCESS *)NULL)
        return(FAIL);                            /* No Connection */
```

```
    DBLOCKLIB();

  if (SQLText != (char *)NULL) /* Add any text to the command buffer */
       dbcmd( sqlproc, (LPSTR)SQLText );



   if((return_code = dbsqlexec(sqlproc)) != FAIL)   /* execute the */
                                              /* command buffer */
   {
       /* To allow for any possible query, dbresults and dbnextrow */
       /* are called in a loop to account for possibility of data  */
       /* returning from server                                    */

       while(((return_code = dbresults(sqlproc)) != NO_MORE_RESULTS)
                                        && return_code != FAIL)
       {   /* dbresults is called for each query in command buffer */
           if (return_code == SUCCEED)
           {
             while ((return_code = dbnextrow(sqlproc)) !=
             ➥ NO_MORE_ROWS);
                   /* loop through each row (discarding results) */
           }

       }
   }


   DBUNLOCKLIB(); /* Unlock the library */

   return (return_code);   /* Return the status of the execution */


}

/********************************************************************

   FUNCTION: RETCODE SQLTranCount


   PURPOSE:  Check for the number of transactions currently in effect.

   RETURN:   Returns the number of transactions currently in effect for
             the given DBPROCESS * or -1 if error

   COMMENTS:

   This routine is handy for checking if a server error caused a
   rollback in a transaction. If so, a 'rollback transaction'
```

continues

Listing 5.2.5. continued

```
          statement will cause an error. Checking this is a good idea,
          as any database updates occuring after a rollback are permanent!

   ************************************************************************/

DBINT SQLTranCount( sqlproc )
DBPROCESS *sqlproc;
{

     RETCODE return_code;                /* Status Indicator */
     DBINT    no_of_trans = -1;          /* Number of transactions */

     if (sqlproc == (DBPROCESS *)NULL)
          return(no_of_trans);           /* No Connection    */

    DBLOCKLIB();

     dbcmd( sqlproc, "select @@trancount");

     if(dbsqlexec(sqlproc) != FAIL)      /* execute the command buffer */
     {

          if (dbresults(sqlproc) != FAIL)
          {   /* dbresults is called for each query in command buffer */

             /* 1 column should be returned with transaction count */
             dbbind( sqlproc, 1, INTBIND, 0, (DBINT *)&no_of_trans);

             if (return_code == SUCCEED)
             {
                  dbnextrow(sqlproc);     /* Get the result */
             dbcanquery(sqlproc);
                             /* Good idea to ensure buffer is cleared */
          }
        }
     }

     DBUNLOCKLIB();

     return( no_of_trans );    /* return results */
}


/************************************************************************
     End of File SQLUTILS.C
   ************************************************************************/
```

Other Capabilities Available through Open Client DB-Library

In addition to the capability to invoke any custom-designed bit of logic, the Windows display features, and the myriad other advantages that writing your own applications gives, several key functions are provided by Open Client DB-Library that are not otherwise available:

> Cursors
>
> Two-phase commit
>
> Bulk copy

There are several codicils to this list of capabilities.

As mentioned in the section on SQL Server Release 10, support for cursors on the server will be offered with the upgrade to that version. If, however, you are using SQL Server for a 4.9.X or lower version, the only way to use cursors is to develop them with Open Client DB-Library.

Two-phase commit is also available only through the Open Client DB-Library functions. However, also with SQL Server Release 10, the Replication Server product is being offered to address applications in which two-phase commit is not desirable or entirely applicable.

Last, bulk copy is provided with each SQL Server as a utility for moving data in and out of the server. This topic has been covered in greater detail elsewhere in the book. However, you can use bulkcopy functions specific to DB-Library to build discrete applications that perform the bulkcopy function from within a program. For many developers, this capability is much more desirable than relying on users or operators to manually invoke bulkcopy as part of some data transfer procedure.

These extensions to the functionality offered by Open Client DB-Library translates into a capability to accomplish some tasks that would be simply impossible through stored procedures or T-SQL alone. For example, the following programs demonstrate how cursors, bulkcopy, and two-phase commit can be implemented within C/C++ programs.

The cursor program shows how you can use the Open Client DB-Library for PC/ Windows, whereas the two-phase commit example is for the DOS environment.

If you take the Open Client DB-Library course from Sybase, they have an exercise for creating a sample two phase commit application. For those of you who want to see the example now, it is included in Listing 5.2.6.

Listing 5.2.6. A sample two phase commit program.

```
/*      Sample Program for Two Phase Commit */
#include <stdio.h>
#include <sybfront.h>
#include <sybdb.h>
int err_handler();
int msg_handler();

char    cmdbuf[256];
char    xact_string[128];

main()

{
DBPROCESS               *dbproc_server1;
DBPROCESS               *dbproc_server2;
DBPROCESS               *dbproc_commit;
LOGINREC                *login;
int                     commid;
RETCODE         ret_server1;
RETCODE         ret_server2;

dberrhandle(err_handler);
dbmsghandle(msg_handler0;

printf("Demonstration of Two Phase Commit\n");

login = dblogin();
DBSETLUSER(login,"sa");
dbproc_server1 = (login, "SERVER_A");
dbproc_server2 = (login, "SERVER_B");
dbproc_commit  = (open_commit,login "SERVER_A");

if(     dbproc_server1==NULL¦¦
        dbproc_server2==NULL¦¦
        dbproc_commit==NULL)
{
        printf("Connection failed!\n");
        exit (-1);
}
/* Use the Pubs Database */
sprintf(cmdbuf, "use pubs");
dbcmd(dbproc_server1,cmdbuf);
dbsqlexec(dbproc_server1);
dbcmd(dbproc_server2,cmdbuf);
dbsqlexec(dbproc_server2);
/* Start the distributed transaction on the Commit Manager */
commid = start_xact(dbproc_commit,"sample","test",2);

/* Build the Transaction Name */
```

```
build_xact_string ("test","SERVER_A",commid,xact_string);

/* Build the first command buffer */

sprintf(cmdbuf,"BEGIN TRANSACTION %s", xact_string);

/* Begin the Transactions on each server */

dbcmd(dbproc_server1,cmdbuf);
dbsqlexec(dbproc_server1);
dbcmd(dbproc_server2,cmdbuf);
dbsqlexec(dbproc_server2);
/* Perform Updates */
sprintf(cmdbuf,"update titles set price = $1.50 where");
strcat(cmdbuf, "title_id = 'BU1032'");
dbcmd(dbproc_server1,cmdbuf);
ret_server1 = dbsqlexec(dbproc_server1);
if(ret_server1 == FAIL ||ret_server2 == FAIL)
{
        /*Something went wrong */
        printf("Transaction aborted,sqlexec failed\n");
        abortall(dbproc_server1,dbproc_server2,dbproc_commit,commid);
}
/* Determine if Servers are prepared to commit transaction */

sprintf(cmdbuf,"PREPARE TRANSACTION");
dbcmd(dbproc_server1,cmdbuf);
dbcmd(dbproc_server2,cmdbuf);
ret_server1 = dbsqlexec(dbproc_server1);
ret_server2 = dbsqlexec(dbproc_server2);
if (ret_server1 == FAIL || ret_server2 == FAIL)
{
        /* One or both of the servers failed to prepare */
        printf("Transaction aborted, prepare failed\n");
        abortall(dbproc_server1,dbproc_server2,dbproc_commit,commid);
}

/* Commit the Transaction */
if (commit_xact(dbproc_commit,commid)==FAIL)
{
        /* The commit server failed to record the commit */
        printf("Transaction aborted due to failed commit xact\n");
        abortall(dbproc_server1,dbproc_server2,dbproc_commit,commid);
exit(-1);
}

/* Transaction a Success! Inform each Server */
sprintf(cmdbuf,"COMMIT TRANSACTION");
dbcmd(dbproc_server1,cmdbuf);
if (dbsqlexec(dbproc_server1)!=FAIL)
        remove_xact(dbproc_commit,commid,1);
```

continues

Listing 5.2.6. continued

```
dbcmd(dbproc_server2) !=FAIL)
        remove_xact(dbproc_commit,commid,1);

/* Close connection to Commit Manager */
close_commit(dbproc_commit);
printf( "No Problemo!\n);
dbexit();
exit();
}

/* Function to abort the distributed Transaction */

abortall(dbproc_server1,dbproc_server2,dbproc_commit,commid)
DBPROCESS       *dbproc_serer1;
DBPROCESS       *dbproc_server2;
DBPROCESS       *dbproc_commit;
int             commid;
{
        /* Some part of the Transaction failed */
        /* Inform the Commit Manager of the failure */
        abort_xact(dbproc_commit,commid);

        /* Roll back the Transactions on each Server */
        sprintf(cmdbuf, "ROLLBACK TRANSACTION");
        dbcmd(dbproc_server1,cmdbuf);
        if(dbsqlexec(dbproc_server1) != FAIL)
                remove_xact(dbproc_commit,commid,1);

        dbexit();
        exit(-1);
}
```

In the sample program above, the commit manager is a process which runs on the same server as one of the transactions, Server_A. The Commit Manager may be handled by one of the involved servers or by another server on the network.

Cursors through the Open Client DB-Library API

The cursor program shown in Listing 5.2.7 is supplied with the Open Client DB-Library for PC/Windows. An example of how it looks when executed appears at the end of the source code listing.

Listing 5.2.7. A sample Windows program incorporating a cursor.

```
/***********************************************************************

    PROGRAM: SqlCursw.c
            Copyright (C) 1991 Microsoft Corp.

    PURPOSE: Sql Server sample Windows applications

    COMMENTS:

      Windows can have several copies of your application running at the
      same time. The variable hInst keeps track of which instance this
      application is so that processing will be to the correct window.

      You need to initialize the application only once. After it is
      initialized, all other copies of the application will use the same
      window class, and do not need to be separately initialized.

 ***********************************************************************/

#include "windows.h"          /* required for all Windows applications */
#define DBMSWIN               /* needed to define environment          */
#include "sqlfront.h"         /* standard dblib include file           */
#include "sqldb.h"            /* standard dblib include file           */
#include "sqlcursw.h"         /* specific to this program              */

DBPROCESS *dbproc = (DBPROCESS *)NULL;
DBCURSOR  *hdbcursor = (DBCURSOR *)NULL;

char stmt[] = "select au_lname, au_fname, city, state from authors where
➥contract = 1 ";

/* Status array, and results set */

DBINT      pstat[NROWS];
DBINT      plen[NROWS];
char    au_lname[NROWS][41];
char    au_fname[NROWS][21];
char    au_city[NROWS][21];
char    au_state[NROWS][3];
char    szRowNum[5];
USHORT     rownum = 0;
char    szValues[251];
char    szTable[31];

HANDLE hInst;                 /* current instance                      */
HWND ghWnd;                   /* global window handle for handlers     */
HWND errhWnd;                 /* global window handle for current error */

/***********************************************************************
```

continues

Listing 5.2.7. continued

```
FUNCTION: WinMain(HANDLE, HANDLE, LPSTR, int)

PURPOSE: Calls initialization function, processes message loop

COMMENTS:

    This will initialize the window class if it is the first time this
    application is run. It then creates the window, and processes the
    message loop until a PostQuitMessage is received. It exits the
    application by returning the value passed by the PostQuitMessage.

*************************************************************************/

int PASCAL WinMain(hInstance, hPrevInstance, lpCmdLine, nCmdShow)
HANDLE hInstance;                       /* current instance          */
HANDLE hPrevInstance;                   /* previous instance         */
LPSTR lpCmdLine;                        /* command line              */
int nCmdShow;                           /* show-window type (open/icon) */
{
    HWND hWnd;                          /* window handle             */
    MSG msg;                            /* message                   */


    if (!hPrevInstance)         /* Has application been initialized? */
      if (!SqlTestInit(hInstance))
        return (NULL);          /* Exits if unable to initialize     */

    hInst = hInstance;                  /* Saves the current instance    */

    hWnd = CreateWindow("SQL Test",             /* window class      */
      "SQL Server Sample Windows Application",  /* window name       */
      WS_OVERLAPPEDWINDOW,                      /* window style      */
      CW_USEDEFAULT,                    /* x position     */
      CW_USEDEFAULT,                    /* y position     */
      CW_USEDEFAULT,                    /* width          */
      CW_USEDEFAULT,                    /* height         */
      NULL,                             /* parent handle  */
      NULL,                             /* menu or child ID   */
      hInstance,                        /* instance       */
      NULL);                            /* additional info    */

    if (!hWnd)                          /* Was the window created? */
      return (NULL);

    ghWnd = hWnd;                       /* set global handle       */
    errhWnd = hWnd;

    ShowWindow(hWnd, nCmdShow);                 /* Shows the window       */
    UpdateWindow(hWnd);                         /* Sends WM_PAINT message */
```

```
    while (GetMessage(&msg,        /* message structure            */
        NULL,              /* handle of window receiving the message */
        NULL,              /* lowest message to examine    */
        NULL))             /* highest message to examine   */
    {
     TranslateMessage(&msg);        /* Translates virtual key codes  */
     DispatchMessage(&msg);         /* Dispatches message to window  */
    }
    return (msg.wParam);  /* Returns the value from PostQuitMessage */
}

/**************************************************************************

    FUNCTION: SqlTestInit(HANDLE)

    PURPOSE: Initializes window data and registers window class

    COMMENTS:

    Sets up a structure to register the window class. Structure includes
    such information as what function will process messages, what cursor
    and icon to use, etc.

**************************************************************************/

BOOL SqlTestInit(hInstance)
HANDLE hInstance;                   /* current instance            */
{
    HANDLE hMemory;                 /* handle to allocated memory */
    PWNDCLASS pWndClass;            /* structure pointer          */
    BOOL bSuccess;                  /* RegisterClass() result     */

    hMemory = LocalAlloc(LPTR, sizeof(WNDCLASS));
    pWndClass = (PWNDCLASS) LocalLock(hMemory);

    pWndClass->style = NULL; /*CS_HREDRAW ¦ CS_VREDRAW; */
    pWndClass->lpfnWndProc = SqlTestWndProc;
    pWndClass->hInstance = hInstance;
    pWndClass->hIcon = LoadIcon(hInstance, "SQLITEST");
    pWndClass->hCursor = LoadCursor(NULL, IDC_ARROW);
    pWndClass->hbrBackground = GetStockObject(WHITE_BRUSH);
    pWndClass->lpszMenuName = (LPSTR)"SQLTest";
    pWndClass->lpszClassName = (LPSTR)"SQL Test";

    bSuccess = RegisterClass(pWndClass);


    LocalUnlock(hMemory);                    /* Unlocks the memory    */
    LocalFree(hMemory);                      /* Returns it to Windows */
    return (bSuccess);   /* Returns result of registering the window */
}
```

continues

Listing 5.2.7. continued

```
/***********************************************************************

    FUNCTION: SqlTestWndProc(HWND, unsigned, WORD, LONG)

    PURPOSE: Processes messages

    MESSAGES:

      WM_SYSCOMMAND - system menu (About dialog box)
      WM_CREATE     - create window
      WM_DESTROY    - destroy window
      WM_COMMAND    - application menus (Connect and Select dialog boxes

    COMMENTS:

      To process the ID_ABOUTSQL message, call MakeProcInstance() to get
      the current instance address of the About() function. Then call
      Dialog box, which will create the box according to the information in
      your SqlTest.rc file and turn control over to the About() function.
      When it returns, free the instance address.
      This same action will take place for the two menu items Connect and
      Select.

***********************************************************************/

long FAR PASCAL SqlTestWndProc(hWnd, message, wParam, lParam)
HWND hWnd;                        /* window handle             */
unsigned message;                 /* type of message           */
WORD wParam;                      /* additional information     */
LONG lParam;                      /* additional information     */
{
    FARPROC lpProcAbout;          /* pointer to the "About" function     */
    FARPROC lpProcRowNum;         /* pointer to the "GetRowNum" function  */
    FARPROC lpProcModify;         /* pointer to the "ModifyRow" function  */
    FARPROC lpProcSQL;            /* pointer to the "ConnectSQL" function */

    HMENU hMenu;                  /* handle to the System menu    */
    static FARPROC lpdbwinMessageHandler; /* pointer to message handler */
    static FARPROC lpdbwinErrorHandler;   /* pointer to error handler   */
    RETCODE   rc;                 /* return code                  */

    switch (message) {
      case WM_SYSCOMMAND:         /* message: command from system menu */
          if (wParam == ID_ABOUTSQL) {
            lpProcAbout = MakeProcInstance(AboutSQL, hInst);

            DialogBox(hInst,              /* current instance      */
                "ABOUTSQL",               /* resource to use       */
                hWnd,                     /* parent handle         */
                lpProcAbout);             /* About() instance address */
```

```
        FreeProcInstance(lpProcAbout);
        break;
    }

    else                    /* Lets Windows process it */
        return (DefWindowProc(hWnd, message, wParam, lParam));

case WM_CREATE:             /* message: window being created */

    /* Get the handle of the System menu */

    hMenu = GetSystemMenu(hWnd, FALSE);

    /* Add a separator to the menu */

    ChangeMenu(hMenu,                   /* menu handle          */
      NULL,                             /* menu item to change */
      NULL,                             /* new menu item        */
      NULL,                             /* menu identifier      */
      MF_APPEND | MF_SEPARATOR);        /* type of change       */

    /* Add new menu item to the System menu */

    ChangeMenu(hMenu,                   /* menu handle          */
      NULL,                             /* menu item to change */
      "A&bout SQL Test...",             /* new menu item        */
      ID_ABOUTSQL,                      /* menu identifier      */
      MF_APPEND | MF_STRING);           /* type of change       */

                        /* Now make the message and error */
                        /* handler instances              */
        dbinit();
    lpdbwinMessageHandler =
      MakeProcInstance((FARPROC)dbwinMessageHandler, hInst);
    lpdbwinErrorHandler =
      MakeProcInstance((FARPROC)dbwinErrorHandler, hInst);
                        /* Install the instances into dblib */
    dbmsghandle(lpdbwinMessageHandler);
    dberrhandle(lpdbwinErrorHandler);
    MessageBox(hWnd,
      (LPSTR)"None of the data modifications will be committed",
      (LPSTR)"SQLCURSW", MB_OK);
    break;

case WM_COMMAND :           /* menu selections generate */
                            /* the WM_COMMAND message    */
    switch(wParam)                  /* menu in WORD parameter */
    {
     case IDM_CONNECT :         /* connect to server       */
        lpProcSQL = MakeProcInstance(ConnectSQL, hInst);
```

continues

Listing 5.2.7. continued

```
        DialogBox(hInst,       /* current instance              */
         "CONNECT",            /* resource to use               */
         hWnd,                 /* parent handle                 */
         lpProcSQL);           /* ConnectSQL() instance address */

        FreeProcInstance(lpProcSQL);
        break;
    case IDM_RAND :
    case IDM_RELT :
    case IDM_REFRESH :
        /* Obtain the row number */
        lpProcRowNum = MakeProcInstance(GetRowNum, hInst);
        DialogBox(hInst, "ROWNUM", hWnd, lpProcRowNum);
        FreeProcInstance(lpProcRowNum);

        /* FALL THROUGH */

    case IDM_FIRST :
    case IDM_NEXT :
    case IDM_PREV :
    case IDM_LAST :
        DBLOCKLIB();
        if (wParam == IDM_REFRESH)
         rc = dbcursor(hdbcursor, wParam - UPD_CONST, rownum,
             NULL, NULL);
        else
         /* Do the fetch and display of rows */
         rc = dbcursorfetch(hdbcursor, wParam - FETCH_CONST,
            rownum);
        if (rc == SUCCEED)
         SQLTestProcessResults(hWnd);
        DBUNLOCKLIB();
        rownum = 0;       /* Reset for next fetch */
        break;
    case IDM_DELETE :
    case IDM_LOCK :
    case IDM_UPDATE :
    case IDM_INSERT :
        szValues[0] = '\0';
        szTable[0] = '\0';
        /* Obtain the row number */
        if (wParam == IDM_DELETE ¦¦ wParam == IDM_LOCK)
        {
         lpProcModify = MakeProcInstance(DelLockRow, hInst);
         DialogBox(hInst, "DELLOCK", hWnd, lpProcModify);
        }
        else
        {
         lpProcModify = MakeProcInstance(ModifyRow, hInst);
         DialogBox(hInst, "MODIFY", hWnd, lpProcModify);
```

```
                }
                FreeProcInstance(lpProcModify);
                DBLOCKLIB();
                /* Do the dbcursor call */
                dbcursor(hdbcursor, wParam - UPD_CONST, rownum,
                  szTable, szValues);
                DBUNLOCKLIB();
                rownum = 0;       /* Reset for next command */
                break;


            }
            break;

        case WM_DESTROY:           /* message: window being destroyed */
            dbexit();              /* free any active dbprocesses      */
            FreeProcInstance(lpdbwinMessageHandler); /* release handlers */
            FreeProcInstance(lpdbwinErrorHandler);
                dbwinexit();
            PostQuitMessage(0);
            break;

        default:                   /* Passes it on if unproccessed */
            return (DefWindowProc(hWnd, message, wParam, lParam));
        }
        return (NULL);
}

/***************************************************************************

    FUNCTION: AboutSQL(HWND, unsigned, WORD, LONG)

    PURPOSE:  Processes messages for "AboutSQL" dialog box

    MESSAGES:

     WM_INITDIALOG - initialize dialog box
     WM_COMMAND    - input received

    COMMENTS:

     No initialization is needed for this particular dialog box, but TRUE
     must be returned to Windows.

     Wait for user to click "Ok" button, then close the dialog box.

 ***************************************************************************/

BOOL FAR PASCAL AboutSQL(hDlg, message, wParam, lParam)
HWND hDlg;
```

continues

Listing 5.2.7. continued

```
unsigned message;
WORD wParam;
LONG lParam;
{
    switch (message) {
    case WM_INITDIALOG:          /* message: initialize dialog box */
        return (TRUE);

    case WM_COMMAND:                 /* message: received a command */
        if (wParam == IDOK) {            /* "OK" box selected?     */
          EndDialog(hDlg, NULL);         /* Exits the dialog box   */
          return (TRUE);
        }
        break;
    }
    return (FALSE);                  /* Didn't process a message   */
}


/**************************************************************************

    FUNCTION: GetRowNum(HWND, unsigned, WORD, LONG)

    PURPOSE:  Processes messages for "ROWNUM" dialog box

    Messages:

     WM_INITDIALOG - initialize dialog box
     WM_COMMAND    - input received

    COMMENTS:

     No initialization is needed for this particular dialog box, but TRUE
     must be returned to Windows.

     Wait for user to click "Ok" button, then close the dialog box.

 **************************************************************************/

BOOL FAR PASCAL GetRowNum(hDlg, message, wParam, lParam)
HWND hDlg;
unsigned message;
WORD wParam;
LONG lParam;
{
    switch (message) {
    case WM_INITDIALOG:             /* message: initialize dialog box   */
        SendDlgItemMessage(hDlg,      /* limit input to 4 characters */
         ID_ROWNUM,EM_LIMITTEXT,4,0L);
        return (TRUE);
```

```
    case WM_COMMAND:                    /* message: received a command   */
        if (wParam == IDOK) {              /* "OK" box selected?         */
         GetDlgItemText(hDlg,ID_ROWNUM,
             (LPSTR)szRowNum,4);           /* Get row number */
         szRowNum[4] = '\0';
         rownum = atoi(szRowNum);
         EndDialog(hDlg, NULL);            /* Exits the dialog box    */
         return (TRUE);
         }
         break;
     }
     return (FALSE);                       /* Didn't process a message   */
}

/*************************************************************************

    FUNCTION: DelLockRow(HWND, unsigned, WORD, LONG)

    PURPOSE:  Processes messages for "DELLOCK" dialog box

    MESSAGES:

     WM_INITDIALOG - initialize dialog box
     WM_COMMAND    - input received

    COMMENTS:

     No initialization is needed for this particular dialog box, but TRUE
     must be returned to Windows.

     Wait for user to click "Ok" button, then close the dialog box.

 *************************************************************************/

BOOL FAR PASCAL DelLockRow(hDlg, message, wParam, lParam)
HWND hDlg;
unsigned message;
WORD wParam;
LONG lParam;
{
    switch (message) {
    case WM_INITDIALOG:            /* message: initialize dialog box */
        SendDlgItemMessage(hDlg,    /* limit row# input to 4 characters*/
         ID_DROWNUM,EM_LIMITTEXT,4,0L);
        SendDlgItemMessage(hDlg, /* limit table input to 30 characters*/
         ID_DTABLE,EM_LIMITTEXT,30,0L);
        return (TRUE);
```

continues

Listing 5.2.7. continued

```
    case WM_COMMAND:                    /* message: received a command  */
        if (wParam == IDOK) {           /* "OK" box selected?           */
         GetDlgItemText(hDlg,ID_DROWNUM,
             (LPSTR)szRowNum,4);        /* Get row number */
         szRowNum[4] = '\0';
         rownum = atoi(szRowNum);
         GetDlgItemText(hDlg,ID_DTABLE,
             (LPSTR)szTable,30);        /* Get table name */
         EndDialog(hDlg, NULL);         /* Exits the dialog box         */
         return (TRUE);
         }
         else if (wParam == IDCANCEL)
         {
         EndDialog(hDlg, NULL);         /* Exits the dialog box         */
         return (TRUE);
         }
         break;
    }
    return (FALSE);                     /* Didn't process a message     */
}

/**************************************************************************


    FUNCTION: ModifyRow(HWND, unsigned, WORD, LONG)

    PURPOSE:  Processes messages for "MODIFY" dialog box

    MESSAGES:

     WM_INITDIALOG - initialize dialog box
     WM_COMMAND    - input received

    COMMENTS:

     No initialization is needed for this particular dialog box, but TRUE
     must be returned to Windows.

     Wait for user to click "Ok" button, then close the dialog box.

 **************************************************************************/

BOOL FAR PASCAL ModifyRow(hDlg, message, wParam, lParam)
HWND hDlg;
unsigned message;
WORD wParam;
LONG lParam;
{
    switch (message) {
     case WM_INITDIALOG:                /* message: initialize dialog box */
```

```
        SendDlgItemMessage(hDlg,    /* limit row# input to 4 characters*/
         ID_MROWNUM,EM_LIMITTEXT,4,0L);
        SendDlgItemMessage(hDlg, /* limit table input to 30 characters*/
         ID_MTABLE,EM_LIMITTEXT,30,0L);
        SendDlgItemMessage(hDlg, /* limit values input to 250 characters*/
         ID_MVALUES,EM_LIMITTEXT,250,0L);
        return (TRUE);

    case WM_COMMAND:                 /* message: received a command */
        if (wParam == IDOK) {             /* "OK" box selected?      */
         GetDlgItemText(hDlg,ID_MROWNUM,
            (LPSTR)szRowNum,4);        /* Get row number    */
         szRowNum[4] = '\0';
         rownum = atoi(szRowNum);
         GetDlgItemText(hDlg,ID_MTABLE,
            (LPSTR)szTable,30);        /* Get table name    */
         GetDlgItemText(hDlg,ID_MVALUES,
            (LPSTR)szValues,250);      /* Get values string */
         EndDialog(hDlg, NULL);        /* Exits the dialog box    */
         return (TRUE);
         }
         else if (wParam == IDCANCEL)
         {
         EndDialog(hDlg, NULL);        /* Exits the dialog box    */
         return (TRUE);
         }
         break;
    }
    return (FALSE);                   /* Didn't process a message    */
}

/**************************************************************************

    FUNCTION: ConnectSQL(HWND, unsigned, WORD, LONG)

    PURPOSE:  Processes messages for "Connect" dialog box

    MESSAGES:

     WM_INITDIALOG - initialize dialog box
     WM_COMMAND    - input received

    COMMENTS:

     No initialization is needed for this particular dialog box, but TRUE
     must be returned to Windows.

     Wait for user to click "Ok" button, then close the dialog box.

    *************************************************************************/
```

continues

Listing 5.2.7. continued

```
BOOL FAR PASCAL ConnectSQL(hDlg, message, wParam, lParam)
HWND hDlg;
unsigned message;
WORD wParam;
LONG lParam;
{
    char szSQLServer[31];
    char szServerMess[81];
    static LOGINREC *LoginRec;
    RETCODE   rc;

    *szSQLServer = NULL;
    switch (message) {
     case WM_INITDIALOG:          /* message: initialize dialog box */
        SendDlgItemMessage(hDlg,      /* limit input to 30 characters */
         ID_SQLSERVER,EM_LIMITTEXT,30,0L);
        return (TRUE);

     case WM_COMMAND:                    /* message: received a command */
        errhWnd = hDlg;
        switch(wParam)
        {
         case IDOK :                  /* "OK" box selected?     */
            GetDlgItemText(hDlg,ID_SQLSERVER,
             (LPSTR)szSQLServer,
                MAX_SERVERNAME);    /* get Server name */
            if(*szSQLServer != NULL) /* was something input     */
            {
             DBLOCKLIB();            /* lock down library       */
             if(dbproc != (DBPROCESS *)NULL) /* if an active    */
                                             /* process close it */
             {
                dbclose(dbproc);
                dbproc = (DBPROCESS *)NULL;
             }
             if((LoginRec = dblogin()) != (LOGINREC *)NULL)
                                             /* get loginrec      */
             {
                DBSETLUSER(LoginRec,(char far *)"sa"); /* set user */
                    /* now open the connection to server */
                if((dbproc = dbopen(LoginRec,(LPSTR)szSQLServer))
                    == (DBPROCESS *)NULL)
                {
                    /* if NULL couldn't connect   */
                 dbfreelogin(LoginRec);
                }
                else /* got connect so use the pubs database */
                {
                 dbuse(dbproc,(LPSTR)"pubs");
```

```
                    dbfreelogin(LoginRec);
                    LoginRec = (LOGINREC *)NULL;
                    }
                }
            else /* memory allocation problem */
                MessageBox(hDlg, "Could not allocate Login Record",
                 "System Error", MB_ICONHAND | MB_OK);

            /* Open the cursor, bind variables */
            if (SQLInitCursor() == FALSE)
                MessageBox(hDlg, "Cursor open failed",
                 "System Error", MB_ICONHAND | MB_OK);
             DBUNLOCKLIB(); /* done unlock library */
            }
            EndDialog(hDlg, NULL);        /* Exits the dialog box        */
            return (TRUE);
            break;
        case IDCANCEL :
            EndDialog(hDlg, NULL);
            return(TRUE);
            break;

        }
        break;
    }
    return (FALSE);                          /* Didn't process a message    */
}

/***************************************************************************

    FUNCTION: SQLInitCursor(void)

    PURPOSE:  Initialize cursor, bind variables

    PARAMETERS: NONE

    RETURN:   NONE

    COMMENTS:

***************************************************************************/

BOOL PASCAL SQLInitCursor()
{
    int     i, j= 0;
    RETCODE  rc;

    /* Open the cursor */
    hdbcursor = dbcursoropen(dbproc, stmt,
     KEYSET, CONCUROPT, NROWS, pstat);
    if (hdbcursor == (DBCURSOR *)NULL)
```

continues

Listing 5.2.7. continued

```
{
 return FALSE;
}

/* Start a transaction block. We will exit without
** committing, so the pubs database will
** not be altered.
*/
if ((dbcmd(dbproc, "begin tran") != SUCCEED) ¦¦
  (dbsqlexec(dbproc) != SUCCEED))
{
 /* Error! Close the connection and exit */
 dbclose(dbproc);
 dbproc = (DBPROCESS *)NULL;
 return FALSE;
}
while ((rc=dbresults(dbproc)) != NO_MORE_RESULTS)
{
 if (rc == FAIL)
 {
   /* Error! Close the connection and exit */
   dbclose(dbproc);
   dbproc = (DBPROCESS *)NULL;
   return FALSE;
 }
}
/* Bind variables */
rc = dbcursorbind(hdbcursor, 1, NTBSTRINGBIND, 41, NULL,
 (char far *)au_lname);
if (rc == FAIL)
{
 return FALSE;
}
rc = dbcursorbind(hdbcursor, 2, NTBSTRINGBIND, 21, NULL,
 (char far *)au_fname);
if (rc == FAIL)
{
 return FALSE;
}
rc = dbcursorbind(hdbcursor, 3, NTBSTRINGBIND, 21, NULL,
 (char far *)au_city);
if (rc == FAIL)
{
 return FALSE;
}
rc = dbcursorbind(hdbcursor, 4, NTBSTRINGBIND, 3, NULL,
 (char far *)au_state);
if (rc == FAIL)
{
```

```
    }
    return (TRUE);
}

/***********************************************************************

    FUNCTION: CheckForScroll(HWND, int, int, int)

    PURPOSE:  Check if next output line will be out of client area

    PARAMETERS: hWnd - Handle to the window.
            CurrentPosition - Current y coordinate for the line of
                text just written to the client area.
            Spacing - The height of the line (including the space
                separating lines) of the text just written.
            Length - The length of the line just written in device
                units.

    RETURN:   Returns the y coordinate for the next line of text.

    COMMENTS:

    Will determine if the next line of text will be out of the client
    area. If so will scroll the window for the next line. Also validates
    the current line of text so that a WM_PAINT will not clear it.

***********************************************************************/
int CheckForScroll(hWnd,CurrentPosition,Spacing, Length)
HWND hWnd;
int CurrentPosition;
int Spacing;
int Length;
{
    RECT rect;                   /* RECT structure for validation   */
    rect.top = CurrentPosition;     /* top of last line of text     */
    rect.bottom = CurrentPosition+Spacing+1; /* bottom of last line */
    rect.left = 1;                  /* left-most column of line     */
    rect.right = Length+1;          /* right-most column of line     */
    ValidateRect(hWnd,(LPRECT)&rect);   /* validate line so that it is */
                                        /* not blanked on next paint   */

    GetClientRect(hWnd,(LPRECT)&rect);  /* get rect for current client */
    if(CurrentPosition + (Spacing*2) > rect.bottom) /* will line fit   */
    {
                        /* if not scroll window and    */
                        /* update client window        */
      ScrollWindow(hWnd,0,-(Spacing+1),NULL,NULL);
      UpdateWindow(hWnd);
      return(CurrentPosition);
    }
```

continues

Listing 5.2.7. continued

```
        return(CurrentPosition+Spacing);
}

/*************************************************************************

    FUNCTION: SQLTestProcessResults(HWND)

    PURPOSE:  If a valid dbprocess is present, process all results from
              pending select statement, output each field to client area.
              Whenever a new line is written to client area it is checked to
              see if the client area needs to be scrolled.

    PARAMETERS: hWnd - Handle to the window.

    RETURN:   Returns the y coordinate for the next line of text.

    COMMENTS:

    This function will bind the fields in the select statement
    to local variables, format an output string, then
    write that string to the client area via TextOut.

*************************************************************************/

BOOL SqlTestProcessResults(hWnd)
HWND hWnd;
{
    HDC hDC;                     /* display context        */
    TEXTMETRIC tm;               /* text metric structure  */
    char szOutputString[81];     /* general output string  */
    int Y;                       /* y coordinate for text output */
    int Spacing;                 /* Spacing between lines   */
    unsigned short i;

    errhWnd = hWnd;
    hDC = GetDC(hWnd);                    /* get display context        */
    GetTextMetrics(hDC, (LPTEXTMETRIC)(&tm)); /* get font info          */
    Spacing = tm.tmExternalLeading + tm.tmHeight; /* set up spacing     */
    Y = 1;                               /* start at line 1            */
    if(dbproc == (DBPROCESS *)NULL)   /* if process null, no results   */
    {
     ReleaseDC(hWnd,hDC);                     /* free resources and return  */
     return(TRUE);
    }
    SendMessage(hWnd,WM_ERASEBKGND,hDC,0L); /* always erase background */
    UpdateWindow(hWnd);          /* force painting of window   */
    DBLOCKLIB();                 /* lock down library          */
```

```
      /* Convert from OEM to ansi */
      for (i=0 ; i < NROWS ; i++)
      {
        if (pstat[i] & FTC_SUCCEED)
        {        /* Print only if fetch succeeded */
        OemToAnsi((LPSTR)(au_lname[i]), (LPSTR)(au_lname[i]));
        OemToAnsi((LPSTR)(au_fname[i]), (LPSTR)(au_fname[i]));
        OemToAnsi((LPSTR)(au_city[i]), (LPSTR)(au_city[i]));
        OemToAnsi((LPSTR)(au_state[i]), (LPSTR)(au_state[i]));

        /* here we format each field and write it to client */
        /* area checking to see if the client area needs to */
        /* be scrolled after each line is written           */
        sprintf(szOutputString,"Last Name: %s",au_lname[i]);
        TextOut(hDC,1,Y,szOutputString,strlen(szOutputString));
        Y = CheckForScroll(hWnd,Y,Spacing,strlen(szOutputString) *
        ➥tm.tmMaxCharWidth);

        sprintf(szOutputString,"First Name: %s",au_fname[i]);
        TextOut(hDC,1,Y,szOutputString,strlen(szOutputString));
        Y = CheckForScroll(hWnd,Y,Spacing,strlen(szOutputString) *
        ➥tm.tmMaxCharWidth);

        sprintf(szOutputString,"City:  %s, State:  %s",au_city[i],
        ➥au_state[i]);
        TextOut(hDC,1,Y,szOutputString,strlen(szOutputString));
        Y = CheckForScroll(hWnd,Y,Spacing,strlen(szOutputString) *
        ➥tm.tmMaxCharWidth);

        Y = CheckForScroll(hWnd,Y,Spacing,0); /* add extra line   */
                                              /* after each results */
        }
        else if (pstat[i] & FTC_MISSING)
        {
        sprintf(szOutputString,"Row %d is missing.", i+1);
        TextOut(hDC,1,Y,szOutputString,strlen(szOutputString));
        Y = CheckForScroll(hWnd,Y,Spacing,strlen(szOutputString) *
        ➥tm.tmMaxCharWidth);

        Y = CheckForScroll(hWnd,Y,Spacing,0); /* add extra line */
        }
      }

    DBUNLOCKLIB();                   /* unlock library    */
    ReleaseDC(hWnd,hDC);             /* free resource     */
    return(TRUE);
}

/***********************************************************************
```

continues

Listing 5.2.7. continued

```
    FUNCTION: dbwinMessageHandler(DBPROCESS *, DBINT, DBSMALLINT,
              DBSMALLINT, LPSTR)

    PURPOSE:  When the Data Server returns a message to dblib, this
              function will be called to process that message. This function
              is installed into dblib via MakeProcInstance. It must be
              declared as a FAR cdecl function, not as a FAR PASCAL function,
              unlike other call-back routines, as dblib conducts all of its
              calls in the cdecl fashion. You must return 0 to dblib.

    RETURN:   Returns 0

    COMMENTS:

****************************************************************************/

int FAR dbwinMessageHandler(dbproc, msgno, msgstate, severity, msgtext)
DBPROCESS       *dbproc;
DBINT           msgno;
DBSMALLINT      msgstate;
DBSMALLINT      severity;
LPSTR           msgtext;
{
    MessageBox(errhWnd,msgtext,(LPSTR)"SQL DataServer Message",MB_OK);
    return(0);
}


/****************************************************************************

    FUNCTION: dbwinErrorHandler(DBPROCESS *, int, int, int, LPSTR, LPSTR)

    PURPOSE:  When dblib returns an error message to the application, this
              function will be called to process that error. This function is
              installed into dblib via MakeProcInstance. It must be declared
              as a FAR cdecl function, not as a FAR PASCAL function, unlike
              other call-back routines, as dblib conducts all of its calls
              in the cdecl fashion. You must return INT_CANCEL,
              INT_CONTINUE, or INT_EXIT to dblib.

    RETURN:   Returns continuation code.

    COMMENTS:

****************************************************************************/

int FAR dbwinErrorHandler(dbproc, severity, errno, oserr, dberrstr,
➡oserrstr)
DBPROCESS *dbproc;
int severity;
```

```
int errno;
int oserr;
LPSTR dberrstr;
LPSTR oserrstr;
{
    MessageBox(errhWnd,dberrstr,(LPSTR)"DB-LIBRARY error",MB_ICONHAND ¦
    ➥MB_OK);

    if (oserr != DBNOERR)      /* os error */
    {
     MessageBox(errhWnd,oserrstr,(LPSTR)"Operating-System error",
     ➥MB_ICONHAND ¦ MB_OK);
    }

    return(INT_CANCEL);   /* cancel command */
}
```

When successfully compiled and executed, this program launches the screen shown in Figure 5.2.1.

FIGURE 5.2.1.

The SQL Server Connect dialog box for the Windows cursor sample application.

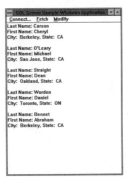

There are essentially three main screens: the main screen offering the choice of Connect, Fetch, and Modify, as well as a SQL Server connect screen; a response window to specify a specific row number to fetch; and another response window to capture row number, table name, and string values to modify, insert, or delete the values retrieved by the cursor.

When activated, the Fetch menu option looks as shown in Figure 5.2.2.

FIGURE 5.2.2.
*The Fetch menu
and Row Number
Response window.*

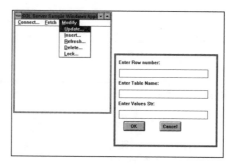

Finally, the Modify menu option offers you additional functionality. As discussed in the chapter dealing with cursors and transactions, these cursors are especially useful when you want to deal with a retrieved result set one row at a time.

Bulk Copy Functions in DB-Library

You have already been introduced to the use of the bulk copy utility. Here you will see specifically what you can accomplish by writing your own bcp utility functions as opposed to using the bulk copy utility itself. The bulk copy extensions to the Open Client DB-Library include the following functions:

Table 5.2.1. Bulk copy functions in the Open Client DB-Library.

Function	Description
bcp_batch	Saves rows already sent to the SQL Server through the bcp_bind and bcp_sendrows functions
bcp_bind	Binds data from a program variable to a defined SQL Server table
bcp_colfmt	Defines the user file format for the bulk copy application
bcp_collen	Defines the length of the program variable to be copied into the SQL Server table
bcp_colptr	Sets the data address of a program variable
bcp_columns	Defines the number of columns to be affected by the user file
bcp_control	Changes the control parameter default values
bcp_done	Completes a bulk copy operation from program variables to the SQL Server

Function	Description
bcp_exec	Executes a bulk copy of data between a database table and user file
bcp_init	Initializes bulk copy
bcp_moretext	Sends a portion of text or image value to the SQL Server
bcp_sendrow	Sends a row of data from program variables to the SQL Server
bcp setl	Defines the login record for bulk copy operations

You might choose to automate the uploading of data from a portable computer to a central office SQL Server by writing your own bulkcopy routines. Listing 5.2.8 is an example of a bulk copy program for the PC/DOS environment downloaded from CompuServe.

Listing 5.2.8. Handling Bulk Copy operations from a C program.

```
define DBMSDOS
#include <sqlfront.h>
#include <sqldb.h>
#include <stdio.h>
#include <string.h>
#include <stdlib.h>

int err_handler();
int msg_handler();

void main(int argc, char *argv[])
{
FILE    *data_file;
int rec_count=0;
int rec_batch=0;

struct inrectype
{char year[2];
 char f1[1];
 char grant10[10];
 char f2[1];
 char term[8];
 char f3[1];
 char emph[3]; };
struct inrectype inrec;
DBTINYINT year;
long int term;
```

continues

Listing 5.2.8. continued

```
LOGINREC *log-in;
DBPROCESS *dbproc;
DBINT rows_sent;
DBBOOL  more_data;
char    *terminator = "\n";

dberrhandle(err_handler);
dbmsghandle(msg_handler);

log-in = dblogin();
DBSETLUSER(log-in,"sa");
DBSETLPWD(log-in,"mogambo");
DBSETLAPP(log-in,"bcpload4");
BCP_SETL(log-in, TRUE);
dbproc = dbopen(log-in,"SQL");

if (bcp_init(dbproc,"abstract..coding",(BYTE *)NULL,(BYTE *)NULL,
    DB_IN) == FAIL)  exit(ERREXIT);

if (bcp_bind(dbproc, (BYTE *)&year, 0, (DBINT)-1, (BYTE *)NULL,0,48,1)
    == FAIL)
{
    fprintf(stderr, "bcp_bind, column 1, failed.\n");
    exit(ERREXIT);
}

if (bcp_bind(dbproc, inrec.grant10, 0, 10, (BYTE *)NULL,0,47,2)
    == FAIL)
{
    fprintf(stderr, "bcp_bind, column 2, failed.\n");
    exit(ERREXIT);
}

if (bcp_bind(dbproc, (BYTE *)&term, 0, (DBINT)-1, (BYTE *)NULL,0,56,3)
    == FAIL)
{
    fprintf(stderr, "bcp_bind, column 3, failed.\n");
    exit(ERREXIT);
}

    if (bcp_bind(dbproc, inrec.emph, 1, (DBINT)-1, terminator,1,39,4)
    == FAIL)
{
    fprintf(stderr, "bcp_bind, column 4, failed.\n");
    exit(ERREXIT);
}

if ( (data_file = fopen(argv[1],"r")) == NULL)
    {fprintf(stderr, "Cannot open file %s\n",argv[1]); exit(1); }
```

```
while (fgets(inrec.year,100,data_file) != NULL)
  {
   year = atoi(inrec.year);
   term = atol(inrec.term);
/* printf("%s %s %s %ld\n",inrec.year,inrec.term,inrec.emph,term); */
   if (bcp_sendrow(dbproc)==FAIL) exit(ERREXIT);
   if (++rec_count == 10000)
      {rec_count=0; bcp_batch(dbproc); ++rec_batch;
       fprintf(stderr,"Committed batch %d of 10000
records\n",rec_batch);}
  }

if ((rows_sent = bcp_done(dbproc)) == -1)
   printf("Bulk-copy unsuccessful.\n");
else printf("%ld rows copied.\n", rows_sent);


dbexit();
}

int err_handler(dbproc, severity, dberr, oserr, dberrstr, oserrstr)
DBPROCESS *dbproc;
int  severity;
int  dberr;
int  oserr;
char *dberrstr;
char *oserrstr;
{
    if ((dbproc == NULL) || (DBDEAD(dbproc)))
        return(INT_EXIT);
    else
    {
        printf("DB-LIBRARY error:\n\t%s\n", dberrstr);

    if (oserr != DBNOERR)
        printf("Operating-system error:\n\t%s\n", oserrstr);

    return(INT_CANCEL);
    }
}

int msg_handler(dbproc, msgno, msgstate, severity, msgtext)
DBPROCESS *dbproc;
DBINT     msgno;
int  msgstate;
int  severity;
char *msgtext;
{
    printf
    ("SQL Server message %ld, state %d, severity %d:\n\t%s\n",
    msgno, msgstate, severity, msgtext);
    return(0);
}
```

One advantage to writing your own bulkcopy routines is the capability to trap and return error messages to the user. For applications in which users require uploading or downloading data in a controlled fashion, writing your own bulkcopy routine sometimes makes more sense than working through a third-party tool.

Summary

I promised at the outset of this chapter that you would not be trained in C/C++ programming by reading through this material. (See, I was true to my word!) However, you should now have a much better grasp of both the advantages of writing your own Open Client DB-Library applications and the challenges involved.

As you have noticed reinforced from the beginning of this book, the strength of the Sybase client/server solution is the capability to integrate a vast array of technological products at many diverse levels.

By segregating DB-Library from the communications layer, your custom applications can be deployed across many different networks. And by enabling you to incorporate DB-Library function calls into multiple languages, you have many new options for tying existing code or apps back to your SQL Server.

The ease of use and market growth of good MS Windows applications are highly exciting. Hopefully, this chapter has helped you shape your expectations of the complexities involved in developing these GUI-based client programs.

5.3

Connecting Personal Computers to a SQL Server

As discussed in the first section, one of the biggest benefits of using a Sybase database engine is its connectivity. Unquestionably, the single largest population of end-user computers is the IBM-compatible personal computer. The price and performance features of XT- and AT-compatible machines, and more recently the 386- and 486-based systems, have led to an explosion of computer-literate non-systems professionals in organizations throughout the world. These people are moving beyond being mere users and are quickly becoming a force in organizations everywhere, demanding faster access to more data. In many cases, end-user departments are installing their own LANs and databases. The backroom IS shop, once in the position of dictating what data would be had by whom, is now struggling to keep up with the explosion of data and technology.

Although client/server solutions can help address these issues, the complexity inherent in the client/server model is nowhere more apparent than in connecting PCs to a SQL Server.

First, each machine is as different as its users. And each user has his or her own suite of personal productivity tools, application programs, TSRs, screen savers, and such. Compatibility issues abound, between hardware and software interrupts; memory types, sizes, and speeds; and software versions. Not to mention the tremendous range in technical awareness on the part of these end users, from naive newcomers to sophisticated power users. Ask anyone responsible for providing PC support in any good-sized organization, and you will likely be told, "It's a nightmare out there."

Well, that might be. But the capability to leverage existing investments in personal computer hardware and time spent in the learning of applications software is too attractive for most organizations to ignore. From a user's perspective, to be able to point and click or use the Lotus 1-2-3 /File Retrieve process to access departmental data as if it were on the local disk is the kind of service that computers have been promising for years.

Recently, some large PC companies have spent a fortune advertising their view that the next few years will be the era of the workgroup. As products that facilitate client/server computing are brought to market, organizations begin to see the benefits of combining personal computing, networking, GUIs, and relational database management software into an integrated solution. What most of these users want is transparent access to networked corporate data. That's where your SQL Server comes in.

Sybase Networks—A User's Perspective

In many organizations in which Sybase has been used to implement a true client/server system, a user sits down at the PC, starts Windows, and launches three or four icons. One icon might be the company's internal e-mail system, running on an office automation server under, say, NetWare. Another might be a spreadsheet, Improv or Excel. Then again there would be the company's own custom developed program.

Evaluating a spreadsheet with data supplied by Accounting's OS/2-based SQL Server, writing a report incorporating that data on the company's local PC, and sending a copy of the report through e-mail based on a third server is becoming a reasonable, achievable expectation on the part of corporate users.

In this case, the user need only be computer-capable enough to deal with the application programs he intends to use. Accessing remote applications and database servers needs to be made no more technical than mounting that server by name. As with an iceberg, the visible part represents the least of it.

The International Standards Organization has specified a seven-layer model for networks called the Open Systems Interconnection model. The OSI model has the following components:

> Application—This is the layer the user sees.
>
> Presentation—This is the desktop environment, such as Windows or PM.
>
> Session—This establishes a valid login and connection between the client and server.
>
> Transport—This layer manages the assembly of the bytes into packets and streams.
>
> Network—The software in this layer establishes the end-to-end network connection.
>
> Data Link—These software or hardware controls manage the physical transmission of frames over the data link.
>
> Physical—The physical connection manages the electrical interface that makes up the network.

Most networks do not completely adhere to each layer of this model. It serves, however, as a useful illustration of how the various components of the network fit together. Most of the time spent in bringing up a client PC is involved in configuring that specific machine to successfully accommodate the various software that makes up the necessary protocol stack.

I will use the OSI model to illustrate how the various software components "stack up" for several SQL Server networks. Most client/server solutions based on a SQL Server involve components at every level in the model. You can see each of these constituent parts in Figure 5.3.1.

FIGURE 5.3.1.
The ISO Open Systems Interconnection model.

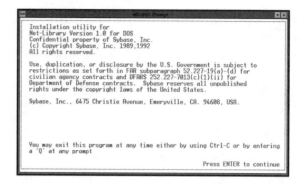

How a PC Client Talks to the SQL Server

Most users see a network as a "black box" that keystrokes go into and data comes out of. For purposes of planning and integrating a SQL Server into a networked environment, it will be necessary to go into some detail about networks.

To accomplish this task, I must first define in general terms how a PC connects to a network. A network consists of at least two computers, one a server and one a client. Each must have a compatible network card such as Ethernet and be linked through a properly terminated cable. Sybase supports various networking platforms and is not dependent on any particular network configuration.

The PC treats the network card as a device that software can talk to by loading device drivers in the config.sys at boot time or by loading Terminate and Stay Resident (TSR) drivers at the command prompt. When properly configured, the PC sends packets of data out to the network in search of a server address to receive them. These packets are assembled into a stream and passed by the server's operating system to the program to which they are addressed. In the case of a SQL Server request, the PC issues, say, a T-SQL call for data. The PC breaks the SQL code into packets, addresses them, and wraps check characters around the packets, then passes them through the network card. The server, seeing packets addressed to it, receives the packets, checks for any corruption, reassembles them into a stream of bytes, and directs the assembled stream to the SQL Server as appropriate. The TransAct SQL is processed, and the results are directed back to the PC's network address.

As the PC receives packets from the server, they are first received into the RAM buffer of the network card. Depending on the size of the packet stream, the speed of the network, and the size of the buffer, the PC might off-load the packets into PC RAM before filling the card buffer, or packets might overflow and have to be retransmitted.

Several factors affect the performance of the network node. For example, if packet loss and retransmission rates are substantial and chronic, it might appear to the end user that the link is slow.

Communications Hardware

It will be helpful to take a network from the ground up. The most prevalent physical LAN options traditionally implemented in organizations have been these:

- Ethernet
- Token Ring
- FDDI
- ArcNet

Generally, your organization will already have made some investment in networking technology before acquiring and installing a SQL Server. Because it is unlikely that you will be making an investment decision in network hardware and software based on this book, I will not spend a lot of time comparing and contrasting the various networks available. This section, however, will cover several representative configurations of network cards for a PC that will be connecting to a SQL Server network.

For those interested in buying network cards specifically for new SQL Server clients, the following configuration recommends what would typically be the best combination of price and performance for a network card:

- 16-bit card
- 16K RAM buffer
- Software configurable
- External lights to indicate connection status and traffic

Network Card Notes

Although 32-bit bus master cards are beneficial for servers, they do not generally provide sufficient increases in performance for SQL Server clients to warrant the cost due to performance factors other than network card throughput. Eight-bit bus cards function acceptably, although 16-bit cards do provide better throughput on large transfers of data.

A software configurable card is easier to install and troubleshoot, because it is not necessary to take the card out of the PC to find a suitable interrupt and memory setting.

Wherever practical, you should standardize on one make of network card, because the configuration settings for the various levels of software must all be set differently for each vendor. By working with the same make and type of card, you greatly reduce the number of variables to be managed from one machine to the next.

Communications Drivers

Applications that run over networks, such as client/server systems, are significantly more complex than traditional host/terminal-based communications. The application sits at the highest level of a stack of protocols and layers, and each must be installed and properly working for the application to function properly. In most cases, it is not desirable to have the user understand the various layers and software involved in allowing their PC-based application to talk to the SQL Server over a network. However, when the user is a developer responsible for Sybase solutions involving PCs, it is critical for them to have a complete grasp of the concepts and procedures involved.

To have a PC recognize an installed network card, a communications driver must be loaded. Even simple networks with one server and a few nodes or workstations (or peer-to-peer networks) require this software.

Application-Supplied Board-Specific Drivers

Years ago, when a software package was developed for networking personal computers, it usually required sole access and complete control over the network board. Switching from one application to another involved changing lines in the config.sys file and adding new ones or loading and unloading TSRs. It was, to say the least, a pain. As networks have become more sophisticated and PCs more prevalent in organizations, newer approaches have been developed to allow multiple applications to use the same network card. In some cases, this capability has been expanded to allow more than one protocol and framing type to be supported simultaneously. In keeping with its client/server orientation, Sybase does not provide any board-specific communications drivers, but rather provides Net Libraries that talk to other communication drivers.

Sybase Net-Lib Explained

One of the greatest strengths of the Sybase database architecture is its capability to manage logins and user connections independent of the operating system the SQL Server is running on. With Novell, for example, you could install an 8-user version of Sybase on a 5-user version of NetWare and have as many as 13 users logged on to the server at once. The real benefit of this arrangement, as discussed in Section 2, is the capability of the SQL Server to manage many users without significant degradation in response time. The reverse side of this coin is that Sybase requires its own connectivity software in order to integrate client software with the SQL Server. This requirement effectively divorces SQL Server accounts from operating system logins, which provides an additional level of security as well. These benefits, however, come at the price of increased complexity.

After you have successfully connected your personal computer to the network, you still must install an additional software program to allow PC-based clients to communicate with the SQL Server. These products are called Open Client Net-Libraries. They must be acquired from Sybase for the specific PC communications driver you want to load for each of your connected PCs.

In the personal computer arena, separate and distinct Sybase Net-Libs are available for DOS and Windows applications. Net-Library for DOS does not allow Windows Applications to talk to a SQL Server, and vice versa. It is important to note that each copy of Net-Lib you buy provides the necessary DLLs and programs to link with specific supported communications drivers (sometimes called middleware). You must buy one copy of Net-Lib for each PC client and each environment (that is, DOS and Windows) that you want to attach to your SQL Server.

When installing Net-Lib you will be presented with a menu similiar to the diagram in Figure 5.3.2.

FIGURE 5.3.2.

Screen capture of Net-Library installation routine.

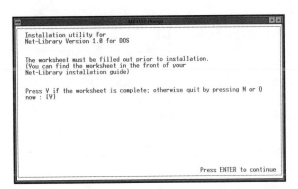

The Net-Lib install routine creates the necessary directories and copies the library programs to the PC in the SQL directory as a default. Additionally, the routine makes changes in the autoexec.bat to place the SQL directory in the path and to set the value of DSQUERY to the name of your SQL Server. The Net-Libraries pass requests for SQL Server access or resources through to the communications drivers and pass the resulting messages or data back to the requesting application program.

The Net-Library Installation Utility prompts you for the following information:

> The location of your Windows directory
>
> The serial number of your diskette
>
> The source drive for the files
>
> The target drive
>
> The name of the target directory
>
> The IP address of your SQL Server
>
> The Query Port number for your SQL Server

To complete the installation process, you must establish a number of questions as displayed in the install programs worksheet checklist shown in Figure 5.3.3.

FIGURE 5.3.3.

Screen capture of completed Net-Library worksheet.

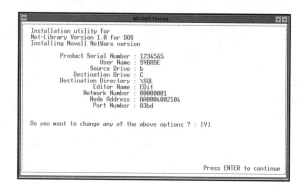

Sybase supplies a Ping utility for both DOS and Windows that you can use to ensure that your software has been correctly loaded and configured. The Ping utility behaves like the dbopen() routine of DB-Library when it is given a sqlserver name string. You do not have to have a valid login or account on the SQL Server to use Ping. You must, however, have one if you want to connect any third-party applications.

PC Communications Software Options

As of June 1993, Sybase has provided Net-Libraries for the following communications driver software:

Novell LAN Workplace for Windows

Novell LAN Workplace for DOS

PATHWORKS (DECnet)

HP ARPA Services

AT&T StarGroup

Named Pipes Networks

FTP PCTCP for DOS

These specific networks are based on several communications network approaches. Of course, there are specific technical differences in vendor implementations of even the same general approach. However, the four most common types of communication approaches for the transport, network, and data link layers of PC networks are Packet Drivers, ODI, NDIS, and Named Pipes, which are explained in the following subsections. ODBC drivers are supplied with an increasing number of Windows applications, which allow those programs to find the net-library software and attach to the SQL Server through it.

Packet Drivers

Packet Drivers owe their origin to work done at Carnegie Mellon University during the 1980s. As befits an academically developed product, many packet drivers are in the public domain, which means they are essentially free and unsupported. Commercial products such as FTP Software's PC/TCP for DOS provides copies of packet drivers and communications kernels for Ethernet, token ring, serial links, and X.25. These are not free but come with technical support and updates. Sybase does not talk directly to packet drivers, but to the communications kernel loaded on top of the packet driver.

ODI (Open Data-Link Interconnect)

This standard was developed by Novell, Inc, to accommodate clients who wanted concurrent connections between Novell and TCP/IP servers. Novell offers LAN Workplace for DOS and Windows, both of which support SQL Server connectivity.

NDIS (Network Data Interchange Specification)

Microsoft has developed NDIS as part of its LAN Manager Network Operating System product. More recently, products such as Windows for Workgroups have incorporated NDIS as part of their communications architecture. A Net-Library is available for 3Com 3+ Open TCP that uses NDIS drivers.

Named Pipes

Named Pipes was also developed as part of the OS/2 LAN Manager Architecture. It serves as a high-level application programming interface supported by OS/2. The Named Pipes API insulates the client software from the transport layer protocols. The Microsoft version of SQL Server, which runs on the OS/2 platform, uses Named Pipes independent of the network it is running on. Sybase provides a Net-Library for Named Pipes.

Your choice of communications software will most likely be dictated by the server environment in your organization: Packet Drivers for TCP/IP, ODI for NetWare, NDIS for LAN Manager, or Named Pipes for OS/2. It should be noted, however, that advanced configurations of products from any of these families can be configured to support the servers on the networks mentioned previously.

Installation Scenarios

There are great differences in the way each type of communication driver can be configured. Perhaps the clearest way to demonstrate configuration of the various PC clients would be to show the steps one would take for a specific example. The following scenarios demonstrate the installation approach one would take for various server installations.

Sybase Client Scenario #1: Novell Only with a DOS Client

Connecting a DOS-based PC to a Novell-based Server running Sybase NLM gives the user access to both the NetWare Server as drive F:\ and the SQL Server named as DSQUERY. To achieve this, you would perform the following steps:

1. Install the network card.
2. Use WSGEN to generate an IPX.

   The WSGEN utility for NetWare 3.11 generates an IPX shell for the specific interrupt and memory settings used on the network card.
3. Install Net-Lib for DOS, Novell on the PC.

   The install routine copies dbnovsp.exe and dbping.exe to the \sql\binr subdirectory.

Modify your autoexec.bat by adding \sql\binr to your path, and set DSQUERY=1,1,83bd (or whatever your network, node, and query port specifications are for your SQL Server).

4. Reboot (or rerun autoexec.bat) to activate the new path and environment variables.

5. At the command line, enter `DBPING DSQUERY`.

   You should get an affirmative response from your dbping.

6. Switch to drive F:\. You can now login to Novell and connect your DOS applications to your SQL Server.

Sybase Client Scenario #2: Novell Only with a Windows Client

This scenario demonstrates how to connect a Windows-based PC to a SQL Server NLM. MS-Windows connectivity uses different communications drivers than a DOS connection uses.

1. Install the network card.

2. Use WSGEN to generate an IPX.

3. Install the Net-Library for Windows, Novell.

   After creating a SQL directory with binr, dll, install, and lib subdirectories, and copying the wdbnovsp files, the routine modifies your win.ini and adds

   ```
   [SQLSERVER]
   DSQUERY=wdbnovsp,1,1,83bd
   ```

   The autoexec.bat is modified and has \sql\dll added to the path.

4. Reboot.

5. Load IPX.

6. Load NETX.

7. Change to the F:\ drive and log in to NetWare.

8. Start Windows and run \sql\binr\wdbping.exe.

9. You can now connect to your SQL Server or access the NetWare Server.

As you can see from these steps, the Net-Library for Windows is completely different than the product for MS-DOS. However, you can load both the DOS and Windows Net-Libraries in the same directory on the PC and load either Net-Library depending on whether you want to run Windows- or DOS-based SQL Server clients. In both cases, the IPX loaded remains the same.

You can also see that it is not necessary to load NETX or login to the Novell Server to access the SQL Server. In fact, it is not necessary for SQL Server clients to even have a valid NetWare login in order to connect. Of course, they must have a valid SQL Server login to accomplish anything more than a simple dbping.

Sybase Client Scenario #3: UNIX Host Only

This scenario demonstrates how to connect a Windows PC to a UNIX-based SQL Server using FTP Software packet drivers. Other vendors use the same approach but have different names for the drivers and kernel software. To install FTP's PCTCP software and use packet drivers to connect the PC to your SQL Server, you would perform the following steps:

1. Install the network card make a note of the interrupt and memory settings.
2. Install FTP's PCTCP software which modifies the path statement in your autoexec.bat to include \pctcp; specifically, this adds `set pctcp=\pctcp\pctcp.ini`.
3. Install the Net-Library for Windows, FTP.
4. Modify \windows\system.ini to include

   ```
   [386Enhanced]
   Device=c:\pctcp\vpctcp.386
   ```
5. Reboot.
6. Load the packet driver for the network card by typing

   ```
   ne2000.com
   ```
7. Load the Ethernet kernel by typing

   ```
   ethdrv.exe
   ```
8. Start Windows.
9. Run \sql\binr\wdbping.exe.

   You should see that DSQUERY is alive!

Similar to when you load Net-Library for Novell, the SQL Server client need not have a UNIX account. Conversely, UNIX host account holders cannot connect to the SQL Server. The greatest advantage to using this approach is the capability to change the underlying communications hardware and packet drivers and keep the remaining drivers and configuration intact. This enables a network administrator to migrate a PC from one network card to another or even to substitute Wide Area

Network communications gear in place of the LAN without having to completely reconfigure the PC.

Sybase Client Scenario #4: Concurrent Access to a UNIX Host, NetWare, and SQL Server from a Windows-Based PC

This scenario demonstrates how to configure a PC to support access to three distinct servers, on different platforms, using one network card under Windows. To achieve this, you could perform the following steps:

1. Install the network card.

2. Load the appropriate Packet Driver.

3. Generate IPX for the Packet Driver.

4. Install communications kernel for the Packet Driver.

5. Install Net-Library for the communications software.

6. Edit win.ini and system.ini (see scenario 3).

7. Load PDIPX and NETX.

8. Switch to F:\ and log in into the NetWare Server.

9. Start Windows.

10. Run wdbping, which should return a message indicating that your SQL Server is alive.

11. Run Wtelnet or other UNIX host related software.

12. Start the SQL Server client software.

The specific options for loading each driver are documented in the vendor-supplied manuals for the specific make and version of software you choose. These scenarios, however, should convey a sense of how the various products work together to allow SQL Servers to be integrated with complex existing networks and give your users transparent access to their SQL Server data.

Summary

This is not (obviously) intended to be an exhaustive review of the methods you can use to connect your client PC's to a SQL Server over a local area network. Even since this chapter was drafted, new and different ways of connecting have been introduced.

What you should now have a better grasp of is the components that you must manipulate in order to connect to SQL Server. The move to NetWare's ODI was not covered, for example, as the access method from the Net-Library for SPX has not changed.

No matter which connectivity scheme you choose, you will find that the Net-Library products are quite flexible and work in a variety of communications channel and software driver combinations and configurations.

5.4

Troubleshooting Net-Lib Connections

Throughout this section, you have been introduced to client-side software and connectivity utilities necessary to connect front-end applications to SQL Servers. At this point, you will be shown a methodology for evaluating problems in connecting and will be provided with several alternatives for resolving those problems.

Each network has its own unique characteristics, which make it difficult to lay down any tried-and-true formulas for resolving network connection problems. It is possible, however, to identify some of the more common problems as well as to lay out the step-by-step approach a troubleshooter would take to resolve problems at a specific site.

As you have heard many times already in this book, the biggest drawback to a client/server environment is complexity. This chapter will promote a series of methods you can use to help you resolve problems in a complex, multivendor environment. Increasingly, client/server customers are becoming frustrated with the lack of support offered by vendors and are discovering that they must be responsible for the systems integration aspects of their own environment. In a way, this responsibility actually makes sense. Vendors of a single product, or even a set of products, cannot be expected to know all the implications and permutations of the various other products on the market that you might be trying to work with. When it comes right down to it, you are the one who stands the most to gain from knowing the products used in your environment, and that puts the onus for support squarely on your shoulders.

On the other hand, it is asking a lot of you as a client/server customer not only to develop and support your own users and applications, but to become experts in the inner workings of the various products that make up your environment. To be fair, often you pay for support, and what you get is the dreaded finger pointing—the support staff for product x is always blaming product y for your particular difficulties. An effective SQL Server solution involves many different technologies at different levels. To be able to develop and support applications based on these technologies, you have been taken on a high-level view of the server side, client-side, and systems integration issues involved. At this point, I will assume that you have implemented at least your first few client/server products and are now interested in gaining a better grasp of what you need to know to support the operation of these products.

This chapter will cover each of these areas by walking you through a typical problem and by listing common complaints and recommending a course of action. By reading this chapter, you should be able to reinforce your understanding of how SQL Servers are accessed by programs across a network. However, the primary objective of this chapter is to give you an effective reference to assist you in diagnosing and fixing connection problems when they arise at your site.

Diagnosing Network Problems

Frequently, network problems are not a straightforward case of a user being unable to connect to the SQL Server. Often, network problems masquerade as software bugs, causing flaky, inconsistent problems such as hanging the machine or displaying weird results. It would be impossible to list all the bizarre behaviors the system can present to the user as a result of network problems. All too often, the problem is simply an hourglass that won't go away. This aggravates the user and only indicates to you that something is wrong without giving you any meaningful pointers.

You can use the following methodology to evaluate and diagnose network problems with the client machines you work on or support. In the event of a problem, you should take the following steps:

1. Start from the ground up.

   Avoid the temptation to start looking first at the program being used. In terms of percentages, when a system previously has been connected to a SQL Server and has been working fine, and it can no longer access the Server, it is almost always hardware failure. Check the network connection at the back of the machine to ensure that it is properly seated. Trace all connections from the machine to the wall or ceiling. Double-check that the link has not been broken between your machine and the server. Check the status of any hubs, repeaters, or concentrators along the network path. Are they all functioning? Is the SQL Server up?

   The reason for walking through the physical link that the network runs over is simply to ensure that you do not make any changes you might regret later. It is all too easy to think that you know what the problem is, and change a configuration setting, only to find that the network still does not work. By double-checking the physical status of the network, you avoid making unnecessary alterations to the client's config.

2. When in doubt, reboot.

   I would like to be able to tell you that the degree of quality assurance and standards compliance is such that all the components of a client/server solution will work together effectively, easily, and reliably. The unpleasant truth, however, is that it just ain't so. Client machines from any and all hardware vendors are subject to strange, unrepeatable complaints. With the number of diverse components involved in these solutions, it might be more practical to adopt the philosophy that it is amazing that any of this stuff works at all, rather than expecting perfection.

My point here is that you can sometimes resolve a client connection problem by rebooting the machine. When this does occur, there *might* be a pattern of software loaded and conflicts generated within the client machine itself. I have noticed this kind of conflict more often since people began adding sound and CD-ROM controllers to their existing systems. If nothing is wrong with the network, try rebooting the machine. Note that hardware lockups are sometimes not cleared with a soft boot (Ctrl-Alt-Del) or even by punching the reset. If you are going to reboot, power down the machine, wait a minute, and power it back up again. This should give you a clean starting point to work from.

3. What have you done to me lately?

   Rare indeed is the system that just stops working for no apparent reason. Usually, someone has been playing around, and a configuration setting has been changed or something has been commented out of the startup files. If you can find out what new software has been added to the machine, you can more easily track down the files that might have been modified as part of its installation. New cards or modified hardware settings are also frequent culprits. The key here is that when you add something new to a system, the existing services can easily be affected. You will sometimes find that you need to resolve network problems as a result of changes that you yourself have made to the client workstation.

   Part of the challenge facing you as a client/server developer is dealing with the rapidly changing releases of the tools with which you work. Even within relatively stable environments, there is an ongoing requirement to incorporate upgrades and new versions as they are released. Installing a new operating system version on either the server or the client side can quickly turn into a nightmare of troubleshooting and reconfiguring machines. By identifying recent changes, you are in a much better position to determine where the origin of any given problem lies.

4. Isolate the problem.

   If you have determined that there is nothing physically wrong with either the machine or the network, and the user swears that no systems configuration changes were made, you need to draw as tight a circle around the problem area as possible. This approach necessarily restricts your efforts to the most likely causes of the problem, which is more efficient than simply taking a shotgun or hierarchical approach.

   Determine whether the machine is the only one on the network experiencing the problem. Duplicate addresses, a malfunctioning concentrator, or various other problems might affect software operation or server access for more than one machine. If more than one client machine is experiencing the same problem, you can determine the common denominator and focus on that.

Problem isolation is not simply to determine the number of machines involved. Assume that only the one client PC is unable to access the server. The problem has been isolated to the one machine. The next step is to isolate exactly where in the machine's environment the problem is occurring.

5. Take one step at a time.

   Never make more than one change to an environment at a time. Of course, I say that not knowing just how familiar you are with your environment, and perhaps you do know vastly more than either I or any of the other tech support people I have discussed this with. But let's just say that we have all done it and regretted it at some point.

   When you make a series of changes and then try to connect to the server, you run two risks: one, that one of your changes will work and you won't know exactly what you did to fix the problem, and two, that one of the changes will work, but another will cause a new problem. The way to minimize the complexity of the problem is to reduce your problem-solving methodology to a series of single-step activities. Try something and evaluate the outcome. If that change does not work, put it back the way it was.

6. Use the process of elimination.

   Even from the preceding list you can get a sense of the troubleshooting approach using the process of elimination. Naturally, you want to eliminate the most common problems first. That is one of the reasons for performing a hardware check, or ensuring that the server is up, from the outset. Troubleshooting takes you away from your more pressing development activities, and especially when the workstation was working previously, there is little glory to be gained from getting something back to the point where it was before. Systematically identify and eliminate each element of the client/server equation as the source of the problem.

7. Take notes.

   As obvious as it might seem, this step is one that many client/server troubleshooters skip over—and live to regret! When you are working on something, it seems natural to remember the last few steps or changes you made. There is a real temptation to just keep making changes, thinking you will remember what you did and put it back if the change does not fix the problem. Real life being what it is, however, you end up getting called away, go for lunch, break for the day, or go on a holiday, and the next thing you know, you can't quite remember exactly what it is you did (or changed). You end up going back to square one.

An integral part of an effective troubleshooting methodology is ensuring that you do not make the same mistake twice. By taking notes (and they don't have to be submitted to the teacher for marking, they just must be good enough for you to decipher), you can create an audit trail of what you tried to resolve the problem and what changes you made. Keep in mind that if you end up involving some other technical support person in resolving your problem, your notes can be invaluable for discussing what you did and did not try to do.

8. Document version sets.

   As you determine which components of your client/server solution are actually compatible, you should take the time to list the compatible version sets. Frequently, you will find that older versions of operating systems will not work with 100 percent compatibility with new releases of Net-Lib, transport software, and so forth. The key is that you need to establish which versions do, in fact, work together, and then when possible, upgrade/downgrade/modify the stack of software in use by a particular client workstation to be able to take advantage of the compatible versions.

If possible, you should assign someone to test compatibility of new software releases before allowing users to upgrade their own machines, or having a PC support group do it when it is not responsible for supporting access to Sybase.

Use the list of compatible version sets to determine whether a problematic machine actually uses the right versions of the various layers of software. Sometimes you just can't get two versions to work together, and knowing that in advance can save you a lot of time and effort.

An Example Case

You should now have at least a general sense of the approach to solving your client/server problems. However, it is sometimes difficult to understand how these principles can be applied without a specific example to demonstrate. Following is a treatment of a recent troubleshooting problem I faced. This example identifies what specific steps need to be taken to diagnose and resolve a problem in the context of this troubleshooting methodology.

The Problem

A PowerBuilder developer who had been working with a system for several months complained that she could no longer connect to the SQL Server.

The Approach

The SQL Server was running under Novell 3.11. Because the F: drive was still available and working fine, there was no question of a network cabling problem. In fact, rebooting the PC showed that the connection worked fine; the user could log into the file server without difficulty. A quick review of the NetWare console showed that the SQL Server was up and running, also proven by the capability of other workstations to connect.

An interview with the user indicated that no new software had been installed. Using the WDB Ping utility verified that the workstation could not see the SQL Server. However, because the workstation had both IPX and TCP/IP access to the server, I tried WDB Ping using the TCP/IP drivers—and it worked! The problem then was in the Net-Library for IPX connections.

The [SQL Server] entries in the win.ini looked fine; they both explicitly pointed to the drive and path where the client software was to find the .dll to use for establishing the connection. By all rights, everything looked fine—it should have been working.

After rebooting again, I noticed that the version and date on the ipx being loaded looked a little old. When I used the file manager to search for ipx.com, it reported two copies of the ipx file on the user's hard disk. Investigating each of these ipx versions turned up that one was an old version of ipx that had been left in a subdirectory. I changed the autoexec.bat routine to load the newer ipx.com explicitly. After I loaded Windows and ran WDB Ping, it worked. PowerBuilder, too, could again find the SQL Server.

After I explained to the user what I had found, it turned out that someone had loaded a demonstration version of a new package on that system. The person hadn't thought to mention it because he had taken it off soon afterward. While the other package was being installed, however, the path statement in the autoexec.bat routine had been changed a little, and as a result, the first ipx.com found was the older version. As it turns out, to use wdbnovsp.dll to connect a workstation to a Novell file server, you must use version 3.10 or newer of ipx.com. Other versions will enable you to access Novell services without difficulty, but you have difficulty connecting to a SQL Server from a Windows-based client program.

More Problem-Solving Approaches

One of the points you should get from the preceding example is that the specifics surrounding any given SQL Server networking problem will vary greatly from site to site and from machine to machine. Especially with PCs, the various configuration options, software versions, and hardware components can range dramatically. Each problem must be taken case by case. Of course, that is not a lot of consolation when you're the one trying to resolve a particularly thorny problem. To assist you, following is a representative problem and potential solutions.

Symptom

The message `SQL Server is unavailable or does not exist` is received by an application or is displayed when you try to ping the server.

Action Steps

1. Check win.ini for the `[SQL Server]` entry. Correct the entry to read:

   ```
   [SQL SERVER]
   DSQUERY=drive:\path\netlib ,address,query port
   ```

   For example, to connect with FTP's PCTCP transport software, I have the following entry:

   ```
   [SQL SERVER]
   DSQUERY=c:\sql\binr\wdbftptc,192.9.200.69,4096
   ```

   For LAN Workplace for DOS to connect to a Novell-based server, I use this:

   ```
   [SQL SERVER]
   SYBASE=c:\sql\binr\wdbnovsp,1,1,83bd
   ```

2. Check that your system.ini has been pointed to the correct drivers.

   For FTP Version 2.1, I use this:

   ```
   [386 Enh]
   device=c:\pctcp\vtcptc.386
   ```

   For Lan Workplace for DOS, I use this:

   ```
   [386 Enh]
   device=c:\net\bin\vtcpip.386
   ```

   Windows should notify you that it has loaded these devices immediately after it displays the Windows logo (if you still load that) when MS-Windows first starts.

3. Ensure that your path statement points to the appropriate communications subdirectories. Frequently, path statements become longer than 128 characters or are modified (mangled) by automatic installation routines. Type `path` at the command line and determine whether your system can see the subdirectories needed. If you do not explicitly point to the subdirectories for your win.ini and system.ini devices, you *must* ensure that the path is set correctly.

4. For TCP/IP connections to the server, ensure that the IP address set for your machine is valid and unique. Duplicate numbers on the network will work somewhat and for a while. Unpredictable results will occur. The first three sets of numbers in the IP address refer to subnets. Ensure that you have specified the correct network path for your PC. Also, if you are using a router, ensure that it is functioning correctly.

5. Check that you have specified the query port. The SQL Server not only must have a machine address to connect a client to the server, but it also looks for a specific query port for Sybase services. The query port is defined in the interfaces file on the server.

Summary

In this chapter you were introduced to a way to approach problem solving and troubleshooting of client/server networks. One key point stressed was the uniqueness of each site due to the sheer number of variables involved. Although this may fill some of you with fear and trepidation, take heart. Like most complex machines, your client/server network will seem to take on characteristics and idiosyncracies of its own and, over time, you will become familiar with them. The purpose of this chapter was to simply provide you with an overview of troubleshooting considerations.

Unlike developing systems under a more traditional computing model, client/server developers are greatly affected by and, in turn, can have a tremendous effect on all aspects of the computing environment. I have met many software developers who feel strongly that understanding and dealing with networking and administration issues is "not my job."

It is important to keep in mind that increasingly, companies are becoming their own systems integrators. This makes sense when you consider that no external vendor can be as concerned with the successful integration of your particular set of third-party products as you, the customer, will be. As a result, organizations are placing a greater requirement on all systems people to understand and manage the entire computing environment.

This chapter was intended to assist those of you having to deal with the alligators, while trying to remember that your objective is to drain the swamp.

Section Summary

This section covered the specific functions and operations handled by the two cornerstone products in client-side connection to SQL Server: DB-Library and Net-Library.

From this section, you should now have a clear view of the purpose and role of these two products, as well as the specific considerations involved when configuring them to work with either DOS or Windows.

Many of you may not find it necessary to deal with DB-Library or even Net-Library issues as part of your projects. You can see from this section, however, just how much power is available to you through these products. You should also now be in a much better position to understand how third-party products such as PowerBuilder actually work with SQL Server.

To those of you who will be taking advantage of DB-Library and Net-Library to write your own applications, good luck. I hope this section has helped make clear some of the approaches and issues involved in using the DB-Library and Net-Library products.

6

Front-End Tools and Utilities

Introduction

THIS SECTION MOVES TOWARD A GREATER EMPHASIS ON THE relationship of the front-end client process as a part of the overall Sybase client/server solution. Until now, I have focused almost exclusively on the technical architecture and features of the SQL Server database engine itself. This section introduces the kinds of client tools that have been incorporated into SQL Server environments—from shrink-wrapped PC packages to end-user query tools and custom-built client applications. Because of the openness of the SQL Server architecture, a tremendous number of client software packages has been or can be integrated with a SQL Server.

The purpose of this section is to cover representative examples of products, and to give you as a developer a sense of how these tools can fit into your client application suite and just how they work with SQL Server. Necessarily, not all effective tools are discussed here. I do not intend to promote a particular third-party package over another, and any slight or offense is not intended and should not be taken. My objective in this section is to introduce a range of solutions, which you can choose or reject, simply to illustrate the various levels of client application interaction with SQL Server databases.

Where possible, the products discussed are natural contributors to a SQL Server solution. Products from Sybase, Inc., for example, are not necessarily the best development products, but the range of options presented by them is covered in this section because many of your organizations have acquired server and client development tools from Sybase. In other cases, I have opted to discuss market leaders, trend setters, or simply hot products, such as PowerBuilder.

In some examples, high visibility has been the key rationale for choosing a particular product as an example. Excel is known as a spreadsheet in Mac and UNIX environments, for instance, and it can be connected transparently to a SQL Server. I have no wish to debate the relative merits of Excel versus Quattro Pro, or any other packages. The objective of this section is to provide a meaningful treatment with practical examples of client software options for developing client/server solutions. To accomplish this, I have chosen to be product specific.

Does everybody get the idea? In this section I am not pushing one set of client solutions over another. The objective is to make the discussion restricted and specific enough to provide some information that will be meaningful to you as a developer even if you do not use the products described in this section.

6.1

Sybase-Supplied Utilities

Not everything that you will find useful about your SQL Server is provided as part of the internal database architecture. Several utilities that operate as client programs running against the database are shipped along with the SQL Server database engine. The most prevalent and often-used utility is ISQL—the Interactive Structured Query Language utility for interpreting T-SQL commands. This is shipped for all platforms on which SQL Server runs. Another useful client program is the bulk copy utility for moving data in and out of tables, to and from operating systems files. Like ISQL, the bcp utility is shipped with every SQL Server. Several other programs also interface to SQL Server, although they are available only on certain platforms.

This chapter introduces each of these utilities, shows the syntax and options available, and covers the implications of using the various flags. By the end of the chapter, you should have a good idea of just how to use SQL Server utilities to accomplish some of the most frequently required administration and development tasks.

ISQL is provided with every SQL Server shipped. It is a necessary part of the initial installation and is used for many systems administration purposes. Every SQL Server site uses ISQL, and, like vi in the UNIX world and edlin in the antique DOS arena, a great many people truly hate it. Not that you can blame them. ISQL is an unforgiving, display-poor, and highly mnemonic command-line interface to your SQL Server. It is also the first client to come up and the easiest to connect, and it lets you do anything and everything to the SQL Server. For many, a relationship with ISQL is a marriage either of convenience or of mutual inconvenience. As a developer, you will no doubt be forced to use it on an occasional basis at least and a daily basis at worst. If you work exclusively with ISQL, forget this entire section, because it will only make you jealous. In any case, this chapter covers the basics of using ISQL to access SQL Server database objects.

ISQL

The Interactive Structured Query Language utility is provided with every SQL Server for all platforms. It is really a server utility and frequently executes directly on the host platform on which the server runs, but it is nevertheless a client program. The ISQL application operates through a character-based command-line interface, and as such it is used on the console terminals or windows. ISQL provides no editing, formatting, or scrolling capabilities, which means that the retrieved results frequently scroll off the top of the screen and disappear into the ether. Keying errors mean that you must rekey the command entirely, although on some platforms, like Novell, you can use the up-arrow key to recall previous commands. ISQL tips and tricks are discussed later in the chapter.

Results are displayed lengthwise by row. When the row is longer than 80 characters, the line wraps, which can make the results difficult to interpret. Typically, an ISQL session involves typing a number of SQL statements to form a batch and then issuing the command to execute the batch. The default execution command is go, but you can change it to anything you like. The parameters that can be passed to ISQL are shown in Table 6.1.1.

Table 6.1.1. Description of ISQL Options

Parameter	Description
-e	echoes input
-c \<word>	changes execution command
-U \<Username>	defines the SQL Server login ID
-P \<Password>	supplies the password for the login ID
-S \<Servername>	defines the server to connect to (default is DSQUERY)
-i \<filename>	takes a filename as the batch input
-o \<filename>	writes results to the specified text file name

You can use the slash (/) instead of the hyphen (-) to separate the parameters when starting ISQL. A typical startup command to connect through ISQL to a SQL Server that had been defined already with the DSQUERY environment variable would look like this:

```
isql -Usa -Popensesame
```

On some systems a space is not acceptable between the flag and the value, so it is probably easier to get in the habit of entering the command in this way. You should keep in mind that for systems that keep a buffer of past commands, entering the command in this way will show the password for the login ID. To make your ISQL session more secure, try entering this command:

```
isql -Usa
```

In the following example, the -P tells ISQL to prompt you for a password, which is hidden from prying eyes and is not kept in the command history either. When the password is currently null and is undefined, you must enter the -P flag on the command line:

```
isql -Usa -P
```

You do this when first installing the SQL Server, or when logging in as a new user with no password. You can also just hit return when prompted for a password.

When you have successfully established an ISQL session, you are presented with a simple line counter that looks like this:

```
1>
```

The number increments for each command you enter. To clear the buffer and begin at 1>, type reset. To execute the commands in the buffer, type go. A sample ISQL session could look something like this:

```
1>select * from syslosers
2>where uid = 1
3>reset
1>select * from sysusers
2>where uid = 1
3>go
```

You can choose to output the results of your ISQL statements to a text file. Unfortunately, when you use the -o flag with ISQL, you lose the line numbers, and results are directed only to the file and not to the screen where you are entering commands. You are flying blind. The most straightforward way to deal with ISQL is to write your SQL statements into a text file and redirect the results to an output file. When doing this, be sure to include the necessary execute commands in your text file, especially at the end of the file, or ISQL will read your script and exit without executing it. The command line to take input and redirect the output would look like this:

```
isql -Usa -i/usr/sybase/inputfile -o/usr/sybase/outputfile
```

At this point, ISQL would prompt you for a password and execute the commands contained in the input file.

ISQL allows you to define an editor that can be called from within your ISQL session for editing your SQL scripts. On some platforms, you can also execute operating systems commands from within ISQL with the !! command.

BCP Bulk Copy

Every development effort requires the ability to get data in and out of the SQL Server at some point. Although this cannot be achieved using the SQL Server feature set directly, the bulk copy (bcp) utility is provided with each server to enable you to perform these transfers. To move data in and out of the server itself, you would use the dump database and transaction log features. Although these can also be used to transfer databases between SQL Servers, some restrictions exist. Bulk copy can be used to transfer data not only between SQL Servers with incompatible character sets and sort orders but also between your SQL Server and other programs and databases through flat files. These flat files are simple operating system files, either in character or os_native character format, and they can be fixed length or delimited with a special column and row terminator, such as a comma. The user can configure these for a particular bulk-copy session.

The bulk-copy utility operates in two modes: fast and slow. Each mode has distinct characteristics.

Fast Bulk Copy

As you might expect from the name, fast bulk copy is the high-performance option. The high performance is achieved by limiting bulk copy to the straightforward insertion of data into SQL Server tables. No transaction log is maintained, and data entered into the table is not indexed. When you expect to populate 80 percent or more of the overall table size with the bulk-copy operation, it is generally faster to drop any indexes or triggers defined on the table and use the fast bulk-copy option. To successfully execute bulk copy in fast mode, you must get the db_owner to set the db_option bulk copy to true. The default for newly created databases is false; without changing this option, bulk copy will execute only in slow mode.

If you choose to populate a table using fast-bulk-copy, you must dump the database after bulk copy completes. This enables you to execute the DUMP TRAN command for the database. After using bulk copy in fast mode, you will get an error message if you try to dump the transaction log before dumping the database entirely.

Slow Bulk Copy

Slow bulk copy enables you to continue logging and building indexes as the data is inserted into the tables, albeit at the expense of performance. When less than 20 percent of the table size is being inserted through bulk copy, you should use the slow mode. You should also use it in situations where recoverability is important. In slow mode, bulk copy logs each transaction as it takes place. In the event of a systems failure, the log can be used for recovery. You should also use slow bulk copy rather than re-creating your clustered indexes if you are short on disk space. Because a clustered index is at the base level a physical sorting of the table, you must have approximately 2.2 times the table size in available disk space to successfully complete the re-indexing of the table.

Interactive Bulk Copy

You can also enter your bulk copy specifications interactively through ISQL. You can use this mode to set the storage types, prefix length, and terminator characters for variable-length text files. For character and binary datatypes, bcp prompts you to set a field length. You can define and use format files to make bcp easier to operate.

defncopy

Elsewhere in this book, you learned that you cannot edit and recompile database objects such as stored procedures and triggers. Although that is true in the strictest sense, you can find ways around it. The defncopy utility is one of the utilities provided by Sybase for the UNIX, VMS, and OS/2 versions. defncopy copies definitions for specified views, rules, defaults, triggers, and procedures from the database where they are stored out to an operating system. You can also use defncopy to create database objects from OS script files, rather than using ISQL.

Like ISQL and bcp, defncopy is a front-end client program that must connect to a SQL Server through Net-Lib. To successfully execute defncopy, you must have already established a valid connection to a SQL Server and have a login and permissions to a database. You invoke defncopy from the operating system and specify any of the optional parameters on the command line. The parameters that can be passed to defncopy include

```
defncopy -U username -P password -S server
```

Additional settable options are as follows:

-I Interfaces_file	Sets this parameter to reference a specific interfaces file
-J client_charset	Displays the retrieved definitions in a local character set and handles the translation of the client and server character sets if they are different
-z language	Displays defncopy output in the alternate language specified
-X	Encrypts the client-side password during the login sequence

defncopy is a noninteractive method used to copy complete create statements for views, rules, defaults, triggers, or procedures in or out of operating-system files. You must have select permission on the sysobjects and syscomments tables to copy out definitions, although you do not need to have permission for the object itself.

You cannot use defncopy to get around restrictions in create permissions. If you wish to use defncopy to create a stored procedure, you must have the appropriate create permission for the target database, or defncopy will fail. If you use defncopy as SA, the permissions set for the created object will default to the systems administrator. To create objects as a user, you should log in as that user prior to creating objects using defncopy.

You can use defncopy to reverse-engineer a script file from objects you have already created, then drop the object, modify the script, and use defncopy to create the new object. By using this approach, you can work around the lack of a direct editing process for database objects within your SQL Server.

Summary

Sybase is isolated and insulated from the operating system of the host machine on which it runs. Although this is a benefit for performance and portability reasons, it does create some minor problems when you wish to move data, text, or object definitions between the operating system and SQL Server. The utilities covered in this chapter show how Sybase has elected to address this requirement.

These products are undeniably inelegant, especially for developers and administrators used to full-featured, GUI-based interfaces. These products have the advantage of ubiquity, however. That is, you can sit down at virtually any SQL Server running on any platform and use these utilities to accomplish your goals.

For this reason, I recommend that you spend the time necessary to become comfortable with the capabilities and syntax of the utilities covered in this chapter. After all, you never know when you might have to slip down to the lowest common denominator in the tool set.

6.2

Build Momentum

Over the past few years, Sybase has been criticized for the lack of features and capabilities delivered in its development tools. Although many applications designers and developers liked the power afforded by their SQL Server, the reaction of many developers to the APT and DWB tools was less than enthusiastic. With the recent acquisition and integration of the Momentum tools, Sybase is preparing to address these criticisms with a vengeance.

The two tools, Gain Momentum and Build Momentum, are very different products targeted for completely separate sets of applications and users. The Gain Momentum product is specifically oriented to applications such as interactive television. The World Cup, for example, is using the product to build an application that will allow a user to touch a player on the television and retrieve statistics and data on that player as the game progresses. These applications are addressing what Bob Epstein sees as the future of data services: delivering data to the doorstep. Sybase has stated that the company wants to be a player in this marketplace.

For those of you with a pressing requirement for more mainstream, leading-edge, client/server, GUI-based, object-oriented systems solutions, the Build Momentum offering will have greater appeal and applicability for your requirements.

Build Momentum is a complete GUI applications development environment. It is intended to compete head to head with the now-entrenched products such as PowerBuilder, Uniface, and SQL Windows. Build Momentum is quite different from these products in a number of ways. The key architectural differences that set Build Momentum apart revolve around its approach to object orientation and handling large teams with many developers.

Build Momentum and Object Orientation

Often, people who know object-oriented technology can be rather narrow-minded about the characteristics that qualify a product for object-oriented status. They believe that SmallTalk is object-oriented, but C++ is not, for a variety of reasons. More recent debates about the relative nature of these products has led to a differentiation between being object-oriented and object-based. However strictly you define your terms, Build Momentum qualifies for true object orientation. In comparison, other Windows GUI development tools are object-based.

What exactly do these labels mean, and what can you accomplish with the product? Specifically, Build Momentum enables you to modify the behavior of the tool itself. Products such as PowerBuilder or SQL Windows are shipped as compiled programs with which you develop applications that in turn are compiled. Build Momentum is constructed entirely out of Object Momentum, the language used by developers working with the tool. In the same way that the UNIX operating system can be extended because it is written in C, Build Momentum can be tailored, refined, and customized because it is written in Object Momentum.

Of course, true object orientation goes further than this, and Build Momentum remains consistent with that object orientation. Everything built with the Build Momentum development environment is represented as data (including Build Momentum itself, as described earlier). This data is defined in two categories, either as classes or as methods.

Classes are an object-oriented concept defined as a template that specifies the structure and capabilities of an object instance. An object is the combination of a class and a method. Methods are defined as the services provided by, or the behavior of, a class. The object "duck" is an object because it looks like a duck, walks like a duck, and quacks like a duck. (If it just looks like a duck, but doesn't quack or waddle, it might be a decoy, not a duck!)

Hunting-oriented or hunting-based analogies aside, Build Momentum also works within the object-oriented parameters of incorporating encapsulation, inheritance, and polymorphism, as you see in more depth a little further on in this chapter.

First, you should understand how Build Momentum fits into the client/server architecture, remembering that the purpose is to explore representative tools that can be integrated with your SQL Server to enable you to develop client/server solutions. As such, this review provides you with an overview of what an object-oriented, GUI-based development tool can provide as part of your client/server toolset in a SQL Server environment.

Build Momentum is a Sybase product (at least it is now that Sybase bought the company that developed it). As such, it provides the necessary open-client libraries to interface Build Momentum to a SQL Server. However, it can also talk to a number of different relational and nonrelational database management products. Build Momentum provides native connectivity support for Oracle, Ingres, Informix, and OBDC-based database systems. The database connectivity is provided as an underlying component of the development environment, which is managed by a multithreaded kernel. Other services on which the kernel is based include support for international languages and character sets and multiplatform support that allows Build to be run on Windows, Mac, and Motif platforms as well the object repository. The object repository manages both the master repository, where all the ancestor and systems objects are stored, and the user repositories, where user-specific objects are maintained. The kernel manages these services transparently to the developers who use Build Momentum. The development environment provides a set of services to a team of developers.

Dynamic Compilation

The Build Momentum kernel differs from what you might be used to thinking of as a kernel (the UNIX or SQL Server database kernel, for example), because the kernel is not a precompiled piece of code shipped by Sybase. The Build Momentum source code is shipped as part of the development environment and is compiled as it is executed. Through this process you can actually refine and revise the Build Momentum product and execute those refinements online. After a portion of the product has been compiled, it remains available in compiled form for the remainder of the session. Part of the Build Momentum kernel monitors and evaluates the frequency of access for certain features and determines which program pages should be compiled accordingly. As a result, the performance of this dynamic compilation actually exceeds that of precompiled development products, while providing the additional advantage of allowing you to use Build Momentum to modify the product itself.

Stratification of Systems Skills

The concept of multiple developers and users is an integral part of the design of Build Momentum. The development team builds applications using three distinct sets of objects, comprised of graphical objects, developer services, and language support. This includes graphical controls, which are the Windows widgets necessary to build GUI-based applications such as list box structures and scroll bars, and the various Build Momentum services and programming language support which are managed by the kernel for the development team.

As part of the commitment to reusability and inheritance, Build Momentum allows developers to inherit their C++, Visual Basic, and APT-SQL applications and migrate them into the Build Momentum environment. Not only can much of the logic and code then be reused as part of the GUI development effort, but Build Momentum can also be tailored to allow the scripts behind its various objects to be written in a syntax resembling one of these three languages. The scripts do not use identical syntax; it simply resembles the syntax of the language they are used to working with.

You can also work with the 3GL software services that are part of the Dynamic Link Libraries in Windows and Windows NT, shared resources in the Mac world, and shared libraries under UNIX. By creating an object wrapper in Build Momentum, thereby defining a global object, you can then call those services like any other object in the development environment. In this way, it becomes unnecessary to reinvent the wheel to take advantage of features or services already provided as part of the targeted client platform. This again demonstrates the extent of reusability designed into the Build Momentum product.

In many ways, the development environment in Build Momentum resembles that of any GUI-based power tool, such as PowerBuilder, SQL Windows, or Interface Builder. It has a main menu panel with toolbars and services. Along with browsers to view the objects held in the various repositories, the development environment includes editors for viewing and changing the syntax describing any of the application classes or methods. A powerful debugger utility allows the developer to step through single or multiple breakpoints in the code to evaluate how and if it works and determine exactly what it is doing when it fails.

The inherent team management facilities in the product mean that version control and promoting objects across projects, applications, or the entire development environment are built in.

Team Development Facilities

The Build Momentum product is specifically geared toward large scale development shops that require an object-oriented development environment capable of managing a large number of developers with different projects and skill levels.

A key concept underlying the Build Momentum product is the stratification of skill sets within the development team.

Centralized database operating system staff provide ongoing administration and technical support to a development team. However, as systems development efforts move toward the object-oriented model, a new class of systems professional is emerging—that of object guru. Of course, in many situations each developer is a guru of some set of objects. Because an object is both data and the methods for affecting the data encapsulated into a single entity, an application developer with the greatest familiarity with the real-world entity that the object represents is the best person to become that object's guru. In such cases, the owner of the object can promote the object to the other members of the development team, who can be aware of the object and its services without being responsible for the creation and maintenance of the object. Build Momentum is designed to support just this kind of delegated responsibility across a large team of developers. Build Momentum uses a single system to manage objects and relationships throughout the development environment.

Each user has his or her own objects and has access to the master repository. In addition, multiple developers can work concurrently on a single repository for a particular application. By choosing between the repositories, any developer can work in as integrated or independent a fashion as is appropriate for the application being developed. By working on a local repository, a Build Momentum developer doesn't have to be connected to a database to continue work on the application. The work done locally can be checked back into the shared repository later.

Through this process, the Build Momentum development environment is structured to manage the participation of a large number of developers working together and separately on multiple projects while sharing the objects that have been developed and perfected by specialists within the organization.

The Application Development Environment

In Build Momentum, the application developers work with the product as an environment with services and resources. The primary view of the environment is the options panel, where the various features and functions of Build Momentum are maintained.

The resources are the objects held in the various repositories. Build Momentum uses a project metaphor to store objects; it requires only that the objects be named uniquely within their project or subproject. As a developer, you can define as many subprojects as you require. If you specify an object that doesn't exist within your current project or subproject, Build Momentum will search the parent projects to the highest level in the hierarchy to find the declared object. You can also establish search trees of projects to access objects to share or use within an application. You can easily move objects between projects with the graphical drag-and-drop interface.

Several browsers and editors are available to a developer who is working with various components of an application. These are described in the sections that follow.

Database Browser

The Database Browser enables you to view all objects in connected databases, to edit data in tables, to modify database objects as permitted, and to perform simple database administration services. This feature depicts all relevant database names and ownership data on databases to which Build Momentum has been connected.

When you have identified a table in the Database Browser, you can click on the table and drag it to a window, where you can begin to incorporate it into an application object.

As soon as you release the mouse button and drop the table into the browser, the table is represented as a default form. You can tie metadata descriptions of column names to the application windows (for example, au_lname could be referenced as lastname). When this has been specified, the default form shows the metaname for the column as part of the default form.

The toolbar provided with the menu editor enables you to drag and drop widgets or Windows controls onto the screen. These controls are logical: the defaults are one screen forward, one screen back, scroll up, scroll down. As soon as you drop the button onto the menu editor, these controls can be used to retrieve data from the table you selected from the Database Browser. The real power behind this feature is not just how quickly you can build prototypes that retrieve and display form representations of tables, but that you can build your own custom buttons, with their own logic, and release those to developers as part of their toolbar. This logic can be developed using Build Momentum scripts, or it could be a stored procedure or even some imported 3GL software service. The object's services are made instantly available to the developers who drop the control onto the form with the table.

In this way, you can completely customize and streamline the development process on your client/server site, using a product like Build Momentum.

Development Features

Along with the Database Browser, and providing comparable levels of functionality, are several editors that are used by developers when creating applications using Build Momentum. These include the following:

- **Bitmap Editor:** This editor allows you to perform straightforward manipulation and cleanup of imported bitmaps to be displayed in your application.
- **Custom Object Editor:** You can use this editor to create and manage any customized objects developed for your project or environment.
- **Keymap Editor:** This editor provides the ability to define keymaps and associated function key processes across the multiple keyboard layouts supported by the Windows, Mac, and Motif platforms.
- **Menu Editor:** This editor gives you the facility to create and manage menu bars across the multiple platforms over which your applications are deployed.
- **Method Editor:** This editor enables you to define and edit any processing invoked as the result of an event occurring within the application.
- **Query Editor:** All SQL queries can be created, stored, and called using the query editor.
- **SQL Editor:** With this editor, you can create, edit, and delete database objects or send dynamic SQL code to the server and view the results.

Applications Deployment

Much of the focus on this evaluation of the Build Momentum product has been on the services it provides to you as a developer and where it fits into your client/server systems architecture. Ultimately, Build Momentum is intended to generate a production application that is rolled out to organizational users. This is accomplished through the creation of a stripped-down version of the repository (containing only the object required by the application) and a run-time Build Momentum environment. This environment enables users to store and execute only the components of the Build Momentum environment and the objects required to support their application. This keeps the size of the applications to a minimum. Through the dynamic compilation feature, any enhanced objects or revised Build Momentum features can be rolled out to the user, allowing them to upgrade while their application is online.

Build Momentum comes with a Deployment Utility to assist you in managing this rollout process.

Summary

Using Build Momentum promises that your investment in skills, knowledge, and development can not only be easily shared across a large team, but can also be maintained and controlled on an ongoing basis. By appointing key systems people as object-oriented tool makers, you no longer need to make everyone an object-oriented development expert or see widely varying development practices across any given set of developers. On a Build Momentum team, developers inherit the tools created for them specifically to meet their development objectives, which makes each member of the team more productive. The developers create client/server applications that take advantage of the multiserver, multiclient object-oriented GUI-based systems features and release these applications to the organization's end users.

As a result of this stratification, people interact with the technology at a level appropriate for their level of expertise and the job given to them to perform. The tool objects and the applications objects developed and deployed through Build Momentum enable you to encapsulate data and methods into any given object. Through the extensive use of inheritance provided in Build Momentum, you can automatically reflect ongoing enhancements and changes to any of the objects throughout the developers' and end-users' applications. All of this is transparent to the staff below the level where the changes take place.

Reuse of objects is supported throughout the development environment, and you can declare an object available in any shared repository or even the master repository. Developers can use the object as a base, make changes to it, and incorporate it into a completely different use or application. This is how Build Momentum supports the object-oriented principle of polymorphism.

The Build Momentum product demonstrates that your SQL Server can be used as a hub for powerful client/server applications that use new technology and techniques such as object-oriented software development. Just as importantly, this product clearly supports the stated Sybase objectives of interoperability of products outside the SQL Server and client software lines and the company's commitment to providing tools that develop enterprise-wide client/server solutions.

6.3

**PowerTools for Microsoft
Windows Development**

No doubt many of you who are new to the whole client/server architecture have heard about PowerBuilder and related "PowerTools" and wondered what the fuss was about. As I write this in early 1994, PowerBuilder and SQL Server are considered "the dynamic duo" for client/server development. In this chapter, you see why.

As with other chapters addressing adjunct technologies working in conjunction with Sybase, my objective is to give you a better idea of what kind of third-party options are available for your client/server development toolset. Not only is PowerBuilder generating the greatest amount of interest in the development community at this time, but it is also the environment that I personally have the most Windows development experience with. As such, it makes the most sense for me to use PowerBuilder as a representative development tool in this book.

It is not my intent to recommend PowerBuilder over the other Windows development tools on the market. I have seen some pretty marvelous Windows client programs running against SQL Server that have been built with other packages. Conversely, some seriously ugly applications have been developed with PowerBuilder (my personal favorite was the single giant purple close button in the middle of a pink screen). It is up to you to determine what development environment makes the most sense for your requirements.

This chapter gives you a pretty good idea of what you can do with a Windows Power Tool, specifically PowerBuilder. You will learn what it looks like and what traps have been found by first-time developers. To compensate for the glowing reports of the PowerBuilder product line, I point out some of the failings and weaknesses as well.

These development tools work with many different database environments. Like any tool that crosses a number of platforms, there are advantages to learning one product and making the database distinctions transparent. However, because this is a SQL Server book, I address PowerBuilder as you would use it in a Sybase environment, rather than opting for the more generally applicable, lowest common denominator approach.

By the end of this chapter, you should have a good idea of what PowerBuilder is and how it can be incorporated into your client/server environment. This chapter also introduces two companion products: PowerMaker and PowerViewer. PowerSoft has introduced the three as a set to provide more services than you would get from PowerBuilder alone. Again, these are not the be-all and end-all of query tools, decision support assistants, and Windows development environments, but they are a highly visible representative set.

This chapter shows you just how extensive the third-party tool support is for Sybase databases and gives you an idea of what kind of applications you can build using them. This chapter also discusses in general terms some of the critical success factors for developing Windows-based client software. You should be able to apply these observations to any development tool you choose—PowerBuilder, SQL Windows, Uniface, Build Momentum, or even Visual Basic or C++.

Windows Client Development

If you remember the summer of 1990, you probably remember some of the discussions about the future of PC and workstation development environments. Within the UNIX world, it was Motif versus Open Look; for PCs it was Windows versus OS/2. For Apple it was the Mac, the whole Mac, and nothing but the Mac.

The dust has pretty much settled on those arguments. Technical capabilities and superiorities aside, Windows has been massively adopted by customers over OS/2. Although Motif has pushed ahead of Open Look for UNIX user acceptance, both of these platforms have been dwarfed by the sheer volume of Windows seats and applications. Whether you like it or not, Microsoft Windows has become the GUI of the masses.

In previous chapters, you saw how SQL Server has been structured to take advantage of various LAN topologies and provide open access to client software through the open client application programming interface. PowerBuilder is just one of the third-party products that has emerged for Windows client application development that takes advantage of those features.

Released in 1992, PowerBuilder has ridden the wave of Windows buyers and grown, releasing two subsequent versions of the product in 1992 and 1993. Early adopters of the technology raved about the ability to automatically generate T-SQL code for complex Windows-based applications. This in a nutshell is what PowerBuilder provides; it allows a developer to build Windows-based applications that retrieve, manipulate, and report data from SQL Servers where the database access is totally transparent to the users of the applications and largely transparent to PowerBuilder developers. As search criteria are specified on tables and views, PowerBuilder generates T-SQL code that is shipped off to the attached SQL Server. The results are returned to the PowerBuilder application, where they are manipulated by the application user on the local PC.

Connecting PowerBuilder to a Database

PowerBuilder is a self-contained client development environment that provides a transparent interface to SQL Server and other database management systems. This is achieved through PowerBuilder metaphors for database objects, which are connected directly to the physical database objects running on the server. The PowerBuilder architecture divides each major activity such as database connections and Windows screen development into what PowerSoft terms "painters." Each painter contains a set of services that relate to the major activity. For example, after first starting PowerBuilder, you might choose to work with Windows and other local client-side objects that do not issue any SQL calls to the database. To accomplish this, you would select the windows painter. You could also choose to connect to a database and directly manipulate the database objects. PowerBuilder allows you to define a list of default databases, or you can enter a new database name and address into the Connect Database dialog box.

Figure 6.3.1 illustrates the first screen you see when you start PowerBuilder.

FIGURE 6.3.1.

The PowerBuilder 3.0 PowerPanel and menu options.

Figure 6.3.2 illustrates the process by which you connect to your database.

FIGURE 6.3.2.

The Database Profile Setup dialog box.

When you have successfully connected and logged in to the database, the database objects contained in that database are displayed in PowerBuilder, as shown in Figure 6.3.3.

As you can see from this figure, PowerBuilder provides its own graphical representations for the database objects held in the database to which it is connected. As long as the user name you used to log into the database through PowerBuilder has appropriate permissions, you can take almost all the actions on the database that you could through ISQL. For example, you can create and drop indexes or tables and views.

FIGURE 6.3.3.

The pubs database contents seen from PowerBuilder's database painter.

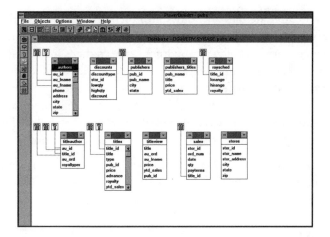

However, PowerBuilder does not let you specify different devices or segments for logs and indexes. As such, any tables created through PowerBuilder will reside entirely on the default device for that database. In some cases, such as development environments, this might not be much of a problem. In other situations, however, you will want to maintain control over the creation of tables and indexes to ensure that they use the correct devices.

With PowerBuilder, you don't need to be familiar with the syntax to be able to create tables, indexes, views, and other database objects. Although PowerBuilder allows a developer to access database objects through the database painter, it is not suitable for database administration purposes, as it is too restrictive in scope.

The GUI Development Environment

On the other side of the equation, PowerBuilder has extensive tools and options for creating GUI database applications. By selecting the windows painter, a PowerBuilder developer can design and lay out the various windows, dialog boxes, and screens necessary to build an entire application. The windows painter is shown in Figure 6.3.4.

As you can see, PowerBuilder allows you to incorporate all the buttons and scroll bars typically associated with Windows.

An important aspect of the PowerBuilder development environment is the facilities it provides for inheritance. Although the argument rages on regarding the definitive features for an object-oriented development tool, no one would dispute that PowerBuilder does provide some of the inheritance characteristics typically associated with an object-oriented development environment. What this gives to you as a developer is the ability to define ancestor windows with certain characteristics. Users can incorporate these windows into their applications, and if you decide to change the root or ancestor window, the descendent windows will subsequently display those changes automatically. As you might expect, there are several caveats and rules about which changes are automatic and when descendent windows have been modified or customized. These features have been implemented in an intelligent manner so that you don't lose the customized aspects in your application windows. However, you should refer to a more detailed treatment of PowerBuilder for further discussion on the extent and nature of the product's object orientation.

For your purposes, you need to know simply that PowerBuilder lets you create GUI applications that retrieve, manipulate, and modify database data in a client/server application.

FIGURE 6.3.4.
The windows painter with several widgets displayed.

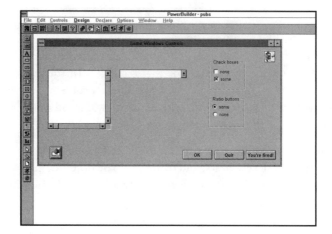

PowerBuilder's DataWindows

The reason for presenting PowerBuilder as first a way of connecting to a database and secondly for Windows application development is to highlight the single most powerful feature of PowerBuilder: DataWindows.

DataWindows is a PowerBuilder construct or metaphor for graphical representation in the PB environment of database data. On one level, a datawindow is similar to a view; the data can come from several tables and appears as one straightforward collection of columns and rows. However, the implementation of DataWindows goes far beyond simply displaying data.

At the heart of any PowerBuilder application are the datawindows that access the database. Datawindows are usually contained within windows that have been created with the windows painter. If the windows painter provides tools, options, and services for manipulating the screen, DataWindows enables you to encapsulate methods for retrieving and manipulating the data in the database itself.

As a datawindow is defined, PowerBuilder automatically generates SQL code to be associated with that datawindow. For a SQL Server environment, that SQL is the T-SQL code the Sybase server needs to properly process the commands. PowerBuilder also supports several other database environments and generates the SQL code appropriate for the database connection selected.

As a developer, you need to understand PowerBuilder well enough to know what selection criteria you want and which fields you wish to update, insert, or delete. You don't need to understand SQL syntax. As you might imagine, this opens up a whole world of development opportunities for developers who cannot build C++, Windows SDK, and SQL applications themselves. PowerBuilder manages all of these functions through the datawindows.

One of the reasons the extent of PowerBuilder's object orientation is questioned is the lack of inheritance support for DataWindows. With PowerBuilder version 3.0, the ability to manage descendent datawindows is not supported. However, given the power and functions provided by DataWindows, this is an omission that many developers are willing to overlook.

For each column defined in the datawindow, you can associate validations and styles. Using the PowerScript language supplied by PowerBuilder, you have a great deal of control over the acceptable values that can be entered into a datawindow. Conversely, you can define how you want data displayed and formatted after it has been retrieved from the database. Using PowerBuilder, you can develop code tables that map retrieved codes to more English language (or other language) responses. All of this executes on the client workstation running the PowerBuilder application and takes advantage of the local processing power in true client/server fashion.

Figure 6.3.5 better illustrates the functions provided by DataWindows.

FIGURE 6.3.5.
The datawindow painter.

When you create a datawindow, you can set the display format as either tabular or free form. A tabular datawindow presents the data from the table or view as a straight-forward column and row format. The free form option represents the datawindow as a screen form. Within the datawindow painter, you can move the fields around to create the layout that best suits your application requirements. A title is associated with each displayed column value. This title defaults to the name of the column taken from the table. However, you can edit, reformat, or delete this title to suit yourself. One of the datawindow painter's features is the ability not only to retrieve and ma-nipulate table data according to predefined or user-prompted selection criteria, but also to create forms that act as masks for displaying the data. The user's navigation within this screen form can be through a mouse event, such as clicking the mouse within the field, or by specifying a tab order for keyboard users. The PowerBuilder developer has a great deal of control over the order, format, and access of the values retrieved or entered through the datawindow. In Figure 6.3.6 you can see how tables are represented by PowerBuilder. Note that the names have been modified to be easier to read by a user/developer.

FIGURE 6.3.6.

Datawindow with free-form display of books table from pubs database.

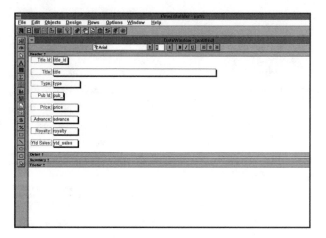

Because datawindows can be contained within windows, or even within other datawindows, the PowerBuilder developer can display and capture data from and for many tables within the same operation. Front-end validations on the datawindow can be written to ensure that the transaction will be successfully committed to the database.

Structures, Cursors, and Functions within PowerBuilder

As well as providing some object-oriented features, PowerBuilder enables the client/server developer to use more traditional programming methods. Functions can be written in C or other lower-level languages and then called from within the PowerBuilder application. Cursors are also supported, and complex structures can be developed to hold retrieved data being operated on as part of the application or development.

Drag-and-Drop and Other Windows Features

For those of you who are not completely familiar with the user interface advantages offered by a GUI environment such as Windows, you will be interested in some of the advanced Windows functions that can be handled from within PowerBuilder.

Drag-and-drop is a Windows operation in which you click the mouse button on an item on the screen and hold the button down and drag that item until it is where you want it to be, then you release the mouse button. One of the most widely known examples of this operation is the way the Apple Macintosh allows you to delete files by clicking on the file and dragging it over to the trash can icon. When the mouse button is released, the file is deleted. On an applications level, this feature can be used to retrieve data with a minimum of user intervention. For instance, with two datawindows on the screen, the user could retrieve details about an item picked from a list using drag-and-drop. This saves typing or cutting and pasting the column value you wish to retrieve into the detail screen before initiating a query.

Other advanced Windows functions such as Object Linking and Embedding (OLE) and Dynamic Data Exchange (DDE) are supported by PowerBuilder, allowing developers to include these features in their applications services. You would use OLE to launch another third-party application from within your PowerBuilder application. One of the more interesting applications that uses this feature is the creation of mail-aware applications using PowerBuilder. In such an application, where a predefined operation should be communicated to another person or group of people, the application calls the electronic-mail program specified and automatically initiates an e-mail message. Other OLE applications start word processing or spreadsheet applications simply by clicking on the document in the application. Through OLE, you as the developer can bring a multitude of options to bear on the application, without requiring the user to exit your application. OLE allows integration of applications on the desktop.

Dynamic Data Exchange, on the other hand, allows your application to use data that is generated and updated from another application. In the same way that the database is accessed and data displayed to the application, you can use PowerBuilder to access documents from other sources besides a database. This enables you to specify a document (a form, for example) stored on the network and kept up-to-date by other users. DDE ensures that any changes made to that document are reflected in the one you work with as part of your application. It avoids copying or replication timing and duplicate storage issues by simply identifying a source document and then pulling that data into the application dynamically when called.

PowerBuilder's support for advanced Windows features such as these enables you to create highly effective Windows applications without ever writing a line of C code. This is great news for shops with developers who already have their hands full with client/server and GUI issues, with no time, energy, or money to learn a new language. Even for those of you who are already solid C programmers, you might find that an applications development tool like PowerBuilder cuts the time required to develop applications.

A Practical Example

Here is an example of how you might develop an application using PowerBuilder that incorporates DataWindows and some of the other advanced Windows functions.

In this case, consider the pubs database. Although the database structure and model are provided with every copy of SQL Server distributed, you really have no clear example or statement of what you would use this data for. Many of the queries and examples in this book and in the Sybase product documentation refer to the pubs database simply to illustrate the "how to" of particular T-SQL commands. As you have seen so far in this chapter, with a PowerBuilder application the user is completely isolated from the SQL code itself. However, the code can be reviewed and even edited for users or developers who are comfortable with T-SQL syntax (so don't worry, you haven't wasted your time following all the T-SQL examples).

Assume you have decided to use PowerBuilder to develop a bookstore point of sale and inventory control application. Obviously, you have decided to deploy this in the Windows environment. What your user would see when looking for the specifics on a particular book, for example, is shown in Figure 6.3.7.

FIGURE 6.3.7.

A PowerBuilder application screen showing a listbox of book titles and a detailed description of the book.

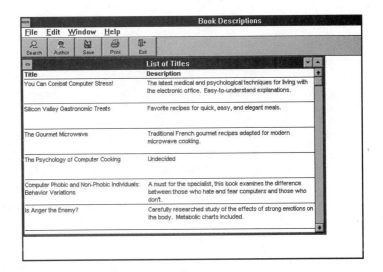

The application user can scroll through the listbox to identify the particular book for which details will be requested. By isolating the first listbox to one or two columns, the query performance is better and the amount of traffic on the network is reduced. Using drag-and-drop, the user highlights the book for which a detail query will be executed and then drags the book over to the detail window. By dropping the column value into the window, the retrieve is initiated with the select criteria equal to the column value dropped into the window. You don't need to click Go or perform any other operation to initiate the query. It all happens with one step. Figure 6.3.8 shows you the relationship between the two windows when using drag-and-drop.

FIGURE 6.3.8.

The listbox and associated detail window with retrieved values.

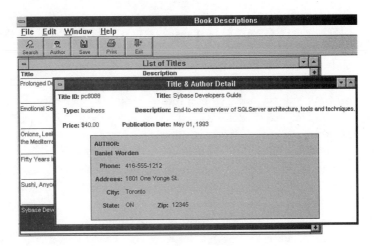

Keep in mind that the second datawindow can be an updatable view or a combination of tables. You can see the performance implications of segregating the list of all possible values from the multi-table joins and retrieves that must be performed to populate the detail datawindow. Using PowerBuilder in this way, you can structure the access of the database for performance and to best fit the application requirements and the way the users work.

Behind this GUI interface masking the database access, the PowerBuilder developer has gone to a certain amount of work. The listbox in this example can actually retrieve two values: the name of the book and its associated unique book ID. Although the book ID is not displayed, it can be the value passed to the detailed window for the select criteria using the drag-and-drop function. Naturally, you would want to avoid retrieving on the basis of name, because the index for the book table is keyed on unique ID number.

To accomplish this, the PowerBuilder developer must write scripts that are activated as soon as an event occurs. Events in the Windows world include such things as "clicked" and "get focus." These terms refer to the mouse activity taken when the cursor is placed on a specific icon or region of the screen. When the event occurs, the script executes.

You should have a clear idea of how PowerBuilder can be used to create client applications that are tightly integrated with the data in your SQL Server. Additionally, you should have taken from the example an understanding of what applications developed in PowerBuilder actually look like. You can see why products of this nature are becoming an integral part of the client/server developer's toolset.

The PowerSoft Product Suite and Target Market

With the commercial success of PowerBuilder, the PowerSoft corporation quickly released two other products—Power Maker and PowerViewer—to complement their flagship product. Build Momentum is designed to leverage the skills of a few development and systems experts as well as build applications. PowerSoft then focused on the other end of the spectrum, allowing ad hoc reporting and power users to create and modify applications. The Power Maker and PowerViewer products are intended to augment the applications produced by PowerBuilder developers. PowerViewer offers powerful features and ease of use for users who wish to simply retrieve data from the database and work with a combination of stored and ad hoc reports. Power Maker has been developed for those users who have sufficient levels of skill to manipulate data but are not in a position to learn the PowerScript language integral to PowerBuilder.

PowerSoft has structured these products to allow PowerBuilder developers to pass along objects to users of Power Maker and PowerViewer. The products can essentially inherit objects from each other. This has been incorporated into the design of the products to reinforce the value that each user gains from working with the entire suite of products. Put another way, efforts to develop reports in PowerViewer can be passed up to Power Maker, where more features can be added. These applications can in turn be opened by a PowerBuilder developer and modified. The objective is to maximize the amount of work that any given user can do, and minimize duplication of development efforts.

As a client/server developer using Sybase, this is relevant to you from the standpoint of getting many different organizational levels involved in the database application process. In the past, database development was a job for professionals, but now products are being brought out on the market that allow less sophisticated users and systems staff to work directly with the data. This is very significant for two reasons. First, you can offload some of the basic reporting and more straightforward applications to the people who want to use them. Second, as a Sybase developer you will have entire populations of users who have no idea that the SQL Server is even there, let alone how to use ISQL or write SQL code to access it. It is no longer necessary for everyone involved in the development process to know the structure of the database or how to work with a structured query language. The implication of this is clear: although more people can participate in data access, the structure and integrity requirements for those working with the back-end database server have never been greater.

Someone in the organization has to be responsible for database integrity and security. Rules, defaults, and privileges take on a much greater importance when access is being granted to developers and users who have no clear idea of the database objects they might be affecting with their operations.

Products like PowerBuilder and its companions are clearly enjoying a great deal of acceptance in the marketplace. Certainly the opportunity to allow access for users and individuals of varying skill levels and expertise is a more attractive alternative to organizations than increasingly adding systems developers to the payroll. However, these user/developers bring with them a requirement for you as a client/server software developer to be even more aware of your development environment and to look for ways to insulate these users from any potential damage they might do to your database environment.

PowerBuilder and Third-Party Products

Several other products are being offered to the market that integrate to some extent with PowerBuilder. PVCS is a version control and development environment manager that works with PowerBuilder. Er-Win has developed a version of their data-modeling tool that automatically generates certain PowerBuilder constructs and defaults as defined in the data model. Other products are being announced regularly that offer support for the environment. PowerSoft is not the only company enjoying this kind of support. Increasingly, vendors are demonstrating their commitment to integration by developing their products to work tightly with products from other companies. More than any other event, this should illustrate to you the power of the client/server architecture. Instead of trying to be the one vendor solution, client/server product vendors are looking for ways to link their products with the other software tools that you as a client/server developer need to manage every aspect of the development process.

In the same way that Sybase has created a whole greater than the sum of its parts by allowing easy open access to the data held within a SQL Server, the vendors of the tools you use for client/server applications development are incorporating support for each other. Even the software vendors recognize that in client/server, there is no one key technology. Everything has to work together or it doesn't work at all.

Summary

This chapter has introduced one of the most popular third-party development environments for MS-Windows client software applications that are tightly integrated with SQL Server back-ends. To demonstrate the power and flexibility of these tools, I selected PowerBuilder to describe in detail. Please keep in mind that this is not a recommendation for the product or for its fitness for any specific purpose. As a consultant, I charge for those kinds of recommendations, so I am not going to make them here! You should take this chapter as an exploration into some of the things that are possible using third-party tools where the vendor has integrated their product with the SQL Server. Product integration of this nature was not available on the market six or seven years ago. It is a phenomenon that is being driven by the move to client/server and by market acceptance of products that provide these hooks and levels of integration.

You can expect to see many more of these kinds of products and alliances in the future.

The last few pages explained the way a development tool such as PowerBuilder isolates the developer and user from the underlying database and structure. Also emphasized was the need to ensure that these users and developers were managed appropriately for access permissions. Finally, I mentioned the importance of familiarity with backend database objects such as stored procedures. When developers do not have sufficient knowledge of the database, serious downstream implications can result.

You should have gained a sense of the PowerBuilder product line as being stratified across the levels of developers, power users, and data browsers found in any organization. The idea is to place an appropriate amount of data access and applications power in the hands of everyone in the organization. The technology exists for you to do this; however, the management and coordination issues are increased, not minimized. Although transparent access to the database might be a godsend for many of your users, it can create extraordinary demands for support. That's the bad news. The good news is that these products allow you to develop robust and powerful applications while minimizing the learning curve for some of the underlying technologies, such as T-SQL and C. This might not appeal to the experienced hard-core developers who want to get right in and start coding applications in a "real" language, but for many of you it is the way you can actually build and deploy your first few client/server applications for the MS-Windows environment.

I wish to emphasize once again that a great many products on the market provide similar and competing services to PowerBuilder, Power Maker, and PowerViewer. Many options are available, or you can choose to develop competitive products yourself. Gone are the days when you had to program in traditional languages to create a database application.

Go forth and multiply, divide, add, and perform whichever database operations your users require. Sybase supports third-party tools that will help you get the job done.

6.4

Database Publishing

Some of the more enthusiastic advocates of client/server technology and its online transaction processing capabilities lose sight of one of the more mundane but valuable systems services: batch reporting. In the same way that technology was intended to provide a paperless office but ended up proliferating laser printers and using even more paper, client/server is and will be used to produce printed reports.

As a developer, you should be interested in this for a couple of reasons. First, batch reports can eliminate performance complaints about queries with multiple joins and large tables. Second, the reality of today's business world is that not everyone who is integrally involved with the system is computer literate (senior management, for example). Last, everyone at some point wants to be able to look at, touch, and feel a hard copy of data and programs.

This chapter looks at several methods that you can use to create printed documents from your SQL Server. Some of these incorporate products and services that have just hit the market in early 1994. Others represent standard methods to produce output from SQL Server that are readily accessible and widely available throughout organizations.

You will see that users can be put to work creating their own reports. Whereas this was discussed in a conceptual framework in the first section of the book, here you will see practical suggestions for how this theory can be implemented.

By reading this chapter, you will become familiar with the concerns and issues felt by the clerical and managerial users of SQL Server data. Although this might not be as technical or even as interesting as some of the database administration or SQL Server internal-feature sections, these users represent a large constituency in SQL Server sites. It pays to take advantage of the Sybase client/server architecture to ensure that their needs are met.

The Requirement

A great many of the uses for data stored on a centralized server go beyond customized, mission-critical applications. Obviously, the same benefits that apply to those applications can also be enjoyed by more casual users of data. Mailing lists that are derived from up-to-date and validated customer tables are often significantly more useful than duplicate and redundant data maintained in departmental mail-merge files.

Organizations need the efficiency that come from reduction of duplicate efforts. Replication Server notwithstanding, when you have two separate databases maintaining the same data, one of them is invariably wrong. And it costs real money to create, maintain, and use this wrong data. Even if your SQL Server has been justified for some glamorous mission-critical strategic prototype application, you can become a hero by rolling it out and making it useful to legions of secretaries, clerks, and managers.

Many of these people are loathe to involve IS. They have learned from bitter experience that corporate systems applications frequently drive their business practice and not the other way around. Systems people frequently behave as if their system is more important than the users they serve. As a result, some departments and individuals have looked for ways to help themselves.

The requirement, then, is to provide all that great back-end security, integrity, and concurrency without making the users feel that they are jumping through hoops.

You can accomplish this in two ways: create and deliver batch reports for users to employ at their leisure, or let them have access to the data themselves.

Seamless Transparency

Those of us who are paid to navigate systems often forget how difficult it is to keep straight all the rules and variances in syntax. A great many corporate citizens are not paid to acquire these skills and have no interest in doing so. We tend to think of seamless applications as being a convenient, few-keystrokes way of jumping from application to application and from service to service. Less sophisticated end-users do not want to have to deal with any keystrokes at all. When they say seamless integration, they mean absolutely invisible to them.

Of course, even with seamless and transparent integration (or virtual transparency), a user still has to learn a few things. Unless you are providing someone with a printed report, all technology requires at least some rudimentary training and specialized procedures to take advantage of the service. To be fair, most users expect to have to jump through a few hoops, but they generally want the minimum number at the least degree of difficulty.

Completely eliminating the need to understand or work with the underlying aspects of the system from the user is difficult, if not impossible. With capability comes complexity. The best way to bring it down to the lowest possible degree of difficulty is by taking advantage of the flexible connectivity options provided as part of the SQL Server architecture.

Third-Party Software

As you may remember from the first section, the assertion was made that one of the most appealing features of SQL Server is the inherent interconnectibility of various shrink-wrapped products out there on the market. Although power tools for development, such as PowerBuilder or Build Momentum, can leverage the skills, expertise, and time of highly trained IS staff, most end users never get to the point where they can create supportable applications. And there is no reason to expect them to do so. In fact, if you can get them to work with the tools with which they are already familiar, your SQL Server can earn its keep and pay off its investment costs even if your mission-critical project fails.

This might seem like a terribly pessimistic thing to say, but the fact of life in organizations today is that some factors that affect client/server projects are beyond the developer's control. As such, you can protect your investment in time and effort (not to mention your job) by providing value to the company in less glamorous ways, such as providing transparent access to centralized data to PC users throughout the company.

The early 1990s have demonstrated that PCs are neither a fad nor a luxury. Companies are acquiring and installing GUI-capable machines in unprecedented numbers. Learning to work with them is becoming a condition of employment throughout corporate North America and the rest of the world.

Many people are working very hard to upgrade their DOS-based Lotus and Word Perfect to their Windows counterparts. If you say client/server to these people, you are likely to be met with a glazed look and a blank stare. But if you can show them just how easy it is to connect back to a great store of data *that someone else maintains*, you can get not only their attention but also their support.

The following is a practical example of just how easy this can be.

The Microsoft Office

Wherever I have reviewed specific products in this book, I have explained that these examples are not to be taken as slurs against their competitors. The reason for using the Microsoft office as an example is simply the fact that it is the most prevalent offering—and therefore the one most likely to be applicable to you. I have seen these examples actually work; they are not just suggestions based on theoretical assumptions. In addition, this is the suite of office software that I use, so why wouldn't I use it as an example?

The most recent release of Excel (version 5.0) replaces the older Q+E software with a utility called MSQuery. Once MSQuery is installed on your machine, other Microsoft products such as Word and Access can utilize it. Because I have been discussing user access to SQL Server data from word processing, I will use Word for this example.

To pull data from SQL Server into a word processing document, simply perform the following steps:

1. From within a document, select Insert from the main menu bar.
2. Select Database.

   The database dialog box is displayed.
3. Select Get Data.

   The data source dialog box is displayed.
4. Select MSQuery.
5. Select Data Source - Other ODBC Server.
6. Provide your Login and Password.

   The tables from your default SQL Server database are displayed.
7. Select Tables.
8. Use the mouse to click desired Columns.
9. Exit with Return Data to Document Option.
10. Copy into your document with the Auto Format Table.

With these 10 steps, a word-processing user can attach to a SQL Server across the network, log into a database, choose tables that are joined automatically, and select desired columns. When the user returns to the document, the data is pasted in as a preformatted table containing the retrieved column values. All this can be performed quickly by using a mouse to click and select options presented in dialog boxes and representations of the data.

Additionally, the user can select the modify data option and return data to the SQL Server through the same mechanism. The formats and settings can be saved to automate the retrieval of the data whenever a particular document is opened.

From this it should be clear that even the most narrowly focused computer users can take advantage of access to a SQL Server through their faithful old office program, whether that is a word processor, spreadsheet, or whatever.

Naturally, the SQL Server must be set up to support ODBC (see Microsoft SQL Server). The user must be given access to the data with the appropriate permissions, and the client software (including MSQuery) must be installed and configured. Once that's done, it's easy!

Data from the SQL Server can then be formatted and printed using all the features supported by MS-Word, including table of contents, cross-referencing, page numbering, and table formatting.

Batch Printing

This still might not be what you need. In some cases, as I mentioned earlier, operator intervention alone is not sufficient. You want the capability to retrieve data, format it, and print it completely through a batch process. Fair enough. Powerful document-processing solutions are available for you to use.

For those of you who want to get into some really complicated stuff, you might want to look at the new application programming interface to FrameMaker.

FrameMaker is a workstation document publishing company that has produced software for heavy-duty publishing requirements since 1986. Currently, the company has offerings on UNIX Workstations, (including Sun, HP, RS6000, and X-terms), MS-Windows, and Macintosh. The most recent version of FrameMaker (version 4.0) offers an API, which functions in many ways like the Sybase Open Client DB-Library. In fact, if you wish to write Windows programs in C/C++ and have access to a version 4.0 of Frame, which supports the Sun-based API, you can exploit the provided capabilities to retrieve data from SQL Server and apply Frame formatting capabilities to it, directing the resulting output to a nearby PostScript printer. Naturally, you can create applications that are interactive to the user as well as batch programming.

Explaining how to accomplish this would require more room than the DB-Library chapters and is beyond the scope of this book.

The point here is that you can access SQL Server and integrate it with a range of publishing options from the simplest word processing package to industrial strength, custom-designed applications.

Summary

To paraphrase the ancient Roman speech, client/server has not come to bury batch reporting, but to praise it. The major idea behind this chapter is the ease of matching online retrieval and formatting of SQL Server data.

In your enthusiasm for the new capabilities of the online client/server environment, especially GUI-based applications, don't forget the tried-and-true methods of yesterday. Although many batch reporting requirements are really online access applications in disguise, you may still find the old-fashioned overnight batch to be a reasonable and practical response to the requirement.

Using a SQL Server allows you a myriad number of new ways to accomplish this, as well as supporting the proven practices of the Jurassic Era of computing.

6.5

Using CASE Tools
with SQL Server

One of the most confusing things about getting into client/server systems is sorting out the plethora of seemingly integrated technologies. By now you should have a reasonably strong grasp of the distinction between client and server. (Clients run on diverse platforms and share the processing load with a transparently connected, centralized server.) If you remember from the first section of the book, a SQL Server client/server solution involves much more than just those two components. The integration or networking aspects are involved as well—putting the clients in touch with the server. You learned about SQL Server Net-Library products and how they talk to the various third-party software transports in the last section.

Now it is time to introduce an ancillary, yet important, systems development technology that you can use as part of your client/server toolset: Computer-Assisted Software Engineering (CASE) tools.

This chapter introduces the features generally available with CASE tools and shows how they can be integrated with your SQL Server development effort. Specifically, you are shown how a representative tool, E-R Win, generates SQL Server-compatible Data Definition Language that creates tables, indexes, triggers, and other database objects. Sybase provides a CASE tool as part of its product suite. The DEFT product runs on the Apple Macintosh platform and provides similar features to its competitors. Once again, I do not intend to tout any given product over another. For purposes of this book, I thought it best to introduce you to one of the most powerful, lower-cost CASE tools available for the Windows platform.

Many strong products in the marketplace can provide you with appropriate data modeling and CASE tool services. None of them are perfect, but most of them can be highly effective for certain aspects of the client/server design and development process.

The purpose of this chapter is to expose you to the use of these tools in creating and managing your database objects. Earlier in the book you learned about the syntax and methods you might use to create tables directly from the command line. Using scripts to assist in revising and re-creating these objects was recommended. In this chapter, you will see how CASE tools help you design your application and feed your SQL Server with automatically generated scripts.

In many development shops, CASE tools are used not only to save time and help document the project, but also as a method of controlling and directing database changes.

By the end of this chapter, you should have a solid grasp of what a CASE tool can be used for as part of your SQL Server project and how you could integrate it with the rest of your development effort.

Why Use CASE?

Those of you who worked in larger Information Systems shops in the mid- to late 1980s might remember that CASE tools were heralded as the savior of systems development projects. It was almost as if, by using a computer to assist in the development of software code itself, the programs would be developed automatically, resulting in the end of programmers and application developers. Of course, nothing of the sort occurred and the marketing hype moved on to a different set of products.

Taken at face value, CASE tools are self-explanatory; they are tools that provide computer-assisted software engineering. The emphasis is on the process, not the result. (For those of you who are wondering where I am going with this, stay with me. It will be worth it!) The use of the word engineering is no accident. Many applications developed over the past few decades have been crafted rather than engineered. Craftsmen, like artisans, develop their products with an almost personal vision and approach. Engineers apply proven principles and accepted practices. CASE tools were developed to reinforce a consistent, disciplined, and formula-based approach for developing software. Such tools are critical to success in a client/server environment.

As you now can see from the earlier coverage of the SQL Server architecture, your client/server development environment can quite easily get out of control. The sheer number of variables and components to be managed presents a complexity that can reduce your applications to anarchy. You can use CASE tools to help you prevent this.

Where Do CASE Tools Fit in the Development Cycle?

If you remember the discussion of the role of physical and logical data modeling, you can recall the importance of up-front design. One of the key roles played by a CASE tool is as a method of documenting the entity-relationship diagrams. If you flip back and look at some of the examples used in this book, you will see that they were generated using E-R Win. Tools such as E-R Win, Silverrun, DEFT, System Architect, Excelerator, and IEF can be highly useful as front-end diagramming tools to assist you in the modeling process. As you proceed through the design phase, the tool captures more and more information about the entities and their attributes that you intended to reflect in a database. CASE tools enable you to tie detailed descriptions to the entities and attributes until you finally have a complete data dictionary for your database.

Some of you might be thinking that this is what the Sybase system catalogs are intended to provide. Although you can use the systems catalogs to document which objects are contained in the database, it is not practical to model your database with any internal SQL Server features, nor can you relate business descriptions to data in the systems catalogs. A CASE tool provides specially designed data dictionary management and reporting features.

You realize the greatest payback in the ongoing management of the development environment. By channeling changes in your database objects through the CASE tool, you have a central point of control and the capability to provide up-to-date documentation on the status of your database. In a multideveloper environment, this can result in a major productivity gain by dramatically reducing wasted time and effort.

Naturally, using a CASE tool to accomplish this is not mandatory. It is part of the way in which you structure and manage your development environment. The use of a CASE tool, however, provides you with the opportunity to move beyond the yellow stickies and mental notes methods of recording database design, structure, objects, and modifications.

Who Uses CASE Tools?

Although you might appoint a single person to develop the expertise in using the actual CASE tool itself (sometimes called a scribe), everyone involved in the development team will likely refer to output from the CASE tool. The users and user developers will evaluate the initial data model for completeness as they review the entity-relationship model defined at the beginning of the project. Applications developers and programmers will use the physical data model diagrams to determine which database objects are available to them, the column names and lengths, and key relationships between tables. The database administrator will use the DDL to generate database objects defined in the CASE tool. On an ongoing basis, the DBO might use successive versions of the DDL to drop and re-create modified tables. Last, you can use the output from a CASE tool to impress management, who will have no idea what it means but will approve of the volume and professionalism of the documentation. (I am only somewhat kidding about this. Management knows that staff turnover presents a risk, and anything that makes documentation easier and more complete insures against the potential impact of this risk.)

What Is a CASE Tool?

Now that you know why you would use one and where it fits in, perhaps this is a good time to tell you what a CASE tool is.

Strictly speaking, CASE is a process and a CASE tool is any software or system service that supports that process. On a more practical level, this translates to data modeling. Most CASE tools, and E-R Win and its competitors in particular, deal with the translation of the business requirements into a high-level data model and the various levels of detail from there down to the physical table, column, datatype, and key definitions for the database.

CASE tools are not generally tightly integrated with the databases. The creation of database objects from a CASE tool is not automatic; it is in the form of DDL, which is the complete set of statements necessary to create a database object. You must run the DDL into the SQL Server through something like ISQL or defncopy. As you will see later in this chapter, you also can create CASE tool schema from script definitions from database object create scripts that you might have created and run manually. Using this feature, you can reverse-engineer a data model from an existing database, which saves a lot of tedious typing and deciphering!

From this you can see that a CASE tool is simply a program used to create a model that translates user perspectives of the entities and relationships manipulated by the application into a description of the actual database contents needed to support those views. A good CASE tool provides ways to mask, filter, or report the various levels of detail with the click of a mouse button. In this, a CASE tool differs greatly from any drawing program you might otherwise use to create your entity-relationship diagrams.

Using a CASE Tool

For those of you who gain the best understanding from practical illustrations, this chapter includes a sample application, as the various aspects of the application development effort would be affected by a CASE tool. As mentioned earlier, the CASE tool demonstrated here is E-R Win; however, almost all the tools on the market provide directly analogous services. (Choose whichever one you want on the basis of platform requirements, program look and feel, and internal politics.)

The first thing you see on starting the program is a blank work area and a master menu. The toolbox is also displayed. To create entities, click the entity box and then click again in the work area. You create a new entity for each click in the work area.

After you have created a few entities, you can edit them to enter the names and make them more meaningful to you. Click on the line to link two entities, establishing the existence and nature of a relationship between the two.

As you learned in the section on data modeling, the creation of parent and child relationships between two tables is the first step in defining a table's foreign keys.

Managing foreign key relationships is an integral part of maintaining referential integrity. By using a CASE tool, you can document foreign key dependencies in a way that can be easily used by a developer who might be dealing with insert, update, and delete operations on that data as part of an application. For pre-System 10 versions of SQL Server, these relationships must be managed by the developers or through explicit triggers, because declarative referential integrity for Sybase is newly incorporated in SQL Server Release 10. By detailing these primary and foreign key relationships in a CASE tool, you provide developers with a quick reference for viewing all the relationships in the tables as they work with them.

A Practical Example

Because you should now have a clear conceptual picture of what a CASE tool is and where it fits into a client/server development project, the following is a practical example to demonstrate these features.

As discussed earlier, the CASE tool can be used to build your data dictionary as you design your project. Another important point is that the CASE tool can be used to capture these considerations when meeting with end users or developers. You could use a CASE tool to determine what domains are to be defined for a particular attribute. When moving into the physical database, domains must be defined as rules that are then bound to specific columns. SQL Server does not support domains as such, and it is much easier to use a CASE tool to identify where and what they should be than to use Sybase features for managing domains.

Using CASE to Model a Bookstore Application

Working with the bookstore analogy, imagine a normalized entity-level display of the bookstore data model. Picture this model emerging as part of a joint application development session with the users and the development team. As you can appreciate, there is no real reason for a DBA to be present, since the data model being worked with is at the logical rather than the physical level. As part of the JAD session with the users, a corporate standard for identifying the bookstores emerges, and there are a finite number of stores. If you consider that the domain for the store ID could include a letter designating the type of store (mall, airport, kiosk, or superstore, for example) and a sequential number after that, this attribute of the bookstore entity is a likely candidate for defining a domain.

Defining Domains for the Column Values

Some people might argue that the store type should be a separate column and the store ID should be a unique number on its own. If you were building the entire organization from scratch, you might want to do this. Real life being the rather messy place that it is, however, codes and IDs were often developed and used extensively by organizations long before relational systems showed up. In some cases it is easier to work with what already exists instead of trying to retrain a horde of clerks in a new series of store numbers. For your purposes, the domain includes a letter code that points to a store type along with the identifying number. Even if it were a separate column, it would still be a candidate for a domain, but I am not going back and redefining the data model for the purposes of this example, just to be a purist!

To finally get on with the example, you could define the domain for the column by using the SYBASE Domain option in the editor menu. In ER-Win you can select the SYBASE Domain option from directly within the CASE tool (other CASE tools have comparable features).

As soon as the CASE tool user selects this option, a dialog box pops up to provide the user with the facility to define the rule. In this case, the users have identified that there are half a dozen alphabetic codes for each type of store, and that every store ID must start with one of those letters. You could choose to define the rule as a list of the exact store IDs that are acceptable for this column. Although that might work for a dozen stores, it would prove impractical for a very large chain. To demonstrate the most straightforward domain, this example defines the following domain for the store ID column:

A   Airport Store

B   Discount Store

C   Premium Mall Store

D   Drugstore

E   Department Store

F   Kiosk

To define a domain for this column using these allowable values, you might use the domain editor to create a list of allowable values; it will then create a default SQL Server expression. If the DBA (or anyone knowledgeable about Sybase) were using the CASE tool, he or she would recognize that the default expression would have to be modified to allow other values to be appended to the store type. (I am starting to wish I had gone back and created a unique column for store type.) However, the point here is that as long as the need for the domain has been identified and documented in the CASE tool, it can be added to or expanded by someone with the appropriate expertise.

Generating Data Definition Language from a CASE Tool

Using a CASE tool such as ER-Win allows the data modeler to capture and document database components such as domains without being knowledgeable about the specific syntax for a particular database. As well as Sybase support, ER-Win provides default data definition language for a number of other SQL databases.

You might notice two interesting options in the target DBMS list: SQL Server and SYBASE. ER-Win does not differentiate between the two for any of the built-in datatypes supported or the defaults for object name lengths and user data-type support. Although I have been using SQL Server and Sybase interchangeably, it appears from the ER-Win option list that they are different products. Presumably, this is to allow any Microsoft SQL Server users to feel that their RDBMS is supported. The differences between Microsoft SQL Server and Sybase SQL Server are primarily version-specific and related to the connectivity of the underlying platform. For more information about this, see the chapter on installing and configuring SQL Server. From a Data Definition Language standpoint, they are the same.

Continuing to work with the sample bookstore data model, now look at what you could do with the domain specification you entered in the previous example.

CASE tools provide much stronger reporting than the administrative reports you can obtain from the database itself. The biggest advantage to using a CASE tool is the opportunity to define these database objects as part of the design process, and then to output the reports and hand them off to others for implementation. The CASE tool generates specifications for the physical data model, if you like. Actually, the output reports can be used for reference, or as scripts to automate the creation of the database objects themselves.

Figure 6.5.1 is an example of the constraints defined for the bookstore data model. You can see that the ER-Win constraints include domains, defaults, and user-defined datatypes in the diagram below.

When the options have been established for the constraints, you can very flexibly report some or all of the constraints that have been set, as shown in Figure 6.5.2.

FIGURE 6.5.1.

The constraint options screen.

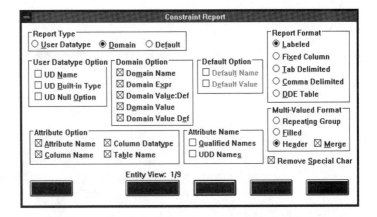

FIGURE 6.5.2.

A sample screen print of the domain's constraint report.

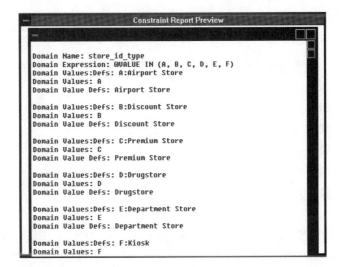

You can use the reporting option to list the entire set of defined constraints for a particular database. It may be viewed on screen or sent to print. This output is what a developer might refer to when looking for the range of values to be found in a column against which his application is working.

The database schema reports are what make these CASE tools really interesting. For example, Figure 6.5.3 gives you a preview of the syntax generated when you select the database schema generation option in the report menu.

As you can see, the whole point to this exercise is the generation of scripts that can be run directly through ISQL to create the database objects. Not only does this save a great deal of typing, but the required syntax for the creation of the database objects is handled by the CASE tool.

FIGURE 6.5.3.

A sample of the database schema generated by ER-Win for the bookstore database.

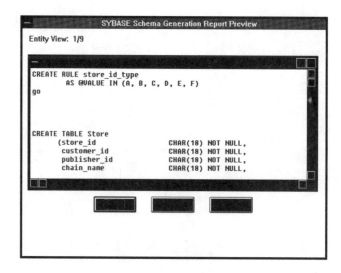

ER-Win, in particular, gives you the opportunity to define the following:

■ Tables

■ Indexes

■ Triggers

■ User-defined datatypes

■ Defaults

■ Rules

Designing and Documenting Referential Integrity

In spite of the fact that declarative referential integrity is supported only in SQL Server Release 10.0, you can use CASE tools to define referential integrity constraints to be placed on tables within your database. Identifying parent and child tables helps in identifying these constraints, as does the explicit identification of primary and foreign keys in the E-R diagrams. However, ER-Win also allows you to define referential integrity through rules placed on the tables defined in the data model. These rules enforce the referential integrity constraints in the database as they were specified in the data model.

You can use the CASE tool as a means of automatically generating complex rules that enforce the cascade or restrict delete, insert, or update constraints. This depends on the status of the column in the table as a foreign key and whether you want any such changes to be made as a complete set to more than one table. You remember from the section on building referential integrity into Sybase that this can be pretty tough to manage.

SQL Server Release 10.0 implements declarative referential integrity, which makes managing this process easier. Although it might be a while before the CASE tools support the latest SQL Server release, for those working with pre-System 10 database engines, this feature might prove highly attractive.

You can also use ER-Win and other CASE tools to generate entity-relationship diagrams in a variety of detail and specificity. As a design tool, CASE can be extremely effective in helping your team cut down on the amount of time it takes to design your application, and in creating useful documentation. In the minds of most of the client/server developers I know, however, the single most important service provided by a CASE tool is the creation of this DDL.

The objective of this chapter was to talk about CASE tools, define what they are, and show you practical examples of what they can be used to accomplish. If you are already knee-deep in client/server, you should probably look at the services provided by a CASE tool as well. Necessarily, this chapter is oriented more toward developers, designers, and project leaders. If you are already quite familiar with CASE tools, you skipped over this chapter anyway. For those of you who stayed with me, thanks. I hope this gives you a fair idea of the main features provided by a representative CASE tool, ER-Win.

Managing Multiple Databases

Before closing, there is one more key feature to some CASE tools that I believe should not go unnoted. Many CASE tools on the market today support reverse-engineering and cross-relational database schema translation.

If you incorporate a CASE tool such as ER-Win, Silverrun, or DEFT into your project, you can build your data model from the table and database object create scripts that you already ran when you first defined your database objects. If you did not use scripts, or they are no longer available, you could use the defncopy utility to create text files that reflect your database objects. From these text files, you can have the CASE tool automatically generate an entity-relationship diagram for you, which you can revise and refine and then generate new DDL for your database.

If you are involved in a multidatabase vendor application, you can use this process to create scripts for one environment from the definitions of the objects in the other. In this way, you can take your existing database structures from DB2 or another database and migrate it to SQL Server. This can prove highly useful for projects in which an existing application is being downsized to client/server.

Obviously, a tool of this nature will have quirks, bugs, restrictions, and frequently a steep learning curve. The other proviso I will add is that creating good data models is not as easy as it looks. However, the objective of this chapter was simply to provide you with a description of how a CASE tool can be integrated into your client/server development toolset. I cannot stress enough that the successful incorporation of CASE technology is entirely contingent on the degree of discipline you take to the technology. Although the generation of DDL is automatic and relatively painless, training a team of more or less independent developers to channel all database changes through a central point and documenting those changes in your CASE tool will determine how useful the product really is for you.

This is almost entirely a management issue rather than a technical process. It is the central issue in the successful use of CASE to support a client/server development effort. Getting the benefits from a CASE tool is neither automatic or axiomatic. You don't get them just because you got one. At the same time, with some planning and discipline, you can incorporate computer-assisted software engineering tools and techniques and realize a significant payback. Like the SQL Server relational database system itself, you must design and develop your applications to take advantage of the features provided.

Summary

One of the biggest problems with client/server development projects is the complexity of integrating so many diverse technological components. This chapter extended the definition of the client/server toolset to include CASE tools, as well as all the other bits of mortar and glue used to pull a multivendor solution together.

One of the things stressed in this chapter was the role played by a CASE tool. Without a key individual assigned responsibility for creating the original model and keeping it up to date, a CASE tool can easily become just another piece of shelfware. On the other hand, with some commitment to consistency, you can use a CASE tool to ensure that your data model is kept up to date and that you can produce voluminous and accurate documentation at whim. Perhaps the most important point is that you can produce this documentation during the design phase, even before installing your SQL Server.

From this chapter you should also have gained a sense of the scope of the services provided by CASE tools. The creation of data definition language (DDL) is one of the most used features, and the capability to reverse-engineer data models from scripts and existing database objects is also welcomed by anyone who has to deal with multiple database environments or migrations from one to another.

The screen captures showed many of the options that can be set in ER-Win. This flexibility translates directly to complexity and, like a project manager, a database design tool can take some time to master. However, from this chapter you should have a better understanding of what the key features of a CASE tool are and how you might be able to capitalize on them for your development project. For those who spend a great deal of time with the design process, a CASE tool can be a great method for capturing the user's perspective of the data model and translating that into a physical data specification.

If you choose not to use a CASE tool, you will still have to perform all the same steps in the design process. You simply won't have the ability to easily change your documentation or to generate scripts with which to create the database objects.

As more client/server solutions are developed, the need for a CASE tool of some sort is becoming increasingly obvious. For those of you who have shied away from the investment because of past (unkept) promises, now is the time to take another look. There are many good tools to choose from, and once you put it to work, you might find yourself wondering how you did without it. At the very least, you will find that it provides sufficient return to make the investment worthwhile.

New Products and Emerging Trends

Introduction

BY NOW, YOU SHOULD HAVE A DEFINITE SENSE THAT THE environment in which you will be developing client/server systems is very volatile. The extreme degree of leverage among the component parts of the systems components you integrate, and the rate of change from new releases and new products, both combine to create a rapidly changing landscape.

The purpose of this section is to isolate two of the most significant developments on the horizon; SQL Server Release 10.0 and Wide-Area Networking.

SQL Server Release 10.0 is already released for some platforms and in production at some sites. For those of you who are currently at 4.9.*x*, however, or on a platform for which Release 10.0 is not yet available, this section will let you know what you are missing.

The impact of evolving communications channels is somewhat more subtle and less immediate. Throughout this book, I have stressed the need to understand the end-to-end processes that make up your client/server solution. With the following chapter on communications, I hope to sensitize you to one of the greatest areas of potential growth in systems: remote client/server computing.

This book began with a review of the history behind Sybase the company. It seems only fitting to close it with an eye to the future, both for SQL Server itself and client/server solutions at large.

7.1

What's New in SQL Server Release 10.0

Introduced in 1993, SQL Server Release 10.0 represents more than just a new version of the SQL Server database engine. Along with the enhancements and improvements you would expect from a maturing product are new products, all of which are offered under the name System 10.0. This new term encompasses SQL Server Release 10.0 and a suite of new products that significantly extend the range of services provided by Sybase.

This chapter gives an overview of the new features and enhancements that have been built into the SQL Server product itself. In Section 4 of this book, SQL Server features, along with their limitations and restrictions, have been discussed in detail. In this chapter, you can see how those features are affected by System 10.

The leapfrogging of version numbers from 4.x to 10.0 is no accident. With this release, Sybase is laying the foundation for the direction the SQL Server and companion products will take for the rest of the decade. As you remember from the discussion of the Sybase product line and the company's vision for the future, Sybase is committed to providing products that enable you to build enterprise-wide client/server solutions. These capabilities have been released with the System 10 product line. By the end of this chapter, you should have a solid idea of the extent and nature of the enhancements to SQL Server that have been incorporated into Release 10.0. Also, you will have some idea of the impact of moving any existing SQL Server databases into the System 10 world.

As you will see, the improvements to the SQL Server database engine address many of its deficiencies and provide powerful new capabilities to help you build your client/server solution.

New Features

For those of you already familiar with the SQL Server architecture and its terminology, the following is a high-level list of the new features of SQL Server Release 10.0:

New installation, upgrade, and configuration utility

25 new systems procedures

Backup Server

Full cursor support

New built-in functions

New configuration options

New systems tables

Declarative referential integrity

Along with these new capabilities, existing SQL Server features have been revised and enhanced. Areas of the SQL Server that have extended capabilities include the following:

Data definition language extensions

Trigger modifications

Transactions

Query optimizer

Create index

Bulk copy utility

SQL Server Release 10.0 is unquestionably more than a maintenance release. The new features and extensions support operations that simply could not be done with previous versions of the product. The extensions to transactions and triggers are the result of feedback from existing clients, and many of you can put these new capabilities to work immediately.

So that you can better understand exactly what these terms mean and the new functionality that is supported by SQL Server in Release 10.0, I cover each new feature in some detail. Before breaking the list down into its components, first I will discuss how the changes have affected the SQL Server environment as a whole.

SQL Server Architecture Changes

The new features incorporated into SQL Server Release 10.0 have made it necessary to include new tables and procedures with the server. In previous versions of SQL Server, this would have required extending the size of the master database. In many customer sites, the devices on which the master database resides cannot easily be altered to expand the device size. Sybase decided that rather than making customers rework their existing database structures and sizes, they would revise their internal architecture.

Although this doesn't affect those of you installing SQL Server (Release 10.0) for the first time, for others the impact could be severe. The master database no longer contains the systems procedures used in the various user databases. Instead they have been moved into a new database: sybsystemprocs. Whenever a stored procedure with the prefix sp_ is called from a batch, application, or transaction, the SQL Server automatically looks in this database for the procedure. Because this search path is set up as part of the architecture, system procedures are found even if they are fully specified with the master database prefix (master.dbo.sp_who).

Several new user databases are covered as part of the features that they support. The key point here is that the master database remains fixed at the approximately 20M size and should not need to be extended in the future to hold Sybase-supplied database objects. This is significant when you consider recovery time for the master database. For sites with high up-time requirements, a large master database can take too long to dump and restore. By minimizing the contents of the master database, the recovery time is greatly minimized also.

The SQL Server itself has been segmented into a number of components. For example, all backup and recovery (dump and load) functions are now handled through a set of processes called the Backup Server. This is not a new product you must purchase from Sybase; it is just a way of referring to and isolating the backup process to increase the dump devices supported and make the operation easier to perform. There is also now a Threshold Manager, which monitors available disk space for databases. When a particular threshold is reached, the Threshold Manager fires a user-defined stored procedure that can perform numerous functions, from allocating more space for the segment to writing warning and error messages.

This allocation of functions to discrete servers and managers is consistent with a move to object orientation. Although SQL Server Release 10.0 is not itself object-oriented, the encapsulation of methods and data needed to support a function within a named entity like Backup Server or Threshold Manager is consistent with an object-oriented outlook.

As well as separating server functions into discrete servers, SQL Server Release 10.0 has changed the administrator role and created three separate login identities to address the new security and administration functions provided. Now look at each of the new features in more detail.

New Installation Utility

The older sybconfig utility has been replaced with sybinit. This is also a menu-driven interface for the installation of the software, setting configuration value, installing and configuring the master and systems devices and databases, and creating appropriate interface files.

Backup Server

The SQL Server Release 10.0 Backup Server incorporates all the dump and load database functions that were previously handled through explicit statements issued by the database owner or SA. The console utility that allowed messages for tape changing to be displayed on the host's console terminal is no longer supported. Backup Server provides for managing the dump and restore process from any client machine that logs onto the server using the `sp_volchanged` stored procedure.

Additionally, Backup Server allows several new features, including the following:

Dump striping   You can now dump to as many as 32 separate dump devices in parallel.

Multiple devices   You can write a single dump across multiple files or tapes.

Network dump   You can specify a tape device on a machine across the network as a valid dump device.

Backup Server is compatible with dump and load scripts, procedures, or transactions that you might have developed and used for SQL Server versions prior to Release 10.0. However, any dump or load commands issued from such scripts are trapped and issued through the Backup Server process. You must install and configure the Backup Server to successfully dump and load databases and transaction logs. Pre-Release 10.0 dumps cannot be loaded onto SQL Server 10.0 through Backup Server. Use bulk copy instead.

Security Features

Several new security features installed with SQL Server Release 10.0 bring the product to the C2 trust level defined by the U.S. Government. For all SQL Server clients, this translates into working with two new roles in the administration of your server and databases. Whereas the login ID SA was previously responsible for all superuser activities on the server, now an SSO (systems security officer) and an operator identity manage the dump and load database and transaction log functions. In SQL Server Release 10.0, SA manipulates disk space and memory allocation, and grants and revokes permission for users to execute the create database command. The SSO looks after such security issues as creating logins, changing passwords, granting/revoking roles, and determining the password change interval after which a user is prompted to enter a new password. Passwords of NULL are not acceptable under SQL Server Release 10.0, and passwords are now encrypted on the system (SA could view all users' passwords as textfiles by selecting * from syslogins). Features such as these provide a higher level of security than previous versions of SQL Server. However, for valid and authorized users of a database, you can now audit much more tightly changes made to data under SQL Server Release 10.0.

Audit Server

Like Backup Server, Audit Server is an incorporated component of the overall SQL Server Release 10.0. However, the audit trail monitoring and reporting features provided through Audit Server are completely new to the SQL Server environment.

Through Audit Server, you can now track all operations taken by anyone on a defined database object, or you can track all actions taken on any database object by a defined user. When you have specified that an audit trail is to be maintained by Audit Server, all database activities are logged to a separate systems database called sybsecurity. This database tracks all logins and logouts to the SQL Server, flags use of special roles such as SA or SSO, and flags the use of objects or IDs as mentioned earlier. It records all delete operations taken on the database, as well as the execution of stored procedures and firing of table triggers. Through a combination of these monitoring and reporting facilities, you can be sure of finding and shutting down anyone looking for your particular caramilk secret.

Cursors

Full cursor support is now available on the SQL Server side of the client/server equation. In previous versions of SQL Server, cursor support was provided as an extension to the open client libraries. With SQL Server Release 10.0, you can now declare and manipulate cursors as part of a stored procedure, trigger, or transaction, as well as within an application. Cursors declared in SQL Server Release 10.0 enable you to manipulate the result set of a select on a row-by-row or multiple row basis.

Declarative Referential Integrity

One of the greatest criticisms of SQL Server versions prior to Release 10.0 was the need to explicitly manage foreign key and primary key relationships through stored procedures and triggers. With the System 10 product, support for declarative referential integrity as part of the table create statement is supported. This means that you can define a table with the constraint that to insert or update a column in the table, a row with that value as a primary key must already exist in another table. For example, to add a book title to the store's inventory table, an entry for that book_id must already exist in the publishers table, where the book_id is a primary key. Through declarative referential integrity, you can now manage the cascading deletes and entry of new table rows in a predetermined manner. You can define referential integrity constraints when you first create the table, or you can add or modify them with the alter table command.

New Datatypes

SQL Server Release 10.0 has provided a new datatype—the numeric datatype. Also known as decimal or dec, this datatype specifies the exact numeric values to the left and right of the decimal place. This is an exact datatype that adds to the tinyint, smallint, and int datatype family of exact numbers; however, only the numeric datatype allows the storage of decimal points. The float, double precision, and real datatypes also support decimal points, but those datatypes are approximate because they allow rounding during arithmetic operations.

When specifying a numeric datatype, you provide two arguments to the type: the precision and the scale. For a numeric datatype, precision defines the maximum number of decimal digits that can be stored in the column. That is the total number left and right of the decimal place. The scale determines the number of digits to the right of the decimal place. Thus the syntax for a column defined as a numeric datatype would be column1 numeric (10,2). The maximum value that could be stored in a column so defined would be 99999999.99 and the minimum value (other than zero) would be .01

Based on the numeric datatype is a new column type—the IDENTITY column. Each table can have one IDENTITY column used to store unique sequential numbers allowing you to generate a number to serve as a primary key for a column. This addresses the difficulty in previous SQL Server versions in automatically generating unique transaction or order numbers. Before the inclusion of the IDENTITY column, this could be achieved only through stored procedures or other application code.

IDENTITY columns begin numbering at 1 for the first row and increment automatically for each new row. Rolled-back rows or server failures can result in gaps in the numbering. Within the table, the IDENTITY column can be referred to by the column name or with the syb_identity keyword, by which the IDENTITY column is also known for every table.

These constitute the major new features in SQL Server Release 10.0. In addition to these new features, significant enhancements have been made to the existing features and functions available within SQL Server. I will go into a little more detail on the enhancements that come with the System 10 SQL Server.

Changes to Keywords Allowed in Transactions, Triggers, and Stored Procedures

Previous releases of SQL Server placed several restrictions on which T-SQL keywords could be used in stored procedures, transactions, and triggers. Although they were still powerful features, there were certain things you simply could not do. In the System 10 release of SQL Server, the set of allowable keywords has been expanded to include the following:

alter table	create table	drop procedure
create default	create trigger	drop rule
create index	create view	drop table
create procedure	drop default	drop trigger
create rule	drop index	drop view
create schema		

Like these, the grant and revoke commands can be incorporated into user-defined transactions. You are still restricted from dumping either the database or transaction log from within transactions. To use these data definition language statements within a transaction (including stored procedures or triggers), you must enable the ddlintran option through db_option.

As you can see, a whole new range of services can now be written into stored procedures. Whereas previously you had to execute such commands as create view on the first line of a batch, now you can create much more complex transactions that take parameters, create database objects named from the parameters, and grant rights to users or groups. The implication of incorporating these DDL commands into user-created transactions is the ability to more tightly encapsulate the methods used to access data with the data held in underlying tables.

Trigger Behavior

Triggers have been modified to operate somewhat differently than in previous versions of SQL Server. In SQL Server 4.X and earlier, when a trigger was fired by a transaction and the trigger's conditions were not passed, the entire transaction was aborted. With SQL Server Release 10.0, you now have the ability to simply roll back the trigger to the point where the transaction fired it. From within your transaction, you can branch to a new operation based on the trigger failing or succeeding.

Also, triggers now fire themselves if the trigger performs the operation for which it was defined. Previously a trigger could fire only once and then not be invoked again by the same transaction, no matter how many rows were updated.

With this new behavior, your trigger continues to enforce business rules, even if a new row being added is part of the logic of the trigger itself. For example, if a delete trigger was fired by a transaction and that trigger called a stored procedure that deleted yet another row in the table, the trigger would be fired again and the stored procedure called once more, recursively. This allows you to define triggers that continue to enforce the business rules for which they were defined, under all circumstances.

Changes to Views

You can now use the distinct keyword within the select statement that defines a view, thereby suppressing retrieval of duplicate rows. As noted earlier, views can be created from within transactions and a new option, the with check option, has been added to the create view statement. The with check option ensures that any rows inserted or updated through the view must match the select criteria for which the view was created, adding an additional level of validation to the written rows.

Create Schema

This new command allows you to create multiple database objects and to grant permissions to those objects as a single set that can be committed or rolled back as a unit. This command can also be incorporated into transactions, triggers, and stored procedures and makes administration of access to newly created objects easier.

Datatype Conversion Changes

The rules governing implicit and explicit conversion of datatypes have been modified in SQL Server Release 10.0. Conversions to and from binary datatypes are now supported. These conversions are handled implicitly and do not require a convert statement in the select with which they are being retrieved and manipulated.

Query and Data Modification Changes

There have been a number of changes to some of the "down and in" details that govern how T-SQL can be used to access and manipulate data. Many of these can be covered by the general heading ANSI SQL compatibility enhancements.

Previous versions of SQL Server were compatible with ANSI SQL standards defined in 1986 and 1988. SQL Server Release 10.0 is compatible with SQL ANSI 1989, which is a more mature and robust definition of how the Structured Query Language should behave. The TransAct SQL extensions are necessary to develop real-world applications. The ANSI standards still do not provide for control-of-flow capabilities, which are necessary for writing database programs. However, for those of you who are developing applications that must also run against SQL databases other than

SQL Server, you might be interested in using the FIPS Flagger to indicate non-ANSI-compliant code. The modifications toT-SQL to provide ANSI SQL 1989 compatibility are covered in this section (Section 7) of this book.

Set FIPS Flagger

For those applications that must fully conform to ANSI SQL conventions, you can use the SET FIPS FLAGGER ON option to identify incompatible syntax in your transactions. The FIPS Flagger generates an error message when it encounters T-SQL extensions that have no direct ANSI SQL counterpart.

Chained Transactions

You can now set your SQL Server session to support ANSI Standard chained transaction behavior. This allows SQL Statements beginning with delete, insert, update, open, and fetch to implicitly begin a transaction. Without chained transactions set on, all transactions in T-SQL must begin with an explicit Begin Tran command.

If you have T-SQL applications that were not specifically written to take advantage of chained transactions (they have Begin Tran statements in them), they will not operate properly if you set the chained transaction option on. When you first begin a session with your SQL Server Release 10.0, the default is T-SQL mode. You must be careful not to mix the two modes in your applications. Stored procedures and triggers do not behave predictably when written for one mode and executed in another.

Both chained and T-SQL transaction modes require explicitly offsetting Commit Tran or Rollback Tran commands to successfully execute the operation defined in the transaction. This means that for every Begin Tran you must have a Commit or Rollback Tran statement in T-SQL mode, and in chained mode you must have a commit/rollback for every delete, insert, or update operation.

Transaction Isolation Levels

The ANSI SQL 1989 standard defines three levels of isolation for SQL transactions. Each level defines actions that cannot be performed while concurrent transactions are executed.

> **Level 1: Prevent Dirty Reads**   These are deemed to have occurred when Transaction 1 modifies a row or rows and Transaction 2 reads the row before the first transaction is committed. In the event of a rollback of

Transaction 1, the data retrieved by Transaction 2 would be invalid. Level 1 isolation prevents this from taking place and is the default isolation level for SQL Server Release 10.0.

Level 2: Prevent Nonrepeatable Reads   These occur when Transaction 1 reads and Transaction 2 subsequently modifies the rows read by the first transaction. After Transaction 2 commits, the rows read by Transaction 1 cannot be repeated using the same query. Level 2 isolation prevents this from taking place.

Level 3: Prevent Phantoms   A phantom occurs when Transaction 1 performs a retrieve with search conditions and Transaction 2 commits modifications to the values in a row. Subsequent retrieves by Transaction 1 with the same search conditions would yield different results.

ANSI SQL 1989 standards require transaction isolation Level 3 as a default. This is the equivalent of issuing all select operations with a holdlock, ensuring that no other transaction can request an exclusive or demand lock on the data being read until the entire transaction is completed. This can affect concurrency and perceived performance, and depending on your application requirements might not be what you want. In any case, SQL Server Release 10.0 now supports all three transaction isolation levels with a set option.

Other ANSI Standard Features

Comments   The System 10 SQL Server now supports ANSI-style comments in addition to the comment symbols traditionally used by SQL Servers. The ANSI-style comments consist of two minus signs without a space between them (--). Each commented line must begin with the -- characters.

Null Operands   You can use the set ansinull option to determine ANSI compliance for evaluation of null-valued operands used in equal to or not equal to comparisons.

Systems Administration

Beyond ANSI compliance, datatypes, and audit features, there are several enhancements to the systems administration functions in SQL Server Release 10.0:

Permissions   Users can now grant permission to grant permissions on their objects. This means that if Joe creates a table and grants all rights to June, she can in turn grant all rights to Jody. Previously, only Joe could grant rights on his database objects. As you can imagine, this makes it much easier to allow access to shared database objects in a development environment, for example, and you can still grant subsets of the permissions if you choose.

Packet Sizes   For your SQL Server, ISQL, and bcp utilities, you can now configure the packet sizes to best fit your requirements. Larger packet sizes provide faster throughput of large data files across the network or communications channel, because overhead for addressing and check control characters is fixed. This means that the smaller the packets, the greater the percentage of overhead, and the larger the packet size, the smaller percentage of overhead.

Chargeback Statistics

It is now possible to maintain statistics on CPU and I/O usage for particular users. These reports allow you to allocate costs on the basis of usage for chargeback and financial administration purposes.

DBCC Option

You can now use DBCC to fix some allocation errors rather than simply checking the consistency of a particular database or database object.

Kill Command

Sleeping processes can now be killed without requiring you to shut down and reboot the SQL Server. Previous versions of the kill command waited until sleeping processes woke up before killing them, essentially meaning that you could not kill sleeping processes.

Space Monitoring

When using the sp_help <database_name> or sp_helpsegment <segment_name> systems procedure, you can now see how much space is left on the device or segment and how much is already taken up with objects.

Create Index Performance Enhancements

SQL Server Release 10.0 incorporates changes that have boosted the speed at which the create index command executes. Additionally, there is a new sp_configure option that yields a net decrease in the amount of time it takes to create indexes.

These changes address the process by which SQL Server physically sorts the data pages while the index is being created. Previous versions of SQL Server have read, sorted, and then written out a new index one data page at a time. With Release 10.0, you can now choose to allocate buffers to the create index command so that it reads and writes an extent (eight data pages) at a time, making better use of the SQL Server disk and memory resources and increasing the execution speed of the create index command.

You should keep in mind that these memory buffers are on top of the memory already allocated by SQL Server and that it is possible to define the variable so high that insufficient physical memory exists, making it impossible to boot your SQL Server.

Also, the extent-at-a-time allocation is available to only one create index command at a time; if two or more create index commands are issued concurrently, only the first one uses the extent option—all others revert to the single-page-at-a-time process. In some cases, this makes it desirable for users to monitor who is creating indexes to take advantage of the increased memory option, and wait their turn, rather than opting for the slower approach.

Query Optimizer Enhancements

SQL Server Release 10.0 includes a more accurate query optimizer. This allows the optimizer to better choose least cost indexes when evaluating a submitted query. If you are migrating previous SQL Server databases to System 10, you must run update statistics on all indexes to have the query optimizer calculate with the new efficiency. Previous versions' indexes still work on SQL Server Release 10.0.

Bulk Copy Performance Improvements

The underlying bulk copy code has been rewritten to provide better performance. As mentioned earlier, you can also set the size of the packets used by bulk copy to gain increased throughput. Between these two enhancements, bulk copy provides you with noticeably faster execution.

Set Options

Following is a summary of the specific changes made in SQL Server Release 10.0 as detailed in the Sybase documentation:

Table 7.1.1. New SQL Server Release 10.0 options.

Command	*Description*
`set ansinull {on ¦ off}`	When ON, NULL value operands are treated as ANSI 1989 type for equality and inequality comparisons
`set arithabort [arith_overflow ¦ numeric_truncation] {on ¦ off}`	Determines whether SQL Server aborts a query when an arithmetic overflow or numeric truncation occurs
`set arithignore [arith_overflow] {on ¦ off}`	Determines whether SQL Server displays a warning message after any query that results in arithmetic overflow
`set role {"sa_role" ¦ "sso_role" ¦ "oper_role"} {on ¦ off}`	Toggles the specified role during the current SQL Server session
`set fipsflagger {on ¦ off}`	Toggles the FIPS flagger; when ON, the option prints warning messages when encountering T-SQL extensions to ANSI 1989 SQL
`set identity_insert <table_name> {on ¦ off}`	Determines whether a user can explicitly insert a value into the specified table's IDENTITY column
`set chained {on ¦ off}`	Toggles the chained transaction mode in SQL Server
`set transaction isolation level {1 ¦ 3}`	Sets the transaction isolation level. An isolation level of 3 is equivalent to performing select with holdlock. Default is level 1

Command	Description
`set cursor rows # for` `<cursor_name> (where # = an integer > 0)`	Sets the number of cursor rows returned for each fetch for the specified cursor; the default is 1
`set close on endtran {on ¦ off}`	Forces all open cursors to be closed when the transaction ends (on) or to remain open across multiple transactions (off)
`set quoted_identifier {on ¦ off}`	Determines whether SQL Server treats strings enclosed in quotation marks as identifiers
`set self_recursion {on ¦ off}`	Switches trigger self-recursion ON or OFF so that triggers that modify data cause the trigger to fire again

Additionally, there are new and modified built-in functions as shown in Table 7.1.2:

Table 7.1.2. New built-in functions in SQL Server Release 10.0.

Function	Description
`inttohex`	New datatype conversion function that returns the platform-independent hexadecimal equivalent of an integer.
`hextoint`	New datatype conversion function that returns the platform-independent integer equivalent of a hexadecimal string.
`lct_admin`	New systems function that adds a last-chance threshold on the log segment of a pre-Release 10.0 database. Can also report on status or wake up processes waiting for a threshold.

continues

Table 7.1.2. continued

Function	Description
proc_role	New system function that checks to see if the user possesses the specified role. Can be used to restrict execution of procedures.
show_role	New system function. Shows the user's current and active roles.
col_name	Changed to allow the database name as an optional third parameter.
index_col	Changed to accept a user name as an optional fourth parameter.
object_name	Changed to accept a database name as an optional second parameter.
user	New ANSI-compatible system function returns the user name.

SQL Server Release 10.0 has also introduced significant new systems procedures. These are identified and described in Table 7.1.3.

Table 7.1.3. New systems procedures in SQL Server Release 10.0.

System Procedure	Description
sp_addauditrecord	Allows users to enter user-defined audit records (comments) into the audit trail.
sp_addthreshold	Creates a free-space threshold to monitor space remaining on a database segment.
sp_auditdatabase	Establishes auditing of different types of events within a database, or of references to objects within that database from another database.
sp_auditlogin	Audits a user's attempts to access tables and views and/or the text of a user's commands.
sp_auditobject	Establishes auditing of accesses to tables and views.
sp_auditoption	Enables and disables system-wide auditing and global audit options.
sp_auditsproc	Audits the execution of stored procedures and triggers.

System Procedure	Description
sp_bindmsg	Binds a user message to an integrity constraint.
sp_checkreswords	Checks for reserved words used as identifiers. This procedure is run as part of pre-upgrade.
sp_configurelogin	Initializes the security-relevant information for new Secure SQL Server logins.
sp_cursorinfo	Reports information about a specific cursor or all active cursors.
sp_dbremap	Forces changes made by alter database to be recognized by SQL Server. Run this procedure when instructed explicitly by SQL Server messages.
sp_displaylogin	Displays information about a login account.
sp_dropthreshold	Removes a free-space threshold from a segment.
sp_estspace	Estimates the amount of space needed for a table and its indexes.
sp_helpconstraint	Reports information about any integrity constraints specified for a table.
sp_helpthreshold	Reports information on all thresholds in the current database or all thresholds for a particular segment.
sp_locklogin	Prevents a user from logging in, or displays a list of all locked-in accounts.
sp_modifylogin	Modifies default database, default language, and full name information for a SQL Server login account.
sp_modifythreshold	Changes parameters for existing thresholds in a database.
sp_procxmode	Displays or modifies the transaction modes associated with stored procedures.
sp_remap	Upgrades a Release 4.8 or higher stored procedure, trigger, rule, default, or view and makes the object compatible with Release 10.0. Use if upgrade procedure fails to remap an object.
sp_role	Grants or revokes roles to a specified SQL Server login account.

continues

Table 7.1.3. continued

System Procedure	Description
sp_thresholdaction	Default threshold procedure that is executed automatically when remaining space on log segment falls below specified threshold level. This procedure must be user-created.
sp_unbindmsg	Unbinds a user-defined message from a constraint.
sp_volchanged	Notifies SQL Server that the operator has performed the requested volume handling during a dump or load operation.

Two new procedures are used for chargeback monitoring and reporting. Previously, these features were available only for SQL Servers shipped for VMS platforms. They are now available for all SQL Server platforms.

sp_clearstats	Initiates a new accounting period for all users of a server, or for a specified user. Prints out statistics for the previous period by invoking sp_reportstats.
sp_reportstats	Reports statistics on system usage.

Modifications have been made to several systems procedures as well. Table 8.1.3 summarizes the affected systems procedures for SQL Server Release 10.0.

Table 7.1.4. Modified systems procedures in SQL Server Release 10.0.

System Procedure	Description
sp_addsegment, sp_dropsegment, sp_extendsegment	These procedures now require a database name as the second argument. This change prevents users from accidentally affecting segments in the wrong database.
sp_defaultdb, sp_defaultlanguage	These procedures have been superseded by sp_modifylogin (see new systems procedures table).
sp_helpdb	Now displays information about the amount of space left on each disk assigned to the database.
sp_lock	Now displays information about whether the lock is associated with a cursor.

System Procedure	Description
`sp_who`	Displays different status values for sleeping processes: recv sleep, send sleep, lock sleep, and alarm sleep to assist in debugging.
`sp_helpsegment`	Now displays information about the amount of free space left on the segment.

Several new options can be set on specified databases. The following list identifies these new options, which are executed in conjunction with the `sp_dboption` command.

Table 7.1.5. New database options in SQL Server Release 10.0.

Option	Description
abort tran on log full	Determines whether user processes are suspended (the default) or aborted when the last-chance threshold on a database log segment is reached.
allow nulls by default	Changes the default null type for create table statements from not null (T-SQL default) to null (ANSI 1989 default).
ddl in tran	Allows data definition language in user transactions. The allowed commands are all create/drop database (except create/drop database), plus all grant and revoke commands.
no free space acctg	Suppresses free-space accounting and the execution of threshold actions on non-log segments of a database.

Additionally, several new systems tables support the new features described in this chapter. Because you do not access systems tables directly, I leave coverage of the systems changes to the discussion on the services and operation of the new systems procedures.

Upgrading to SQL Server Release 10.0

So far, this chapter has introduced you to the new features and services provided with SQL Server Release 10.0. For anyone considering moving to SQL Server for the first time, you would probably choose to implement System 10 from the outset. However, some of you have already invested in an earlier version of SQL Server, or perhaps are limited to an earlier release due to the platform on which you must run your SQL Server. The following part of the chapter addresses the implications of upgrading your current SQL Server to System 10. From this discussion, you should be in a position to determine not only the new features of SQL Server Release 10.0 and their applicability to your site, but also the impact of upgrading on your current operation.

Prerequisites for Upgrading

You can upgrade only a Sybase SQL Server Release 4.8 or later to System 10. Data from other versions must be bulkcopied into the new SQL Server.

Changes to Existing Database Objects

Possibly the single most dramatic change is in the stored procedures. Although you do not have to explicitly rename any of the references to the systems procedures now moved to a new database, you do have to migrate any customized stored procedures you developed for your own site. To accomplish this, you must change all references to system tables or any other objects that exist only in the master database to refer to the master prefix explicitly, for example master.syslogs.

Additionally, you should add a line of logic to any of your custom systems procedures to ensure that they are not run from within a transaction, because doing so can create difficulties with recovery of the master database.

In virtually all other cases, however, the new SQL Server Release 10.0 features are enhancements that you can take advantage of when you choose, and you can continue to operate in exactly the same fashion as previous releases. Even the new Backup Server continues to execute pre-System 10 scripts for dump and load database and transaction logs.

Summary

SQL Server Release 10.0 is a strong product offering showing that Sybase is committed to addressing its product weaknesses and extending its already considerable strengths. New products, such as the Replication Server, work in tandem with SQL Server Release 10.0, forming a heavy-duty set of products to address enterprise client/server requirements.

That's the marketing hype. The nuts and bolts of the SQL Server engine especially withstand closer scrutiny. The enhancements to stored procedures greatly extend the range of tasks that can be programmed to run on the database engine itself. The audit and security features definitely go a long way toward increasing corporate comfort zones when it comes to confidential data. The declarative referential integrity constraints remove the biggest and most frequent criticism of SQL Server in one fell swoop.

Unlike some network operating systems, Sybase has maintained the consistency of previous commands and architecture, even while developing a greatly enhanced product. Most of the skills and efforts you have invested in pre-System 10 releases of SQL Server can be maintained and migrated. At the same time, the new services and features provide capabilities that significantly extend what can be achieved through stored procedures and triggers.

In this chapter, you have been given a high-level treatment of the new features in SQL Server Release 10.0, as well as some discussion on the modifications made to existing aspects of the database engine. At this point you should be able to identify whether these features can provide you with services that would be useful for your applications. You were also taken through the implications for existing transactions and what aspects of them might have to be reviewed and modified. Overall, Sybase has made it possible for you to continue working with your applications, scripts, and transactions from one release version to the other. The real changes come from making your SQL Server environment ANSI 1989 compliant, which you may or may not decide to do.

7.2

Remote Client/Server Solutions

In this book, you have seen client/server solutions discussed within the context of local area networks. This is not so much a deliberate assumption as it is implicit. Anyone seriously considering taking advantage of the MIPS on the desktop as part of an architecture generally assumes that those desktop units will be linked to his or her servers through a network. Those networks are usually in the same local vicinity as the server itself. The key difference between local and wide-area networks is data transmission speed and capacity, not geographic distance.

Depending on the type of network you are using, a LAN may be capable of linking machines up to a kilometer in distance. Repeaters, backbones, and other internetworking devices have been used in many sites to extend networks and connect machines across organizations and campuses everywhere. In this chapter, I cover the significant issues and implications of communications channel speed when designing client/server solutions. I also introduce the methods and services used to link computers in distant sites. Last, I look at how future developments in communications technologies will affect the systems you build today and the solutions you will be able to create eventually, when they become technically feasible.

As stated at the very beginning of this book, one of my main objectives was to cover the range of issues posed by the Sybase approach to client/server computing. This chapter rounds out that discussion by introducing you to the distinct capabilities and requirements of wide-area networking as it relates to SQL Server solutions.

The Remote Client

If there is anywhere that technology is responding to a real-life requirement rather than driving change, it is in the field of communications. (How's that for an assertion!) Globalization alone is a trend that is forcing all of us to find ways to connect and communicate with people outside our own geographic area. In fact, in the past few years, e-mail, faxes, and overseas calls have become so common that many of us take the global village for granted.

Yet the overwhelming emphasis when developing client/server solutions is on deployment within a local area. As the rest of the computer and communications technologies press forward toward integration at the global level, our client/server projects have most typically revolved around users connected to their SQL Server via a local area network. Contrast the number of local SQL Server solutions you can think of with the number of more traditional applications that access a mainframe located miles away.

By now, you should be more than familiar with the differences between host/slave computing and the client/server model. Yet, think about the systems you have seen and worked with that involve remote databases. Are they not either store-and-forward applications, such as e-mail, which involves batch transmissions that can be read off-line; or terminal-based solutions, where the actual work is performed on a remote server? As you have seen, true client/server applications split the processing between the two systems. This split is greatly affected by the capability of the two machines to send data back and forth. And that capability is a function of the communications channel or network by which the client and server are linked.

As you develop successful client/server solutions at the departmental level, many of you will be asked to export these applications to users who are not located in the same geographic vicinity. The best example of this is probably software developers who work from home. Disconnecting from the development server can often make it impossible to develop and test client/server applications, let alone access databases as part of a production system.

Sybase has endorsed the concept of enterprise client/server computing as a corporate direction. However, products such as the Replication Server are quite distinct from the concept of remote client/server applications. Replication involves updating data held by multiple servers across a network. A remote client, on the other hand, is actually participating in a client/server session over a wide-area network. For purposes of this chapter, you can consider a remote client to be a single user who wants to access data and applications from home in exactly the same manner as he or she would from the office. If I extend this picture to include a definition of the kind of technology in the user's home, the need for a remote client/server application will become more clear.

Assume that the user has a 486 DX 66 personal computer in the den. Just how attractive does a terminal emulation session become to a user with access to this level of technology? Of course, most initial remote client/server applications involve branch offices rather than those who work from home. However, I want you to visualize the work-from-home user as the remote client because it makes it somewhat easier to understand why replication is not the way to go for this type of application. When we start talking about branch offices, it is easy to try to solve the problem by holding the data on a local server and updating it from another office or data source. What we are looking for here are the issues involved in linking a remote client, not two servers.

The Significance of Bandwidth and Speed

As soon as you start discussing networks and communications, one of the first terms you come across is bandwidth. It gets bandied about (nudge, nudge) so frequently that many people end up taking the meaning from context instead of having a firm understanding of its meaning and implications. This is especially true now that Vice President Gore has electrified the media and nontechnical members of society with his support of the National Information Superhighway.

Bandwidth can be defined as the difference between the upper and lower frequencies of a specific analog signal carrier. The bandwidth of a voice call on a telephone line is approximately 3khz (kilohertz). For purposes of comparison, the bandwidth of AM radio is 5 Khz and FM radio is 18 khz. Rather than discuss the physics that affect this, consider the practical implications. Music sounds better on FM radio than on either AM or when your telephone call is placed on hold. This is a direct result of the higher bandwidth available to FM radio and not just the difference between your favorite band and Muzak. The greater bandwidth translates into a fuller reproduction of the original sound. Even though FM is superior to the other transmission methods, the music itself can be perceived by the human ear in a range from below 20 hz to upwards of 20 khz.

The bandwidth of a carrier also has a direct implication for the amount of data that can be transmitted on the line. Although fast modems will allow a regular voice grade telephone line to send and receive data at speeds up to 19.2 kbps (kilo bits per second or baud), the speed pretty much tops out at that point. To get higher transmission rates, you need a different service, with correspondingly higher capacity and speed as well as pricing.

This brings me to the point. Bandwidth affects speed and throughput of the signal. From a client/server developer's perspective, it is the effective communications rates that matter, not the bandwidth. Voice, data, cable TV, and other communications vehicles are all looking for more bandwidth in order to offer increased speed and capacity. Depending on the underlying communications media used by the various services (or put in place by your networking people), you will have data rates at which you may link your clients and server.

It is these data rates that affect how quickly your commands and data are transferred from one machine to another. Because the bandwidth—and hence the speed—are functions of the media involved in transmitting the signal, you will see how the various emerging communications technologies are affected by their underlying media (copper wire, fiber optic, microwave, and so on).

The Relationship Between Speed and Capacity

At the simplest level, you can visualize your communications channel as a data train moving along a track between source and destination. Speed is naturally the rate at which the train is moving from point A to point B. This speed can be the same whether the train is fully, somewhat, or not loaded with cargo. In the case of data communications, the loading factor, or throughput, has a critical bearing on the overall performance of an application. As discussed in the chapter on performance tuning, this applies not only to networks but to hard drives as well. Performance is a factor of how long it takes to get to the data and how much data can be moved at that speed.

Modem manufacturers make a big deal out of the various compression schemes they use to increase performance. In such cases, the speed remains constant but the throughput is increased, giving you an effective rate of 38.8kpbs or whatever they claim. The point is that the train is not moving any faster, although overall performance is increased. This will become an important concept as you consider the effect of the various communications options available for your remote client/server application. To give you a better idea of exactly how the speed of the communications channel affects the performance of your application, consider the following example.

The query "select * from tablename" is 23 bytes long. In an ethernet local area network running at the theoretical maximum of 10 megabits per second (which nothing does, but anyway...), it would take .0000184 seconds to move from the client to the server. At 9600 baud (9.6 kilobits per second), the same query would take .019 seconds. All in all, it will still take the user the usual .75 seconds to react to the information that the query was sent, so the transmission speed is not an issue or constraining factor. However, a select * statement could yield some pretty horrifying results, depending on the table size. For purposes of illustration, assume that the result set is 1 megabyte of data. Again, under the theoretical maximum in a local setting, it would take .8 seconds to move the result set from the server to the client. At 9600 baud it takes 833 seconds or 13.8 minutes.

These numbers show the importance of speed to the user's perception of how long it takes to get results. Obviously, if the queries and result sets are small, the impact of channel speed is minimized. When overhead, traffic, retries, and network card speeds are taken into account, a 1 megabyte file might take more like 10 seconds to move across an ethernet link, not the .019 seconds that would be theoretically possible at 10 megabaud. A megabyte of data is still a significant unit of work from a communications standpoint, even in local area applications.

Remote Client/Server Defined

From a practical perspective, the quickest and most effective way to create a remote client/server system is to implement an off-the-shelf solution or subscribe to a commercial service. Each of these options has performance and pricing implications. For example, the fastest and cheapest way to connect two systems is over an asynchronous dial-up line using a regular voice line and readily available modems. Typically, you are looking at a 9600 baud connection between the two machines. Figure 7.2.1 represents such a connection.

FIGURE 7.2.1.

Topology of a straightforward terminal/host dial-in connection.

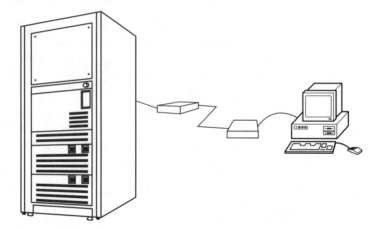

As this has worked fine for terminal sessions, what then is the problem for client/server? The key difference between the two approaches is the amount of data that is retrieved and displayed. In a terminal session, you submit your command as you type the characters; the work is performed on the host and the output is displayed only on the remote terminal. This is the equivalent of dialing into a remote host and bringing up ISQL running against a SQL Server. The same communications topology works when you connect two hosts over a communications channel. Figure 7.2.2 has been included to help you visualize this topology.

These may provide access to a remote host, but they are not remote client/server solutions. The remote solution sends data to the client, where it can be processed using the resources of the local machine. Although this functions effectively in a LAN setting, however, the same result sets can be unacceptably large when the communications channel is much more constrained. This situation is represented in Figure 7.2.3.

FIGURE 7.2.2.

Topology of two hosts connected over a dial-in connection.

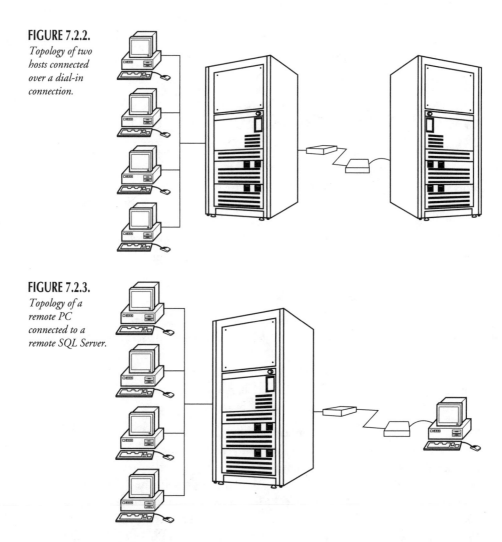

FIGURE 7.2.3.

Topology of a remote PC connected to a remote SQL Server.

As you can see, the communications link between a true remote client running against SQL Server is virtually identical to that of the more traditional host/slave configuration. The differences are in which software is run on the client, and how much of the processing is split between the two machines. For our purposes, if the remote client simply displays results processed on the host, then it is not a remote client/server solution, even if it does allow access to a remote SQL Server. This will become more apparent as you are introduced to the application driven trade-offs when calculating which machine to perform the work on—the client or the server. With a true remote client/server solution, you can tune or modify this balance, whereas with the more traditional approach, the work is all performed remotely. This may not be the optimum way to meet your application requirements. (Though to be fair, it often works just fine.)

Wide-Area Communications Options

There are many very clear and comprehensive books available that explain in much more detail how wide-area networks function. From an introductory standpoint, however, you will now see the most commonly used methods to link systems across a wide area, as well as their effective speeds and pricing implications. Actual billing rates will vary from place to place depending on your local service providers. The point here is the method by which the costs are calculated and when you might choose one billing method over another.

Asynchronous Dial-Up Lines

This communications method was mentioned earlier. It is by far the most common way to gain access to a remote machine, and for remote client/server functions much the same way at the communications level as does a dial-in session to CompuServe or a bulletin board. All you need is a local machine with a communications program, a modem, and access to a telephone line. Charges are incurred for distance and time in accordance with your local telephone company.

To link any Open Client DB Library-enabled application to a remote SQL Server over an asynchronous dial-in line, you configure the underlying transport software to talk to the serial port rather than to a local area network card. The relationship between Net-Library and the communications transport software was covered in more detail in the chapter on Net-Library. Most of the communications packages with which Net-Library works support Serial Link Internet Protocol (SLIP) and PPP (Point to Point Protocol). These allow you to connect your local PC to a remote server and run a true client/server session.

You would use this connection method when you had remote clients that were not considered long distance by the phone company. This allows you to connect remotely for the price of a local call. Connecting in this fashion may also be effective for very casual connections for a remote client. Consider the amount of connection time carefully, however, because the costs work exactly the same as making a long distance telephone call: if you are connected, you pay. For a five-day-a-week, eight-hours-a-day link over a long distance, this option can be prohibitively expensive.

Packet-Switching Networks

An alternative to asynchronous dial-up is to use a packet-switching topology. There are several variations within this method; however, the most common and straight-forward is to subscribe to a public service such as Tymnet in the U.S. or Datapac in Canada. These services are usually offered by the local telephone companies, and frequently there are third-party service providers as well.

In a packet-switching network, you are charged only a nominal amount for connection time, say a few cents a minute. However, as you move data between the two (or more) systems, you are charged for the volume of the packets sent. Under this scheme, a query would be broken up into packets consisting of 256 bytes (this can be configurable depending on the specific scheme you are using). The packets also contain source and destination addresses as well as some control characters. This means that a 256-byte query would be processed as two packets.

This work is performed by a Packet Assembly/Disassembly device (PAD) and the packets are routed through the network. This is often referred to as "the cloud" because of the way the network is represented in topologies, and because it might as well be a cloud, you will have very little idea and no control over what happens in there. A PAD at the destination reassembles the packets into a byte stream and they are routed to the appropriate server. The query is executed and the result set returned in the same manner. The results are also broken up into packets and sent. Your bill at the end of the month reflects the fixed costs of the PADs and circuit, the connect time per minute, and the volume of traffic sent in kilopackets. A topology of this nature is represented in Figure 7.2.4.

FIGURE 7.2.4.

A packet-switching topology showing client, server, and linking devices.

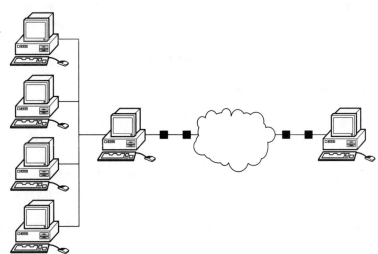

This has proven to be much more cost effective than asynchronous dial-in links for connect time intensive links with small to moderate transmission size requirements. The highest speeds currently offered by public packet-switching network service providers is 9600 baud.

Private Packet-Switching Networks

You may also choose to build your own network, either by leasing dedicated equipment and lines from a third-party provider or by buying and installing the gear yourself. At some point you will have to acquire lines from a third party, because privately installed communications lines are exceedingly rare.

In any case, the reason for pursuing this approach can be found in the increased speeds available to you, generally up to 56 kpbs or almost six times faster than 9600 baud. Additionally, with leased lines you pay only for the line lease. The actual volume of packets does not affect your bill. Depending on the number of users and the volume of data to be sent between systems, this approach could be the most cost effective. You could also choose to implement a combination of public and private services, using public services for smaller branches and a dedicated line with equipment installed at more major sites across the country.

New Products and Services

This is where things start to get interesting. The traditional (non-IBM) wide-area communications networks have been built using X.25 for packet switching. Recently, however, the network service providers have been working on new methods of providing WAN connectivity. Many of you will have come across these terms in the systems press and possibly wondered what they were about. A quick summary of the more significant networking technologies follows.

Frame Relay

Frame Relay is commonly used to link LANs across a wide area. Like X.25, the protocol also uses packet-switching techniques to move data from one site to another. It is considered to be a faster, more efficient access protocol than X.25. Many service providers now support commercial Frame Relay network services or are in beta programs. The technology is available today. When comparing performance statistics between Frame Relay and X.25, be sure to check the vintage of the networking hardware itself. In many cases, a Frame Relay solution is significantly faster because it has been built using new technology that supports higher access and trunk speeds, and not because of the superiority of the protocol itself. Frame Relay Network speeds are available to 56 kbps.

Integrated Services Digital Network (ISDN)

This service has been promoted conceptually since the 1980s; however, commercial products and services are only just becoming available in some areas now. ISDN provides two 64-Kpbs channels and one regular voice line to what looks a lot like a set of regular wall plugs. Unlike regular voice lines, the network provides digital communications, as is implied by the name.

Switched Multimegabit Data Service (SMDS)

SMDS is more oriented to connecting LANs within a metropolitan area rather than across wider geographic distances. SMDS offerings currently operate at speeds up to 1.544 Mbps, and these rates may increase over time. This service is particularly useful for interconnecting a large number of LANs that undergo frequent changes.

Asynchronous Transfer Mode (ATM)

ATM provides a means of carrying packetized data and real-time traffic such as voice and video on the same network. Speeds of 45 Mbps and higher are available with ATM services. Although it may eventually be used to link desktop units to remote LANs, ATM is currently oriented to linking either Ethernet or Token Ring LANs. ATM combines packet-switching efficient use of bandwidth with the minimized delays inherent in circuit switching.

Each of these services has varying application and availability. And once you get past a cursory overview, the specifics of any one of these technologies is highly involved. The point here is not to try to turn you into a network designer, but rather to give you an appreciation for the direction toward which such networks are heading.

As a client/server developer, you can no longer limit your thinking to a local group of users. Increasingly, clients will be remote and they will need to be provided with the same level of service as your local user population. Although communications services like the ones listed above will help narrow the gap between remote and local communications channel speeds, it is unlikely that the two will ever be at a uniform rate. This leads us to the impact of remote clients on your client/server systems design.

Designing for Remote Clients

The reality of most remote client connections is the restriction to a 9.6 Kbps link. And this has serious implications for throughput, especially when you consider larger file sizes. Even with the 45 Mbps and higher speeds potentially available with the newer communications services, it is unlikely that you will ever want to provide full multimedia database access across a wide area. Large image and other binary retrieves could bring an application to its knees in short order.

This is not likely to be a problem for most of you. After all, how many people are only just acquiring CD-ROMS and sound cards for their local machines? The need to provide multimedia database access is not prevalent even in local environments, let alone remotely.

Though some day in the not-so-distant future these may become client/server systems issues, today there are more pressing concerns. As mentioned earlier, branch offices, home-based employees (including systems developers), and other remote users have a need to access centralized data in a functional manner. And once you have gone to the bother of implementing a client/server system locally, you are not going to want to develop an entirely new application for remote users.

This brings me to the design considerations for your applications when considering connection of remote clients.

With Open Client DB-Library programs you write yourself, and even with some of the third-party packages, it is possible to connect to a SQL Server, retrieve the data, drop the connection, and still work with the data. This is especially true of select-intensive applications. Depending on the nature of your communications connection, this may be one of the key aspects of your application: connecting, retrieving, and disconnecting.

A more important consideration from a user's perspective is the response time to the user's queries. This is the central question to address when determining how best to structure your client/server application for remote users.

On the surface, the optimum method of structuring queries for remote clients would be through the use of stored procedures. The communications traffic would be limited to passing the name of the stored procedure along with the parameters and, of course, the result set. Also, the procedure is already compiled, which cuts down on the host processing time required. You could then build your application in such a way as to extensively use stored procedures, design a specific procedure for each anticipated query, and possibly limit the size of the result set in the stored procedure as well.

But in some cases, it may actually make more sense to retrieve a larger result set once and use the local power of the client system to filter, sort, report, and otherwise manipulate the retrieved data. By retrieving a superset of the data once, you allow your user to enjoy immediate access to the results without the delay of reconnecting and issuing a retrieve. From a traffic and cost standpoint, it also makes sense to retrieve a superset once as opposed to half the set more than twice. As we all know, users frequently need to look at previously retrieved results for purposes of comparison or other analysis. By retrieving all that data into a local application, you make it available to them for the duration.

Inserts and updates are separate issues again. As discussed in the chapter on concurrency, it is possible to retrieve the results to be updated into a cursor and check the timestamp value before actually writing the changes back to the database. It is more likely, however, that you will want to opt for the shorter, faster, stored-procedure approach when performing remote client inserts or updates.

Summary

No one is in a better position for analyzing, designing, and developing client/server applications than you are yourself. Certainly, it would not be practical for me to cover all the considerations involved in developing a specific application for remote client/server access. The purpose of this chapter is twofold: one, to give you a better appreciation for what enterprise client/server computing means in the context of remote clients; and two, to give you a heads-up on the direction and potential impact of emerging communications technologies.

Software developers and client/server systems people are often unaware of the complexity of their computing environment as a whole. Yet, client/server systems are based on that end-to-end provision of systems services. It is not practical to isolate yourself as a developer to a particular component of the technological mix. What you do as a client/server developer is greatly affected by all the aspects of the systems environment and, in turn, the design decisions you make will affect those components as well.

The National Data Superhighway is not a reality today. But continual strides are being made in providing the communications infrastructure necessary to link people and systems, not only across the country but globally. These services are there for you to take advantage of. But before you can do that, you must be aware of their existence.

The purpose of this chapter specifically and this book in general has been to provide you with a high-level tour of SQL Server-based systems in their entirety. I hope you feel this tour has provided you with some measure of insight that you can turn into practical value for yourself and your organization.

Section Summary

In this section you have been introduced to emerging trends on two levels. Sybase is continuing to evolve and grow, bringing the future to market in terms of SQL Server Release 10.0 and its new features. Although this version is not yet released for all platforms, it provides a pretty good idea of what you as developers can look forward to working with, even if you can't use Release 10.0 today.

On another level, I wanted to tie in one of the most important developments I perceive occurring today. The communications infrastructure is being developed throughout North America and the rest of the world. As client/server developers, this will pose opportunities and challenges like nothing we have seen before. The capability to integrate with powerful local and remote machines, incorporating software and utilities from many vendors, all over high speed communications channels, will dramatically change the face of computing a few short years from now. I hope that by introducing the potential applicability of this communications infrastructure, I help you become a little more sensitized to how you can use your Sybase client/server skills to take advantage of these emerging technologies.

8.1

Glossary

No book on client/server technology would be complete without a full definition of terms in quick-reference format. The following should provide you with definitions for all the terms used throughout this book.

aggregate function   A built-in SQL Server function that generates a single summary value from all the rows within a column. These include AVG, SUM, MIN, MAX, ANY, and COUNT.

alias   1. A short, temporary name declared for a table in a SELECT statement (for example, select blah, blah1, blah2 where p.pub_id = t.title_id). 2. A mapping of a SQL Server login ID to a database user name to allow that login to assume the user's name and privileges.

allocation unit   The base measurement for database sizing. Each allocation unit equals 256 2K pages (.5 megabytes).

ANSI   The American National Standards Institute is a standards body that is responsible (among other things) for the definition of the ANSI standard SQL, which determines the basic minimum components of the query language.

API   Applications Programming Interface. A specification and set of functions that allow third-party and custom programs to access databases and other services directly.

application generator   A software program that translates specifications into a third or fourth generation language syntax. PowerBuilder can be considered an application generator for T-SQL and Windows code.

application server   As relates to OS/2 SQL Server, an application server is an OS/2-based workstation running SQL Server that is accessible to Novell clients under NetWare Requester.

argument   A value passed to a function or procedure necessary for it to execute. *See also* parameter.

arithmetic operators   The basic math operations that can be taken on numbers, including addition, subtraction, division, and multiplication. SQL Server also supports modulo operators.

attributes   Those characteristics belonging to or describing an entity in the relational model.

automatic recovery   SQL Server performs an automatic recovery on startup. This involves rolling forward any committed but unguaranteed database changes or rolling back transactions incomplete at the time of systems failure.

base date   The default for SQL Server datetime fields: January 1, 1900.

base tables   The data tables on which views or a select with browse mode are based.

batch   A single set of TransAct SQL statements that are executed when terminated by an end-of-batch keyword, such as go.

built-in functions   SQL Server functions that allow extra operations to be taken on strings and numbers. These include mathematical, system, string, date, text, and conversion functions. They are built into T-SQL.

browse mode   An option when issuing a SELECT statement from within an application that affects the locking of the base tables.

cardinality   The zero-to-many, one-to-many, or many-to-many relations that are specified for an entity in an Entity-Relationship diagram.

Cartesian product   When a table join is performed, a Cartesian product is the primary calculation, yielding a number of rows equal to multiplying the number of rows in the first table by the number of rows in the second table. The joined table is made smaller than the Cartesian product by eliminating rows that do not satisfy the WHERE clause specified in the join definition.

cascading deletes   These are deletes of rows in many tables with the same key value. When a row in a table with a primary key is deleted, a cascading delete ensures that no orphaned references to that key remain in other tables.

CASE tools   Computer-Assisted Software Engineering tools are software products that support the disciplined practice of software development through extensive use of data modeling and code generation.

checkpoint   An operation within a transaction to ensure that all changes performed to that point are written to the database pages in the base tables.

client   A separate and distinct process or application that uses services provided by the SQL Server (or other server). Often runs on its own computer across a network from the database.

client/server architecture   A method of organizing computing resources that connects two processes, each with their own services, requirements, and resources. The total processing requirement is balanced between the client and the server. Frequently, though not necessarily, the two are linked over a communications network.

clustered index   An ordering of a database table so that the rows are physically stored in order of values within a particular column, such as department number.

column   A constituent part of a table. Tables are constructed of columns, which equate to fields, and rows, which represent records.

command   An instruction consisting of a keyword along with mandatory and optional parameters or clauses.

comparison operators   The symbols used to represent a relationship between two expressions, such as column names or variables. In SQL Server, the comparison operators are equal to (=), less than (<), greater than (>), less than or equal to (<=), greater than or equal to (=>), not equal to (!=), not greater than (!>), and not less than (!<). Frequently used in WHERE clauses, such as `where a.column <= b.column`.

compiler   The part of the database engine that generates an executable version of a query or procedure.

concatenation   Adding character or binary strings, column names, or combinations together to form a single expression.

control-of-flow   Refers to the extensions in TransAct SQL that allow programming logic to be built into SQL statements. Includes IF, ELSE, WHILE, PRINT, and RAISERROR.

correlated subquery   The inner part of a nested query that passes its results to the outer query. This query executes once for every row to be processed by the outer query.

cursor   An extension to DB-LIB and SQL Server 10 that allows results to be stored in a structure that processes rows one at a time.

data definition language (DDL)   The output of a CASE tool that allows the creation of tables and other database objects automatically.

data manipulation language (DML)   T-SQL is an example of a data manipulation language.

data modeling   The process by which a database environment is designed and defined prior to actual implementation. *See also* logical data model and physical data model.

database   A separate and complete collection of tables, views, indexes, and other objects with a different name, users, storage allocations, and permission profiles than any other database on a SQL Server.

database dump   The process and output of copying the contents of a SQL Server database to a designated backup device.

database object   A table, column, view, stored procedure, rule, trigger, or index held within a database.

database owner   The user who is assigned all controls and permissions over a particular database. Only one user can be designated as the DBO.

datatype   A fundamental definition of the values allowed for a column. Each datatype has its own characteristics, some of which can be set by the creator of the table when the column is defined.

date function   A built-in function that operates on values stored in columns defined with the datetime datatype. Displays information or manipulates date and/or time components.

DB-Library   An applications programming interface (API) supplied by Sybase to allow applications and programs to access SQL Server databases directly.

deadlock   An event that occurs when two transactions each attempt to access the same locked page of a table or index.

default database   The database that a user is automatically deemed to be in when first logged on, such as master for the systems administrator (SA).

demand lock   Issued by a transaction waiting for read or shared locks to be relinquished when preparing for an update. The demand lock ensures that no more than four shared locks are allowed before the exclusive lock is granted for the write transaction.

dirty page   A data page that has been modified but whose changes have not yet been written to disk is deemed to be dirty.

distributed database   An integrated set of data resources that reside on multiple, physically segregated machines.

domain   Refers to the range of values considered legal or valid for a particular column. The domain of human ages is 0 to 980 (if you count Methuselah).

dump device   A tape or disk device specified to hold the contents of a database or transaction dump.

embedded SQL   This refers to the process of accessing a relational database management system by surrounding SQL code within a set of programming language statements.

entities   The real-world items that have characteristics or attributes and that relate to other entities. These form the basis for the groupings of the data maintained in tables in the database.

equijoin   A straightforward joining of two tables where the values in a column on one table equal the values held in a column on the other.

error messages   Messages describing the nature of a problem or complaint about an operation taken on SQL Server data. Described as a number, state, and level with a text description to allow investigation for debugging purposes.

exclusive locks   A lock held on a data page when a write operation takes place on a table.

expression   Expressions are the complete statements that execute on a SQL Server and return a value of some sort (including success or failure status). Expressions can be combined to create complex T-SQL queries and transactions. (`Select * from titles` is an expression, whereas SELECT by itself is a keyword.)

extent lock   A special lock maintained by SQL Server when allocating or deallocating database or index pages as the result of an operation on the table.

fatal errors   Any return status code of 19 or higher indicates a fatal error, which terminates the user's session.

field   The traditional term field (meaning discrete element of data) corresponds to a column value in relational databases.

foreign key   A column used as a key that depends logically on the existence of that column as a primary key in another table is considered to be a foreign key.

functions   Operations that can be taken on data. The range of functions depends on which programming environment or language is being discussed. SQL Server provides built-in functions. *See also* built-in functions.

global variables   These system-wide variables contain overall status information that can be accessed by any application or SQL Server user. Some global variables can be accessed within a transaction or application and are set for a specific session, such as `@@error`.

groups   All database users belong to a group (Public by default). Permissions can be set at one time for every user within a group, speeding account setup systems administration.

guest   An identity set up optionally that enables any user to log into a database to which they have not been established as a user. The guest account has restricted access and privileges associated with it.

hierarchical   A formal structure of levels. Typically refers to more traditional approaches to systems design and database software.

identifier   Unique identifiers are the name of the database object, which can be up to 30 characters long, must start with a letter, #, or _, contain legal symbols, and cannot contain spaces.

implicit conversion   For datatypes that are not identical but are compatible, SQL Server performs the conversion without being told.

inner query   In a nested query, the inner query or subquery is performed first, passing its results to the outer query.

integrity constraint   A rule or relationship that must be enforced on a column or table to ensure data integrity is called an integrity constraint.

intent lock   A read or write operation places an intent lock on a data page when other locks are already placed on the same page. The intent lock reserves the next available lock for that operation.

ISQL   The Sybase-supplied command-line interface to SQL Server.

JAD   Joint Application Development is a process by which users and systems developers work together to define and design a system.

join   A cornerstone of relational databases, the join operation allows two separate tables to be treated as one by combining the two where a common column value matches predefined criteria (equal to, not equal to, greater than, or less than).

kernel   The central database engine itself (the dataserver program) is the RBDMS kernel that runs all the tasks and processes of the SQL Server.

key   A column value that identifies the other columns in a table, keys are used by indexes for sorting and retrieving data.

keyword   A reserved TransAct SQL word or phrase used for operations on SQL Server data (SELECT, for example).

leaf level   Refers to the bottom level of an index. In a clustered index, the leaf level consists of the physical data as they are stored on the hard disk.

livelock   Exclusive locks for write operations cannot be granted while successive shared locks for reads are in place. This is known as a livelock, which is detected automatically by the SQL Server and corrected after four new shared locks are granted.

locking   A concurrency control mechanism that manages multiple users engaging in both read and write operations on the same data.

logical data model   The high-level view of the entities, attributes, and relationships of a database prior to its physical implementation.

logical database device   The name by which physical disk space is known to Sybase. This is defined with the DISK INIT command.

logical operators   AND, OR, and NOT are the logical operators that can be used to build the desired set of expressions in a WHERE clause. Logical operators define the select criteria by combining conditions to be met by the query.

login   The account name set for a user on the SQL Server itself. This is the first component of establishing a successful database connection. The login name need not be the same as the user name defined in a particular database.

master database   The systems database set up during the initial installation of SQL Server containing all users, databases, and operation of the server as a whole.

master device   The logical device name for the disk on which the master database is installed.

master table   A table containing high-level data for which detailed data is maintained in another table. The master table contains the primary key, which links to the foreign key in the detail table.

messages   In SQL Server, the system communicates status information to users and applications through messages.

metadata   Data about the data. Can include dictionary definition, scope notes, formatting options, and display preferences.

modulo   An arithmetic operator that expresses division with remainders rather than decimals. (31/3 is 10 with a remainder of 1 rather than 10.3333333333.)

natural join   When two tables can be linked by stating that the values in the columns are equal, the join is considered natural when only one of the identical columns is displayed rather than the full contents of both tables, including the redundant column.

nested queries   Multiple levels of queries are considered nested. These queries are used to retrieve one set of data and then perform other T-SQL operations on that subset.

Net-Library   The name of the Sybase products that allow DB-Library applications to talk to network transport software and connect to SQL Server across the network.

nonclustered index   This form of index stores the key values and pointers to the data pages where the rows are held.

normalization   Refers to the extent to which data is segregated or duplicated in tables. Database design defines rules for specific degrees and stages of normalization.

null   This is a unique status for a column value that does not mean zero. Null indicates that the value for that column is unknown or not yet established and does not equate to any existing value in the column.

object   A term for a database element including table, view, stored procedure, trigger, default, rule, and datatype. In object-oriented programming, an object is seen as a tightly integrated set of data and methods that has behaviors and responds to messages.

object owner   The user who is considered the creator and has all rights to the specific object.

object permissions   The privileges or permissions provided to database users for a specific object.

operating system   The system control program for a host computer. The operating system type and version determine which SQL Server can be loaded onto the host platform.

outer join   A special join type that returns all the rows of one table and only those rows matching a WHERE clause criteria from another. This is useful for selecting all employees, and license information for those employees with parking spaces. Outer joins are specified with *= or =* to return all rows from the first or second table respectively.

outer query   Refers to the first query that contains a query within it.

parameter   A value that is passed to a program or stored procedure. Parameters specify names and options when running commands. For example, OPEN <filename> where filename is a parameter. Parameters can be optional or mandatory.

permission   The necessary allocation of rights or authorization to perform certain tasks.

physical data model   Describes the specific structures of tables and other database objects as they exist and relate to devices in the database.

primary key   The column or columns by which each row in a table is uniquely identified.

project   To project. A fundamental aspect of relational systems. To project over a table is to pull a subset of the table.

qualifier   A naming convention that specifies the database and/or owner of a particular object. The qualified name of the sysusers table in the master database is master.dbo.sysusers.

query   A SQL statement that selects, inserts, or deletes data in the database.

referential integrity   Like normalization, referential integrity refers to the rules defined as part of the relational model. Referential integrity is the area of database practice that ensures that tables with primary keys contain rows for which other tables have foreign keys. This prevents lost or meaningless data from being proliferated through many tables.

restriction   Works with projection and is synonymous with selection. A SELECT statement is a means of restricting the values retrieved by a query.

rollback transaction   A T-SQL extension to SQL, rollback transaction is a control-of-flow statement that performs an "Undo" for all changes made within a transaction when an error or other defined condition has occurred.

row   The complete set of column values for one unique record in a relational system is considered a row. Fields and Records are referred to as Columns and Rows in Sybase.

row aggregate functions   These built-in functions create a summary row when you issue compute sum, avg, min, max, and count within a SELECT statement.

rule   A definition that determines the format and/or content of data entered into a specific column or user-defined datatype.

SA   The systems administrator role in SQL Server. This is the root account that performs all system-wide administration and configuration functions.

savepoint   A savepoint sets up a marker to allow a rollback to undo changes made since the last savepoint rather than from the beginning of the transaction.

scalar aggregate   A built-in function that returns a single value from a SELECT statement without using the GROUP BY clause.

select list   The columns specified to be retrieved within the main portion of a SELECT statement.

self-join   A type of join that compares a table to itself. Useful for determining data on the basis of comparisons of column values within the same table.

server   A computer based service available to other machines and programs. May provide access to files, applications, printing, communications, and myriad other services. A single machine may be both a client and a server.

severity level number   Error messages from SQL Server identify the severity of the error as part of the returned status code. Error 666 indicates Armageddon.

shared lock   SELECT statements place shared locks on data pages that allow other queries to select data but that block write operations which require exclusive locks on pages to be affected.

SSO   The systems security officer role in SQL Server Release 10.0. This role functions similarly to SA, with specific responsibility for assigning rights and permissions.

statement   T-SQL commands and parameters are defined as statements that begin with keywords and specify the SQL operations to be performed.

statement block   The T-SQL statements that make up a single transaction.

stored procedure   T-SQL statements that have been stored as a script and compiled into an executable routine on the SQL Server.

string function   Built-in functions that perform operations on strings of characters or binary data.

SQL   Acronym meaning Structured Query Language. SQL is the accepted basis for writing queries against relational databases.

subquery   An inner query or complete and legal SELECT statement that is called from within another query.

suid   Server user ID. The internal number that identifies a logged-in user.

system databases   The initial installation of SQL Server sets up three databases (more for SQL Server 10.0). The master, model, and tempdb systems databases are used as part of all ongoing user database setup and operation.

system functions   A built-in function that retrieves information from the SQL Server and system tables.

system procedures   These stored procedures are supplied with the SQL Server to ensure that administrative tasks that affect the system tables are performed completely and accurately.

system tables   These tables reside in the master and other databases and contain rows reflecting all users, database objects, and permissions. The system tables in master contain the data dictionaries about the SQL Server as a whole, whereas the system tables within each database contain the data dictionary for that specific database.

table   A single complete set of columns and rows within a database.

TCP/IP   Transmission Control Program/Internet Protocol. This transport layer communications specification is used to link computers over a network. Prevalent in the UNIX/Ethernet environment, but no longer restricted to this.

theta join   These joins incorporate comparison operators when specifying the join condition. Comparisons include where table 1 is equal to, not equal to, greater than, or less than table 2.

transaction   A set of statements that are treated as a single task and can be undone or committed according to certain conditions, such as encountering an error.

transaction log   A record of all changes made to a database. The transaction log is used in conjunction with a database dump to restore the database and replay any actions taken on the database.

trigger   A special stored procedure defined once for insert, delete, and update operations on a specific table. Triggers are executed automatically rather than called as are stored procedures.

type conversion function   An explicit or implicit conversion of data manipulated in a statement from one datatype to another. Formatting datetime information requires a conversion of the value to character type, for example.

update   Any change to a value within a database table can be considered an update. The update command modifies one or more column values within an existing row. Delete, insert, and truncate table statements can also be considered update operations.

user-defined datatype   The Sybase-supplied datatypes can be defined to contain defaults and rules and named as unique datatypes. A postal code datatype, for example, might be based on the character datatype but include a rule to ensure that the right number of characters is entered.

variable   A variable is a logical mapping of an event, value, or values to a name that can be accessed by a T-SQL program or client program. Variables can be user-defined or supplied by the system.

vector aggregate   A value that is obtained through the use of an aggregate function in conjunction with the GROUP BY clause.

view   A method for presenting columns from one or more tables as if it were a single, complete table. Useful for security and presenting data to users unfamiliar with joins.

view resolution   All queries accessing a view must be processed to ensure that the objects referenced by the view exist and appropriate permissions have been granted to the user of the view.

wildcard   A special character that represents any character in that position. Wildcards allow retrieval of nonexact matches within a single statement, such as `select * from tablename`.

Index

Symbols

!= (not equal to) operations, table scans, 406

% symbol, wildcard (TransAct SQL), 324

/* ls_table systems table, 381

/* symbols as comments in batches, 357

@@error global variable, 362

@@trancount variable, 361

1.544 mbps (megabits per second), SMDS speed, 641

18 khz (kilohertz), FM radio bandwidth, 634

19.2 kbps (kilobits per second), transmission speeds of modems, 634

3khz (kilohertz), telephone bandwidth, 634

45 mbps (megabits per second), speeds in ATMs, 641

5 khz (kilohertz), AM radio bandwidth, 634

56 kbps (kilobits per second), Frame Relay Network speeds, 641

64-kpbs (kilobits per second) channels in ISDN, 641

9.6 kbps (kilobits per second), remote server connection speed restriction, 642

A

abort_xact() function, 367

access
commands in SQL Servers, 284-293
unauthorized, and data security, 175

access time, server optimization, 424

accounting spreadsheets, SQL Server storage, 72

active data, denormalizing databases, 411

ad hoc queries, 143, 157

add sp_ procedures, 285

addresses
IP, 191-192
network, 190
two-phase commit, 365

adduser command, 264

administration of systems, TransAct SQL, 323

administration systems procedures, 297

advantages
CASE tools, 595
SQL Servers, 6

aggregate
functions, 330-332, 646
vectors, 656

AIX OS (IBM) SQL Server installation, 205

aliases/aliasing users, 267, 646

allocation units, 646

allow duplicate rows parameter, clustered indexes, 257

alter database command, 227, 243

alternate keys, linking tables, 147

AM radio bandwidth (5 khz), 634

analog signal carriers, bandwidth, 634

ancestor windows, PowerBuilder, 573

ANSI (American National Standards Institute) SQL, 320, 646

API (Application Programming Interface) Open Client DB-Library, 6, 62, 432, 646

application development
Build Momentum tool, 564
client/server models, 36-37

application generators, 646
application logic bugs, 182
application servers, 646
application specifications
    development processes, 140
    models and processes, 114-116
applications
    analysis
        key questions, 121
        objects as classes in CRC cards, 127
    bookstore example with CASE tools,
        598-604
    budget-forecasting example for systems
        development, 87
    classes of objects in CRC card analysis,
        128
    closing connections to SQL Servers,
        440
    cursor operations, 390-392
    data model support and database
        structures, 139-141
    database publishing with client/server
        systems, 171-172
    DB-Lib (Open Client DB-Library),
        433-442
        command buffer, 435-436
        creation process, 433
        error handling, 441-442
        returned results, 437-440
        sample (listing 5.2.3.), 469-483
        templates (listing 5.2.4.), 484-491
    developing
        for client/server systems, 112
        JAD sessions, 119
        various methods, 129-135
    form-based, 171
    incomplete transactions and data
        integrity, 180-181
    queries, 156-158
        end-user, in conflict with data models,
        145
    questionnaires, 171
    representing with CRC Cards, 127
    specifications for client/server systems,
        112-114
    SQLTEST3.C (listing 5.2.3.), 468-483
    systems failure, data integrity, 176
        threats and dangers to data security and
            integrity, 174-176
        transactions, two-phase commit, 181
        transparency of operations, 587
        using browse mode, 375
applications analysts and client/
    server systems, 103
APT (A Productivity Tool), 8
areas of performance in SQL Server
    design optimization, 400-402
arguments, 646
arithmetic operators, 646
artificial keys, tables, 147
ascending sort order, ORDER BY
    clause, 335
assigning logins to users/groups for
    SQL Servers, 262-268
asynchronous dial-ups
    remote client/server systems, 636
    WANs, 638
asynchronous I/0, SQl Server disk
    partitions, 194
AT&T StarGroup network driver,
    533
ATM (Asynchronous Transfer
    Mode), 641
attributes, 646
Audit Server, 614
autoexec.ncf file (SQL Server
    NLM), TCP/IP services, 214
automatic recovery, 646

B

back-end processes and SQL
    servers, 5
backbones, internetworking
    devices, 632
backup plans
    data security/integrity, 174, 184
    designing systems, 174
Backup Server, 612-613

backups, 274-276
  databases, 272
  dump devices, 272
  scripts, 274
  transaction logs, 273
bandwidth, analog signal carriers, 634
base dates, 646
base tables, 647
batch commands, 357
batch delimiters, 356
batch reports, 170-172, 586
  forms, 171
  printing with FrameMaker, 590
  questionnaires, 171
  statements, 356, 647
    comments, 357
    containing within transactions, 358
    stored procedures, 357
baud (kilobits per second), 634
bcp utility (bulk copy), 54, 554-556
BEGIN statement, blocks, 356
begin tran statement, 358-361
benefits
  client/server applications, 37-42
  normalization of databases, 395, 411
  Sybase Servers, 19-21
binary datatypes, 248
binary sort order, databases, 193
binding
  column values with dbbind command, 438
  rules to columns and datatypes, 316
bit datatypes, 249
Bitmap Editor, Build Momentum tool, 565
BLOBS (binary large objects), database publishing, 172
blocks of statements, 356
books table example, 241
  data_disk1 device/data_disk2 device, 241
  database1 script, 241

database10_device, 242
database9_device, 241-242
two_device_seg segment, 243
bookstore application
  CASE tools, 598-604
  domain and column values, 599-600
bottom-up method of systems development, 76-77
branch office systems, 77-78
browse mode, 647
  select statements, 375
  using in applications, 375
bubble diagrams in example applications, 130
budget-forecasting application example for systems development, 87
buffers, command in DB-Lib applications, 435-436
bugs, application logic, 182
Build Momentum tool, 560
  application development environment, 564
  Database Browser, 564-565
  Deployment Utility, 566
  development facilities, 563-564
  kernel, 561
    dynamic compilation, 562
  OOP (object oriented programming), 560-561
  reusability/inheritance, 562
building application features in systems development, 86
buildmaster utility, 197
built-in functions (TransAct SQL), 249, 647
  aggregate values, 330
  dates and time, 327
  mathematical operations, 333
  new for SQL Server Release 10.0, 623-624
  string manipulation, 326-327
  systems functions, 334-335

bulk copy utility
  enhancements, 621
  functions, Open Client DB-Library,
    520-524
  operations in C programs (listing
    5.2.8.), 521-523
  Windows programs, 497
businesses
  connecting related departments with
    Open Client software, 72
  functioning of current systems and
    actual needs of users, 118-119

C

C programs, bulk copy operations
  (listing 5.2.8.), 521-523
C/C++ programs and Open Client
  DB-Library functions, 454
calculating table sizes and data
  pages, 414-423
cardinality, 142, 647
Cartesian Product of tables, JOIN
  statements, 162, 647
cascading deletes, 350-351, 647
CASE tools (Computer Assisted
  Software Engineering), 647
  advantages, 595
  bookstore application example,
    598-604
  data modeling, 597
  database diagram development,
    595-596
  database schema reports, 601
  DDL generation, 600-602
  defining/managing logical data models,
    141-142
  ERD design, 127
  multiple database management,
    603-604
  referential integrity, 602-603
  scribes, 596
  SQL Servers, 594
chained transactions, 618
character datatype, 246-248

character set and sort order, SQL
  Server databases, 192-193
checkpoints, 647
checkpoint command, 298
Chen, Peter P., entity relationship
  diagrams, 122
child tables, 126, 147
cl command, SQLTESTR.C
  program, 460
classes
  Build Momentum tool, 561
  objects in CRC card applications
    analysis, 127
clauses (SQL), 320
  COMPUTE, dbbind command, 322,
    439
  COMPUTE BY, 337-338
  FROM, FORCEPLAN statement,
    407-408
  GROUP BY, aggregate function, 331
  HAVING, aggregate functions, 331
  ORDER BY, select statement, 335
  WHERE
    aggregate functions, 331
    column indexes, 396
    JOIN command, 162
    SELECT command, 159
client/server applications
  and relevance to work to be performed,
    37-38
  benefits of, 37-42
  developing with C/C++ and Open
    Client DB-Library function calls, 454
client/server architecture, 647
  relational databases, 4-5
  users, 35
client/server model development,
  36-37, 81-84
client/server platforms, 13-14
client/server projects using Sybase,
  24-33
client/server systems
  client emphasis, 401
  complexity of development, 47-48

data administrators, 104-105
data retrieval for forms, 171
DBA (database administrator), 103-104
defining roles/responsibilities, 96-109
development, side-by-side models,
  83-84, 112
documentation specialists, 107-109
end users, 101-102
example application development with
  various methods, 129-135
explanation of operations to users, 401
form following function, 112-114
integration of users, 39-40
interface designer, 105-106
network architects, 106
query example, 64-65
systems architects, 102-103
technical specialists, 100
technology transfer, 46-47
integrated systems, 70-75
interviewing user groups during
  applications development, 119-122
JAD sessions in applications development, 119
modeling based on application
  specifications, 114-116
performance optimization, 402
potential problems and risks, 43-48
project leader/manager/sponsor, 98-100
remote
    clients, 632-633
    connections, 632
    operations divisions between PCs,
      636-638
throughput, 635
traditional development models, 74
usefulness of system, 401
user involvement in deleopment, 44-45
using existing resources in new Sybase
  systems, 70
clients, 647
development for Windows, 571
remote, in client/server systems,
  632-633
close_xact() function, 367
closing applications connections,
  440

clouds, *see* PADs
clustered indexes, 255-257,
  406, 647
optimization of use, 397
SQL Server design optimization, 396
unique, 256
coding in systems development, 76
column-level data integrity,
  177-178
columns, 647
adding to tables, 243-244
as database objects in physical data
  model, 151
binding rules, 316
binding values with dbbind
  command, 438
data integrity defaults, 311
deleting from tables, 243
IDENTITY, 615
indexes, WHERE clauses, 396
not null, tables, 243
storage datatypes, 246
tables, 240
    timestamp, 375
unbinding defaults from, 312
values, bookstore application example,
  599-600
command buffer, DB-Lib applications, 435-436
commands, 648
accessing SQL Servers, 284-293
adduser, 264
alter database, 227
ALTER TABLE, 243
batches, 357
checkpoint, 298
cl, SQLTESTR.C program, 460
create index, 257
    Release 10.0 enhancements, 620
    writing extents, 621
create rule, 313
create schema, 617
DB-Library, 442-449
dbbind, binding column values, 438
DUMP TRAN, 275

exec, stored procedures in batch statements, 357
INSERT, SQL queries, 164-165
JOIN, SQL queries, 162
kill, 620
RECONFIGURE, 232
RECONFIGURE WITH OVER-RIDE, 232
rollback tran, 360
RUNSERVER, 197
save tran, 360
SELECT, SQL queries, 159-160
SET SHOWPLAN ON, 404-407
setuser, user permissions, 268
sp_addalias, 288
sp_addgroup, 290
sp_addserver, 199
sp_adduser, 288
sp_bindefault, 312
sp_changedbowner, 287
sp_commonkey, 306
sp_configure, 194, 233
sp_dboption, 298
sp_defaultdb, 286
sp_defaultlanguage, 287
sp_depends, 294
sp_dropalias, 292
sp_dropgroup, 292
sp_dropuser, 292
sp_extendsegment, 299-301
sp_foreignkey, 305
sp_help, 291
sp_helpdevice, 300
sp_helpgroup, 289
sp_helpindex, 295
sp_helpjoins, 296
sp_helpkey, 305
sp_helplog, 302
sp_helprotect, 290
sp_helpsegment, 299
sp_helpsort, 293
sp_helptext, 294
sp_helptext ziprule, 313
sp_helpuser, 285
sp_locks, 372
sp_logdevice, 302
sp_placeobject, 303

sp_primarykey, 304
sp_rename, 296
sp_renamedb, 297
sp_unbindefault, 312
sp_who, 285
UNIX, 403
use model, 316
see also stored procedures, statements
comments
    batch statements, 357
    SQL Servers, 619
Commit Manager facility, 365
Commit Servers, two-phase commit, 181
COMMIT TRANSACTION statement, 358
commit_xact() function, 367
communication drivers, 534-537
communication with remote servers, 199-200
communications, PCs to SQL Servers, 528-529
communications drivers
    software, 532-534
    SQL Server/PC networks, 530
communications hardware in LANs, 529-530
Communications layer, Open Client Net-Library, 64
comparison operators, 159, 648
Compiler, 62-64
compilers/compiling, 648
    dynamic, Build Momentum kernel, 562
    SQLTESTR.C program, 460-465
complexity of client/server systems, 47-48
components of SQL Servers, 60-63
compression, transmission speeds on networks, 635
COMPUTE BY clause, 337-338
COMPUTE clause, dbbind command, 322, 439

concatenation, 648
  keys, entity identifiers, 147
  string functions, 250
concurrency
  control of SQL Server, 370
  cursors, 389-390
  optimistic control, 390
condition testing, 359
confidential data protection, 175
config_value variable, 233
configuration options, 222-227, 232, 384
conflicts, systems resources, 402
Connect Database dialog box, PowerBuilder, 572
connections to SQL Servers, closing for applications, 440
connectivity options, SQL Servers, 587
context diagrams in example applications, 130
contrived columns, denormalization for databases, 413
control-of-flow language, 321, 648
convert function, 249
convert statements, 251
converting datatypes, 251
corporate management, client/ server systems, 73-75
correlated subqueries, 648
corruption, checking database objects with DBCC, 275
cost efficiency of client/server systems, 41-42
costs of data model modifications, 144-145
cperrlog utility, 198
CRC (Class, Responsibility, and Collaborator), 127
  CRC Cards representing applications, 127
  in example applications development, 133

create database syntax, 227
create index command, 257-258
  Release 10.0 enhancements, 620
  writing extents, 621
create information, HP-UX platform, 211-212
CREATE permissions, limiting for indexes/tables, 149
create procedure ls_proc procedure, 382
create procedure ls_rule procedure, 383
create procedure ls_table procedure, 381
create procedure ls_trig procedure, 381
create procedure ls_view procedure, 383
create procedure pwd procedure, 382
create procedure whoami procedure, 382
create rule command, 313
create schema command, 617
create statement, books table example, 241
create table permissions, 243
create view statement, 253
cursor program, Open Client DB-Library API, 500
cursors, 648
  concurrency, 389-390
  defining with select statement, 388-390
  dynamic, 389
  keyset-driven, 389
  locking methods, 390
  obtaining row position with fetch function, 391
  operations in applications, 390-392
  positioning current row of, 389
  PowerBuilder, 577
  restrictions, 391
  row operations, 388

SQL Server feature set, 388
static, 389
support
   DB-Library (Open Client function library), 390-392
   SQL Servers, 614
with Windows programs (listing 5.2.7.), 501-519
Custom Object Editor, Build Momentum tool, 565
Customer Authorization String, 195

D

dangers to data security and integrity, 174-176
data, modifying with views, 254
data administrators and client/ server systems, 104-105
data definition language (DDL), 648
data dictionaries, 58-60
data domains, logical data models, 142
data flow diagrams
   lower-level, 124
   nested detail levels, 123
data integrity
   applications and incomplete transactions, 180-181
   backup plans, 174
   column-level, 177-178
   defining defaults, 311-312
   in databases, 174
   in databases with datatypes, 244
   network failure, 176
   referential integrity, 176-179
   rules, 312-315
   rules and defaults, 310-315
   systems failure, 175-176
   table-level, 178-179
   transaction logs, 180
data manipulation language (DML), 648

data modeling, 597, 648
data models
   ad hoc queries, 143
   applications support and database structures, 139-141
   conflicts with end-user query applications, 145
   data-retrieval activities, 143
   developing for SQL Server environments, 138
   entity identifiers, 147
   logical
      defining/managing with CASE tools, 141-142
      for SQL Server environments, 142-143
      identifying database members, 139
   logical and physical, 125
   new database requirements in applications development, 141
   physical
      database objects, 151-152
      implementing elements in databases, 145-149
      integrity/security issues, 144
   primary keys, 146
   risks/costs of modifications, 144-145
   user review, 144
   user walkthroughs, 143-144
data pages, 370
   calculating, 414-423
   performance optimization, 414
data retrieval
   and views, 252
   batch reports, 172
   queries, TransAct SQL, 324
   query specifications, 158
   table views, 252-254
   with SQL in relational databases, 320
data security
   backup plans, 174
   unauthorized access, 175
data-retrieval activities, data models, 143
data_disk1/data_disk2 devices, books table example, 241

database administrator, developing
data models, 138
database backup and restoration,
272
database backups script, 274
Database Browser
Build Momentum tool, 564-565
toolbar, 565
database catalogs, 59
database devices, 55
database dump file, 274
database dumps, 193, 648
database engines, 5, 60-63
as dataservers, 53
OLTP (On-Line Transaction Processing), 52
database information, systems
tables, 379
database mirroring, TransAct SQL,
323
database modeling
E-R Win tool, 597-598
testing with queries, 157
database normalization, design
optimization, 395
database object metaphors,
PowerBuilder, 571
database objects, 57-58, 648
changes to in Release 10.0, 628
checking for corruption with DBCC,
275
creation permissions, 149-150
data model development, 138
performance optimization, 413-414
physical data models, 151-152
procedures for manipulation, 293-306
views, 252
database objects and structures,
240
database operations, lock requirements, 372
database owners, 648

database publishing, 171-172, 586
database schema reports, CASE
tools, 601
database security, 174
stored procedures, 183-184
system backup plans, 184
database size, SQL Server configuration, 235
database structures
data model applications support,
139-141
data models, 125
referential integrity, 126
database systems and Sybase
developers, 18
database-level integrity, 179
database1 script, books table
example, 241
database1_device, logical disk
device script, 223-224
database10_device, books table
example, 242
database9_device, books table
example, 241-242
databases, 648
adding users to, 263
and logs, 56-57
benefits of normalization, 395
binary sort order, 193
cardinality between entities in
development, 142
character sets/sort order, SQL Servers,
192-193
corporate management on OmniSQL
Gateway, 74
creating views for retrievals, 149
data integrity with datatypes, 244
denormalization, 411-413
diagram development, CASE tools,
595-596
dictionary sort order, 193
expanded format rules, 313
expanding size, 227

identifying members with logical data models, 139
identifying new requirements in applications development, 141
implementation of elements with physical data models, 145-149
intersection tables for relationships, 151
linking tables with foreign keys, 146
managing with physical data models, 148
master, 57
   restoring, 278-279
   SQL Server configuration, 222
   systems tables, 383-385
mirroring system security, 184
model, 57
multilingual, 193
multiple management, CASE tools, 603-604
new options in SQL Server Release 10.0, 627
permissions, 183
physical implementation plans, 200-201
PowerBuilder connections, 571-573
privileges granted by systems administrator, 183
programmable, 6
pubs
   data retrieval with stored procedures, 341
   transactions, 359
referential integrity, 178
relational, data retrieval with SQL, 320
reloading from dump devices, 276-278
resource balancing in design, 152
restoring from DISKINIT scripts, 276
splitting across disks, 241
storing dumps, 179
sybsystemprocs, 611
system, 55
tempdb, 57, 222
updates, 656
utility/value to users, 139
writing transactions to, 356
Datapac packet-switching networks, 639

dataserver program, 55
dataservers, SQL Server engines as, 53
datatype conversion, 617
datatypes, 649
   binary, 248
   binding rules, 316
   bit, 249
   char, 247
   character, 246-248
   column storage, 246
   columns, data integrity, 177
   converting, 251
   date/time, 248-249
   float, 246
   floating-point, 246-247
   image, 248
   int, 246
   integer, 246
   money, 245, 247
   numeric, SQL Server Release 10.0, 615
   real, 247
   small money, 245
   smalldatetime, 249
   smallint, 246
   smallmoney, 247
   tables, 240, 244-249
   text, 246-248
   tinyint, 246
   user-defined, 58, 316-317, 656
   varbinary, 248
   varchar, 246-247
DataWindows, PowerBuilder, 574-576
dataypes, 244-245
date functions, 315, 649
date/time datatypes, 248-249
dateadd function, 329
datediff function, 328
datename function, 328
datepart function, 328
dateparts function, 329
datetime functions, 327-330

DB-Lib applications (Open Client DB-Library), 433-442
   command buffer, 435-436
   DB-LIB API (Application Programming Interface), 6, 62
   dbsqlexec() function, 436-437
   error handling, 441-442
   returned results, 437-440
   second sample template (listing 5.2.5.), 491-496
   templates (listing 5.2.4.), 484-491
DB-Library (Open Client function library), 649
   cursor support, 390
   dbcursoropen function, 390
   functions, 442-449
   sample program, listing 5.1.1., 450-451
DB2 databases in OmniSQL Gateways, 74
DBA (database administrator), and client/server systems, 103-104
dbaltbind() function, 439
dbbind command/function, 438
   binding column values, 438
   COMPUTE clause, 439
DBCC (database consistency checker), 275
dbclose() function, 440
dbcmd() function, 435
dbcursoropen function, DB-Library, 390
dbdata() function, 439
dbdataready() function, 438
dbexit() function, 440
dbfcmd() function, 436
dblogin() function, 434
DBO (database owner), 58
dbopen() function, 434
dbproc function, 433
DBPROCESS structure, 434
dbresults() function, 437-439
DBSETLPWD statement, Windows test program, 468

dbsqlexec() function, DB-Lib applications, 436-437
dbuse() function, 434
dbwintst program, 468
DCE (Distributed Computing Environment), 12
DDE (Dynamic Data Exchange), PowerBuilder, 577
DDL (Data Definition Language), 594
   generation with CASE tools, 600-602
   table create scripts, 127
deadlocks, 373, 649
debugger utility, Build Momentum tool, 563
declarative referential integrity, 348, 614
default databases, 649
default permissions, users, 182
defaults
   data integrity, 310
   defining for data integrity, 311-312
   for parameters in stored procedures, 342
   SQL Server datatypes, 244
   TransAct SQL, 322
   unbinding from columns, 312
   user-defined datatypes, 316-317
defining
   cursors with select statements, 388-390
   defaults for data integrity, 311-312
   dump devices for databases, 272-274
   logical data models with CASE tools, 141-142
   screen specifications in systems development, 85
defncopy utility, 556-557
DEFT tool, 9, 594-595
deleted table, triggers, 349
deleting columns from tables, 243
deletions of data, 175
delimiter, batch statements, 356
demand locks, 372, 649

denormalization for databases
   active data, 411
   contrived columns/redundancy/table
      segmentation, 412-413
   summary values, 411
   temporary tables, 411
departmental/branch office systems, 77-78
departments, integrating systems
   with SQL Server, 71-73
dependent tables, *see* child tables
Deployment Utility, Build Momentum tool, 566
descendent windows,
   PowerBuilder, 574
design optimization
   database normalization, 395
   queries, 395
   SQL Servers, 394-396
      guidelines for improvement, 408-410
design solutions, remote client/
   server systems, 642-643
designing client/server applications,
   form following function, 113
detail in client/server systems,
   eliminating in new systems, 79
developer services, Build Momentum tool, 562
developing client/server systems,
   112
developing data models for SQL
   Server environments, 138
development facilities, Build
   Momentum tool, 563-564
development models for client/
   server systems, 81-84
development process for application specifications, 140
development tools, GUI-based,
   561

device drivers
   communications, SQL Server/PC
      networks, 530
   communications software, 532-534
   SQL Server/PC communications, 530
devices
   disk, 56
   dump, 56
   logical, 55-56
   SQL Server configuration, 236
DFDs (data flow diagrams),
   122-124, 132
diagnosing problems for SQL
   Server connections, 540
diagrams
   bubble, in example applications, 130
   context, in example applications, 130
   data flow, 122-124
   development for databases, CASE tools,
      595-596
   entity relationship, 124-127
dialog boxes
   Connect Database, PowerBuilder, 572
   SQL Server Connect, Windows cursor
      program, 519
dictionary sort order, databases,
   193
directories, Sybase home, interfaces
   file, 192
dirty pages, 649
disks
   configurations, server configurations,
      423
   disk-based dump devices, 273
   devices, 56
   dump devices, syntax for backups, 274
   failures, data integrity, 175
   mirroring, database security, 184
   partitions, HP-UX platform, 207
   storage, SQL Servers, 194
DISKINIT script, restoring
   databases from, 276
distinct keyword, views, 617
distributed databases, 649

distributed database support and
  Replication Servers, 23-24
distributed transactions, 365
documentation specialists and
  client/server systems, 107-109
documenting key relationships
  with systems procedures, 304-306
documents, word processing,
  accessing data, 589
domains, 599-600, 649
DOS, Sybase NLMs and PCs, 534
drag-and-drop, PowerBuilder
  support, 577
drop sp_ procedures, 285
dropping procedures, syntax for,
  342
DSLISTEN environment variable,
  191
dump device file, 273
dump device script, 273
dump devices, 56, 649
    defining for databases, 272-274
    disk-based, 273
    reloading databases from, 276-278
    restoring master devices, 278
    storage, 179
    transaction logs, 272
dump striping, 613
DUMP TRAN command, 275
dumping multiple devices,on
  networks, 613
DWB (DataWorkBench), 8
dynamic compilation, Build
  Momentum kernel, 562
dynamic cursor, 389

E

E-R Win tool, 582, 594, 597-598
embedded SQL, 649
encapsulation of objects in OOP,
  82

encryption of passwords, 613
END statement, blocks, 356
end users
    and client/server systems, 101
    developers and client/server systems,
      101-102
    interviewing for applications updating,
      117
    query applications in conflict with data
      models, 145
    solutions in systems development, 76
engine for SQL Server, 60-63
enhancements and new options,
  SQL Server Release 10.0,
  622-623
enterprise client/server computing,
  633
enterprise client/server systems, 70
entities, 649
    cardinality between, in database
      development, 142
    intersection, for tables in databases, 151
    linking through physical data models,
      146
    many-to-many relationships in logical
      data models, 151
    with identifiers in data models, 147
entity identifiers, concatenated
  keys, 147
entity relationship diagrams (Peter
  P. Chen), 122
entity relationship modeling, 124
environment variables
    DSLISTEN, 191
    Sybase, 190-191
EPSS (electronic support systems),
  11
Epstein, Robert, Sybase co-
  founder, 4
equi-joins, joining tables, 162, 649
ERD (entity relationship diagrams), 124-127
    designing with CASE tools, 127
    first-level diagrams, 125

identifying objects in databases, 142
in example applications development, 134

err_handler() function, 441

error and message handlers, 441

@@error global variable, 362

error handling
applications, Open Client DB-Library, 441-442
stored procedures, listing 4.6.1., 362-363
TransAct SQL, 322
transactions, 361-364

error messages, 546-547, 650

errorlog file, 198

/etc/checklist file, HP-UX platform, 212

Ethernet LANs
ATM, 641
performance example, 635

evaluating SQL Server system needs, 33-37

event-driven triggers, 7

example client/server applications, 129-135

examples of queries, 165-166

Excelerator tool, 595

exclusive locks, 371, 650

exec command, stored procedures in batch statements, 357

existing resources, using in Sybase systems, 70

expanding database sizes, 227

expressions, 650

extending segments with sp_helpdevice procedure, 299-301

extent locks, 373, 650

extents, writing with create index command, 621

F

failure
hardware, 541
networks, 175-176

fast bulk copy utility, 555

fatal errors, 650

feedback in systems development, 86

fetch function, cursor row position, 391

fields, 650

files
autoexec.ncf, SQL Server NLM with TCP/IP services, 214
database dump, 274
dump device, 273
errorlog, 198-200
/etc/checklist, HP-UX platform, 212
installation, 190
interfaces, Sybase home directory, 192
Open Client DB-Library for PC/DOS, 456
Open Client DB-Library for PC/Windows, 466
termcap, 55

fill factor, SQL Server configuration, 235

first normal form normalization, 410

first-level ER diagrams, 125

float datatype, 246

floating-point datatypes, 246-247

flow charts, application specifications, 114

FM radio bandwidth (18 khz), 634

FORCEPLAN statement, FROM clause, 407-408

foreign exchange companies and SQL Servers, 31-33

foreign key triggers, 351

foreign keys, 650
    child tables, 147
    in tables, referential integrity, 348
    linking tables in databases, 146
form following function, client/
    server system applications,
    112-114
forms
    client/server retrievals, 171
    reviewing manuals for query modeling,
      158
Frame Relay network services,
    640-641
FrameMaker, batch printing, 590
FROM clause, FORCEPLAN
    statement, 407-408
front-end processes, 5-6
FTP PCTCP for DOS network
    driver, 533
FTP Software packet drivers,
    UNIX-based SQL Servers,
    536-537
functions, 650
    abort_xact(), 367
    aggregate, 330-332
    built-in, 249, 647
    bulk copy, 520-524
    close_xact(), 367
    commit_xact(), 367
    convert, 249
    date, 315
    dateadd, 329
    datediff, 328
    datename, 328
    datepart, 328
    dateparts, 329
    datetime, 327-330
    DB-Library, 442-449
    dbaltbind(), 439
    dbbind(), 438
    dbclose(), 440
    dbcmd(), 435
    dbcursoropen, 390
    dbdata(), 439

    dbdataready(), 438
    dbexit(), 440
    dbfcmd(), 436
    dblogin(), 434
    dbopen, 434
    dbproc, 433
    dbresults(), 437-439
    dbsqlexec(), 436-437
    dbuse(), 434
    err_handler(), 441
    fetch, 391
    for Windows programs from Open
      Client DB-Library, 497-500
    IF UPDATE, 350
    ISNULL systems, 335
    mathematical, 315, 332-334
    msg_handler(), 441
    new built-in, 623-624
    object_name(), 373
    Open Client DB-Library, 432
      and C/C++ programs, 454
      cursor support, 391-392
      programming, 442-449
    open_commit(), 367
    PowerBuilder, 577
    remove_xact, 367
    start_xact(), 367
    string, 249-250
    string manipulation, 326-327
    substring, 250-251
    system, 334-335, 655
    tsequal(), 375
    type conversion, 656

G

Gain Momentum client/server
    tools, 10
Gain Momentum tool, 560
global consulting and SQL Servers,
    24-27
global variables, 362, 650
grant statements
    permissions for stored procedures, 266
    permissions to users, 265
    rights to groups, 264
    setuser command, 268

graphical objects, Build Momentum tool, 562
GROUP BY clause, aggregate functions, 331
GROUP BY modifier, SELECT command, 160
groups, 650
    assigning logins for SQL Server, 262-268
    granting rights, 264
    permissions, 264-265
    revoking permissions, 266
    setting up on SQL Servers, 262
guests, 650
GUIs (graphical user interfaces)
    client/server systems, 105
    development tools, 561
    PowerBuilder development environment, 573-574

H

hard disk configurations, servers, 423
hard disk failures, data integrity, 175
hard disk storage, 194
hard disks, splitting databases across, 241
hardware
    communications in LANs, 529-530
    server performance optimization, 423-425
hardware failures, 541
hardware resources and logical device names, 153
HAVING clause, aggregate functions, 331
health care facilities and SQL Servers, 30-31
help documentation, 107
help sp_ procedures, 285
hierarchical, 650

Hoffman, Mark B., Sybase co-founder, 4
holdlocks, 374
home users, remote client/server systems, 633
host platform performance in systems optimization, 403
HP ARPA Services network driver, 533
HP-UX platform
    /etc/checklist file, 212
    logical volume subdirectories, 206
    ownership and create information, 211-212
    SQL Server installation on logical volumes, 205-213
    volume group manager, 207-211
human ear bandwidth, 634

I

IBM AIX OS, server installation, 205
IBM-compatibles, server connections, 526
identical disk devices, scripts, 226-227
identical disk/database structure, server configuration, 223
identifiers, 651
    entities in tables, concatenated keys, 147
    of entities in data models, 147
IDENTITY column, 615
IDs
    for login, 263
    suid (Server user ID), 655
IEF tool, 595
IF UPDATE function, update triggers, 350
image datatype, 248
implicit conversion, 651

in-house experts and client/server
systems, 100
incomplete transactions and data
integrity, 180-181
indexes
    clustered, 255-257, 406
    clustered/nonclustered, server design
        optimization, 396-397
    columns, WHERE clauses, 396
    limiting CREATE permissions, 149
    locking, 371
    nonclustered, 257-259, 652
    SQL Server tables, 255-259
    unique clustered, 256
information gathering techniques,
    client/server systems construction,
    115-129
inheritance
    Build Momentum tool, 562
    of objects in OOP, 83
inner queries, 651
INSERT command, SQL queries,
    164-165
INSERT statement, adding values
    to tables, 164
inserted table triggers, 349
inserting rows in tables with views,
    254
installation
    communication drivers, 534-537
    HP-UX platform, 205-213
    manual, SQL Server 4.2, 216-220
    Net-Libraries, 531
    Open Client DB-Library, 455
        Open Client DB-Library for PC/
        DOS, 455-460
        Open Client DB-Library for PC/
        Windows, 466-468
    OS/2 SQL Servers, LAN Manager,
        215-216
    SQL Servers, 190-202
        IBM AIX OS, 205
        Novell NLM, 213-214
        Solaris OS, 205
        SunOS 4.x, 204
        UNIX, 204
    Sybase, 195-197
    sybload utility session, 196-197
installation files, 190
int (integer) datatypes, 246
integrated client/server systems, 70
integrated management systems
    and Open Server technology, 74
integration
    client/server systems into current
        systems, 40-41
    departmental systems with SQL Server,
        71-73
    systems across departments, 71-75
    users in client/server systems, 39-40
integrity
    data backup plans, 174
    database-level, 179
    security issues in physical data models,
        144
integrity constraints, 651
intent locks, 372, 651
interaction locks, 371-374
interactive bulk copy utility, 556
interface designers and client/server
    systems, 105-106
interfaces file, Sybase home
    directory, 192
internetworking devices, 632
interoperability of Sybase products,
    22-23
intersection entities for tables in
    databases, 151
intersection tables for relationships
    in databases, 151
interviewing user groups when
    developing new applications,
    117-122
IP addresses, 191-192
IPX/SPX networking number
    (Novell default), 190

ISDN (Integrated Services Digital Network), 641
ISNULL systems function, 335
ISO (International Standards Organization), Open Systems Interconnection model (OSI), 527
isolation levels, transactions, 618-619
ISQL (Interactive Structured Query Language) utility, 54, 214, 218, 552-554, 651

J

JAD (Joint Application Development), 81-82, 119, 651
joining tables, 651
    Cartesian Product, 162
    equi-joins, 162
    JOIN command/statement, 162
    not-equal joins, 163
    outer joins, 163
    SELECT command, 160
    self-joins, 163

K

kernel, 651
    Build Momentum, 561-562
    SQL Server, 53, 60
    memory allotment, 201
key questions in applications analysis, 121
key relationships, documenting with systems procedures, 304-306
keyboard shortcuts/quick keys in client/server systems, 105
Keymap Editor, Build Momentum tool, 565
keys, 651
    alternate, linking tables, 147
    artificial, tables, 147

concatenated, entity identifiers, 147
foreign, linking tables in databases, 146
primary, data models, 146
tables, 240
keyset-driven cursor, 389
keywords, 651
    distinct, views, 617
    holdlock, 374
    LIKE, 246, 330
    SQL, 320
    SQL Server Release 10.0, 616
khz (kilohertz), 634
kill command, 620
kilopackets in packet-switching networks, 639

L

LAN Manager Network Operating System (Microsoft), 215-216, 533
language support, Build Momentum tool, 562
languages
    Object Momentum, Build Momentum tool, 560
    PowerScript, PowerBuilder, 575
LANs
    communications hardware, 529-530
    Ethernet ATM, 641
        performance example, 635
    remote client/server systems, 632
    Token Ring ATM, 641
leaf levels, 651
legacy systems, 77-78
libraries, Open Client DB, 432-433
LIKE keyword, 246
LIKE qualifier, TransAct SQL, 323
LIKE statement, datetime functions, 329
linking entities through physical data models, 146

linking tables
    alternate keys, 147
    foreign keys, 146
listings
    3.4.1. sp_configure output, 232-233
    4.6.1. error handling and stored
        procedures, 362-363
    5.1.1. sample DB-Library program,
        450-451
    5.2.1. SQLTESTR.C program supplied
        with Open Client DB-Lib, 456-459
    5.2.2. modified sqltestr.c program,
        462-465
    5.2.3. sample DB-Library Windows
        application, 469-483
    5.2.4. template for DB-Lib applica-
        tions, 484-491
    5.2.5. second sample template, DB-Lib
        applications, 491-496
    5.2.6. sample two phase commit
        program, 498-500
    5.2.7. sample Windows program with
        cursor, 501-519
    5.2.8. Bulk Copy operations in C
        programs, 521-523
livelocks, 651
locks, 370-371, 651
    configuration, 235
    cursor methods , 390
    environment interaction, 371-374
logic bugs, applications, 182
logical data models, 125, 651
    data domains, 142
    defining/managing with CASE tools,
        141-142
    entities with many-to-many relation-
        ships, 151
    for SQL Server environments, 142-143
    identifying database members, 139
    in example applications, development,
        134
    parent-child relationships, 147
logical devices, 55-56
    databases, 228-229, 652
    disks
        database1_device script, 223-224
        naming physical hard disks, 152

logical operators, 159, 652
logical volumes, HP-UX platform,
    205-213
login ID SA, 613
login IDs, 55
login record, Windows test pro-
    gram, 468
LOGINREC structure, 434
logins, 652
    assigning to SQL Server users, 262-268
    DB-Lib applications, 433
logs
    and databases, 56-57
    SQL Server configuration, 222
    transactions
        backups, 275
        dump devices, 272
long-term evaluation of client/
    server systems, 38-39
lower-level data flow diagrams, 124
ls procedure, 378
ls_proc systems table, 381
ls_rule systems table, 381
ls_table systems table, 381
ls_trig systems table, 381
ls_view systems table, 381

M

management of corporations and
    server systems, 73-75
managing logical data models with
    CASE tools, 141-142
manipulating database objects,
    293-306
manipulating strings, built-in
    functions, (TransAct SQL),
    326-327
manuals, reviewing for query
    modeling, 158
many-to-many relationships, 151

mapping
  databases to processes in systems
    development, 85
  physical data models to SQL Server
    environment, 152-153
  process logic in systems development,
    88
Martin, James, RAD process
  (Rapid Application Development), 81
master databases, 55-57, 652
  configuration, 222
  restoring, 278-279
  systems tables, 58-59, 383-385
master devices, 652
master systems catalogs, 384
master tables, 652
master.dat (master database), 55,
  59
mathematical functions (TransAct
  SQL), 332-334
mathematical functions as rules,
  315
memory, 201
  configuration, 234
  kernel allotment, 201
  server optimization, 425
  system, 190, 194-195
memory model switches,
  SQLTESTR.C program, 461
Menu Editor, Build Momentum
  tool, 565
message handlers (Sybase), 441
messages, 652
metadata, 652
metaphors, database objects
  (PowerBuilder), 571
Method Editor, Build Momentum
  tool, 565
Microsoft
  LAN Manager Network Operating
    System, 533
  Microsoft Office, MSQuery utility,
    589-590

MSVC (Microsoft Visual C/C++),
    compiling Windows test program,
    467
  NDIS (Network Data Interchange
    Specification), 533-534
mirroring databases, system
  security, 184
model databases, 55-57
modeling
  based on application specifications,
    114-116
  databases
    E-R Win tool, 597-598
    systems development, 85
  entity relationships, 124
  existing processes in systems develop-
    ment, 85
  improved processes in systems
    development, 85
  queries, 158
modem transmission speeds, 19.2
  kbps (kilobits per second), 634
modifications
  data models, risks and costs of, 144-145
  problems in populated tables, 145
modified sqltestr.c program, listing
  5.2.2., 462-465
modified systems procedures, SQL
  Server Release 10.0, 626-627
modifiers
  GROUP BY, SELECT command, 160
  ORDER BY, SELECT command, 160
modulo, 652
money datatypes, 245-247
monitoring corporate management
  with client/server systems, 73-75
MS-Windows, Uniface, 10
msg_handler() function, 441
MSQuery utility, Microsoft Office,
  589-590
MSVC (Microsoft Visual C/C++),
  compiling Windows test program, 467
multilingual databases, 193

multiple database management,
CASE tools, 603-604
multiple devices
dumping, 613
tables located on, 241
multiple PCs, server connections,
537
multiple servers
transactions, 361
two-phase commit, 364
multiple tables
SELECT command, 160-161
SQL statements, 321
multiprocessor server platforms,
disk mirroring, 184
multithreading in SQL server
architecture, 7-8, 53

N

Named Pipes Networks network
driver, 533-534
natural joins, 652
NDIS (Network Data Interchange
Specification), Microsoft,
533-534
nested commit tran statement, 361
nested detail levels in data flow
diagrams, 123
nested queries, 398, 652
nested select statements as
subqueries, 159
nested stored procedures, tables,
150
nested triggers, 179, 233, 236, 353
nesting transactions, 361
Net Libraries (Sybase), 62-63,
530-532, 652
connecting related departments, 72
Net-Library Installation Utility, 532
Open Client DB-Library server
connections, 433

Net-Library for DOS, 531
Net-Library for Windows, 531
NetWare servers and SQL Server,
TCP/IP connectivity, 214
network addresses, 190
network architect and client/server
systems, 106
network cards, 529-530
network connections to SQL
Servers, 62
network dumping, 613
Network Handler, 61, 64
networking numbers
IPX/SPX (Novell default), 190
pipes (OS/2 default), 190
networking protocol, Novell IPX/
SPX, 213-214
networks
compression and transmission speeds,
635
failure and data integrity, 176
model, OSI (Open Systems Interconnection model), 527
optimizing performance, 425-426
packet-switching, 639-640
problem diagnosis for SQL Servers,
541-544
Sybase, from user perspective, 526-528
transport software, 63
Netx versions, SQL Server NLM,
214
new database options/systems
procedures, SQL Server Release
10.0, 624-627
new WAN solution options,
640-641
newtable table, 243
NO EXEC statement, query plans,
406
NO_MORE_ROWS condition,
dbresults() function, 439
non-rewinding tape devices,
loading Sybase, 195

nonclustered indexes, 257-259, 652
  optimization of use, 397
  SQL Server design optimization, 396
  unique, 258
normalization, 652
  benefits, 411
  databases
    and design optimization, 395
    benefits of, 395
  forms of, 410
not equal to (!=) operations, table scans, 406
not null columns, tables, 243
not-equal joins, joining tables, 163
Novell
  IPX/SPX
    default networking number, 190
    networking protocol, SQL Server NLM, 213-214
  ODI (Open Data-Link Interconnect), 533
  Sybase operating system files, 200
  sybinst utility, 197
Novell LAN Workplace for DOS network driver, 533
Novell LAN Workplace for Windows network driver, 533
Novell NLM, SQL Server installation, 213-214
null-valued operands, 619, 653
numeric datatypes, SQL Server Release 10.0, 615

O

object, 653
Object encapsulation (OOP), 82
object inheritance in OOP, 83
object lists with sp_help command, 291-292
Object Momentum language, Build Momentum tool, 560

object names (SQL), 320
object owners, 653
object permissions, 653
object polymorphism, 83
object reusability (OOP), 82
object_name() function, 373
objectives in example application, 129
objects
  as classes in CRC card applications analysis, 127
  database, 57-58
    creation permissions, 149-150
    data model development, 138
    physical data models, 151-152
  graphical, Build Momentum tool, 562
ODI (Open Data-Link Interconnect), Novell, 533
office systems, departmental/branch, 77-78
older development models and client/server systems, 44
OLE (Object Linking and Embedding), PowerBuilder, 577
OLTP (On-Line Transaction Processing)
  database engines, 52
  RDBMS, 356
Omni Server Gateway, multiple server transactions, 361
OmniSQL Gateway, 9
  corporate management databases, 74
  interoperability of, 22
  tying systems together, 70
OOP (object-oriented programming)
  Build Momentum tool, 560-561
  systems development, 82-83
open architecture
  DB-LIB, 33
  SQL Servers, 21

Open Client DB Libraries, remote client/server systems, 432-433, 638
  application error handling, 441-442
  applications creation process, 433
  bulk copy functions, 520-524
  DB-Lib applications, 433-442
  functions for Windows programs, 497-500
  including calls in Windows programs, 465-466
  installation, 455
  language versions, 432
  programming functions, 442-449

Open Client DB-Library
  API cursor program, 500
  functions, 432, 454
    cursor support, 391-392
    software, 364

Open Client DB-Library for PC/DOS, 432, 455-460

Open Client DB-Library for PC/Windows, 466-468

Open Client Net-Libraries, 62, 531

Open Client software
  connecting related departments, 72
  two-phase commit transactions, 366

open databases default, SQL Server configuration, 235

open objects, SQL Server configuration, 235

Open Server technology and integrated management systems, 74

Open Server toolkit, 8, 70

Open Solutions Catalog (Sybase), 42

Open Solutions Directory, 14

open_commit() function, 367

operating system files (Sybase), 200

operating systems, 52-54, 653

operations, != (not equal to), table scans, 406

operations divisions between PCs in remote client/server systems, 636-638

operations of cursors in applications, 390-392

operators
  comparison, WHERE clause, 159
  logical, WHERE clause, 159
  UNION, SELECT command, 160

optimistic concurrency control, 390

optimization
  performance
    client/server systems, 402
    data pages, 414
    database objects, 413-414
    server hardware, 423-425
    WANs (Wide-Area networks), 426
  query examples, 410
  query structure in SQL Servers, 397-399
  SQL Server design, 394-396
    guidelines for improvement, 408-410
    performance issues, 400-402
    performance measures, 399-400
  SQL Servers, 394
  systems, host platform performance, 403

Optimizer, 61, 64

optimizers, query processing, 404

options
  ISQL utility, 553
  SET FIPS FLAGGER ON, 618

Oracle 7, 9-10

Oracle servers in OmniSQL Gateways, 74

ORDER BY clause
  ascending sort order, 335
  select statement, 335

ORDER BY modifier, SELECT command, 160

orphans in tables, 147

OS/2
  default networking numbers, pipes, 190
  LAN Manager installation, 215-216

SQL Server version 4.2, 214-216
Sybase operating system files, 200

OSI (Open Systems Interconnection model), network model, 527

outer joins, 653

outer queries, 653

output, changing order for queries, 335

overview of components when installing SQL Servers, 54-60

overwriting tape drives, 273

ownership and create information, HP-UX platform, 211-212

P

packet drivers, FTP Software, 533, 536-537

packet-switching networks, 639-640
  privately developed, 640
  X.25, 640

PAD (Packet Assembly/Disassembly device), 639

page locking
  concurrency control for data access, 370
  table locking, 374

painters, PowerBuilder, 572

parameters, 653
  allow duplicate rows, clustered indexes, 257
  defaults in stored procedures, 342
  defncopy utility, 556
  stored procedures, 342
  unique, clustered indexes, 256

parent tables, 126, 147

parent-child relationships, logical data models, 147

Parser, 61, 64

partitions
  HP-UX platform, 207
  SQL Server databases, 194

passwords
  encryption, 613
  user logins, 263

PATHWORKS (DECnet) network driver, 533

PCs
  device drivers for SQL Server communications, 530
  LAN communications hardware, 529-530
  multiple server connections, 537
  Open Client DB-Library for PC/DOS, 432
  SQL Server communications, 528-529
  SQL Server connections, 526
  Sybase NLMs and DOS, 534

performance
  host platforms in systems optimization, 403
  issues in SQL Server design optimization, 400-402
  LAN Ethernet example, 635
  measures, SQL Server design optimization, 399-400
  networks
    optimizing, 425-426
    compression, 635
  optimization
    data pages, 414
    database objects, 413-414
    in client/server systems, 402
    server hardware, 423-425
    SQL Servers, 404

permissions, 653
  CREATE, limiting for indexes/tables, 149
  create table, 243
  databases, 183
  defaults, 182
  for database object creation, 149-150
  for groups, 264
  granting by systems administrator, 262, 265-268
  group scripts, 265
  revoking from groups, 266

physical data models, 125, 653
  database objects, 151-152
  implementation of elements in
    databases, 145-149
  integrity/security issues, 144
  linking entities, 146
  managing databases, 148
  mapping to SQL Server environment,
    152-153
physical database implementation
  plans, 200-201
Ping utility, 532
pipes, OS/2 default networking
  number, 190
platforms, SQL Server installation,
  204
polymorphism of objects in OOP,
  83
populated tables, modification
  problems, 145
ports, query, 190
positioning current row of cursor,
  389
potential problems and risks of
  client/server systems, 43-48
Power Maker (PowerSoft), 580-
  581
PowerBuilder tool (PowerSoft), 10,
  570-571
  ancestor windows, 573
  Connect Database dialog box, 572
  cursors, 577
  database object metaphors, 571
  DataWindows, 574-576
  DDE (Dynamic Data Exchange), 577
  descendent windows, 574
  drag-and-drop support, 577
  functions, 577
  GUI development environment,
    573-574
  OLE (Object Linking and Embedding),
    577
  PowerScript language, 575

structures, 577
  Windows program development,
    578-580
  Windows client software development,
    571
PowerScript language,
  PowerBuilder, 575
PowerViewer (PowerSoft), 580-
  581
PPP (Point to Point Protocol), 638
predefined values as rules, 314
prepare transaction statement, 367
Prevent Dirty Reads isolation level,
  618
Prevent Nonrepeatable Reads
  isolation level, 619
Prevent Phantoms isolation level,
  619
primary keys, 653
  data models, 146
  for tables
    physical data model, 151
    referential integrity, 348
  parent tables, 147
PRINT statement (TransAct SQL),
  322
printing batch reports, 586, 590
private packet-switching networks,
  640
privileges
  databases, granted by systems adminis-
    trator, 183
  user tables, 182
problems
  diagnosing for server connections, 540
  modifications to populated tables, 145
  networks, diagnosing for servers,
    541-544
procedure cache, SQL Server
  configuration, 235
procedures
  create procedure ls_proc, 382
  create procedure ls_rule, 383

create procedure ls_table, 381
create procedure ls_trig, 381
create procedure ls_view, 383
create procedure pwd, 382
create procedure whoami, 382
database object manipulation, 293-306
ls, 378
pwd, 378
remote, 344
sp_addgroup, 290
sp_bindefault, 312
sp_clearstats, 626
sp_commonkey, 306
sp_dboption, 298
sp_defaultlanguage, 286
sp_depends, 294
sp_depends trigger_name, 352
sp_dropalias, 292
sp_dropgroup, 292
sp_dropuser, 292
sp_estspace, 416-422
sp_extendsegment, 299-301
sp_foreignkey, 305
sp_getitle, 342
sp_getitlebydate, 342
sp_help, 291, 620
sp_helpdevice, 300
sp_helpgroup, 289
sp_helpindex, 295
sp_helpjoins, 296
sp_helpkey, 305
sp_helplanguage, 287
sp_helplog, 302
sp_helprotect, 290
sp_helpsegment, 299, 620
sp_helpsort, 293
sp_helptext, 294
sp_helptext trigger_name, 352
sp_helptext ziprule, 313
sp_locks, 372
sp_logdevice, 302
sp_placeobject, 303
sp_primarykey, 304
sp_rename, 296, 352, 378
sp_renamedb, 297
sp_reportstats, 626
sp_spaceused, 415

sp_unbindefault, 312
stored
    created by developers, 150
    data integrity, 179
    nested in tables, 150
    performing tasks for developers, 150
    referential integrity, 152
    writing, 340
syntax for dropping, 342
use model, 316
whoami, 378
process logic, mapping in systems
    development, 88
processes in application specifica-
    tion models, 114-116
program development and client/
    server models, 36-37
programmable databases, 6
programming functions, Open
    Client DB-Library, 442-449
programs
    C bulk copy operations (listing 5.2.8.),
        521-523
    C/C++, and Open Client DB-Library
        functions, 454
    cursor, Open Client DB-Library API,
        500
    dataserver, 55
    DB-Library sample (listing 5.1.1.),
        450-451
    dbwintst, 468
    modified sqltestr.c (listing 5.2.2.), 462-
        465
    SQLTEST3.C (listing 5.2.3.), 468-483
    SQLTESTR.C (Open Client DB-Lib)
        listing 5.2.1., 456-465
    TSRs (Terminate and Stay Resident
        programs), 528
    two phase commit sample (listing
        5.2.6.), 498-500
    Windows
        cursor, 519
        development with PowerBuilder,
        578-580
        including Open Client DB-Library
        calls, 465-466

Open Client DB-Library functions,
497-500
test, compiling in MSVC (Microsoft
Visual C/C++), 467
with cursors (listing 5.2.7.), 501-519
Windows/DB-Library templates, 484-
496
project leader/manager/sponsor of
client/server systems, 98-100
projects, 24-33, 653
protocol
Novell IPX/SPX networking SQL
Server NLM, 213-214
two-phase commit, 365
prototyping applications in systems
development, 86
ps -ef command (UNIX), 403
pseudo-coding in systems development, 76
PSTAT.EXE utility, Windows 32
SDK, 216
publishing databases, 586
pubs database
data retrieval with stored procedures,
341
transactions, 359
PVCS manager, 582
pwd procedure, 378
pwd systems table, 381

Q

qualifications, SELECT command,
159
qualifiers, 323, 653
queries, 654
ad hoc, 157
data models, 143
data retrieval, 324
design optimization, 395
determining plans with NO EXEC
statements, 406
example for client/server systems
operations, 64-65

examples of approaches, 165-166
nested, server optimization, 398
optimization examples, 410
placing into stored procedures, 340
resource-intensive, 398
results sets, 398
round function, 333
single character retrieval, 324
sorting results, 335-337
SQL, 156, 159-160
SQL Server processing optimizers, 404
string functions, 327
view resolution of, 656
WHERE clause, 325
Query Editor, Build Momentum
tool, 565
query optimizer, 162
enhancements, 621
indexing options, 396
query plans, 62
query ports, 53, 64, 190
query specifications, data retrieval,
158
query structure, server optimization, 397-399
query types, 158-165
questionnaires, 117, 171
quick keys and interface designers
in client/server systems, 105

R

RAD process (Rapid Application
Development), 81
RAISERROR statements,
TransAct SQL, 322
RAM, server optimization, 424
raw partitions
SQL Server configuration, 225
UNIX systems, 200
RDB servers in OmniSQL Gate-
ways, 74
RDBMS (Remote Database
Management Systems), 320

read locks, 371
read-only cursors, 388
real datatypes, 247
rebooting, troubleshooting SQL
  Server problems, 542
RECONFIGURE command, 232
RECONFIGURE WITH OVER-
  RIDE command, 232
recovering databases from dump
  devices, 276
recovery flags, SQL Server configuration, 236
redundancy, denormalization for
  databases, 412
redundant data storage, 410-411
referential integrity, 654
    CASE tools, 602-603
    data integrity, 176-179
    database structures, 126
    declarative, 348
    keys in tables, 147
    stored procedures, 152
    table-level, 178
    triggers, 348-353
relational databases
    and client/server architecture, 4-5
    data retrieval with SQL, 320
relational models in systems
  development, 88
relationships, many-to-many, 151
release notes, Sybase, 190-191
reloading databases from dump
  devices, 276-278
remote access, 236
remote client/server systems, 632
    connection speed restriction (9.6 Kbps),
     642
    design solutions, 642-643
    Open Client DB Libraries, 638
    operations divisions between PCs, 636-
     638
    WANs, 638-640

remote clients in client/server
  systems, 632-633
remote logins, 236
remote procedure calls, transactions, 360-361
remote procedures, 344
remote servers, communication
  with, 199-200
remove_xact function, 367
repeaters, internetworking devices,
  632
Replication Server (System 10), 11,
  633
    distributed database support, 23-24
    multiple server transactions, 361
reports
    batch, 586
    batch and user-generated, 170-172
    database schema, CASE tools, 601
requirements, software, program
  development, 455
resource balancing in database
  design, 152
resource requirements, Sybase
  installation, 201-202
resource-intensive queries, 398
resources, hardware and logical
  device names, 153
responsibilities in client/server
  systems, 96
restoration, databases, 272
restoring databases
    from DISKINIT scripts, 276
    master databases, 278-279
restricting privileges, 183
restrictions, 654
    cursors, 391
    stored procedures, 344
    transactions, 364
result codes, SQL statements, 321
results of queries, sorting, 335-337

results sets of queries, 398

retrieving data for batch reports, 172

retrieving data from datetime functions, 329-330

return codes (status messages), 321

returned results, DB-Lib applications, 437-440

returning status messages from stored procedures, 343-344

returning values from stored procedures, 343-344

reusability
Build Momentum tool, 562
of objects in OOP, 82

review/refinement of systems development, 86

reviewing manuals and forms for query modeling, 158

revoking permissions from groups, 266

rewinding/non-rewinding tape device, loading Sybase, 195

rights, granting to groups, 264

risk management (insurance) and SQL Servers, 29-30

risks/costs, data model modifications, 144-145

roles and responsibilities, defining in client/server systems, 96-109

rollback, transaction processing, 356

rollback statements
stored procedures, 360
triggers, 361

rollback tran command, 360

rollback transaction, 654

ROLLBACK TRANSACTION statement, 358

root user, UNIX Sybase user, 191

row aggregate functions, 654

row retrieval structures, 324

row-level locking, 370

rows, 654
cursor operations, 388
inserting in tables with views, 254
obtaining cursor position with fetch function, 391
positioning cursors in, 389
timestamps, optimistic concurrency control, 390

rules, 654
binding to database columns for data integrity, 178
data integrity, 310-315
date functions as, 315
expanded database formats, 313
mathematical functions as, 315
predefined values as, 314
TransAct SQL, 322
user-defined datatypes, 316-317

rules for configuration of servers, 222-227

run_value variable, 233

RUNSERVER command, SQL Server startup, 197

S

SA systems administrator, 191, 613

sample DB-Library program (listing 5.1.1.), 450-451

sample DB-Library Windows application (listing 5.2.3.), 469-483

sample two phase commit program (listing 5.2.6.), 498-500

sample Windows program with cursor (listing 5.2.7.), 501-519

sar command (UNIX), 403

save tran command, 360

SAVE TRANSACTION statement, 358

savepoint, 654

scalability of SQL Servers, 22

scalar aggregate, 654

scribes, CASE tools, 596

scripts
  adding users to SQL Servers, 262
  aliasing users, 267
  database backups, 274
  database1, books table example, 241
  database1_device, logical disk device, 223-224
  DISKINIT, restoring databases from, 276
  dump device, 273
  dump devices, 272
  granting rights to groups, 264
  group permissions, 265
  identical disk devices, 226-227

SDMs (systems development methodologies), 75

second normal form normalization, 410

security
  client/server systems, 182-185
  data, unauthorized access, 175
  data backup plans, 174
  databases, 174, 183-184
  mirroring databases, 184

security features, SQL Server Release 10.0, 613

security issues in physical data model, 144

segments
  database9_/10_devices, books table example, 242
  extending with sp_helpdevice procedure, 299-301
  logical database devices, 228-229
  specified, creating tables on, 242
  two_device_seg, books table example, 243

SELECT command
  modifiers, 160
  multiple tables, 160-161
  qualifications, 159
  SQL queries, 159-160

UNION operator, 160
  WHERE clause, 159

select list, 654

SELECT statement, 160-161

SELECT statements, triggers, 352

select statements
  browse mode, 375
  creating views, 252
  defining cursors, 388-390
  nested as subqueries, 159

self-join, 654

self-joins, joining tables, 163

serial number, SQL Server configuration, 236

servers, 654
  multiple PC connections, 537
  Open Client DB-Library/Net-Library connections, 433
  programmable, 7
  sybase name, 192
  UNIX, SQL Server installation, 190

SET FIPS FLAGGER ON option, 618

SET SHOWPLAN ON command, 404-407

SET statement, 322

setuser command, user permissions, 268

severity level number, 654

shared locks, 371, 655

short-term evaluation of client/server systems, 38-39

side-by-side development models, 83-84

Silverrun tool, 595

single character retrieval queries, 324

sizes of teams for systems development, 83

sleeping processes, kill command, 620

SLIP (Serial Link Internet Protocol), 638

slow bulk copy utility, 555
smalldatetime datatype, 249
smallint datatype, 246
smallmoney datatype, 245, 247
SMDS (Switched Multimegabit Data Service), 641
software
  communications drivers, 532-534
  components of server development environment, 52
  development for client/server systems, 116
  Open Client DB-Library, 364
    connecting related departments, 72
    two-phase commit transactions, 366
  requirements, SQL Server program development, 455
  SQL Servers, 54-55
  third-party for SQL Servers, 588
  Windows-based clients, PowerBuilder, 571
Solaris OS, SQL Server installation, 205
sort order
  ascending, ORDER BY clause, 335
  SQL Server databases, 192-193
  SQL Server version 1.X, 217
sorting query results, 335-337
sp_ procedures, add, help, drop, 285
sp_addalias command, 288
sp_addgroup systems procedure, 290
sp_addlogin statement, user logins, 263
sp_addsegment stored procedure, 228
sp_addserver command, 199
sp_addumpdevice statement, dump devices, 272
sp_adduser command, 288
sp_bindefault system procedure, 312

sp_changedbowner command, 287
sp_clearstats procedure, 626
sp_commonkey procedure, 306
sp_configure command, 194, 233
sp_configure stored procedure (listing 3.4.1.), 232-237
sp_dboption procedure, 298
sp_defaultdb command, 286
sp_defaultlanguage procedure, 286
sp_depends system procedure, 294
sp_depends trigger_name procedure, 352
sp_dropalias procedure, 292
sp_dropgroup procedure, 292
sp_dropuser procedure, 292
sp_estspace procedure, 416-422
sp_extendsegment procedure, 301
sp_extendsegment system procedure, 299
sp_foreignkey system procedure, 305
sp_getitle stored procedure, 342
sp_getitlebydate procedure, 342
sp_help command, 291-292
sp_help systems procedure, 620
sp_helpdevice procedure, 300
sp_helpgroup procedure, 289
sp_helpgroup stored procedure, 289
sp_helpindex systems procedure, 295
sp_helpjoins systems procedure, 296
sp_helpkey procedure, 305
sp_helplanguage procedure, 287
sp_helplog systems procedure, 302
sp_helprotect procedure, 290
sp_helpsegment procedure, 299
sp_helpsegment systems procedure, 620

sp_helpsort system procedure, 293

sp_helptext command, 294

sp_helptext trigger_name procedure, 352

sp_helptext ziprule procedure, 313

sp_helpuser command, 285

sp_locks systems procedure, 372

sp_logdevice systems procedure, 302

sp_placeobject systems procedure, 303

sp_primarykey procedure, 304

sp_rename procedure, 352, 378

sp_rename system procedure, 296

sp_renamedb procedure, 297

sp_reportstats procedure, 626

sp_spaceused procedure, 415

sp_unbindefault systems procedure, 312

sp_who command, 285

specifications for client/server systems
   development, 45-46
   form following function, 112-114

splitting databases across disks, 241

spreadsheets, accounting, SQL Server storage, 72

sprintf program variable types, dbfcmd() function, 436

SQL (Structured Query Language), 320, 655
   clauses, 320
   keywords, 320
   queries, 156
      INSERT command, 164-165
      JOIN commands, 162
      SELECT command, 159-160
      user data requests, 158

SQL Editor, Build Momentum tool, 565

SQL LifeCycle graphical tools, 8-10

SQL object names, 320

SQL Servers
   concurrency control, 370
   design optimization
      nonclustered indexes, 396
      performance issues, 400-402
      performance measures, 399-400
   feature set, cursors, 388
   integrating departmental systems, 71-73
   integrating systems, 71-74
   locks, 370-371
   software components of development environment, 52

SQL Server 4.2 manual installation, 216-220

SQL Server configuration, raw partitions, 225

SQL Server Connect dialog box, Windows cursor program, 519

SQL Server kernel memory allotment, 201

SQL Server NLM, Novell IPX/SPX networking protocol, 213-214

SQL Server NLMs, Windows, 535-536

SQL Server query optimizer, indexing options, 396

SQL Server Release 10.0
   Backup Server, 612-613
   declarative referential integrity, 614
   enhancements and features, 610
   enhancements and new options, 622-623
   keywords, 616
   modified systems procedures, 626-627
   new built-in functions, 623-624
   new database options, 627
   new systems procedures, 624-626
   numeric datatypes, 615
   security features, 613
   support architecture changes, 611-627

SQL Server version 1.X
  sort order, 217
  strict compatibility code page, 217
SQL statements
  multiple tables, 321
  return codes (status messages), 321
  typical example, 321
SQLTEST3.C program (listing 5.2.3.), 468-484
SQLTESTR.C program (listing 5.2.1.), 456-465
SQLTESTR.C program, modified (listing 5.2.2.), 462-465
SSO (systems security officer), 613, 655
standardization in client/server systems, 78-79
start_xact() function, 367
statement batches, 356
statement blocks, 356, 655
statements, 655
  as stored procedures, 340
  batch, 647
  begin tran, 360-361
  BEGIN TRANSACTION, 358
  BEGIN/END, blocks, 356
  COMMIT TRANSACTION, 358
  COMPUTE BY, 337-338
  convert, 251
  create, books table example, 241
  create index, 258
  create view, 253
  DBSETLPWD, Windows test program, 468
  FORCEPLAN, FROM clause, 407-408
  grant, granting permissions to users, 265
  INSERT, adding values to tables, 164
  JOIN, Cartesian Product of tables, 162
  LIKE, datetime functions, 329
  nested commit tran, 361
  NO EXEC, query plans, 406
  prepare transaction, 367

RAISERROR (TransAct SQL), 322
rollback
  stored procedures, 360
  triggers, 361
ROLLBACK TRANSACTION, 358
SAVE TRANSACTION, 358
SELECT, 160-161
select
  browse mode, 375
  creating views, 252
  nested as subqueries, 159
SET SHOWPLAN ON (TransAct SQL), 404-407
sp_addlogin, user logins, 263
sp_addumpdevice, dump devices, 272
Table Scan, 405
transaction control, 358-364
typical SQL example, 321
view, SELECT * command, 163-164
see also commands
static cursors, 389
status messages
  returning from stored procedures, 343-344
  SQL statements, 321
stock exchange and SQL Servers, 27-28
storage of redundant data, 410-411
storage of accounting spreadsheets, 72
stored procedures, 284, 655
  accessing SQL Servers, 284-293
  and security, 183-184
  batch statements, 357
  created by developers, 150
  data integrity, 179
  default parameters, 342
  error handling (listing 4.6.1.), 362-363
  granting permissions for, 266
  in transactions, 360-361
  nested in tables, 150
  parameters, 342
  performing tasks for developers, 150
  placing queries into, 340
  referential integrity, 152
  restrictions, 344

returning status messages from, 343-344

returning values, 343-344

rollback statements, 360

sp_addsegment, 228

sp_configure, 232-237

statements as, 340

syntax, 341-342

systems table access, 381-383

systems tables, 379

TransAct SQL, 322

user data retrieval, 341

writing, 340

see also commands

storing database dumps, 179

strategies for indexing design optimization, 396

strict compatibility code page, SQL Server version 1.X, 217

string functions, 249-250, 326-327, 655

structured analysis methodologies in systems building, 121

structured diagramming techniques in systems development, 75

structures

database, data model applications support, 139-141

DBPROCESS, 434

LOGINREC, 434

PowerBuilder, 577

queries, SQL Server optimization, 397-399

row retrieval, TransAct SQL, 324

subdirectories, HP-UX platform, 206

subqueries, 655

aggregate functions, 331

nested select statements, 159

server optimization, 398

WHERE clauses, 159

substring functions, 250-251

suid (Server user ID), 655

summary values, denormalizing databases, 411

Sun Solaris OS, SQL Server installation, 205

SunOS 4.x operating system, SQL Server installation, 204

super-user identity, Sybase user, 191

support architecture changes in SQL Server Release 10.0, 611-627

support program for SQL server products, 10

switches

clustered indexes, 256

memory model, SQLTESTR.C program, 461

Sybase

API (Application Programming Interface), Open Client DB-Library, 432

Build Momentum, 561

client/server projects, 24-33

developers and database systems, 18

error and message handlers, 441

installation, 195-197

resource installation requirements, 201-202

TransAct SQL, 156

Sybase devices, 55-56

Sybase environment variables, 190-191

Sybase home directory, interfaces file, 192

Sybase Net Libraries, 530-532

Sybase NLMs, DOS PCs, 534

Sybase Open Solutions Catalog, 42

Sybase operating system files, 200

Sybase release notes, 191

sybconfig utility (UNIX), 197

sybinit utility, 612

sybinst utility, 197, 213

sybload utility, 195-197

sybsystemprocs database, 611

Syman utility, 54

syntax
cascading delete triggers, 350-351
clustered indexes, 255, 406
create database, 227
creating views, 252
data integrity defaults, 311
disk dump devices, 274
dropping columns from tables, 243
dropping procedures, 342
nonclustered indexes, 257
return status stored procedure, 343
SET SHOWPLAN ON command, 404-407
stored procedures, 341-342
Titleview view, 253
triggers, 349-350
unique nonclustered indexes, 258
sysalternates systems table, 379
syscolumns systems table, 379
sysconfigures systems table, 384
syscurconfigs systems table, 384
sysdatabases systems table, 384
sysdepends systems table, 380
sysdevices systems table, 384
sysindexes systems table, 379
syskeys systems table, 380
syslocks systems table, 384
syslogins systems table, 384
syslogs table, 180, 274
sysmessages systems table, 384
sysobjects systems table, 379
sysprocedures systems table, 380
sysprocesses systems table, 384
sysprotects systems table, 379
sysremotelogins systems table, 384
syssegments systems table, 380
sysservers systems table, 384
System 10 product package, 10
Navigation Server, 22
Replication Server, 11, 23
System Architect tool, 595
system databases, 655
system functions, 655

system memory for SQL Server, 190, 194-195
system procedures, 655
system requirements in example application, 130
system security, 182-185
system tables, 655
systems, integrating with SQL Server, 71-74
systems administration, TransAct SQL, 323
Systems Administration Facility, OS/2 SQL Server version 4.2, 214
systems administration tools, 24
systems administrator
database privileges, 183
granting permissions, 265
nested trigger support, 353
restoring master devices, 278
SA, 191
see also SA
systems architects and client/server systems, 102-103
systems catalogs, 58, 378
systems development
models, 74-80
OOP (object-oriented programming), 82-83
users as participants in, 78
systems failure, data integrity, 175-176
systems functions (TransAct SQL), 334-335
systems modeling, 75-77
systems optimization, host platform performance, 403
systems procedures
documenting key relationships, 304-306
modified for SQL Server Release 10.0, 626-627
new for SQL Server Release 10.0, 624-626

systems resource conflicts, 402

systems table, syslogs, 274

systems tables
  database information, 379
  in master database, 58-59
  master databases, 383-385
  SQL Server, 378-385
  stored procedures, 379
  stored procedures for access, 381-383

systypes systems table, 380

sysusages systems table, 384

sysusers systems table, 379

T

table create scripts, DDL (Data Definition Language), 127

table locking
  concurrency control for data access, 370
  page locking, 374

Table Scan statement, 405

table scans, != (not equal to) operations, 406

table segmentation, denormalization for databases, 412-413

table sizes, calculating, 414-423

table triggers and referential integrity, 152

table-level data integrity, 178-179

tables, 58, 655
  adding columns, 243-244
  adding values to INSERT statement, 164
  artificial keys, 147
  as database objects in physical data model, 151
  books example, 241
  cardinality relationships, 142
  Cartesian Product, JOIN statements, 162
  child, 126
    foreign keys, 147

contents, 240
create scripts, DDL (Data Definition Language), 127
creating on specified segments, 242
data retrieval with views, 252-254
database structures, 240-251
datatypes, 244-249
deleted (triggers), 349
deleting columns, 243
entity identifiers, concatenated keys, 147
indexes, 255-259
inserted (triggers), 349
inserting rows in with views, 254
intersection for relationships in databases, 151
joining
  equi-joins, 162
  not-equal joins, 163
  outer joins, 163
  SELECT command, 160
  self-joins, 163
limiting CREATE permissions, 149
linking
  alternate keys, 147
  foreign keys, 146
located on multiple devices, 241
multiple
  SELECT command, 160-161
  SQL statements, 321
nested stored procedures, 150
newtable, 243
not null columns, 243
orphans, 147
parent, 126, 147
populated, modification problems, 145
primary keys in rows (data models), 146
referential integrity, 348
referential integrity of keys, 147
syslogs, 274
systems, 378
timestamp columns, 375
transaction changes, commits, 358
trigger operations and referential integrity, 349
updating with views, 254

user privileges, 182
views, 656
tape devices
   database dumps, 179, 272
   overwriting as dump devices, 273
   rewinding/non-rewinding, loading
      Sybase, 195
tape retention, SQL Server configuration, 236
TCP/IP connectivity, 655
   NetWare/SQL Server, 214
   SQL Server NLM autoexec.ncf file, 214
technical specialists and client/
   server systems, 100
telephone bandwidth, 3khz
   (kilohertz), 634
tempdb database, 55-57, 222
templates
   DB-Lib applications (listing 5.2.4.),
      484-491
   second sample for DB-Lib applications
      (listing 5.2.5.), 491-524
   Windows/DB-Library programs,
      484-496
temporary tables, denormalizing
   databases, 411
termcap files, 55
terminal/host dial-in connections,
   636
terms of reference in example
   application, 129
testing database models with
   queries, 157
text datatypes, 246-248
theta joins, 656
third normal form normalization,
   410
third-party products for SQL
   Servers, 14-15, 588
threats and dangers to data security
   and integrity, 174-176
Threshold Manager, 612

throughput, data in network
   systems, 635
TIFF images, database publishing,
   172
time command (UNIX), 403
time datatypes, 248-249
time slice variable, 235
timestamp columns, tables, 375
timestamps on rows, optimistic
   concurrency control, 390
tinyint datatypes, 246
Titleview view, syntax, 253
Token Ring LANs and ATM, 641
toolbar, Database Browser, 565
tools
   Build Momentum, 560
   CASE (Computer-Assisted Software
      Engineering), 594-595
   DEFT, 594-595
   Er-Win, 582, 594
   Excelerator, 595
   Gain Momentum, 560
   IEF, 595
   PowerBuilder, 570-571
   Silverrun, 595
   System Architect, 595
top-down approach to systems
   modeling, 75-76
topologies, remote client/server
   systems, 636
@@trancount variable, 361
TransAct SQL, 156, 320
   compute clauses, 322
   control-of-flow language, 321
   data retrieval queries, 324
   datetime functions, 327-330
   defaults, 322
   defining cursors with select statements,
      388-390
   error handling, 322
   mathematical functions, 332-334
   rules, 322
   SET SHOWPLAN ON statement,
      404-407

SQL server query support, 158-165
statements, RAISERROR/PRINT/
  SET, 322
stored procedures, 322
systems administration, 323
systems functions, 334-335
transactions, 181
triggers, 322
wildcards, 323-325
writing stored procedures, 340
transaction logs, 656
  backups, 273
  data integrity, 180
  dump devices, 272
  syslogs systems table, 274
transactions, 656
  applications, two-phase commit, 181
  backups, 275
  chained, 618
  condition testing, 359
  containing batch statements within,
   358
  control statements, 358-364
  deadlocks, 373
  distributed, 365
  error handling, 361-364
  incomplete, and data integrity, 180-181
  isolation levels, 618-619
  multiple servers, 361
  nesting, 361
  pubs database, 359
  remote procedure calls, 360-361
  restrictions, 364
  stored procedures in, 360-361
  table changes, commits, 358
  TransAct SQL, 181
  two-phase commit, Open Client
   software, 366
  writing to databases, 356
transfer rates, server optimization,
  424
transmission speeds of modems,
  9.2 kbps (kilo bits per second),
  634

transparency of applications
  operations, 587
transport software, 63
triggers, 656
  as event-driven, 7
  cascading delete, 350-351
  data integrity, 178
  foreign key, 351
  guidelines for use, 352-353
  modifications to in Release 10.0,
   616-617
  nested, 179, 233, 353
  referential integrity, 348-353
  rollbacks, 361
  SELECT statements, 352
  syntax, 349-350
  table operations and referential
   integrity, 349
  TransAct SQL, 322
  update, IF UPDATE function, 350
  update example, 65
troubleshooting
  error messages, 546-547
  example, 544-545
  SQL Server problems, 544
tsequal() system function, 375
TSRs (Terminate and Stay Resident programs), 528
two-phase commit
  application transactions, 181
  for Windows programs, 497
  Open Client software transactions, 366
  sample program (listing 5.2.6.),
   498-500
  SQL Servers, 364-367
two_device_seg segment, books
  table example, 243
Tymnet packet-switching networks, 639
type conversion functions, 656
typical SQL statement example,
  321

U

unauthorized access, data security, 175

unbinding defaults from columns, 312

Uniface for MS-Windows/X-Windows, 10

UNION operator, SELECT command, 160

unique clustered indexes, 256

unique nonclustered indexes, syntax, 258

unique parameter, clustered indexes, 256

UNIX
   ps -ef command, 403
   raw partitions, 200
   sar command, 403
   SQL Server installation, 190, 204
     FTP Software packet drivers, 536-537
   sybconfig utility, 197
   time command, 403
   vmstat command, 403

unrecoverable deletions of data, 175

update locks, 371

update triggers
   example, 65
   IF UPDATE function, 350

updates
   databases, 656
   tables with views, 254

upgrading to SQL Server Release 10.0, 628

use model procedure, 316

user connections, servers, 234

user data requests, 158

user devices, 60-61

user groups, interviewing for application development, 117-122

user input/feedback in client/server systems, 101

user review of data models, 144

user walkthroughs of data models, 143-144

user-defined datatypes, 58, 316-317, 656

user-generated reports, 170-172

user.dat. (user device), 61

userdata database, 61

users
   adding to databases, 263
   aliasing, 267
   aliasing script, 267
   and client/server architecture, 35
   as focus in client/server systems, 114
   as participants in systems development, 78
   assigning logins for SQL Servers, 262-268
   data retrieval with stored procedures, 341
   default permissions, 182
   granting permissions, setuser command, 268
   integration in client/server systems, 39-40
   login passwords, 263
   observing interaction with current systems for application development, 116
   perspectives of Sybase network, 526-528
   remote client/server systems, 633
   reviewing data models, 144
   root, UNIX Sybase user, 191
   setting up on SQL Servers, 262
   side-by-side development of client/server applications, 84
   sybase, 191
   table privileges, 182
   value and utility of database, 139

utilities
   bcp (bulk copy), 54, 554-556
   buildmaster, 197
   bulk copy, 621

cperrlog, 198

debugger, Build Momentum tool, 563

defncopy, 556-557

Deployment, Build Momentum tool, 566

fast bulk copy, 555

interactive bulk copy, 556

ISQL (Interactive Structured Query Language), 54, 214, 218, 552-554

MSQuery, Microsoft Office, 589-590

Net-Library Installation, 532

Ping, 532

PSTAT.EXE, Windows 32 SDK, 216

slow bulk copy, 555

SQL Servers, 552

sybinit, 612

sybinst, 197, 213

sybload, 195-197

Syman, 54

V

values

adding to tables, INSERT statement, 164

binding for columns with dbbind command, 438

domain and column, bookstore application example, 599-600

returning from stored procedures, 343-344

varbinary datatype, 248

varchar datatype, 246-247

variables, 656

@@trancount, 361

config_value, 233

environment

DSLISTEN, 191

Sybase, 191

global, @@error, 362

run_value, 233

sprintf program types, dbfcmd() function, 436

SQL Server configuration, 232

Sybase environment, 190

time slice, 235

vector aggregates, 656

view resolution of queries, 656

view statement, SELECT * command, 163-164

views, 252-254

creating for retrievals in databases, 149

data retrieval in tables, 252-254

distinct keyword, 617

modifying data, 254

SELECT statement, 161

tables, 656

Titleview syntax, 253

VMS, Sybase operating system files, 200

vmstat command (UNIX), 403

volume group manager, HP-UX platform, 207-211

W

walkthroughs of data models by users, 143-144

WANs (Wide-Area Networks), 633

asynchronous dial-ups, remote client/server systems, 638

new solution options, 640-641

optimizing network performance, 426

remote client/server systems, 638-640

WHERE clause

aggregate functions, 331

comparison operators, 159

JOIN command, 162

logical operators, 159

SELECT command, 159

WHERE clauses

column indexes, 396

queries (TransAct SQL), 325

subqueries, 159

whoami procedure, 378

whoami systems table, 381

wildcards, 323-325, 656

Windows

client development, 571

development tools, PowerBuilder, 570

PowerBuilder program development,
578-580
SQL Server NLMs, 535-536
windows, ancestor/descendent,
PowerBuilder, 574
Windows 32 SDK, PSTAT.EXE
utility, 216
Windows NT SQL Server installation, 216-220
Windows programs
bulk copy, 497
cursor program Connect dialog box,
519
Open Client DB-Library
calls, 465-466
functions, 497-500
templates, 484-496
sample DB-Library (listing 5.2.3.),
469-483
two-phase commit, 497

test program
compiling in MSVC (Microsoft Visual
C/C++), 467
DBSETLPWD statement, 468
interpreting SQLTEST3.C, 484
word processing documents
accessing SQL Server data, 589
workstations, connecting PCs to
SQL Servers, 526
write locks, SQL Servers, 371
writing extents
create index command, 621
stored procedures, 340-342
transactions to databases, 356

X-Y-Z

X Windows, Uniface, 10
X.25 packet switching, 640

Wordⁿ
SYSTEMS

1801 One Yonge St.

Toronto On. M5E 1E5

Canada

phone:
(416) 597-9258

fax:
(416) 599-7942

Word N Systems, Inc...

Consulting

Word N Systems provides experienced team leaders and technical specialists to augment your client/server project. By working closely with your technical staff, users and management, WnS consultants can help you pull off that critical first or high visibility project.

Skills Transfer:

Organizations throughout the U.S. and Canada have gained valuable skills transfer and conceptual insight through WnS training courses. WnS provides both customized and standard courses in server and client software development tools and techniques.

DBA & Developer Tools

As experienced developers and administrators of client/ server systems, WnS staff know the practical day to day difficulties and challenges you face. To help you meet and beat them, we have developed a number of software tools and utilities.

Support:

Getting up to speed with new technology and practices is often not enough. The trick is to stay on top of them, as they evolve. WnS supplies on-going support to clients, based on their platforms, level of expertise and application requirements.

Contact us today for more info!

Add to Your Sams Library Today with the Best Books for Programming, Operating Systems, and New Technologies

The easiest way to order is to pick up the phone and call

1-800-428-5331

between 9:00 a.m. and 5:00 p.m. EST.

For faster service please have your credit card available.

ISBN	Quantity	Description of Item	Unit Cost	Total Cost
0-672-22804-1		Reorganizing MIS: The Evolution of Business Computing in the '90s	$34.95	
0-672-30153-9		Downsizing Information Systems	$39.95	
0-672-30382-5		Understanding Local Area Networks, Fourth Edition	$26.95	
0-672-30173-3		Enterprise Wide Networking	$39.95	
0-672-30180-6		Insider's Guide to Personal Computing and Networking	$29.95	
0-672-30119-9		International Telecommunications	$39.95	
0-672-30005-2		Understanding Data Communications, Third Edition	$24.95	
0-672-30293-4		TOP SECRET: Data Encryption Techniques (book/disk)	$24.95	
0-672-22790-8		Data Communications, Networks and Systems, Second Edition	$49.95	
0-672-30473-2		Client/Server Computing, Second Edition	$40.00	
0-672-30209-1		Netware Unleashed (book/disk)	$45.00	
0-672-30191-1		DB2 Developer's Guide	$59.95	

❏ 3 ½" Disk

❏ 5 ¼" Disk

Shipping and Handling: See information below.	
TOTAL	

Shipping and Handling: $4.00 for the first book, and $1.75 for each additional book. Floppy disk: add $1.75 for shipping and handling. If you need to have it NOW, we can ship product to you in 24 hours for an additional charge of approximately $18.00, and you will receive your item overnight or in two days. Overseas shipping and handling adds $2.00 per book and $8.00 for up to three disks. Prices subject to change. Call for availability and pricing information on latest editions.

201 W. 103rd Street, Indianapolis, Indiana 46290

1-800-428-5331 — Orders   1-800-835-3202 — FAX   1-800-858-7674 — Customer Service

Book ISBN 0-672-30467-8

Installing Your Disk

What's on the Disk

The disk contains DBA@Win, a powerful DBA tool that automates procedures such as grant/revoke rights and viewing stored procedures, rules, and triggers. It also contains an extensive help system.

Installing the Floppy Disk

The software included with this book is stored in a compressed form. You cannot use the software without first installing it to your hard drive. The installation program runs from DOS.

> **Note:**
>
> To install the files on the disk, you'll need at least 4.5M of free space on your hard drive.

1. Log onto the drive that contains the installation disk and type INSTALL drive, where *drive* is the letter of your hard drive. For example, INSTALL C: will copy the files from the installation disk to your C hard drive.
2. You many want to create a Windows Program Manager icon for the DBA@Win application. Please refer to your Windows documentation for instructions.

The files will be installed to the \SDG directory.

> **CAUTION:**
>
> *Get SA to run the PBSYB.SQL script on your SQL Server.*
>
> DBA@Win won't really work properly without certain stored procedures being installed on your server. SA must run the PBSYB.SQL script contained on the DBA@Win release diskette. To accomplish this,
>
> ```
> isql  -Usa -Pyourpassword -Syourservername <pbsyb.sql
> ```
>
> (Naturally, pbsyb.sql must be copied to your server or be otherwise accessible to ISQL!)